Cases on Internationalization Challenges for SMEs

António Carrizo Moreira
University of Aveiro, Portugal

IGI Global
PUBLISHER of TIMELY KNOWLEDGE

A volume in the Advances in Business Strategy and Competitive Advantage (ABSCA) Book Series

Published in the United States of America by
IGI Global
Business Science Reference (an imprint of IGI Global)
701 E. Chocolate Avenue
Hershey PA, USA 17033
Tel: 717-533-8845
Fax: 717-533-8661
E-mail: cust@igi-global.com
Web site: http://www.igi-global.com

Library of Congress Cataloging-in-Publication Data

Names: Moreira, António Carrizo, editor.
Title: Cases on internationalization challenges for SME / Antonio Carrizo Moreira, editor.
Description: Hershey : Business Science Reference, 2020. | Includes bibliographical references and index. | Summary: "This book provides a set of case studies to share empirical research on the Internationalization of Small and Medium-sized firms (SMEs) in the context of a globalized world, and considering a highly competitive international business setting. It offers a variety of reasons leading to the success or failure of the process of internationalization of SMEs and their inherent activities"-- Provided by publisher.
Identifiers: LCCN 2020023243 (print) | LCCN 2020023244 (ebook) | ISBN 9781799843870 (hardcover) | ISBN 9781799864844 (paperback) | ISBN 9781799843887 (ebook)
Subjects: LCSH: Small business. | International business enterprises.
Classification: LCC HD2341 .C3777 2020 (print) | LCC HD2341 (ebook) | DDC 338.8/8--dc23
LC record available at https://lccn.loc.gov/2020023243
LC ebook record available at https://lccn.loc.gov/2020023244

This book is published in the IGI Global book series Advances in Business Strategy and Competitive Advantage (ABSCA) (ISSN: 2327-3429; eISSN: 2327-3437)

British Cataloguing in Publication Data
A Cataloguing in Publication record for this book is available from the British Library.

Advances in Business Strategy and Competitive Advantage (ABSCA) Book Series

Patricia Ordóñez de Pablos
Universidad de Oviedo, Spain

ISSN:2327-3429
EISSN:2327-3437

Mission

Business entities are constantly seeking new ways through which to gain advantage over their competitors and strengthen their position within the business environment. With competition at an all-time high due to technological advancements allowing for competition on a global scale, firms continue to seek new ways through which to improve and strengthen their business processes, procedures, and profitability.

The **Advances in Business Strategy and Competitive Advantage (ABSCA) Book Series** is a timely series responding to the high demand for state-of-the-art research on how business strategies are created, implemented and re-designed to meet the demands of globalized competitive markets. With a focus on local and global challenges, business opportunities and the needs of society, the **ABSCA** encourages scientific discourse on doing business and managing information technologies for the creation of sustainable competitive advantage.

Coverage

- Globalization
- Joint Ventures
- Strategic Management
- Tacit Knowledge
- Co-operative Strategies
- Foreign Investment Decision Process
- Strategic Alliances
- Adaptive Enterprise
- Differentiation Strategy
- Entrepreneurship & Innovation

IGI Global is currently accepting manuscripts for publication within this series. To submit a proposal for a volume in this series, please contact our Acquisition Editors at Acquisitions@igi-global.com or visit: http://www.igi-global.com/publish/.

The Advances in Business Strategy and Competitive Advantage (ABSCA) Book Series (ISSN 2327-3429) is published by IGI Global, 701 E. Chocolate Avenue, Hershey, PA 17033-1240, USA, www.igi-global.com. This series is composed of titles available for purchase individually; each title is edited to be contextually exclusive from any other title within the series. For pricing and ordering information please visit http://www.igi-global.com/book-series/advances-business-strategy-competitive-advantage/73672. Postmaster: Send all address changes to above address.

Titles in this Series

For a list of additional titles in this series, please visit:
http://www.igi-global.com/book-series/advances-business-strategy-competitive-advantage/73672

Handbook of Research on Nascent Entrepreneurship and Creating New Ventures
António Carrizo Moreira (University of Aveiro, Portugal) and José Guilherme Leitão Dantas (CARME, School of Technology and Management, Polytechnic of Leiria, Portugal)
Business Science Reference • © 2021 • 483pp • H/C (ISBN: 9781799848264) • US $295.00

Reshaping Entrepreneurship Education With Strategy and Innovation
Ayansola Olatunji Ayandibu (University of Zululand, South Africa)
Business Science Reference • © 2021 • 422pp • H/C (ISBN: 9781799831716) • US $205.00

Emerging Business and Trade Opportunities Between Oceania and Asia
Angus Hooke (Australian Institute of Higher Education, Australia) Hardik Vachharajani (Crown Institute of Higher Education, Australia) Harpreet Kaur (Australian Institute of Higher Education, Australia) and Kevin E. Dow (University of Auckland, New Zealand)
Business Science Reference • © 2021 • 325pp • H/C (ISBN: 9781799841265) • US $195.00

Global Challenges and Strategic Disruptors in Asian Businesses and Economies
Patricia Ordóñez de Pablos (The University of Oviedo, Spain) and Miltiadis D. Lytras (American College of Greece, Greece & Effat University, Saudi Arabia)
Business Science Reference • © 2021 • 358pp • H/C (ISBN: 9781799847878) • US $195.00

Global Business Leadership Development for the Fourth Industrial Revolution
Peter Smith (The Leadership Alliance Inc., Canada) and Tom Cockburn (Center for Dynamic Leadership Models in Global Business, Canada)
Business Science Reference • © 2021 • 425pp • H/C (ISBN: 9781799848615) • US $195.00

Advanced Models and Tools for Effective Decision Making Under Uncertainty and Risk Contexts
Vicente González-Prida (University of Seville, Spain & UNED, Spain) and María Carmen Carnero (University of Castilla-La Mancha, Spain)
Business Science Reference • © 2021 • 423pp • H/C (ISBN: 9781799832461) • US $195.00

Knowledge Management for Corporate Social Responsibility
Gregorio Martín-de Castro (Complutense University of Madrid, Spain) and Jaime González-Masip (Rey Juan Carlos University, Spain)
Business Science Reference • © 2021 • 388pp • H/C (ISBN: 9781799848332) • US $195.00

IGI Global
PUBLISHER of TIMELY KNOWLEDGE

701 East Chocolate Avenue, Hershey, PA 17033, USA
Tel: 717-533-8845 x100 • Fax: 717-533-8661
E-Mail: cust@igi-global.com • www.igi-global.com

Table of Contents

Detailed Table of Contents

to facilitate internationalization, that is, the commitment to corporate social responsibility (internal factor) and the support of export promotion programmes (external factor).

Due to recent economic, social, and public health drawbacks, social enterprises (SEs) play an increasingly important role in addressing a wide range of social problems, as part of their market-based approach to social value creation. Since SEs operate mainly in challenging contexts characterized by scarce resource environments, they need to develop strategies in order to effectively accomplish their missions while achieving organisational sustainability. Often, SEs expand their activity overseas within an internationalisation strategy. The purpose of this study is to examine the role of resources in the internationalisation strategy undertaken by SEs. The study applies the resource-based view (RBV) to understand how the type and nature of resources may influence the international activities pursued by these organisations. The findings highlight the important role of different key resources in the growth, sustainability and internationalisation of SEs.

This chapter analyzes the internationalization strategy of a Portuguese knowledge-based service firm. It is based on a case study and the main objective is to discuss what internationalization theory best explains the company's internationalization strategy. The literature reviews the main internationalization patterns—Uppsala model, born globals, born again globals, and born regionals—so that a comparison of the main characteristics of each theory is discussed and analyzed. At the end of the chapter, a table summarizes the main characteristics of the internationalization process of each model presented. The case study is based on the analysis of both primary data from the firm and data obtained from an interview obtained with the CEO.

Re-internationalization represents a research challenge for the internationalization process. Many companies withdraw from international operations go through a period of interregnum time, and then reenter in the international arena. Little is known about this process and whether re-internationalizers opt for the same entrepreneurial orientation or behave differently than they began with the first approach, allowing for faster re-entry and take-off. This chapter follows a qualitative methodological approach, based on the case study, using semi-structured interview with the top manager of the wine company. This work is intended to serve as a basis for future studies related to the internationalization of SME, based on the profile of CEO, and as a basis for reflection by company managers. This exploratory study aims to contribute to the emerging literature on entrepreneurial orientation and re-internationalization using the SME case study.

Video game studios are an example of born global firms, companies that operate in international markets from the moment they are created. After providing an overview of the video game industry and a description of the video games business model, the Barcelona ecosystem is presented. A multiple case study is the chosen methodology and primary and secondary qualitative data are collected and analyzed. The purpose of the research is twofold: On the one hand, using the context of the effectuation theory to examine how video game developers transform means into effects. The first outcome of this study is a process model describing the mentioned transformation. On the other hand, the research explores the connection between microfoundations of routines and capabilities and international entrepreneurship (IE) to increase the understanding of how startups with scarce resources achieve launching games that have an international reach and, hence, become international entrepreneurs. The second outcome of this research is a model that sheds light on how microfoundations affect IE.

This chapter will present a series of university-industry collaboration (UIC) projects between a university industrial design research unit and various small-medium (manufacturing) enterprises (SMEs) with a focus on the facilitators role in these projects. Previous research has referred to ‘innovation intermediaries’ as a term to define (service) firms that proactively facilitate collaboration between two or more parties in innovation projects. In terms of technological development these have been exemplified as research and technology organisations (RTOs). The authors suggest an adjacent term ‘intermediary interpreters’ to describe the key facilitator by bringing together the term ‘intermediaries’ and the term ‘interpreters’ as they are defined by Roberto Verganti. These individuals have specialised external expertise and ability to take part in the ‘design discourse; to support innovation. The authors argue that intermediary interpreters are an important third party in UIC projects that provide unique support that can help SMEs embrace innovation strategy and more effectively internationalise.

flow of the process in SMEs have been included. With this method, it is aimed to prevent losses and leaks, provide data flow towards accounting internal control system, sustain competitive advantage and contribute to the internationalization efforts.

Preface

Historically, internationalization is one of the key elements that firms use to expand their activities abroad and to widen their future perspectives.

With the globalization process, firms are not only seeking to expand their activities to international markets but are also "feeling" competitors from abroad competing in their own markets. Small and medium-sized enterprises (SMEs), although seeking to expand abroad, have particularities that hinder their natural international expansion path due to particular barriers and challenges that most multinational firms have already overcome as a result of their large resource endowments.

Cases on Internationalization Challenges for SMEs is not meant to be the typical book that seeks to answer common aspects such as: What is business internationalization?; What are the main business internationalization strategies?; What to do to internationalize a company; How to export products?; What requirements are necessary to export products?; What is the difference in the internationalization of products and services? Rather, this book seeks to address the case of SMEs that play an important role in the contemporary society as they behave heterogeneously and face a variety of international expansion modes that deserve to be analyzed from plural perspectives. This book also seeks to explore avenues regarding important aspects of internationalization that can have important consequences for SMEs.

Taking into account the importance of internationalization, this book sought the contribution of researchers and academics that deal with challenges of the internationalization process of SMEs. Some studies explore important case studies of SMEs in their international quest. Some involve parametric analysis, with important learning outcomes for SMEs.

The objective of this publication is to provide scholars and graduate and undergraduate students in the management field with a set of case studies — but not limited to it — on the internationalization of SMEs in order to share the latest empirical research findings in the context of a globalized world, considering a highly competitive international business setting. This includes examining the main reasons leading to the success or failure of the process of internationalization of SMEs and their inherent activities.

This book consists of 13 chapters that encompass different topics and different research methods. Chapter 1 covers an underesearched topic: inward internationalization. It was prepared by Alexandra Alves, Carolina Rodrigues, Cristiana Gonçalves, Joana Conceição, and António Carrizo Moreira. *Inward Internationalization. A Case study from the Hotel Industry* aims to explore a gap in the literature on internationalization in the Hotel industry. It analyzes the behavior of the internationalization process of a small hotel located in Portugal and discusses which internationalization theory best explains the company's strategy. A qualitative methodology was carried on through a semi-structured interview with the head of the hotel marketing department and was complemented with data obtained from secondary information from public sources. Both Uppsala and Network models play an important role in the hotel internationalization process. The Uppsala model can be used to explain how the hotel behaved to gather a gradual and sequential knowledge of the international markets it seeks to achieve. However, it was important for the company to build new partnerships and relationships with suppliers, competitors, or other institutions involved in the business environment, especially abroad, to increase their international presence. Since research on inward internationalization activities in the hotel industry has been ignored, this chapter fills an important gap in the literature, contributing to a better understanding of how a small service-based firm of the hotel industry manages its inward internationalization process.

An International and Socially Responsible SME Based on Tailored Innovative Products: empakando from El Salvador is the title of Chapter 2. Its main purpose is to analyze the internationalization process of a small and medium-sized firm founded El Salvador. Antonia García-Cabrera, Gracia García-Soto, and Deybbi Cuéllar-Molina used a qualitative methodology based on a single case study of a firm in a developing country that successfully internationalized towards Central America. The following main factors favored the successful internationalization of this SME: (1) the choice of a gradual internationalization model; (2) the commitment of the firm to implementing a corporate social responsibility strategy; (3) the support offered by public export promotion programs; and (4) the complementarity of the founding team members' backgrounds. This chapter addresses the following practical implications: SMEs may accelerate the entry into foreign markets looking for local distributors with experience in the same industry and a good reputation in the target country. Governments in developing countries should offer export promotion programs and financial support to facilitate SMEs' internationalization.

Drawing on the Resource-Based View (RBV), Chapter 3 examines the influence of key resources, namely human capital, management, and experiential and industry know-how on the internationalization strategy undertaken by social enterprises. For that, *Resourced-based View and Internationalisation of Social Enterprises: An Exploratory Study* adopts a multiple case study research design. A qualitative methodology was applied to collect data from four case studies belonging to the Ashoka's Globalizer Program in Brazil, operating in different fields of social entrepreneurship. In this chapter José Carlos Pinho, Isabel Macedo, and Marcelo Dionísio highlight the fact that internationalisation strategies are greatly influenced by the quality of the social enterprise business model and by the social impact these organizations are able to provide. This chapter contributes to the current body of knowledge in the area of social enterprises by examining how key managerial resources and capabilities influence the SE internationalization strategy. The main contribution of the chapter is the understanding that resources, contact networks, and management know-how capabilities play an important role leading to more effective processes within internationalisation strategies in the SEs setting.

Chapter 4 analyzes the internationalization strategy of a Portuguese knowledge-based service company. Authored by Carolina Carlos, Nicole Bento, Raquel Henriques, and António Carrizo Moreira, *Challenges of the Internationalization Process. A Case Study of a Knowledge-intensive Service Company* reviews the main internationalization patterns of four distinct theoretical approaches — Uppsala Model, Born Globals, Born Again Globals, and Born Regionals — to compare the main characteristics of each theory is discussed and analyzed. The chapter summarizes the main characteristics of the internationalization process of each model presented and models are compared. Through an empirical investigation, a semi-structured interview was conducted within a case study. The case study is based on the analysis of both primary data from the firm and data obtained from an interview obtained with the CEO. The present chapter added a new perspective to the internationalization models' literature. With the application of a practical case, the different internationalization models were explored, and the combination of their results applied in a more comprehensive and holistic perspective.

SMEs' Re-internationalization Strategy: An Analysis based on Multiple Cases, authored by Rui Martins, Luís Farinha, and João Ferreira, presents a model proposal that shows the important role played by the CEO's entrepreneurial orientation in the process of re-internationalisation of a company in the wine industry. Following a qualitative methodology approach, based on a case study, using a semi-structured interview with the top managers of a wine company, it is possible to conclude that the profile of the CEO is fundamental for the enhanced competitive advantages of the firms. Chapter 5 is intended to serve as a basis for future studies related to the internationalization of SMEs, based on the profile of CEO, and as a basis for reflection by companies' managers. The decision to re-enter international markets is complex and dynamic and depends on the match between the internal factors of the company and its CEO and the international context.

International Entrepreneurship in the Video Game Industry in Barcelona is the title of Chapter 6. Prepared by Yeda Swirski de Souza and Antoni Olive-Tomas, this chapter examines how creative individuals and teams transform means into effects using the context of the effectuation theory. Using qualitative methodology through the use of multiple case studies based on semi-structured interviews with founders-managers as instruments to collect primary data, the chapter increases the understanding of how startups with scarce resources achieve launching products and services that have an international reach and, hence, become international entrepreneurs. There are two main findings that deserve to be released: firstly, video game studios transform means into effects following an effectual process; their working method and partnerships with stakeholders play crucial roles in the process; and secondly, video game studios enter the market if they succeed at launching a first game; managerial capabilities are required to survive after this first game.

The main purpose of Chapter 7 — *Intermediary Interpreters in University-Industry Collaboration to Support Manufacturing SMEs* — is to understand key individuals, defined by Roderick Walden and Anton Nemme as 'intermediary interpreters', involved in the success of university-industry collaboration (UIC) projects between university industrial design research units and manufacturing SMEs. Through a case study research analysis, the chapter establishes the intermediary interpreter as central to industrial design UIC projects. The authors classify five features that define their role along with five profile attributes that emerged from the analysis. An overview of the intermediary interpreter is provided along with how they positively influence building internationalization competency. The research presented may be beneficial to university research units and manufacturing SMEs in the formation of UIC projects. Identifying and establishing a clear role for the intermediary interpreter in such projects can help to ensure a successful project outcome for both partners and support the internationalization efforts of the manufacturing SME. The significance of the research is that a clear definition of the role of these 'intermediary interpreters' has not, to our knowledge, been previously established for UIC projects with manufacturing SMEs in the industrial design field

Cultural Intelligence. German Expatriates as Managers in Portugal, authored by Carolin Roehl, is the title of Chapter 8. The purpose of this chapter is to show the influence of culture on international business. It demonstrates the necessity for employees to be culturally literate and selecting and training expatriates in regard of cultural intelligence. Based on a mixed research method, in addition to a survey, three German expatriate managers in Portugal are interviewed. It was found that culture is barely given importance in today's internationalized environment and companies are very passive during the expatriation process not providing sufficient support. Expatriate managers would benefit from mastering cross-cultural communication strategies and leadership skills. Preparation for potential culture-based conflicts increases the expatriates' adjustment and performance and increase the companies' chances for success. German managers in Portuguese projects should especially prepare to be confronted with (moderately) high-context workers who prioritize interpersonal harmony over performance and to deal with a strong emotional connection between a task and an employee. The emotional identification may lead to difficulties when feedback is given, something German managers tend to do (very directly). Adjustment may be problematic and managers will have to actively try to integrate themselves in Portugal.

International Effect on Family SME's Financial Distress Prediction is the title of Chapter 9. Its purpose is to analyze the impact of internationalization on firm's probability of distress. Inês Lisboaand Magali Costa, the authors of the chapter, used an unbalanced panel data of 10,832 Portuguese family SMEs over the period from 2012 to 2018. The stepwise method is applied to select more accurate variables to explain the default risk. The Logit model is applied to develop the distress prediction model for family SMEs. The results show that international SMEs have a lower probability of default than domestic firms, and compliant firms export more. Moreover, the ratios of export intensity, liquidity, profitability, size, leverage, efficiency, cash flow, and age are relevant to explain default probability. The proposed model has an accuracy of 92.9%, increasing to 95.6% if only export SMEs are analyzed.

Chapter 10 analyzes the relationship between brand image and competitive advantage through differentiation and market orientation. Orlando Rua and Catarina Santos used a sample of 86 exporting companies of the footwear industry, where they applied a quantitative methodological approach based on a questionnaire survey. They concluded that: (a) brand image has a positive direct effect on both market orientation and competitive advantage through differentiation; and (b) market orientation has a significant impact on competitive advantage through differentiation. The main contribution of this chapter — *Assessing the Relationship between Brand Image, Market Orientation, and Competitive Advantage* — is that if companies of the footwear industry wish to increase their competitive advantage, they need to start investing in their brand images.

The main purpose of Chapter 11 — *Internationalization of Family Businesses: Does size really matter?* — is to examine whether internationalization performance does vary according to firm size, and its link to the innovative performance in multiple dimensions along with conventional characteristics such as age and turnover. Joana Costa applied logistic regressions to a purposeful database of 1148 family businesses with heterogeneous characteristics. Non-parametric tests were run to appraise the significant differences according to size sub-sampling reinforcing the importance of dimension as a threshold. This chapter demonstrates that the determinants do change depending on the firm dimension, providing valuable insights about the connection between globalized operation and innovation, for the different organisations. This chapter also evidences the role of size and innovation towards internationalization performance. As such, policies need to address these links given their importance for firm growth and survival, notwithstanding its advantages and disadvantages.

The main purpose of Chapter 12 is to analyze the connection between intangible resources and export performance, considering the mediating effect of innovation. *Predictive Strategic Factors in Export Performance in the Automotive Industry*, authored by Orlando Rua and Ana Ferreira, conclude that intangible resources have a direct positive effect on export performance and innovation mediates this relationship. Through the application of the structural equation using Partial Least Squares (PLS-SEM) applied to a sample of Portuguese exporting companies from the automotive industry they defend that intangible resources leveraged by innovation are important to improve and differentiate firms' products and services.

Chapter 13, authored by Engin Meriç, is entitled *Using Main Courante and Daily Revenue Report Methods in Accounting of Daily Revenues in Touristic Accommodation Enterprises.* Its purpose is to track income and internal control mechanisms among small and medium-sized accommodation enterprises. Using the case study method applying *Main Courante software*, the chapter demonstrates how accommodation enterprises prevent losses and leaks and provide data flow towards accounting internal control system. This chapter shows how a tool helps firms to sustain their competitive advantages and contributes to the inward internationalization efforts of those small and medium-sized businesses. Through the application of this software and accounting method, it is possible to account for the real profit (or loss) of each month by recording the revenues to the month they belong to. Moreover, with this easy-to-apply method, it is possible to recognize the revenues in a correct and timely manner, to prevent losses, to contribute to the strengthening of internal control, and to create an infrastructure for cost control, which is a very important factor in international competition.

Once the chapters are presented, a word of appreciation is mandatory to those who were of added value during this journey: the reviewers. They play a silent, important role for the outcome of this book. For all of them — Alexandra Alves, Ana Gomes, Antoni Olive-Tomas, Antonia García-Cabrera, Carolina Carlos, Carolina Rodrigues, Cristiana Gonçalves, Deybbi Cuéllar-Molina, Inês Lisboa, Joana Conceição, Joana Costa, João Ferreira, José Carlos Pinho, José Noroño Sánchez, Luís Moreira, Marcelo Dionísio, María Gracia García-Soto, Orlando Rua, Raquel Henriques, Roderick Walden, Rui Martins and Yeda Swirski de Souza — my heartedly appreciation.

This book is the result of a tremendous effort from all the authors involved in the preparation of the chapters. It is exiting to witness the added value of all the chapters which contribute to the common topic of the book: Cases on Internationalization. Challenges for SMEs. Moreover, there is a clear complementarity among the chapters of this book.

I sincerely hope the readers find it very pleased to read Cases on Internationalization. Challenges for SMEs and that the compilation of chapters hitherto presented are of added value and insightful. Last but not the least, I would like to thank all the authors for their effort in contributing to this book.

Finally, it is expected that this book can be of added value for scholars and graduate and undergraduate students in the management field. It is expected this book could also be of interest to managers and executives concerned with the international business environment.

Chapter 1
Inward Internationalization: A Case Study From the Hotel Industry

Alexandra Almeida Alves
University of Aveiro, Portugal

Carolina Ferreira Rodrigues
University of Aveiro, Portugal

Cristiana Durães Gonçalves
University of Aveiro, Portugal

Joana Conceiçao
University of Aveiro, Portugal

António Carrizo Moreira
https://orcid.org/0000-0002-6613-8796
University of Aveiro, Portugal

EXECUTIVE SUMMARY

This chapter analyzes the internationalization strategy of a small hotel firm of Central region of Portugal. It is based on a case study and the main objective is to discuss what internationalization theory best explains the company's internationalization strategy. This chapter explores a gap in the literature on inward internationalization involving a player of service-based firm of the hotel industry. The literature reviews the main internationalization patterns—Uppsala model, network-based model, and inward internationalization—in order to analyze behavior of small hotel and its internationalization. At the end of the chapter, a table summarizes the main characteristics of the internationalization process of each model presented. This chapter adds value by explaining how a small service-based firm of the hotel industry manages to address its inward internationalization process.

DOI: 10.4018/978-1-7998-4387-0.ch001

INTRODUCTION

Internationalization of enterprises is a phenomenon often related to the entry in international markets and a process of growing international involvement (Moreira, 2009; Ribau, Moreira, & Raposo, 2018a). Normally, Small and Medium-sized Enterprises (SMEs) seek to exploit their competitive advantages in overseas markets (Ribau, Moreira, & Raposo, 2018a; Stanisauskaite & Kock, 2016), which involves outward internationalization processes. However, inward internationalization processes are not as extensively analyzed as outward internationalization processes (Moreira, Ferreira, & Silva, 2018).

Research on inward internationalization activities have been neglected given the scarce number of studies in this area when compared to outward internationalization (Karlsen, Silseth, Benito, & Welch, 2003; Moreira, Ferreira, & Silva, 2018). One of the possible explanations is that most of the theory analyzing internationalization is based on the typical industrial large companies, on one hand, in which the service perspective is marginally analyzed, and, on the other hand, the internationalization of the hotel industry players has been largely overlooked. Moreover, inward activities are more frequent in the early life of firms, particularly through the imports of raw materials, components, and machinery.

Companies must refine their resources and capabilities to operate internationally, in order to achieve a good export performance (Leonidou, Palihawadana, & Theodosio, 2011). This upgrade can lead to the development of an effective export marketing strategy, which will help companies win a competitive advantage. Therefore, companies look forward to improving their market and financial performance in both international and domestic markets. In the Hotel Industry, the flexibility of options presents challenges that differ from country to country and hotel to hotel. Thus, each country and hotel should evaluate their industry and establish the most appropriate way for its international market (Correia, Lengler, & Mohsin, 2019).

Although several theories have been put forward to explain the different internationalization strategies implemented by SMEs (Ribau et al., 2015; 2018a; 2018b), the Uppsala theory has been extensively used to explain the incremental perspective SMEs tend to use to become gradually involved in international markets despite their passive or active internationalization behavior (Ribau et al., 2015; Moreira et al., 2018a). SMEs also need to develop their capabilities and competitive advantages and assume a proactive behavior to internationalize (Ribau et al., 2017; 2019), which might involve a network-based approach to reach overseas markets.

The provision of services, namely in the hotel industry, means that internationalization represents the development and improvement of skills and competences of institutions that seek to exploit their competitive advantages in international markets. However, the provision of services in the hotel industry means that the service provider not only needs to have certain competitive advantages to outcompete their local rivals but also needs to be internationally competitive in order to attract international tourists. As such, service providers of the hotel industry face quite specific challenges in international markets in order to arrange inter-organizational activities so that they can generate a continuous flow of tourists so that they can 'export' their services. The same occurs in the higher education industry (Nogueira & Moreira, 2018).

This chapter aims to investigate the internationalization of a Portuguese company – named GAMMA for confidentiality reasons, established in the market since 1902 – that competes in the hotel industry and seeks to provide its services to international guests. As a Portuguese company, GAMMA belongs to the group of inward internationalizers that desires to expand their activities and embraced export promotion programs to achieve their goals.

Based on the literature on internationalization, this chapter aims to examine the internationalization process of GAMMA from a historical perspective and debate the intricacies of the internationalization process. As such, the following objectives were defined:

1. To analyze how GAMMA is preparing the internationalization process.
2. To analyze how this company embraced new restructuring opportunities and export promotion programs to successfully embrace inward internationalization.
3. To analyze what led this company to choose its strategy.
4. To contribute to a better understanding of how small companies competing in the hotel industry manage their inward internationalization process.

The chapter is structured in six sections. After the first introductory section, the second section reviews the literature on internationalization. The third section presents the methodology used. The fourth section briefly describes GAMMA business activities. While the fifth section presents the results obtained, the sixth section discusses the results. Finally, section seven presents the conclusions.

LITERATURE REVIEW

Internationalization

The international environment is very complex since both SMEs and multinationals firms adopt various forms and strategies of internationalization to serve global markets, adapt and quickly develop new products in many countries and adapt their brands in the global situation (Ribau, Moreira, & Raposo, 2015; 2018a; 2018b). The internationalization process can be described as a dynamic, multidimensional process that depends on the accumulation of business knowledge in international markets and has the consequence of the increasing presence of enterprises in overseas markets. Internationalization has been defined as the process that increases the involvement of international operations (Karlsen et al., 2003), which is consistent with an outward internationalization process.

The world has witnessed rapid internationalization of markets, industries, and companies that have led to different theoretical and analytical perspectives regarding the evolution of internationalization and their main theories (Ribau et al., 2015; 2018a; 2018b; Ietto-Gillies, 2012). Although there is no single definition about internationalization, it is normally understood as a business activity across countries, which involve both outward and inward perspectives of internationalization (Olejnik & Swoboda, 2012; Chetty & Campbell-Hunt, 2003; Moreira, 2009, Moreira, Ferreira, & Silva, 2018).

SMEs face two main challenges during the internationalization of their activities (Johanson & Vahlne, 2009): liability of outsidership, and liability of foreignness. The former is related with the lack of knowledge about international target markets and their players. The latter is related with uncontrollable factors such as (different) laws of destination markets and language barriers.

Despite the risk assumed when competing abroad in unknown environments, markets and clients, the decision not to internationalize is seen as an even riskier decision (George, Wiklund, & Zahra, 2005) as firms that do not internationalize can lose competitiveness as they rely excessively on their domestic markets (Hilmersson, 2014).

Different international entry modes have been proposed to explain how companies compete abroad. The internationalization of enterprises is a phenomenon that normally assumes an entry mode into international markets and a growing process of international involvement and exposure. Firms are able to choose between a wide range of entry modes, which suggests there are several levels of commitment, control and risk in international engagement (Fernandes, Simões, Pereira, & Moreira, 2019; Furtado, Pereira, Pereira, & Moreira, 2019; Moreira, Ramos, Ferraz, & Martins, 2018; Ribau et al., 2015).

Following a historical timeline, Ribau et al. (2015) provide a schematic analysis of the main internationalization theories, their focus, and underlying assumptions. They claim there are two well-known approaches explaining the internationalization processes of SMEs (Hakansson & Snehota, 2006; Johanson & Vahlne, 2009): the Uppsala Model and the network-based view.

The Uppsala model defends that internationalization takes place in a gradual and linear form (Johanson & Vahlne, 2009; Rhaiem, 2015). In other words, the company increases its international participation (knowledge and experience) gradually (Johanson & Vahlne, 2009; Ribau et al., 2015) and has four main phases (Rhaiem, 2015; Ribau et al., 2015): (1) non-regular export activities; (2) exports through independent representatives (agents and distributors); (3) establishment of international sales subsidiaries and (4) establishment of international production units.

The Uppsala model argues that firms follow a sequential path in their international operations and is based on a linear cumulative path in which the absence of international experience reduces the propensity of the firm to engage in unknown international markets. For firms to get involved in far-flung international markets they have to internalize knowledge of different cultures, languages, laws and industrial competitive ecosystems (Ribau et al., 2015), which might force SMEs to internationalize their activities to low psychic distant markets and as soon as they internalize form the experience they expand their activities to more psychic distant markets.

The logic of this model is based on the evolution of the internationalization process because of the increased knowledge and operations in international markets, as well as a result of the increased commitment of resources in international markets (Ribau et al., 2015). The gradual acquisition, integration, and use of knowledge about operations and overseas markets are considered vital for the internationalization process since it leads to a greater commitment to those markets (Karlsen et al., 2003).

Following a network-based perspective, Johanson and Mattsson (2015) argue that internationalization is the outcome of the development of (internal and external) inter-organizational relationships among individuals and/or firms that have resources and experience/knowledge. This inter-organizational network helps explain different internationalization paths, based on an interactive perspective among different players (suppliers, buyers, competitors, or other institutions) involved in the business environment (Moreira & Alves, 2016; Durão & Moreira, 2019).

The network theory states that the development of firms occurs in context-based relationships. For this purpose, firms establish long-term relationships among them. The firms' domestic network and the relationships within it can be a starting point for companies to go international. When entering new countries, companies establish new relationships to get access to other international markets. Therefore, internationalization is a process led by relationships and by the evolution of a firm's network (Johanson & Mattsson, 2015; Ribau et al., 2015).

Johanson and Mattsson (2015) claim that the number and depth of relationships increase among clients, suppliers, distributors, and competitors as firms internationalize. As such internationalization, according to the network approach, takes place when firms: (a) build inter-organizational relationships in new countries (i.e., involving international expansion); (b) increase their commitment in international networks (i.e., international penetration); and (c) integrate their position in several networks in various countries (i.e., international integration).

Many service companies, namely in the tourism industry, support their competitive advantage in resources connected to locations, which are used to provide services to international clients in the domestic market (Turunen & Nummela, 2017). A well-succeed tourist product tends to be based on network cooperation between companies, organizations, and public authorities. In short, one can argue that tourist firms internationalize through and within the networks in which they are inserted. Those networks can be social, institutional, technological, regional, and/or virtual ones (Turunen & Nummela, 2017).

As the business environment changes, inter-organizational relationships become more and more important; as such companies must have in mind the use of relational marketing to compete more efficiently. Although traditional marketing is necessary, it is no longer enough for companies to remain successful (Sin et al., 2006). Moreover, the literature suggests that in order to acquire and maintain a competitive advantage, the organization providing the service must develop long term relationships with clients (Sin et al., 2006). Sin et al. (2006) outlined five strategic elements for practicing relational marketing: the development of core activities around building a relationship with the customer; the customization of the relationship for each client; the introduction of service-based benefits; the creation of specific services to increase customer loyalty; and training employees to achieve better performance and satisfy customers. Sin et al. (2006) shows that relationship marketing has a bigger effect than traditional marketing in overall performance, marketing performance (retention of clients, customer satisfaction and trust) and financial performance (sales growth, market quotation, return on investment, and return on sales). These results suggest that relationship marketing is crucial to determine the performance of the hotel industry (Sin et al., 2006).

There are two different kinds of motivations for firms to internationalize (Westhead, Ucbasaran, & Binks, 2004; Ribau et al., 2017): proactive and reactive. When firms initiate the internationalization process drawing on their own internal competencies in order to exploit market opportunities, one is before typical proactive motivations. On the other hand, when firms react to some events, internationalization is closely linked to a passive attitude. Some examples of proactive motivations are the following (Westhead et al., 2004; Ribau et al., 2017): the creation of unique products for certain target markets; managerial commitment to entering new markets abroad; and a clear focus on product/market diversification. Reactive motivations are the result of competitive pressures, excess production capacity, and saturation of the domestic market. Although both types of strategies are common among SMEs, the performance of proactive internationalizers is better than that of reactive internationalizers (Ribau et al., 2017).

Business internationalization encompasses two processes (Li, Yi, & Cui, 2017): inward and outward activities. Inward activities refer to activities in which companies get involved with international companies in their own country, namely, technology and product import activities, internal franchising, and the provision of services to international tourists. Inward activities can create a good opportunity for companies to learn about international trade techniques, operations characteristics, and other ways to use different operation modes. Through the active use of the knowledge acquired in international markets, the company can achieve a better positioning and assume operations in overseas markets. On the other hand, outward activities refer to activities that companies have in international markets, namely, franchising and licenses for international enterprises, mergers, and acquisitions in the exterior and the establishment of subsidiaries in external markets (Li et al., 2017).

Internationalization Incentives

Previous studies have shown that the participation of companies in export activities can be stimulated by internal and external agents of change (Seringhaus & Rosson, 1994; Naidu et al., 1997; Ayob & Freixanet, 2014). The first emerges within the organization, as is the case of possessing unique resources and capabilities that confer businesses competitive advantages, while the second refers to external forces, such as export promotion programs (EPPs) organized by the governments that drive companies to embrace higher risks abroad. It was also observed in several studies that, among SMEs, the involvement in exporting activities is more influenced by external than internal incentives (Ayob & Freixanet, 2014).

In a study involving SMEs, Francioni, Pagano, and Castellani (2016) distinguish two types of internationalization drivers: internal and external drivers. Several authors have recognized that the internal drivers can be related to companies Human Resources, I&D, innovation, and productivity activities, Marketing and Purchasing (Holmlund et al., 2007; Frishammar & Andersson, 2009; D'Angelo, 2012; Onkelinx et al., 2015).

As for the Human Resources, three different categories of factors that stimulate export activities in SMEs are emphasized: competencies (proficiency in foreign languages and international experience), cognitive factors (risk attitude, cost perception and benefits, commitment and global mentality) and sociodemographic factors (origin of shareholders, entrepreneurs, or owners). Human Resources, R&D, and Marketing are the factors most positively associated with the beginning of the SME internationalization process (Rundh, 2007; Francioni, Pagano, & Castellani 2016).

The external drivers can originate from factors related with the home country and the host country as well as the business networks (Francioni, Pagano, & Castellani 2016). Networks have been stated as the most influencing factor in driving the export activities of SMEs, bearing in mind that the more involved in established international networks executive directors are, the better their understanding and knowledge about foreign markets, which eases the internationalization process. Relationships and networks play an important role, mainly when SMEs carry out projects of international expansion in countries with less social and institutional diversity, such as emerging markets.

Additionally, once in a declining domestic market, there is a bigger chance of SMEs' success in internationalization, even if this is a secondary factor. Regarding the host country, several studies point out that the role of identifying better opportunities abroad in the development of export activities is very important.

The combination of proactive, internal, and external stimuli has led Portuguese hotels to internationalize (Correia et al., 2019). The internal or organizational incentives are sustained by marketing actions and interpersonal capabilities. On the other hand, external stimuli are supported by the identification of market opportunities based on confidential and institutional information gathered by participating in trade fairs and commercial missions, by formal and informal networks with commercial associations, by the privileged knowledge of managements and by the target country's initiatives. Moreover, the managers' resources, entrepreneurial capabilities, and international attitude also help Portuguese hotels to internationalize (Correia et al., 2019).

Destinations and strategies for entering foreign markets are decisions that can be conditioned by the company's family nature (Andreu, Claver, Quer, & Rienda, 2020). Some reasons for the growth strategy are (Andreu et al., 2020): improving the company's image and reputation, ensuring business continuity, achieving greater prestige and renown, seeing the internationalization effort recognized, and increasing the company's value for the next generation.

In order not to lose control, Andreu et al. (2020) argue that both family businesses and most SMEs prefer to go to geographically or culturally close destinations.

Additionally, Bianchi (2011) proposes the following drivers of export performance: market orientation, service quality, cultural sensitivity of service providers, organizational communication strategy, business networks, government support, and the image of the service of the home country. Regarding market orientation, the author argues that it is important that the company has a complete knowledge of the preferences and individual needs of the international market and adapts itself adequately to the market variation to obtain a good performance in the long term. Furthermore, in order to properly compete at an international level, the provision of quality service needs to be set and maintained at international quality standards.

Cultural sensitivity is an important stimulus. According to Bianchi (2011), due to the inseparable nature of services, service providers need to interact with consumers from different cultures. Dealing properly with cultural differences is a core competence for the performance of service exports.

In addition, Bianchi (2011) mentions the international activities – visits done by managers to the target countries, the participation in fairs, the use of international agents, the use of internet and merchandising development of communication – as important drivers. Another important driver is "domestic" networking, which is the exchange of information and marketing practices between tourist establishments and joint promotional efforts abroad. Government support is also an important factor. Industrial associations, export promotion companies, etc. (national and regional) can provide essential support for travel and participation in fairs. Finally, Bianchi (2011) refers to the image of the home country. This plays a significant role in providing a tangible suggestion to shape the service's perception and assess its quality in an international context. Thus, the brand and promotion of the country are relevant for these companies.

Barriers to Inward Internationalization of Services

In general, barriers to the internationalization of enterprises can consist of high costs, strong competition, protectionist regulation, lack of information, difficulties in locating or obtaining representation abroad, among others (Ayob & Freixanet, 2014).

Regarding consumer services, these generally require a high degree of face-to-face contact and interaction between service providers and consumers for the service to be produced and consumed. Therefore, there is a greater probability of problems arising due to cultural differences and communication errors during the service meeting (Bianchi, 2011).

The inward internationalization of services faces some barriers and factors of international performance unique to the service industry. Bianchi (2011) identifies three main barriers to inward internationalization of services: government regulations, exchange rate fluctuations, and cultural differences.

Finally, cultural differences are barriers that strongly influence the internationalization of services, especially if they arise in the domestic market where the service is provided. In addition, Bianchi (2011) also highlights the importance of the difference that exists between the expectations of the service between the provider and the consumer, as these aspects may differ, depending on the culture of each country. Thus, there are Export Promotion Programs (EPPs) whose main purposes are to reduce or eliminate export barriers, motivate companies to internationalize, assist planning and preparation for export and provide financial and non-financial assistance (Ayob & Freixanet, 2014).

EPPs' main objective is helping firms overcome the barriers to the entry of new international markets (Freixanet, 2012). These services include seminars, trade fairs and trade missions, consultancy, export financing advice, and information on foreign markets (Freixanet, 2012; Jalali, 2012).

Trade fairs are one of the promotional programs that aim to provide empirical knowledge supporting companies in international markets. These fairs are considered a marketing and information platform that allows international expansion of companies. They are also an important promotional tool for marketing products and services and an opportunity to contact directly with potential international buyers and therefore create new relationships (Haddoud, Jones, & Newbery, 2017).

These trade fairs are positively related to the satisfaction and export performance of firms since firms that use fairs promoted by governments tend to have positive export performance results. (Geldres-Weiss & Monreal-Pérez, 2018; Wilkinson et al., 2009). Additionally, the use of sponsored fairs and trade missions is related to a wide range of export areas, improvements in product marketing, cooperation agreements, and better internationalization planning (Francis & Collins-Dodd, 2004; Freixanet, 2012).

METHODOLOGY

This chapter is based on a case study – GAMMA – and involves a qualitative analysis of a Hotel in São Pedro do Sul, Portugal, whose core business is based on providing SPA activities for two different market segments – Portuguese and foreign nationals – through two different activities – hotel and aparthotel premises. GAMMA was chosen for their choice in looking for export promotion programs in order to increase their inward based internationalization strategy.

The case study method was selected to analyze GAMMA, as this allows the analysis of particular situations, the combination of known theories with new empirical results drawn from the specific situations under analysis, investigating phenomena within their real life contexts, the analysis and interpretation of retrospective information and the possible development of new theoretical and practical insights (Chetty, 1996; Eisenhardt, 1989; Ghauri, 2004; Ribau et al., 2019; Yin, 2008). Moreover, the case study method is particularly adequate for analyzing a dynamic perspective over time that involves a complex nonlinear internationalization process (Vissak & Francioni, 2013; Silva & Moreira, 2019; Welch & Welch, 2009).

As this chapter is based on a single case study, it is possible to deepen the analysis of the object of study (Piekkari et al., 2009; Voss et al., 2002), as well as to use a research method with inductive/deductive approaches. Those approaches are particularly appropriate: firstly, when addressing explanatory and exploratory aspects (trying to deal with the 'why' and 'how'); and secondly, when uncovering relational aspects that take place over time (Yin, 2008).

GAMMA was selected based on judgmental/purposive sampling (Patton, 2015). This sampling method involves the selection of cases that meet four important requirements for this research: (a) being involved in the exploration of the idiosyncrasies associated with inward international business activities; (b) the participation in the provision of service-based activities in the hotel industry; and (c) having core activities aimed at different market segments; and (d) actively seeking to increase the international market segment.

A semi-structured interview with the head of GAMMA's marketing department in May 2019 was used to collect data, typical of a qualitative methodology. Data collection involved obtaining primary and secondary information both from interviews and public sources, such as the firm's website, marketing information from industrial associations, and multiple observations, which was important to ensure the validity and reliability of data (Ghauri, 2004). The interview lasted approximately one hour and thirty minutes, complemented by a visit to the hotel facilities and environmental atmosphere where the hotel was located. The interview allowed us to understand the internationalization activities and strategies and supported our goal of studying the business transformation the hotel is going through and the active seeking incorporation of internationalization activities. This procedure helped the interviewee feel more comfortable while speaking in her own environment and enabled events to be observed in their natural setting. The researchers maintained a passive and unobtrusive presence, not to interfere with on-going events and activities.

The visit to the hotel facilities and environmental atmosphere where the hotel was located was important for the interviewers to aware of both the different types of segments and strategies the hotel was seeking to implement. After the visit, the researchers' impressions were attached to the summary of the interview.

In order to facilitate the interviewing process, the interviewers began by explaining the research, guaranteeing anonymity, and requesting authorization to audio-record the interview. The interview script sought to explore the evolution of international paths, the importance of the restructuration process the hotel was going through, and activities used by the hotel in its internationalization process. The interview script included questions to triangulate the information obtained from informants with additional information obtained through the firm's website and public sources (e.g. firm size, age, international presence/experience, main current markets, etc.).

Data from all sources were collected and transcribed into a single case story, helping to identify missing information.

PRESENTATION OF THE COMPANY

Over the years, Portugal has witnessed a progressive increase in the demand of rural areas for tourism and leisure activities, mainly by urban populations (Silva, 2007). Moreover, tourism has been increasing worldwide, with the number of international tourists reaching 1235 million in 2016 (Carrasqueira, Garcia, & Carrasqueira, 2018). As such, companies seek to follow this growth through not only the consolidation of their domestic market but also developing new tourist destinations. In 2016, Portugal received 21.3 million guests (INE, 2017; Carrasqueira et al., 2018).

Although there is a growing demand for rural tourism, it is still very seasonal. Seasonality of demand is generally considered a challenge within the tourism business – particularly ecotourism, rural, nature, and adventure tourism – potentially jeopardizing its development. This is predominantly true for tourist destinations that are more vulnerable to systematic fluctuations of demand, typically those related to climate, as in the case of Portugal (Kastenholz & Almeida, 2008).

In Portugal, as in some other European countries, the therapeutic use of hot springs is very common, known as "thermalism" or "water cures". The most famous area in Portugal is São Pedro do Sul, located in the Centro region of Portugal (Quintela, 2011).

The GAMMA hotel, in São Pedro do Sul, Portugal, has a great strength in terms of its geographical location because it is in a specific and unique thermal area. However, like this hotel, there are others that are located in the same area. Thus, in order to respond to the seasonality of demand and to be able to attract different target audiences in both low and high season, adding an indoor SPA to its services not only makes the customer experience more complete but also differentiates this hotel from its competitors.

GAMMA is a family-run hotel founded in 1902 and, until today, remains managed by family members. It is in the São Pedro do Sul thermal area and consists of a Hotel, now with 48 rooms and an Aparthotel with 20 rooms.

GAMMA's core strategic pillars are essentially SPA and health tourism, and its target audience is the senior market, which, for health reasons, needs thermal treatment. Regarding the number of employees, during the normal season they have around 20 employees, however, during the high season they have around 30 to 40 employees, considering the holding of events such as christening and wedding celebrations at the Hotel.

The hotel has partnerships with nature and adventure companies in the nearest geographic area and with the transport company Vale do Vouga to take and pick customers up at Porto's airport. They are the first Hotel in São Pedro do Sul to have these kinds of partnerships.

Located in a touristic area, GAMMA has direct and indirect competitors. Some examples are Hotel Lisboa, Pensão David, Monte Rio, among others. However, competition is not considered strong nor a negative factor, because each hotel has a different strategy.

The main markets GAMMA reaches are Portuguese, Spanish, Dutch, French, English, and German. According to its clients' evaluations, the Hotel has as main differentiating factor the food and friendliness of staff. GAMMA's internationalization is quite recent and emerged to increase the average annual occupancy, both for the hotel and the aparthotel. As the occupation of its regular (senior) customers is much lower in the low season, GAMMA aims to attract a younger market, especially in this season.

It is important to mention that senior clients have specific needs and look for specific accommodations when they're looking for a hotel, such as quietness and comfort, and health treatments. However, to be able to attract a younger market it requires almost the opposite. The younger clients belong to the adventure segment that seeks pleasure and fun. Comfort is important but younger customers also look for a hotel that can provide dynamic and adventurous activities in the nearest areas, a SPA to relax in and a restaurant and/or a bar to have some fun. In short, the two segments the GAMMA hotel looks to get to are quite different and the hotel must take that into account.

RESULTS

GAMMA started its internationalization strategy in 2018. At that time the Hotel participated in two projects, co-financed by Portugal 2020. One of the projects consists of remodeling the Hotel for health and well-being activities. The second project consists of the internationalization of GAMMA.

Portugal 2020 "is a partnership agreement between Portugal and the European Commission that includes activities of the 5 European Structural and Investment Funds – ERDF, Cohesion Fund, ESF, EAFRD and EMFF – which was adopted in order to apply the principles of the Europe 2020 strategy and to focus on the economic, social, environmental and territorial development policy that could stimulate growth and job creation in Portugal for the upcoming years" (Portugal 2020, n.d.).

The first project includes the qualification, innovation, and modernization of the services GAMMA offers. Thus, the company added two strategic pillars, in addition to its main ones – thermal and health tourism: (1) physical and mental wellbeing (SPA); (2) Nature and adventure tourism. These pillars' main goal is to have a broader offer of thermal and wellness tourism activities and to become more attractive for other kind of audience, namely a young and "urban" customer – couples who appreciate nature, adventure and rural environments and have the need to take a break from the city life.

To attract the new target audience, the hotel building underwent a renovation of the exterior and common spaces, transforming it into a sophisticated and modern space in terms of design and decoration. To focus more on their quality, the company invested less on the wedding/christening celebration services hitherto performed. Furthermore, GAMMA created a new floor, modernized the existing rooms, and added five new rooms (48-53). They also created a SPA, a bar ("Guarda-Rios"), a restaurant ("1902"), a gym, and an indoor pool. These changes made it possible for the Hotel to go from 3 stars to 4 stars.

The renovation project of GAMMA adds crucial value for the second perspective – internationalization – to have better results. Since the strategic pillar of the Hotel is thermal and health tourism, with a mostly senior target audience, over 65 years, it is easy having maximum occupancy during high season, due to the good weather. However, throughout the low season, it is difficult to have this audience's presence, due to the weather conditions and their negative impact on elder people's health. Therefore, the company feels the need to increase the affluence during the low season.

Through a market research, it has been possible to determine that even though Portuguese customers do not search much for activities such as those mentioned above during winter, people with different cultures have a different mindset. For example, northern Europeans do not mind carrying out activities in the rain and cold weather. However, Portugal is not ready to receive these customers in low season. Maybe that is why there is not a great influx of foreign people in this season either.

The company used Portugal 2020 to co-finance the investment in the participation of business fairs. For this project, the hotel aims to achieve the following objectives: (1) to achieve a solid position in international markets; (2) to increase turnover, occupancy rate, and number of foreign guests; (3) to internationalize its activities related to welfare.

The project includes the involvement in four foreign tourism fairs, namely the World Travel Market (WTM), in which they obtained thirty contacts, and the World Tourism Fair, in Paris, FITUR, in Madrid and BTL, in Berlin. Until the moment of the interview, the company had participated in the WTM fair and the World Tourism Fair. All the fairs were considered as interesting; however, the WTM is more oriented towards the goals that GAMMA wants to achieve, while the World Tourism Fair is more focused on Business to Consumer kind of business. In these fairs, the company can obtain contacts, for example, with Destination Management Companies (DMC) – tourism companies that plan trips. There will also be four trips made with the purpose of doing some market research, collecting data on how the hotels are positioned, among other aspects. Additionally, the Hotel offered vouchers to the new partners/contacts they found, for them to have a post-remodeling hotel experience.

Additionally, the GAMMA redesigned the company's website. The marketing plan also includes an online blog which will post interviews to the inhabitants of São Pedro do Sul about the positive and negative aspects they find in living in this place, with the purpose of providing testimonials about the rural environment to potential clients.

In terms of social media, the Hotel has Instagram and Facebook pages, in which they publish the latest news and seek to attract new customers. GAMMA has also collaborated with influencers: an older couple with a daughter to promote calmer activities, and a younger couple, more adventurous. This way they reach the different audiences they aim to attract. The website is available in more than two languages. They also invested in language training for their employees, as another aspect of the internationalization project. For example, the French market is sensitive to language barriers, and hotel's staff feels the need to be fluent in order to establish a better communication.

From the very beginning, word of mouth among its network of contacts has been the hotel's main marketing strategy. Since it is a family business, the sharing of contacts happened naturally, contributing to greater customer loyalty. At that time, the company did not feel the need to invest in its online brand image.

However, in the past few years, the GAMMA hotel wanted to balance out the low occupancy rate during the low season, so it had to create a new target audience, which includes young adventurous people who enjoy nature. In addition, the company perceived the need to attract foreign visitors, due to cultural differences.

Given the evolution of the market through the years, for example, urban tourist's search for calm and relaxing environments and for health and well-being tourism, it became necessary for the hotel to reinvent itself in order to respond to the new market needs and to be able to attract their new target audiences. Thus, it was necessary to adopt and invest in new strategies. The new strategies also allowed the GAMMA hotel to become more competitive.

Considering that GAMMA started the new projects in 2018, and they will end in 2020, it is only possible to have access to some short-term results. So far, it has only been possible to determine that there are already some measures that have been implemented in relation to social networks and the website. In relation to other strategies, the company expects to achieve other results in the medium/long term.

A summary of the main objectives and strategies adopted can be found in Table 1.

Table 1. Summary of main objectives and strategies

<table>
<tr><th>Projects – Portugal 2020</th><th>GAMMA 4*- Health and Well-being</th><th>GAMMA - Internationalization</th></tr>
<tr><td>Main objectives</td><td>- Increase the number of rooms;
- Have a more complete offer in terms of SPA and wellness;
- Attract another type of audience, namely a young and urban one;
- Balancing revenue during the low season.</td><td>- Achieve a consolidated position in international markets;
- Increase turnover;
- Increase the occupancy rate;
- Internalization of activities associated with Wellness, such as Gymnasium and SPA;
- Increase the number of foreign guests.</td></tr>
<tr><td rowspan="2">Implemented Strategies</td><td>- Add strategic pillars: physical and mental well-being and nature and adventure tourism;
- Remodeling of outdoor and common spaces - creating more rooms, SPA, open bar, restaurant, gym, and indoor pool.</td><td>- Investment in participation in business fairs: four business fairs (WTM - World Travel Market, World Tourism Fair, FITUR, and BTL) and four prospecting trips.</td></tr>
<tr><td colspan="2">- Partnerships with nature and adventure organizations;
- Remodeling of the website and online blog;
- Dissemination through Social Networks;
- Collaboration with influencers.</td></tr>
<tr><td>Results Achieved</td><td></td><td>- 30 contacts made at the WTM fair</td></tr>
</table>

DISCUSSION

Geldres-Weiss and Monreal-Pérez (2018) describe trade fairs as one of the export promotion programs that aims to provide experiential knowledge. These trade fairs are an instrument that can be used to market products and services and it offers the opportunity to create new relationships (Haddoud, Jones, & Newbery, 2017). Geldres-Weiss & Monreal-Pérez (2018) and Wilkinson et al. (2009) also consider that the use of trade fairs positively affects the export performance of companies.

It is possible to observe that GAMMA acquires experiential knowledge and new contacts and develops partnerships with travel agencies through its participation in trade fairs. Although it is not yet possible to determine the success of the use of trade fairs by this company, since it is still a process in development, it can be verified that GAMMA has already managed to establish some contacts. This demonstrates a plausible positive effect of fairs in its process of internationalization.

According to Ribau (2015) and Nummela (2017), companies that have their national networks already consolidated will find it easier to create networks internationally. This will consequently develop new relationships and make the company network evolve. This, in turn, will contribute positively to the success of the internationalization process. Thus, it can be argued that GAMMA could be an example of these authors' perspective. The offer of vouchers at trade fairs enhances the loyalty of international partners since, using vouchers, partners have the possibility to first-hand experience the various hotel services. If they consider it a good business opportunity, they will ask GAMMA for a profit margin for each recommendation given to their customers. The investment in transactional relations with different intermediaries is essential not only to increase the number of international guests but also to publicize the hotel in foreign markets.

Li et al. (2017) define inward export activities as internationalization activities in the company's country of origin. They consist mainly of importing products, knowledge or technology, and joint ventures. The authors argue that these activities can be advantageous for the company's learning about foreign markets, foreign trade techniques, among others. As a service organization, GAMMA does not have products that can be exported abroad. This acts according to the inward perspective, choosing to travel to other markets, through trade fairs for tourism and prospecting trips. Hence, the company not only attracts new customers but also acquires knowledge about foreign markets.

According to Correia et al. (2019), in the hotel industry, each hotel must evaluate its own industry and establish the most appropriate way to enter its international market since the challenges may vary by country. Additionally, Andreu et al. (2020) also argue that family businesses in this sector tend to internationalize to culturally close countries. However, this theory does not apply to GAMMA, which is a family business, since the company intends to reach different markets in order to resolve its low occupancy rate in the colder seasons. For example, the French market does not mind carrying out nature activities in the winter. Nonetheless, GAMMA must be cautious in this change of position. When trying to attract a new target audience it is possible to drive away and lose its current audience. At the moment, the company's target audience is senior customers who need a sober and calm environment and, by involving a more dynamic and young audience, they can interfere with the needs of the senior audience and thus lose them.

Currently, customer relations are increasingly important, especially in the hotel industry. Consequently, hotels should pay special attention to marketing since, according to several authors, traditional marketing is no longer sufficient to attract and retain customers (Sin et al., 2006). Thus, it can be argued that GAMMA should strengthen its relationship marketing, standing out not only for the special and personalized service offered but also for the lasting connection they create by doing so. Since relationship marketing, in comparison with conventional marketing, leads to an increase in the business performance in general, as confirmed by Sin et al. (2006).

CONCLUSION

Many companies fail in their internationalization process as they believe that this is a solution to the poor results they present. This perspective is not ideal. GAMMA can be considered a good example to follow since before starting its internationalization process, they decided and invested in improving not only its infrastructure but also its attitude in the market.

Despite always obtaining successful results, this company was not settled and decided to seek out new opportunities that would increase its competitive advantage. The GAMMA hotel saw internationalization as a good opportunity to increase its average annual occupancy rate and to reaffirm itself in the market. This situation was what led the company to choose its strategy, which includes not only the strategic restructuring and physical remodeling of the hotel but also its internationalization process. Therefore, the hotel applied to the Portugal 2020 Project in order to acquire financial support for participating in business fairs and prospecting trips. With the participation in these export promotion programs, they expect not only to reach new markets but also to create new relationships and consequently achieve success in their internationalization process.

GAMMA was proactively motivated to start its export activities, which typically leads to a greater performance among SMEs and, as part of the hotel industry, this company's internationalization process was clearly based on inward activities.

One can affirm that the hotel's restructuring along with the use of export promotion programs, such as trade fairs, was essential for the company to successfully embrace inward internationalization.

GAMMA is the first hotel in the São Pedro do Sul area to have so many partnerships and to offer a wide range of activities to its customers – from sports and adventure activities to rural experiences. Thus, it changes and increases its offer, modifying the idea that São Pedro do Sul is only a place for SPA tourism and trying to make the public associate this tourist destination with adventure, nature and youth. GAMMA considers that the change of the company's image in the mind of the consumer, after all its remodeling and internationalization process, may take some time. In other words, the hotel expects to achieve positive results only in the long term – five or six years.

It is also important to mention the role that the UPPSALA and Networks models play in the GAMMA's internationalization process. The UPPSALA model can be used to explain how the Hotel behaved to gather a gradual and sequential knowledge of the international markets it seeks to achieve. The Hotel is starting to internationalize to countries with less psychic distance such as Spain, France and the UK. The fact that these countries have close cultural aspects to Portugal helps GAMMA to acquire knowledge and experience in international markets investing and allocating resources that will be needed once they decide to internationalize to other countries.

Furthermore, being a family-based business allowed the hotel to build, from the start, a network of contacts only through word of mouth. However, it was important for the company to build new partnerships and relationships with suppliers, competitors or other institutions involved in the business environment, especially abroad, in order to increase their international presence.

We cannot fail to highlight GAMMA's efforts to be the first hotel in the area to internationalize and to innovate a large part of its processes in order to create more lasting international connections. However, during this process, GAMMA should pay careful attention to the problems they may face in terms of positioning, financial, and linguistic barriers.

REFERENCES

Andreu, R., Claver, E., Quer, D., & Rienda, L. (2020). Family ownership and Spanish hotel chains: An analysis of their expansion through internationalization. *Current Issues in Tourism*. Advance online publication. doi:10.1080/13683500.2019.1620186

Ayob, A., & Freixanet, J. (2014). Insights into public export promotion programs in an emerging economy: The case of Malaysian SMEs. *Evaluation and Program Planning*, *46*, 38–46. doi:10.1016/j.evalprogplan.2014.05.005 PMID:24907593

Carrasqueira, H., Garcia, C., & Carrasqueira, M. (2018). A internacionalização da hotelaria portuguesa para os mercados emergentes. *Revista Investigaciones Turísticas*, *15*(15), 34–48. doi:10.14198/INTURI2018.15.02

Chetty, S. (1996). The case study method for research in small- and medium-sized firms. *International Small Business Journal*, *15*(l), 73–85. doi:10.1177/0266242696151005

Chetty, S., & Campbell-Hunt, C. (2003). Paths to internationalisation among small to medium-sized firms: A global versus regional approach. *European Journal of Marketing*, *37*(5/6), 796–820. doi:10.1108/03090560310465152

D'Angelo, A. (2012). Innovation and export performance: A study of Italian high-tech SMEs. *The Journal of Management and Governance*, *16*(3), 393–423. doi:10.100710997-010-9157-y

de Correia, R., Lengler, J., & Mohsin, A. (2019). Entrepreneurial approaches to the internationalisation of Portugal's hotel industry. *International Journal of Contemporary Hospitality Management*, *31*(3), 1141–1165. doi:10.1108/IJCHM-09-2017-0567

Durão, V., & Moreira, A. C. (2019). Critical and inhibiting success factors in inter-organizational networks: A case study. In S. Teixeira & J. Ferreira (Eds.), *Multilevel Approach to Competitiveness in the Global Tourism Industry* (pp. 63–86). IGI Global. doi:10.4018/978-1-7998-0365-2.ch005

Eisenhardt, K. M. (1989). Building theories from case study research. *Academy of Management Review*, *14*(4), 532–550. doi:10.5465/amr.1989.4308385

Fernandes, L., Simões, D., Pereira, C., & Moreira, A. C. (2019). Challenges of the internationalization strategy of a technology-based international new venture. In N. Teixeira, T. Costa, & I. Lisboa (Eds.), *Handbook of Research on Entrepreneurship, Innovation, and Internalization* (pp. 467–489). IGI Global. doi:10.4018/978-1-5225-8479-7.ch018

Francioni, B., Pagano, A., & Castellani, D. (2016). Drivers of SMEs' exporting activity: A review and a research agenda. *Multinational Business Review*, *24*(3), 194–215. doi:10.1108/MBR-06-2016-0023

Francis, J., & Collins-Dodd, C. (2004). Impact of export promotion programs on firm competencies, strategies and performance: The case of Canadian high-technology SMEs June. *International Marketing Review*, *21*(4/5), 474–495. doi:10.1108/02651330410547153

Freixanet, J. (2012). Export promotion programs: Their impact on companies' internationalization performance and competitiveness. *International Business Review, 21*(6), 1065–1086. doi:10.1016/j.ibusrev.2011.12.003

Frishammar, J., & Andersson, S. (2009). The overestimated role of strategic orientations for international performance in smaller firms. *Journal of International Entrepreneurship, 7*(1), 57–77. doi:10.100710843-008-0031-9

Furtado, J., Pereira, A., Pereira, I., & Moreira, A. C. (2019). Does theory really fit real life situations?: A case study on the internationalization process of a technological service-based firm. In N. Teixeira, T. Costa, & I. Lisboa (Eds.), *Handbook of Research on Entrepreneurship, Innovation, and Internationalization* (pp. 419–438). IGI Global. doi:10.4018/978-1-5225-8479-7.ch016

Geldres-Weiss, V. V., & Monreal-Pérez, J. (2018). The effect of export promotion programs on chilean firms' export activity: A longitudinal study on trade shows and trade missions. *Journal of Promotion Management, 24*(5), 660–674. doi:10.1080/10496491.2018.1405519

George, G., Wiklund, J., & Zahra, A. (2005). Ownership and the internationalization of small firms. *Journal of Management, 31*(2), 210–233. doi:10.1177/0149206304271760

Ghauri, P. (2004). Designing and conducting case studies in international business research. In R. Marschan-Piekkari & C. Welch (Eds.), *Handbook of Qualitative Research Methods for International Business* (pp. 109–124). Edward Elgar. doi:10.4337/9781781954331.00019

Haddoud, M. Y., Jones, P., & Newbery, R. (2017). Export promotion programmes and SMEs' performance: Exploring the network promotion role. *Journal of Small Business and Enterprise Development, 24*(1), 68–87. doi:10.1108/JSBED-07-2016-0116

Hilmersson, M. (2014). Small and medium-sized enterprise internationalisation strategy and performance in times of market turbulence. *International Small Business Journal, 32*(4), 386–400. doi:10.1177/0266242613497744

Holmlund, M., Sören, K., & Vanyushyn, V. (2007). SMEs' internationalization and the influence of importing on exporting. *International Small Business Journal, 25*(5), 459–477. doi:10.1177/0266242607080655

Ietto-Gillies, G. (2012). *Transnational corporations: Fragmentation amidst integration*. Routeldge.

Jalali, S. H. (2012). The effect of export promotion programmes on export performance: Evidence from Iranian food manufacturers. *International Journal of Business and Globalisation, 9*(2), 122–133. doi:10.1504/IJBG.2012.048955

Johanson, J., & Mattsson, L. G. (2015). Internationalisation in industrial systems — A network approach. In M. Forsgren, U. Holm, & J. Johanson (Eds.), *Knowledge, Networks and Power* (pp. 111–132). Palgrave Macmillan. doi:10.1057/9781137508829_5

Johanson, J., & Vahlne, J. (2009). The Uppsala internationalization process model revisited: From liability of foreignness to liability of outsidership. *Journal of International Business Studies, 40*(9), 1411–1431. doi:10.1057/jibs.2009.24

Karlsen, T., Silseth, R., Benito, G., & Welch, L. S. (2003). Knowledge, internationalization of the firm, and inward – outward connections. *Industrial Marketing Management, 32*(5), 385–396. doi:10.1016/S0019-8501(03)00012-9

Kastenholz, E., & Almeida, A. (2008). Seasonality in rural tourism – the case of North Portugal. *Tourism Review, 63*(2), 5–15. doi:10.1108/16605370810883905

Leonidou, L. C., Palihawadana, D., & Theodosiou, M. (2011). National export-promotion programs as drivers of organizational resources and capabilities: Effects on strategy. *Journal of International Marketing, 19*(2), 1–29. doi:10.1509/jimk.19.2.1

Li, H., Yi, X., & Cui, G. (2017). Emerging market firms' internationalization: How do firms' inward activities affect their outward activities? *Strategic Management Journal, 38*(13), 2704–2725. doi:10.1002mj.2679

Moreira, A. C. (2009). The evolution of internationalisation: Towards a new theory? *Global Economics and Management Review, 14*(1), 41–59.

Moreira, A. C., & Alves, C. (2016). Commitment-trust dynamics in the internationalization process: A case study of market entry in the Brazilian market. In Information Resources Management Association (Ed.), International business: Concepts, methodologies, tools, and applications, (vol. 3, pp. 1206–1229). Hershey, PA: IGI Global. Doi:10.4018/978-1-4666-9814-7.ch057

Moreira, A. C., Ferreira, L., & Silva, P. (2018). Inward internationalization. Important challenges among SMEs. In R. Pérez-Uribe, C. Salcedo-Pérez, & D. Ocampo-Guzman (Eds.), *Handbook of Research on Intrapreneurship and Organizational Sustainability in SMEs* (pp. 250–275). IGI Global. doi:10.4018/978-1-5225-3543-0.ch012

Moreira, A. C., Ramos, M., Ferraz, L., & Martins, D. (2018). The internationalization process of a born global: A case study of a beverage firm. In O. Rua (Ed.), *Entrepreneurial Orientation and Opportunities for Global Economic Growth* (pp. 46–68). IGI Global. doi:10.4018/978-1-5225-6942-8.ch003

Naidu, G. M., Cavusgil, S., Murthy, B., & Sarkar, M. (1997). An export promotion model for India: Implications for public policy. *International Business Review, 6*(2), 113–125. doi:10.1016/S0969-5931(96)00041-8

Nogueira, R., & Moreira, A. C. (2019). Internationalization and higher education: The case of the University of Aveiro. In C. Machado & P. Davim (Eds.), *Higher Education and the Evolution of Management, Applied Sciences, and Engineering Curricula* (pp. 87–119). IGI Global. doi:10.4018/978-1-5225-7259-6.ch004

Olejnik, E., & Swoboda, B. (2012). SMEs' internationalisation patterns: Descriptives, dynamics and determinants. *International Marketing Review, 29*(5), 466–495. doi:10.1108/02651331211260340

Onkelinx, J., Manolova, T. S., & Edelman, L. F. (2016). Human capital and SME internationalization: Empirical evidence from Belgium. *International Small Business Journal, 34*(6), 818–837. doi:10.1177/0266242615591856

Patton, M. Q. (2015). *Qualitative Evaluation and Research Methods.* Sage.

Piekkari, R., Welch, C., & Paavilainen, E. (2009). The case study as disciplinary convention: Evidence from international business journals. *Organizational Research Methods, 12*(3), 567–589. doi:10.1177/1094428108319905

Portugal 2020. (n.d.). *Portugal 2020.* Retrieved from https://www.portugal2020.pt/Portal2020

Quintela, M. M. (2011). Seeking "energy" vs. pain relief in SPAs in Brazil (Caldas da Imperatriz) and Portugal (Termas da Sulfúrea). *Anthropology & Medicine, 18*(1), 23–35. doi:10.1080/13648470.2010.525875 PMID:21563001

Ribau, C., Moreira, A. C., & Raposo, M. (2015). Internationalisation of the firm theories: A schematic synthesis. *International Journal of Business and Globalisation, 15*(4), 528–554. doi:10.1504/IJBG.2015.072535

Ribau, C., Moreira, A. C., & Raposo, M. (2017). SMEs innovation capabilities and export performance: An entrepreneurial orientation view. *Journal of Business Economics and Management, 18*(5), 920–934. doi:10.3846/16111699.2017.1352534

Ribau, C. P., Moreira, A. C., & Raposo, M. (2018a). SME internationalization research: Mapping the state of the art. *Canadian Journal of Administrative Sciences, 35*(2), 280–303. doi:10.1002/cjas.1419

Ribau, C. P., Moreira, A. C., & Raposo, M. (2018b). Categorising the internationalisation of SMEs with social network analysis. *International Journal of Entrepreneurship and Small Business, 35*(1), 57–80. doi:10.1504/IJESB.2018.094264

Ribau, C. P., Moreira, A. C., & Raposo, M. (2019). Multidyadic relationships: A multi-stage perspective. *Global Business and Economics Review, 21*(6), 732–755. doi:10.1504/GBER.2019.102553

Rundh, B. (2007). International marketing behaviour amongst exporting firms. *European Journal of Marketing, 41*(1/2), 181–198. doi:10.1108/03090560710718175

Seringhaus, F. H., & Rosson, P. J. (1994). International trade fairs and foreign market involvement: Review and research direction. *International Business Review, 3*(3), 311–329. doi:10.1016/0969-5931(94)90008-6

Silva, L. (2007). A procura do turismo em espaço rural. *Etnográfica (Lisboa), 11*(1), 141–163. Advance online publication. doi:10.4000/etnografica.1896

Silva, P., & Moreira, A. C. (2019). Subsidiary survival: A case study from the Portuguese electronics industry. *Review of International Business and Strategy, 29*(3), 226–252. doi:10.1108/RIBS-10-2018-0094

Sin, L., Tse, A., Chan, H., Heung, V., & Yim, F. (2006). The effects of relationship marketing orientation on business performance in the hotel industry. *Journal of Hospitality & Tourism Research (Washington, D.C.), 30*(4), 407–426. doi:10.1177/1096348006287863

Turunen, H., & Nummela, N. (2017). Internationalisation at home: The internationalisation of location-bound service SMEs. *Journal of International Entrepreneurship, 15*(1), 36–54. doi:10.100710843-016-0167-y

Vissak, T., & Francioni, B. (2013). Serial nonlinear internationalization in practice: A case study. *International Business Review, 22*(6), 951–962. doi:10.1016/j.ibusrev.2013.01.010

Voss, C., Tsikriktsis, N., & Frohlich, M. (2002). Case research in operations management. *International Journal of Operations & Production Management*, *22*(2), 195–219. doi:10.1108/01443570210414329

Welch, C. L., & Welch, L. S. (2009). Re-internationalisation: Exploration and conceptualization. *International Business Review*, *18*(6), 567–577. doi:10.1016/j.ibusrev.2009.07.003

Westhead, P., Ucbasaran, D., & Binks, M. (2004). Internationalisation strategies selected by established rural and urban SMEs. *Journal of Small Business and Enterprise Development*, *11*(1), 8–22. doi:10.1108/14626000410519065

Wilkinson, T. J., Brouthers, L. E., Salazar, D., & McNally, M. (2009). The strategic impact of international trade shows and trade missions for entrepreneurial firms. *Journal for Global Business Advancement*, *2*(3), 207–220. doi:10.1504/JGBA.2009.028701

Yin, R. (2008). *Case Study Research: Design and Methods*. SAGE.

ADDITIONAL READING

Moreira, A. C., Silva, P., Mota, J. H., & Gadim, H. (2019). De-internationalization of SMEs: A Case Study. In A. C. Moreira & P. Silva (Eds.), *Handbook of Research on Corporate Restructuring and Globalization* (pp. 143–169). IGI Global., doi:10.4018/978-1-5225-8906-8.ch007

Mota, J. H. & Moreira, A. C. (2017). Determinants of the capital structure of Portuguese firms with investments in Angola. *South African Journal of Economic and Management Sciences, 20*(1), a885. doi: . v20i1.885 doi:10.4102ajems

Ribau, C. P., Moreira, A. C., & Raposo, M. (2017). Export performance and the internationalisation of SMEs. *International Journal of Entrepreneurship and Small Business*, *30*(2), 214–240. doi:10.1504/IJESB.2017.081438

Ribau, C. P., Moreira, A. C., & Raposo, M. (2018). Internacionalização de PME no Continente Americano: Revisão da Literatura. *Innovar (Universidad Nacional de Colombia)*, *28*(67), 59–73. doi:10.15446/innovar.v28n67.68613

Ribau, C. P., Moreira, A. C., & Raposo, M. (2019). The role of exploitative and exploratory innovation in export performance: An analysis of plastics industry SMEs. *European Journal of International Management*, *13*(2), 224–246. doi:10.1504/EJIM.2019.098149

KEY TERMS AND DEFINITIONS

Case Study: It is a qualitative methodology, normally used in social sciences, that seeks to interpret a reality through a particular perspective. It is normally used to answer questions like "how" and "why." It is commonly used to addresses constructivist research processes.

Internationalization: It is normally associated with a strategy carried out by firms that decide to operate in foreign markets. It involves the implementation of goods and services that can be easily adapted and adopted in different countries. It could involve business to consumer activities, as well as business to business activities. It may involve cross border transactions of goods, services, or resources between two or more firms or organizations that belong to two different countries, as well as foreign direct investment.

Inward Internationalization: Inward internationalization activities pertain to internationalization activities in which the firm is the buyer in a business exchange situation. It normally involves indirect imports, direct imports, purchasing office overseas, and license in Portugal for overseas firms.

Network-Based Approach: It based on the industrial networks theory, which states that firms evolve on the basis of established relationships. It considers the companies' internationalization process through their integration into networks and relationships. Following this perspective, the internationalization process occurs in interactive environments where companies of a well-established network of companies have an opportunity to develop new relationships that give them access to broader markets in other countries.

Outward Internationalization: Outward internationalization activities pertain to internationalization activities in which the firm is the seller in a business exchange situation. It normally involves indirect exports, direct exports, sales branch overseas, license overseas, and production activities overseas.

Uppsala Model: It has been one of the most discussed dynamic theories in Nordic School and International Business Studies. It explains the process of internationalization of companies. It explains how organizations learn and the impact of learning on the companies' international expansion. This theory defends that the companies' internationalization process is carried out in stages, from non-regular exports to the establishment of companies abroad.

Chapter 2
An International and Socially Responsible SME Based on Tailored Innovative Products:
empakando From El Salvador

Antonia Mercedes García-Cabrera
Universidad de Las Palmas de Gran Canaria, Spain

María Gracia García-Soto
Universidad de Las Palmas de Gran Canaria, Spain

Deybbi Cuéllar-Molina
Universidad de Las Palmas de Gran Canaria, Spain

EXECUTIVE SUMMARY

In view of the many studies carried out on multinational firms and, to a lesser degree, the internationalization of SMEs based on developed countries, it is surprising to find that so little attention is being paid to the internationalization process of SMEs based on developing countries. There is scarce evidence and knowledge available on the circumstances underlying these processes or the decisions made to successfully address internationalization. The case of the company Empakando, founded in the developing country of El Salvador in 2000 and successfully internationalized toward countries in Central America, allows the authors to make a contribution to this field. Based on the company's experience, the authors addressed a range of important aspects to understand this phenomena: (1) the internationalization process and the entry modes chosen and (2) two key elements in gaining access to the resources and connections needed to facilitate internationalization, that is, the commitment to corporate social responsibility (internal factor) and the support of export promotion programmes (external factor).

DOI: 10.4018/978-1-7998-4387-0.ch002

THEORETICAL BASIS FOR THE STUDY

Literature on international business has prioritized the study of large international companies rather than SMEs. Furthermore, studies on SMEs have primarily focused on companies based in developed countries (García-Cabrera, García-Soto, & Durán-Herrera, 2016). Consequently, the internationalization process of SMEs settled in developing and emerging countries has scarcely been analyzed (Zahra, Newey, & Li, 2014), and the evidence available is not conclusive. For instance, there is consensus over these economies being characterized by the weakness and instability of their institutional frameworks, and some authors have determined that such weakness hampers the international performance of SMEs (Latin-American SMEs, for example). Conversely, other authors suggest that, so as to reduce their exposure to these unstable institutional environments, SMEs often put increasing emphasis on their international expansion (Gil-Barragan, Belso-Martínez, & Mas-Verdú, 2020), consequently improving their internationalization.

The absence of studies on this issue limits our understanding of these processes (e.g. disadvantages associated with socioeconomic and institutional conditions of the country of origin, property advantages facilitating the company's internationalization), decisions made around the internationalization process (e.g. adopting an international strategy, choosing the target country and the entry mode), and the consequences of such decisions.

In an attempt to bridge the knowledge gap somewhat, this work studies a number of key topics on a company's internationalization process. These key elements will be empirically discussed for an SME based in a developing economy. The study addresses the stages of the internationalization process and its main characteristics (e.g. availability of resources for the company, choosing the target country, entry modes, and so on). In addition, two factors that may contribute to having access to the necessary information, resources and connections to facilitate the SME's internationalization are analyzed. From a company-based perspective, the commitment to corporate social responsibility and its impact on the access to valuable resources for international expansion (e.g. qualified human resources, reputation, information) are studied. Then, from an external perspective, export promotion programs available in the country are analyzed, with a particular emphasis on trade shows and commercial missions.

The Internationalization Process and the Entry Modes Chosen by the SME

Among the key variables that have been traditionally identified as key factors determining companies' international expansion, the literature highlights having property advantages (Cheng & Yu, 2008), local geographical resources (e.g. natural resources in the country, weather, geographic location) (Gilmore, O'Donnell, Carson, & Cummins, 2003), the institutional framework's level of development (e.g. property rights, corruption) (Demirbag, Tatoglu, & Glaister, 2009), and economic openness (incoming direct investments, imports) (Luo & Tung, 2007). When analyzing the international expansion of companies based in developing and emerging economies, there has been significant criticism around the emphasis that the literature has placed on property advantages. The literature seems to ignore the difficulties that these companies are faced with when developing property assets (Yan, Zhu, Fan, & Kalfadellis, 2018). In addition, Valliere and Peterson (2009) found that incoming direct investment flows have no impact on developing economies' growth. It can be partly explained by barriers such as local companies' limited capacity to absorb the knowledge transferred by foreign multinationals (Cantwell, Dunning, & Lundan, 2010). The spillover effect caused by multinationals' investments has been proven to only materialize when these acquire a shareholding in local companies (Damijan, Knell, Majcen, & Rojec, 2003). But such practices only cover a limited number of SMEs in developing economies. Consequently, Valliere and Peterson (2009) suggested that, in order to understand internationalization for SMEs based in developing economies, future research should explore variables which are different from those used in developed economies.

As such, it is important to consider the challenge that international expansion poses for SMEs in general. Among other reasons, this is due to their limited resources (Dimitratos, Amorós, Etchebarne, & Felzensztein, 2014), lack of knowledge in international markets (Fletcher & Harris 2012), risk aversion (Laufs & Schwens, 2014) and the difficulties involved in accessing international networks (Johanson & Vahlne, 2009). These barriers increase when the SME comes from a developing country. Taking these difficulties into account, many SMEs, as well as larger-sized companies, decide to internationalize gradually, on a step-by-step basis.

The Uppsala model proposed by Johanson and Vahlne (1977) analyzes this process based on the company's accumulated expertise, increasing resources and incremental, sequential learning process. According to the model, after the company is established, it provides a range of products in the local market to start the business. Only after the company has established itself in the local market does it decide to address its international expansion (Gabrielsson, Kirpalani, Dimitratos, Solberg, & Zucchella, 2008).

However, there are several important factors influencing the decision around which markets the company should expand to (Johanson & Wiedersheim-Paul, 1975), for example, the distance between the company's country of origin and the target countries for internationalization. Ghemawat (2001) suggests distance has four aspects: (1) geographic (e.g. physical distance between countries, lack of access); (2) economic (e.g. differences in consumers' rents); (3) political (e.g. institutional differences); and (4) cultural (e.g. language differences, social values). Taking into account the postulates of the gradual Uppsala model, companies initially set up their external activities in countries in close geographical proximity (i.e. countries that are similar to the country of origin), and then expand towards more distant countries (Johanson & Vahlne, 1977; Johanson & Wiedersheim-Paul, 1975). In this way, they can avoid uncertainty, costs and mistakes (Welch & Loustarinen, 1993).

Johanson and Wiedersheim-Paul (1975) structured the internationalization process into four stages, taking into consideration the company's increasing commitment of resources and its accumulation of experience in the international market: (1) non-regular (sporadic) export activities where the company does not commit resources to the host market and lacks any direct and regular information flows to and from such a host market; (2) export activities through independent intermediaries (agents), where the company assumes a certain degree of commitment in the host market and, through the agent, gains access to an indirect channel to receive regular information about market characteristics; (3) establishment in foreign countries by means of sales subsidiaries, where the company commits economic resources and becomes part of a controlled and direct information channel, enabling access to information flows from the market to the company; and (4) establishment in foreign countries by means of production subsidiaries whereby the company commits a large number of resources abroad. At each stage of the internationalization process, the company accumulates resources and experience before progressing to the next stage. As such, at each stage of the process, it increases its knowledge of international markets and foreign activity management. At the same time, the company's increasing commitment at each stage (i.e. investing its own resources) involves greater levels of activity control and risk, as well as diminishing flexibility (Knight & Cavusgil, 2004; Rialp, 1999).

Based on the above model, Cerviño, Arteaga and Fernández (2017) described the different modes of entry available for international expansion. These are as follows, in order of the increasing resource commitment taken by companies:

1. Indirect export. The exporting company hires an intermediary who sells its products to retail companies or the end consumer abroad. The intermediary is responsible for managing the internationalization process, in the form of a sales representative or distributor, among others.
2. Export through cooperation agreements. The company shares the investment, duties and profits of the export activity with its partners. These agreements include licenses, franchises or joint ventures, among others.
3. Direct export. The company manages the internationalization process on its own, selling its products abroad via the Internet, directly to retail companies or with the help of its own sales team.
4. Establishment abroad. The company commits financial resources abroad to manage the sale of its products, for instance, starting up a commercial delegation, a sales subsidiary or even its own production facilities.

For SMEs, exports are the most frequently used mode of entry (Wright, Westhead & Ucbasaran, 2007). This is because exports are faster (Wright et al, 2007), and the effort required is gradual, as they adapt to the increasing demand the company achieves in the international market (Rialp, 1999). Overall, exports require less investment of resources (financial resources and knowledge), which SMEs usually lack (Dimitratos et al, 2014; Fletcher & Harris, 2012). As such, the modes of entry which involve establishing subsidiaries abroad might not be appropriate for all SMEs undergoing internationalization (Wright et al, 2007), given that they require greater investment and increased risk (Agarwal & Ramaswami, 1992). Therefore, choosing the most appropriate mode of entry is one of the most important decisions an SME must make (Kruesi, Hemmington, & Kim, 2018). In order to make informed decisions, the company needs to thoroughly evaluate its resources, including its knowledge and capabilities (Elbanna, Hsieh, & Child, 2020).

Using Corporate Social Responsibility to Support the Internationalization Process

If a company aims to achieve long-term success, that final goal may converge with the creation of shared value. Shared value allows a company's interests to match society's interests in general. Specifically, generating shared value implies that the company creates the financial value it needs to survive and to meet its owners' interests, whilst at the same time generating social value (Porter & Kramer, 2006). According to Grant (2016), reconciling both objectives is possible. Firstly, if the company's profit converges with society's interests as a whole, the company's profit-seeking actions become oriented towards the common good. Secondly, the benefits earned by businesspeople and stakeholders depend on the company's long-term profit, so setting up business goals within this time frame would make it easier to create shared value.

In economic and strategic terms, having a goal of shared value creation, and the socially responsible behavior related to it, are relevant for the company (Uzhegova, Torkkeli, & Saarenketo, 2019). For example, it contributes to guaranteeing the necessary sustainability of the ecosystem in which the company must thrive, to build a positive reputation amongst consumers and other stakeholders, or to facilitate the obtaining of authorizations for the operation of a particular business activity (Porter and Kramer, 2006). From a financial standpoint, the company's socially responsible behavior is also associated with diminishing costs and greater efficacy (Uzhegova et al, 2019), as well as increasing activities in international markets (Torkkeli, Saarenketo, Salojärvi, & Sainio, 2017).

SMEs may be motivated to adopt the philosophy of social responsibility by the following reasons: (1) their relationships with different stakeholders within the networks they participate in; (2) the tough circumstances of the environment they operate in; and (3) the enterprise's characteristics (Ayuso & Navarrete-Báez, 2018; Uzhegova et al, 2019). These SME motivating factors are relevant to our case study because, depending on the type of corporate social responsibility involved, each can create different valuable utilities for their international operations. These potential connections will be analyzed as follows:

Firstly, stakeholders include a wide range of collectives, e.g. employees, investors, local communities, NGOs, government institutions, industry associations or consumers (Yang & Rivers, 2009). The interaction between the company and these groups, within the business or social networks they participate in, is based on their shared notion of what is valuable. As such, each network's participants are expected to collaborate with the shared objective of creating this value.

In this context, social responsibility allows the SME to build and preserve the trust of these networks' members, whilst also making it easier to develop their intangible assets such as reputation and legitimacy (Uzhegova et al, 2019). For instance, if the company carries out corporate social activities in the networks it has established with its clients or consumer associations, the company can then share their expertise with them, in the context of a network collaboration. Thus, it becomes easier to gain the knowledge necessary to support the company's international expansion (Torkkeli et al, 2017), such as expertise related to product improvement and best market practices.

Secondly, social responsibility may be motivated by the circumstances or deficiencies of the company's environment (Uzhegova et al, 2019). It reflects the company's willingness to meet the needs of a wider audience, either in the immediate local community or at a national level, taking into account (particularly given aim of this study) the audiences in the country of origin and the target country that the company will expand to (Torkkeli et al, 2017).

From this point of view, not only does social responsibility allow the company to build stronger relationships with other local actors, but it also attracts resources (Spence, 1999), such as valuable human resources, therefore facilitating the internationalization of its operations. Additionally, if socially responsible practices are implemented in the countries that the SME wishes to expand to, it is more easily able to gain a deep insight into the host local culture. This contributes to building brand reputation and legitimacy and facilitates the company's integration in the target markets (Jahdi & Acikdilli, 2009).

Thirdly, with regard to the entrepreneurs themselves, variables such as personality, business orientation, and ethical and moral values (Ayuso & Navarrete-Báez, 2018; Porter & Kramen, 2006; Uzhegova et al, 2019) have been identified as elements which promote the adoption of corporate social responsibility, which facilitates successful internationalization. For instance, a greater entrepreneurial orientation leads businesspeople to establish continuous innovation strategies. Combined with entrepreneurs' ethical values and so the will to minimize the ecological footprint of the company and its products, this can give rise to new, highly competitive ecological products in international markets (Torkkeli et al, 2017). In fact, the SME's capacity for innovation has been identified as an essential factor both for a successful international expansion and the development of corporate social responsibility practices (Ayuso & Navarrete-Báez, 2018).

Export Promotion Programs and International Trade Shows to Support the Internationalization of SMEs in Developing Countries

When companies want to begin exporting, the steps they need to take are not always easy to carry out, for instance, collecting information on the conditions of entry in foreign markets, or seeking reliable commercial partners. SMEs are undoubtedly more sensitive to these processes (Comi & Resmini, 2019). Given both these needs and the government's interest in facilitating the company's foreign operations as a contribution to their country's economic development, Export Promotion Programs (EPP) are developed. EPPs are an institutional tool used by governments to stimulate exports and enhance the company's performance when exporting (Geldres-Weiss, Etchebarne, & Bustos, 2011; Leonidou, Samiee, & Geldres, 2015).

EPPs bring together a large number of very diverse activities, including training sessions on export procedures, providing information to companies on market opportunities, holding meetings with potential clients, providing advice on the different stages of the export process, organizing commercial missions abroad, or international trade shows (Lederman, Olarreaga, & Payton, 2010). Having EPPs in countries is important as companies find that participating in these programs has a positive effect on their performance in international markets, such as the financial gains made from exports (Geldres-Weiss & Monreal-Pérez, 2018).

Research has recognized the positive effects that participating in EPPs has on SMEs' international performance. Firstly, EPPs allow SMEs to overcome the export barriers they are usually faced with due to their size (Kalafsky, 2017), e.g. limited financial resources, lack of expertise, insufficient connections. Secondly, such programs help SMEs achieve competitive advantages and improve export performance (Coudounaris, 2018). The positive effect of EPPs on SMEs' international performance is significant even when the potential impact of other financial aids or grants is considered (Comi & Resmini, 2019).

The positive influence of EPPs on SMEs' international operations is derived from a number of factors. For instance, within promotion programs, it is common for export promotion agencies to hold meetings with companies participating in the programs (Haddoud, Jones, & Newbery, 2017). In this way, SMEs become members of a "club" of export companies or firms intending to export. They therefore have the opportunity to develop networks with other companies, have access to foreign networks by establishing connections within the "club", and share expertise and information on foreign markets with other "club members."

Among the several actions and activities associated with EPPs, commercial missions and international trade shows are particularly important. Both allow SMEs to acquire direct expertise (Geldres-Weiss & Monreal-Pérez, 2018; Kalafsky, 2017), in addition to indirect knowledge derived from access to commercial reports, lessons learned by others, etc. According to the Uppsala model, expertise represents a great source of support when entering international markets.

1. Commercial missions consist of scheduled visits to focus countries, aimed at building connections that will go on to support the development of international operations. Such missions help companies connect to markets in these focus countries and support them in conducting field missions to gain a greater insight into the potential operating context. From this point of view, EPPs provide relevant tools for export-oriented SMEs to obtain direct information, enabling them to evaluate the market's suitability for their products. Such programs also provide companies with potentially useful connections who can support the introduction and distribution of their products in new markets.

These commercial missions are also beneficial for SMEs with greater experience as exporters. Participating in the programs provides experienced companies with an opportunity to maintain and strengthen their relationships with their existing local clients (Spence, 2003). Additionally, for exporting companies, missions also represent a chance to survey new markets and countries.

2. Secondly, international trade shows are the perfect stage for SMEs that are already exporting or have the intention to export, to present their products to potential clients based in other markets. As such, these trade shows are an important marketing tool (Evers & Knight, 2008; Geldres-Weiss & Monreal-Pérez, 2018). They also offer companies the chance to form direct connections with potential foreign buyers, carry out negotiations and make commercial agreements (Haddoud et al, 2017). In the case of a company's existing markets, trade shows are also useful as a way of increasing exports (Geldres-Weiss & Monreal-Pérez, 2018).

The previous literature provides evidence on the benefits that participating in international trade shows have on SME internationalization. The literature states that by participating in trade shows, SMEs can generate interest in their products from potential clients, and consequently boost their international performance (Osei, Forkuoh, Shao, & Osei, 2016). These benefits are even more evident in the case of SMEs based in developing countries with less experience in international markets (Martincus & Carballo, 2010). Despite the benefits, there are only a few SMEs participating in international trade shows in these countries, because there are fewer events, the associated costs with attending international events are high, and because companies are not aware of the opportunities and benefits that trade shows offer them (Osei et al, 2016).

Given the evidence supporting the benefits of EPPs, and in an attempt to help SMEs to overcome specific challenges they are faced with when entering international markets, governments are increasingly trying to expand the offer of such markets (Pickernell, Jones, Thompson, & Packham, 2016). When developing these policies, authorities should be aware that the benefits of EPPs on companies' international performance are not direct. The quality of the companies' resources and capabilities to operate at an international level are also important determinants (Leonidou, Palihawadana, & Theodosiou, 2011). It is also dependent on the industry in which the company operates, and on its experience as an exporter. EPPs are likely to provide fewer opportunities for international expansion to companies which are already well-established in foreign markets (Geldres-Weiss & Monreal-Pérez, 2018). In this sense, the suggestions made by Comi and Resmini (2019) are increasingly relevant, as there is a need for new studies which allow researchers to better understand the operation and mechanisms underlying the effects of EPPs on companies' international performance.

THE CASE: EVIDENCE FROM THE SME EMPAKANDO IN THE DEVELOPING COUNTRY OF EL SALVADOR

The SME *empakando* produces and sells tailored products to small, medium, and large international firms in El Salvador, as well as to firms located in other countries in Central America, among them Guatemala, Honduras, Nicaragua, Costa Rica, and Panama. This company was founded in 2000 and currently is a leader in the design and manufacture of semiautomatic and automatic machines for filling, dosing, labeling, and packaging, and conveyor belts, for the food, cosmetic, chemical, and pharmaceutical industries.

The Stage: The Developing Country of El Salvador

El Salvador is a democratic, presidential republic country located in Central America. The country has a surface of 21,040 km^2 divided into 14 municipalities. According to CEPALSTAT (2019), as of 2019, it had a population of 6,654,000 inhabitants, with a resulting population density of 316 inhabitants per km^2. When compared with other countries in Central America (Belize, Costa Rica, Guatemala, Honduras, Nicaragua, and Panama), it is one of the smallest countries in terms of surface, while also being the densest in terms of population. A high proportion of people live in an urban area (72.4%) with an average annual growth rate of 1.37 per 100 inhabitants from 2015 to 2020 (DIGESTYC, 2020). In El Salvador highlights are coffee plantations and a mangrove ecosystem on the coast (The World Bank in El Salvador, 2019).

The country's productive industry consists mostly of SMEs, being the main contributors for the domestic economy, which suffers low economic growth rates (CEPALSTAT, 2019). E.g. its GDP decreased from 2.58% to 2.09% between 2016 and 2018. Additionally, its yearly GDP was €22,064,000, and its per capita GDP €3,321, which is lower than the average in Central America. In particular, the composition of its GDP in 2018 points to an economy based on the manufacturing industry that went from €860,060 in 2017 to €897,190 in 2018, which represented 18.17% of the gross value added in the latter year. The fiscal collection, which is inefficient, leads the country to resort to indebtedness to complete many of its investment programs (The World Bank in El Salvador, 2019).

With regard to the external sector, total exports rose 2.5% and total imports rose 10.7% in 2018 compared to 2017. According to the Central Reserve Bank of El Salvador (2020), the main exports are textile goods (€200.9 million) and food products (€93.98 million), followed by rubber and plastic items (€28.85 million). Industry represents 18.2% of the country's exports, according to data from the third quarter of 2018 (PROESA, 2019a). In particular, the sub-sector of machinery and mechanical devices accounts for 5% of the country's total exports (elsalvadortrade.com.sv). The National Directory of Exporting Companies (PROESA, 2019a) includes 373 companies registered in total in 2019, of which only 7 companies (1.88%) belong to the sub-sector of machinery and mechanical devices, including *empakando*. The country's principal trading partners for exports are the USA, as well as other neighboring countries in the region such as Honduras, Guatemala, Nicaragua, and Costa Rica; but El Salvador has signed commercial agreements with 44 countries in America, Europe and Asia (PROESA, 2019a).

As for social indicators, the country ranked 124 out of 189 countries on the Human Development Index (HDI) in 2018. With a score of 0.667, it is placed among the countries with medium human development levels, along with other Central American countries such as Guatemala, Nicaragua, and Honduras, but El Salvador presents higher levels than the latter. Taking into account that it had an HDI of 0.674 in 2017, the situation in El Salvador has deteriorated slightly in the last year. On the other hand, the Gini coefficient, which measures the inequality of income distribution, was 0.398 in 2017 and 0.389 in 2018. Given that a Gini coefficient near 0 suggests income and consumption are distributed equitably among the population, El Salvador is becoming a more equitable country. If compared to other Central American countries, El Salvador ranks among the least inequitable countries along with Nicaragua (Gini=0.432), whereas coefficients than 0.44 can be found in the rest of the countries. Despite that, 34.5% of the population live in poverty, and 7.6% in extreme poverty, compared to 29.6% on average in the region (The World Bank in El Salvador, 2019). Additionally, the level of illiteracy among people older than 10 is 10.1%, and the level of school attendance for people older than 18 is only 21.3%, according to household survey data collected by the Ministry of Economy of El Salvador (2018). With regard to the labor market and taking into account the urban employed population, 56.5% of people were salaried workers for hire or reward in 2018, 28.2% are self-employed workers, and only 4.5% are employers.

Corruption, and crime and violence in El Salvador are two of the most important factors influencing the country's growth and job creation, which has led to high emigration levels among the population (World Bank in El Salvador, 2019). In this sense, 1.600.739 people have emigrated from El Salvador (24.1% of the population), a medium-high level according to the emigration raking (Expansión, 2019).

However, being a developing economy with so weak and unstable institutional framework, the country's characteristics are challenging for any firm, particularly new and small ventures, or those trying to sell products abroad. For example, some of El Salvador's attributes may harm firms' credibility at the beginning of its internationalization process when they are yet unknown firms in the international markets, so becoming an obstacle. The distrust towards the country by customers abroad extend to firms for being founded and located in El Salvador. It also happens to *empakando*, as detailed below.

Organization Background: Origins of *empakando* and Its Entrepreneurial Team

The company *empakando* was founded by Regina Olmedo, from El Salvador, and Nick Bienz from Switzerland. When they got married, she moved to Switzerland to live with him. She joined the local labor market on a "hire or reward" basis. However, Regina was faced with the reality that neither the country nor her job made her happy. She dreamt of returning to her beloved homeland, El Salvador. In addition, coming from a long line of entrepreneurs, Regina also wanted to set up her own business.

The couple decided to give it a try and moved to El Salvador. They had a clear idea in mind——they wanted to found their own company, which would be different from and hold no ties to the business that Regina's parents ran at that time. Her family's company sold scales and balances to differently-sized businesses from a wide range of industries and was a leading company in the field in El Salvador. However, they had not formed a clear business concept yet, so they took a year to assess their options before deciding on the focus of their future. During that year, they traveled, visiting different trade shows in countries such as Colombia, the Netherlands, and so on. They even thought about importing products that had not been sold in El Salvador yet.

Regina and Nick had saved up money to set up a business, but it was not enough to become manufacturers and build industrial facilities that were suited for production. For this reason, their first business activity revolved around importing water purification filters from Switzerland and distributing them in El Salvador. This first attempt was a complete failure, even though they had bet on the Katadyn brand, one of the leading companies in the market. After this mishap, Regina and Nick carried on looking for business opportunities until in one of the trade shows they used to attend (specifically in Colombia) the field of packaging machinery caught their attention. Thus they found their second business opportunity. They would buy these machines and start up a company to provide semi-automated packaging services to industrial clients focused on wholesale distribution in El Salvador.

Their idea was to buy innovative machines fitted to satisfy their clients' packaging needs based on their manufacturing operations, and it was hugely successful!

After giving shape to their idea, Regina and Nick started the company in 2000 (Figure 1), based on two central pillars: (1) the target market and client acquisition, and (2) providing high-quality services adapted to the clients' needs. The venture provided both the machinery that the industrial client needed and the staff to operate the machines and manage the entire packaging process. The clients achieved faster packaging compared to traditional processes. Regina remembers the time, when they had no employees yet, and she, herself, used to visit prospective clients. Service quality was an essential factor for new venture's strategy. In their view, high service quality meant rigor in process development, punctuality when meeting commitments with clients, and working with responsible staff. For example, the company used to teach and explain the processes to *empakando*'s staff, who would then apply them at the clients' facilities. According to Regina and Nick, good image in the clients' eyes depended on it.

Figure 1. The entrepreneurs: Nick Bienz and Regina Olmedo

As a result of this initial strategy, *empakando* started working with large clients, leading companies in the Salvadoran market. When negotiating with these companies, Regina noticed that their managers developed a wrong idea about *empakando*. They started believing that *empakando* was a big company with large production facilities when it only had a 4-m^2 room where Nick and Regina worked. In any event, those important clients decided to hire *empakando*'s services, and little by little, by promoting client trust in their company, other businesses started contacting Regina and Nick, too. As a result, in only a year *empakando* had become a leading company in the packaging market of El Salvador.

However, the company's first steps were not exactly devoid of problems. The main difficulty was financial. The venture did not have enough economic resources at first, and banks are reluctant to grant loans to recently founded businesses that have no experience and are not well-known. In El Salvador, only a few institutions, such as the Development Bank-Bandesal, are oriented to SMEs and slightly more flexible. This flexibility means they are more willing to grant loans, but only if entrepreneurs are supported by guarantors or mortgage guarantees, which is not always possible.

The entrepreneurs Regina and Nick, however, accepted the challenge to create a successful company. As an entrepreneurial team, they enjoyed a solid trajectory, training, and complementarity. For example, as Regina's parents were entrepreneurs and Nick's parents self-employed, they shared a common background about businesses. However, given the fact that she came from El Salvador and he came from Switzerland, their cultural origins could not be more different. Nick was a mechanical engineer specialized in machinery manufacturing. During the time he lived in Switzerland, he worked at a company that manufactured robots, specifically assigned to the robot design department. Mercedes Benz was included in Nick's client portfolio. So he became experienced designing robots for the German automobile company. On the other hand, Regina specialized in business administration. Having grown up in a family of entrepreneurs, she had high organizational and commercial skills. Therefore, Nick and Regina's educational backgrounds complemented each other.

Thus, they are a couple with an ideal combination of knowledge and abilities——e.g. they have different cultural origins (El Salvador and Switzerland) and different specializations (commercial and technological), which allows them to create valuable synergies. This complementarity of their backgrounds has been the main factor in the success of their business project.

As for their other personality traits, Regina thinks they share several characteristics with other successful business people: "We entrepreneurs have to be stubborn people. We have to be fighters and take risks. It's got to be in your blood." In regards to her and Nick, she highlights their ability to take risks given the characteristics of El Salvador.

Managing a Company in a Developing Country: Challenges Faced by *empakando* in El Salvador

Due to the socioeconomic and institutional characteristics of El Salvador, entrepreneurs are faced with high levels of uncertainty. All the decisions and investments are subject to high levels of risks, so entrepreneurs can never take for granted what the final result will be. Discussing decision-making and the risks assumed by companies in El Salvador, Regina said, "In our country, sometimes you make plans, you devise a perfect strategy, you think this and that will be the results and you believe everything will be fine for you because you have thought out every little detail, but everything is a mess here, and your entire strategic plan might fall apart at the end of the day." As an entrepreneur in the country, she knows that if she makes a bad decision, it will have consequences. That is why she carefully considers the steps she takes, but in the end, she still has to take big risks and keep fighting to achieve success based on her decisions.

Indeed, *empakando* has faced and overcome difficult economic circumstances in the country, problems with clients and employees, problems derived from crime in El Salvador, and so on. That is why Regina believes that, in a country such as El Salvador, entrepreneurs must be able to make the majority of decisions instinctually and take risks, and that this way of doing things is shared by all entrepreneurs who manage to have successful businesses.

But at the same time, starting up a firm is a way to contribute to job creation, wealth and development for the country. This brings satisfaction to entrepreneurs, but there is also a factor of concern and responsibility at play for them. In this sense, Regina said: "When you create a company, many families start depending on you. That is why you need to manage your business very carefully. Setting up a business in El Salvador is a very complex process, but it is a beautiful, very rewarding challenge at the same time. It can bring you a lot of joys but also cause you many, many headaches and difficulties." They are the two sides of the same coin.

Globally considering their 20 years managing *empakando*, Regina and Nick have assimilated that the day-to-day operation of the company is a challenge in itself. But they have accepted such challenge and with their qualities and good practices, they have been able to create a global industrial company. Nick and Regina work at the company as Chief Executive Officer (CEO), and Administrative Manager-Legal Representative, respectively, and they provide high-quality jobs to 18 other Salvadoran people. Despite conditions in El Salvador, Regina and Nick were never less enthusiastic about carrying on with their company: "We are together in this boat and we want to keep growing. We want to keep innovating, diversifying our products and creating more jobs," she says, her voice filled with excitement and conviction.

Preparing the SME for Internationalization: Consolidation in the Local Market and Acquisition of Increasing Resources and Capabilities

From the operations based on the first idea to *empakando*'s current business, Regina and Nicks faced many challenges that required them to make decisions in order to adapt the venture to the competitive context and so survive. Meanwhile, they took advantage of such experiences to increasingly learn about the clients, the products, the local market and the foreign markets due to import activities, as well as to build social and business networks.

Looking at the company's origin, the packaging services that *empakando* focused on were very dynamic and inspiring. The company had to manage a wide range of processes and it was quite a challenge (they had to understand the client's processes, design packaging processes adapted to the client's industrial practices and products, train the staff, organize the provision of services at the client's facilities, and so on). As for the inconveniences, the profit earned from this operation heavily depended on the clients' business volume. Additionally, margins were minimal, only amounting to a few cents. Moreover, *empakando*'s activities were highly stressful. They required a lot of staff to provide the services to the clients punctually, while staff turnover for this type of business in El Salvador (mainly, laborers) is quite high. Another problem that Regina and Nick had to overcome sooner than expected was that many small Salvadoran businesses started imitating *empakando* after noticing their success. Competition appeared quickly, and the tariffs for these services, which were already low, to begin with, experienced an even sharper drop. All of this was taking quite a heavy toll on Regina and Nick.

The name "*empakando*" (Figure 2) led to favorable business alternatives for Regina and Nick. Industrial companies associated it with everything related to filling operations, not merely packaging. For instance, clients contacted Regina and Nick to request services related to sealing and filling machines, and so on, and some even asked if they could buy the machines themselves. Thus, Regina and Nick identified additional business growth opportunities. Selling machinery, in addition to providing packaging services, could be an interesting option for the company!

Figure 2. The logo of empakando

empakando
Maquinaria de empaque

Making a global assessment of the competition and the market, Regina and Nick concluded they had already made great progress. The company had valuable, well-structured processes in place, had earned recognition in the market, and made large investments, mainly in machinery. For these reasons, they decided against lowering their margins more than they had already to address the growing competition in their initial field of operations. This situation, along with the fact that they were addressing other types of demands in the market, led Regina and Nick to gradually move away from packaging services and closer to the market of design, manufacturing processes, and sale of machinery in the same industry.

Initially, Regina and Nick imported sealing machines, packaging materials, and other tools from Taiwan for the industry, but their clients had other insistent ideas: "Look, the truth is that I have these ideas. Don't you know more about sealing machines? I would require something that more closely meets my needs." Nick had acquired extensive experience in Switzerland during the years he worked in a robot manufacturing company, so he accepted the challenge and started designing machines. When he had arrived in El Salvador, he did not imagine he would ever operate with those services, because the Salvadoran market, given its limited development, did not offer many opportunities in the field in 2000. For this reason, Nick could not put his skills and experience to much use.

The company's new course, making use of Nick's abilities, would not only allow *empakando* to benefit from its founder's training but also strengthen Nick's hopes for the company even more. Nick started designing very basic, completely mechanical machines, what the clients demanded most at the time. In 2003 *empakando* built its first machine, a bag-filling tubular machine, which was basic and 100% mechanical as well. From 2005 on, the company took a very important step forward by building semi-automated liquid-filling machines. Up until now in 2020, the company has mainly focused on this. Its core strength has been the design and manufacture of the semi-automated and fully automated packaging and filling machines, in addition to importing other types of machinery that they do not build, from the USA and several Asian countries.

Now, this decision has been based on the same principles that supported Regina and Nick's initial project——paying attention to the target market and client acquisition, and product quality and meeting the clients' needs. This is along with two additional principles that, albeit present from the beginning of Regina and Nick's business, became more and more important as the company progressed: the importance of staff training, and management based on the principles of corporate social responsibility.

These four pillars have been supporting the company's operations up until know and have also offered the basis to successfully carry out its international expansion process.

Target Market and Client Acquisition

When Regina and Nick started their business, they prioritized acquiring the biggest companies set up in El Salvador (e.g., Kellogg, Kraft, Jugos del Monte, Leche de Lactome) as clients. Currently the entrepreneurs aim their offers to very small, small, medium-sized, and large companies, including multinational companies based and operating in El Salvador. While initially Regina and Nick offered them complete packaging services, currently clients demand a wide range of products, although there are some patterns in their requests. Very small businesses mostly require packaging solutions, whereas SMEs want to optimize their resources and operation efficiency, so they usually decide to invest in full-process automation. Concerning industries, Regina and Nick assist companies in the food manufacturing, for instance, nostalgic products such as *pupusas*[1], or typical foods from El Salvador such as *tortillas,* tamales[2], tropical fruits, and so on. All of these companies export large amounts of products to other countries, mainly the USA. Over time, as the company increased its operations, *empakando* expanded its target market incorporating companies from the pharmaceutical, chemical, and cosmetic industries.

Aiming its products and services to industrial clients with export capabilities and facilities has allowed *empakando* to adopt an international view for its operations, as well as knowledge about the procedures and sometimes difficulties involved in these processes. For instance, when *empakando*'s clients want to export products, they must comply with the conditions required by each country of destination. For instance, in 2017 the USA established new standards that foreign food products had to meet to enter the country. However, many export Salvadoran companies that had been selling their products in the USA did not satisfy these requirements. To carry on exporting products to America, these companies had to introduce automation, sanitization, and sterilization processes in their operations. The company *empakando* provided these companies from El Salvador with personalized solutions that allowed them to keep operating in the USA, and at the same time, *empakando* was able to acquire necessary expertise in international processes.

As for client acquisition, *empakando* carries out its marketing activities through two main channels: its website (www.empakando.com) and its sales force. For Regina and Nick, the website is an essential component of the business because it helps the company showcase *empakando*'s brand image. That is why they take care of the website, making sure that it is based on and fully communicates the company's core values, such as professionalism, quality, innovation, and functionality. For instance, in the machinery section, each model that the company sells is accompanied by a PDF file carefully designed as a presentation tool, including a description of the machine, its characteristics, specifications, potential applications, and so on. Thus, the company also presents the technical expertise supporting the machinery it produces, and the professionalism that serves as a core principle for its business operations.

empakando also relies on a two-person sales team. One of its sales representatives focuses on the sale of import products, specifically sealing and labeling machines, as well as spare parts. The second representative is in charge of selling machinery built by *empakando* itself: filling machines, tanks, tunnel machines, capping machines, rinsers, and bakery machines. Now, in the case of large-scope projects, clients can discuss their needs and negotiate directly with Nick. Therefore, he collaborates with the sales team for bigger projects. Some of the company's traditional clients, such as the Spanish company Calvo, are always served by Nick.

Offered Products

While initially *empakando* designed the packaging process based on the peculiarities of its clients' products, currently the offer is focused on manufacturing more than the provision of services. The company's portfolio includes semiautomatic and automatic machines for filling, dosing, labeling, packaging, and conveyor belts (Figure 3). From a global point of view, the company's offer includes a first, pre-sale stage, supported by the premise "We transform your idea." The company helps the client materialize its ideas by designing plans, making first drafts, among other things. Next, *empakando* builds the machine, makes an inspection, and installs the equipment at the client's facilities. Finally, *empakando* provides the client with after-sales technical services, on-the-field training, and continuous support.

When designing and manufacturing these products, *empakando* follows the principles of quality, innovation, and complete adaptation to the client's needs. Thus, clients can expect high quality and precision throughout the entire purchase process, from machine design to final assembly and installation. Additionally, because these products are manufactured locally, prices are competitive, which clients appreciate. This is all possible largely thanks to Nick's experience in Switzerland and his technological skills. This allows *empakando* to develop new and unique products that meet high European manufacturing standards. *empakando*'s machines are so competitive compared to those built in the USA or Europe that sometimes it is questioned whether they were manufactured in El Salvador.

Figure 3. Automatic machine for filling designed by empakando

Regarding the services provided by *empakando*, these are also of very high quality. For instance, technical services are provided by highly qualified, specialized staff. Moreover, in comparison to the competition, Regina and Nick meet their clients' demands with faster response times, reducing downtime caused by the failure of machinery owned by the company's clients. On the other hand, because *empakando* is a manufacturer, it always has an available stock of spare parts, which allows the company to quickly repair the client's equipment. Furthermore, as the spare parts themselves are manufactured by *empakando*, they are high quality, which helps preserve the clients' machines longer and ensures optimal performance. By providing after-sales support, *empakando* offers its clients complete solutions, minimizing downtime and subsequent losses of productivity.

Staff Training

Regina and Nick, who make up a highly qualified founding team, have always placed great emphasis on staff training at *empakando*. As the company's administrative director, Regina relies on a graduate in Business Administration whom she considers "her right hand" without a doubt. On the other hand, Nick works with the support of a team of mechanical and industrial engineers. The entire staff in the Production Department is made of specialists who hold degrees in Mechanical Engineering. Regina and Nick think that it is much easier to work with qualified personnel, which also allows them to learn from their employees. In Regina's opinion, the new generations have quick minds, are fast, and have high technological skills. By contrast, she and Nick have started becoming slower due to their age. Their experience as managers of a company is valuable, but they also need the support of talented, younger generations. The emphasis that the entrepreneurs place on the staff's specialized training is a key element of *empakando's* growth. Technological expertise is an essential requirement to develop and market innovative products and processes, which, at the same time, is a necessary requisite for industrial SMEs' international expansion (García-Cabrera, García-Soto y Suárez-Ortega, 2017).

Business Social Responsibility

Empakando's socially responsible operations are based on three pillars: the difficulties many Salvadoran people are faced with due to the country's circumstances; relationships with different stakeholder groups with whom the company collaborates; and Regina and Nick's passion for education and human values (e.g., empathy, solidarity, responsibility).

First, and regarding the country, El Salvador is characterized by its harsh, difficult conditions. Thus, having the opportunity to receive high-quality training is extremely valuable for the population. A good education allows people to have access to decent, regulated jobs, hence why this activity is considered so valuable. The students and mechanical engineers welcomed into the company feel that *empakando* is a paradise for them in terms of training because they can receive a lot of specialized expertise from Nick.

Secondly, the company's interactions with several local and foreign stakeholder groups that it shares common goals with also contribute to developing the activity of corporate social responsibility. For example, in regards to training, *empakando* is currently collaborating with the Central American Technical Institute (ITCA), which imparts several degrees (e.g. mechanical engineering, industrial engineering, computer science, business administration, and management) applying a dual training system. ITCA's dual system, which is similar to the training provided in Switzerland, is unique in El Salvador. More specifically, *empakando* collaborates with the School of Engineering ITCA-FEPADE by granting scholarships to students so that they can study at this university while also pursuing an internship with the company within the framework of their dual training. A student with a scholarship from *empakando* spends alternate months at the company and ITCA, in addition to receiving the money to pay the entirety of their university fees. Many of these students are subsequently hired by *empakando*, therefore joining the labor market after finishing their studies. It is a good process for the company to hire talented people which are necessary to maintain the company's levels of quality and innovation and, therefore, the competitiveness of its products; and for graduates to join a company that provides them with a job suited to their training. Thus, both the company and the community benefit from this activity; that is, the company adds shared value. In addition, within the framework of its social business program and cooperation with stakeholders, *empakando* supports charity organizations. At Christmas, it also provides support to organizations that help minors with oncological problems.

Finally, at a more personal level, Nick and Regina are members of the Management Board of the Sociedad de Beneficiencia Suiza (Swiss Charity Society), where Nick is president. Every year this organization holds three large fundraisers so that they can offer scholarships to financially challenged, young people with great academic records. Moreover, Nick is also the president of the Fundación Educación (Education Foundation), which is based in Switzerland and has branch offices in different countries in Latin America. This foundation also provides funding for scholarship programs, specifically in the university context. For instance, it grants scholarships so that students can get their degrees at the universities of ESEN, Don Bosco, or ITCA. In this case, Regina and Nick participate in the screening process for scholarship candidates, whose progress they track throughout the entire degree. This is relevant because most students are faced with severe financial and family-related problems. Throughout their university years, they often feel overwhelmed by these difficulties and so they want to give up their studies. Regina and Nick provide them with emotional support to keep trying. They have taken it as a personal challenge to help these students graduate, to improve their lives and that of their families.

In addition, Regina is a member, along with five other female entrepreneurs, of the Advisory Committee of the international organization Voces Vitales. This organization proves support to business women and female entrepreneurs. For over a year, the organization has been implementing a program with funding provided by FOMILENIO[3] from the USA. The program offers technical and practical training to women who want to start businesses and thrive in life. Given that, in El Salvador, many theoretical seminars and workshops are already provided, Voces Vitales only provides real, practical training and counseling to women who wish to set up a business. Regina has a very positive opinion of the work carried out at Voces Vitales. By offering female participants valid connections for their own companies and practical training, the organization makes a relevant contribution to the Salvadoran society.

Thus, *empakando*'s commitment to corporate social responsibility has benefitted the local business and social environment, which requires help in El Salvador. This has been recognized by customers and many stakeholders, which helps reinforce the company's positive image and reputation. Also, it has benefitted *empakando*, in terms of acquiring qualified, highly committed employees who value the company's corporate social responsibility, as well as its slightly reduced hiring and turnover costs. All this has helped consolidate *empakando's* business project in the local Salvadoran market, therefore generating sufficient financial resources and experience to address the challenges posed by international markets.

Going Gradually into International Markets

The local Salvadoran market is small. Regina had already contacted all the companies that she thought would be interested in *empakando's* machinery. However, many of these companies did not want to invest in improving their production processes. The company was founded in 2000. Three years later it had already reached maximum capacity in the local market, and sales began to diminish (2003). It was time to consider increasing the company's operations entering foreign countries.

Regina and Nick thought of *empakando*'s international expansion as a regional process, aimed at Central America, including Belize, Costa Rica, El Salvador, Guatemala, Honduras, Nicaragua, and Panama. For the couple, the Central American region was so small that it did not make sense for them to keep growing sequentially across these countries. In Regina and Nick's opinion, it was better to target these countries simultaneously. As such, after three years, between 2004 and 2007, the company was already present across Central America.

Given its resources at that time, the company carried out the process in a rudimentary way. From its headquarters in El Salvador, Regina and Nick sought companies operating in industries that were the most suitable for *empakando*, in order to sell their machines to them. They used telephone directories and information requests submitted to the relevant embassies. Once they had located the companies, they called them by phone, arranged meetings, and travelled to visit them in their home countries. In general, these foreign companies gave a warm welcome to Regina and Nick and appreciated *empakando*'s offer. A few years after *empakando*'s entry into the region, Regina and Nick's visits were complemented by the company's participation at trade shows. Regina and Nick yielded excellent results from these given that such events provide networking opportunities to connect with potential clients from foreign countries

The below information provides more detail about the motives and methods of entering each country.

- **Belize and Nicaragua.** Belize was the first foreign country where the company sold its products. *empakando* chose it to seize an opportunity: Belize's ambassador in El Salvador contacted the company believing that its products and services could be of value to Belizean businesses. After the initial contact, Regina and Nick visited Belize in person to engage clients following the procedure described above. That is how they made their first sales in Belize in 2004. After two years in the country, *empakando* decided to stop operating there for two main reasons: (1) the food and pharmaceutical industries in the country were very limited and work is mostly done manually, so there were few potential clients; and (2) the country's political situation was very sensitive. There was a similar situation in Nicaragua which *empakando* entered in 2006, because there were no other machinery manufacturers that could compete with it in the country. The company's entry followed the same procedure as in Belize, directly contacting other businesses as potential clients. After many years operating in Nicaragua, *empakando* decided to cease its activities there in 2013, again due to the country's political situation, which had made negotiations more complicated.

- **Panama.** The SME entered the country in 2005, knowing that there were no competitors that manufactured similar machinery. To make the entry easier, based on their previous positive experience in Belize, Regina and Nick made prospecting visits to the country. Afterwards, to accelerate *empakando*'s launch in the country, the company's owners visited international trade shows in 2010 and 2013. Both procedures allowed them to engage customers and close sales deals.
- **Guatemala**. *empakando* entered the country in 2005. Although entering Guatemala would have been easier because geographically it is the closest country to El Salvador, it was the third country where they sold their products. Guatemala was an interesting market, not only because it was close to El Salvador, but also because its food and cosmetics industry is highly developed. Therefore, there were many potential clients for *empakando*. The SME entered Guatemala just as it had done with Panama. After a few years operating in the country, *empakando* started participating in international trade shows between 2009 and 2014. However, unlike in Panama, the trade show visits were not as productive in terms of engaging customers and closing deals. As an alternative, Regina and Nick decided to find a Guatemalan distributor to represent the company's brand in-country. This was most beneficial for *empakando*, with an increase in sales in Guatemala.
- **Costa Rica**. Given the country's high potential for engaging customers, *empakando* entered in 2006. Just as on previous occasions, the procedure stayed the same: visits, direct contact with potential clients, followed by participation at trade shows. Following its recent positive experience in Guatemala, the company located a distributor in Costa Rica, a company focused on similar operations which agreed to sell *empakando*'s products.
- **Honduras**. Finally, *empakando* entered Honduras in 2007. It was a strategic and potentially valuable country given the potential market available for the company to sell its products. After its previous experiences in other countries and the results obtained with the help of a local distributor, *empakando* made slight modifications to the entry procedure. The company directly contacted a Salvadoran firm with a subsidiary in Honduras. As such, they agreed that the firm would represent *empakando* and sell its products in Honduras.

However, when *empakando* initially entered the country they experienced a lot of difficulties. Some potential clients regarded them as an unknown company based in El Salvador, offering a product that is rarely manufactured in Central America. Indeed, El Salvador is known for its textile and agro-industrial products. As previously stated, *empakando* had almost no competition in the country and the region as a whole. Thus, being a Salvadoran company did not open many doors in foreign countries, resulting in prospective clients having doubts about *empakando*'s reliability. These circumstances were barriers to the company's beginnings as an exporter.

The company started operating abroad by selling liquid-filling machines (its strongest products) and then gradually increased its range of exported products (e.g. piston fillers, conveyor belts and rotary tables). Because *empakando* manufactured these machines adapting them to the clients' needs (e.g. size, capacity, speed), Regina and Nick requested an advance on 50% of the machines' value to start production. Because the clients doubted that the machinery was being produced in El Salvador, they were reluctant to advance money for a purchase they regarded as highly uncertain. Despite that, in 2005, the same year *empakando* started manufacturing semi-automated (not solely mechanical) machinery, the company also made its first sales in Panama and Guatemala. Gradually, potential clients in Central America researched and became more familiar with *empakando*. Thanks to initial product sales, *empakando* was able to demonstrate the high quality of its machines and the company's first clients became strong ambassadors. "The fact that local clients had an excellent opinion of our team and work helped increase people's trust in our company and our sales volume, as well," Regina remembers.

However, the procedure they chose to enter those countries (direct exports based on client engagement carried out by Regina and Nick, and recommendations made by their first clients) led to a slower entering than expected. As a faster alternative, the company used indirect exportation, sealing deals with companies based in Central American countries to enhance customer acquisition. Regina and Nick's first experiences with some of these distributors were not positive and they soon realized that, unless these companies' own operations were related to machinery, they were not effective. This made *empakando* waste a great deal of time. Regina and Nick learned that it is essential for the local distributor to operate in the same industry as *empakando* and to have a good reputation in the target country. Furthermore, a specialization in machinery meant that these representatives could provide installation and maintenance services for *empakando*'s products. When Regina and Nick started working with specialized intermediaries, and as an additional measure to guarantee service quality for customers (a distinguishing mark for *empakando*), Nick started training their local distributors' technical staff. On the other hand, when *empakando* had no local distributor in some host countries (for instance, when an intermediary failed and had to be replaced by another), *empakando* sent a technical specialist from El Salvador. This procedure for the company's foreign operations has been retained over the years, so Regina and Nick have not established delegations for the company abroad.

empakando's exports started growing gradually, accounting for 23%-52% of its production over the last 5 years, with an annual average of 31.4% between 2015 and 2019. However, the level of implementation varies between these countries. For instance, in Panama and Guatemala, sales are continuous, with the latter being *empakando*'s best customer abroad. On the other hand, in Honduras and Costa Rica, exports are sporadic. After providing the company with significant profit for a long time, over the last four years, sales in Honduras have greatly diminished, which is why *empakando* is preparing to strengthen its presence there. In Costa Rica, the company is currently looking for a new distributor because the previous one failed to meet their expectations.

When evaluating entry barriers in these countries, Regina does not identify other relevant obstacles. They certainly had to deal with the differences in some target countries' legislations, but this was not a problem. For instance, Panama is the only Central American country that requires a certificate of origin for its products, but *empakando*'s papers were already in order in El Salvador which made it easy to obtain the document and submit it to Panamanian customs so that the company's clients could import *empakando*'s products.

Concerning the negotiation processes needed to operate in the international context, Regina found them to be very similar to clients from Belize, Guatemala, Honduras, Nicaragua, Costa Rica, or Panama. In her opinion, the negotiating process has always been the same. The SME *empakando* first identifies the client's needs to find the product best suited to them. As for the steps where the client accepts the planes, the offer, and so on, there were no significant difficulties either. For Regina, the fact that *empakando* offers solutions aimed at improving the client's processes and clearly provides the relevant information from the beginning, which the client also notices, makes it easier to hold smooth negotiations that benefit all the parties involved. In addition, all Central American countries speak the same language and have similar cultures, which also simplifies the process. In any event, when contacting people from other cultures who also operate in Central America, negotiations have been held and agreements have been implemented successfully as well, without relevant incidents.

Finally, in geographical terms, exporting products to other countries in the region has been easy. Given that Central America is a relatively small region and there are reliable transport services in place, shipment time also meets the requirements. In fact, all of these products have always been sent from El Salvador by land, using specialized transport companies. In this regard, the company faces no problems. The only exception comes from situations outside the company's control, such as customs, strikes, etc. However, such difficulties can appear at any time and affect both *empakando* and its clients.

The Support of Export Promotion Programs Offered by Public Institutions and Non-profit Business Unions in El Salvador

El Salvador has a number of institutions that provide support to local companies wishing to internationalize. Some of them are public institutions and others are non-profit business unions (elsalvadortrade.com.sv). Among the first are: PROESA, responsible for strengthening Salvadoran companies' export operations; the Centro de Trámites de Importación y Exportación (CIEX) (Import and Export Center), which expedites the necessary export and import procedures; and the Ministry of Foreign Affairs, which manages El Salvador's foreign policy. Some non-profit business unions are the Corporación de Exportadores de El Salvador (COEXPORT) (Salvadoran Exporters Corporation), which promotes the production and export of products and services, and other organizations such as the Asociación Salvadoreña de Industriales (ASI) (Salvadoran Industry Association), El Salvador's Chamber of Commerce and Industry (CAMARASAL), the Salvadoran Chamber of the Construction Industry (CASALCO) or the Salvadoran Coffee Council (CSC).

With the help of these public and private institutions, the Salvadoran Ministry of Foreign Affairs presents an events plan each year based on the Government and business associations' industrial strategic interests. The plan comprises national and international trade shows, missions and investment fora organized to help Salvadoran companies to market their products and services. For instance, El Salvador's Event Plan 2019 (PROESA, 2019b) includes 50 events, including a description of the events, how and how many companies can participate, the benefits for companies, etc. Among the scheduled events, highlights include multi-sectoral commercial missions to countries such as Guatemala, Honduras and the Dominican Republic; the presentation of business opportunities El Salvador-Belgium; Design & Manufacturing Pacific in the USA, related to developments made with regard to engineering, computer science, electronics, automation, etc.; AGITRADE in Guatemala on agro-industrial matters; the EXPOCOMER multi-sectorial trade show in Panama; 6th Multi-Sectorial Business Meetings in El Salvador; as well as several trade shows related to tourism, fashion or the automotive industry.

However, the expenses associated with participating at trade shows and international missions (e.g. plane tickets, hotel reservations, and meals) make them inaccessible for some companies, especially for newly established ones. For example, companies sometimes attend trade shows because they are invited by the organizers, yet they still have to pay the expenses involved in attending. In some cases,

Salvadoran institutions help local companies participate in these international trade shows. They help companies book a space or stand to represent El Salvador so that the companies do not have to pay to rent it. Other expenses incurred to attend the show are the companies' responsibility. In Regina's opinion, these expenses can be very high depending on where the event is held.

Several factors determine the requirements to participate at an international trade show: whether the company wants to attend individually or as part of a commercial mission, the size, and relevance of the show, and whether it is a general or specialized trade show in a specific industry. To attend a trade show individually, if the company can cover all its expenses, including the reservation of the stand for its products, it simply has to submit a request and the relevant forms. Additionally, when the trade show is specialized, all the products being exhibited must belong to the same industry. *empakando* attended both general and specialized international trade shows to market their products, acquire customers and seal sales deals shortly after starting its internationalization process, in order to enter Central American countries faster. It participated in general trade shows in 2010 and 2013 independently to facilitate its entry in Panama, in specialized trade shows from 2009 to 2014 independently to acquire customers and business opportunities in Guatemala, and in a commercial mission to facilitate its entry in Costa Rica. In the latter case, the SME was supported by the Salvadoran Chamber of Commerce, which organized commercial missions so that local entrepreneurs could attend international trade shows. The company was also supported by FONDEPRO, which financed 50% of the costs.

Nevertheless, for a few years there have not been any relevant specialized trade shows for the Central American market, which is why *empakando* does not currently attend such events. Although general trade shows are available, they provide fewer business opportunities. For specialized events in *empakando*'s areas of interest, highly renowned trade shows, such as a machinery trade show, are held every year, but these take place in other geographic areas such as the USA and Brazil. Given that most companies in the industry want to participate in such trade shows, aspiring companies are evaluated according to their product portfolio, country of origin, among other criteria. To ensure high standards, the organizers decide which companies the stands should be assigned to. As *empakando* has not yet considered internationalizing to other countries outside of Central America, it has limited interest in these trade shows.

If companies participate in a trade show within the framework of a commercial mission, there are also specific requirements. Again, it depends on who the organizers of the mission are and on whether there is partial or complete financial support available for companies. In these cases, it is quite difficult to access these programs. Companies must include their legal registration certificate as well as their financial information. Entrepreneurs are not considered for these programs. As such, if a potential entrepreneur has a business idea and has carried out the necessary analyses to establish their project, but their company has not yet become a legal entity, they will not be able to receive support to participate in a commercial mission. Once the necessary information has been collected from the candidates, the organizers will evaluate the companies that have submitted the correct information. They then decide which companies they should support and authorize to participate in the mission.

Earning a place within a commercial mission is not easy, as the organizers usually establish a maximum number of participants, i.e. five to ten companies. In El Salvador, these missions are mainly aimed at different Central American countries, but some are also organized to attend trade shows in the USA, Europe, and Asia. As Regina and Nick registered their company and followed all the legal procedures since the inception of their business, they were able to participate in some commercial missions, as described above. However, they are currently not particularly interested in such programs given that they are now established in Central America and not aiming to sell their products in the USA, Europe or Asia.

For companies entering foreign markets for the first time, commercial missions offer great support. Regina suggests that finding clients and initial negotiations are a very different experience as part of a commercial mission, compared to doing so independently. That is why their participation in these missions was so useful for them in the initial years of their internationalization process. As part of a commercial mission, the company introduces itself as a member of its country's delegation. Simply being chosen to participate in a country's commercial mission is proof of the company and its management's reliability. Moreover, on many occasions, organizers provide additional support to business people who are taking their first steps in the international context. For instance, during negotiations, they offer guidance about which countries are most suitable for them depending on the type of products they wish to export and each country's tax law.

Regarding the general advice provided to companies in commercial missions, organizers usually provide useful oral and written information related to closing successful deals. For instance, when a company participates in a commercial mission, the organizers usually provide handbooks and pamphlets on how to negotiate or export products to countries which might be of value to El Salvador. Organizers usually supply information on the available Free Trade Agreements (e.g. Central American free trade agreements, Panama-Central America Free Trade Agreement, Dominican Republic-Central America Free Trade Agreement) and how to benefit from them, important factors in specific countries, and tips related to networking and negotiations. All this information was very useful for *empakando*. It is particularly necessary for companies participating in the mission for the first time because they need more support. As such, organizers usually provide them with additional help. When a company participates in a commercial mission, it can ask the organizers for support in arranging meetings with potential clients. The organizers then contact the potential clients, inform them that the company is going to attend the trade show, and request a meeting. This process ensures professionalism and security for both the companies participating in the mission and the potential clients themselves.

If companies attend international trade shows individually, as *empakando* did when it had already acquired enough experience, they lack the support that commercial missions usually provide, because the trade shows do not offer such services. The company must prepare on its own, collecting all the necessary information to ensure the productivity of attending the event. Regina remembers that, on one occasion, they wanted to do business in China, but they initially got the impression that the company they wanted to collaborate with was not very reliable. As such, they sought information about the company, yet what they found did not allay their doubts. Regina then contacted COEXPORT, who informed her about China's situation at the time. Their recommendation was for her not to carry out the negotiation. The entrepreneurs did not hesitate to follow COEXPORT'S suggestions. Situations like this can affect both importers and exporters. That is why every company should carry out a thorough investigation before attending trade shows.

When considering their general experience with commercial missions and trade shows, Regina believes that each company should make an analysis individually, as they did. Even if the company participates in the trade show as a member of a commercial mission, the conclusion of the negotiations is still their responsibility. At a trade show, many clients can approach the company without it expressly seeking them, and therefore prior to the show, the company must develop strong criteria to assess potential collaborations on-site. This is key to forging a long-term relationship based on a "win-win" principle, i.e. a mutually beneficial relationship.

All things considered, the support of export promotion programs in a country like El Salvador, although less important than *empakando*'s products and principles, is still important.

FINDINGS FROM *EMPAKANDO*'S EXPERIENCE AND CURRENT CHALLENGES FACING THE FIRM

The current case study aims to address a gap in the current literature: the lack of evidence with regard to the internationalization process of SMEs based in developing countries. We provide details on the circumstances underlying these processes and the decisions made to successfully address internationalization. Our case study is based on the SME *empakando*, which was founded in the developing country El Salvador in 2000. The case study analyzes a range of important aspects in order to understand the phenomenon: firstly, the internationalization process and the entry methods chosen; and secondly, two key elements in gaining access to the resources and connections needed to facilitate internationalization, that is, the commitment to corporate social responsibility (as an internal factor) and the support of export promotion programs (as an external factor).

Regarding the internationalization process, we note that like many SMEs, *empakando* follows the internationalization process based on a gradual model. After the SME was established in the local market, it began its international expansion by entering new countries step by step, based on an incremental, gradual learning process. During this process, the firm adopted the most common entry mode used by SMES, i.e. using exports with or without intermediaries, as such avoiding having to commit a high level of resources.

The case also demonstrates the main challenges *empakando* experienced when entering foreign countries as an SME based in a developing country. It also highlights the primary factors favoring its successful internationalization.

The country the SME is based in can provide challenges. Some are challenges usually faced by SMEs during internationalization (e.g., lack of experience on foreign markets, lack of financial resources, reputation when entering foreign countries, etc.), and some are country-level factors related to the conditions in a developing economy such as El Salvador. The country's characteristics harmed *empakando*'s credibility at the beginning of the process and became an obstacle. The distrust towards the country by customers abroad was extended to *empakando* because of it being an SME founded and located in El Salvador.

On the other hand, factors that favored its successful internationalization include the following:

- The complementarity of the founding team members' backgrounds. They are a couple with an ideal combination of knowledge and abilities, e.g. they have different cultural origins (El Salvador and Switzerland) and different specializations (commercial and technological), which provide valuable synergies. Such complementarity allows them to nurture the SME with (1) market capabilities and the ability to develop tailor made products; and (2) technological capabilities, particularly innovation, which allows *empakando* to develop new and unique products that meet high European manufacturing standards.
- The SME's commitment to corporate social responsibility, which has helped *empakando* recruit qualified and committed employees, as well as resulting in slightly reduced hiring and turnover costs. This social commitment also benefits the firm's environment, which requires great support in El Salvador.
- The support offered by public export promotion programs has also been relevant, albeit to a lesser degree.

However, *empakando's* internationalization process does not end with the experience described in this case study. For the next few years, *empakando* has set itself new challenges to expand its operations in two ways:

Concerning the market, Regina and Nick have decided to strengthen the company's international presence in Central America, specifically in Guatemala, Honduras and Costa Rica, given that their operations are scarce in these countries. *empakando* has a very large margin for growth and it therefore hopes to achieve greater market penetration.

Concerning products, Nick has designed a new dosing machine, geared towards bakeries and confectioneries. It is a markedly innovative and competitive product. *empakando* has already hired new staff to manufacture and distribute it. Additionally, Regina and Nick intend to use the new machine as a way of reaching the South American region, a new market which has remained unexplored by the company until now. This product provides a highly valuable competitive advantage to help the company enter the regional market, even if Regina and Nick's aim is to sell its entire range of machinery there once the company enters the region. They have said they are very excited about this challenge. Although they know that 2020 will involve a lot of work and uncertainty due to the pandemic generated by COVID-19 and their inexperience in South America, they remain positive as to the potential of their product to be successful in this new region.

In fact, Regina and Nick are working on an aggressive plan to enter into the entire South American market. The company is preparing to seek and establish connections with potential clients in the region. They will enter the market through Colombia, which they chose for two reasons. Firstly, *empakando* has previous commercial experience with Colombian companies, meaning that they have knowledge and connections for that market, despite not having previously operated in the country. Secondly, there is a large market in Colombia for *empakando*'s products, and the company already has a list of potential clients there.

To speed up its entry into Colombia, and later other South American countries, *empakando* will use the same methods which have previously helped it to expand internationally. The company will attend commercial trade shows in target countries to market their products and seek new clients and look for suitable local distributors. Given the company's extensive international experience, *empakando* will not use export promotion programs, choosing only targeted trade shows, particularly specialized events (e.g. a trade show in Brazil), which the company will attend individually. As for distributors, to save on travel expenses and particularly to protect *empakando*'s distinguishing mark, these distributors will have to be local, well-established companies, with a relevant trajectory and a strong reputation in their respective countries, as well as working with similar products to *empakando*. They will also have to rely on a technical department to provide customers with optimal assembly and repair services. Given that *empakando*'s aim is to have a wide distributor network, the company will not enter exclusivity agreements for the distribution of their products. Regina and Nick know that establishing this sales network will be a difficult and lengthy process. As such, their first sales will be made via direct exports if necessary, because they have no distribution agreements in the target countries. In such cases, installation and maintenance services for the machinery will be provided directly by *empakando*.

Regina and Nick are aware of the challenges that they will have to address in the upcoming months. Their experience, good principles and practices employed over the 20 years they have been running *empakando,* will be essential in meeting their new objectives.

ACKNOWLEDGMENT

This research was supported by the Spain's Economy, Industry and Competitiveness National Department [grant number ECO2016-80518-R].

REFERENCES

Agarwal, S., & Ramaswami, S. N. (1992). Choice of foreign market entry mode: Impact of ownership, location and internalization factors. *Journal of International Business Studies*, *23*(1), 1–27. doi:10.1057/palgrave.jibs.8490257

Ayuso, S., & Navarrete-Báez, F. E. (2018). How does entrepreneurial and international orientation influence SMEs' commitment to sustainable development? Empirical evidence from Spain and Mexico. *Corporate Social Responsibility and Environmental Management*, *25*(1), 80–94. doi:10.1002/csr.1441

Cantwell, J., Dunning, J. H., & Lundan, S. M. (2010). An evolutionary approach to understanding international business activity: The co-evolution of MNEs and the institutional environment. *Journal of International Business Studies*, *41*(4), 567–586. doi:10.1057/jibs.2009.95

Central Reserve Bank of El Salvador. (2020). Retrieved from https://www.bcr.gob.sv/comex/

CEPALSTAT. (2019). Retrieved from https://estadisticas.cepal.org/cepalstat/WEB_CEPALSTAT/estadisticasIndicadores.asp?idioma=e

Cerviño, J., Arteaga-Ortiz, J., & Fernández-del Hoyo, A. (2017). Marketing internacional. In J. Arteaga Ortiz (Ed.), *Manual de internacionalización. Técnicas, herramientas y estrategias necesarias para afrontar con éxito el proceso de internacionalización* (pp. 218–372). ICEX-CECO.

Cheng, H. L., & Yu, C. M. J. (2008). Institutional pressures and initiation of internationalization: Evidence from Taiwanese small and medium-sized enterprises. *International Business Review*, *17*(3), 331–348. doi:10.1016/j.ibusrev.2008.01.006

Comi, S., & Resmini, L. (2019). Are export promotion programs effective in promoting the internalization of SMEs? *Economics and Politics*, 1–35.

Coudounaris, D. N. (2018). Export promotion programmes for assisting SMEs. *Review of International Business and Strategy*, *28*(1), 77–109. doi:10.1108/RIBS-06-2017-0050

Damijan, P. J., Knell, M., Majcen, B., & Rojec, M. (2003). The role of FDI, R&D accumulation and trade in transferring technology to transition countries: Evidence from firm panel data for eight transition countries. *Economic Systems*, *27*(2), 189–204. doi:10.1016/S0939-3625(03)00039-6

Demirbag, M., Tatoglu, E., & Glaister, K. W. (2009). Equity-based entry modes of emerging country multinational. *Journal of World Business*, *44*(4), 445–462. doi:10.1016/j.jwb.2008.11.009

DIGESTYC -Dirección General de Estadístico y Censos. (2020). Retrieved from http://www.digestyc.gob.sv/index.php/foro/2-bienvenido-mat/16-pib.html

Dimitratos, P., Amorós, J. E., Etchebarne, M. S., & Felzensztein, C. (2014). Micro-multinational or not? International entrepreneurship, networking and learning effects. *Journal of Business Research, 67*(5), 908–915. doi:10.1016/j.jbusres.2013.07.010

Elbanna, S., Hsieh, L., & Child, J. (2020). *Contextualizing internationalization decision-making research in SMEs: Towards an integration of existing studies*. European Academy of Management. doi:10.1111/emre.12395

Evers, N., & Knight, J. (2008). Role of international trade shows in small firm internationalization: A network perspective. *International Marketing Review, 25*(5), 544–562. doi:10.1108/02651330810904080

Expansión. (2019). Retrieved from https://datosmacro.expansion.com/paises/el-salvador

Fletcher, D., & Harris, S. (2012). Knowledge acquisition for the internationalization of the smaller firm: Content and sources. *International Business Review, 21*(4), 631–647. doi:10.1016/j.ibusrev.2011.07.008

Gabrielsson, M., Kirpalani, V. H. M., Dimitratos, P., Solberg, C. A., & Zucchella, A. (2008). Born globals: Propositions to help advance the theory. *International Business Review, 17*(4), 385–401. doi:10.1016/j.ibusrev.2008.02.015

García-Cabrera, A. M., García-Soto, M. G., & Durán-Herrera, J. J. (2016). Opportunity motivation and SME internationalisation in emerging countries: Evidence from entrepreneurs' perception of institutions. *The International Entrepreneurship and Management Journal, 12*(3), 879–910. doi:10.100711365-016-0386-7

García-Cabrera, A. M., García-Soto, M. G., & Suárez-Ortega, S. M. (2017). Macro-level spillovers and micro-level capabilities as antecedents of young SMEs' propensity to export and to become a born global. *The International Entrepreneurship and Management Journal, 13*(4), 1199–1220. doi:10.100711365-017-0451-x

Geldres-Weiss, V. V., Etchebarne, M. S., & Bustos, L. H. (2011). The impact of governmental export promotion on the firm's export performance. *Academia (Caracas), 47*, 1–17.

Geldres-Weiss, V. V., & Monreal-Pérez, J. (2018). The Effect of Export Promotion Programs on Chilean Firms' Export Activity: A Longitudinal Study on Trade Shows and Trade Missions. *Journal of Promotion Management, 24*(5), 660–674. doi:10.1080/10496491.2018.1405519

Ghemawat, P. (2001). Distance still Matters. *Harvard Business Review, 79*(8), 137–145. PMID:11550630

Gil-Barragan, J. M., Belso-Martínez, J. A., & Mas-Verdú, F. (2020). When do domestic networks cause accelerated internationalization under different decision-making logic? *European Business Review, 32*(2), 227–256. doi:10.1108/EBR-11-2018-0191

Gilmore, A., O'Donnell, A., Carson, D., & Cummins, D. (2003). Factors influencing foreign direct investment and international joint ventures – A comparative study of Northern Ireland and Bahrain. *International Marketing Review, 20*(2), 195–215. doi:10.1108/02651330310470401

Grant, R. M. (2016). *Contemporary strategy analysis: Text and cases*. Reino Unido: John Wiley & Sons.

Haddoud, M. Y., Jones, P., & Newbery, R. (2017). Export promotion programmes and SMEs' performance. *Journal of Small Business and Enterprise Development, 24*(1), 68–87. doi:10.1108/JSBED-07-2016-0116

Jahdi, K. S., & Acikdilli, G. (2009). Marketing communications and corporate social responsibility (CSR): Marriage of convenience or shotgun wedding? *Journal of Business Ethics, 88*(1), 103–113. doi:10.100710551-009-0113-1

Johanson, J., & Vahlne, J. (1977). The internationalization process of the firm: A model of knowledge development and increasing foreign market commitments. *Journal of International Business Studies, 8*(1), 23–32. doi:10.1057/palgrave.jibs.8490676

Johanson, J., & Vahlne, J. (2009). The Uppsala internationalization process model revisited: From liability of foreignness to liability of outsidership. *Journal of International Business Studies, 40*(9), 1411–1431. doi:10.1057/jibs.2009.24

Johanson, J., & Wiedersheim-Paul, F. (1975). The internationalization of the firm - four Swedish cases. *Journal of Management Studies, 12*(3), 305–323. doi:10.1111/j.1467-6486.1975.tb00514.x

Kalafsky, R. V. (2017). Export programs and SME market choice: Evidence from North West England. *GeoJournal, 82*(6), 1135–1144. doi:10.100710708-016-9733-z

Knight, G. A., & Cavusgil, S. T. (2004). Innovation, organizational capabilities, and the born-global firm. *Journal of International Business Studies, 35*(2), 124–141. doi:10.1057/palgrave.jibs.8400071

Kruesi, M. A., Hemmington, N. R., & Kim, P. B. (2018). What matters for hotel executives? An examination of major theories in non-equity entry mode research. *International Journal of Hospitality Management, 70*, 25–36. doi:10.1016/j.ijhm.2017.11.005

Laufs, K., & Schwens, C. (2014). Foreign market entry mode choice of small and medium-sized enterprises: A systematic review and future research agenda. *International Business Review, 23*(6), 1109–1126. doi:10.1016/j.ibusrev.2014.03.006

Lederman, D., Olarreaga, M., & Payton, L. (2010). Export promotion agencies: Do they work? *Journal of Development Economics, 91*(2), 257–265. doi:10.1016/j.jdeveco.2009.09.003

Leonidou, L., Samiee, S., & Geldres, V. V. (2015). Using national export promotion programs to assist smaller firms' international entrepreneurial initiatives. In P. N. Ghauri & V. H. M. Kirpalani (Eds.), *Handbook of Research on International Entrepreneurship Strategy: Improving SME Performance Globally* (pp. 239–252). Edward Elgar Publishing Ltd. doi:10.4337/9781783471584.00023

Leonidou, L. C., Palihawadana, D., & Theodosiou, M. (2011). National export-promotion programs as drivers of organizational resources and capabilities: Effects on strategy, competitive advantage, and performance. *Journal of International Marketing, 19*(2), 1–29. doi:10.1509/jimk.19.2.1

Luo, Y., & Tung, R. L. (2007). International expansion of emerging market enterprises: A springboard perspective. *Journal of International Business Studies, 38*(4), 481–498. doi:10.1057/palgrave.jibs.8400275

Martincus, C. V., & Carballo, J. (2010). Beyond the average effects: The distributional impacts of export promotion programs in developing countries. *Journal of Development Economics, 92*(2), 201–214. doi:10.1016/j.jdeveco.2009.02.007

Ministry of Economy of El Salvador. (2018). *Household survey data*. Retrieved from http://www.digestyc.gob.sv/index.php/temas/des/

Osei, A., Forkuoh, K. S., Shao, Y., & Osei, M. A. (2016). The impact of institutional support in SMEs marketing, and growth—A case study of retail SMEs in Ghana. *Open Journal of Business and Management*, *4*(3), 408–426. doi:10.4236/ojbm.2016.43043

Pickernell, D., Jones, P., Thompson, P., & Packham, G. (2016). Determinants of SME exporting: Insights and implications. *International Journal of Entrepreneurship and Innovation*, *17*(1), 31–42. doi:10.5367/ijei.2016.0208

Portal[REMOVED HYPERLINK FIELD]. (n.d.).Retrieved from http://www.elsalvadortrade.com.sv/

Porter, M. E., & Kramer, M. R. (2006). The link between competitive advantage and corporate social responsibility. *Harvard Business Review*, *84*(12), 78–92. PMID:17183795

PROESA. (2019a). *Directorio Nacional de Empresas Exportadoras*. Retrieved from http://www.proesa.gob.sv/

PROESA. (2019b). *Plan de Eventos El Salvador (2019).* Retrieved from http://www.proesa.gob.sv/

Rialp-Criado, A. (1999). Los enfoques micro-organizativos de la internacionalización de la empresa: Una revisión y síntesis de la literatura. *Información Comercial Española, ICE. Revista de Economia (Curitiba)*, *781*, 117–128.

Spence, L. J. (1999). Does size matter? The state of the art in small business ethics. *Business Ethics: A European Review, 8*(3), 163-174.

Spence, M. M. (2003). Evaluating export promotion programmes: UK overseas trade missions and export performance. *Small Business Economics*, *20*(1), 83–103. doi:10.1023/A:1020200621988

The World Bank in El Salvador. (2019). Retrieved from https://www.bancomundial.org/es/country/elsalvador/overview#1

Torkkeli, L., Saarenketo, S., Salojärvi, H., & Sainio, L.-M. (2017). Sustainability and Corporate Social Responsibility in Internationally Operating SMEs: Implications on Performance. In Value Creation in IB: An SME Perspective (pp 359-373). Vaasa, Finland: Palgrave MacMillan.

Uzhegova, M., Torkkeli, L., & Saarenketo, S. (2019). Corporate Social Responsibility in SMEs: Implications on Competitive Performance. *Management Review*, *30*(2-3), 232–267.

Valliere, D., & Petterson, R. (2009). Entrepreneurship and economic growth: Evidence from emerging and developed countries. *Entrepreneurship and Regional Development*, *21*(5), 459–480. doi:10.1080/08985620802332723

Welch, L. S., & Luostarinen, R. K. (1993). Inward-Outward Connections in Internationalization. *Journal of International Marketing*, *1*(1), 44–56. doi:10.1177/1069031X9300100104

Wright, M., Westhead, P., & Ucbasaran, D. (2007). Internationalization of small and medium-sized enterprises (SMEs) and international entrepreneurship: A critique and policy implications. *Regional Studies*, *41*(7), 1013–1029. doi:10.1080/00343400601120288

Yan, Z. J., Zhu, J. C., Fan, D., & Kalfadellis, P. (2018). An institutional work view toward the internationalization of emerging market firms. *Journal of World Business, 53*(5), 682–694. doi:10.1016/j.jwb.2018.03.008

Yang, X., & Rivers, C. (2009). Antecedents of CSR practices in MNCs' subsidiaries: A stakeholder and institutional perspective. *Journal of Business Ethics, 86*(S2), 155–169. doi:10.100710551-009-0191-0

Zahra, S. A., Newey, L. R., & Li, Y. (2014). On the frontiers: The implications of social entrepreneurship for international entrepreneurship. *Entrepreneurship Theory and Practice, 38*(1), 137–158. doi:10.1111/etap.12061

KEY TERMS AND DEFINITIONS

Corporate Social Responsibility: The continuing commitment by the business to behave ethically and contribute to economic development while improving the quality of life of the workforce as well as the local community and society.

Developing Country: Nation with a less-developed industrial base and a lower Human Development Index than other countries.

Dual Training: Training system takes place at two learning center, an academy and a workplace. The relationship between the student and the company is organized through a training and learning contract.

Entrepreneur: An individual who creates a new, independent company aiming to exploit business opportunities.

Entrepreneurship: The creation of a new business enterprise.

Entry Mode Strategy: Structural agreement for organizing and conducting international business transactions, by carrying out the marketing and/or production operations, by itself or in partnership with others.

Export Promotion Programs: Support offered by governments to help firms overcome real or perceived obstacles to exporting.

Gradual Internationalization Model: Strategic approach to internationalization based on the offer of products and services aimed at a local market in order to achieve business consolidation and undertake international expansion later.

ENDNOTES

1. Thick flatbread made by hand with cornmeal or rice flour, usually stuffed with one or more ingredients, e.g. cheese, *chicharrón,* squash, fried beans or cheese with *loroco* buds.
2. Made with chicken meat, tamales are a traditional dish for New Year's Eve and almost all kinds of festivities in El Salvador.
3. FOMILENIO is a programme funded with US$277 million donated by the Government of the USA through the Millennium Challenge Corporation (MCC).

Chapter 3
Resourced-Based View and Internationalisation of Social Enterprises:
An Exploratory Study

José Carlos M. R. Pinho
Universidade do Minho, Portugal

Isabel Maria Macedo
University of Minho, Portugal

Marcelo Dionisio
https://orcid.org/0000-0001-6346-2307
Universidade Federal Rio de Janeiro, Brazil

EXECUTIVE SUMMARY

Due to recent economic, social, and public health drawbacks, social enterprises (SEs) play an increasingly important role in addressing a wide range of social problems, as part of their market-based approach to social value creation. Since SEs operate mainly in challenging contexts characterized by scarce resource environments, they need to develop strategies in order to effectively accomplish their missions while achieving organisational sustainability. Often, SEs expand their activity overseas within an internationalisation strategy. The purpose of this study is to examine the role of resources in the internationalisation strategy undertaken by SEs. The study applies the resource-based view (RBV) to understand how the type and nature of resources may influence the international activities pursued by these organisations. The findings highlight the important role of different key resources in the growth, sustainability and internationalisation of SEs.

DOI: 10.4018/978-1-7998-4387-0.ch003

INTRODUCTION

Significant changes have recently occurred in the world with an emphasis on the COVID19 pandemic that is expected to produce a huge economic recession causing significant social and environmental costs in most developed and emerging countries. In the face of this crisis, coordinated global responses are needed at national and international levels, involving the public sector, the market and social economy organisations (Loayza & Pennings, 2020). Social Enterprises (SEs) are often recognised for their capacity to operate in adverse and institutionally-challenging contexts characterized by scarce resource environments. Often, social enterprises are expanding the scope of their strategic interest into the international global sphere. This trend has been particularly noteciable as the increasing global wealth disparity, the corporate social responsibility movement, the market, institutional and state failures along with technological advances have created numerous opportunities for SEs internationalisation (Zahra, Rawhouser, Bhawe, Neubaum, & Hayton, 2008).

Thus, the growing interest in SEs mirrors their promise of reducing long-term public spending in several social related fields like reducing poverty, protecting minorities and immigrants, health and environment related behaviors, community development, among others (Zahra, Gedajlovic, Neubaum, & Shulman, 2009; Chen, Saarenketo, & Puumalainen, 2018). In order to respond adequately to these demands and to successfully accomplish the creation of social value, SEs must leverage their resource-base (RBV) by combining different types of social, human and financial resources in order to create social and economic value (Zahra et al., 2009). This challenge requires crucial managerial capabilities and creativity from SE managers in order to successfully attract resources and accomplish the organisations' mission (Bacq & Eddleston, 2018; Desa & Basu, 2013; Zahra et al., 2009) while achieving organisational and environmental sustainability (Di Zhang & Swanson, 2013).

In the current global crisis, internationalisation strategies are increasingly being adopted by SEs which intend to grow and scale up their operations globally to fulfil unmet social needs. Yet, research addressing the topic of internationalisation among SEs remains limited (Yang & Wu, 2015). Likewise, other authors claim that little is known about the drivers of and the processes underlying SE internationalisation and SE-specific and country-specific consequences of internationalisation (Alon, Mersland, Musteen, & Randoy, 2020). In response to this shortcoming, our study attempts to bridge this void by addressing the following research question: *What is the influence of key founder's SE resources on the internationalisation strategy?*

By providing answers to the above research question, the present study seeks to examine which resources and capabilities are relevant to the internationalisation process of SEs. From a conceptual framework, the study applies the resource-based view (RBV) to explain how the type and nature of resources are relevant to explain the international activities pursued by these organisations. It is widely recognised that the concept of SE has been mostly focused on single country studies, has mostly addresssed local oriented organisations and lacks empirical support (Kerlin, 2010, 2013; Zahra, Newey, & Li, 2014). Moreover, the RBV view has been mainly applied to the for-profit sector with very few empirical studies being applied to the social enterprises setting (Meyskens, Robb-Post, Stamp, Carsrud, & Reynolds, 2010).

With respect to the methodological approach, the study relies on several case studies of social enterprises belonging to the Ashoka's Globalizer Program in Brazil, a global initiative created in 2010 with the objective of supporting the internationalisation of social enterprises, connecting them with experts, supporters and investors (Ashoka, 2016). The authors followed a qualitative approach and conducted several in-depth interviews with the founders and directors of these social enterprises. In selecting the organisations, particular care was taken to ensure that the organisations belong to different segments and represent different stages of internationalisation.

The study findings provide relevant insights regarding the role of key resources-based factors in social enterprises' performance. Further, the study contributes to shed light on the role of these resources leading to more effective processes within internationalisation strategies.

2.THEORETICAL FRAMEWORK

2.1 The Concept of Social Entrepreneurship

Social entrepreneurship is considered as a new phenomenon in the industrialised, emerging and developing economies (Doherty, Haugh, & Lyon, 2014; Seelos & Mair, 2005) and has become a highly relevant topic in different research domains (Yang & Wu, 2015). Luke and Chu (2013) acknowledged that by combining market-based skills and a for-profit mindset associated with social purposes, social entrepreneurs seize market opportunities by offering creative solutions to social issues. According to Doherty et al. (2014) the increasing interest towards social entreprises and social entrepreneurship can be justified by 1) a decrease in philanthropic giving; 2) the emergence of new models of public services; 3) the interest in novel forms of capitalism and; 4) the lack of responses to deficiencies in economies and the consequent growth in inequalities.

The increasing interest in the topic of social entrepreneurship has resulted in multiple meanings and definitions of the term. Zahra et al (2009: 519) reviewed nearly twenty definitions of social entrepreneurship and concluded that social entrepreneurship includes those activities and processes undertaken to "discover, define, and exploit opportunities in order to enhance social wealth". On their part, Mair and Martí (2006: 37) acknowledged that social entrepreneurship involves ''the innovative use and combination of resources to pursue opportunities to catalyze social change and/or address social needs". Although there is a general lack of consensus around the definiton of social enterpreneurship, the creation of social value associated with the provision of solutions to social problems stands as a common theme in most social entrepreneurship definitions (Yang & Wu, 2015). Overall, it can be stated that, although different, social entrepreneurship can be viewed as a special branch within the field of entrepreneurship as it incorporates many basic similarities concerning traditional entrepreneurship (Martin & Osberg, 2007). The major difference relies on social objectives. As Yang and Wu (2015) observed, the creation of social value is arguably the most important feature of SE that distinguishes it from a normal business entity. Another focus regarding the concepualization of social entreppreneurship refers to the conflicting balance between social and economic goals (Peredo & McLean, 2006). For instance, Spieth et al. (2020, in press) assert that social businesses are hybrid businesses that simultaneously seek to achieve a social mission, as well as commercial activities, which involves managing the ambiguity of diverging objectives and values. Accordingly, these organisations need "to balance the expectations of multiple stakeholders, which bears the risks of satisfying the demands of one side while violating others', as well as undermining the stakeholders' social purpose's authenticity (...) In addition, each logic's distinct objectives may compete for bottleneck resources within the firm, such as managerial attention" Spieth et al. (2020: 3). Based on the definitions reviewed, resources are also commonly acknowledged as a critical factor to organisational sustainability. Thus, acquiring resources and developing new capabilities assume crucial importance to SE managers who need to conceive adequate strategies in order to achieve sustainable goals.

2.2 A Resource-Based View (RBV) of Social Entrepreneurship

The resource-based theory explains how firms sustain competitive advantage by focusing on their ability to develop resources and new capabilities as environments change (Barney, 2001). This theoretical framework is considered ''perhaps the most influential framework for understanding strategic management'' (Barney, 2001: 625). Therefore, the use of RBV in the context of social enterprises assumes particular relevance in understanding the type and nature of resources which are critical to the internationalisation processes and to the fulfillment of SEs mission from a global perspective. As it is widely recognised, from a for-profit perspective, RBV explains how firms maintain their competitive advantage. According to Barney, Wright, and Ketchen (2001: 625) "These resources and capabilities can be viewed as bundles of tangible and intangible assets, including a firm's management skills, its organisational processes and routines, and the information and knowledge it controls." Given the diversity of resources, not all firm resources hold the potential to sustain competitive advantages, and to do so, a resource must have four attributes, in particular: 1) it must be valuable; 2) rare; 3) imperfectly imitable; and 4) able to be exploited by a firm's organisational processes. Based on the resource-based view, a firm is considered to have a sustainable competitive advantage when it is creating more economic value than the marginal firm in its industry and when other firms are unable to duplicate the benefits of this strategy (Barney & Clark, 2007). Further, resources constitute the base of the organisation's competitive advantage not only in domestic markets but also in international markets (Prange & Pinho, 2017). This is in line with recent studies that have also emphasised resources and capabilities as important drivers for internationalisation.

2.3 Internationalisation of Social Enterprises

Despite the growing interest in social entrepreneurship, most of the literature in this area is still focused on single countries (or regional analysis) with little attention being given to the international perspective (Chen et al., 2018; Kerlin, 2013; Tukamushaba, Orobia, & George, 2011). The contribution of Zahra et al. (2008) was particularly relevant as they examined the key major drivers that have contributed to the emergence of international social enterprises. Among these drivers they emphasise global wealth disparity, the corporate social responsibility trend, technological advances and institutional voids. As they observed, the majority of the world's poor, illiterate and sick are located in less developed countries, which means that it is in these countries where social needs are less covered and, as a result of that, the awareness of global opportunities are more present. Social entrepreneurship emerged as an economically sustainable alternative that generates social value and alleviates social problems (Chen et al., 2018; Munoz, 2010). According to Alon et al. (2020) it is important to identify what distinguishes SEs internationalisation from for-profit firms. As these authors acknowledge, first, SEs pursue social and financial goals at the same time; second, unlike charitable organisations, which depend on donations and symbolic CSR-related activities, SEs need to be financially sustainable in the long run; third, SEs contribute to filling institutional voids at local, national and global level. In other words, SEs provide services, or goods that are either unavailable, lacking or of poor quality through the public and private sectors. From an international perspective, the emergence of a new type of social entrepreneur, better informed and holding managerial capabilities and resources, contributes to fulfill the SEs mission.

This is in line with Zahra et al. (2008) who maintain that SE managers view internationalisation as a promising strategy to enable the accomplishment of their social vision. Further, such view occurs at an early stage and is aligned with the desire to pursue the organisational vision on a global scale, despite their enduring limited resources. Another characteristic of these organisations is their natural ability to employ social support networks with different stakeholders in order to attract those resources that are essential to pursue their social mission.

2.4 Conceptual Propositions

This study utilises the RBV approach focusing on four resources: human capital, management know-how, industry-specific know-how and capability of the founder to obtain financial resources in accordance with Westhead, Wright, and Ucbasaran (2001).

Human Capital

According to Westhead et al. (2001:339) "Entrepreneurs with more diverse levels of human capital are purported to have the ability to develop relevant skills and contacts and are able to tap into dense resource and information networks". These authors argue that highly educated entrepreneurs have enhanced problem-solving skills and are able to widen social and business networks, which help them to find business opportunities, including entering foreign markets. According to Estrin, Mickiewicz and Stephan (2016) psychological approaches stress that education, and specially higher education has a two-fold socialising effect. It enhances flexibility, openness and independent thinking. Moreover, as these authors claim, higher education instills preferences and motivations which are in line with the core aspiration of social entrepreneurs to contribute to the welfare of others and to create wealth. Clearly, high levels of education may have a distinct effect on social as opposed to commercial entrepreneurs. This can be partly explained by the fact that the authors are in the presence of a more complex nature form of entrepreneurship. Social entrepreneurship deals distinctively with a number of features that are not present in their counterparts, such as social mission, dealing with institutionally challenging environments which are characterized by scarce resources (e.g., poverty, discrimination of women) and ultimately they also deal with the need to make some profit to assure the survival of the SE.

Management and Experiential Know-How

Management know-how may assist social entrepreneurs in acquiring resources through the ability to identify appropriate partners, investors, and advisors. This managerial capability would allow them to introduce better human resource practices, undertake more promising competitive strategies, and identify better market opportunities, including potential internationalisation opportunities (Westhead et al., 2001). In what concerns for-profit organisations, experiential knowledge is an important predictor of international activities as it helps to develop cognitive reasoning that compares previously experienced situations and newly encountered ones (Child et al., 2017). As these authors assert, relying on RBV, from the cognitive perspective, the decision-maker's previous international experience can reasonably inform his decision with regard to the best international strategy to pursue. Prange and Pinho (2017) maintain that experience and knowledge derived from previous activities in international settings expand the decision-maker's knowledge about international markets. In addition, it has been observed that managerial and experiential know-how induces entrepreneurs gradually to use more rational decision-making modes and enhance network connections, that is, it contributes to the accumulation of social capital that facilitates international activities.

Industry-Specific Know-How

Experience in a particular industry provides the founder of social enterprises with valuable resources such as networks, base of stakeholders, and the ability to seek opportunities leading to the success of their social ventures (Westhead et al., 2001). The knowledge of a competitive environment increases the possibility that organisations located in particular industries adopt generic business models that are similar in the way they configure components such as innovation, core competitive strengths, key network connections, among others (Child et al., 2017). To support this rationale, the authors take the United Nations report on inclusive business in Brazil (Programa das Nações Unidas para o Desenvolvimento, 2015) which posits that lower income markets need the necessary knowledge, technology and know-how to function.

Ability to Acquire Financial Capital

Many social enterprises struggle to achieve organisational sustainability. These organisations often need to compete for donors, volunteers, investors and customers. In such a competitive enviroment, the acquisition of resources and the development of capabilities to achieve social goals allow SEs to pursue a broader range of activities and projects (Bacq & Eddleston, 2018; Programa das Nações Unidas para o Desenvolvimento, 2015; Westhead et al., 2001). One great challenge for most SEs is to develop revenue streams that make them less dependent on donations and government funds, so the ability to acquire capital is key for the SEs' success. Due to the nature of their activities, SEs can hardly provide sufficient financial guarantees and warranties to potential and traditional financial supporters, which may explain why banks are often reluctant to support SE activities and particularly to support their international ambitions. However, they may apply to other types of financing that include venture philanthropies, social investment funds and governmental supports or benefits. The ability of social enterprises to obtain financing is critical to pursue their global activities. Considering the above discussion, the following research propositions are put forward:

RP1: Highly educated founders (or top-managers) are more likely to follow an international strategy.
RP2: Founders (or top-managers) who hold high management training tend to follow an international strategy.
RP3: Founders (or top management) evidencing high industry-specific know-how are likely to pursue an international strategy.
RP4: Higher ability to acquire financial capital is likely to lead SEs to pursue an international strategy.

3. METHODOLOGY

Given the complex nature of the topic, resources in social entrepreneurship and consequently its internationalisation path, along with the particularities and challenges faced by the Brazilian market, the authors adopted a qualitative case study research strategy. This approach provides a flexible and iterative process which enabled a detailed access of multiple perspectives within each case, allowing us to contribute to and develop existing theory.

The study reports the findings of four social enterprises indicated by Ashoka as part of their Globalizer Program in Brazil, a global initiative created in 2010 with the objective of supporting the internationalisation of social enterprises, connecting them with experts, supporters and investors (Ashoka, 2016). Founded in 1980 by Bill Drayton, Ashoka is a global, nonprofit organization, present in more than 90 countries, pioneer in the field of social innovation and support to social entrepreneurs that started operating in Brazil in 1986. Ashoka coined the term Social Entrepreneurship and characterized it as a field of work, being considered one of the six most influential NGOs in the world, according to the 2016 ranking of Swiss media organization - NGO Advisor (Ashoka, 2017, 2019).

The Globalizer Program is an Ashoka initiative that supports social entrepreneurs in their internationalisation process to spread their impact more broadly and efficiently. Ashoka fellows from the Globalizer Program were chosen for this analysis because they usually play a very active role in the markets in which they operate. The rationale for studying multiple cases, rather than a single one, was chosen to permit cross-comparisons amongst cases to improve the robustness of the findings (Yin, 2014).

3.1 Data Collection

The study relies on four case studies as information gathered from multiple sources provides more comphreensive and detailed undertanding of the topic under study. The selection of four cases is consistent with the sugested range of four to ten cases to allow an adequate level of construct abstraction from multiple cases (Eisenhardt, 1989). As the objective of this study is to provide useful insights about the nature of personal resources and capabilities to pursue an international strategy and not to test potential relationships between variables, a non-random sample was found appropriate. The sampled organisations also varied in terms of size and the nature of activities regarding their core missions. In Table 3.1 a summary of the organisations main characterists are presented.

The first stage of the research protocol started with an interview with an Ashoka director who indicated the companies that best suited the study objetives. The SE's responsibles were contacted and the purpose of the study was explained. Out of five companies, four accepted to participate in the research. In the second stage, in-depth interviews were conducted with the founders and directors from the social enterprises who agreed to participate in the study. As Rowley (2012:261) acknowledged "interviews are generally used in conducting qualitative research, in which the researcher is interested in collecting facts, or gaining insights into or understanding of opinions, attitudes, experiences, processes, behaviors, or predictions". On average each interview lasted one hour. The major key questions included in the interview addressed the four major dimensions of founder's capabilities: the level of education, the level of management training, the specific knowledge of the industry and the capability to attract financial resources.

A core set of questions guided the interviews (see Appendix B). The interviews typically lasted one hour. Digressions were common, and the participants' lines of thought were followed and probed in depth. All interviews were audiotaped and transcribed for aThe information obtained from the interviews was analysed using thematic content analysis to explore the guiding topics covered in the interviews which included the four major dimensions of the manager's profile: the level of education, the level of management training, the specific knowledge of the industry and the capability of attracting financial resources.

Interviews were registered, transcribed verbatim and analysed prior to undertaking content data analysis. Follow up conversations were also conducted to provide further explanation of less clear ideas found during the data collection. In addition, relevant documents about the organizations under study were collected at the time of interview. These multiple sources of data provided triangulation of reference material for thematic analysis (Cresswell, 2003).

Table 1. Main characteristics of the sampled organisations

Case	Designation	Area of Activity	Size	Revenue Sources	International Presence	Legal Form
Case #1	ISES	Incubator & Business Accelerator; Consulting	Medium	Partnerships & Commercial Activities	Mozambique	SE/SME
Case #2	Preta Hub	Cultural & Business event; Services	Micro	Sponsorship - public & private, Commercial activities	Columbia (TBC)	NGO/SME
Case #3	TdB Turma do Bem	Oral Heath	Micro	Sponsorships - Private, Donnations Commercial Activities	Latin America/ Portugal	SE
Case #4	Vivendas	House reconstruction	Small	Commercial Activities	Not Yet	SME

Source: The own authors

4. DATA ANALYSIS

The data collection process involved multiple sources, allowing the convergence and triangulation of findings (Jick, 1979). Data were analyzed and tested to enhance internal validity and reliability of the constructs (Yin, 2014). Reliability was assured by following a strict protocol of each interview (Eisenhardt, 1989). The qualitative analysis involved within-case and cross case analysis through representation of patterns of quotations and themes as well as comparing emerging patterns of data (Miles & Huberman, 1994). As Rowley (2012) observed there is no universal recipe for success, which means that data analysis can be a confusing and dauting process. Yet, there are a number of rules or steps that needs to be considered, namely: organising the data set, getting acquainted with the data, classifying data, coding, interpreting data and, presenting and writing up the data (Rowley, 2012). Consistent with these ideas, the four social enterprises comprising the sample used in the present study are briefly described, as follows:

Case Study 1: ISES

This organisation emerged from incubator and accelerator programs from the main universities in São Paulo and was sponsored by public authorities to eradicate poverty. ISES (Institute of Socioeconomics Solidary) has worked since its beginning in 2004 with the support and development of inclusive businesses. Between 2005 and 2014, in collaboration with Fundação Getúlio Vargas (FGV) ISES started their first partnerships with large companies interested in qualifying their investments in projects to strengthen local economies through development of inclusive businesses. In 2017, ISES started, in a partnership with Catering International & Serviços (CIS), to work in Mozambique to develop community-based suppliers, with emphasis on family farmers and artisanal fishers to supply CIS-managed restaurants in the country (ISES, 2019).

Case Study 2: Preta Hub - Feira Preta Festival

Preta Hub is an NGO and a commercial enterprise that comprises a network of independent small entrepreneurs seeking to promote business and cultural events with a focus on the Afro Brazilian community. Their main activity is the Feira Preta Festival (black fair), the largest black cultural event in Latin America. The event was born in 2002 as a product fair for African Brazilian entrepreneurs and today is a festival that presents content, products and services that represent the most inventive and innovative in black creativity in different segments. Currently, Preta Hub is negotiating the launch of Feira Preta Festival in Colombia, the second largest population of people of African descent in Latin America after Brazil (Preta, 2019).

Case Study 3: Turma do Bem (TdB)

In 1995 Fabio Bibancos, a well-known dentist, launched the "Dentist for good" project with a group of fellow dentists to work as volunteers to provide dental treatment to young people from the base of the pyramid (BoP). In 2002 he founded the TdB (gang for good), which became the largest specialized network of volunteers in the world, with the objective of promoting and scaling up the access to dental treatments. TdB is an OSCIP (Organisation of Civil Society of Public Interest) that operates with a number of commercial partnerships, sponsorships and donations (they do not take public funds) and mainly it coordinates around 16,000 volunteer dentists in Brazil, throughout Latina America and Portugal.

Case Study 4: Vivenda

Fernando Assad, one of the owners of Vivenda, has worked with his two partners for ten years at the CDHU (Development Company of Housing and Urban Development) in São Paulo carrying out urbanization projects for favelas (shantytowns). He realized that although the government focus had been on building new homes, the inadequacy of existing ones was a problematic issue, so in 2014 they launched the program Vivenda to reform homes of lower income families with solutions that integrate technical advice, specialised labor and installment payments. This is the only social enterprise that depends exclusively on their commercial activities as they are a regular for-profit SME. They have recently opened their first store and they plan to expand through this model which has called the attention of other countries, even though they plan to internationalize only after they consolidate their business model (Vivendas, 2019).

5. DISCUSSION

These four social enterprises represent a very heterogeneous group, evidencing diverse features with respect to size, business segments, stage of internationalisation, sources of revenues and legal forms. By comparing each organisation the authors found many differences and similarities in the way they have managed their resources in order to startup, sustain and develop their businesses and their path to internationalisation.

As previously mentioned, the key variable for small business internationalisation is the decision-maker of the firm. In line with Westhead et al. (2001) four categories of an entrepreneur's human capital are examined: general human capital, management know-how, specific industry know-how and the ability to acquire financial capital. Our main objective was to analyze the SEs resource management and mobilization strategies in order to identify capabilities that contribute to scale their social impact. The findings support the proposed view of social entrepreneurship, as the entrepreneurs in our cases pursued opportunities to address social problems, with the common goal of developing sustainable and independent businesses, in most cases, avoiding the use of government funds. In the case of Brazil, this conduct is an important sign of seriousness that helped them to strengthen their reputation and achieve the legitimacy that, in some cases, allowed their internationalisation. The analysis of each resource provided insights into the management, business models and performance, including their path of internationalisation, and thus contributing to the theoretical development on Social Entrepreneurship.

Considering each managerial resource, the authors observed that education, training as well as the industry-specific know-how were considered as crucial elements to the success of the SEs. In all cases, the role of the founders was crucial for the accomplishment of the organisation's initiatives, along with the active role of their teams, considered very motivated and committed to the success of their SEs. This finding contrasts with the common view according to which there is a conflict between social and economic missions (Desa & Basu, 2013; Tan & Yoo, 2015), leading us to consider that these SEs adopted complementary roles in order to bring together the 'economic' and the 'social' in their business equation and routines (Ormiston & Seymour, 2011). Interestingly, the management and industry know-how of the founders are also perceived as key capabilities to SEs internationalization success. In addition, findings demonstrate that in most cases founders used all their expertise, skills and network for the success of their projects. In the case of Vivenda, this expertise was decisive for the identification of opportunities based on a deep knowledge of the market and the needs of their users, allowing them to develop a specific "product" in a sustainable business model.

The internationalisation strategy topic deserves a special consideration as it varied greatly among the four social enterprises. It is worth noting that the main driver for internationalisation is the managers's intention to address specific marketing failures and at the same time fulfil unmet social needs in different locations around the globe. For instance, Turma do Bem (TdB) is the most international organisation and is present in 12 countries in Latina America and Portugal (TdB, 2019). Its internationalisation is partly explained due to global wealth inequalities, in particular the growing price value of dental treatments for young people and due to the institutional failures in providing such services. This is followed by ISES who started their operations in Mozambique. Nevertheless, Preta Hub already caught the attention of Colombian investors and potential partners and Vivenda has caught the eye of investors from Argentina, who want to replicate their business model. It was also found that personal networks and local connections revealed to be rather important for SEs to establish abroad, share their resources and obtain competitive advantages. This capability can be reflected in the establishment of alliances and partnerships with foreign players. Overall, these organisations are mainly motivated by fulfilling unmet social needs. A relevant issue emerges with regard to international activity. The four SEs stressed that to implement a successful internationally strategy it is crucial to possess high educated entrepreneurs, high training, high industry-specific know-how as well as high capability to access financial capital. It can be concluded therefore that the four proposed research propositions are confirmed by the data.

For instance, in what concerns financial capital, SEs are likely to rely on different sources of financial capital, such as governmental grants, philanthropic donations and social investment funds. In fact, the ability that these organisations have in securing and obtaining financing is a key factor for determining their success abroad. Additionally, in order to succeed these organisations need to maximize their knowledge about different international markets and take full advantage of their social networks and connections internationally. They need to show that they are credible and trustful among potential financiers.

6. CONCLUSION, IMPLICATIONS FOR THEORY AND PRACTICE & FURTHER RESEARCH

This study contributes to enhancing our understanding of the role of different resources in the growth, sustainability and internationalisation of SEs. The findings obtained from the case studies confirm the relevance of the four considered resources, which are human capital, management know-how, industry know-how and capability to obtain financial resources for the achievement of success among SEs. To some extent, the influence of resources on the SEs internationalisation strategy was also evidenced. The study highlights the fact that internationalisation strategies are greatly influenced by the quality of the SEs business model and by the social impact these organisations are able to provide. The authors conclude that creative solutions may work everywhere and that the success of SEs is not necessarily related to the economic or social stage of its original market. This knowledge may provide policy-makers and practitioners with additional insights into the key resource-based factors associated with the SEs decision to internationalize their business. It is also significant to observe that in all cases, the duality of their missions was not an issue, as teams were highly motivated, dedicated and fully committed to the success and impact of their SEs. This study reinforces the importance of balancing the SEs' dual missions by conciliating 'economic' and 'social' goals in their regular functioning, and therefore confronting the common view that there is a conflict between social and economic missions (Desa & Basu, 2013; Tan & Yoo, 2015).

Further, the RBV demonstrated its theoretical relevance to examine the processes through which key resources influence the overall success of SEs. In particular, the study findings demonstrated that SEs whose founders have more resources, larger contact networks and connections, and considerable management know-how are likely to have more propensity to pursue an international strategy which enables them to pursue their social mission. In terms of limitations, the authors recognise that the sample size of four social enterprises may have implications for the results and limit possible generalisations. Therefore, the authors encourage future research addressing this topic, including quantitative studies in order to further confirm our results. Future studies could extend this work by examining either the process of foreign market establishment of SEs and the decision of entry mode. Concerning the later Musteen, Datta, and Herrman (2009) argued that the size and previous experience are important aspects that may influence the choice of entry mode. Ultimately, the question resides in how these processes differ from their for-profit counterparts. Another area that deserves further investigation relates to potential barriers

SEs may face in the course of their internationalisation process. In the case of traditional firms' liability of outsidership, lack of access to relevant networks as well as vital resources and knowledge are considered common barriers for successful establishment in international markets. The question is if these same barriers also apply to SEs. This is another interesting research line that could be further explored.

REFERENCES

Alon, I., Mersland, R., Musteen, M., & Randy, T. (2020). The research frontier on internationalization of social enterprises. *Journal of World Business*, *55*(5), 101091. doi:10.1016/j.jwb.2020.101091

Ashoka. (2016). *the Ashoka Globalizer Program*. Author.

Ashoka. (2017). *Institutional Report - Ashoka Brazil*. Author.

Ashoka. (2019). www.ashoka.org

Bacq, S., & Eddleston, K. A. (2018). A resource-based view of social entrepreneurship: How stewardship culture benefits scale of social impact. *Journal of Business Ethics*, *152*(3), 589–611. doi:10.100710551-016-3317-1

Barney, J. B. (1991). Firm resources and sustained competitive advantage. *Journal of Management*, *17*(1), 99–120. doi:10.1177/014920639101700108

Barney, J. B. (2001). Resource-based theories of competitive advantage: A ten-year retrospective on the resource-based view. *Journal of Management*, *27*(6), 643–650. doi:10.1177/014920630102700602

Barney, J. B., & Clark, D. N. (2007). Resource-Based Theory: Creating and Sustaining Competitive Advantage. Oxford University Press. doi:10.1362/026725708X382046

Barney, J. B., Wright, M., & Ketchen, D. (2001). The resource-based view of the firm: Ten years after. *Journal of Management*, *16*(3), 171–174.

Chen, J., Saarenketo, S., & Puumalainen, K. (2018). Home country institutions, social value orientation, and the internationalization of ventures. *International Business Review*, *27*(2), 443–454. doi:10.1016/j.ibusrev.2017.09.011

Child, J., Hsieh, L., Elbanna, S., Karmowska, J., Marinova, S., Puthusserry, P., Tsai, T., Narooz, R., & Zhang, Y. (2017). SME international business models: The role of context and experience. *Journal of World Business*, *52*(5), 664–679. doi:10.1016/j.jwb.2017.05.004

Cresswell, J. W. (2003). *Research design: Qualitative, quantitative, and mixed methods approaches* (2nd ed.). Sage Publications.

Desa, G., & Basu, S. (2013). Optimization or bricolage? Overcoming resource constraints in global social entrepreneurship. *Strategic Entrepreneurship Journal*, *8*(6), 4517–4524. doi:10.1002ej.1150

Di Zhang, D., & Swanson, L. A. (2013). Social entrepreneurship in nonprofit organizations: An empirical investigation of the synergy between social and business objectives. *Journal of Nonprofit & Public Sector Marketing*, *25*(1), 105–125. doi:10.1080/10495142.2013.759822

Doherty, B., Haugh, H., & Lyon, F. (2014). Social enterprises as hybrid organizations: A review and research agenda. *International Journal of Management Reviews*, *16*(4), 417–436. doi:10.1111/ijmr.12028

Eisenhardt, K. M. (1989). Building theories from case study research. *Academy of Management Review*, *14*(4), 532–550. doi:10.5465/amr.1989.4308385

Estrin, S., Mickiewicz, T., & Stephan, U. (2016). Human capital in social and commercial entrepreneurship. *Journal of Business Venturing*, *31*(4), 449–467. doi:10.1016/j.jbusvent.2016.05.003

ISES - Instituto Socio Economia Solidária. (2019). http://ises.org.br

Jick, T. J. (1979). Mixing qualitative and quantitative methods: Triangulation in action. *Administrative Science Quarterly*, *24*(4), 602–611. doi:10.2307/2392366

Kerlin, J. A. (2006). Social enterprise in the United States and Europe: Understanding and learning from the differences. *Voluntas*, *17*(3), 246–262. doi:10.100711266-006-9016-2

Kerlin, J. A. (2010). A comparative analysis of the global emergence of social enterprise. *Voluntas*, *21*(2), 162–179. doi:10.100711266-010-9126-8

Kerlin, J. A. (2013). Defining social enterprise across different contexts: A conceptual framework based on institutional factors. *Nonprofit and Voluntary Sector Quarterly*, *42*(1), 84–108. doi:10.1177/0899764011433040

Loayza, N., & Pennings, S. (2020). *Macroeconomic Policy in the Time of COVID-19: A Primer for Developing Countries*. Research & Policy Briefs, 28. Washington, DC: World Bank Group. https://documents.worldbank.org/curated/en/951811585836124198/Macroeconomic-Policy-in-the-Time-of-COVID-19-A-Primer-for-Developing-Countries

Luke, B., & Chu, V. (2013). Social enterprise versus social entrepreneurship: An examination of the 'why' and 'how' in pursuing social change. *International Small Business Journal*, *31*(7), 764–784. doi:10.1177/0266242612462598

Mair, J., & Martí, I. (2006). Social Entrepreneurship Research: A Source of Explanation, Prediction, and Delight. *Journal of World Business*, *41*(1), 36–44. doi:10.1016/j.jwb.2005.09.002

Martin, R. L., & Osberg, S. (2007). Social entrepreneurship: The case for definition. *Stanford Social Innovation Review*, *5*(2), 28–39.

Meyskens, M., Robb-Post, C., Stamp, J. A., Carsrud, A. L., & Reynolds, P. D. (2010). Social ventures from a resource-based perspective: An exploratory study assessing global Ashoka fellows. *Entrepreneurship Theory and Practice*, *34*(4), 661–680. doi:10.1111/j.1540-6520.2010.00389.x

Miles, M. B., & Huberman, A. M. (1984). Drawing valid meaning from qualitative data: Toward a shared craft. *Educational Researcher*, *13*(5), 20–30. doi:10.3102/0013189X013005020

Munoz, J. M. (2010). *International Social Entrepreneurship: Pathways to Personal and Corporate Impact*. Business E. doi:10.4128/9781606491072

Musteen, M., Datta, D. K., & Herrmann, P. (2009). Ownership structure and CEO compensation: Implications for the choice of foreign market entry modes. *Journal of International Business Studies*, *40*(2), 321–338. doi:10.1057/jibs.2008.63

Ormiston, J., & Seymour, R. (2011). Understanding Value Creation in Social Entrepreneurship: The Importance of Aligning Mission, Strategy and Impact Measurement. *Journal of Social Entrepreneurship*, *2*(2), 125–150. doi:10.1080/19420676.2011.606331

Peredo, A. M., & McLean, M. (2006). Social entrepreneurship: A critical review of the concept. *Journal of World Business*, *41*(1), 56–65. doi:10.1016/j.jwb.2005.10.007

Prange, C., & Pinho, J. C. (2017). How personal and organizational drivers impact on SME international performance: The mediating role of organizational innovation. *International Business Review*, *26*(1), 1114–1123. doi:10.1016/j.ibusrev.2017.04.004

PretaF. (2019). https://pretahub.com/festival-feira-preta

Programa das Nações Unidas para o Desenvolvimento. (2015). *Mercados inclusivos no Brasil*. Retrieved from http://www.br.undp.org

Rowley, J. (2012). Conducting research interviews. *Management Research Review*, *35*(3/4), 260–271. doi:10.1108/01409171211210154

Seelos, C., & Mair, J. (2005). Social entrepreneurship: Creating new business models to serve the poor. *Business Horizons*, *48*(3), 241–246. doi:10.1016/j.bushor.2004.11.006

Tan, W. L., & Yoo, S. J. (2015). Social entrepreneurship intentions of nonprofit organizations. *Journal of Social Entrepreneurship*, *6*(1), 103–125. doi:10.1080/19420676.2014.954260

TdB – Turma do Bem. (2019). http://turmadobem.org.br

Tukamushaba, E. K., Orobia, L., & George, B. P. (2011). Development of a conceptual model to understand international social entrepreneurship and its application in the Ugandan context. *Journal of International Entrepreneurship*, *9*(4), 282–298. doi:10.100710843-011-0079-9

VivendasP. (2019). http://programavivenda.com.br

Westhead, P., Wright, M., & Ucbasaran, D. (2001). The internationalization of new and small firms: A resource-based view. *Journal of Business Venturing*, *16*(4), 333–358. doi:10.1016/S0883-9026(99)00063-4

Wright, M., Westhead, P., & Ucbasaran, D. (2007). Internationalization of small and medium-sized enterprises (SMEs) and international entrepreneurship: A critique and policy implications. *Regional Studies*, *41*(7), 1013–1030. doi:10.1080/00343400601120288

Yang, Y., & Wu, S. (2015). An exploratory study to understand the internationalization strategies of social enterprises. *Journal of Social Entrepreneurship*, *6*(1), 31–41. doi:10.1080/19420676.2014.954255

Yin, R. K. (2014). Applied social research methods series: Vol. 5. *Case study research : Design and methods*. doi:10.1097/FCH.0b013e31822dda9e

Zahra, S. A., Gedajlovic, E., Neubaum, D. O., & Shulman, J. M. (2009). A typology of social entrepreneurs: Motives, search processes and ethical challenges. *Journal of Business Venturing, 24*(5), 519–532. doi:10.1016/j.jbusvent.2008.04.007

Zahra, S. A., Newey, L. R., & Li, Y. (2014). On the frontiers: The implications of social entrepreneurship for international entrepreneurship. *Entrepreneurship Theory and Practice, 38*(1), 137–158. doi:10.1111/etap.12061

Zahra, S. A., Rawhouser, H., Bhawe, N., Neubaum, D., & Hayton, J. (2008). Globalization of social entrepreneurship opportunities. *Strategic Entrepreneurship Journal, 1*, 11–26. doi:10.1002ej

KEY TERMS AND DEFINITIONS

Financial Capital: Can be defined as a tangible (economic asset) consisting of both personal and third-party funding. Personal funds includes entrepreneur's personal savings, financial assistance from family and friends as well as banking loans obtained through personal relationships. Third party funding includes government loans and grants or funds, seed capital, business angels or venture capitals.

Human Capital: It is mainly related with education, skills, tacit knowledge, which play an important role in instigating entrepreneurial activity, productivity, and the relative success of SE ventures.

Industry-Specific Know-How: Experience derived from having worked in the same industry before starting a new business provides the founder of social enterprises with valuable resources, such as networks, base of stakeholders and the ability to seek new opportunities.

International Strategy: A social enterprise (SE) commits and plans to operate in overseas markets. This may occur at two levels. First, the SE focuses its marketing strategy on a single market. Second, the SE treats a global region or the global market as potential markets.

Managerial and Personal Know-How: Several entrepreneurs exhibit some characteristics or, at least, some talents that contribute to his predisposition to leverage the SEs resources and competencies for success.

Resource-Based View: This theory explains how firms keep and maintain their competitive advantages by developing resources and new capabilities as environments change.

Social Entrepreneurship: It is mainly related to the provision of solutions to social problems and the creation of social value.

Chapter 4
Challenges of the Internationalization Process:
A Case Study of a Knowledge-Intensive Service Company

Carolina Teixeira Carlos
University of Aveiro, Portugal

Nicole Bento de Jesus
University of Aveiro, Portugal

Raquel Nogueira Henriques
University of Aveiro, Portugal

António Carrizo Moreira
https://orcid.org/0000-0002-6613-8796
University of Aveiro, Portugal

EXECUTIVE SUMMARY

This chapter analyzes the internationalization strategy of a Portuguese knowledge-based service firm. It is based on a case study and the main objective is to discuss what internationalization theory best explains the company's internationalization strategy. The literature reviews the main internationalization patterns—Uppsala model, born globals, born again globals, and born regionals—so that a comparison of the main characteristics of each theory is discussed and analyzed. At the end of the chapter, a table summarizes the main characteristics of the internationalization process of each model presented. The case study is based on the analysis of both primary data from the firm and data obtained from an interview obtained with the CEO.

DOI: 10.4018/978-1-7998-4387-0.ch004

INTRODUCTION

Internationalization is of key importance for small and medium-sized firms (SMEs) to grow, as domestic markets are sometimes very restricted. Internationalization helps SMEs to exploit their competitive advantages abroad (Ribau, Moreira, & Raposo, 2017; Stanisauskaite & Kock, 2016). Internationalization is normally known as the process of increasing involvement in international activities and is related to how companies explore international markets (Ribau et al., 2015; 2018a; 2018b).

Although internationalization has been traditionally considered an incremental process in which companies gradually increase their involvement in overseas markets through a series of evolutionary stages (Bell, McNaughton, & Young, 2001; Ribau et al., 2015), several companies follow different international paths as a consequence not only of their capabilities, but also as a result of their active behavior (Pinto, Ribeiro, & Moreira, 2018; Moreira, Alves, Martins, Pereira, & Conceição, 2018; Ribau et al., 2017; 2018a).

Although the Uppsala model—which advocates an evolutionary, sequential and linearly growing international involvement (Ribau et al., 2015)—and the network-based view of the firm—based on relations among market players (Hakansson & Snehota, 2006)—have been extensively used to explain how some firms internationalize, there have been new models—known as born global and born again global in which firms internationalize rapidly or suddenly, based on entrepreneurial behaviors empowered by powerful, open-minded entrepreneurs/managers (Bell, McNaughton, & Young, 2001; McDougall & Oviatt, 2000)—that explain internationalization from a different perspective.

In the last decades, major changes have led to a global socio-economic climate. Globalization, emergence of new markets, advances in technology and a constant need for novelty are examples of those changes (Engelman, Zen, & Fracasso, 2015). Thus, and related to this paradigm, governments have acknowledged the inherent benefits of increasing exports, in order to improve the balance of payments, among other indicators and indexes (Bayfield, Dana, & Stewart, 2009).

Nowadays, in an increasingly global world economies are constantly growing. Several countries recognize the importance of the internationalization process, as this allows increased productivity and economic growth (Marin, 1992; Bayfield, Dana, & Stewart, 2009), as well as reduced costs and the exploitation of economies of scale (Jornal de Negócios, 2019).

Based on a case study analyzing a Portuguese knowledge-intensive firm—known as EPSILON for confidentiality reasons—that seeks to internationalize its activities, the objective of this chapter is to examine the internationalization process from a historical perspective and to debate the intricacies of the main internationalization theories: the Uppsala perspective; the born global; born-regional; and born again global theories. The aim is to confront these four theories in order to address the firm's particularities within them.

Despite the criticism associated with case studies, fundamentally due to the impossibility of generalizing the results obtained, such studies undeniably contribute to the acquisition and construction of knowledge (Mariotto, Zanni, & Moraes, 2014). Therefore, this case study aims to explore, understand and analyze the strategic formulation combined with the internationalization process, framing the perspective and processes conducted by EPSILON.

The case study shows how EPSILON addresses new market entry opportunities abroad, based on the firm's strategy to deploy their new services in international markets, which is a very significant advance for this company. Accordingly, the aim of this chapter is to examine EPSILON from a business historical perspective and the internationalization process. In order to achieve that goal, several theories about internationalization are presented and discussed throughout this chapter.

The chapter is structured in five main sections. After the introduction, the second section addresses the importance of internationalization. To do so, a literature review addresses four internationalization theories: the Uppsala model, born globals, born regionals and born again globals. The third section presents the methodology implemented. The case study is presented in the fourth section, with section five containing the results. Finally, the discussion and conclusions are presented in sections six and seven.

LITERATURE REVIEW

Internationalization

Globalization is seen to involve great complexity, observing several internationalization strategies adopted by firms, when entering global markets (Bayfield, Dana, & Stewart, 2009; Ribau et al., 2015).

The internationalization process leads to benefits within the organization, namely growth opportunities and value creation. Furthermore, firms that expand into foreign markets increase their technological expertise, as they also increase their knowledge of the market. All these improvements lead to better performance and allow the firm to continue its innovation process, and to build a stronger presence within the market (Engelman, Zen, & Fracasso, 2015).

Nowadays, firms are increasingly involved in internationalizing their businesses, making this an inherent and essential process to improve business performance (Zhang, Beatty, & Walsh, 2008). Moreover, in the business world the internationalization process is embedded in a globalized and constantly changing environment (Johanson & Vahlne, 1990).

Although it may be crucial for firms to expand to overseas markets, they need to develop internal competencies and knowledge about foreign markets before embarking on the internationalization process, as well as the concomitant international contacts and partnerships. Nevertheless, the ultimate challenge in a global market is the rapid learning and adaptation vis-à-vis firms' main competitors (Schueffel, Rico, & Amann, 2014).

The internationalization process can occur based on two dichotomous situations (Ribau et al., 2017): reactive or proactive reasons. In the former, internationalization is the reaction to an event, where changes happen during a period of time. The latter, proactive motivation, represents strategic changes and the firm's own will to internationalize (Braga, Marques, & Serrasqueiro, 2018). Some of the reasons underlying the firm's intention to internationalize quickly can be: new opportunities in global markets, favorable exchange rates, and adverse, negative conditions in the domestic market. In contrast, the intention to remain in the domestic market may be motivated by difficulties in commercial conditions in international markets and unfavorable exchange rates (Bell, McNaughton, & Young, 2001).

The internationalization of services can take place through five not mutually exclusive strategies (Grönroos, 1999): (1) direct exports; (2) systems exports; (3) direct market entry; (4) indirect market entry; and (5) electronic marketing. It is also important to take into account that a first step towards the commercialization of services at an international level involves looking for a way to allow access to the services in the chosen market (Johanson & Vahlne, 1990). The internationalization of services has emerged as a relevant research area as a result of firms' intention and need to be present in international markets (Javalgi & Martin, 2007).

Knowledge-intensive Business Services

Knowledge-intensive business services (KIBS) are considered to be at the top of technological development and innovation (Acs & Audretsch, 2005; Jenssen & Nybakk, 2013). The innovations resulting from those firms are transferred to the innovation ecosystems they belong to (Battisti, 2012). Considering the importance of technology for the success of innovation-based services (Hipp, 2008), it is worth mentioning that KIBS must be designed based on the complexities of the technology-based systems that are part of innovation ecosystems (Djellal & Gallouj, 2008; Battisti, 2012).

Adopting an international and rapid orientation has become increasingly relevant for KIBS (Karagozoglu & Lindell, 1998; Arenius, Sasi & Gabrielsson, 2005). This is a key premise as KIBS need to create procedures that allow better protection of their business value, in order to avoid negative outcomes such as knowledge expropriation (Oviatt & McDougall, 1994; Arenius et al, 2005).

KIBS refer to services involving economic activities that are expected to result in: creation, accumulation or dissemination of knowledge (Braga et al., 2018). These firms' growth comes not only from the firms' demand for knowledge and inputs to overcome both technological and social changes, but also from organizational and outsourcing strategies (Miles, 2005).

Uppsala Model

The Uppsala model is one of the most studied in the literature on internationalization (Coviello & McAuley, 1999; Ribau et al., 2015). This model explains that internationalization is a sequential process. It also states that it takes a learning process for firms to evolve and develop their marketing strategy abroad (Furtado, Pereira, Pereira & Moreira, 2019; Ribau et al., 2015), and that internationalization takes place, firstly in foreign markets geographically and culturally close to the domestic market, and only afterwards in geographically and culturally distant markets (Bayfield, Dana, & Stewart, 2009). Therefore, after solid consolidation in the domestic market, firms begin their process of internationalization (Chetty & Campbell-Hunt, 2004).

This internationalization model is based on two premises: the importance of the knowledge-based approach regarding the foreign markets targeted as well as resource commitment to that market (Johanson & Vahlne, 1990). That is why, unequivocally, the key point of this model lies in a learning process regarding the new market, which leads to greater commitment through investment in that new market (Chetty & Campbell-Hunt, 2004; Johanson & Wiedersheim-Paul, 1975).

Born Global

Research concerning born globals began to appear during the 1990s (Cavusgil & Knight, 2015; Ribau et al., 2015). This type of firm is defined as being international from inception (Knight & Cavusgil, 1996). In order to explore this phenomenon, born globals can be analyzed taking into account four parameters (Oviatt & McDougall, 1994): (1) speed of internationalization from inception; (2) percentage of exports; (3) foreign market scope; and (4) firm size. Born global firms are considered to be strongly innovative, aiming to break new ground as they challenged the traditional theories on internationalization (Eurofound, 2012; Fernandes, Simões, Pereira, & Moreira, 2019), not going through an incremental internationalization process centered first in the domestic market. Therefore, born globals seek to exploit their multiple competitive advantages in foreign markets, right from their inception (Knight & Cavusgil, 1996).

Generally, born globals are SMEs that have operations in several international markets and are present in technological sectors (Fernandes et al., 2019; Furtado et al., 2019). Indeed, these firms would not exist if they did not have a foreign presence (Bayfield, Dana, & Stewart, 2009) and due to their limited resources, exporting activities are the most common form of entry (Cavusgil & Knight, 2015).

Chetyy and Campbell-Hunt (20014) advocate that the main characteristic of a born global's internationalization process is based on the global economic transformation which leads to and enables greater competition in foreign markets. They also state that born globals are fast learners, constantly looking for solutions as difficulties and problems arise in the internationalization process. Once again, born globals contrast strongly with the traditional internationalization process model which corresponds to a slow / gradual accumulation of experience and knowledge in each foreign market and country.

Born global firms compete through a knowledge-based competitive advantage, which they use to exploit the dynamics of an increasingly global market environment (Bell et al., 2001). Therefore, globalization helps leverage the position held by born global firms, as they share a vision that the world is their market (Cavusgil & Knight, 2015).

Born Again Global

Born again globals are normally well-established firms in their domestic markets, with no great motivation to start an internationalization process (Furtado et al., 2019; Pinto et al., 2018). Suddenly, born again globals embrace a rapid and dedicated internationalization process. Changes in administration and management roles, acquisition and ownership of the firm are some of the reasons that both enable and trigger the internationalization process (Bell et al., 2001; Pinto et al., 2018). One of the main motivations to enter foreign markets is to exploit both new networks and resources (Baum, Schwens & Kabst, 2015). Overall, born again globals are firms focused on the domestic market which, when facing strategic changes, metamorphose into firms with a focus on foreign markets (Schueffel et al., 2014).

Born again globals are frequent in technological industry, and regarding their internationalization process, there are no pre-defined time criteria for that process to happen, as opposed to born global firms. These firms are late internationalizers that begin the process by choosing to enter several markets and adapt their products accordingly (Baum, Schwens, & Kabst, 2015). Schueffek et al. (2014) consider born again globals as innovative firms, as they adapt to changes. Furthermore, the sustainability of these firms is based on their preparation and adaptation, which allow them to get their products to new foreign markets.

Born Regional

Born regional companies have an internationalization process similar to born global companies, and are characterized by restricting their internationalization process and activities to geographical areas where there are similar cultures and business approaches (Baum, Schwens, & Kabst, 2015). They are associated with a lower probability of learning orientation, considering that they do not need to spend much time getting to know the markets in which they wish to be present (Baum, Schwens, & Kabst, 2011). Born regional companies are initially focused on the domestic market, and later, when identifying opportunities abroad, start a rapid process of internationalization—and are therefore similar to a born global company (Maciejewshki & Wach, 2019).

Born regional companies aim for a quick entry into foreign markets in the early stages of their existence. Nevertheless, considering that they are restricted to a geographical area and close cultures, it is difficult for them to have the necessary resources to implement a broadly global strategy (Baum, Schwens, & Kabst, 2015). Moreover, although born regional companies focus on geographically close markets, they aim for internationalization on a global scale, and it is relevant for them to have knowledge, through early investment, of global markets and their complexity (Rugman & Verbeke, 2007).

RESEARCH METHOD

This chapter is based on a case study of an intensive knowledge-based service firm—EPSILON—which is a spinoff of the University of Aveiro, in Portugal. It involves a qualitative analysis based on both an interview carried out with EPSILON's CEO and previous knowledge of the firm, gained from public presentations. EPSILON's core business is based on providing intensive knowledge-based service activities in the areas of software and hardware to the business sector, and it seeks to internationalize its business activities. The choice of EPSILON was based on its commitment and success as a service provider seeking to expand activities abroad.

As the case study method allows analysis of particular situations, it was selected to analyze EPSILON, as this can combine known theories with new empirical results drawn from specific situations under analysis. The case study also allows the investigation of particular phenomena within their real-life contexts, analysis and interpretation of retrospective information and the possible development of new theoretical and practical insights (Eisenhardt, 1989; Ghauri, 2004; Ribau et al., 2019; Yin, 2008). Moreover, the case study method is particularly appropriate to analyze a dynamic perspective over time involving a complex nonlinear internationalization process (Durão & Moreira, 2019; Nogueira, & Moreira, 2019; Vissak & Francioni, 2013; Silva & Moreira, 2019; Welch & Welch, 2009).

The case study method, based on a single case study, makes it possible to adapt the particularity of the analysis according to the object of study, as well as the use of inductive and deductive approaches (Piekkari et al., 2009; Voss et al., 2002). These approaches are particularly useful when addressing explanatory and exploratory aspects (trying to deal with the 'why' and 'how') and when uncovering relational aspects that take place over time (Durão & Moreira, 2019; Nogueira & Moreira, 2019; Yin, 2008).

EPSILON was selected from a purposive sampling perspective, which involves the selection of cases that meet four important requirements for this research (Patton, 2015): (a) being involved in the exploration of the idiosyncrasies associated with inward international business activities; (b) participation in the provision of service-based activities; (c) having core activities aimed at different market segments; and (d) actively seeking to increase the international market segment.

Typical of a qualitative methodology, a semi-structured interview was arranged with EPSILON's CEO to collect data. This took place in May 2019 and lasted approximately one hour. This semi-structured interview aimed especially to obtain primary information form the interviewee. Secondary information from public sources—such as the firm's website, marketing information from industrial associations and multiple observations—complemented primary data from the interview and was important to ensure the validity and reliability of data (Ghauri, 2004). The interview was complemented by a visit to EPSILON's premises to get a deeper understanding of EPSILON's *modus operandi.* The interview allowed us to understand EPSILON's internationalization strategies and supported our goal of debating EPSILON's internationalization activities and the applicability of the different theoretical perspectives.

This procedure helped the interviewee feel more comfortable while speaking in his own environment. The researchers maintained a passive and unobtrusive presence, not to interfere with on-going events and activities. After the interview, the researchers' impressions were summarized for subsequent analysis.

To facilitate the interviewing process, the interviewers began by explaining the research, guaranteeing anonymity and requesting authorization to audio-record the interview. The interview script was developed to explore the evolution of international paths, the importance of the internationalization process EPSILON was going through, and the different modes of entry to international markets. The interview script included questions to triangulate the information obtained from informants with additional information obtained through the firm's website and public sources (e.g. firm size, age, international presence/experience, main current markets, etc.).

Data from all sources were collected and transcribed into a single case story, helping to identify missing information.

CASE STUDY PRESENTATION

EPSILON is an organization that operates in the business to business (B2B) market. It was founded in March 2010 and operated in the market as a spin-off of the University of Aveiro. Originally, it resulted from a research project (Mathematics Teaching Project—PmatE).

EPSILON focuses on consultancy and professional training, providing assistance with computer-based solutions in education and in producing and editing pedagogical content. Moreover, EPSILON's operations are based on differentiation activities through innovation in providing solutions that meet the specific needs of its target audience.

The products and services offered by EPSILON are based on the development of software and hardware for the education sector. Examples of its important service activities are, among others: the SIGA (Integrated Management and Learning System) project and the SEI (Integrated School System) project, both within the scope of school management software; mobile applications for municipalities and community councils, within the scope of municipal school management software; and the commercialization of multi-brand computer equipment (computers, interactive whiteboards, printers, among others). All school management software seeks to reduce operational costs for their client institutions throughout the educational process, as EPSILON is focused on the provision of fast and reliable online processes. Since the technological solutions presented by EPSILON are designed and built as brand new solutions, all products developed and marketed by EPSILON are customized according to their clients' specific needs.

At an early stage, EPSILON had only two main core activities: one in the area of computer programming and another in education support services. In 2014 it adopted a growth strategy based on those two main core activities, and ever since those two main business activities have been responsible for 98% of EPSILON's sales volume.

EPSILON's main target markets are municipalities and schools, both nationally and abroad, especially Brazil, Spain and Mozambique. For greater success, EPSILON is involved in several partnerships with science and technology-based institutions. EPSILON's partners include both higher education institutions, such as the University of Aveiro, Portugal, and other companies operating in the Information and Communication Technology sector, as is the case of Altice Portugal.

The year 2012 was a very important milestone in EPSILON's evolution as it became a national leader in the segment of school management platforms, with more than 120 solutions implemented in several municipalities. Also, due to the growth of its innovative capacity and entrepreneurial spirit, in 2012 EPSILON was awarded the prize of Best Start-Up Company 2012 by TecParques—Portuguese Association of Science and Technology Parks.

RESULTS

EPSILON is a company with headquarters at the Aveiro Science Park. Originally it started at the University of Aveiro Incubator. It emerged in 2010 as a result of a spin-off of a research project of the University of Aveiro. The company's CEO stated during the interview that they were growing so rapidly that "*we couldn't respond to the requests from customers*." Thus, there was a need to create the company so that the project could "*grow at the business level*" and be able to provide "*a much more agile response to customers*."

EPSILON operates in the software industry and its clients, in Portugal, are "*the public sector, that is, councils and municipalities, schools, central government and the autonomous regions*." Internationally their work was "*primarily for schools (both in the public and private sectors) or for governments*." It currently has around "*45 employees*" and in 2018 the sales volume was approximately "*3.300.000 euros*." Recently the company applied to two programs offering financial support for the internationalization processes "*QREN and Portugal 2020*."

EPSILON was focused first on serving the domestic market, which proved possible as a result of two factors: firstly, due to the "particular product type" they sell, and, secondly, as a result of the legal demand for these products/services that "*require municipalities to have a certain number of solutions*."As a result, EPSILON managed to internalize technology and market knowledge that allowed the company to rapidly win over the Portuguese market. This enabled massive growth at a national level and, consequently, pushed the firm"into the international market."

The internationalization process emerged between 2011 and 2012, "*mainly in Portuguese-speaking African Countries*", and began with "*Mozambique and Brazil*." Considering the date of the company's creation, 2010, this was a rapid process. This speed was thanks to "*contacts and relationships with a number of countries*", during their involvement in the"*research project of the university*" (PmatE). The CEO also stated that the "*first markets*" conquered by the company were connected to the networks established previously during the university project. Entry into these markets was fostered by relationships, as "*several entities knew*" their work and due to their attendance at trade fairs.

To achieve success in the internationalization process, the importance of "*adapting the product to the particular market*" is crucial, as a product standardization strategy was not possible due to the particularities of each market. The Brazilian market and the particularity of its form of Portuguese are presented as an example, considering that "*if the solution is not presented in Brazilian Portuguese*" a "*serious problem*" exists, despite the cultural and linguistic proximity between the two countries.

In 2018 the percentage of exports was between 10% and 12% of the company's total sales volume, although EPSILON had managed to reach a percentage of 30% in previous years. The reason for the decline in this percentage is related largely to one factor: the decrease in revenues from two countries, Brazil and Mozambique, with a greater emphasis on the Brazilian market, where invoicing in the last two years "*has been close to zero*." Therefore, it is possible to point out some difficulties experienced by the company in those two markets. The complexity of the Brazilian market for a highly successful internationalization process is highlighted, as the CEO states that this is one of the "*most complex markets*" he knows, despite the existence of greater facility with the language. He states that there are apparent facilities at the beginning of the process, but that ultimately, "*it is one of the markets where success is very difficult to attain*". Additionally, it is a market with a "*problem of payment restrictions*", generating various adversities. Regarding the Mozambican market, the difficulties experienced corresponded to the "*hidden debts of Mozambique*". This situation caused EPSILON a number of problems, resulting in the largest projects the company had "*with the government*" being "*entirely cancelled due to lack of money.*"

Despite the difficulties felt in these markets, EPSILON is not deterred from trying to enter those markets, as they are still actively involved with partnerships in both countries. It is noted that the investment made, especially in Brazil, were too significant to consider withdrawing from the country, even if it no longer represents "*an investment priority*" for the company in the near future.

There were other difficulties experienced by EPSILON at the beginning of their internationalization process, which are closely linked to operating in the European market. Firstly, the fact that Portugal was considered a less-favored technologically-based country made it difficult to enter European markets. As a result, the company was motivated and willing to concentrate "*on Africa and on Latin America*", as Portugal had strong technology that facilitated entering some "*more underdeveloped*" markets. The other inhibiting factor was the language, as in Portuguese speaking countries "*language was no longer a problem.*"

Regarding projects and future goals, The CEO points out that the industry where they carry out their businesses is "*greatly reliant on political issues*", explained by the fact that they create "*solutions for the public sector.*" He believes that the "*decentralization of education to municipalities*", a decision made by the public sector, will positively affect EPSILON's business volume in the Portuguese market in the coming years, given that it will strengthen the need for EPSILON's products.

In terms of internationalization, the company believes that it holds "*strong possibilities*" of conquering the "*African and South American markets*", which is why the company "*continues to bank on them.*" It is further stated that Angola and Equatorial Guinea are growing markets for the company, and that this trend will continue this year, increasing "*invoicing in the foreign markets*" to approximately 15%. Although the growth in these countries represents twice as much as the previous year, EPSILON is expecting to experience very large growth in the domestic market "*and, therefore, growth at international level will not be as noticeable at a percentage level.*"

Finally, the company has no specific goal regarding an export percentage, and that internationalization is considered important for EPSILON, in order to prevent the firm from entering a phase of stagnation. The difficulty rests in the fact that the "*Portuguese market is rather small*" and that, in the CEO's view, a company needs to internationalize in order to stop "*being a microenterprise*" and not to fall behind "*in terms of innovation.*"

DISCUSSION

The literature shows a change of mind in the different approaches to the internationalization process, embracing new paradigms involving SMEs and their internationalization and less emphasis on the internationalization of large companies (Ribau et al., 2015).

Nowadays, the concept of internationalization includes the activities and characteristics of small and medium enterprises, as is the case of EPSILON. This construct also recognizes the differences between the strategies and experiences of these companies when compared to larger ones (Shuman & Seeger,

1986). However, an idea still remains: in an increasingly global and competitive market, internationalization is the determinant step for a promising future (Schueffel et al., 2014).

Knowledge-intensive business services are defined as including significant added value arising from science-based technological knowledge. KIBS generally rely more on human capital than on financial capital (Robertson & Hammersley, 2000). EPSILON can be said to fit in this perspective, with deep technological capital that leads EPSILON to a variety of products based on several technological solutions.

Due to several market limitations and resource constraints, start-ups may need external support to compete properly in international markets. Thus, environments that foster and positively influence the development of new projects should be created, in order to increase the likelihood of success (Engelman, Zen, & Fracasso, 2015). This is the case of EPSILON, which also sought financial assistance to embrace overseas markets that otherwise might not have been reached.

SMEs experience several adversities when competing in international environments, being much more likely to fail when compared to multinational companies as a result of resource constraints and lack of proper market knowledge (Apetrei, Kureshi, & Horodnic, 2015). In the business sector where EPSILON competes, some companies require greater assistance not only in the launching stage, but also in their internationalization process. In this connection, business incubators are defined as shared spaces that provide start-ups with assistance, which can then take the form of a business incubation space, organizational resources or assistance and monitoring of the evolution of the business. Companies located in incubators and science parks obtain numerous advantages, such as a good technological and business environment or the opportunity to create business relationships and networks with other companies in the incubator. These companies benefit from the provision of a wide range of services and processes conceived to ease their internationalization (Engelman, Zen, & Fracasso, 2015). By sharing the business incubator with other companies it was possible for EPSILON to gain the capacity to internalize knowledge that can prove to be beneficial.

It is clear that domestic and international policy issues are important in the process of internationalization affecting the international competitiveness of any company. Those policy issues can function as an enabling or inhibiting factor in the internationalization process. Another important factor is related to firms' capacity to adjust to the cultural differences of the different geographical markets they want to serve (Tesfom & Lutz, 2006; Bayfield, Dana, & Stewart, 2009). EPSILON felt some barriers in the internationalization process related to the Brazilian market's legal system.

In the course of the internationalization process, organizations need to overcome international barriers. To do so, they need to deploy risky strategies that managers are normally not very familiar with. As such, inter-organizational relationships and networks are very interesting solutions in order to reduce the risk of failing in their internationalization process. This path, based on networking activities, in order to reach international markets rapidly, is not new (Chetty & Campbell-Hunt, 2004), involves a great deal of communication and a major knowledge transfer (Styles & Ambler, 1994; Bayfield, Dana, & Stewart, 2009), as in the case of EPSILON. This internationalization process ended up being easier due to the previously developed networks, which helped mitigate the barriers to international market entry.

In order to adapt the product properly to the new international market, companies need to decide whether to modify or improve their existing products. This process can be defined as the adjustment to market conditions in such a way that the product is as suitable as possible for the foreign market's needs. To facilitate the overcoming of natural market barriers, products should be modified in order to meet market expectations and local requirements (Medina & Duffy, 1998). This is the process that EPSILON has undertaken when entering new international markets, namely Brazil, where EPSILON feels that an adaptation strategy plays a crucial role in reaching positive results.

Information and communication technology (ICT) is a vital resource used by EPSILON when developing their products and services. Chetty and Campbell-Hunt (2004) emphasized that the use of ICT did not appear to be a distinctively determinant factor between born global companies and a traditional internationalization process. Even though ICT plays an unquestionable role in supporting the internationalization process, this role is common to both models.

CONCLUSION

Internationalization is a long, incremental process, through which companies are able to increase their involvement in international markets (Johanson & Vahlne, 1977). Contrasting this principle, it is evident in the literature that internationalization is not necessarily a one-way, linear, incremental process as there are cases where companies place a primary focus on their domestic market for a long period of time before rapidly expanding internationally. On the other hand, a de-internationalization process can also be found, followed by withdrawal to the domestic market. Furthermore, there are cases where certain motivations or episodes lead to a "*rapid and dedicated internationalization period*". In this case, there are three main critical success factors in this process (Bell et al., 2001): global market orientation, commitment and experience.

It is always important to understand how a company manages to stay competitive and how its internationalization process takes place. Analyzing this case study, the inherent importance of internationalization was seen in enabling the company's growth, aligned with the need to serve new markets. In addition, it was possible to identify both enablers and barriers during the internationalization path, as well as to understand the strategies that can be used in external environments to facilitate this operation. Today's technological development can raise companies' internationalization capacity, at the same time as being associated with optimizing operations, resources and competences throughout the value chain (Cavusgil & Knight, 2015).

In Table 1, a parallel was established between various internationalization models for the company under analysis. These represent the result of a long process of analysis and inquiry, allowing analysis and debate with greater understanding of firms' internationalization processes. A comparison between the Uppsala, Born Global, Born Again Global and Born Regional models is outlined and overlapped according to EPSILON's internationalization perspective.

The Uppsala model, which implicitly involves a very long internationalization process requiring both great market knowledge and internalization of that knowledge during the ongoing process, does not correspond to the internationalization path followed by EPSILON. On the other hand, the born global perspective suggests a rapid internationalization process, with the company's goal of a significant volume of sales overseas predominating, which also does not correspond to the situation of EPSILON. The born-again global model adds a new perspective to the previous model, where its internationalization objective resides in a "*critical incident*" where there are no time restrictions, which does not reflect the path followed by EPSILON. Lastly, nor does the born regional model fit the company, as this proposes a rapid internationalization process to geographically and/or culturally close markets. The conclusion is that there is no optimal and precise framing between EPSILON and the featured models, as this

Table 1. EPSILON's main characteristics

Characteristics	*Uppsala Model*	*Born Globals*	*Born Again Globals*	*Born Regionals*
Timing of Internationalization	After developing the domestic market	Up to three years after beginning operations	No time limit	Up to three years after beginning operations
	Yes	Yes	Yes	Yes
Motivation behind Internationalization	*Resource-seeking* and *market-seeking*	It is the main objective of the firm	As a result of critical incidents	*Market-seeking*
	No	No	No	Yes
Sales Volume Abroad	No established rule	More than 25% of sales volume	More than 25% of sales volume following the strategic change	More than 25% of sales volume
	Yes	No	No	No
Presence in international markets	Geographically and/or culturally close foreign markets	Global markets	Geographically and/or culturally distant foreign markets	Geographically and/or culturally close foreign markets
	Yes	No	Yes	No
Speed of Internationalization	Slow and incremental	Rapid	Sudden rapid internationalization after a lethargic period. Several markets at the same time.	Rapid
	No	Yes	Yes	No
Modes of Entry	Low export commitment and a gradual evolutionary perspective. First, exports, then foreign presence.	*Local Networks*	Acquisition of distribution and/or market subsidiaries	Exports
	No	Yes	No	Yes

company shows an internationalization pattern that does not properly fit the theories proposed in the literature until now.

Considering the lack of a clear fit with any of the models, two of the models presented are suggested as complementary: Uppsala model and Born Regional, in order to synthesize EPSILON's internationalization process. This mixed model results from the propositions presented in both models, in harmony with that process. Analyzing this according to Table 1, it can be concluded that EPSILON initiated this process within the three-year time frame imposed by the born regional typology, in close cultural markets with low liability of newness, but in an incremental way. This process was initiated with a typical market-seeking behavior, through exporting products and services that currently in an international context, represent less than 25% of the company's total sales volume.

Generally, despite the different models of internationalization, it is clear that EPSILON does not match any one perfectly. As such, it can be argued that the situation is very simple: models are mere representations of the situation, and it can be argued whether the firm 'fits' the typology and not the other way around. It is clear that EPSILON's international path is not uniquely represented by a single typology, which implicitly recognizes the importance of analyzing the firm's international path and the difficulties faced along the way. As such, what really matters is the holistic view of the reality the firm faces and not the typologies commonly used to explain internationalization paths.

REFERENCES

Acs, Z. J., & Audretsch, D. B. (2005). Entrepreneurship, innovation and technological change. *Foundations and Trends in Entrepreneurship*, *1*(4), 1–65. doi:10.1561/0300000004

Apetrei, A., Kureshi, N. I., & Horodnic, I. A. (2015). When culture shapes international business. *Journal of Business Research*, *68*(7), 1519–1521. doi:10.1016/j.jbusres.2015.01.044

Arenius, P., Sasi, V., & Gabrielsson, M. (2005). Rapid internationalisation enabled by the internet: The case of a knowledge intensive company. *Journal of International Entrepreneurship*, *3*(4), 279–290. doi:10.100710843-006-7856-x

Battisti, S. (2012). Social innovation: The process development of knowledge-intensive companies. *International Journal of Services Technology and Management*, *18*(3-4), 224–244. doi:10.1504/IJSTM.2012.052860

Baum, M., Schwens, C., & Kabst, R. (2011). A typology of international new ventures: Empirical evidence from high–technology industries. *Journal of Small Business Management*, *49*(3), 305–330. doi:10.1111/j.1540-627X.2011.00328.x

Baum, M., Schwens, C., & Kabst, R. (2015). A latent class analysis of small firms' internationalization patterns. *Journal of World Business*, *50*(4), 754–768. doi:10.1016/j.jwb.2015.03.001

Bayfield, R., Dana, L. P., & Stewart, S. (2009). Firm characteristics and internationalisation strategies: An empirical investigation of New Zealand exporters. *International Journal of Globalisation and Small Business*, *3*(3), 275–287. doi:10.1504/IJGSB.2009.024571

Bell, J., McNaughton, R., & Young, S. (2001). 'Born-again global' firms: An extension to the 'born global' phenomenon. *Journal of International Management*, *7*(3), 173–189. doi:10.1016/S1075-4253(01)00043-6

Braga, A., Marques, C. S., & Serrasqueiro, Z. (2018). Internationalisation strategy of knowledge-intensive business services. *Journal of the Knowledge Economy*, *9*(2), 359–377. doi:10.100713132-017-0461-5

Cavusgil, S., & Knight, G. (2015). The born global firm: An entrepreneurial and capabilities perspective on early and rapid internationalization. *Journal of International Business Studies*, *46*(1), 3–16. doi:10.1057/jibs.2014.62

Chetty, S., & Campbell-Hunt, C. (2004). A strategic approach to internationalization: A traditional versus a 'born-global' approach. *Journal of International Marketing*, *12*(1), 57–81. doi:10.1509/jimk.12.1.57.25651

Coviello, N., & McAuley, A. (1999). Internationalisation and the smaller firm: A review of contemporary empirical research. *Management International Review*, *39*(3), 223–256.

Djellal, F., & Gallouj, F. (2008). A model for analysing the innovation dynamic in services: The case of 'assembled' services. *International Journal of Services Technology and Management*, *9*(3-4), 285–304. doi:10.1504/IJSTM.2008.019702

Durão, V., & Moreira, A. C. (2019). Critical and inhibiting success factors in inter-organizational networks: A case study. In S. Teixeira & J. Ferreira (Eds.), *Multilevel Approach to Competitiveness in the Global Tourism Industry* (pp. 63–86). IGI Global. doi:10.4018/978-1-7998-0365-2.ch005

Eisenhardt, K. M. (1989). Building theories from case study research. *Academy of Management Review, 14*(4), 532–550. doi:10.5465/amr.1989.4308385

Engelman, R., Zen, A. C., & Fracasso, E. M. (2015). The impact of the incubator on the internationalization of firms. *Journal of Technology Management & Innovation, 10*(1), 29–39. doi:10.4067/S0718-27242015000100003

Eurofound. (2012). *Born global: The potential of job creation in new international businesses*. Luxembourg: Publications Office of the European Union.

Fernandes, L., Simões, D., Pereira, C., & Moreira, A. C. (2019). Challenges of the internationalization strategy of a technology-based international new venture. In N. Teixeira, T. Costa, & I. Lisboa (Eds.), *Handbook of Research on Entrepreneurship, Innovation, and Internalization* (pp. 467–489). IGI Global. doi:10.4018/978-1-5225-8479-7.ch018

Furtado, J., Pereira, A., Pereira, I., & Moreira, A. C. (2019). Does theory really fit real life situations?: A case study on the internationalization process of a technological service-based firm. In N. Teixeira, T. Costa, & I. Lisboa (Eds.), *Handbook of research on entrepreneurship, innovation, and internationalization* (pp. 419–438). IGI Global. doi:10.4018/978-1-5225-8479-7.ch016

Ghauri, P. (2004). Designing and conducting case studies in international business research. In R. Marschan-Piekkari & C. Welch (Eds.), *Handbook of Qualitative Research Methods for International Business* (pp. 109–124). Edward Elgar. doi:10.4337/9781781954331.00019

Hakansson, H., & Snehota, I. (2006). "No business is an island" 17 years later. *Strategic Management Journal, 22*(3), 271–274.

Hipp, C. (2008). Service peculiarities and the specific role of technology in service innovation management. *International Journal of Services Technology and Management, 9*(2), 154–173. doi:10.1504/IJSTM.2008.018433

Javalgi, R., & Martin, C. (2007). Internationalization of services: Identifying the building-blocks for future research. *Journal of Services Marketing, 21*(6), 391–397. doi:10.1108/08876040710818886

Jenssen, J. I., & Nybakk, E. (2013). Inter-organizational networks and innovation in small, knowledge-intensive firms: A literature review. *International Journal of Innovation Management, 17*(2), 1350008. doi:10.1142/S1363919613500084

Johanson, J., & Vahlne, J. E. (1977). The internationalization process of the firm–a model of knowledge development and increasing foreign market commitments. *Journal of International Business Studies, 8*(1), 23–32. doi:10.1057/palgrave.jibs.8490676

Johanson, J., & Vahlne, J.-E. (1990). The mechanism of internationalism. *International Marketing Review, 7*(4), 11–24. doi:10.1108/02651339010137414

Johanson, J., & Wiedersheim-Paul, F. (1975). The internationalization of the firm - four Swedish cases. *Journal of Management Studies*, *12*(3), 305–323. doi:10.1111/j.1467-6486.1975.tb00514.x

Jornal de Negócios. (2019). *Internacionalização da economia portuguesa: é possível pedir mais?* Retrieved from: https://www.jornaldenegocios.pt/opiniao/colunistas/detalhe/internacionalizacao-da-economia-portuguesa-e-possivel-pedir-mais

Karagozoglu, N., & Lindell, M. (1998). Internationalization of small and medium-sized technology-based firms: An exploratory study. *Journal of Small Business Management*, *36*(1), 44–59.

Knight, G. A., & Cavusgil, S. T. (1996). The born global firm: A challenge to traditional internationalization theory. *Advances in International Marketing*, *8*, 11–26.

Maciejewski, M., & Wach, K. (2019). International startups from Poland: Born global or born regional? *Journal of Management and Business Administration. Central Europe*, *27*(1), 60–83.

Marin, D. (1992). Is the export-led growth hypothesis valid for industrialized countries? *The Review of Economics and Statistics*, *74*(4), 678–688. doi:10.2307/2109382

Mariotto, F. L., Zanni, P. P., & Moraes, G. H. S. M. (2014). What is the use of a single-case study in management research? *Revista de Administração de Empresas*, *54*(4), 358–369. doi:10.1590/S0034-759020140402

McDougall, P. P., & Oviatt, B. M. (2000). International entrepreneurship: The intersection of two research paths. *Academy of Management Journal*, *43*, 902–908.

Medina, J. F., & Duffy, M. F. (1998). Standardization vs globalization: A new perspective of brand strategies. *Journal of Product and Brand Management*, *7*(3), 223–243. doi:10.1108/10610429810222859

Miles, I. (2005). Knowledge intensive business services: Prospects and policies. *Foresight*, *7*(6), 39–63. doi:10.1108/14636680510630939

Nogueira, R., & Moreira, A. C. (2019). Internationalization and Higher Education: The Case of the University of Aveiro. In C. Machado & P. Davim (Eds.), *Higher Education and the Evolution of Management, Applied Sciences, and Engineering Curricula* (pp. 87–119). IGI Global. doi:10.4018/978-1-5225-7259-6.ch004

Oviatt, B., & McDougall, P. (1994). Toward a theory of international new ventures. *Journal of International Business Studies*, *25*(1), 45–64. doi:10.1057/palgrave.jibs.8490193

Pinto, L., Ribeiro, M., & Moreira, A. C. (2018). Challenging the theoretical lenses of internationalization: A case study analysis. In C. Machado & P. Davim (Eds.), *Enhancing Competitive Advantage with Dynamic Management and Engineering* (pp. 112–137). IGI Global. doi:10.4018/978-1-5225-5360-1.ch005

Ribau, C., Moreira, A. C., & Raposo, M. (2017). SMEs innovation capabilities and export performance: An entrepreneurial orientation view. *Journal of Business Economics and Management*, *18*(5), 920–934. doi:10.3846/16111699.2017.1352534

Ribau, C. P., Moreira, A. C., & Raposo, M. (2015). Internationalisation of the firm theories: A schematic synthesis. *International Journal of Business and Globalisation*, *15*(4), 528–554. doi:10.1504/IJBG.2015.072535

Ribau, C. P., Moreira, A. C., & Raposo, M. (2018a). SME internationalization research: Mapping the state of the art. *Canadian Journal of Administrative Sciences*, *35*(2), 280–303. doi:10.1002/cjas.1419

Ribau, C. P., Moreira, A. C., & Raposo, M. (2018b). Categorising the internationalisation of SMEs with social network analysis. *International Journal of Entrepreneurship and Small Business*, *35*(1), 57–80. doi:10.1504/IJESB.2018.094264

Ribau, C. P., Moreira, A. C., & Raposo, M. (2019). Multidyadic Relationships: A Multi-stage Perspective. *Global Business and Economics Review*, *21*(6), 732–755. doi:10.1504/GBER.2019.102553

Robertson, M., & Hammersley, G. O. M. (2000). Knowledge management practices within a knowledge-intensive firm: The significance of the people management dimension. *Journal of European Industrial Training*, *24*(2-4), 241–253. doi:10.1108/03090590010321205

Rugman, A., & Verbeke, A. (2007). Liabilities of regional foreignness and the use of firm-level versus country-level data: A response to Dunning et al. (2007). *Journal of International Business Studies*, *38*(1), 200–205. doi:10.1057/palgrave.jibs.8400242

Schueffel, P., Rico, B., & Amann, W. (2014). Behavioral patterns in born-again global firms: Towards a conceptual framework of the internationalization activities of mature SMEs. *Multinational Business Review*, *22*(4), 418–441. doi:10.1108/MBR-06-2014-0029

Shuman, J. C., & Seeger, J. A. (1986). The theory and practice of strategic management in smaller rapid growth firms. *American Journal of Small Business*, *11*(1), 7–18. doi:10.1177/104225878601100101

Silva, P., & Moreira, A. C. (2019). Subsidiary survival: A case study from the Portuguese electronics industry. *Review of International Business and Strategy*, *29*(3), 226–252. doi:10.1108/RIBS-10-2018-0094

Styles, C., & Ambler, T. (1994). Successful export practice: The UK experience. *International Marketing Review*, *11*(6), 23–47. doi:10.1108/02651339410072999

Tesfom, G., & Lutz, C. (2006). A classification of export marketing problems of small and medium sized manufacturing firms in developing countries. *International Journal of Emerging Markets*, *1*(3), 262–281. doi:10.1108/17468800610674480

Yin, R. (2008). *Case Study Research: Design and Methods*. SAGE.

Zhang, J., Beatty, S. E., & Walsh, G. (2008). Review and future directions of cross-cultural consumer services research. *Journal of Business Research*, *61*(3), 211–224. doi:10.1016/j.jbusres.2007.06.003

ADDITIONAL READING

Moreira, A. C., Brandão, F., Longa, I., Campolargo, L., & Lopes, A. R. (2019). A Discussion on Transnationality and Globalness of HEI Internationalization. In C. Machado & P. Davim (Eds.), *Higher Education and the Evolution of Management, Applied Sciences, and Engineering Curricula* (pp. 27–58). IGI Global., doi:10.4018/978-1-5225-7259-6.ch002

Moreira, A. C., Silva, P., Mota, J. H., & Gadim, H. (2019). De-internationalization of SMEs: A Case Study. In A. C. Moreira & P. Silva (Eds.), *Handbook of Research on Corporate Restructuring and Globalization* (pp. 143–169). IGI Global., doi:10.4018/978-1-5225-8906-8.ch007

Mota, J. H., & Moreira, A. C. (2017). Determinants of the capital structure of Portuguese firms with investments in Angola. *South African Journal of Economic and Management Sciences, 20*(1), a885. doi: . v20i1.885 doi:10.4102ajems

Ribau, C. P., Moreira, A. C., & Raposo, M. (2017). Export performance and the internationalisation of SMEs. *International Journal of Entrepreneurship and Small Business, 30*(2), 214–240. doi:10.1504/IJESB.2017.081438

Ribau, C. P., Moreira, A. C., & Raposo, M. (2018). Internacionalização de PME no Continente Americano: Revisão da Literatura. *Innovar (Universidad Nacional de Colombia), 28*(67), 59–73. doi:10.15446/innovar.v28n67.68613

Ribau, C. P., Moreira, A. C., & Raposo, M. (2019). The role of exploitative and exploratory innovation in export performance: An analysis of plastics industry SMEs. *European Journal of International Management, 13*(2), 224–246. doi:10.1504/EJIM.2019.098149

KEY TERMS AND DEFINITIONS

Born Again Globals: Characterized as being focused on the domestic market and suddenly being able to change their strategic focus radically in order to increase their sales volumes in international markets.

Born Global: A type of company that, from its inception, seeks to derive a competitive advantage to compete in many countries. It normally pursues a vision of becoming global and globalizes rapidly without any preceding long-term domestic or internationalization period or experience. Usually born globals are small, technology-oriented companies that operate in several international markets.

Case Study: A qualitative methodology, normally used in social sciences, that seeks to interpret a reality through a particular perspective. It is normally used to answer questions like "how" and "why." It is commonly used to address constructivist research processes.

Globalization: A worldwide movement toward economic, financial, trade and communication integration. It is usually envisaged as a lack of trade barriers between nations, these being removed through free trade agreements throughout the world and between nation-states. It implies the opening up of local and nationalistic perspectives to a broader outlook of an interconnected and interdependent world with free transfer of capital, goods and services across national frontiers, in which investment opportunities soar.

Internationalization: Normally associated with a strategy formed by firms that decide to operate in foreign markets. It involves the implementation of goods and services that can be easily adapted and adopted in different countries. It could involve business to consumer as well as business to business activities. It may involve cross -border transactions of goods, services or resources between two or more firms or organizations belonging to two different countries, as well as foreign direct investment.

Internationalization Process: This emphasizes a company's trajectory in its transition from a national market to a particular foreign market. It normally involves several entry modes (exports, FDI, franchising, etc.) that exert a critical influence on the subsequent trajectory, as well as on the cost related to the internationalization process. The two most important theories explaining the internationalization process are the Uppsala model and the network-based approach.

Uppsala Model: One of the most discussed dynamic theories in the Nordic School and International Business Studies. It explains the process of companies' internationalization, how organizations learn and the impact of learning on their international expansion. This theory defends that companies' internationalization process is carried out in stages, from non-regular exports to establishing companies abroad.

Chapter 5
SME Re-Internationalization Strategy:
An Analysis Based on Multiple Cases

Rui Centeno Martins
https://orcid.org/0000-0001-5002-8907
Instituto Superior de Gestão e Administração de Santarém (ISLA), Portugal

Luis Farinha
https://orcid.org/0000-0003-1705-5000
Polytechnic Institute of Castelo Branco, Portugal & NECE Research Center in Business Sciences, Portugal

João Ferreira
https://orcid.org/0000-0002-5928-2474
University of Beira Interior, Portugal

EXECUTIVE SUMMARY

Re-internationalization represents a research challenge for the internationalization process. Many companies withdraw from international operations go through a period of interregnum time, and then reenter in the international arena. Little is known about this process and whether re-internationalizers opt for the same entrepreneurial orientation or behave differently than they began with the first approach, allowing for faster re-entry and take-off. This chapter follows a qualitative methodological approach, based on the case study, using semi-structured interview with the top manager of the wine company. This work is intended to serve as a basis for future studies related to the internationalization of SME, based on the profile of CEO, and as a basis for reflection by company managers. This exploratory study aims to contribute to the emerging literature on entrepreneurial orientation and re-internationalization using the SME case study.

DOI: 10.4018/978-1-7998-4387-0.ch005

INTRODUCTION

Re-internationalisation represents a huge research challenge for internationalisation in the area of international entrepreneurship, as many SMEs withdraw from international operations for a limited period and then re-enter the international arena again, yet little is known whether they act in the same way or approach the market in another way.

Re-internationalization is a process that involves a period of international business activity, and then there is an interregnum of operations for a certain period until there is again an international re-entry process, where international operations are successfully renewed (Welch & Welch, 2009), based on learning, entrepreneurial orientation, the behavior of the re-internationalizer and also his ability to resilience in the face of obstacles that were not initially transposed.

Entrepreneurial orientation is fundamental in the process of re-internationalization, there is a change of managers/owners who are bolder and more experienced internationally than their predecessors, international networks more sustainable than before, and human resources are better equipped and better documented to successfully approach re-entry into international markets.

The entrepreneurial orientation of SME managers who strive for internationalization should be in organizational innovation, as their companies are better equipped to exploit the opportunities that the international market provides and improve their performance and performance in these markets (O'Cass & Weerawardena, 2009).

Thinking precisely about the challenges that CEO's often face when choosing or not to re-nationalise, this study was concerned with broadening this theme, the profile of the CEO, and his participation in the entrepreneurial strategies that organizations use when choosing to embrace the opportunities that arise, as well as the possible obstacles they encounter in re-nationalising the wine sector. Given the few studies that have focused on the re-internationalisation of the CEO in the wine sector in the Ribatejo region, we intend to fill this gap by analysing this sector that is so fundamental in our economy and that has never been studied in this region.

In this line, the purpose of this chapter was based on three points, first of all it presented a proposal for a model that would demonstrate the role of the CEO's entrepreneurial orientation in the process of re-internationalisation of the company in the wine sector. Secondly, it presented how these variables together, obstacles to Internationalization and entry into new markets, are related within a single *framework*.

Finalizing the analysis of this study, thirdly, it was demonstrated that within this panorama that is the business environment, the profile of the CEO is fundamental and presents its positive side in the matrix of competitive advantages.

Our chapter is structured in several stages. After the literature review, case studies on the re-internationalisation of SMEs and the survival of companies in the wine sector in the Ribatejo region will be analysed. In this study, conclusions, limitations and future lines of research will also be pointed out.

This chapter is organized into six sections: (i) Introduction; (ii) Literature review; (iii) Methodology; (iv) Case Studies; (v) Conclusions and (vi) Limitations and future Research.

LITERATURE REVIEW

Re-Internationalisation

Vissak (2010) said that "re-internationalisation can be followed by several re-internationalisations", also Axinn and Matthyssens (2002) concluded that SMEs use combinations of entry and exit strategies, a company can also experience several exits and re-entry Javalgi et al. (2011) for a certain period, until they opt again for an international re-entry process, with renewed international operations (Welch & Welch, 2009).

SMEs can also re-enter the market by assuming new network relationships (Hadjikhani, 1997; Welch & Welch, 2009), where they choose different resources and capabilities (Javalgi et al., 2011), other entry costs (Roberts & Tybout, 1997) and divergence from previously established strategies (Jones & Khanna, 2006) in international market entry decisions.

Some authors identify other factors that influence and lead to the re-internationalisation of SMEs, such as: change of ownership (Welch & Welch,2009), acquisition of additional experience (Benito & Welch, 1994), reduction of trade barriers (Javalgi et al., 2011) and improvement of market conditions (Akhter & Choudry, 1993; Crick, 2004; Swoboda et al., 2011).

According to Ellis and Pecotich (2001), many SMEs rely on sporadic export orders because they export in an unsystematic way, thus becoming more flexible and quite common among SMEs (Kalinic & Forza, 2012), this behaviour, thus fulfilling international orders as they enter, but there may be too long periods between each order. The longer this period is, the more likely it is that re-entry will increase (Welch & Welch, 2009).

Companies with greater knowledge of the market, due to the international experience of the entrepreneur have a greater ability to learn to gather more foreign knowledge (McDougall & Oviatt, 2003), we can thus state that entrepreneurs feel encouraged to make more inroads into internationalization due to its benefits, both in productivity and profitability of the enterprise, so an entrepreneur with entrepreneurial orientation, relational capital and human capital directly influences the international performance of the SME, and it is shown that entrepreneurial orientation and relational capital play a fundamental role as mediators in strengthening the performance of human capital.

According to Malhotra and Hinings (2010), re-internationalisation happens when the rate of the commitment of resources continuously expands and shrinks, depending on the scale and flow of SME projects.

According to Freeman (2007) the international activity oriented to the interior, with foreign networks created and maintained, can be the springboard for the renewal of international sales.

Hadjikhani (1996) also stated that re-internationalization is more likely for companies that were previously highly committed to the international markets where they already operated, as they benefit from the knowledge, contacts and experiences already established before (Welch & Welch, 2009; Javalgi et al., 2011), and may complement the evolutionary process of internationalization of the company

(Ribau et al., 2018) however, the experience accumulated through failure does not guarantee the success of re-entry (Aguzzoli et al., 2020).

Entrepreneurial Orientation

The entrepreneurial orientation plays a fundamental role and favors re-internationalization, according to Bell et al. (2001) there are entrepreneurial guidelines that opt for rapid re-internationalisation, although periods of consolidation or containment then arise, Welch and Welch (2009) point out that re-internationalisation becomes less likely, the longer SMEs stay away from the international arena, opting for de-internationalisation should not be seen as a failure, but as an opportunity to grow again and return to international markets, with an even stronger value (Turcan, 2019).

Conversely, other entrepreneurial guidelines choose to approach other international markets (Crick, 2004; Javalgi et al., 2011; Vissak, 2010), this option results essentially from the negative circumstances of leaving the markets where they initially operated (Welch & Welch, 2009), as the lack of knowledge about the current state of these markets, lack of trust and fear of prejudice because of the activities previously developed (Javalgi et al., 2011).

Entrepreneurial orientation influences not only how a company is organised for the discovery and exploitation of opportunities, but also how the SME acquires and organises the implementation of resources for its growth, which can create a unique organisational capacity. There is research that shows that entrepreneurial experience tends to have a positive effect on the probability of a new beginning for entrepreneurs (Stam et al., 2006), as they will be able to learn positively from failure, relying on a return to entrepreneurial activity in the future (Stam & Schutjens, 2006), however, in the opposite direction, the international entrepreneurial orientation retreats when there are international hostility and personal pressures to the detriment of good management practices in SMEs (Thanos et al., 2017).

According to Malhotra and Hinings (2010), re-internationalisation happens when the rate of the commitment of resources continuously expands and shrinks, depending on the scale and flow of SME projects, also Hadjikhani (1996) said that re-internationalisation is more likely for companies that were previously highly committed to the international markets where they were already operating, as they benefit from the knowledge, contacts and experiences already established before (Javalgi et al., 2011; Welch & Welch, 2009).

Family businesses tend to build relatively strong relationships with key players in foreign markets. These relationships can last after the company has stopped exporting to the market, facilitating the re-entry of family businesses compared to non-family businesses (Naldi & Kuiken, 2016).

Family ownership is a critical factor in wine companies in distinguishing between the different export patterns of these companies. Most of the companies that have continued with export strategies over time are mostly family-owned. Family firms re-entering export markets are much more resilient than non-firm firms, which is somewhat surprising as family firms are often described in the literature as more risk-averse and less prone to re-internationalization (Gomez-Mejia et al., 2010)

The Role of the Wine Entrepreneur

The entrepreneur is the individual who carries out entrepreneurial actions, such as entering international markets, according to Schumpeter (1911, 1942). His/her characteristics are fundamental for SMEs, as they influence entrepreneurial orientation, both through their personality traits and their motivational and personal characteristics.

The entrepreneur as a leader has several paths to entrepreneurial orientation based on a social and organizational context (Del Giudice et al., 2011). Entrepreneurs are also sources of knowledge at various levels, such as in management, internationalization, industry and linguistics (March, 1991).

This knowledge makes the entrepreneur a great bearer of knowledge within SMEs. This knowledge is previously acquired and manages to reduce the psychic distance from other markets and, as such, facilitates the internationalization of their companies. The development of internationalization strategies is therefore based on the rationality of the choices made by the entrepreneur and based on his knowledge (Pla-Barber & Escriba-Esteve, 2006).

The role of the entrepreneur is successful when he can make calculated risk decisions, set realistic goals, have the strong conviction to produce new products and expand into international markets (Ngoma et al., 2012). Entrepreneurs, while attracted by risk, are also able to manipulate, measure and deal with it (Hron, 2006).

In the interconnection with his knowledge, is still his international orientation. However, recognizing this opportunity may not be enough, what is relevant is that entrepreneurs are motivated to exploit it (Dubravská et al., 2015).

Entrepreneurs who have lived abroad probably have a greater export appetite than others (Zucchella et al., 2007). Entrepreneurs also have a global mindset, which makes them proactive and therefore constantly seek and explore international business opportunities, as well as being able and able to create innovative products (Demel & PotuGuáková, 2012), which translate into a competitive advantage for their company (Suarez-Ortega & Alamo-Vera, 2005).

The entrepreneur's personality and his need for self-realization lead him to take risks in businesses that hold his attention, thus proactively dealing with the risks inherent to them (Hutchinson et al., 2006).

The entrepreneur is, without a shadow of a doubt, a true public relations of his company and, therefore, ends up being closer to the markets and his potential clients, therefore, his reputation has to be that of an honest and credible individual, because the entrepreneur is also the reflection of his company and, as such, it is his image that passes to the outside (Belak & Duh, 2012).

The knowledge that through the absorption capacity will become learning, is verified in the face of the knowledge acquired at the international level, by the entrepreneur, and also by his contact networks (Mura & Rózsa, 2013). Due to its importance, the SME entrepreneur is interested in understanding how, through his experiences abroad, but also as a person, manager and visionary, he contributes to the development of the enterprise (Ruzzier et al., 2006).

We can stress that these entrepreneurs are imbued with an ambitious spirit, based on previously lived experiences, have a high level of education and high knowledge of foreign languages. There is, therefore, a strong international orientation in terms of export capacity (Swoboda et al., 2011; Fernández et al., 2015) and that represents a competitive advantage against all the competition.

The role of the entrepreneur's strategic intention becomes therefore fundamental, since his ability to define and communicate the strategy, for the whole company, allows it to be better prepared and available to accumulate knowledge in the foreign market (Ciszewska-Mlinarič, 2016).

Although there are several theories presented to explain the process of internationalization (Ribau et al., 2015), the understanding of internationalization has changed over time as a result of different interpretations of structures, theories and basic premises (Ribau et al., 2015) such as the increasing instability of the contextual environment in which companies operate and the growing specialization of wine companies around core competencies (Moreira & Alves, 2016).

An analysis of the wine industry's internationalisation strategies should also consider the changes in global wine consumption patterns, especially as wines develop and facilitate the re-entry of new producers into foreign markets (Dalmoro, 2013), the pace of internationalization of the company should also develop a long-term strategy that maximizes its sustainability and profit growth (Naldi & Kuiken, 2016), the role of CEO's being fundamental to the development of wine companies and are involved in two clear processes: the recognition of market opportunities and the implementation of strategies through resource and capacity development (Torres & Kunc, 2016).

Analysis Model

The wine sector is a growing industry in Portugal, with high economic development in rural areas, and its success is closely linked to viticulture, wine tourism, wine routes and festivals (Molina et al., 2015), this analysis model intends to explore the role played by the CEO's entrepreneurial profile in removing the main obstacles faced by SMEs during the whole process of re-internationalisation and in choosing ways to enter new international markets. Based on the literature review presented above, a new conceptual analysis model is presented in Figure 1, however, this model does not cover all plausible combinations and explanations for the distinct realities and needs that exist in all wine enterprises, particularly at a time when markets and challenges are constantly evolving (Ribau et al., 2015).

Figure 1. Analysis model for the study of CEO wine entrepreneurs
Source: Own Elaboration

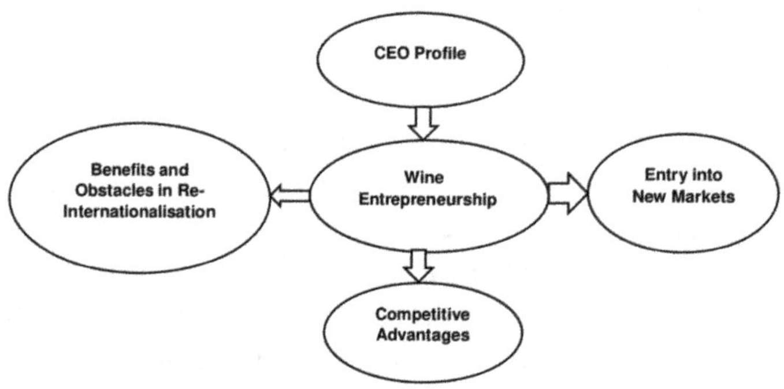

METHODOLOGY

Type of Study and Case Selection

Our study will take the qualitative approach as it offers the researcher adaptability in data collection, where ideas can be followed, answers can be further examined, and motives and feelings can be further explored (Cheuk, 2010).

In the qualitative approach, our research will follow the case study method. Research through Case Studies is increasing. However, the biggest criticisms in the use of this method are the problems of "validity" and "reliability" of the process used (Dubois & Gibbert, 2010). It is therefore important to identify and analyse the main recommendations produced, combining them with the design of the methodological process of this research. A single case was examined (Yin, 2014), which consists of examining the role of entrepreneurial orientation in the success of the re-internationalisation of a wine SME in the process of approaching international markets to boost the business.

Data Collection and Analysis

Following the objective of this work, in-depth interviews were conducted with the CEO of wine companies. The interview allowed the collection of more complete and spontaneous answers through the interaction between the interviewer and the interviewee, preventing an incorrect interpretation of the questions by the interviewee (Minichiello, Aroni, & Hays, 2008).

We analyzed the cooperation between winemakers, the benefits and obstacles they face in re-internationalising their companies, the associated competitive advantages, the search for new markets for current products, products for the current market, the development of a new product for new markets, and improving business effectiveness (Schott & Jensen, 2016). Given the importance of taking a qualitative approach, we have studied a sector that has been little studied in the literature on re-internationalization as the wine sector. The data collected during the interviews were subject to content analysis (Weber, 1990) to define and analyze categories of information. Following the Franco and Haase (2015) procedure, we delimited segments of information, coded the relevant information with a word or a short sentence and, finally, synthesized and compared the codes obtained during the interviews.

CASE STUDIES

Study Context

The Ribatejo region has undeniable natural conditions for the development of wine-growing activities, being a temperate South-Mediterranean climate, influenced by the Tagus River, which runs all over the region, being in the same three distinct wine-growing areas in the Ribatejo, known as "o Campo", "o Bairro" and "Charneca". The "Campo" has extensive plains, adjacent to the River Tagus, which is also known as the "Lezíria do Tejo" and is, par excellence, the area of white wines, where the varieties Casal Branco and Quinta da Alorna are queens. The district located between the Tagus Valley and Montejunto, where the clayey soils prevail. The Charneca, located south of the Campo, on the left bank of the Tagus River, has sandy and fertile soils where the wines from Quinta do Arrobe stand out, both in white and red wines.

Selection of Case Studies

The selection of the following cases was the result of research from several sources, ***Quinta Casal Branco*** was chosen for its importance in the sector and the Ribatejo region, since it is the largest exporter of national wine, with decades of existence, recognition and for being the owner of a brand established nationally and internationally.

The company Quinta do Arrobe, located in Casével, Santarém, is a family property, currently run by Maria and Alexandre Gaspar, who are professionals specialized in their areas and currently have a strong export vocation and are dedicated to wine production. The family's connection to the wine sector started in 1882, resulting from a tradition of several generations. Nowadays his CEO is a young person with 7 years of international experience when he replaces his father in the role of manager.

The company **Quinta do Arrobe** started in 2001 and sporadically entered international markets, but after some time it had to leave those markets, mainly due to the few human resources to ensure the needs of the markets and unsustainable management.

Quinta do Arrobe is a more recent project and is beginning to enter a more in-depth and serious re-internationalization process. Research shows that sales to foreign markets are still a small part of the business.

The CEO interviewed has a high level of *know-how* regarding the sector where they operate and they try to promote Portugal's image as a producer of great wines and it is in this sense that they have been working, however, they are the ones who point the way to markets where they can grow, but the investment decision is always theirs.

We demonstrate the profile of the CEO of each of the companies, the obstacles in the re-internationalisation of their companies and the entry into new markets. We coded the information considered pertinent to the study, with a short and elucidative sentence, finally, we synthesized and compared the answers of the two CEO according to the analysis model throughout the interviews (Figure 2), the results of the research made during the case studies to the CEO of the companies are described, namely, the primary data obtained through the interviews.

Quinta do Casal Branco was a pioneer in technological innovation in Ribatejo, as it was the first steam cellar in the region. The CEO is a person with high art experience in the sector, who knows very well the international markets where his company has been operating for 30 years and now operates in 28 countries.

The CEO's interviewed have a high level of *know-how* regarding the sector where they operate and try to promote Portugal's image as a producer of great wines and it is in this sense that they have been working, however, they are the ones who point the way to markets where they can grow, but the investment decision is always theirs.

Barriers vary from market to market, although there are common problems. In the East (Chinese market), knowledge about wine is a barrier to entry for National wines, as CEO B said. In European countries, the main obstacles are cultural, particularly with consumers' preference for wines produced in their own country. In the USA, the main obstacle is the way the market is segmented in terms of legislation, as each state has its own rules of operation, which makes the market extremely complex and hinders the export process as the two CEO shared in the interview, identified yet another obstacle to the internationalization of their wines, which are the high rates it has to bear mainly in Latin American countries and the difficulty in finding reliable strategic partners in those countries.

Companies also approach international markets at certain times through an agent, such as the company Quinta do Casal Branco, which helps them build new relationships and trust the foreign capital of the partner network (Goel & Yang, 2015b). In developing economies, they are the preferred investment destinations for companies, mainly due to the advantages they offer, such as access to potential markets, low abundant cost, a supply of human capital and natural resources (Frost, 2001). The way to enter the international markets of both *Quinta do Casal Branco* and Quinta do Arrobe is mostly through direct export, using importers and distributors in the destination market, which in some cases is done by people who were even born here, and in most cases, there is no connection to our country. Quinta do Casal Branco has a 90% percent of sales abroad, which says a lot about the importance to the company's business of foreign markets. With a presence in 28 countries, Quinta do Casal Branco's main markets are: South Africa, Angola, Belgium, Brazil, Canada, China, Denmark, Finland, Philippines, Holland, Hong Kong, Japan, Venezuela, Macau, Malaysia, Mozambique, Poland, Russia, Singapore, Sweden and

Figure 2. CEO approaches according to the proposed analysis model
Source: Own Elaboration

APPROACHES	CEO A	CEO B	COMPARATIVE ANALYSIS
Location and age of the Company.	They are located in the Almeirim area and are over 200 years old.	They are located in Casével and have 13 years of activity.	Company A is century-old, while Company B has only 13 years of stock.
Percentage of sales volume to international markets.	91% of production is absorbed by international markets.	35% of production is absorbed by international markets.	Huge dependence on company A in the process of Internationalization.
Where did the CEO of the company start the internationalization process?	It started in the UK when I went to study in London and later in the USA because my family went to live there and from there, our wines started to be awarded and known by the world.	First China, then business began, the next importer was from Norway, it was a *trend* and later, the ease of language and markets of nostalgia (France, Luxembourg and Germany).	The CEO in face of his initiative and at risk started the process of re-nationalisation, CEO B came up through customer contact and the opportunity came initially by mere chance.
Did the possibility of developing an approach to markets arise through a partnership or a decision outlined by the CEO of the company?	From a decision of the CEO of the Company, given the low internal demand for our wines.	At the CEO's initiative, to broaden horizons and try to create greater profitability for the company.	The CEO's were proactive in the face of the low demand in the internal market and tried to leverage the results by focusing on internationalization
What are the biggest disadvantages your company faces in internationalization projects?	The biggest disadvantage we face in the re-internationalization project is the high rates in certain countries and the back labels, which is where all the wine information comes from, and which for each country has its specification.	As a disadvantage, I would point out that government aid should be greater, that another is a cultural and organisational problem, that we work little together, that there is no cooperative work and that we do not share costs.	CEO A is concerned with the sector's problems, while CEO B is also concerned with organizational and cultural issues.

Switzerland. The main customers of this farm, during the initial process of sales abroad, was the so-called market of nostalgia, but currently, with the growth of the business and gaining a name in its main wine, the purchase began to be made by natives of the various countries where the company is already. The way Quinta do Arrobe entered, initially, was to resort to the *Trader* and the networks of distributors in the target market, which served to spread the bet in those markets. Currently, the Brazilian and German market share is 30% each and in the Chinese market, it is 14%. This means that these three markets together absorb more than 74% of exports, which corresponds to 40% of their production.

Quinta Casal Branco started its commercial transactions with foreign markets as early as the 20th century when it started the process of selling wines to foreign markets. The beginning of this internationalization happened to countries where there was a great concentration of the Portuguese community, countries like Brazil, the former colonies in Africa (Angola, Mozambique, Cape Verde) and European countries like England and France, have always been the main destinations, due to their proximity to the Portuguese culture and language. Quinta do Arrobe only started its re-internationalization process in 2007 and, at this moment, it is already present in 12 markets, in the Premium and Superpremium ranges, which are exported to countries such as Germany, Brazil, Luxembourg, Czech Republic, Norway and China. Quinta do Casal Branco started selling to foreign markets, by mere chance, a client admired its product and wanted to market it in China. Nowadays the internationalization works for this SME as an anchor to more easily sell the product and obtain a higher income. Finally, Quinta do Arrobe wanted to internationalize to gain international projection and it is a clear bet of the family to expand the business.

The two CEOs try to get their companies into new markets by using their Internationalization strategy and the support of some national entities that through their consultants make it possible to enter unknown markets, organizing for such action the positioning of the brand and education of professionals to increase the perception of markets for the quality of Portuguese wines, currently, a great example is the Asian market, thus creating competitive advantages.

The company Quinta Casal Branco has a greater diversification of brands and has been operating in international markets for more years and is also present in 28 markets while the Quinta do Arrobe company is only present in 12 international markets, however, both companies are adapted to what the client demands and to meet the demands made of them, for example, in the Chinese market.

CONCLUSION AND IMPLICATIONS

Taking into account the absence of qualitative studies of the profiles of wine CEO's, our study aimed to fill this gap by conducting case studies of the survival of their re-internationalised wine companies in the Ribatejo region. Agricultural CEO's have contributed to the sustainable development of the studied area since, besides economic benefits, they contribute to landscape conservation, job creation and preservation of traditions. Both CEO's demonstrate their knowledge about the wine tradition and the specificities of the product.

Professional experience helps the CEO to recognize possible valuable business opportunities, this factor has been identified by wine studies as being especially important in recognizing opportunities (Torres & Kunc, 2016). The space relationship between farms is the main determinant of cooperation in the area of production, not only between farms with a reduced area (Colombo & Perujo-Villanueva, 2017), but also between farms with a larger area where certain conditions such as the scarcity of human and financial resources, and the use of the same production system, are present. The cooperation between the CEO's also materializes in the sharing of labour and more expensive agricultural equipment. The Portuguese wine sector has improved substantially in the Ribatejo region mainly, with a new generation of entrepreneurial CEO's who are committed to re-internationalisation, a new generation of oenologists with more training and better knowledge of international tastes.

The opportunity recognition process is the result of the CEO's management experience and training or simply a good network means being in the right place at the right time and meeting the right people to do new business within the wine industry (Torres & Kunc, 2016).

A new management strategy also leads to increasing dissemination of Ribatejo wines abroad, either through a presence in international fairs of the sector or through participation in competitions with other foreign producers, which results in the awarding of numerous prizes for wines and a consequent promotion to the international market. Despite these excellent results for the sector, it is necessary to continue to invest in modernisation if they wish to increase their market shares in the various importing countries and give increasing importance to the continuity of the international dissemination of Ribatejo wines.

The company's structures are based on its CEO, and as such, this is what defines the company's positioning and is based mainly on its intuition, being able to successfully undertake entrepreneurial actions and re-internationalisation depends on its success or failure, it has to overcome the obstacles faced by its SMEs in the search for internationalisation by transposing external factors, procedures and exchange barriers, followed by tasks and socio-cultural factors to achieve success in international markets (Roy et al., 2016)

According to the study by Tuija et al. (2018), the focus has to be on the logic of the activity as a producer of international opportunities, instead of putting the main blame on the honor in the entrepreneurs, we can conclude that the CEO's interviewed, are individuals with a global mentality, are much more alert and available to constantly seek international opportunities.

The decision to re-enter a company is a complex and dynamic process that depends on internal factors consisting of the characteristics of the companies and their CEO, who play a significant role in the decisions to re-enter a foreign market.

As a result, the re-internationalisation of your companies is closely linked to the CEO's intuition.

LIMITATIONS AND FUTURE RESEARCH

This chapter has some limitations, on the one hand, the sample is of convenience and focuses on only one region. On the other hand, the adoption of the case study method does not allow the conclusions drawn to be generalized to all the CEOs of the region.

Future research may include other regions to compare the results obtained. In larger regions, they will probably be more CEO's involved in re-internationalisation of the wine sector.

REFERENCES

Aguzzoli, R., Lengler, J., Sousa, C. M. P., & Benito, G. R. G. (2020). Here We Go Again: A Case Study on Re-entering a Foreign Market. *British Journal of Management*, *00*, 1–19. doi:10.1111/1467-8551.12407

Akhter, S. H., & Choudry, Y. A. (1993). Forced withdrawal from a country market managing political risk. *Business Horizons*, *36*(3), 47–54. doi:10.1016/S0007-6813(05)80148-X

Armario, J., Ruiz, D., & Armario, E. (2008). Market Orientation and Internationalization in Small and Medium Sized Enterprises. *Journal of Small Business Management*, *46*(4), 485–511. doi:10.1111/j.1540-627X.2008.00253.x

Axinn, C., & Matthyssens, P. (2002). Limits of internationalization theories in an unlimited world. *International Marketing Review*, *19*(5), 436–449. doi:10.1108/02651330210445275

Belak, J., & Duh, M. (2012). Integral Management: Key Success Factors in the MER Model. *Acta Polytechnica Hungarica*, *9*(3), 5–26.

Bell, J., McNaugthon, R., & Young, S. (2001). Born-again global' firms: An extension to the 'born global' phenomenon. *Journal of International Management*, *7*(3), 173–189. doi:10.1016/S1075-4253(01)00043-6

Benito, G. R. G., & Welch, L. S. (1994). Foreign market servicing: Beyond choice of entry mode. *Journal of International Marketing*, *2*(2), 7–27. doi:10.1177/1069031X9400200202

Cheuk, S., Liew-Tsonis, J., Ing, G. P., & Razli, I. A. (2010). An Establishment Of The Role Of Private And Public Sector Interests In The Context Of Tourism Transport Planning And Development: The Case Of Malaysia. I*nternational Business &. Economic Research Journal*, *9*(2), 59–68. doi:10.19030/iber.v9i2.522

Ciszewska-Mlinarič, M. (2016). Foreign Market Knowledge and SME's International Performance: Moderating Effects of Strategic Intent and Time-to-Internationalization. *Entrepreneurial Business and Economics Review*, *4*(4), 51–66. doi:10.15678/EBER.2016.040404

Colombo, S., & Perujo-Villanueva, M. (2017). Analysis of the spatial relationship between small olive farms to increase their competitiveness through cooperation. *Land Use Policy*, *63*, 226–235. doi:10.1016/j.landusepol.2017.01.032

Crick, D. (2004). U.K. SMEs' decision to discontinue exporting: An exploratory investigation into practices within the clothing industry. *Journal of Business Venturing*, *19*(4), 561–587. doi:10.1016/S0883-9026(03)00032-6

Dalmoro, M. (2013). The formation of country wineries networks for internationalization: An analysis of two new world wines regions. *Journal of Wine Research*, *24*(2), 96–111. doi:10.1080/09571264.2012.747086

Del Giudice, M., Arslan, A., Scuotto, V., & Caputo, F. (2017). Influences of cognitive dimensions on the collaborative entry mode choice of small- and medium-sized enterprises. *International Marketing Review*, *34*(5), 652–673. doi:10.1108/IMR-05-2016-0098

Demel, J., & Potužáková, Z. (2012). FDI and the Liberec Region: The Case of the Labour Market. *E&M Economics and Management Journal*, *4*, 4–18.

Dominguez, N., & Mayrhofer, U. (2017). Internationalization stages of traditional SMEs: Increasing, decreasing and re-increasing commitment to foreign markets. *International Business Review*, *26*(6), 1051–1063. doi:10.1016/j.ibusrev.2017.03.010

Dubois, A., & Gibbert, M. (2010). From complexity to transparency : Managing the interplay between theory, method and empirical phenomena in IMM case studies. *Industrial Marketing Management*, *39*(1), 129–136. doi:10.1016/j.indmarman.2009.08.003

Dubravská, M., Mura, L., Kotulič, R., & Novotný, J. (2015). Internationalization of entrepreneurship - Motivating factors: Case study of the Slovak Republic. *Acta Polytechnica Hungarica*, *12*, 121–133.

Ellis, P., & Pecotich, A. (2001). Social factors influencing export initiation in small and medium-sized enterprises. *JMR, Journal of Marketing Research*, *38*(1), 119–130. doi:10.1509/jmkr.38.1.119.18825

Fernández-Mesa, A., & Alegre, J. (2015). Entrepreneurial orientation and export intensity: Examining the interplay of organizational learning and innovation. *International Business Review*, *24*(1), 148–156. doi:10.1016/j.ibusrev.2014.07.004

Franco, M., & Haase, H. (2015). University-industry cooperation: Researchers' motivations and interaction channels. *Journal of Engineering and Technology Management*, *36*, 41–51. doi:10.1016/j.jengtecman.2015.05.002

Freeman, S. (2007). An integrated framework of de-internationalization strategies for smaller born-globals. *Exploiting the B2B knowledge network: New perspectives and core concepts, 23rd IMP conference proceedings.*

Freeman, S., Deligonul, S., & Cavusgil, T. (2014). Strategic re-structuring by born-globals using outward and inward-oriented activity. *International Marketing Review*, *30*(2), 156–182. doi:10.1108/02651331311314574

Frost, T. S. (2001). The geographic sources of foreign subsidiaries' innovations. *Strategic Management Journal*, *22*(2), 101–123. doi:10.1002/1097-0266(200101)22:2<101::AID-SMJ155>3.0.CO;2-G

Furtado, J. V., Pereira, A. R., Pereira, I., & Moreira, A. C. (2019). Does theory really fit real life situations: A case study on the internationalization process of a technological service-based firm. In Handbook of Research on Entrepreneurship, Innovation, and Internationalization (pp. 419-438). IGI Global. doi:10.4018/978-1-5225-8479-7.ch016

Goel, A., & Yang, N. (2015a). Internationalization and performance of Indian born globals. *European Journal of Marketing*, *24*(5), 41–49. doi:10.1108/EL-01-2014-0022

Gomez-Mejia, L.R., Makri, M., & Kintana, M.L. (2010). Diversification decisions in family-owned companies. *Journal of Management Studies*, *4* (2), 223-252. doi:10.1111 / j.1467-6486.2009.00889.x

Hadjikhani, A. (1996). Project marketing and the management of discontinuity. *International Business Review*, *5*(3), 319–336. doi:10.1016/0969-5931(96)00013-3

Hagen, B., Zucchella, A., Cerchiello, P., & De Giovanni, N. (2012). International strategy and performance—Clustering strategic types of SMEs. *International Business Review*, *21*(3), 369–382. doi:10.1016/j.ibusrev.2011.04.002

Hambrick, D., & Mason, P. (1984). Upper Echelons: The organization as a reflection of its top managers. *Academy of Management Review*, *9*(2), 193–206. doi:10.5465/amr.1984.4277628

Hron J. (2006). Knowledge and Strategic Management. *Agricultural Economics – Czech, 52*(3), 101-106.

Hutchinson, K., Quinn, B., & Alexander, N. (2006). The role of management characteristics in the internationalization of SMEs, Evidence of from the UK retail. *Journal of Small Business and Enterprise Development*, *13*(4), 513–534. doi:10.1108/14626000610705723

Javalgi, R. G., & Todd, P. R. (2011). Entrepreneurial orientation, management commitment, and human capital: The internationalization of SMEs in India. *Journal of Business Research*, *64*(9), 1004–1010. doi:10.1016/j.jbusres.2010.11.024

Jones, G., & Khanna, T. (2006). Bringing history (back) into international business. *Journal of International Business Studies*, *37*(4), 453–468. doi:10.1057/palgrave.jibs.8400198

Kalinic, I., & Forza, C. (2012). Rapid internationalization of traditional SMEs: Between gradualist models and born globals. *International Business Review*, *21*(4), 694–707. doi:10.1016/j.ibusrev.2011.08.002

Lipparini, A., & Sobrero, M. (1994). The glue and the pieces: Entrepreneurship and innovation in small-firm networks. *Journal of Business Venturing*, *9*(2), 125–140. doi:10.1016/0883-9026(94)90005-1

Mainela, T., Puhakka, V., & Sipola, S. (2018). International entrepreneurship beyond individuals and firms: On the systemic nature of international opportunities. *Journal of Business Venturing*, *33*(4), 534–550. doi:10.1016/j.jbusvent.2018.04.002

Malhotra, N., & Hinings, C. R. (2010). An organizational model for understanding internationalization processes. *Journal of International Business Studies*, *41*(2), 330–349. doi:10.1057/jibs.2009.75

March, J. G. (1991). Exploration and exploitation in organizational learning. *Organization Science*, *2*(1), 71–87. doi:10.1287/orsc.2.1.71

McDougall, P. P., & Oviatt, B. M. (2005). Some fundamental issues in international entrepreneurship. *Entrepreneurship Theory and Practice*, *29*(5), 537–553.

Minichiello, V., Aroni, R., & Hays, T. (2008). *In-depht interviewing* (3rd ed.). Pearson/Prentice-Hall.

Molina, A., Gómez, M., González-Díaz, B., & Esteban, Á. (2015). Market segmentation in wine tourism: Strategies for wineries and destinations in Spain. *Journal of Wine Research*, *26*(3), 192–224. doi:10.1080/09571264.2015.1051218

Moreira, A., & Alves, C. B. (2016). Commitment-trust dynamics in the internationalization process: A case study of market entry in the Brazilian market. In M. Garita & J. Godinez (Eds.), *Business Development Opportunities and Market Entry Challenges in Latin America* (pp. 224–255). IGI Global. doi:10.4018/978-1-4666-8820-9.ch011

Mura, L., & Rózsa, Z. (2013). The Impact of Networking on the Innovation Performance of SMEs. 7th International Days of Statistics and Economics Location: Prague, 1036-1042.

Naldi, L., & Kuiken, A. (2016). *International market exit and re-entry: An empirical study of export patterns of Swedish SMEs.* Swedish Entrepreneurship Forum.

Ngoma, M., Ernest, A., Nangoli, S., & Christopher, K. (2017). Internationalisation of SMEs: Does entrepreneurial orientation matter? *World Journal of Entrepreneurship, Management and Sustainable Development*, *13*(2), 96–113. doi:10.1108/WJEMSD-08-2016-0039

O'Cass, A., & Weerawardena, J. (2009). Examining the role of international entrepreneurship, innovation and international market performance on sme internationalisation. *European Journal of Marketing*, *43*(11/12), 1325–1348. doi:10.1108/03090560910989911

Pla-Barber, J., & Escriba-Esteve, A. (2006). Accelerated internationalisation: Evidence from a late investor country. *International Marketing Review*, *23*(3), 255–278. doi:10.1108/02651330610670442

Ribau, C. P., Moreira, A. C., & Raposo, M. (2015). Internationalisation of the firm theories: A schematic synthesis. *International Journal of Business and Globalisation, 15*(4), 528–554. doi:10.1504/IJBG.2015.072535

Ribau, C. P., Moreira, A. C., & Raposo, M. (2018). SME internationalization research: Mapping the state of the art. *Canadian Journal of Administrative Sciences, 35*(2), 280–303. doi:10.1002/cjas.1419

Roberts, M. J., & Tybout, J. R. (1997). The decision to export in Columbia: An empirical model of entry with sunk costs. *The American Economic Review, 87*(4), 545–564.

Roy, A., Sekhar, C., & Vyas, V. (2016). Barriers to internationalization: A study of small and medium enterprises in India. *Journal of International Entrepreneurship, 14*(4), 513–538. doi:10.100710843-016-0187-7

Ruzzier, M. R., Hisrich, D., & Antoncic, B. (2006). SME internationalization research: Past, present and future. *Journal of Small Business and Enterprise Development, 13*(4), 476–497. doi:10.1108/14626000610705705

Schott, T., & Jensen, K. W. (2016). Firms' innovation benefiting from networking and institutional support: A global analysis of national and firm effects. *Research Policy, 45*(6), 1233–1246. doi:10.1016/j.respol.2016.03.006

Schumpeter, J. A. (1911). The Theory of Economic Development. São Paulo: Cultural April.

Schumpeter, J. A. (1942). Capitalism, Socialism and Democracy. Zahar.

Stam, E., & Schutjens, V. (2006). *Starting anew: Entrepreneurial intentions and realizations subsequent to business closure*. ERIM Report Series Reference No. ERS-2006-015-ORG. https://ssrn.com/abstract=902744

Suarez-Ortega, S. S., & Alamo-Vera, F. (2005). SMES' internationalization: Firms and managerial factors. *International Journal of Entrepreneurial Behaviour & Research, 11*(4), 258–279. doi:10.1108/13552550510603298

Swoboda, B., Olejnik, E., & Morschett, D. (2011). Changes in foreign operation modes: Stimuli for increases versus reductions. *International Business Review, 20*(5), 578–590. doi:10.1016/j.ibusrev.2010.11.005

Thanos, I. C., Dimitratos, P., & Sapouna, P. (2017). The implications of international entrepreneurial orientation, politicization, and hostility upon SME international performance. *International Small Business Journal: Researching Entrepreneurship, 35*(4), 495–514. doi:10.1177/0266242616641749

Torres, J. P., & Kunc, M. H. (2016). Market opportunity recognition in the Chilean wine industry: Traditional versus relational marketing approaches. *Journal of Wine Research, 27*(1), 19–33. doi:10.1080/09571264.2016.1144584

Turcan, J. C. (2019). De-internationalization: A business model perspective. *Journal of Business Models, 7*(4), 39–44.

Vissak, T. (2010). Nonlinear internationalization: A neglected topic in international business research. In T. Devinney, T. Pedersen, & L. Tihanyi (Eds.), *The past, present and future of international business & management* (pp. 559–580). Emerald. doi:10.1108/S1571-5027(2010)00000230029

Vissak, T., & Francioni, B. (2013). Serial nonlinear internationalization in practice: A case study. *International Business Review*, *22*(6), 951–962. doi:10 1016/j.ibusrev.2013.01.010

Weber, R. P. (1990). *Basic Content Analysis*. Sage Publications. doi:10.4135/9781412983488

Welch, L., & Welch, C. (2009). Re-internationalisation: Exploration and conceptualization. *International Business Review*, *18*(6), 567–577. doi:10.1016/j.ibusrev.2009.07.003

Yin, R. (2014). *Case study research: Design and methods*. Sage Publications.

Zucchella, A., Palamara, G., & Denicolai, S. (2007). The drivers of the early internationalization of the firm. *Journal of World Business*, *42*(3), 268–280. doi:10.1016/j.jwb.2007.04.008

KEY TERMS AND DEFINITIONS

Benefits: In this context represent the advantages for the company when it chooses the path of re-internationalisation.

CEO: In this context, is the person with the greatest operational hierarchical authority in an organization. He is responsible for the strategies and vision of the company.

Knowledge: In this context, is the capacity that the CEO has on certain topics.

New Markets: Is the expansion of the market is a strategy of business growth, through the identification of other markets that are possible to be reached.

Obstacles: In this context mean the difficulty in re-internationalising companies.

Quinta Casal Branco: Is a very important estate in the wine sector and in the Ribatejo region it is currently the largest exporter of the region.

Quinta do Arrobe: Is located in Casével, Santarém, is a family property and currently have a strong export vocation and are dedicated to wine production.

Ribatejo: Is a wine region situated in Portugal, with a geographical area for the cultivation and harvesting of vines on a large scale.

Wine Entrepreneurship: Is the one that takes the initiative and knows how to identify the opportunities and transform them for your company.

Wine Sector: In this context is characterized by its high-quality wine and, associated to a well-defined and structured strategy involving the agents of the promotion sector in foreign markets.

Chapter 6
International Entrepreneurship in the Video Game Industry in Barcelona

Yeda Swirski de Souza
Unisinos University, Brazil

Antoni Olive-Tomas
IQS, Universitat Ramon Llull, Spain

EXECUTIVE SUMMARY

Video game studios are an example of born global firms, companies that operate in international markets from the moment they are created. After providing an overview of the video game industry and a description of the video games business model, the Barcelona ecosystem is presented. A multiple case study is the chosen methodology and primary and secondary qualitative data are collected and analyzed. The purpose of the research is twofold: On the one hand, using the context of the effectuation theory to examine how video game developers transform means into effects. The first outcome of this study is a process model describing the mentioned transformation. On the other hand, the research explores the connection between microfoundations of routines and capabilities and international entrepreneurship (IE) to increase the understanding of how startups with scarce resources achieve launching games that have an international reach and, hence, become international entrepreneurs. The second outcome of this research is a model that sheds light on how microfoundations affect IE.

INTRODUCTION

This study aims to contribute to two research problems: On the one hand, examine how creative individuals and teams transform means into effects using the context of the effectuation theory. On the other hand, increase the understanding of how startups with scarce resources achieve launching products and services that have an international reach and, hence, become international entrepreneurs.

DOI: 10.4018/978-1-7998-4387-0.ch006

A central point of the effectuation theory (Sarasvathy, 2001) is the transformation of means into effects (Sarasvathy & Dew, 2005; Dew, Read, Sarasvathy, & Wiltbank, 2011).

The transformation of means into effects is the implementation of the effectual prescriptions of "think about what you can do based on what is available to you," or "do the doable and then push it; and then push it even further." It has to do with non-predictive strategies to answer the question: "What to do next?" (Wiltbank, Dew, Read, & Sarasvathy, 2006).

Dew et al. (2011) view *"new market creation as a result of transformation processes"* (p. 246) rather than as a result of *"search and selection among a universe of exogenously given market opportunities"* (p. 233). Entrepreneurs *"generate usable innovations"* (p. 235) out of *"a series of transformations of the particular stakeholders' means-at-hand into new goods and services that are often* unanticipated residual artifacts *of the effectual process"* (p. 236). They list a variety of transformation types: deletion and supplementation, composition and decomposition, exaptation, manipulation, deformation, among others. Olive-Tomas and Harmeling (2019) propose the working method of the creators of Cubism as a new type of transformation of means-at-hand into usable innovations (Dew et al., 2011).

There is abundant literature explaining how effectuation works (McKelvie, Chandler, DeTienne, & Johansson, 2019). However, there are few articles describing how entrepreneurs transform means into effects. The prescriptions of "think about what you can do based on what is available to you" or "do the doable and then push it; and then push it even further" merit further research efforts, and the list of transformation types (Dew et al., 2011) should be refined and extended.

While Olive-Tomas and Harmeling (2019) examine artistic creation within the framework of effectuation, in this research effectuation is used to examine how video game developers transform means into effects.

Although studies on International Entrepreneurship (IE) have been carried out for almost thirty years, revisions of this process (Rialp, Rialp, & Knight, 2015; Cavusgil & Knight, 2015) highlight further research on IE is needed. Its shortcomings justify more in-depth inquiry and a renewed focus. Several strategic management studies consider microfoundations as a way to unpack collective concepts to understand how individual-level factors impact organizations, how the interaction of individuals leads to emergent, collective, and organization level outcomes and performance, and how relations between macro variables are mediated by micro actions and interactions (Abell, Felin, & Foss, 2008; Felin, Foss, & Ployhart, 2015; Barney & Felin, 2013). The researchers believe that studies on microfoundations of routines and capabilities can add explanations to the phenomenon of fast internationalization, which is not totally covered by existent literature in on IE. Capabilities and dynamic capabilities represent an explicative approach to innovation and competitiveness in uncertain environments such as those faced by startups that internationalize in their early stages (Teece, Pisano, & Shuen, 1997; Teece, 2007). Indeed, in the IE process, studies on resources, routines and capabilities have contributed to a better understanding of how companies with scarce resources can operate and grow in a global market (Weerawardena, Mort, Liesch, & Knight, 2007; Butler, Doktor, & Lins, 2010; Autio, George, & Alexy, 2011). However, as Fellin, Foss, Heimeriks, and Madsen (2012) state, while much progress has been made in understanding routines and capabilities, the underlying microfoundations or micro-level origins of these constructs require more attention. In this regard, Autio et al. (2011) observed the lack of studies focusing on the development of capabilities in IE.

In another vein, one of the objects of study of IE is the so-called born global firms, companies that internationalize early and rapidly. Despite their growing importance, our understanding of how and why these companies develop and implement their internationalization strategies, and what makes them successful, remains incomplete (Zander, McDougall-Covin, & Rose, 2015).

This research follows the suggestion of Felin et al. (2012) that microfoundations of routines and capabilities can be clustered into three main categories: (1) individuals, (2) processes and interactions, and (3) structures. A central question is how microfoundations of routines and capabilities affect IE. To answer this question, qualitative data from video game startups that were born global despite being small independent studios were collected and analyzed.

The chapter starts with a literature review that introduces the constructs involved in the research: International Entrepreneurship (IE), effectuation, and microfoundations of routines and capabilities. The researchers justify the use of the case study as the research methodology employed and present the video game industry in Barcelona. The results were obtained using the literature review as a template to analyze the data collected. In the discussion, the results are linked to the theory in order to identify the main findings. The chapter ends with the conclusions of the research study.

BACKGROUND

This section provides a review of the literature on International Entrepreneurship (IE), effectuation, and microfoundations of routines and capabilities.

International Entrepreneurship (IE)

IE has emerged as a branch in the field of international business to cover a new and growing phenomenon which existent theories on internationalization have not addressed. Since the late 1980s, the establishment of new ventures that went international the moment they were founded or soon after has been at the forefront (Oviatt & McDoughall, 1994). These startups were able to raise capital, manufacture, and sell products in several continents, particularly in advanced technology industries. They seemed to be managed by entrepreneurial visionaries who saw the world as a single marketplace from the time of their firm's founding (Oviatt & McDoughall, 1994; Knight & Cavusgil, 1996). The phenomenon of fast internationalization has also been labeled with the expression *born global*, defined by Knight and Cavusgil (1996, p. 11) as *"small, technology-oriented companies that operate in international markets from the earliest days of their establishment."* This article has played an important role in the development of the growing body of research on firms that choose to operate internationally practically from the start of their operations (Zander et al., 2015). The dimension of the research has been shown by Dzikowski (2018) who conducts a bibliometric analysis of 453 scientific papers on born global firms from the Thompson Reuters's Web of Science™ Core Collection database for the period 1994–2016. Knight and Liesch (2016) summarize the evolution of internationalization research over time and provide evidence to suggest that the field has attained legitimacy in scholarly research. They also contrast the incremental internationalization characteristic of older multinational enterprises with the early, rapid internationalization of born global firms. Gerschewski, Rose, and Lindsay (2015) develop and test a model of early performance for born global firms, and suggest that international entrepreneurial orientation, focus on product/service quality, and competitor orientation are critical drivers of international performance for born global firms. Bouncken, Muench, and Kraus (2015) state that born global firms differ in their business models. Their ability to adapt conventional business models to foreign markets acts as the main accelerator of their rapid internationalization.

In contrast to the traditional stage model suggesting that firms learn experientially as they penetrate foreign markets, accumulating knowledge and growing incrementally, Oviatt and McDougall (1994) observe that international new ventures can omit those stages and enter foreign markets using higher order entry modes (Knight & Cavusgil, 1996; Zahra, 2005). Technological innovation is key when opening up new opportunities for small companies with scarce resources to fast internationalization. Oviatt and McDougall (1994, p. 46) highlight that *"the facile use of low-cost communication technology and transportation means that the ability to discover and take advantage of business opportunities in multiple countries is not the preserve of large, mature corporations. New ventures with limited resources may also compete successfully in the international arena."* Autio (2005) lists four factors triggering and giving significance to this growing phenomenon: (1) new market conditions in many sectors of economic activity (including the increasing importance of niche markets for small and medium enterprises worldwide), (2) technological developments in the areas of production, transportation, and communication, (3) the increased importance of global networks and alliances, and (4) the more sophisticated entrepreneurial skills of people, including those of the founder/entrepreneur who starts an early internationalizing firm.

Oviatt and McDougall (2005) suggest a new definition of IE: *"international entrepreneurship is the discovery, enactment, evaluation, and exploitation of opportunities—across national borders—to create future goods and services"* (Oviatt & McDougall, 2005, p. 54). They take into consideration the approach put forward by Shane and Venkataraman (2000), which focuses on two parts of entrepreneurship: opportunities and individuals who strive to take advantage of them.

One core issue in IE is related to how international new ventures develop resources and capabilities enabling them to be competitive in an uncertain environment. Zahra (2005) considers the key role played by knowledge-based resources and (dynamic) capabilities in the early internationalization process needs to be highlighted. Emphasis should to be given to how knowledge-based organizational learning processes impact information seeking and foreign market research.

Studies on routines, resources, capabilities, and dynamic capabilities have contributed to a better understanding of how companies with scarce resources can operate and grow in a global market. Although globalization of markets and technological advances in information and communication technologies can be considered as external drivers for early adoption of internationalization, they are not sufficient to explain why some companies are capable to internationalize during their early stages. Early internationalization takes place despite scarce company resources and experience. Operating under conditions of asset parsimony, startups overcome constraints leveraging unique capabilities and strengths related to a high degree of entrepreneurial orientation, persistence, innovation, and differentiated offerings. These can be attributed to non-traditional organizational assets, such as proactive orientation, dynamic capabilities, and skillful strategy (Knight & Cavusgil, 2004).

Knight and Cavusgil (2004) consider that, besides entrepreneurial and marketing orientation, the knowledge possessed by born global firms appears to be a critical resource in the early internationalization process as managers in young, internationally oriented companies should develop knowledge that is both relatively unique and inimitable. They stress that knowledge generates appropriate organizational capabilities that become embedded into the firm's cultures via ongoing replication of routines, producing a unique configuration of resources.

Ten years after their influential article, Cavusgil & Knight (2015) recognize that many unresolved research questions remain to explain the issue of why some companies internationalize early, others late, and still others choose to remain local. They consider that studies should contribute to the understanding of how entrepreneurial firms capture, develop, share, and optimize knowledge conducive to internationalization and superior performance.

Several studies focused on exploring the role of knowledge resources and capabilities in IE (Weerawardena et al., 2007; Autio et al., 2011). The central idea in Weerawardena et al. (2007) is that companies aspiring to rapid internationalization need to develop a strategic set of dynamic capabilities. The process of capacity building in born global firms is driven by entrepreneurs that are learning-oriented and have a global mindset. These authors argue that the learning orientation of the born global owner-manager influences the development of specific learning capabilities within the firm, moving it rapidly to internationalization. According to them, three learning capabilities are instrumental to early internationalization in born global firms: market-focused learning capability, internally-focused learning capability, and networking capability. As a result, these capabilities influence the capacity to develop knowledge-intensive products or services and the rapid internationalization of companies. Autio et al. (2011) contribute with propositions about the dynamics of capability development in international entrepreneurial firms, calling attention to features of situational uncertainty faced by these companies. In line with these studies, the researchers assume microfoundations of routines and capabilities can shed light on and unpack key dimensions defining IE (discovery, enactment, evaluation, and exploitation of opportunities across national borders) (Oviatt & McDougall, 2005).

Recent research on IE explores the intersection of digital platforms and ecosystems (DPE) and international business. Nambisan, Zahra, and Luo (2019) focus on three overarching themes: cross-border DPEs as affording new ways of internationalization, as facilitating new ways of building knowledge and relationships, and as enabling new ways of creating and delivering value to global customers.

Effectuation

Effectuation consists in taking a given set of means and selecting between possible effects that can be created with them. The means are characteristic of the entrepreneur and the effects are sought but not preselected. *"Characteristics of decision makers, such as who they are, what they know, and whom they know, form the primary set of means that combine with contingencies to create an effect that is not preselected"* (Sarasvathy, 2001, p. 249). Effectuation is a coherent set of five heuristic principles grounded in expert entrepreneurial practice for decision-making under uncertainty (Read, Song, & Smit, 2009) useful in the creation of human artifacts (Sarasvathy, Dew, Read, & Wiltbank, 2008). The five principles, listed as prescriptions to potential entrepreneurs, are: 1) Start with your means (think about what you can do based on what is available to you); 2) focus on the downside risk (affordable loss); 3) leverage contingencies; 4) form strategic alliances; and 5) control versus predict (the future cannot be predicted). In contrast, causation contends that goals determine actions and entails selecting the best action to achieve a given goal, subject to the available means. It also suggests that the future can be predicted.

Businesses created using the effectual logic are usually unexpected businesses because in effectuation processes the venture cannot be envisioned from the beginning. In contrast, in causation processes the venture is envisioned from the beginning (Chandler, DeTienne, McKelvie, & Mumford, 2011), goals are set beforehand, and all efforts are directed at achieving the pre-set goals. Furthermore, *"effectuation processes do not set a specified end point, but focus on what can be done (given the capacity to influence and means at hand) to move toward a yet-to-be-determined near-term future end point"* (Welter, Mauer, & Wuebker, 2016, p. 7).

The effectuator's pool of resources (what I have) is composed of three categories of means: identity (who I am: traits, tastes, and abilities), knowledge (what I know: education, training, expertise, and experience), and network (whom I know: social and professional networks).

The principle of affordable loss states that decision-makers avoid risking more than what they can afford to lose (Read et al., 2009).

Using the same starting point, contingencies shape the artifact that is finally created (Sarasvathy, 2001; Harmeling, 2011). Entrepreneurs exploit contingencies rather than preexisting knowledge, and manage failures rather than trying to avoid them. They do not merely react to contingencies but rather actively seek to transform them into resources (Harmeling & Sarasvathy, 2013).

Effectuation allows for the co-creation of ventures with nothing more than the available resources and stakeholders who self-select into the process and make pre-commitments (Read, Sarasvathy, Dew, & Wiltbank, 2016). New stakeholders provide additional means (Read et al., 2009). Pre-commitments are provisions of resources made early in the process by self-selected stakeholders who engage a priori (Wiltbank et al., 2006). Stakeholders do not only provide resources, they also set agendas. Courses of action are co-determined by stakeholders who commit resources to particular actions (Sarasvathy et al., 2008). Indeed, "who comes on board *determines what the new market will look like*" (Sarasvathy & Dew, 2005, p. 558). The contribution of stakeholders causes an expanding cycle of resources and a converging cycle of constraints on goals (Wiltbank et al., 2006).

The essence of effectuation is a non-predictive way of coping with uncertainty (Sarasvathy, 2001). High uncertainty reduces the accuracy and usefulness of prediction, requiring alternative approaches (Wiltbank, Read, Dew, & Sarasvathy, 2009). Effectuation refers to Knightian uncertainty, for which the future is unknowable because it is impossible to calculate probabilities since distributions do not exist (Sarasvathy et al., 2008).

Effectuators focus on the controllable aspects of an unpredictable future rather than on the predictable aspects of an uncertain future. The logic of non-predictive control suggests that to the extent you can control the future you do not need to predict (Wiltbank et al., 2009).

Sarasvathy (2001) asserts that the available set of means restricts the possible effects that can be created and that the decision-maker uses the heuristic principle of affordable loss for selecting between the means. She also says that, although the assumption of preexistent goals is eliminated, the entrepreneur is guided by a generalized end goal or aspiration in the sense that effectuation is not a theory of trial-and-error and the effectual process is purposeful and propelled through high level goals (Read et al., 2016).

Effectuation is about creating human artifacts and designing the environments in which entrepreneurs live and work. Harmeling and Sarasvathy (2013) claim entrepreneurs must not passively accept the rules of the game (the prevailing norms and modes of operation in their environments), but rather seek to influence and transform their environments. Effectual artifacts may take on shapes that are unanticipated and sometimes even unimagined (Sarasvathy et al., 2008; Harmeling, 2011). Moreover, *"the end-product (...) is inherently unpredictable at the beginning of the process because the process is actor-centric: it depends on which actors come on board with what commitments"* (Sarasvathy & Dew, 2005, p. 544).

Figure 1 shows a dynamic model that describes how new markets as effectual artifacts are created by means of the effectual interactions of their creators (Sarasvathy & Dew, 2005). Effectuators consider what they can do based on all the resources available to them. By engaging self-selected stakeholders who commit resources to the endeavor, the available means are increased. In exchange for the additional resources they commit, these stakeholders help shape the artifact by narrowing the scope of the goals.

Figure 1. Dynamic model of Sarasvathy and Dew (2005)

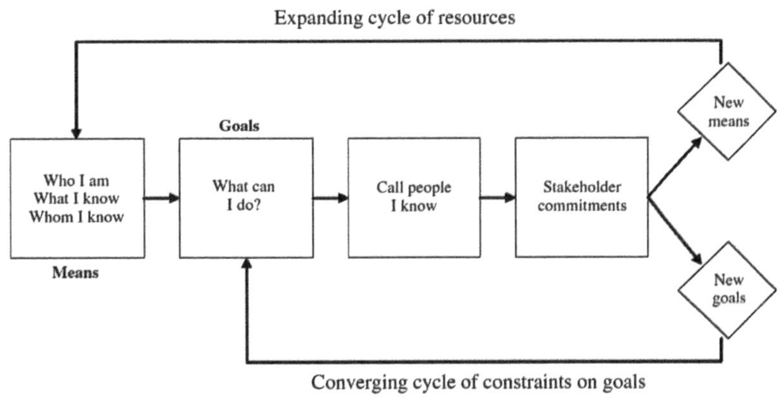

Dew et al. (2011, pp. 235–236) view new market creation as a result of transformation processes rather than as a result of search and selection in a universe of exogenously given market opportunities. Entrepreneurs *"generate usable innovations"* out of *"a series of transformations of the particular stakeholders' means-at-hand into new goods and services that are often unanticipated residual artifacts of the effectual process."* They list a variety of transformation types: Deletion and supplementation, composition and decomposition, exaptation, manipulation, deformation, among others. Exaptation, similar to bricolage, occurs when a resource characteristic that once served a function has evolved to serve another function (Welter et al., 2016).

Several authors have explored the connection between effectuation and internationalization. For instance, Galkina and Chetty (2015) employ the effectuation theory to examine how small and medium-sized enterprises (SMEs) network during internationalization. They show how entrepreneurs network with interested partners, instead of selecting international partners according to predefined network goals. Entrepreneurs who network effectually enter markets wherever an opportunity emerges, and commit to network relations that increase their means.

Microfoundations of Routines and Capabilities

Microfoundations are defined as *"the underlying individual-level and group-level actions that shape strategy, organization and, more broadly, dynamic capabilities, which can lead to the emergence of superior organization-level performance"* (Eisenhardt et al., 2010, p. 1263).

A routine is a distinctive mode of organizational action and its micro-level enables closer observation of the underlying individual processes that generate routine action (Cohen, 2012).

An organizational capability is defined as a high-level routine (or collection of routines) that, together with implementing input flows, confers upon an organization's management a set of decision options for producing significant outputs of a particular type. It is associated with putting resources and other inputs into action (Winter, 2003).

Studies on routines and capabilities are rooted in evolutionary economics and in the resource-based view of the firm, central in strategic management literature. They have played a prominent role in the analysis of organizational and competitive heterogeneity and are linked to the "knowledge-based" emphasis in the field of management (Felin et al., 2012; Barney & Felin, 2013). Research on microfoundations provides a deeper understanding of routines and capabilities that correspond to an aggregate organizational level. This aggregate level can be explained in terms of the actions and interactions of lower level entities, individuals, or other agents (Foss, 2016). Research on capabilities needs microfoundations that capture more fully what is known about cognition and action within organizations (Gavetti, 2005).

The microfoundations literature asserts that macro-outcomes need to be understood in terms of the underlying actions, interactions and characteristics of micro-level entities, such as individual actors and managers (Contractor, Foos, Kundu, & Lahiri, 2019). Studies on microfoundations propose deepening the understanding of how to relate strategical management, dynamic capabilities, and organizational performance in dynamic environments (Eisenhardt, Furr, & Bingham, 2010; Argote & Ren, 2012).

Felin et al. (2012) highlight that while much progress has been made in understanding routines and capabilities, the underlying microfoundations or micro-level origins of these constructs have not received adequate attention.

Felin et al. (2012, p. 1357) suggest that *"microfoundations of routines and capabilities can be clustered into three core or overarching categories: (1) individuals, (2) processes and interactions, and (3) structures."* These authors observe that each category may have main effects on routines and capabilities, and that they do not operate in a vacuum. Instead, they are involved in different interactions within an organization (for example, individuals and individuals, individuals and processes, etc.). Building on Felin et al. (2012), the researchers consider the first category, *individuals*, refers to choices and agents' actions, characteristics, abilities, or cognition. Individuals may have different beliefs, goals, and interests that affect their decisions, and differ in human capital (skills, knowledge, experience, cognitive capacities). The second category, *processes and interactions*, refers to sequences of interdependent events which require the intervention of individuals to become effectual. They correspond to an extensive range of organizational practices, from those related to repeating procedures to others associated with flexibility and adaptation such as experiential learning, *ad hoc* problem solving, situated learning, and human and non-human interactions. The third one, *structures*, concerns the conditions that enable and constrain individual and collective action. They establish the context for interactions within an organization such as the design of decision-making activities within organizations, of organizational structure, and the founder's logic for organizational design.

Experiential learning deserves further attention. Pellegrino and McNaughton (2015) explore the learning modes, including experiential learning, in firms that internationalize incrementally and firms that internationalize rapidly, and also in different stages of internationalization processes. Bunz, Casulli, Jones, and Bausch (2017) investigate the dynamics of experiential learning and adaptation in the internationalization process of international new ventures, and conclude that firms apply deliberate experiential learning. Weerawardena, Mort, Salunke, Knight, and Liesch (2015) examine the relationship between organization learning, innovation and early internationalization. They suggest that early internationalizing firms employ a dual subsystem of dynamic capabilities: a market subsystem and a socio-technical subsystem comprised of network learning capability and internally focused learning capability.

Studies relating capabilities to strategic management recognize hierarchies and layers in routines and capabilities. The dynamic capabilities framework has been used to explain how firms successfully adapt to changing environments (Nayak, Chia, & Canales, 2020). Dynamic capabilities are beyond operational capabilities or technical fitness. They correspond to high-level activities and are more likely to be attributed to entrepreneurial actions than to managerial ones. Indeed, entrepreneurial actions are connected to sense and seize opportunities, shaping future and transforming processes and structures (Teece, 2007).

Teece (2007) provides an umbrella framework that highlights the most critical capabilities management needs to sustain, and proposes that, at least analytically, dynamic capabilities can be separated into different components: (1) identification and assessment of an opportunity (sensing), (2) mobilization of resources to address an opportunity and to capture value from doing so (seizing), and (3) continued renewal (transforming).

Felin and Powell (2016) examine how organizations can put dynamic capabilities into practice. In particular, they show how managers can harness new organizational forms to build a capacity for sensing, shaping and seizing opportunities.

Foss and Linder (2019) provide a characterization of microfoundations and discuss its manifestations in management research over the last decades.

Foss and Pedersen (2019) document the lack of attention on microfoundations in international management research by focusing on knowledge sharing. Contractor et al. (2019) discuss the relevance of microfoundations to global strategy, less impacted by the microfoundations literature than general strategy. Bingham, Howell, and Ott (2019) say that little is known about the individual-level origins of capabilities (e.g., microfoundations) and explore how firms develop internationalization capabilities. Fallon-Byrne and Harney (2017) provide a conceptual overview of the microfoundations of dynamic capabilities for innovation that highlights the importance of incorporating the perspectives and motivation of employees as a basis for more direct managerial interventions in building capabilities. Helfat and Peteraf (2015) focus on microfoundations at the level of the individual manager. They identify specific types of cognitive capabilities that are likely to underpin dynamic managerial capabilities for sensing, seizing, and reconfiguring, and explain their potential impact on strategic change of organizations.

A growing focus of policymakers is the promotion of entrepreneurial ecosystems: the interconnected systems of forces that generate and sustain regional entrepreneurship (Roundy & Fayard, 2019). These authors state that studies draw attention to the positive effects of entrepreneurial ecosystems on the creation and functioning of early-stage ventures, but do not consider the specific mechanisms through which ecosystems influence entrepreneurs. They create a theoretical framework building on dynamic capabilities.

As mentioned in the introduction, except for the work of Dew et al. (2011), Sarasvathy and Dew (2005), and recent research by Olive-Tomas and Harmeling (2019), there is no literature on the effectual transformation of means into effects. The following research question is thus put forward: "How do entrepreneurs transform means into effects?" This study aims to answer the question by examining the development of video games in the context of effectuation.

As said earlier, there is not much literature with regard to the influence of microfoundations of routines and capabilities on IE. We thus propose the following research question: "How do microfoundations affect international entrepreneurship?" Video game studios are considered to be an illuminating example of born global firms.

METHODOLOGY

The researchers adopted a qualitative methodology because they closely examined a series of actions, decisions, choices, and events with the aim of generating models (Eriksson & Kovalainen, 2015). The case study was chosen as the research method because the research questions start with "how" (Yin, 2017). The purpose of the inquiry is to understand a specific phenomenon and to build theory using qualitative evidence, rather than test hypotheses and generalize findings. Because of the exploratory nature of this study, the researchers opted for a qualitative approach based on semi-structured interviews with founders-managers of video game studios headquartered in Barcelona. Models describing the relationships between certain constructs were the expected outcomes of this research.

An analytical approach was used following Gioia, Corley, and Hamilton (2012), who put forward a method to develop new concepts and derive models designed to provide qualitative rigor to the conduct and presentation of inductive research. Applying this method allowed converting the content of the semi-structured interviews into a process model, as shown in Figure 2.

Figure 2. Analytical approach following Gioia, Corley, and Hamilton (2012)

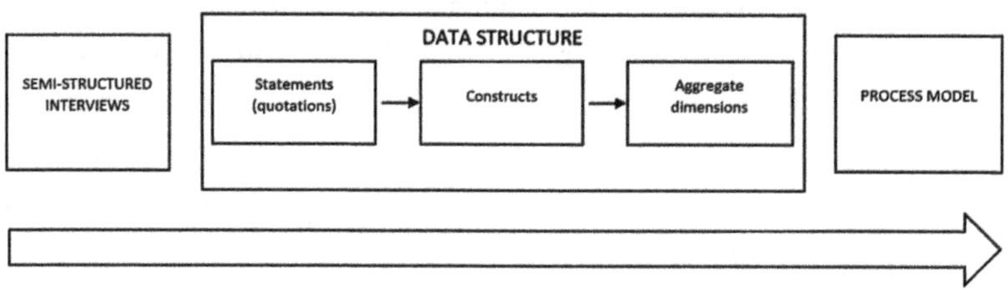

The following sequence was used: quotations from the semi-structured interviews ® constructs used by the researchers to codify the quotations ® dimensions that aggregate the constructs. The quotations taken from the semi-structured interviews ("statements" in the data structure) are not literal. They were reformulated by the researchers. Sometimes, identical statements by different interviewees were integrated. The set of statements, constructs and dimensions was the basis for the data structure, which represents the progression from raw data to the derived model. The model that shows the dynamic relationships between the emergent concepts and clarifies the relevant data-to-theory connections is depicted in graphical form. Using this method allowed maintaining a chain of evidence (Yin, 2017) for external observers to be able to follow the derivation of evidence from the research question to the case study conclusions. The set of constructs used by the researchers to codify the content of the semi-structured interviews was selected from the literature review on IE, on effectuation, and on microfoundations of routines and capabilities. Initially, the codes were the aggregate dimensions of the data structure. The analysis of the statements allowed the researchers to identify additional codes, the ones that correspond to the constructs of the data structure.

As described before, primary data was collected through semi-structured interviews with founders-managers of video game studios. Although the interviews were open, a questionnaire based on the literature review was prepared to guide the interviews and keep the focus on the research questions. All the interviews were recorded, transcribed, and coded. Secondary data came from archival documents including website information, newspaper clippings, internal documents, and public reports.

After the review of the literature, a research protocol was created to guide the researchers in their interactions with the interviewees. The protocol includes a detailed list of data to gather and questions to ask with regard to the topics to cover.

The context of this study is the video game industry in Barcelona. Two reasons justify the choice of context: the features of the industry and the urban setting. Video game development and marketing requires skills in software programming, art, commercial distribution, and monetization of digital products, and video games combine technology, art, and business management in a unique way. Regarding the characteristics of the industry, there is a clear international orientation in the video game sector. Barcelona is an urban setting which corresponds to the pool of resources needed in the knowledge and creative industry. Key resources in the video game industry as well as in other cultural and knowledge-based industries are embedded in an urban context which encompasses a creative hub (an urban ecosystem that enables the connection of diverse and talented people) (Florida, 2011).

The unit of analysis are video game studios that launched a game for mobile, console, or PC played by gamers at the time of data collection.

Thirteen people were interviewed. Nine interviews were conducted with individuals occupying key positions in the startups (founders or key managers). Four interviews were with other stakeholders in the video game sector: (1) the director of Cultura Digital, Institut Català de les Empreses Culturals (ICEC-Catalan Institute for Cultural Companies), a regional government agency; (2) the director of GameBCN, a video game incubator supported by the local and regional governments; (3) the CEO of the Barcelona business unit of a multinational video game company; (4) the CEO of the most prestigious video game company in Barcelona.

THE ECOSYSTEM OF VIDEO GAME STUDIOS IN BARCELONA[1]

Video game studios are a clear example of born global firms, companies that operate in international markets from the earliest days of their establishment (Knight & Cavusgil, 2004). According to Autio, Nambisan, Thomas, and Wright (2018), entrepreneurial ecosystems differ from traditional clusters by their emphasis on the exploitation of digital affordances, by their organization around entrepreneurial opportunity discovery and pursuit, by their emphasis on business model innovation, and by voluntary horizontal knowledge spillovers.

The Video Game Industry

Private and public agents are generating a lot of statistical information relating to both the Catalan and the Spanish video game industries (AEVI, 2020; DEV, 2020a, 2020b). The economic impact of the industry has also been quantified (AEVI, 2018). Egenfeldt-Nielsen, Smith, and Tosca (2019) detail the economics of the video game industry.

Console manufacturers, developers, service providers, publishers, and distributors are vital actors in the video game industry. Console manufacturers (for example Sony, Microsoft, and Nintendo) organize and dominate the production of hardware (consoles) with massive procurement strategies and provision of technological standards. Besides console games, digital platforms (such as Apple Store, Google Play, Microsoft Store, Steam) have increasingly been getting the most significant share of this market. Games are developed by studios that seek to sign contracts with a publisher to obtain the financing necessary to create the game (Tschang, 2005; Gandia, 2012; Bossom & Dunning, 2015). The publisher is often the primary funder, and developers must ensure their resources have the required flexibility to meet the demands and requirements of the publisher. Depending on the funding provided to the developer, the publisher can appropriate a significant share of revenues from the sale of the game. When the game is completed, the publisher works with a distributor to supply wholesalers and retailers. The distributor also captures a significant share of revenues related to sales.

From the moment they are founded, video game studios are connected to a global market spread in five continents. English is the primary language for any game developer. While the domestic market is not a target, North America is recognized as a significant market. Product adaptations to different languages and cultural contexts is one of the tasks of game development.

Many of the video game studios do not survive their first year. Most of them are created by individuals or small teams. However, those with a more organized structure, where functions and roles are clearly defined, are more likely to raise funds and develop more sophisticated projects. Cabra et al. (2017) suggest that investing in managerial resources increases studios' survival rates.

Apart from the advance payments made by publishers, funding also comes from long term loans with low interest rates offered by banks and other financial institutions. In the case of Catalonia, these loans are provided by means of agreements between the regional government and private and public banks. They usually cover the development period of the first game, and the average amount is one hundred thousand euros.

A passion for games is usually mentioned as a must to work at a video game studio. Formal education plays a crucial role in video game development. However, learning processes in this industry are rooted in a set of experiences, connected or not to entrepreneurship decisions, including having played video games since childhood.

Video Games Business Models

Osathanunkul (2015) presents two classifications of business models in the video game industry, the first according to customers' accessibility and the second according to publishers' revenue model. Sandqvist (2015) traces the evolution and adaptation of new business models within the video game industry. Li (2020) suggests that a firm may use multiple business models to serve different market segments or sell different products, and may use different business models over time. Komorowski and Delaere (2016) show that business models designed for video games are inspiring business models for other online media offerings.

There are two basic monetization methods (Bossom & Dunning, 2015). The first model is that of games for iOS and Android. The launch of iPhone in 2007 was decisive for the studios that began operations when iOS and Android platforms started to distribute video games for smartphones. Today, one thousand games are released every day. Games for smartphones are usually "free to play" in the first stage, and monetization is linked to marketing actions inside the game. Competition from video games for mobile platforms has increased fast in a very short period of time, raising entry barriers for small studios. The second model is the one of games for PC and consoles such as Nintendo Switch, Sony PlayStation, and Microsoft Xbox. These platforms provide visibility to games with a good narrative and design. Games for consoles follow a certification process by the owner (for instance Sony) to ensure compliance with quality and ethical standards, and consoles seem to be the best opportunity for small studios.

Pricing varies from "premium" models (selling price per download) to "free to play" (or "freemium") models (micropayments for integrated purchases). The "free to play" model follows the philosophy "game as a service:" after the launch, the actions of the players are monitored and analyzed, and the game is continuously upgraded (Hanner & Zarnekow, 2015; Rietveld, 2018; Tomić, 2018). In recent years the industry has shifted toward "open" ("free to play") video games (Dale & Green, 2017).

Studios may market their video games through publishers or not. Publishers connect developers to the market and fund studios through advance payments. Thanks to the advance payments of the publisher there is no need to borrow from banks.

Publishers are selected by studios on the basis of their game portfolio and their genre specialization.

Technology—the consoles and platforms, the software that powers games and the software that facilitates game development—plays a vital role in this industry (Bossom & Dunning, 2015). Unity, a cross-platform game engine with a built-in integrated development environment, is used by many studios. Additionally, some consoles such as Nintendo have specific requirements for game developers and allow them to use their development engine.

Video Game Development

McAllister and White (2015) remark the relevance of two interrelated tasks: video game development and evaluation of the user experience.

A design document guides the development of the video game. It is continuously updated as the game is developed. Online tools facilitate planning and organizing jobs and activities.

There are different sections in a studio: game design, software development, art, marketing and monetization. The role of producers in the video games sector is similar to their role in the music industry. They provide technical knowledge, artistic sensitivity, and market knowledge. They also connect technology, art, and business.

In order to enter and stay in the market, studios must succeed at launching at least one game. Developing a video game requires a combination of skills in software development, design and graphic arts, music production, and storytelling. Paying close attention to changing technology, market trends, and consumer behavior is also necessary. These skills must be combined with managerial capabilities. They are required to survive after the launch of the first video game. Many startups do not survive because they exceed time and budget during the development of the game.

The trial-and-error method is often used in marketing, project management, fund-raising, and balancing existent activities with innovation and new releases. Most of the entrepreneurs do not have a business-oriented profile and need to develop new competencies in communication and networking to switch from a game developer identity to an entrepreneurial one.

Experiential learning is required and trial-and-error is an intrinsic process in video game development. Abilities are acquired after a lot of hours of practice. For instance, programmers are generalists, and specialization in game development has to be acquired through a trial-and-error approach.

Knowledge related to project management is required to optimize time-to-market. Studios need to find a balance between achieving a good finishing of the game and keeping it on a reasonable development lead time. Some studios successfully achieve time-to-market by launching simple games that can be developed in a short period of time while a longer and more value-added project is in progress.

In the video game industry, there are a lot of small teams of two or three people without an enterprise structure. They do not want to establish a video game company, but want to develop a video game.

Software that facilitates development is essential, as pointed out before. Some specific tasks (audio, certain programming and artistic tasks that are mechanical and do not involve decisions) are outsourced.

The video game case suggests that experiencing, learning, and networking are daily practices among gamers. These practices are intrinsic to the video game sector and evolve in a community of practice where borders between fun, entertainment, work, and business are ill-defined.

The Barcelona Ecosystem

Barcelona is a cluster for knowledge and creativity industries, particularly the video game industry. The city fits the description of a creative ecosystem and hosts a considerable number of independent studios, local small and medium-sized companies, multinational companies, and several public and private supporting agents (Gristai, 2010). Indeed, the region is advertised as "the best place for the video game industry" based on the fact that Catalunya is attractive to both the local and international video game industry[2]. It offers a wide range of specialized video game training programs, competitive labor costs, R&D facilities, a strategic location, and access to markets. Barcelona also hosts international trade fairs and events such as the Mobile World Congress, which receives more than 100,000 visitors, the One Nice Barcelona[3] (formerly the Barcelona Games World), and a myriad of business incubators and accelerators. There are about 120 companies developing video games in Barcelona. The city is home to one of the five biggest pools of companies in the industry in continental Europe, representing the leading video game cluster in Spain (Gamedevmap[4]). Barcelona also concentrates a significant offer of higher education opportunities in the video games sector.

An educational background in engineering, some experience in other industries, and additional training in software and video game development is common among the entrepreneurs. The teams in video game startups also include people with degrees in music, arts, and design. Competencies to professionally succeed in the video game industry can be acquired in specific programs in several higher education institutions.

Institutional agents operating public policies have also been key to the creation of video game studios in Barcelona. New leadership in the regional government agency ICEC has propelled a new mindset regarding digital culture and video games. Under this new mindset, video game studios began to be considered as candidates to receiving public support besides other cultural industries.

Public and private banks from Catalonia, as part of an agreement with ICEC, have been offering loans to studios under incubation or acceleration processes. These loans have been crucial to allow the teams to be dedicated to a project full-time.

The first video game studios established in Barcelona in the late 1990s were the result of initiatives of young engineers passionate about games since childhood who achieved to launch a game after various attempts in a process of trial-and-error. Video game players decided to set up a studio, in general in partnership with former fellow students from university. Many games are spillovers of final year projects. In 2014, an incubator that was specific for video game studios was created. It began as a joint initiative between regional governments and a private agency called Peninsula, the company that runs Canòdrom Creative Research Park[5]. Their premises, including an auditorium, offices, and co-working spaces, were transformed into a tech-based incubator and open innovation lab. Peninsula serves as a meeting point for entrepreneurs with ideas and companies willing to invest in their projects. GameBCN[6] is an incubation program offering video game studios the necessary training and mentoring to make a successful launch onto the market. The objective is to professionalize small studios and to provide them with a business mentality. The incubated teams are trained to improve their production pipeline in order to minimize the risks associated with market launches. The incubator does not take any equity or royalties from incubated teams.

Developers working in Barcelona easily join a community of entrepreneurs who hardly consider other members as competitors. Collaboration among these entrepreneurs became common practice and has been supporting several learning needs related to game development and managerial capabilities.

Information about publishers, trends, fairs, etc., circulate in informal meetings of the social network of this community.

RESULTS

Table 1 shows the data structure for this research related to the transformation of means into effects. The column "Statements" shows the quotations taken from the semi-structured interviews. The column "Constructs" shows the constructs used by the researchers to codify the quotations. The constructs in the second column are grouped in "Aggregate dimensions." The researchers list the statements from the semi-structured interviews, classified according to the codes *means*, *transformation of means into effects*, and *effects*. This data structure follows the process model depicted in Figure 3. In Table 1, the means are *who I am*, *what I know*, *whom I know*. The code transformation of means into effects was split into sub-codes related to the *working method* of video game studios: *studio set-up*, *video game planning*, *video game development*, *team management*, and *outsourcing*. The effects code was also divided into several sub-codes: *discovery of opportunities*, *enactment of opportunities*, *evaluation of opportunities*, and *exploitation of opportunities*, following the definition of IE by Oviatt and McDougall (2005). During the research, two new codes were included: *strategic alliances* and *contingencies*. The strategic alliances code was split into sub-codes: *funding partnerships*, *marketing partnerships*, *technology partnerships*, *institutional partnerships*, and *Barcelona ecosystem*. Figure 3 depicts the process model for the video game industry in Barcelona.

Figure 3 follows from Table 1 and is a graphical representation of the derived model. It summarizes the results of this research:

1. The founders, managers, and employees of the video game studios possess resources (what I have) comprised of three categories of means: identity (who I am), knowledge (what I know), and network (whom I know)
2. They transform contingencies (sudden technology, marketing, and business changes, sometimes shocks) into additional resources
3. They combine their set of means with the contingencies to create video games, opportunities for IE (effects that are preselected or not)
4. They transform means into effects through a working method
5. The working method requires partnerships forged thanks to strategic alliances of self-selected stakeholders
6. The partnerships arise from the founders' *whom I know*

Although some statements seem to suggest the use of causation ("the industry and market research determine the type of game to be developed"), other statements support that video game developers are using an effectual approach to product development ("the final video game differs from the original design" or "there is not a particular methodology to develop video games").

Sometimes, the resulting video games are non-preselected effects and the process is more effectual than causal. The final version does not look like the initial description. Other times, when the development has followed a design document with little changes, the resulting video games are preselected effects and the process is more casual than effectual.

Table 1. Data structure

Statements*	Constructs	Aggregate Dimensions
Founders developed video games during adolescence Founders developed video games in high school or university Founders studied engineering or software development Founders studied other disciplines (business, audiovisual communication) Founders studied a master's degree related directly or indirectly to video game development Founders have been exposed to entrepreneurship The expertise (in number of years) of developers is reduced as technology life cycles become shorter Skills are acquired through practicing When no formal education programs were available, learning was a matter of self-education (learning from failures) Software developers were not specialists in video games Founders were working as software developers Founders were working in other jobs (project management, engineering) Founders had prior jobs related to video game development Founders established a video game studio after graduating Founders established a video game studio for lack of job opportunities in the industry Founders established a video game studio after leaving a former job in the industry Founders joined the video game industry by chance Founders may leave the studio and the industry after a failure Founders have always been passionate gamers Founders play for fun but also to monitor the industry	Who I am, what I know, whom I know	Means
Advance payments from publishers allow studios not to borrow from banks External investors pay attention to the team and the track record of its members, to the ability to innovate the industry, and to the ability to think big and promise a high return on investment Success cases enhance investors' trust Funds are needed to develop the video game as well as to market it Spanish investors are reluctant to invest in video game studios Most Spanish investors are not specialized in video games Recommendation: Show investors the metrics of video game tests Prior experience in large projects and video game studios enhance investors' trust Possessing proprietary technology (e.g. engine) is valued by external investors Investors that are international and specialized in video games may also provide studios with strategic advice	Funding partnerships	Strategic alliances
Platforms (Sony, Microsoft, Nintendo) may require some features (online, multiple-player, characters' customization, etc.) Games for consoles follow a certification process by the proprietor (for instance Sony) to ensure compliance with quality and ethical standards Studios may market their video games through publishers or not Publishers are in charge of product launch, marketing, user acquisition, and channel management Publishers are selected on the basis of their game portfolio and their genre specialization Publishers contribute with funds, know-how, and contacts Finding a publisher for appealing games is not difficult There is the dilemma of "more margin" (without a publisher) or "more reach" (with a publisher) Some studios prefer to devote the publisher's margin to market the video game by themselves (including user acquisition and customer support) Some studios believe that they will sell a lot more relying on a publisher Some studios believe that publishers will help them to create strong IPs because they have resources, contacts, and a portfolio of successful video games Distribution also involves online user acquisition Pricing varies from "premium" models (selling price per download) to "free to play" models (micro-payments for integrated purchases)	Marketing partnerships	
Videogame developers can co-create with technology providers	Technology partnerships	
Studios in Barcelona are part of a community of practice to share information and know-how, exchange experiences with publishers, platforms, etc., look for advice, and cooperate in some tasks Although the community is not a formal association, there is an annual award ceremony with prizes funded by the members themselves Studios do not perceive other studios as competitors, unless they develop very similar products	Community partnerships	
Agents: local, regional, and national governments Policies: financing lines (participatory loans) to develop video games or to establish new ventures, subsidies to attend international trade fairs and meet with international publishers, benefit from incubation and acceleration, tax benefits, visas for foreign employees Proposed action: Offer programs on visibility and monetization of video games Proposed action: Not letting students graduate unless they have published a video game Proposed action: Connect video game education and management education Founders are teaching video game development at universities	Institutional partnerships	
The Barcelona ecosystem is an example of the triple helix: industry, university, government The Barcelona ecosystem benefits all the agents Agents: studios, universities, local and regional governments, investors, etc. Big international studios (for example King, the developer of Candy Crush) with a lot of employees betting on Barcelona was the very trigger of the emergence and consolidation of the industry Big companies ("unicorns") create synergies Senior professionals are coming to Barcelona Local and regional governments are helping "indie" studios (participatory loans, incubation, trade fairs) Barcelona offers talent, a brand, good weather, international schools, quality of life, lower wages and rents, universities, small companies professionalizing students graduating from universities Barcelona does not offer tax benefits Barcelona is not attractive to foreign investors due to the Spanish tax regime There will not be enough jobs for all the students graduating from university "Indie" studios are better at developing than at marketing (the market is saturated and video games do not have visibility) Some "indie" studios focus on the domestic market only In Barcelona there are neither publishers nor investors because the Spanish mindset requires a high return on investment in a short period of time Proposed action: Provide the banking system with tools to invest in studios Access of studios to Spanish publishers would be easier (language, timetable, distance, currency, culture) Studios are concerned about increases in salaries and office rents There should be an equilibrium of small ("indie"), medium, and large firms	Barcelona ecosystem	
The technology available influences the development of the game Videogame developers must anticipate technology breakthroughs Some technologies (such as software for video game development) may enjoy a boom in the industry	Contingencies	Contingencies

continued on following page

Table 1. Continued

Statements*	Constructs	Aggregate Dimensions
Some studios have been established by classmates to further develop and market video games initially developed as academic projects Some studios have been established following a conventional business venturing pattern: market analysis, business plan, product prototype, personal savings, external fund-raising, team making "Indie" studios have been established without an enterprise structure Some studios have been established after being incubated Incubators train the founders and monitor production and marketing	Studio set-up	Transformation of means into effects
An ongoing design document guides the development (mechanics of the game, number of levels, target audience) The design document is continuously updated as the game is developed (design document and video game evolve together, in parallel) The final video game differs from the original design Changes are due to development "shortcuts," users' feedback, and unplanned integration of new features Extras (micro-payments for integrated purchases) are designed and planned beforehand and staged Online tools facilitate planning and organizing jobs and activities Activities must be planned to avoid bottlenecks and ensure team coordination	Video game planning	
In the "premium" model the game is not upgraded The "free to play" model follows the philosophy "game as a service:" after the launch, the reactions of the players are monitored and analyzed, and the game is continuously upgraded There is no particular methodology to develop video games Platforms do not provide studios with developing guides The success of the first video game allows "indie" studios to hire employees to develop a second video game Recommendation: Before starting the development, choose the genre and the target audience, and check the fit with your resources and capabilities and your know-how Design starts with an idea (from a brainstorming process or from gaming experiences of the team members); the second step is a market research Game mechanics are tested The game is tested to check for programming errors, but also to explore different game options and make decisions about the final design, but also to monitor and analyze the reaction of gamers The design document allows team members to work independently, without personal interaction with other members Studios may develop small projects in parallel to a large project; small projects help studios to fund the large project Video game development requires a firm properly managed and organized Video game development requires team coordination Video game development is an artistic genre Video game development is an art in itself	Video game development	
Sections in a studio: game design, software development, art, marketing and monetization The "free to play" model requires continuous service and upgrades and, hence, a dedicated team Some studios follow certain routines (daily and weekly meetings to exchange information about problems and solutions, achievement of deadlines, delays on deadlines, etc.) Most of the members are engineers Some studios hire apprentice students Some studios hire people without formal education For most of the studios English is the company's language The video game designer is the cinema screenwriter (he/ she envisions what the game, the features and the characters will look like) The role of producers in the video games sector is similar to their role in the music industry (they provide technical knowledge, artistic sensibility, and market knowledge. They connect technology, art, and business) Decisions can be made by the team or by a single individual In Spain most of the studios are "indie": two or three people create and own a studio Founders were not paid a salary or were paid a low salary during the development of the first game	Team management	
Some specific tasks (audio, some programming and artistic tasks that are mechanical and do not involve decisions) are outsourced Outsourcing allows studios to work in parallel and reduce the development time Decision-making and some roles (for instance art direction) cannot be outsourced Platforms are also partners; they provide studios with the metrics generated by the players Localization firms are in charge of translating the video game and warning about sensible cultural issues Some studios sign license agreements to develop video games for third parties (global brands)	Outsourcing	
Industry and market research determine the type of game to be developed Goal: Identify non-saturated markets where a new video game can have visibility Some video game developers believe that in creative industries there is always room for innovation, while others believe that almost everything has already been invented Some opportunities emerge due to breakthroughs (e.g. the iPhone and the Apple store launches) The go-to-market strategy determines the design of the game	Discovery of opportunities	Effects
All games are developed to be played by gamers from all over the world (there are no barriers for digital downloads) Video games are in English and translated into many languages Gamers' behavior differs country by country Country versions only differ in language, but sensible cultural issues are also taken into account "Blockbuster" games require a lot of development and marketing resources The market of video games for mobile phones is saturated and new video games require a lot of marketing resources to have visibility For "indie" studios the mobile phone opportunity disappeared when big developers entered the market by "buying" thousands of users at a cost of 3$ Some studios classify the players in patterns of behavior and analyze them Game development and "market intelligence" are linked Some studios can track the runs played by the gamers and the activity in forums "Indie" studios do not have the resources (infrastructure, technology) to apply the "game as a service" philosophy (online, multi-player, integrated purchases) The first game can be a success because the development cost is low. Most studios do not survive after the second game because the development cost is higher In the "free to play" model the secret is getting people hooked, and studios are using playfulness techniques	Enactment of opportunities	
A video game works if it generates revenues (rather than if it is downloaded or if it is played) A video game does not work if it does not achieve the expected metrics Metrics are the best feedback Recommendation: Do not develop the video game you like, but the video game the market accepts Games are pre-launched with another brand in a country to experiment with, until the metrics show that the game has proved to be good enough to generate revenues in the target market Recommendation: Identify the countries with more potential players for the game and the countries whose players are willing to pay more	Evaluation of opportunities	
The life of a game depends on the result of marketing campaigns Studios measure the impact on the metrics of technology upgrades and marketing campaigns There is the launch phase and the maintenance phase (technology upgrades, marketing campaigns, and seasonal versions such as Halloween, Christmas, Saint Valentine) User acquisition may cost more than the video game development	Exploitation of opportunities	

* The quotations taken from the semi-structured interviews are not literal. They were reformulated by the researchers.

Figure 3. Dynamic relations among constructs

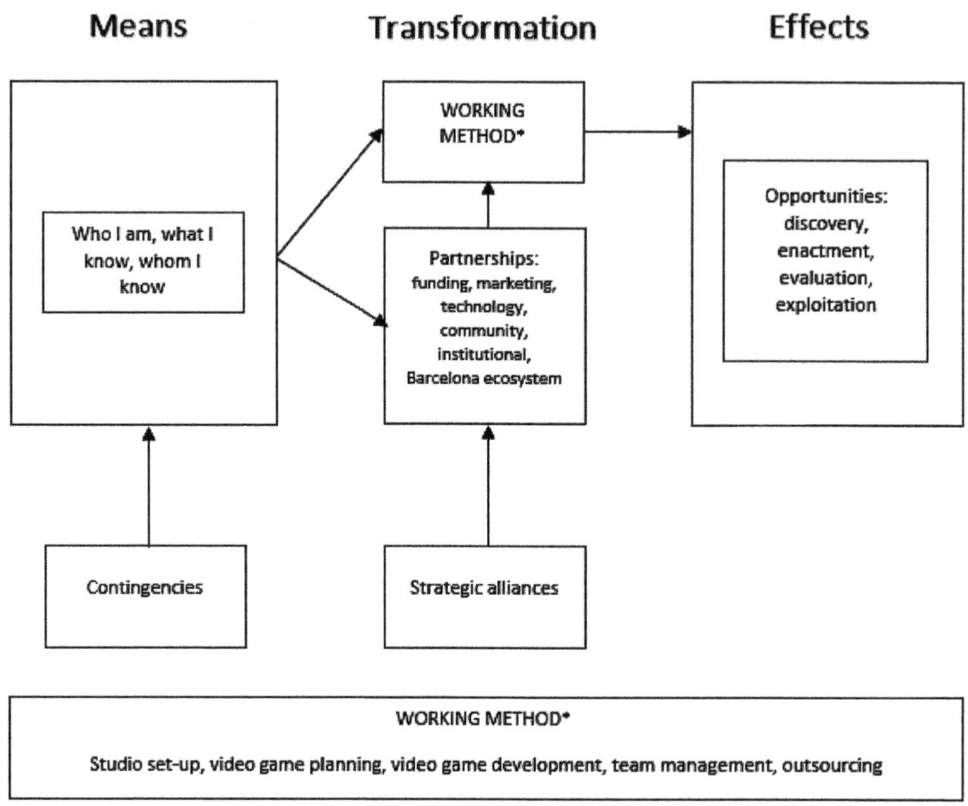

Figure 3 illustrates a process model explaining that the video games were developed by combining a set of means with contingencies. It confirms the dynamic model of Sarasvathy and Dew (2005) shown in Figure 1. The founders attracted the attention of some partners who committed resources and increased the available means (expanding cycle of resources). In turn, in exchange for the resources they committed, the partners influenced the development of the video games (converging cycle of constraints on goals).

The essence of the process model is the working method. It allows video game studios to transform means (what I have and the additional resources provided by contingences) into effects (video games that are opportunities across national borders). The working method consists of establishing a studio, planning and developing a video game, managing a diverse team and outsourcing some non-core operations. The tasks are facilitated by partnerships related to activities such as funding, marketing, and technology. Partnerships with relevant stakeholders (the local community of developers, the local and regional governments, the local ecosystem, etc.) are also created.

Table 2 shows the data structure for this research related to how microfoundations of routines and capabilities influence IE. The column "Statements" shows the quotations taken from the semi-structured interviews. The column "Constructs" shows the constructs used by the researchers to codify the quotations. The constructs are grouped in "Aggregate dimensions." The researchers list the statements from the semi-structured interviews, classified according to the following codes: *personal choices and agents' actions, learning, planning, developing, partnering, networking and cooperating, and team management*

Table 2. Data Structure

Statements*	Constructs
Aggregate Dimension: Individuals and Agents	
Founders developed video games during adolescence Founders developed video games in high school or university Founders studied engineering or software development Founders studied other disciplines (business, audiovisual communication) Founders studied a master's degree related directly or indirectly to video game development Founders have been exposed to entrepreneurship As technology life cycles are short, expertise in number of years is also short Skills are acquired through practicing Learning was a matter of self-education (learning from failures) when there were no formal education programs Software developers were not specialists in video games	Personal choices related to education
Founders were working as software developers Founders were working in other jobs (project management, engineering) Founders had prior jobs related to video game development Founders established a video game studio after graduating Founders established a video game studio for lack of job opportunities in the industry Founders established a video game studio after leaving a former job in the industry Founders joined the video game industry by chance Founders may leave the studio and the industry after a failure Founders have always been passionate gamers Founders play for fun but also to monitor the industry Founders were not paid a salary or were paid a low salary during the development of the first game Founders are teaching video game development at universities	Personal choices related to professional career and lifestyle
Advance payments from publishers allow studios not to borrow from banks External investors pay attention to the team and the track record of its members, to the ability to innovate the industry, and to the ability to think big and promise a high return on investment Success cases enhance investors' trust Funds are needed to develop the video game as well as to market it Spanish investors are reluctant to invest in video game studios Most Spanish investors are not specialized in video games Recommendation: Show investors the metrics of video game tests Prior experience in large projects and video game studios enhance investors' trust Possessing proprietary technology (e.g., engine) is valued by external investors Investors that are international and specialized in video games may also provide studios with strategic advice Platforms (Sony, Microsoft, Nintendo) may require some features (e.g., online, multiple-player, characters' customization, etc.) Games for consoles follow a certification process by the proprietor (for instance Sony) to ensure compliance with quality and ethical standards Studios may market their video games through publishers or not There is the dilemma of "more margin" (without a publisher) or "more reach" (with a publisher) Some studios believe that through a publisher they will sell a lot more Some studios believe that publishers will help them to create strong IPs because they have resources, contacts, and a portfolio of successful video games Some studios prefer to devote the publisher's margin to market the video game by themselves (including user acquisition and customer support) Distribution also involves online user acquisition Pricing varies from "premium" models (selling price per download) to "free to play" models (micro-payments for integrated purchases)	Funding and marketing agents
Agents: local, regional, and national governments Policies: financing lines (participatory loans) to develop video games or to establish new ventures, subsidies to attend international trade fairs and meet with international publishers, benefit from incubation and acceleration, tax benefits, visas for foreign employees Proposed action: Offer programs on monetization and visibility of video games Proposed action: Not letting students graduate unless they have released a video game Proposed action: Connect video game education and management education	Institutional agents
The technology available influences the development of the game Videogame developers must anticipate technology breakthroughs Videogame developers can co-create with technology providers Some technologies (such as software for video game development) may enjoy a boom in the industry	Non-human (technology) agents
Aggregate Dimension: Processes and Interactions	
Some studios have been established by classmates to further develop and market video games initially developed as academic projects Some studios have been established following a conventional business venturing pattern: market analysis, business plan, product prototype, personal savings, external fund-raising, team making "Indie" studios have been established without an enterprise structure Some studios have been established after being incubated Incubators train the founders and monitor production and marketing	Learning
An ongoing design document guides the development (mechanics of the game, number of levels, target audience) The design document is continuously updated as the game is developed (design document and video game evolve together, in parallel) The final video game differs from the original design Changes are due to development "shortcuts," users' feedback, and unplanned integration of new features Extras (micro-payments for integrated purchases) are designed and planned beforehand and staged Online tools facilitate planning and organizing jobs and activities Activities must be planned to avoid bottlenecks and ensure team coordination	Planning

continued on following page

Table 2. Continued

Statements*	Constructs
In the "premium" model the game is not updated The "free to play" model follows the philosophy "game as a service:" after the launch, the reactions of the players are monitored and analyzed, and the game is continuously updated There is no particular methodology to develop video games Platforms do not provide studios with developing guides The success of the first video game allows "indie" studios to hire employees to develop a second video game Recommendation: Before starting the development, choose the genre and the target audience, and check the fit with your resources and capabilities and your know-how Design starts with an idea (from a brainstorming process or from gaming experiences of the team members); the second step is a market research Game mechanics are tested The game is tested to check for programming errors, but also to explore different game options and make decisions about the final design; also, to monitor and analyze the reaction of gamers The design document allows team members to work independently, without personal interaction with other members Studios may develop small projects in parallel to a large project; small projects help studios to fund the large project Video game development requires a firm properly managed and organized Video game development requires team coordination Video game development is an artistic genre Video game development is an art in itself	Developing
Publishers are in charge of product launch, marketing, user acquisition, and channel management Publishers are selected on the basis of their game portfolio and their genre specialization Publishers contribute with funds, know-how, and contacts Finding a publisher for appealing games is not difficult Some specific tasks (audio, some programming and artistic tasks that are mechanical and do not involve decisions) are outsourced Outsourcing allows studios to work in parallel and reduce the development time Decision-making and some roles (for instance art direction) cannot be outsourced Platforms are also partners; they provide studios with the metrics generated by the players Localization firms are in charge of translating the video game and warning about sensible cultural issues Some studios sign license agreements to develop video games for third parties (global brands)	Partnering
Studios in Barcelona are part of a community of practice to share information and know-how, exchange experiences with publishers, platforms, etc., look for advice, and cooperate in some tasks Although the community is not a formal association, there is an annual award ceremony with prizes funded by the members themselves Studios do not see other studios as competitors, unless they develop very similar products	Networking and cooperating
Aggregate Dimension: Structures	
Sections in a studio: game design, software development, art, marketing and monetization The "free to play" model requires continuous service and updates and, hence, a dedicated team Some studios follow certain routines (daily and weekly meetings to exchange information about problems and solutions, achievement of deadlines, delays on deadlines, etc.) Most of the members are engineers Some studios hire interns Some studios hire people without formal education For most of the studios English is the company's language The video game designer is the cinema screenwriter (he/ she envisions what the game, the features and the characters will look like) The role of producers in the video games sector is similar to their role in the music industry (they provide technical knowledge, artistic sensibility, and market knowledge. They connect technology, art, and business) Decisions can be made by the team or by a single individual In Spain most of the studios are "indie": two or three people create and own a studio	Team management and governance

* The quotations taken from the semi-structured interviews are not literal. They were reformulated by the researchers.

and governance. The aggregate dimensions are: *individuals and agents*, *processes and interactions*, and *structures*, following Felin *et al.* (2012). This data structure follows the model depicted in Figure 4.

Figure 4 is the outcome of Table 2 and is a graphical representation of the derived model. It summarizes the results of this research:

1. IE is the result of the interplay of individuals and agents, processes and interactions, and structures.
2. Within *individuals and agents* there are personal choices and agents' actions.
3. Some critical processes and interactions are identified: learning, planning, developing, partnering, and networking and cooperating.
4. Team management and governance refer to the structures in place.
5. IE also influences the personal choices and the agents' actions, the processes and interactions that occur, and the structures in place.
6. IE is characterized by a two-step sequence: an appealing video game is launched and then survival and growth of the video game studio must be managed.

Figure 4. Dynamic relations among constructs

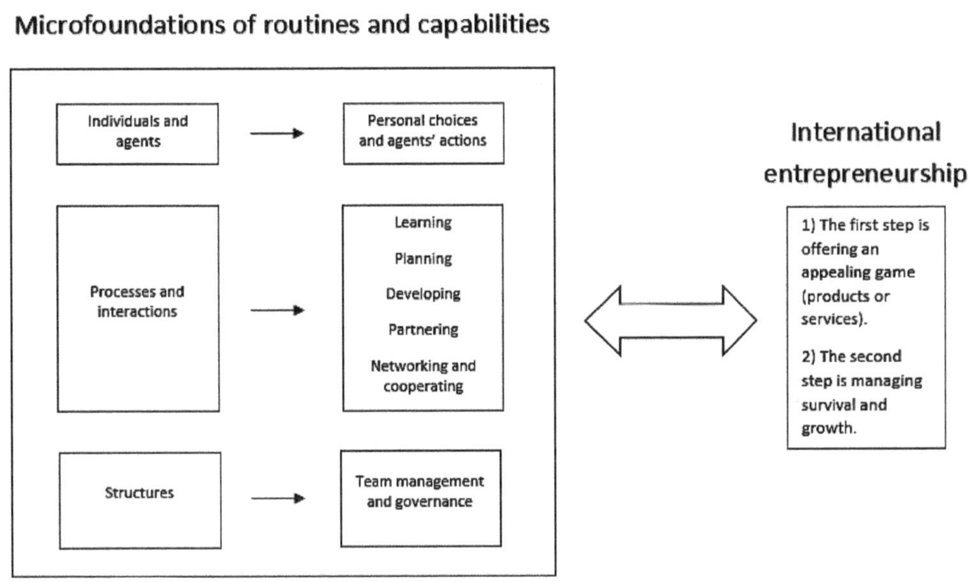

The essence of the model is the bidirectionality of the relationship between microfoundations of routines and capabilities and IE.

DISCUSSION

Some statements seem to suggest the use of causation and other statements seem to support the use of effectuation. This finding is consistent with the notion that firms display both causation and effectuation behavior. During the startup process, there are many decisions to be made and actions to be taken, some using a causation approach, while others an effectuation approach. Reymen et al. (2015), in their retrospective case study on decision events across nine technology-based ventures, show the use of causal and effectual decision-making evolves during the venture creation process and there are certain factors driving the shifts in the use of both decision-making paradigms. The use of either causation or effectuation has to do with the stage of development of the new venture. Effectuation is used during the initial stages of development. As a project progresses uncertainty is reduced and causation is used more frequently. In this vein, McKelvie et al. (2019, pp. 26–28) state that *"we currently have little knowledge as to how long entrepreneurs might use a particular logic, the motivation and factors suggesting when they might switch logics, and the pace and pattern of switching (i.e., concurrently, sequentially, or randomly). (…). The greatest gap in our knowledge is an understanding of how the use of causation and effectuation changes over time throughout the process of venture or project development."*

Connected with the use of causation and effectuation is the realization that effects may be preselected or not. It was also observed that some video games follow the design document with little changes (they are preselected effects and the process is more casual than effectual). In contrast, the final version of other video games does not look like the initial description (they are non-preselected effects and the process is more effectual than causal). This finding confirms the idea that in causation processes the venture is envisioned from the beginning (Chandler et al., 2011), while businesses created using the effectual logic are usually unexpected businesses because in effectuation processes the venture cannot be envisioned from the beginning. Moreover, effectual artifacts may take on shapes that are unanticipated and sometimes even unimagined (Sarasvathy et al., 2008; Harmeling, 2011). As Sarasvathy and Dew (2005, p. 544) say, *"the end-product (...) is inherently unpredictable at the beginning of the process because the process is actor-centric: it depends on which actors come on board with what commitments."* One way to reconcile the debate on the existence or absence of pre-set goals is considering that, although the assumption of preexistent goals is eliminated, the entrepreneur is guided by a generalized end goal or aspiration (Sarasvathy, 2001).

The analysis followed the microfoundations perspective and adopted the three categories for microfoundations of routines and capabilities suggested by Felin et al. (2012): individuals, processes and interactions, and structures. The findings of this research study suggest an interplay among particular elements, relations, hierarchies, and layers corresponding to these categories.

The analysis of data related to the individuals' actions influencing the establishment of video game studios reveals that personal choices related to career and lifestyle can justify the engagement of young professionals to video game startups. This finding is connected to existent literature (Zahra, Korri, & Yu, 2005; Autio, George, & Alexy, 2011) suggesting that analyses of individual cognition contribute to a better understanding of individual choices in IE. However, this study reveals that individual actions are not only related to personal choices but also explained by an interplay among different agents' actions. Agents running educational institutions, private and public policies as well as the presence of funding and marketing agents capable of contributing to this industry also play a pivotal role in enabling the development of video game startups and their IE. Additionally, it was found that non-human agents may influence the launching of video games, in particular the software that facilitates game development. This finding reinforces the idea that the relation between human and non-human agents in routines of technology-based sectors is a crucial element to be considered, as previously stated in Feldmand and Petland (2003).

Regarding processes and interactions, the research confirms the role played by the knowledge of born global firms and their learning capabilities (Autio et al., 2011; Knight & Cavusgil, 2004; Weerawardena et al., 2007), particularly, their experiential learning capabilities (Felin et al., 2012; Tschang, 2005) in the early internationalization process. The findings suggest that learning, networking and collaborating are antecedents to IE. These results reinforce other studies in IE. Weerawardena et al. (2007) consider that the learning orientation of the born global owner-manager influences the development of specific learning capabilities within the firm that move it rapidly to internationalization. The impact of networking and collaboration on IE has also been explored in previous studies. For example, assuming that the relationship in networks generates social capital, an essential resource in access to international opportunities, Coviello (2006) investigates the dynamics of the networks of new international enterprises with respect to the structural patterns of networks and their stages of evolution. Coviello and Cox (2006) examine patterns that exist regarding the types of resources generated by new international enterprises, the nature of the flows of these resources in networks and the development of social capital. The video game case suggests that experiencing, networking, and learning are daily practices among gamers and, eventually, a full game is developed and launched onto the market. They also suggest that these practices are intrinsic to the video game sector and evolve in a community of practice where borders between fun, entertainment, work, and business are ill-defined. Hence, these processes are antecedents to IE given that launching a qualified game is a condition for entering the market.

Findings related to the structure in video game startups suggest that those with a more organized structure, where functions and roles are clearly defined, are more likely to raise funds and develop more sophisticated projects. This finding seems to contradict the understanding taken for granted that horizontal communication in teams is crucial for innovation and creativity.

The models derived have some features that are idiosyncratic of the Barcelona setting. Some constructs in Table 1 such as "Community partnerships," "Institutional partnerships," and "Barcelona ecosystem" and several constructs in Table 2 like "Institutional agents" and "Networking and cooperating" are characteristic of the video game industry in Barcelona. The statements supporting these constructs can provide several clues to understand how and why the sector has boomed in Barcelona and Spain in the last decades.

FUTURE RESEARCH DIRECTIONS

Several opportunities for future research have been identified: 1) with regard to the transformation of means into effects, i) a study of the simultaneous use of causation and effectuation during the development of video games and ii) a more in-depth analysis of the working method as the way to transform means into effects, not only in the video game industry, but also in other knowledge and creativity industries (technology entrepreneurship, arts, etc.); 2) with regard to the influence of microfoundations of routines and capabilities on IE, additional research i) on the role of certain particular agents, ii) on the relationship between networking and growth of video game startups, and iii) on the balance between exploration and exploitation in video game studios.

CONCLUSION

The main contributions of this research are: 1) a process model describing the transformation of means into effects in the video game industry and 2) a model that sheds light on how microfoundations affect IE. Both models fill the previously mentioned voids in the literature. The topics of this chapter may be of interest to entrepreneurs willing to create international new ventures.

This research has concluded that the working method of video game studios plays a crucial role in the transformation of means into effects. As shown in the Results section, the working method consists of establishing a studio, planning and developing a video game, managing a diverse team and outsourcing some non-core operations. The tasks are facilitated by partnerships related to several activities such as funding, marketing, and technology. Partnerships with relevant stakeholders (the local community of developers, the local and regional governments, the local ecosystem, etc.) are also formed.

The findings also highlight that routines and capabilities related to technical skills with regard to game development, design, and narratives are essential to a video game startup. Entering the market depends on succeeding at launching at least one game. Besides capabilities related to technical elements of game development, managerial capabilities are required for a video game startup to survive after launching their first game. This study contributes to identifying microfoundations of routines and capabilities in startups based on knowledge and creativity, particularly in the video game industry. The study recognizes an interplay of individual agents supporting the creation and growth of studios. It identifies experiential learning and networking as antecedent processes to the creation of startups. It also distinguishes patterns of routines and capabilities linked to strategic entrepreneurship to support a balance between performance and innovation.

Finally, the models derived allow understanding the specificities of the video game industry developed in Barcelona since the late 1990s.

REFERENCES

Abell, P., Felin, T., & Foss, N. (2008). Building micro-foundations for the routines, capabilities, and performance links. *Managerial and Decision Economics, 29*(6), 489–502. doi:10.1002/mde.1413

AEVI. (2018). *El sector de los videojuegos en España: impacto económico y escenarios fiscales*. Madrid, Spain: AEVI. http://www.aevi.org.es/web/wp-content/uploads/2018/01/1801_AEVI_EstudioEconomico.pdf

AEVI. (2020). *La industria del videojuego en España. Anuario 2019*. Madrid, Spain: AEVI. http://www.aevi.org.es/web/wp-content/uploads/2020/04/AEVI-ANUARIO-2019.pdf

Argote, L., & Ren, Y. (2012). Transactive memory systems: A microfoundation of dynamic capabilities. *Journal of Management Studies, 49*(8), 1375–1382. doi:10.1111/j.1467-6486.2012.01077.x

Autio, E. (2005). Creative tension: The significance of Ben Oviatt's and Patricia McDougall's article 'toward a theory of international new ventures'. *Journal of International Business Studies, 36*(1), 9–19. doi:10.1057/palgrave.jibs.8400117

Autio, E., George, G., & Alexy, O. (2011). International entrepreneurship and capability development—qualitative evidence and future research directions. *Entrepreneurship Theory and Practice, 35*(1), 11–37. doi:10.1111/j.1540-6520.2010.00421.x

Autio, E., Nambisan, S., Thomas, L. D., & Wright, M. (2018). Digital affordances, spatial affordances, and the genesis of entrepreneurial ecosystems. *Strategic Entrepreneurship Journal, 12*(1), 72–95. doi:10.1002ej.1266

Barney, J., & Felin, T. (2013). What are microfoundations? *The Academy of Management Perspectives, 27*(2), 138–155. doi:10.5465/amp.2012.0107

Bingham, C. B., Howell, T., & Ott, T. E. (2019). Capability creation: Heuristics as microfoundations. *Strategic Entrepreneurship Journal, 13*(2), 121–153. doi:10.1002ej.1312

Bossom, A., & Dunning, B. (2015). *Video games: an introduction to the industry*. Bloomsbury Publishing.

Bouncken, R. B., Muench, M., & Kraus, S. (2015). Born globals: Investigating the influence of their business models on rapid internationalization. *International Business & Economics Research Journal, 14*(2), 247–256.

Bunz, T., Casulli, L., Jones, M. V., & Bausch, A. (2017). The dynamics of experiential learning: Micro-processes and adaptation in a professional service INV. *International Business Review, 26*(2), 225–238. doi:10.1016/j.ibusrev.2016.07.001

Butler, J. E., Doktor, R., & Lins, F. A. (2010). Linking international entrepreneurship to uncertainty, opportunity discovery, and cognition. *Journal of International Entrepreneurship*, *8*(2), 121–134. doi:10.100710843-010-0054-x

Cabras, I., Goumagias, N. D., Fernandes, K., Cowling, P., Li, F., Kudenko, D., Devlin, S., & Nucciarelli, A. (2017). Exploring survival rates of companies in the UK video-games industry: An empirical study. *Technological Forecasting and Social Change*, *117*, 305–314. doi:10.1016/j.techfore.2016.10.073

Cavusgil, S. T., & Knight, G. (2015). The born global firm: An entrepreneurial and capabilities perspective on early and rapid internationalization. *Journal of International Business Studies*, *46*(1), 3–16. doi:10.1057/jibs.2014.62

Chandler, G. N., DeTienne, D. R., McKelvie, A., & Mumford, T. V. (2011). Causation and effectuation processes: A validation study. *Journal of Business Venturing*, *26*(3), 375–390. doi:10.1016/j.jbusvent.2009.10.006

Cohen, M. D. (2012). Perceiving and remembering routine action: Fundamental micro-level origins. *Journal of Management Studies*, *49*(8), 1383–1388. doi:10.1111/j.1467-6486.2012.01078.x

Contractor, F., Foss, N. J., Kundu, S., & Lahiri, S. (2019). Viewing global strategy through a microfoundations lens. *Global Strategy Journal*, *9*(1), 3–18. doi:10.1002/gsj.1329

Coviello, N. E. (2006). The network dynamics of international new ventures. *Journal of International Business Studies*, *37*(5), 713–731. doi:10.1057/palgrave.jibs.8400219

Coviello, N. E., & Cox, M. P. (2006). The resource dynamics of international new venture networks. *Journal of International Entrepreneurship*, *4*(2–3), 113–132.

Dale, G., & Green, C. S. (2017). The changing face of video games and video gamers: Future directions in the scientific study of video game play and cognitive performance. *Journal of Cognitive Enhancement*, *1*(3), 280–294. doi:10.100741465-017-0015-6

DEV. (2020a). *Libro blanco del desarrollo español de videojuegos 2019*. Madrid, Spain: DEV. http://www.dev.org.es/images/stories/docs/libro%20blanco%20dev%202019.pdf

DEV. (2020b). *Llibre blanc de la indústria catalana del videojoc 2018*. Barcelona, Spain: Generalitat de Catalunya, Institut Català de les Empreses Culturals. https://issuu.com/icec_generalitat/docs/200625_llibre_blanc

Dew, N., Read, S., Sarasvathy, S. D., & Wiltbank, R. (2011). On the entrepreneurial genesis of new markets: Effectual transformations versus causal search and selection. *Journal of Evolutionary Economics*, *21*(2), 231–253. doi:10.100700191-010-0185-1

Dzikowski, P. (2018). A bibliometric analysis of born global firms. *Journal of Business Research*, *85*, 281–294. doi:10.1016/j.jbusres.2017.12.054

Egenfeldt-Nielsen, S., Smith, J. H., & Tosca, S. P. (2019). *Understanding video games: the essential introduction*. Routledge. doi:10.4324/9780429431791

Eisenhardt, K. M., Furr, N. R., & Bingham, C. B. (2010). Microfoundations of performance: Balancing efficiency and flexibility in dynamic environments. *Organization Science*, *21*(6), 1263–1273. doi:10.1287/orsc.1100.0564

Eriksson, P., & Kovalainen, A. (2015). *Qualitative methods in business research: a practical guide to social research*. Sage.

Fallon-Byrne, L., & Harney, B. (2017). Microfoundations of dynamic capabilities for innovation: a review and research agenda. *The Irish Journal of Management, 36*(1), 21-–1.

Feldman, M. S., & Pentland, B. T. (2003). Reconceptualizing organizational routines as a source of flexibility and change. *Administrative Science Quarterly*, *48*(1), 94–118. doi:10.2307/3556620

Felin, T., Foss, N. J., Heimeriks, K. H., & Madsen, T. L. (2012). Microfoundations of routines and capabilities: Individuals, processes, and structure. *Journal of Management Studies*, *49*(8), 1351–1374. doi:10.1111/j.1467-6486.2012.01052.x

Felin, T., Foss, N. J., & Ployhart, R. E. (2015). The microfoundations movement in strategy and organization theory. *The Academy of Management Annals*, *9*(1), 575–632. doi:10.5465/19416520.2015.1007651

Felin, T., & Powell, T. C. (2016). Designing organizations for dynamic capabilities. *California Management Review*, *58*(4), 78–96. doi:10.1525/cmr.2016.58.4.78

Florida, R. (2011). *The rise of the creative class*. Basic Books.

Foss, N. J. (2016). Reflections on a decade of microfoundations research. *Revista ADM*, *51*(1), 117–120.

Foss, N. J., & Linder, S. (2019). *Microfoundations: nature, debate, and promise*. Cambridge University Press. doi:10.1017/9781108685498

Foss, N. J., & Pedersen, T. (2019). Microfoundations in international management research: The case of knowledge sharing in multinational corporations. *Journal of International Business Studies, 50*(9), 1594–1621.

Galkina, T., & Chetty, S. (2015). Effectuation and networking of internationalizing SMEs. *Management International Review*, *55*(5), 647–676. doi:10.100711575-015-0251-x

Gandia, R. (2013). The digital revolution and convergence in the video game and animation industries: Effects on the strategic organization of the innovation process. *International Journal of Arts Management*, *15*(2), 32–44.

Gavetti, G. (2005). Cognition and hierarchy: Rethinking the microfoundations of capabilities' development. *Organization Science*, *16*(6), 599–617. doi:10.1287/orsc.1050.0140

Gerschewski, S., Rose, E. L., & Lindsay, V. J. (2015). Understanding the drivers of international performance for born global firms: An integrated perspective. *Journal of World Business*, *50*(3), 558–575. doi:10.1016/j.jwb.2014.09.001

Gioia, D. A., Corley, K. G., & Hamilton, A. L. (2012). Seeking qualitative rigor in inductive research: Notes on the Gioia Methodology. *Organizational Research Methods*, *16*(1), 15–31. doi:10.1177/1094428112452151

Gristai, O. (2010). *Promoting creativity and knowledge in the Barcelona Metropolitan Region*. ACRE.

Hanner, N., & Zarnekow, R. (2015). Purchasing behavior in free to play games: Concepts and empirical validation. In *2015 48th Hawaii International Conference on System Sciences*. IEEE.

Harmeling, S. (2011). Contingency as an entrepreneurial resource: How private obsession fulfills public need. *Journal of Business Venturing*, *26*(3), 293–305. doi:10.1016/j.jbusvent.2009.10.003

Harmeling, S. S., & Sarasvathy, S. D. (2013). When contingency is a resource: Educating entrepreneurs in the Balkans, the Bronx, and beyond. *Entrepreneurship Theory and Practice*, *37*(4), 713–744. doi:10.1111/j.1540-6520.2011.00489.x

Helfat, C. E., & Peteraf, M. A. (2015). Managerial cognitive capabilities and the microfoundations of dynamic capabilities. *Strategic Management Journal*, *36*(6), 831–850. doi:10.1002mj.2247

Knight, G. A., & Cavusgil, S. T. (1996). The born global firm: A challenge to traditional internationalization theory. *Advances in International Marketing*, *8*(1), 11–26.

Knight, G. A., & Cavusgil, S. T. (2004). Innovation, organizational capabilities, and the born-global firm. *Journal of International Business Studies*, *35*(2), 124–141. doi:10.1057/palgrave.jibs.8400071

Knight, G. A., & Liesch, P. W. (2016). Internationalization: From incremental to born global. *Journal of World Business*, *51*(1), 93–102. doi:10.1016/j.jwb.2015.08.011

Komorowski, M., & Delaere, S. (2016). Online media business models: Lessons from the video game sector. *Westminster Papers in Communication and Culture*, *11*(1), 103–123. doi:10.16997/wpcc.220

Li, F. (2020). The digital transformation of business models in the creative industries: A holistic framework and emerging trends. *Technovation*, *92*, 102012. doi:10.1016/j.technovation.2017.12.004

McAllister, G., & White, G. R. (2015). Video game development and user experience. In R. Bernhaupt (Ed.), *Game user experience evaluation. Human-computer interaction series* (pp. 11–35). Springer. doi:10.1007/978-3-319-15985-0_2

McKelvie, A., Chandler, G. N., DeTienne, D. R., & Johansson, A. (2019). The measurement of effectuation: Highlighting research tensions and opportunities for the future. *Small Business Economics*, 1–32.

Nambisan, S., Zahra, S. A., & Luo, Y. (2019). Global platforms and ecosystems: Implications for international business theories. *Journal of International Business Studies*, *50*(9), 1464–1486. doi:10.105741267-019-00262-4

Nayak, A., Chia, R., & Canales, J. I. (2020). Noncognitive microfoundations: Understanding dynamic capabilities as idiosyncractically refined sensitivities and predispositions. *Academy of Management Review*, *45*(2), 280–303. doi:10.5465/amr.2016.0253

Olive-Tomas, A., & Harmeling, S. S. (2019). The rise of art movements: An effectual process model of Picasso's and Braque's give-and-take during the creation of Cubism (1908–1914). *Small Business Economics*, 1–24.

Osathanunkul, C. (2015). A classification of business models in video game industry. *International Journal of Management Cases*, *17*(1), 35–44.

Oviatt, B. M., & McDougall, P. P. (1994). Toward a theory of international new ventures. *Journal of International Business Studies*, *36*(1), 29–41. doi:10.1057/palgrave.jibs.8400128

Oviatt, B. M., & McDougall, P. P. (2005). Defining international entrepreneurship and modeling the speed of internationalization. *Entrepreneurship Theory and Practice*, *29*(5), 537–553. doi:10.1111/j.1540-6520.2005.00097.x

Pellegrino, J. M., & McNaughton, R. B. (2015). The co-evolution of learning and internationalization strategy in international new ventures. *Management International Review*, *55*(4), 457–483. doi:10.100711575-015-0246-7

Read, S., Sarasvathy, S. D., Dew, N., & Wiltbank, R. (2016). Response to Arend, Sarooghi, and Burkemper (2015): Co-creating effectual entrepreneurship research. *Academy of Management Review*, *41*(3), 528–536. doi:10.5465/amr.2015.0180

Read, S., Song, M., & Smit, W. (2009). A meta-analytic review of effectuation and venture performance. *Journal of Business Venturing*, *24*(6), 573–587. doi:10.1016/j.jbusvent.2008.02.005

Reymen, I. M., Andries, P., Berends, H., Mauer, R., Stephan, U., & Van Burg, E. (2015). Understanding dynamics of strategic decision making in venture creation: A process study of effectuation and causation. *Strategic Entrepreneurship Journal*, *9*(4), 351–379. doi:10.1002ej.1201

Rialp, A., Rialp, J., & Knight, G. A. (2015). International entrepreneurship: a review and future directions. In A. Fernhaber & S. Prashantham (Eds.), *The Routledge companion to international entrepreneurship* (pp. 7–28). Routledge.

Rietveld, J. (2018). Creating and capturing value from freemium business models: A demand-side perspective. *Strategic Entrepreneurship Journal*, *12*(2), 171–193. doi:10.1002ej.1279

Roundy, P. T., & Fayard, D. (2019). Dynamic capabilities and entrepreneurial ecosystems: The micro-foundations of regional entrepreneurship. *The Journal of Entrepreneurship*, *28*(1), 94–120. doi:10.1177/0971355718810296

Sandqvist, U. (2015). The games they are a changin': New business models and transformation within the video game industry. *Humanities and Social Sciences Latvia*, *23*(2), 4–20.

Sarasvathy, S. D. (2001). Causation and effectuation: Toward a theoretical shift from economic inevitability to entrepreneurial contingency. *Academy of Management Review*, *26*(2), 243–263. doi:10.5465/amr.2001.4378020

Sarasvathy, S. D., & Dew, N. (2005). New market creation through transformation. *Journal of Evolutionary Economics*, *15*(5), 533–565. doi:10.100700191-005-0264-x

Sarasvathy, S. D., Dew, N., Read, S., & Wiltbank, R. (2008). Designing organizations that design environments: Lessons from entrepreneurial expertise. *Organization Studies*, *29*(3), 331–350. doi:10.1177/0170840607088017

Shane, S., & Venkataraman, S. (2000). The promise of entrepreneurship as a field of research. *Academy of Management Review*, *25*(1), 217–226.

Teece, D. J. (2007). Explicating dynamic capabilities: The nature and microfoundations of (sustainable) enterprise performance. *Strategic Management Journal*, *28*(13), 1319–1350. doi:10.1002mj.640

Teece, D. J., Pisano, G., & Shuen, A. (1997). Dynamic capabilities and strategic management. *Strategic Management Journal*, *18*(7), 509–533. doi:10.1002/(SICI)1097-0266(199708)18:7<509::AID-SMJ882>3.0.CO;2-Z

Tomić, N. Z. (2018). Economic model of microtransactions in video games. *Journal of Economic Science Research*, *1*(1), 17–23.

Tschang, F. T. (2005). Video games as interactive experiential products and their manner of development. *International Journal of Innovation Management*, *9*(1), 103–131. doi:10.1142/S1363919605001198

Weerawardena, J., Mort, G. S., Liesch, P. W., & Knight, G. A. (2007). Conceptualizing accelerated internationalization in the born global firm: A dynamic capabilities perspective. *Journal of World Business*, *42*(3), 294–306. doi:10.1016/j.jwb.2007.04.004

Weerawardena, J., Mort, G. S., Salunke, S., Knight, G., & Liesch, P. W. (2015). The role of the market sub-system and the socio-technical sub-system in innovation and firm performance: A dynamic capabilities approach. *Journal of the Academy of Marketing Science*, *43*(2), 221–239. doi:10.100711747-014-0382-9

Welter, C., Mauer, R., & Wuebker, R. J. (2016). Bridging behavioral models and theoretical concepts: Effectuation and bricolage in the opportunity creation framework. *Strategic Entrepreneurship Journal*, *10*(1), 5–20. doi:10.1002ej.1215

Wiltbank, R., Dew, N., Read, S., & Sarasvathy, S. D. (2006). What to do next? The case for non-predictive strategy. *Strategic Management Journal*, *27*(10), 981–998. doi:10.1002mj.555

Wiltbank, R., Read, S., Dew, N., & Sarasvathy, S. D. (2009). Prediction and control under uncertainty: Outcomes in angel investing. *Journal of Business Venturing*, *24*(2), 116–133. doi:10.1016/j.jbusvent.2007.11.004

Winter, S. G. (2003). Understanding dynamic capabilities. *Strategic Management Journal*, *24*(10), 991–995. doi:10.1002mj.318

Yin, R. K. (2017). *Case study research and applications: design and methods*. Sage.

Zahra, S. A. (2005). A theory of international new ventures: A decade of research. *Journal of International Business Studies*, *36*(1), 20–28. doi:10.1057/palgrave.jibs.8400118

Zahra, S. A., Korri, J. S., & Yu, J. F. (2005). Cognition and international entrepreneurship: Implications for research on international opportunity recognition and exploitation. *International Business Review*, *14*(2), 129–146. doi:10.1016/j.ibusrev.2004.04.005

Zander, I., McDougall-Covin, P., & Rose, E. L. (2015). Born globals and international business: Evolution of a field of research. *Journal of International Business Studies*, *46*(1), 27–35. doi:10.1057/jibs.2014.60

KEY TERMS AND DEFINITIONS

Effectuation: Theory of entrepreneurship that prescribes creating effects from the available means by combining the resources at hand with contingencies.

International Entrepreneurship: Discovery, enactment, evaluation, and exploitation of opportunities across national borders.

Microfoundations of Routines and Capabilities: Underlying individual-level and group-level actions that shape strategy, organization and, more broadly, dynamic capabilities, which can lead to the emergence of superior organization-level performance.

ENDNOTES

1. Except for statements supported with references, this section is based on oral information provided by the founders-managers during their meetings with the researchers.
2. http://catalonia.com/export/sites/catalonia/.content/documents/VideoGames_Sector_Snapshot_2018_EN.pdf. Accessed 3 July 2020.
3. http://www.niceonebarcelona.com/en/. Accessed 3 July 2020.
4. https://www.gamedevmap.com/index.php?location=Barcelona. Accessed 3 July 2020.
5. https://canodrom.com/en/. Accessed 3 July 2020.
6. https://gamebcn.co/. Accessed 3 July 2020.

Chapter 7
Intermediary Interpreters in University–Industry Collaboration to Support Manufacturing SMEs

Roderick Walden
https://orcid.org/0000-0001-8746-7276
University of Technology Sydney, Australia

Anton Nemme
https://orcid.org/0000-0002-7846-9971
University of Technology Sydney, Australia

EXECUTIVE SUMMARY

This chapter will present a series of university-industry collaboration (UIC) projects between a university industrial design research unit and various small-medium (manufacturing) enterprises (SMEs) with a focus on the facilitators role in these projects. Previous research has referred to 'innovation intermediaries' as a term to define (service) firms that proactively facilitate collaboration between two or more parties in innovation projects. In terms of technological development these have been exemplified as research and technology organisations (RTOs). The authors suggest an adjacent term 'intermediary interpreters' to describe the key facilitator by bringing together the term 'intermediaries' and the term 'interpreters' as they are defined by Roberto Verganti. These individuals have specialised external expertise and ability to take part in the 'design discourse; to support innovation. The authors argue that intermediary interpreters are an important third party in UIC projects that provide unique support that can help SMEs embrace innovation strategy and more effectively internationalise.

DOI: 10.4018/978-1-7998-4387-0.ch007

INTRODUCTION

This Chapter will present a series of University-Industry Collaboration (UIC) projects between a University Industrial Design Research Unit and various small-medium (manufacturing) enterprises (SMEs) with a focus on the 'interpreters' role in these projects, broadly responsible for supporting successful collaboration between the university and industry partners. At the University of Technology Sydney (UTS), the Integrated Product Design Research unit (IPD-R) is an Industrial Design Research group made up of four academic members of the Product Design Program in the School of Design. The cases analysed in this chapter are UIC projects worked on by this group. The group members all have experience as professional designers who have transitioned to academia. IPD-R specialises in external research engagement with local SMEs to support innovation development within those organisations and by extension, their ability to compete internationally. The members of IPD-R consider themselves academic design practitioners (2015), a term that has been defined in the following way:

"The academic design practitioner may be defined as a researcher with up-to-date competency in industry-based design practice, enabling them to adapt practice-led research projects that can strategically develop multi-tiered outcomes that supply academic and industry relevant outcomes concurrently." – From the paper: The Academic Design Practitioner, Creative Practices Conference, Arkitektskolen, Aarhus 2015

A very real issue when working with manufacturing SMEs in UIC product design projects is aligning the expectations of the SME with those of the University Research Unit. Research by Doherty, Wrigley, Matthews and Buculo (2013) identified that the integration of design innovation with SMEs faces three challenges:

1. Managing the expectations of the industry partnership. Universities will often be interested in establishing design innovation as a wider strategic benefit for the SME. Whereas the SME may be primarily concerned with a new product design.
2. Conveying the relevance and potential of design innovation across the company. The partnership, wherever possible should attempt to extend beyond the SME director and the designers, to include other departments or relevant partners.
3. Risk averse culture. SMEs can be more reactive than proactive. Proactive management of design innovation across the company can be made possible via "strategic activities to hone the company's core value proposition".

This aligns with research from Bruneel, D'Este and Salter (2010) that finds that orienting the goals of university and those of the industry partner in UIC projects is critical. They note that universities tend to have a leaning toward 'pure science' and a long-term, research focused view compared to the "urgency of implementable industry research". Additionally, Bruneel et al. (2010) recommend that conflicts over Intellectual Property (IP) must be avoided.

UIC projects, most particularly those that are funded, include a facilitator - a third party. For example, the CSIRO[1] SME Connect Scheme has dedicated personnel known as 'Innovation Connections Facilitators'. These are specialists who will have business and technical expertise. They are typically very good at facilitating the negotiation of mutually beneficial goals between the SME and the university research team; and the setting of the scope of the project.

Internationalization of SMEs

Internationalization is a widely used evolving term which requires some clarification, Welch and Luostarinen (1988) provide an extended definition, which is explained as "outward movement in an individual firm's or larger grouping's international operation, (and also), the process of increasing involvement in international operations". Bell et al. (2003) add further specificity to the definition, "internationalization is seen as an entrepreneurial process that is embedded in an institutional and social web which supports the firm in terms of access to information, human capital, finance, and so on". There are two notable aspects that affect an internationalization process which have been explored by Johanson and Wiedersheim-Paul (1975). These are the SMEs 'attitude to foreign activity' and 'the actual carrying out of activities abroad'; the first issue is a key perceptual characteristic, and the second issue, the result of how attitudes can affect internationalization activities in practice.

Internationalization can be viewed as occurring in two distinct modes where an SME might internationalise incrementally or begin as a 'born global' entity (Rennie, 1993). For the former, research by Welch and Luostarinen (1988) is appropriate to introduce here, as they describe that "it is not uncommon for Australian firms to view operations in New Zealand as merely an extension of domestic activities, as also for Finnish firms moving into Sweden". SMEs can be impeded in internationalization activity by the concept of 'psychic distance' (Beckermann, 1956) which means that they may gravitate to markets that are culturally and conditionally similar to their own. Examples of factors that affect 'psychic distance' are "differences in language, culture, political systems, level of education, level of industrial development" (Johanson & Wiedersheim-Paul, 1975).

Welch and Luostarinen suggest a basic way to measure the result of an internationalization process,

"perhaps the simplest objective basis for assessing the degree of internationalization is some measure of foreign sales relative to total sales...although this measure is attractive because of its simplicity and measurability it provides very little information about the nature of and capacity to conduct international operations" (1988).

Welch and Luostarinen (1988) also suggest that a more accurate way to rate internationalization activity rather than focusing on the ratio of foreign sales to total sales would be through observation of data concerning each of the following factors: operation method, sales objects, target markets, organisational capacity, personnel, organisational structure and finance.

'Born global' SMEs are able to exploit niche market opportunities because they "are usually swifter than their larger competitors to adapt product offerings to meet emerging market needs" (Rennie, 1993). In a 1993 study by Rennie of Australia's high value-added manufacturers 'born globals' began exporting on average, 2 years after their inception achieving 76% of total sales, whereas traditional firms (through incremental processes) had an export figure of 20% of total sales much later in their development with the average age after their first export being 27 years.

Challenges of internationalization

Dominguez and Mayrhofer (2017) suggest several other situations that are more reflective of internationalization activities than the two distinct modes described by Rennie (1993) being, born-again globals, acceleration of internationalization, de-internationalization, re-internationalization and serial nonlinear internationalization which suggest far more diversity in internationalization activities over the life of an SME. The SME in question may be involved in several of those internationalization positions of expansion or contraction; particularly after a failed attempt to enter an international market. A discussion of each of those situations is beyond the scope of this book chapter, however it is worthwhile to be aware of their existence.

"We also assume that the most important obstacles to internationalization are lack of knowledge and resources. These obstacles are reduced through incremental decision-making and learning about the foreign markets and operations" (Johanson & Wiedersheim-Paul, 1975).

Being involved in foreign business activities activates a learning process which can provide more knowledge and perceptual adjustments about conducting business external to a familiar local market. Following, the challenges associated with overcoming 'psychic distance' may be mitigated by acquiring knowledge, and a good way to do that might be working with university research units given the international connections and cross-institutional associations that university research typically establish over time.

Rennie goes on to explain that SMEs around the world have been subject to changing conditions, stating that; "broadly, the causes lie in the dynamic interrelationships between changing consumer preferences, changing manufacturing and information technology, and changing competitive conditions" (1993). Dorst (2015) argues that a 'crucial ability' for facing these challenges is to be able to integrate new learnings as active knowledge to enable the organisations to operate proactively rather than only reacting to 'problem situations'.

Business activity may produce an opportunity to expand revenue via the delivery of innovative products and services into new markets. This becomes apparent when traditional SMEs outgrow local markets and attempt to develop an export process. In the case of born global SMEs, entities of this kind could not be satisfied by their local markets, and so from the outset, began their existence with an international focus. A restricted market size is a particular issue for island nations and those countries with smaller populations. McDougall and Oviatt (2000) provide a concise definition of international entrepreneurship and why it might occur, "international entrepreneurship is a combination of innovative, proactive, and risk-seeking behaviour that crosses national borders and is intended to create value in organizations". Entrepreneurs seeking to create value in their own organisations will look beyond a local market for more lucrative possibilities elsewhere.

BACKGROUND

Innovation differs depending on the degree of novelty. Although there are many studies on the differences between innovation types, Dahlin and Behrens (2005) refer to incremental innovation as 'run-of-the-mill' inventions and radical innovations as those that 'break with traditions in the field'. Further, Dahlin and Behrens define radical innovations as (1) novel (dissimilar from prior inventions); (2) unique (dissimilar from current inventions) and (3) having an impact on future technology (must be adopted), based on their study of the technical content of inventions. Roberto Verganti (2009) describes incremental innovations as those that are developed as a result of a market-pull (user-centered) strategy where radical innovations are those that are pushed by technology and represent 'meaning' change. Govindarajan and Trimble

(2010) argue that a move towards developing a practical innovation strategy lies in understanding the differences between ongoing operations and innovation leadership. They state that ongoing operations are *repeatable* and *predictable*; while innovation is *nonroutine*, requiring a different approach to organising; and *uncertain*, requiring a different approach to planning.

Innovative SMEs and Internationalization

A recent, and comprehensive, study of SME internationalization indicates that innovative SMEs involved in the creation of goods have a greater propensity of exporting than non-innovative SMEs (Saridakis, G. et al., 2019). The study uses 'export propensity' as the "operationalisation of internationalization". The study also provides empirical evidence on the role of radical innovation and incremental innovation in the internationalization of SMEs; finding that SMEs that develop and introduce radical innovations that are new to the market are more likely to export than non-innovative SMEs. And that a combination of incremental and radical innovation is more effective than incremental innovation alone.

SME internationalization and competitiveness is often considered dependent on entrepreneurial orientation (Dai et al., 2014), where entrepreneurial orientation is described by Morris et al. (2011) as a firm's capability for emphasizing innovativeness, proactiveness, and risk-taking. Research has found that organisational learning (the process of acquiring and integrating knowledge to improve company performance) and entrepreneurial orientation are important to the success of SMEs and that links with Universities, for external research and knowledge development enables SMEs to enhance these important skills (Dada & Fogg, 2016). Additionally, research has found that management competence defined by a combination of knowledge, qualifications, skills and experience needs to be developed in SMEs/SME managers to overcome the challenge of internationalization (Chandra et al., 2020). These findings suggest that when SMEs work with Universities on UIC projects, that a component of knowledge transferred ought to be geared toward developing management skills and experience in innovation projects; to increase the SMEs internationalization potential.

"The passing structures and systems of the industrial age and the rise of a networked society have resulted in open, complex, dynamic and networked challenges that can only be successfully met by organisations that are ready to become open, complex and networked themselves." – Kees Dorst, Frame Innovation: Create new thinking by design (2015)

Previous research has referred to 'innovation intermediaries' (Howells, 2006) as a term to define (service) firms that proactively facilitate collaboration between two or more parties in innovation projects. In terms of technological development these have been exemplified as Research and Technology Organisations (RTOs) (De Silva, Howells, & Meyer, 2018). We suggest an adjacent term 'intermediary interpreters' that brings together the term 'intermediaries' as defined by Howells (2006) and the definition of 'interpreters' by Verganti (2009). Howells (2006) defines 'intermediaries' as tending to centre on the organisational view (and mostly on technology development) and not on the relationships and role of individuals (Mühlenhoff, 2013). Verganti uses the term 'interpreters' to describe people from broad-ranging areas of expertise that take part in the "design discourse" able to comprehend dynamic changes in socio-cultural models, enabling the 'firm' to move beyond incremental change innovation toward radical innovations (see Verganti, 2009; Norman & Verganti, 2014).

The research indicates that building off Verganti's term enables a more accurate definition of the role of the 'intermediary' in industrial design UIC-SME projects. These are individuals, external to the university and SME organisation, who by initiating the collaborative focus of the project, effectively sows the 'seed' for the partnership with the capacity to influence innovative project directions. A means of tapping into an external expertise that can take a broader view of the design discourse may be achieved using these (non-competing) 'interpreters' enabling the SME to step back from the immediate market and cultivate knowledge across wider technological and cultural concerns (Verganti, 2009). This can lead to innovative products and practices.

UIC projects may work successfully when the research unit adopts the dual role of 'innovation intermediary' and 'interpreter'. However, often the difficulty of working with SMEs is that they expect a project outcome that is implementable soon after completion of the project, either in the form of a (new) product or system. Separately, the academic directives of the university research unit are knowledge driven and therefore more suited to the development of theory or frameworks that inform practice, rather than highly detailed solutions that are immediately implementable. Industry partners are working to generate profit in a sustainable way and to remain competitive in different market segments by solving problems quickly and with minimum risk (Lindemann, 2016). One of the important ways to diminish barriers to UIC, apart from IP (Intellectual Property) and administrative procedures, is to orient the typically 'short-term' goals of industry with the 'long-term' goals of the University (Bruneel, et. al. 2010). We find that for UIC-SME projects, this can be greatly aided by the involvement of an 'intermediary interpreter'. Many Australian manufacturing SMEs are 'trapped by their habits' in a self-made box and have 'shaped their identity around established practices' - two of the five syndromes of conventional organisations that make them resistant to change as outlined by Dorst (2015). Therefore the 'orienting' of goals can be particularly difficult, especially when the industry partner has virtually no internal R&D capability or strategy in place, no specialist designers working inside the organisation and certainly no awareness of design research or theory found in the academic discourse. The 'intermediary interpreter' is a critical member of the project because they are capable of scoping, facilitating (and designing) the project favourably for both the industry and university partner.

Australia's Manufacturing SMEs

Australia has traditionally relied on the export of natural resources, but the area of value-added products is an area of untapped potential and a combination of innovative products and an international focus can be a successful pathway to value creation for born global SMEs. When discussing born globals, Bell et al. (2003) state that, "their main source of competitive advantage is often related to a more sophisticated knowledge base". Cochlear is a great example of a born global company fitting this mould, specialising in the production of implantable hearing devices.

"Based in Australia, it maintains an international technological lead through its strong links with hospitals and research units around the world and through its collaborative research with a network of institutions in Australia, Switzerland, Germany, and the United States (Rennie, 1993)."

The Australian economy is still dependent on natural resources but there has been a strong push to develop our competitive advantage by advancing our ability to manufacture higher value-added products (Engineers Australia, 2009). However, Australia's manufacturing sector is made up, primarily, of small businesses with fewer than 20 employees (PwC, 2019) representing 87% of all employing manufacturing businesses in Australia (Australian Industry Group, 2019). In NSW alone there are 700,000 SMEs, described by the Government as the "engine room" of the state's economy, yet fewer than one in two Australian businesses can be considered innovators in terms of product, processes or strategies (NSW Department of Industry, 2020). With the support of local and federal government, Australia's manufacturing sector is attempting to transition from a 'basic' industry to one that can integrate and collaborate high-value solutions with a stronger connection to the research sector (Foley et al., 2016). International competitiveness for Australian manufacturing SMEs will rely on the ability to purposefully innovate and differentiate; and better collaboration between industry and research institutions is often cited as a key factor (Lydon et al., 2014).

"Manufacturing is a core competency of an educated country. While agriculture and digging up mineral resources may sustain an economy that is growing in a global shortage of unprocessed commodities, a balanced and sustainable economy needs capability to add value and manufacture intelligent technology." – Engineers Australia, 2009

Australia's manufacturing sector is said to be evolving. Part of what has sparked this need to evolve is to account for a combination of factors including; geographical remoteness; a small, dispersed local market; and the fact that there are few multinational companies manufacturing in Australia particularly given the recent closure of some parts of the sector (Foley & McLean, 2016).

A recent report has been released by the Australian Government: Department of Industry and Science, that addresses the closure of the Australian Automotive Industry and provides information for the transitioning of manufacturing competencies, including for those manufacturing SMEs that supplied to the sector (2020). The report also recommends that manufacturers need assistance for a range of activities for successful transition and identifies a number of factors that support these including (but not limited to) awareness of the business landscape, the mindset of company leadership and an inability to manage complex change. These findings align with the research literature.

Research generated via UIC projects to support transition for SMEs that previously made parts for the Australian automotive industry sector, has identified that while these companies have high levels of manufacturing expertise on a technical level, they have not developed the ability to engage innovation strategically and lack the necessary skills and knowledge to enter new markets (Kuys & Kyriazis, 2015). These findings indicate that while Universities can support SMEs develop new designs and R&D practices, the surrounding business of transitioning and combining knowledge into commercialisation strategy is of key importance if the SME is to ultimately develop products for international export.

UIC projects between manufacturing SMEs and design research units, set up to support the SME develop new products or new design strategies, have been encouraged by local and federal government programs in Australia for the past number of years. At the time of writing this chapter, there are quite a number of different programs in place, but we will only discuss two examples here. At the New South Wales (NSW) state level, there is the 'Boosting Business Innovation Program' (NSW Department of Industry, 2020) that provides 'TechVouchers' to fund eligible research collaborations with SMEs up to an amount of 15,000AUD in matched funding. And at a Federal Government level, through the Department of Industry, Science, Energy and Resources, and via the CSIRO 'SME Connect Scheme', there is the 'Innovation Connections Program' (CSIRO, 2020) that provides up to 50,000AUD for eligible research collaborations with SMEs. There are other funding programs for SMEs as well, for specific industries and with different amounts and conditions. To compliment these funding programs, the Federal Government has set up Industry Growth Centers to drive industry-led innovation and competitiveness (Department of Industry, Science, Energy and Resources, 2020). The six Growth Centers in the program are (1) Advanced Manufacturing; (2) Cyber Security; (3) Food and Agribusiness; (4) Medical Technologies and Pharmaceuticals; (5) Mining Equipment, Technology and Services; and (6) Oil, Gas and Energy Resources. Generally, an application for funding is more likely to be successful if the research can be strategically aligned with one of these Industry Growth Centers.

RESEARCH QUESTION

How do we define the role of the 'intermediary interpreter' in industrial design, university-industry collaboration (UIC) projects for manufacturing SMEs; and does their involvement support internationalization of the SME in such projects?

Hypothesis

That the 'intermediary interpreter' is a person - a third party - involved in industrial design UIC projects with manufacturing SMEs that facilitates the negotiation of the terms of the project so that the process (and the outcome) is mutually beneficial for both the university research team and the SME industry partner. The 'intermediary interpreter' is aware of the resource constraints normally associated with such partnerships and is able to focus the project objective to operationalise the project task. They understand the benefits of innovation and understand that university research partnerships can help manufacturing SMEs develop innovative growth strategies for their organisation, beyond new product concepts.

CASE ANALYSIS

Each of the UIC projects discussed in this chapter have benefitted from the involvement of an intermediary interpreter. Five projects are described, and the role of the intermediary interpreter analysed in the context of each project. We identify key attributes of the 'intermediary interpreter' and key functions they perform, particularly in the formation stages of the project and with regard to project facilitation. All projects were conducted with the same industrial design research unit based at an Australian University.

Project 1: Agribusiness Instrument Design

This project developed a new product-system for plant propagation for an Agribusiness Company. The project led to the design of a new apparatus (new IP) that can be made in durable materials using a combination of additive manufacturing (AM) (also referred to as 3D printing) and conventional manufacturing technologies, in limited runs reliably and effectively. The design will enable the industry partner to internationalise their operations and compete more effectively. The successful project outcome has provided the basis for being awarded significant grant funding for commercialisation of the product-system by the industry partner. The intermediary interpreter is an SME research facilitator for the CSIRO (Commonwealth Scientific and Industrial Research Organisation) an independent Australian federal government agency. The CSIRO research facilitator directed the SME to an industrial design research unit as opposed to a science or engineering team, because they understood that 'design' research offered the most appropriate methodologies for generating the right outcome for the industry partner.

As the agribusiness company in question sought to expand their current production techniques, they capitalised on an opportunity via a Department of Primary Industries Innovation Connections Grant that involved them partnering with a university research unit to develop their IP. The agribusiness had an idea for a way to more efficiently expand plant propagation activities but required the development of a suite of hand tools and related equipment to prototype that process. The CSIRO research facilitator was the intermediary interpreter in this case. He set up the Innovation Connections funding arrangement between the SME agribusiness and the IPD-R unit; based on his conceptual understanding of the activities of industrial design and recognition of the need for a user-centred approach to problem solving. This was a choice based on experience and foresight for how external (design) research engagement through Universities operates.

IPD-R created hundreds of prototyped elements and tested the process under laboratory conditions to prove the validity of the new suite of tools (Figure 1). In this process, the university research unit had to acquire knowledge of the plant propagation processes to develop the detailed mechanical features of the hand tools. The way that the product outcome operates is beyond the scope of this chapter. We are able to report that the designs shown performed successfully and verify the use of AM technologies for the production of multiple units in limited runs.

Figure 1. Testing of the hand tools and process for plant propagation

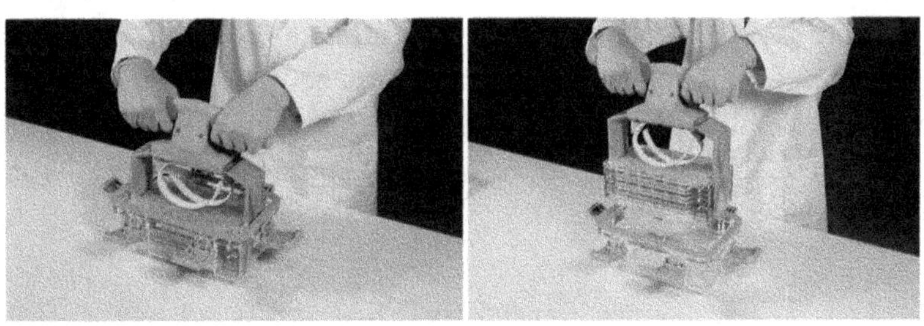

Facilitation of the research process by the CSIRO research facilitator allowed IPD-R to explore new potential for AM technology in end-part production as well as management of prototyping activity using annotated portfolios; and both concepts have been presented in published academic research (Walden et al., 2020; Walden et al., 2018). The agribusiness gained respect for product design activities coupled with a design-led research methodology. Towards the end of the project, the agribusiness was able to advance under their own direction and solve technical issues; education gained through knowledge transfer of the design process exposed to them throughout the partnership.

To ensure that both the University research unit and the SME were satisfied during the process the CSIRO research facilitator managed goal orientation between both parties through a reporting system. Periodically the university research unit was required to report to the Department of Primary Industries and were evaluated against a number of criteria to gauge progress. The agribusiness was also required to provide feedback and from the combination of the two information streams conclusions could be drawn by the facilitators about the current strength and success of the partnership. The project ran successfully, aided by the reporting system and ongoing management of the CSIRO research facilitator; the intermediary interpreter in this case. A lead representative from the SME Agribusiness stated:

"We would recommend IPD-R to everyone except our competitors". – Director of the Agribusiness SME, Industry partner for this project

Project 2: Additive Manufacturing Research

The objective of this UIC project was to assess the potential for additive manufacturing (AM) technology for a commercial outdoor / public furniture company. The industry partner is interested in reducing the amount of inventory stock typically generated when a council orders updated or replacement parts for their installed public furniture. AM could potentially enable the (printed) manufacture of sophisticated parts in very small production quantities as needed. The project developed a series of prototypes that tested (scientifically) the performance of parts made with various additive manufacturing machines and materials. It also provided an outline of various appropriate AM technologies and associated software that could facilitate this transition. The intermediary interpreter for this project is an industrial design (practice) professor at a university with many years of industry experience as director of a leading industrial design firm with a number of high-profile national and international clients.

The deliverables for this project were in the form of a series of prototypes (Figure 2) and a technical report that included the technology assessment, engineering test data and results; and design concepts to indicate future opportunities upon transitioning to AM. Printed versions of selected parts deemed critical in terms of verifying the appropriateness of the AM technology for the company were produced and tested. These parts are typically made from diecast alloy and minimum production quantities for a process such as this often far exceed the number of parts actually needed. Therefore, the company wanted to investigate the feasibility of AM - a technology that would allow small quantities of parts to be produced only when needed. A question on the industry partners mind was "Would it be possible to approach a zero-inventory situation?".

Figure 2. 3D Printed and tested prototypes of selected parts

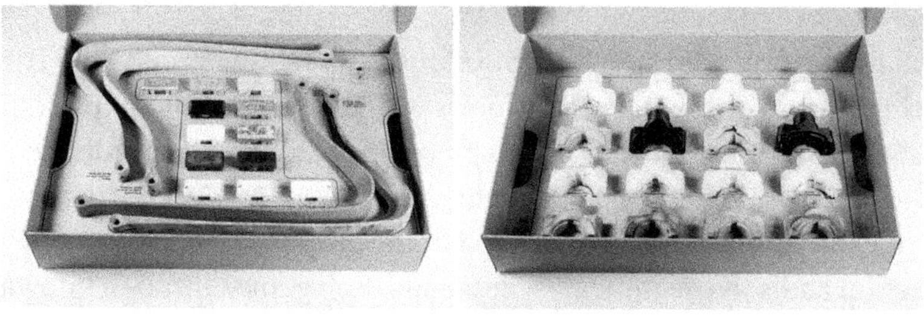

The 3D printed samples acted as a learning tool for the industry partner to self-educate on issues of technology selection, surface finish, post-processing, cost and strength which enabled immediate feedback on how a 3D printing might be implemented. This fresh level of understanding allowed context specific speculation on whether 3D printed parts would be acceptable to their customers now or in the immediate future.

As the role of the intermediary interpreter within this SME was focused on innovation, he advocated the use of a university team to conduct research in this realm and his advice was taken seriously being a person of respect and standing in the design community. This sympathetic attitude to contract research was key to winning the project. Innovation processes can be stifled in many SMEs when directors focus on short term returns on investment and the cost of contract research in these cases often can not be justified internally. Company bottom lines interrupt innovation processes when the cost of that research could be spent on external marketing, training of staff or plant and equipment with immediate results.

Project 3: New Designs for Corrective Services

This project developed a design of a fabrication system to develop office furniture for the commercial arm of a state regional corrective service centre. The industry partner in this project commercialises furniture that is fabricated in workshops inside correctional centres by the inmates. The commercial arm is interested in making their product more competitive (aesthetically and functionally more advanced) while the 'correctional' arm is concerned with rehabilitation, training and reducing recidivism. We define the intermediary interpreter for this project as the director in a (separate) transdisciplinary university research unit that specialises in service-system designs for crime prevention.

The project has led to the design of both a system of fabrication techniques that meet the needs of rehabilitation and training and enables safe and effective construction of a sophisticated range of commercial office furniture products (Figure 3).

Figure 3. Images of the final workstation prototypes with accessories

Within the pre-research phase of this project the university research unit engaged directly with the overseers of the onsite production units distributed state-wide in order to assess production capability. Site visits, interviews and photographic records were made in order to assess the diversity and state of equipment, currently manufactured items and current and potential skill level of the labour force. This information was fed into the design phase so that the ambition of the project could be tempered with the reality of production inside a prison situation.

Following on from the pre-research phase a number of design proposals were presented to the industry partner for possible production. The types of objects included various designs for single and four-person workstations primarily constructed from welded steel tubes, a suite of upholstered breakout furniture and office accessories focused around the storage of small items; a consideration in order to consume sheet metal offcuts. Keeping in mind the parameters established in the pre-research phase, a modular approach to construction was implemented, where there was a focus on repetition of tasks for differing skill levels, which assists inmates to pass the time and also establishes a situation for marked skill level increases.

The intermediary interpreter is both an industrial designer and long-time academic credited with being a founder of a well-known research centre. This individual had the ability to understand the perspectives of both the industry partner and the UIC research unit and functioned in roles of client liaison and project manager throughout the course of the project. The intermediary interpreter worked closely with a director in the partner organisation tasked with advancing the sophistication and design of prison produced products and simultaneously leveraging the benefits in order to occupy inmates and upskill them. Interactions between these key people advanced the project across prototyping enquiry and allowed effective engagement between the university research unit and overseers of the production units. Accordingly, the working relationship built between all parties enabled a level of trust between the UIC team and correctional entity; and facilitated positive working relationships with overseers of the production units and the university research team.

In a project of this scale, the intermediary interpreter performed a crucial management role in mobilising and organising several teams of individuals within each entity. This is evidence to suggest that successful UIC projects that partner with big external government organisations need to be driven with the guidance of an intermediary interpreter with both industry and academic experience. Such experience enables them to confidently function as selectors of key dislocated personnel valuable to the project and furthermore, provide the communication bridge, respectfully interpreting the needs of each party in a way that achieves mutually beneficial outcomes.

Project 4: Battery Technology Research

This project involved assessment of battery technology and battery configuration for a manufacturer of backpack vacuum cleaners. The project comes from a local manufacturing SME that specialises in the design and manufacture of backpack vacuum cleaners for commercial use. The product is sold locally and internationally. In recent years, battery technology has developed and therefore new battery powered (cordless) backpack vacuum cleaners are dominating the market, despite being heavier and having less suction power compared to corded models. The project investigates the state of battery technology and provides innovation pathways for this small company competing in a changing market landscape. The intermediary interpreter for this project is an industrial design consultant that had worked with this SME many years prior and recognised the need for a research phase before launching into the development of new products for their client.

In initial meetings with the industrial designer (intermediary interpreter) it was identified that producing a design for an industrial cordless vacuum cleaner would be well served by a research phase covering battery technology, competitor products/analogues as well as investigation into the ergonomic requirements for daily use and management of the device. Therefore, a university industry collaboration project began with a local cleaning company (as the industry partner), the industrial designer acting as an intermediary or advocate for the process and a university research team.

During the project the industrial designer maintained a clear line of communication with both the industry partner and the university research team. Meetings were conducted in three distinct modes: industry partner and research team, industrial designer and research team and industry partner and industrial designer. At key points in the process, the industrial designer acted as an advocate for the research process and he met with the owner of the cleaning company to discuss the advancement of the project.

The documented research included product autopsy, competitor product analysis, ergonomic exploration and the construction of multiple full-scale mock-up's (Figure 4).

Figure 4. Ergonomic exploration undertaken with full scale mock-up's

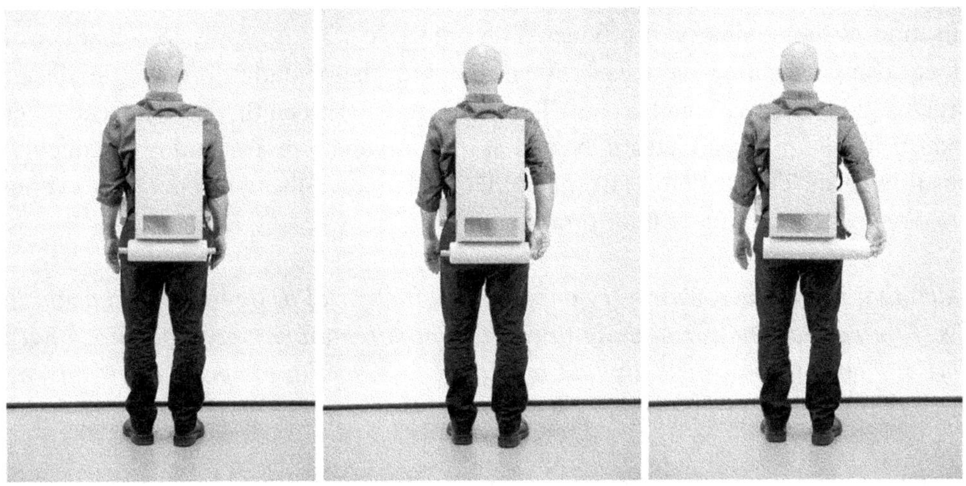

Technical exploration of battery technology was provided by an engineering consultant and this information was used by the research team as a way to reflect on key technical issues that have bearing on the forecasted design: cell type, cost, weight, packaging, cost, runtime, maximum cycles and sustainability. This contract research formed a solid basis from which to begin a product design process particularly for a design team limited by timeframe and personnel.

Project 5: Low Cost Firefighters Cooling Vest

This UIC project developed a design of a firefighter's cooling vest using low-volume, low-cost production for a rural volunteer firefighting service in Australia. The project developed a new form of cooling vest using a technology developed by a science team at another Australian university. The product needs to be very low cost because it is intended for volunteer fire fighting services with very limited access to funding. The design team developed the product so that production of the vest uses low cost, but reliable, manufacturing technology. The intermediary interpreter for this project is a commercialisation director for a company specialising in the commercialisation and IP protection of university generated IP. They have a number of years of experience in commercialising IP with a background in business and science.

The cooling vest is a sheet plastic garment that contains a benign chemical in a dry granulated form. The chemical is held in a pocket located in the upper back section of the vest during production. When the vest is put on the body, it is 'activated' by opening the rear collar section that both accesses the chemical and provides a large orifice used to funnel water poured into the vest from the back. Water rushes through the orifice and upon mixing with the chemical, becomes chilled to around five degrees Celsius, as it passes through the vest, front and back, through specially designed channels. An interior lining helps to make the wearer comfortable as the cooling effect takes place. The rear opening can be sealed after the water has been poured into the vest.

The 'industry partner' in this project was a newly formed business between a team of academics in sports science at James Cook University and a commercialisation company UniQuest. UniQuest was, at the time of the project, operating Australia wide[2] identifying opportunities for the commercialisation of IP developed at Australian Universities. UniQuest formed a new start-up for the development and commercialisation of the cooling vest product. The objective was to supply low-cost cooling vests to rural volunteer bush firefighting services in Australia, with the potential to make the design available to similar organisations internationally. The UIC was formed between this newly formed company and IPD-R an industrial design research team located at the University of Technology Sydney via the University's consulting arm. The academics from both University organisations operating as consultants on the project to develop the cooling vest for production.

"The approach that we adopted was to try and give the industrial designers the freedom they needed to take the vest through an industrial design process whilst retaining the key features that the (sports science team) at James Cook University had identified as essential for product effectiveness." (from Thompson, 2011) Intermediary Interpreter for the project

The Universities are located in different states of Australia; one in Cairns in regional Queensland and the other in Sydney, NSW; more than 2,500km apart. This was a factor as the development of the vest prototypes needed to be evaluated by the science team after each iteration.

"Following initial meetings, updates were provided via brief written reports and by a series of images showing particular aspects or prototype iterations. Distance was still a hindrance since we needed to use touch to evaluate proposed materials and to evaluate the robustness of the prototypes." (from Thompson, 2011) Intermediary Interpreter for the project

The UIC project ran for seven months and during that period the industrial design research team developed 13 prototypes. Each prototype was constructed in pairs; one for testing by the design team and one to be sent to the science team in Queensland. The design outcome is a cooling vest made as a quilted plastic garment that is welded together in a flat form using the same low-cost production technology as that used for making large inflatable pool toys. The production method also adopts some features from the packaging industry as the benign chemical granules that mix with the water to create the cooling effect, are sealed in the vest during the welding process. Design of the orifice for receiving the water, that may be from a hose or bucket, was developed in a form that also maintained the flat pattern on the vest, keeping production costs significantly low (Figure 5). The final design has passed a range of tests in live fire trials with the Queensland Rural Fire Service (Figure 6). There has been interest in the design from a range of other sectors including mining, military and medical industries (Thompson, 2011).

The role of the intermediary interpreter for this UIC project was critical in ensuring that the tasks for each university research team was clearly defined. The interpreter also recognised the opportunity for the eventual design to have wider application beyond its utility as a fire-fighter's cooling vest. In recognising this, he protected the initial design concept as a patented invention with the Australian intellectual property rights and legislation agency, IP Australia. Secondly, he established a separate company to commercialise the IP that duly recognised the sports science team at James Cook University as the

Figure 5. Final prototypes being made in the University workshop and tested

inventors of the technology, but that also enables commercialisation and product development activity to operate more freely than may be possible inside of University 'research and innovation' departments. After these were established, the connection with the industrial design research team at the Sydney based university could be more clearly defined thus enabling a UIC setup in a format where contracts and government support could be seamlessly arranged. During the project he facilitated communication between teams and made arrangements for meetings at either University at key points in the process. There was recognition of the research capability of each team and that was respected and supported throughout the process. This ensured that the academic goals of each team could be met (i.e. the ability to record practice and publish new knowledge) without compromising sensitive information since IP protection was in place; and the contributory role of each of team of researchers had been clearly defined in the contractual terms established at the start of the project. This case indicates the important role of the intermediary interpreter as an independent party that has a business mindset and is able to understand and appreciate the goals of academic enquiry in connection with external industry engagement. It also is a good indicator of the important task of setting up the roles of each party in UIC at the start of the project. The UniQuest organisation invests in University generated IP with an eye toward internationalization. Therefore, IP arrangements and corporate mechanisms to licence IP to international manufacturers is paramount.

Figure 6. Cooling vest tested in live trials

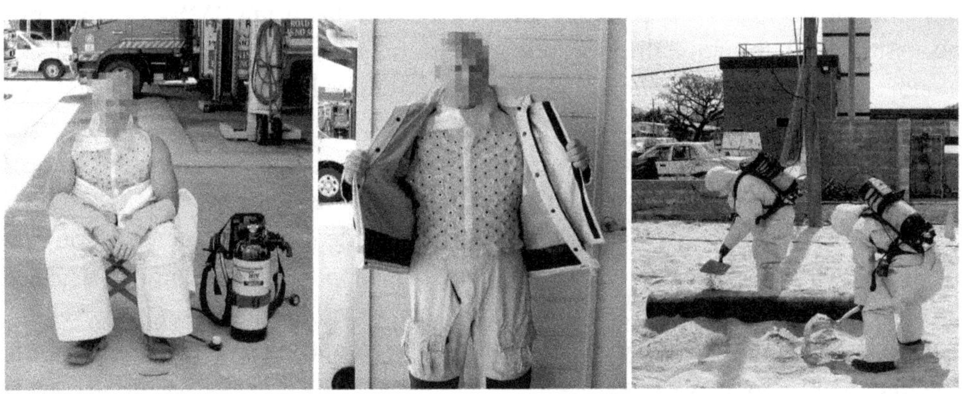

A Description of the Intermediary Interpreter

Analysis of the cases in this Chapter reveals a set of common features that serve to define the intermediary interpreter in UIC industrial design research projects for manufacturing SMEs. In terms of their role, we identify the following tasks that they are primarily responsible for:

1. Set up or enable a mutually beneficial funding arrangement between the university research unit and the manufacturing SME;
2. Setting up a reporting structure to progressively orient the goals of each party, favorably;
3. Enable the university research unit to operate with a degree of autonomy to conduct open enquiry;
4. Secure IP where necessary to make it possible for the university research unit to publish knowledge outcomes;
5. Facilitate knowledge transfer so that the SME can learn from the university research team and take over further R&D work after the UIC project.

Further, the cases, indicate that there are certain profile attributes of the intermediary interpreter that are beneficial in such UIC projects:

1. The intermediary interpreter is someone who is not affiliated with either the university research unit or the manufacturing SME. They operate as a facilitator to bring together the needs of both parties;
2. They are normally a representative of a professional or governmental body that is responsible for improving the competitiveness of SMEs;
3. They understand the role of universities and value the contribution of academic research enquiry;
4. They have an understanding of the underlying methodological principles of practice-led research as it relates to the particular academic field of expertise of the university research unit;
5. They are someone who has practical experience in professional practices associated with the commercialisation of new manufactured products and the securing of new intellectual property and are suitably networked with various organisations that are required to take products to market.

In terms of the internationalization of manufacturing SMEs, these task features and profile attributes are important. Referring again to the Australian Government's report on transitioning the Australian Automotive Industry (2020), one of the barriers for successful transition they identify is an "inability to manage complex change". And we consider that for many manufacturing SMEs, developing innovation capability necessary for internationalisation does represent, for them, a complex change. The report includes a model that identifies the potential roadblocks associated with managing complex change and the effects of not addressing these roadblocks (Figure 7).

The model demonstrates that (1) absence of any one of the five major components can be a roadblock to managing complex change successfully and (2) that each of the five components are interconnected and must be managed concurrently. We identify that the intermediary interpreter is someone who can align the vision of each UIC partner around a project goal; support and channel skills, incentives and resources necessary to meet that vision; and coordinate and supervise an action plan. While the project has a conclusion, it can, with the support of the intermediary interpreter, represent an example of how the SME can engage in future innovation.

Figure 7. Components of the managing complex change model[3]

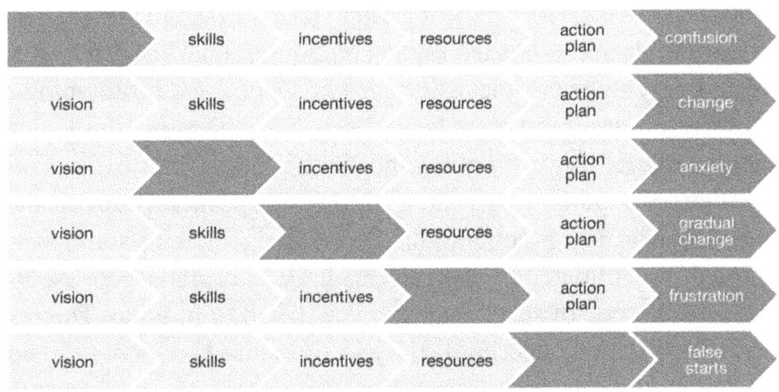

Understanding the Intermediary Interpreter in Practice

According to our analysis, the Intermediary Interpreter is normally the person who is primarily concerned with setting up a mutually beneficial funding arrangement between the research unit and manufacturing SME. Note that this does not mean they are necessarily authorised to access the funding required for the project, though this can be beneficial as in the case with Project 1, where the Intermediary Interpreter was a CSIRO research facilitator and Project 5 where they were a new business manager for a (University IP) Commercialisation firm. In the other projects the Intermediary Interpreters were one step removed from the funding 'agency' but they were uniquely positioned to provide credibility to the project and directly influence the decision on funding. In all cases the Intermediary Interpreter is centrally involved in the framing of the relationship for funding arrangements. In Project 2, 3 and 4, for example, the Intermediary Interpreters come from years of experience in industrial design practice, with a proven track record of understanding the process and of successfully completed industrial designs. In the case of projects 2-4, we might say that their influence encourages the SME to commit funds to the project first and then later, in-kind government funding is arranged (as in normally the case with UIC projects) as a second step. To perform this role effectively we consider it important that the Intermediary Interpreter is someone who is not from within the research unit group or the SME organisation. Being separate from both helps to keep an objective eye on how the funding will be used to complete the project and essentially the scope of work. However, by not being directly affiliated with either the University research unit or the SME, does require, in our assessment, that they are someone that has practical experience in the professional work of bringing products to market, understands the role of universities and values the contribution of academic research enquiry. Our analysis suggests that these qualifications enable the intermediary interpreter to align the expectations of the manufacturing SME with the University research unit; a challenge highlighted by Doherty et al. (2013), and Bruneel et al. (2010). The intermediary interpreter with the right qualifications and experience can instil confidence in the SME and overcome their risk averse culture and facilitate (at times lead) the negotiation of project objectives that enables the SME to operate proactively in the research and invite key members of the organisation into the project at various points. This opens up opportunities for knowledge transfer, and for innovation across the company to take hold and continue to develop after the UIC engagement. This is evident to some degree in all projects but particularly in Project 1 and 3. Project 1 - the agribusiness instrument design led to new knowledge and the potential for further product development that has enabled the company to successfully apply for an additional 1 million dollar Australian Government grant to take the design into higher volume production for international distribution. Project 3 has led to the creation of a new office furniture system that has the capacity to evolve and develop over time, using the knowledge and prototyping methods developed with the University research unit. There have been discussions between the University research unit and the client about new projects to work on together in the future, that expand on the research from the first. Project 2; the battery technology research for the backpack vacuum cleaner interestingly had an Intermediary Interpreter who is a practicing industrial designer with some experience teaching at the University. The project was initiated by the Intermediary Interpreter because it required a level of technical enquiry beyond the scope of service they are qualified to provide. The research unit brought onboard battery experts from the engineering faculty in the same University to complete the findings and provide new knowledge for both the Intermediary Interpreter to carry forward with the necessary design work and for the manufacturing SME to set up a strategic plan for new product development based on emerging battery technologies, suitable for their market goals.

Goal orientation between the manufacturing SME and University research unit is one that needs to be established up front, but also managed throughout. The nature of UIC engagement is normally tied to research enquiry and exploratory in practice. Therefore, a reporting structure that ensures clear lines of communication between both parties is very important. In the IPD-R research unit, this has encouraged the development of new process documentation practices to track prototyping development and to capture 'design thinking'. One such process has been presented and published as new research (Walden et al., 2018) that extends upon annotated portfolio methods as first described by Gaver and Bowers (2012). Particularly during Project 1 and Project 5; the fire fighters cooling vest; documentation of prototyping was critical as the manufacturing SME partner was located a considerable distance from the University. The Intermediary Interpreters is these cases were particularly vigilant with reporting procedure (and methods) as face-to-face meetings were less frequent. The documentation of the project needs to be methodical for the formation of final reports and in some cases is instrumental when applying for IP protection.

Our analysis finds that the Intermediary Interpreter must have an understanding of the way University research units operate. In the case of IPD-R, it helps that the members are academic design practitioners (2015). Regardless, however, university research units operate with the goal of developing knowledge and disseminating knowledge outcomes for general application. Manufacturing SMEs typically want implementable findings that lead to new products. An effective Intermediary Interpreter will be someone that understands the importance for the research unit to have a degree of autonomy but also a basic understanding of how practice-led research operates as a means to verify underlying theory in specific contexts. Where the project leads to new product designs with the potential for commercialisation, an Intermediary Interpreter should be someone who can recognise the point at which IP needs to be secured, allowing a degree of disclosure for the purposes of engaging other expertise, or later, research publication.

Managing these dynamics in the course of an industrial design UIC project for a manufacturing SME does require a level of innovative thinking. Returning to the term 'intermediary interpreter'; as stated above, we have combined the term 'innovation intermediaries' (Howells, 2006) and Verganti's term 'interpreters' (2009). In the cases presented above, the term 'innovation intermediary' may be the government research organisations or (in some cases) the University research unit itself. However, here we hope to demonstrate the more specific role of the individual (who may work for these organisations) in these types of UIC engagements. We suggest that there is a designerly aspect to their involvement in these projects. Verganti's interpreters are people with external expertise that take part in the design discourse and by interpreting the opportunities that arise during the project, facilitate innovation. Verganti's interpreter can be an individual. And in the case of the projects presented above, the interpreters were involved in the design discourse in various ways and did facilitate innovation. Though further to this, the act of facilitating these UIC projects is, in itself, an innovative one. Every project is unique and therefore the constraints and opportunities are always different and evolving. Particularly when working with manufacturing SMEs that may have incredible technical competency, but limited ability to innovate as the data from the NSW Department of Industry (2020) indicates. Tim Brown (2009) refers to the ability of innovative organisations to balance competing constraints. He refers to striking a *harmonious balance* between *desirability* (what makes sense to people for people); *viability* (what is likely to become part of a sustainable business model) and *feasibility* (what is functionally possible within the foreseeable future). If we consider the Intermediary Interpreter's role as the 'designer' of the UIC project, and consider the project as the 'design' that must balance Brown's competing constraints, it makes sense to consider the term *interpreter* in the same way as Verganti does - as an intrinsic part of a design-driven innovation approach. If we consider Brown's competing constraints; *desirability* is about orienting the project favourably for both the university research unit and the manufacturing SME, essentially by scoping the project and facilitating negotiation of project objectives. *Viability* is about ensuring that the project objectives lead to outcomes that can be built upon by the SME (and the research unit) after the UIC engagement is over. And *feasibility* is about ensuring that the objectives are achievable and optimal given the funding available. This encompasses the ability to structure the project as one that can be extended upon in future potential engagements.

FUTURE RESEARCH DIRECTIONS

The research presented in this chapter identifies the 'intermediary interpreter' as an important third-party facilitator in industrial design UIC projects with manufacturing SMEs. Presented here is an overview of projects conducted by the same industrial design research unit that the authors are a member of and have participated in as academic practitioners. Therefore, the chapter constitutes a form of reflective analysis of different UIC projects across a number of years. Future research directions may involve a broader analysis of these types of industrial design UIC projects with manufacturing SMEs at other University institutions. A study of this type could attempt to align 'types' of design engagement (e.g. product outcome, material testing, technology testing, strategic design, etc.) with the role of the intermediary interpreter, specific to those types of projects. Additionally, a more in-depth account of the intermediary interpreter's role could be established with a comprehensive process analysis of a single project, though this study would need to be initiated from the outset and maintained for the length of the project. And would likely need to be conducted by a separate researcher to maintain objectivity.

CONCLUSION

Analysis of the case studies aligns types of expertise with the nature of the projects conducted, particularly in considering the types of outcomes produced, knowledge contributions made, and methodologies adopted. Research indicates that innovation is a necessary component of internationalisation for manufacturing SMEs. However, developing innovation capability for many SMEs is a complex management proposal. UIC projects between an SME manufacturing partner and Industrial Design Research Units can produce innovative new designs with the potential for commercialisation; and while this may place the SME in a better position to internationalise, a design outcome is not enough on its own. Analysis of UIC projects by the IPD-R research unit at the University of Technology Sydney identifies the important role of a third party, often left out of the conversation. The analysis distinguishes the 'intermediary interpreter' as a key individual in the formation of the project, importantly in the 'scoping' phase as this can be particularly difficult to establish and keep under control. Additionally, the chapter demonstrates how the involvement of the intermediary interpreter can influence the role of 'innovation intermediaries' and the make-up of the network of external interpreters for 'design-driven innovation'. The significance of the research presented in the chapter is that it contributes to knowledge on supporting SMEs to navigate internationalization challenges through university-industry collaboration. The research defines the role of key personnel in these projects and the importance of project facilitation of industrial design UIC manufacturing SME partnerships, within the internationalization strategy of SMEs. The chapter is written for the benefit of industry and academia interested in the research and development of new product innovations and innovation strategy.

ACKNOWLEDGMENT

Each of the case study projects presented in this chapter were funded by a combination of Australian Federal or State Government programs and the SME industry partner. We acknowledge the support of the following companies: Lowes TC, Street Furniture Australia, Corrective Service Industries, CleanTech and UniQuest; and the Australian Government Programs, Innovation Connections and NSW TechVoucher Scheme. We also acknowledge the support of key personnel at the University of Technology Sydney, Douglas Tomkin, Jessica Wong, Barry Liu and the staff of the Design, Architecture and Building (DAB) Fabrication and Digital Workshops; and the UTS ProtoSpace. Importantly, we also acknowledge the commitment and expertise of our IPD-R team members, Berto Pandolfo and Stefan Lie in the Product Design Program at UTS.

REFERENCES

Australian Government: Department of Industry, Innovation and Science. (2020). *Australian Automotive Industry: Transition following the end of Australian motor vehicle production*. https://www.industry.gov.au/sites/default/files/2020-01/australian-automotive-industry-transition-following-the-end-of-australian-motor-vehicle-production.pdf

Australian Government: Department of Industry, Science, Energy and Resources. (2020). *Industry Growth Centers*. https://www.industry.gov.au/strategies-for-the-future/industry-growth-centres

Australian Industry Group. (2019). *Australian manufacturing in 2019: local and global opportunities*. Author.

Beckerman, W. (1956). Distance and the pattern of intra-European trade. *The Review of Economics and Statistics*, *38*(1), 31–40. doi:10.2307/1925556

Bell, J., McNaughton, R., Young, S., & Crick, D. (2003). Towards an Integrative Model of Small Firm internationalization. *Journal of International Entrepreneurship*, *1*(4), 339–362. doi:10.1023/A:1025629424041

Brown, T. (2009). *Change by design: How design thinking creates new alternatives for business and society*. Collins Business.

Bruneel, J., d'Este, P., & Salter, A. (2010). Investigating the factors that diminish the barriers to university–industry collaboration. *Research Policy*, *39*(7), 858–868. doi:10.1016/j.respol.2010.03.006

Chandra, A. A., Paul, J., & Chavan, M. (2020). Internationalization challenges for SMEs: Evidence and theoretical extension. *European Business Review*, *ahead-of-print*(ahead-of-print). Advance online publication. doi:10.1108/EBR-08-2019-0164

CSIRO. (2020). *SME Connect - where business meets research.* https://www.csiro.au/en/Do-business/

Dada, O., & Fogg, H. (2016). Organizational learning, entrepreneurial orientation, and the role of university engagement in SMEs. *International Small Business Journal*, *34*(1), 86–104. doi:10.1177/0266242614542852

Dahlin, K. B., & Behrens, D. M. (2005). When is an invention really radical?: Defining and measuring technological radicalness. *Research Policy*, *34*(5), 717–737. doi:10.1016/j.respol.2005.03.009

Dai, L., Maksimov, V., Gilbert, B. A., & Fernhaber, S. A. (2014). Entrepreneurial orientation and international scope: The differential roles of innovativeness, proactiveness, and risk-taking. *Journal of Business Venturing*, *29*(4), 511–524. doi:10.1016/j.jbusvent.2013.07.004

De Silva, M., Howells, J., & Meyer, M. (2018). Innovation intermediaries and collaboration: Knowledge–based practices and internal value creation. *Research Policy*, *47*(1), 70–87. doi:10.1016/j.respol.2017.09.011

Doherty, R., Matthews, J., Wrigley, C., & Bucolo, S. (2013, December). Early challenges of shifting an Australian manufacturer's utilisation of design. In *2013 IEEE Tsinghua International Design Management Symposium* (pp. 259-267). IEEE. 10.1109/TIDMS.2013.6981246

Dominguez, N., & Mayrhofer, U. (2017). Internationalization stages of traditional SMEs: Increasing, decreasing and re-increasing commitment to foreign markets. *International Business Review*, *26*(6), 1051–1063. doi:10.1016/j.ibusrev.2017.03.010

Dorst, K. (2015). *Frame innovation: Create new thinking by design.* MIT Press. doi:10.7551/mitpress/10096.001.0001

Engineers Australia. (2009). *Engineering the Future of Australian Manufacturing*. Author.

Foley, C., & McLean, K. (2016, November 16). The Australian manufacturing industry is not dying, it's evolving CSIRO study. *The Conversation.* https://theconversation.com/the-australian-manufacturing-industry-is-not-dying-its-evolving-csiro-study-69398

Gaver, B., & Bowers, J. (2012). Annotated portfolios. *Interaction*, *19*(4), 40–49. doi:10.1145/2212877.2212889

Govindarajan, V., & Trimble, C. (2010). *The other side of innovation: Solving the execution challenge*. Harvard Business Press.

Howells, J. (2006). Intermediation and the role of intermediaries in innovation. *Research Policy*, *35*(5), 715–728. doi:10.1016/j.respol.2006.03.005

Johanson, J., & Wiedersheim-Paul, F. (1975). the Internationalization of the Firm— Four Swedish Cases. *Journal of Management Studies*, *12*(3), 305–323. doi:10.1111/j.1467-6486.1975.tb00514.x

Kuys, B., & Kyriazis, E. (2015). *It's all about the money: adding value to industry through industrial design-led innovations*. Academic Press.

Lindemann, U. (2016). Impact of Design Research on Practitioners in Industry. In *Impact of Design Research on Industrial Practice* (pp. 223–232). Springer. doi:10.1007/978-3-319-19449-3_14

Lippitt, M. (1987). *The Managing Complex Change Model. Copyright, 1987, by Dr.* Mary Lippitt, Founder and President of Enterprise Management, Ltd.

Lydon, J., Dyer, D., & Bradley, C. (2014). *Compete to Prosper: Improving Australia's global competitiveness*. McKinsey Australia.

McDougall, P. P., & Oviatt, B. M. (2000). International entrepreneurship: The intersection of two research paths. *Academy of Management Journal*, *43*(5), 902–906.

Morris, M. H., Webb, J. W., & Franklin, R. J. (2011). Understanding the manifestation of entrepreneurial orientation in the nonprofit context. *Entrepreneurship Theory and Practice*, *35*(5), 947–971. doi:10.1111/j.1540-6520.2011.00453.x

Mühlenhoff, J. (2013). The Role of Intermediaries in Culture-Driven Innovation and Future Orientation of the Organization. In *ISPIM Conference Proceedings* (p. 1). The International Society for Professional Innovation Management (ISPIM).

New Department of Industry. (2020). *Boosting Business Innovation*. https://www.business.nsw.gov.au

Norman, D. A., & Verganti, R. (2014). Incremental and radical innovation: Design research vs. technology and meaning change. *Design Issues*, *30*(1), 78–96. doi:10.1162/DESI_a_00250

PricewaterhouseCoopers Australia (PwC). (2019). *Transforming Australian manufacturing: preparing businesses and workplaces for Industry 4.0*. Author.

Rennie, M. W. (1993). Born global. *The McKinsey Quarterly*, *45*(4). https://link.gale.com/apps/doc/A15424561/AONE?u=uts&sid=AONE&xid=87dbadf2

Saridakis, G., Idris, B., Hansen, J. M., & Dana, L. P. (2019). SMEs' internationalization: When does innovation matter? *Journal of Business Research*, *96*, 250–263. doi:10.1016/j.jbusres.2018.11.001

Thompson, C. (2011). *Refining Design. U: Magazine*. University of Technology Sydney.

Verganti, R. (2009). *Design driven innovation: changing the rules of competition by radically innovating what things mean*. Harvard Business Press.

Walden, R., Lie, S., Pandolfo, B., & Nemme, A. (2018). Research Prototyping, University-Industry Collaboration and the value of Annotated Portfolios. *Cumulus Paris 2018: To get there together, designing together*.

Walden, R., Lie, S., Pandolfo, B., & Nemme, A. (2020). Developing strategic leadership and innovation capability for manufacturing SMEs transitioning to digital manufacturing technology. In Leadership Styles, Innovation, and Social Entrepreneurship in the Era of Digitalization (pp. 164-189). IGI Global. doi:10.4018/978-1-7998-1108-4.ch007

Walden, R., Pandolfo, B., Lie, S., & Lockhart, C. (2015, September). *The academic design practitioner*. Paper presented at the Creative Practices Conference, Arkitektskolen, Aarhus.

Welch, L. S., & Luostarinen, R. (1988). Internationalization: Evolution of a Concept. *Journal of General Management*, *14*(2), 34–55. doi:10.1177/030630708801400203

ENDNOTES

1. CSIRO: Commonwealth Scientific and Industrial Research Organisation. Australia's national science agency.
2. UniQuest is now situated at University of Queensland (UQ).
3. The original model is from Lippitt, M., 1987, The Managing Complex Change Model.

Chapter 8
Cultural Intelligence:
German Expatriates as Managers in Portugal

Carolin Roehl
Universidade de Aveiro, Portugal

EXECUTIVE SUMMARY

For individuals in management positions, globalization has reinforced contact with foreign cultures and provided opportunities to be assigned to projects abroad. Expatriates encounter additional challenges varying from differently-oriented work forces to building a new life in a foreign country. The organizations must ensure that employees are well selected, prepared, and supported throughout the expatriation process. An exploratory study of German project managers in Portugal is conducted to elaborate the importance of cultural intelligence in business. Current understandings of both national cultures and their potential conflict factors are portrayed and German expatriates questioned about their work environment and private adjustment to Portuguese culture. Performance-orientation and assertive culture on the managers' side and relationship-focus and high-context communication on the employees' side triggered difficulties with work tasks. Differences related to the cultural dimension collectivism versus individualism complicated the expatriates' adjustment to the local culture.

INTRODUCTION

Globalization and multiculturalism have become features of the contemporary world, despite disagreement over how to define them. Globalization defines a very complex development, which in economics refers to the numbers of international corporations and projects which have increased simultaneously with the amount of goods and services, capital, and work force exchanged internationally (Graf, 2004; Kivisto, 2002; Koch, 2012). It is a dynamic process which increases global economic interconnectedness, fosters interdependencies, and makes the world more complex and far-reaching (House et al., 2004; Isidor et al., 2011; Kivisto, 2002). Diffusion of information is accelerated by the expansion and inflation of communication technologies and has increased the importance of information and networks, mak-

DOI: 10.4018/978-1-7998-4387-0.ch008

ing them powerful assets in today's world (Ferreira, 2007; Isidor et al., 2011; Varner & Beamer, 2005; WTO, 2019). This results in the increasing loss of importance of national borders and the intensification of international competition (Koch, 2012; Sambharya et al., 2005; Trompenaars & Woolliams, 2004). Simultaneously with technological advances, the multiplication and intensifying of international relationships have fostered international trade to experience a steep growth over the past few decades (Wild et al., 2006). Koch (2012) states that over the past fifty years the world's trade volume has increased twice as much as the global overall production of goods and services. According to the World Trade Organization (WTO, 2019), in 2018 merchandise trade totaled at 19.48 trillion US dollars with a growth rate of 3% per year, and commercial services at 5.77 trillion US dollars, with a growth rate of 8% per year. Over time, globalization has led to the world's development into "the place of borders and boundaries in a world where capital, production, and peoples are in constant motion" (Dirlik, 2005, p. 49), and an integration of production chains creates "more and more products are 'Made in the World' rather than made in just one economy" (WTO, 2019).

More connections and increasing interdependencies have brought about fundamental changes in global economic and political systems, cultural identities, and reorganized global relations (Dirlik, 2005; Engelen & Tholen, 2014; Kivisto, 2002). International political and economic dependencies have grown and linked the world even tighter. Terms and concepts such as proximity and distance, and place and space have obtained new meanings, as "social relations are no longer necessarily linked to particular places" (Kivisto, 2002, p. 1; see Koch, 2012; Varner & Beamer, 2005). As the borders between nations have come down and multiculturalism has spread, cultural barriers have come up (House et al., 2004; Loth, 2006). In these contexts, the "dependence on a federation of alliances and partnerships with other organizations" (Sambharya et al., 2005, p. 158) has granted more importance to intercultural competencies.

The focus of this chapter is on the influence of cultural intelligence in an international business environment. Firstly, it is important to understand the challenges and opportunities of internationalization in the business context. Special attention is given to expatriation. Definitions of culture and its influence on expatriates' adjustment effecting the success of international business are exposed. Challenges and potential advantages of selecting and training culturally literate managers for international projects are elaborated. In that context an illustrative questionnaire and three interviews were conducted to further understand the current practices of German organizations expatriating managers to Portugal. Complementary information, such as cultural characteristics and conflict potentials are provided. The objective of this chapter is to provide a more specific exemplification of culture's importance in today's business environment and demonstrate the benefits companies profit from when ensuring that their human resources are cross-culturally prepared.

LITERATURE REVIEW

Internationalization of Business

Globalization affects industries and products in different ways so that some companies take advantage of recent developments by maximizing profit from unequal working conditions and local development, while others are fighting for their existence (Feitosa et al., 2014; Wild et al., 2006; WTO, 2019). There is a worldwide competition among locations with respect to the best fiscal system, cheapest workforce, and regional infrastructure (Koch, 2012; Sambharya et al., 2005; Trompenaars & Woolliams, 2004).

It has been intensified by the urge to optimize production chains and business in conjunction with increasingly liberal policies supporting transborder business (Koch, 2012; Sambharya et al., 2005; WTO, 2019). Recently efforts have been made by governments and trends created by local initiatives against the fusion of markets and creating of conglomerates to protect local and small businesses.

When internationalizing, the complexity of a company's actions increases and forces it to restructure by modifying work methods and adapting to local market needs and standards (Deysine & Duboin, 1995; Wild et al., 2006). The big question a company must respond to when internationalizing is, whether they want to standardize their product or service globally or if they need to adapt to the different markets' needs and preferences to be successful (Koch, 2012; Sambharya et al., 2005; Wild et al., 2006). A balance is necessary, and compromises are to be found between global and local requirements (Graf, 2004; Koch, 2012). It is advisable to focus on local particularities but to think globally at the same time (Gesteland, 2005).

The creation of a global market leads to many opportunities, but also confronts companies with a new set of challenges including "the identification and selection of leaders appropriate to the cultures in which they will be functioning, the management of organizations with culturally diverse employees, as well as cross-border negotiations, sales, and mergers and acquisitions" (House et al., 2004, p. 10; see Earley & Peterson, 2004; Varner & Beamer, 2005). Hence, when internationalizing companies should formulate strategies to organize steps and formulate goals and milestones, but "national differences in language, religious beliefs, customs, traditions, and climate complicate strategy formulation" (Wild et al., 2006, p. 322). Cultural discrepancies require detailed attention to local preferences, needs, and business customs. As globalization has increased international economic connections and interdependencies, social and environmental standards, and political systems have adapted accordingly (Kivisto, 2002). International labor markets have appeared and alongside the diffusion of cultures around the globe, the global society has become more complex (Feitosa et al., 2014; Harris & Lievens, 2005; Ng et al., 2009; Vlajčića et al., 2019). These labor markets tend to be more accessible for MNCs than for SMEs due to their extended access to resources and further reach. Even though the importance of culture remains the same, there is a severe lack of research regarding cultural influences on the internationalization process of SMEs (Ribau et al., 2018; Morence et al. 2020).

Furthermore, as employees are of various nationalities and live and work in different countries, a company's Human Resource Management (HRM) becomes a great deal more complicated, yet essential, as everything has to be adapted to local laws and selection practices (Feitosa et al., 2014; Isidor et al., 2011; Loth, 2006). The ethnocentric staffing approach, focused on during this chapter, describes the strategy of taking employees along when internationalizing, assigning employees from its own ranks, and as a result keeping control over all actions abroad at the home-office (Banai & Sama, 2000; Graf, 2004; Wild et al., 2006). As the employees are already loyal to the company, corporate culture is more easily passed on ensuring the conformity of procedures throughout the company and facilitate knowledge transfer (Feitosa et al., 2014; Graf, 2004; Isidor et al., 2011). The sent employee is commonly referred to as an expatriate and commonly fills a highly technical or managerial position.

A manager's job is the goal-oriented leading of individuals and teams with the aim of developing all competencies to top-performance. Team orientation and a successful communication of values and vision that enhance confidence in team members are highly effective leadership skills (House et al., 2004; Koch, 2012). To reach predefined goals, a manager must share information and knowhow, communicate effectively, negotiate successfully, and prevent and solve conflicts, (Koch, 2012; Lauginic, 2009). Gaining others' trust is essential for developing a harmonious social situation within the team and a strong sense of teamwork (Koch, 2012; Rego & Cunha, 2010; Varner & Beamer, 2005). Today it can be assumed, that any managerial position is connected to other cultures (Dirlik, 2005; Isidor et al., 2011; Koch, 2012).

Culture determines the way of thinking and how individuals and groups behave, and influences local consumers' perceptions, preferences, and needs (Dirlik, 2005; Hofstede Insights: Cultural Diversity; Wild et al., 2006). Consequently, knowing how to be culturally appropriate with others can spare businesspeople from (unintentional) mistakes and embarrassment, and is fundamental to achieving positive outcomes and well-functioning business relationships (Engelen & Tholen, 2014; Loth, 2006; Varner & Beamer, 2005). The challenge with leading teams is that employees act on their own personal social and cultural base within an organizational culture. This affects each individual's interests, motivation, commitment, expectations, interpretations, and willingness to perform and how contents, procedures, actions and reactions are understood (Koch, 2012; Wild et al., 2006). The cultural heterogeneity in business projects, namely in international projects and assignments, is commonly more intense than at the hub (Earley & Peterson, 2004; Koch, 2012). Table 1 presents some differential factors between permanent and temporary managers.

Table 1. Differences between permanent and temporary organizations

Distinguishing Criterion	Permanent Organization Line Manager	Temporary Organization Project Manager
Preoccupation of the respective manager	Variety of goals, unique and repetitive, complex and easy	Specific project-oriented goals (often rather complex and unique)
Focus of leadership	Rational and strategic aspects of goal setting	Emotional aspects of goal setting
Hierarchical structure	Several hierarchical levels, power distance, complex and historically grown structures	Flat hierarchies, flexible structures
Resource allocation	Assigned to the company or sub-unit	Assigned to the project
Human resources practices	Long-term investment with relational contracts	Short-term investment with transactional or relational contracts
Life time	Long	Short

Source: Ferreira et al. (2013, p. 3774)

Projects usually involve participants from various organizations. The historic, regional, organizational, and social embeddedness of the environment are therefore very important factors when leading a team (Ferreira et al., 2013). Cultural factors influence the dynamics of a diverse team in various and most complex ways. It is essential that the team has (a) a collective understanding, awareness of possible differences, and (b) everyone has a perception of the others' understandings. As a result, the team's coordination is better, which results in a better team harmony, satisfaction, and performance (Ferreira et al., 2013; Standifer et al., 2015).

Organizational Citizenship Behavior (OCB), for instance, is a concept that can be influenced by managerial practices. It is an individual's behavior promoting efficiency at an organizational level that is beneficial to an organization, but due to being carried out discreetly often remains unrecognized (Ferreira et al., 2013; Rego & Cunha, 2010). High OCB leads to low absenteeism, low turnover rates, high satisfaction, and strong loyalty, resulting in good job performances and influences the team positively

(Ferreira et al., 2013). Ferreira et al. (2013) have analyzed the effects of Project Citizenship Behavior (PCB) comparing Portuguese and German project managers. With PCB the team tends to meet the target of the immediate project, relationships and career related potentials increase, and the parent organization tends to advance in business development (Ferreira et al., 2013; Rego & Cunha, 2010). OCB and PCB have different effects on different cultures. Ferreira et al. (2013) found that the influence on Portuguese project managers regarding project goal achievement, and future individual and organizational opportunities will be more significant than in Germany, where the national culture is more assertive, task-orientated, and aims for high performance, giving less importance to interpersonal relations and social solidarity (Ferreira et al., 2013; House et al., 2004). Creating synergies within a diverse team is beneficial to the project's overall success.

Expatriation of Employees

The number of international projects and businesses has steadily grown over the past years and more professionals are internationally active on a regular basis (Graf, 2004). For some employees, this change's influence is restricted to foreign coworkers at the office or email correspondences. Others may be assigned to work in subsidiaries – expatriates. All "citizens of one country who are living and working in another" (Wild et al., 2006, p. 448) are called expatriates. Some definitions add a temporal factor to expatriation and others leave it open, if plans exist to return to the country of citizenship (Feitosa et al., 2014; Business Dictionary; Lexico). There are different types of expatriation depending on the reason for leaving the home country. Self-initiated expatriates, aiming for personal realization or increasing their professional value by international work experience, for instance, and company assigned expatriates, who are to perform a certain role in a subsidiary or a project outside of their country while remaining with the organization, are the more common forms (Morence et al., 2020). During this chapter, the latter will be focused on as to further understand the companies' involvement in the process of assigning their employees to a project abroad.

The distance to the home-office leaves expatriates more autonomous and with more responsibility (Feitosa et al., 2014). Companies send employees who are technically qualified for the job and often seem to forget about the fact that employees will have to adapt to a completely different way of life. The selection process for positions in international and intercultural environments is seemingly handled like the national one – work and task related – and the ability to deal with people from other cultures is rarely a hiring factor (Feitosa et al., 2014; Graf, 2004). Skills and competencies – such as being open-minded, nonjudgmental, and able to build relationships, to create trust among people, or to have sensitivity, empathy, and interest in others while being confident – are usually not considered (Graf, 2004; Ng et al., 2009). Cultural adaptation only seems to be talked about when the expatriate is being evaluated, despite being the most common reason for failure of expatriation (Feitosa et al., 2014; Graf, 2004). In business the expatriation process usually is temporarily limited and the repatriation, referring to the return of the employee to his/her home nation, concludes the process – especially in the case of company assigned expatriates (Morence et al., 2020; Rodrigues et al., 2020). This phase tends to be reason for many additional difficulties such as reverse culture shock and higher career expectancies leading to higher turnover-rates (Rodrigues et al., 2020). Due to the complexity of the subject, this chapter will focus on the expatriation and not cover repatriation.

On assignment, managers cannot expect that their managers', coworkers', and employees' share or understand their own mindsets and behaviors, leading to the great importance of intercultural skills and the capability to cross-culturally adjust in making transnational business function more smoothly (Koch, 2012; Trompenaars & Woolliams, 2004; Wild et al., 2006). "The inability to speak the foreign language, coping with disorientation in the new environment, understanding the policies, customs, laws, and socializing with host country nationals" (Feitosa et al., 2014, p. 136) are expected barriers that expatriates need to overcome (Graf, 2004; Isidor et al., 2011). Additionally, spending long periods of time away from friends and family at home can be challenging and contribute to expatriate failure (Wild et al., 2006). On one hand, the long-term strategies of an international organization depend on the short-term adaptation capabilities of employees and involved family members (Banai & Sama, 2000; Feitosa et al., 2014; Wild et al., 2006). On the other hand, the effectiveness of strategies depends on how well the internationally active company's processes are adjusted to a heterogeneity of cultures (Koch, 2012; Sousa et al., 2015). The organizational structure of the company needs to encourage knowledge transfer through their expatriates to benefit company practices (Feitosa et al., 2014; Loth, 2006; Trompenaars & Woolliams, 2004). This given, a company's potential benefits include "transfer of managerial and technical knowledge, better control of foreign subsidiaries, improved communication, and more secure business transactions" (Feitosa et al., 2014, p. 135). In contrast, in the case of expatriate failure, the company's image can be harmed, and extremely high financial consequences might ensue depending on the position, location, and family involvement, for instance (Isidor et al., 2011; Wild et al., 2006). Immediate consequences are failed assignments, low performance, or high turnover rates (Feitosa et al., 2014; Graf, 2004). There might be additional consequences to the organization like production setbacks, harmed relationships with business partners, or difficulties for the next generation (Graf, 2004).

Research has yet to discover reliable predictable reasons for expatriates' failures, but many agree that cultural influences are one of the main reasons (Feitosa et al., 2014; House et al., 2004; Isidor et al., 2011). Advances in this area could lead to new strategies increasing the probability of success. There is still no proven model to acquire cultural literacy nor a definition of competencies that are therefore required. Be that as it may, expatriate managers not able to navigate efficiently within a different culture have been shown to be a reason for conflict, leading to instability and failure during international cooperation (Morence et al. 2020; Graf, 2004). For the individuals, adjusting to these differences and being able to work with anyone has become a fundamental skill (Sousa et al., 2015; Varner & Beamer, 2005). While being less obvious to catch on to, these details may also be the most disruptive and the reason for many conflicts (Gesteland, 2005; Wild et al., 2006). To avoid these intercultural conflicts and succeed at business outside of the home-nation, Cultural Intelligence (CQ) is crucial (Graf, 2004; Isidor et al., 2011; Vlajčića et al., 2019).

Culture

Culture is highly complex and many attempts have been made to define it, with no one universal definition being accepted by all (House et al., 2004; Koch, 2012; Williams, 1983). In a famous sentence, Raymond Williams (1983) began his entry on 'Culture' in Keywords by stating: "Culture is one of the two or three most complicated words in the English language" (p. 87). Hall (1976) defines culture as the whole of all details of a certain group's life in a certain place and at a certain time.

Culture is man's medium; there is not one aspect of human life that is not touched and altered by culture. This means personality, how people express themselves (including shows of emotion), the way they think, how they move, how problems are solved, how their cities are planned and laid out, how transportation systems function and are organized, as well as how economic and government systems are put together and function (Hall, 1976, p. 16-17).

According to Hall and Hall (1990), we live in different cultural worlds, with their own dynamics, principles, and laws, where even time and space are different. Then again, Hofstede compares cultures to highly complex computers being programmed: "the collective programming of the mind distinguishing the members of one group or category of people from others" (Hofstede Insights: National Culture). This programmed system then guides human beings through all their actions and responses and determines with which social group people identify themselves (Hall & Hall, 1990; Hofstede Insights: National Culture). Deysine and Duboin (1995) summarize culture as what we still know when we have forgotten everything, because we do it automatically without paying attention to it like intuitions. Indirectly corresponding to Hall and Hall (1990, p. 29) who said that "there is much that is taken for granted in culture that few people can explain but which every member of the culture accepts as given". Forty years and ongoing defining culture remains "a complex argument about the relations between general human development and a particular way of life, and between both and the works and practices of art and intelligence" (Williams, 1983, p. 91). Nevertheless, usually anthropologists agree on three factors when defining culture: culture is learned and not innate, all elements of one culture are connected and inseparable, and finally, culture is shared and defines limits between groups (Engelen & Tholen, 2014; Hall, 1976; Loth, 2006; Varner & Beamer, 2005).

Nation states are highly linked to the connotation of culture, thus within this chapter when culture is mentioned its primary use is referring to national societies. However, there is a great diversity within the 'average' of a national society referred to as subculture (Gesteland, 2005; Hofstede, 1991; Williams, 1983). To understand a local culture it is important to pay attention to a group's national culture and regional subcultures and pay attention to varying contexts along with attitudes towards time, work, and achievements for instance (Boroditsky, 2017; Hofstede, 1991; Wild et al., 2006). A person's ideology and personality are individual factors that must not be forgotten in intercultural situations and determine an individual's "interpretations of meanings of other people's behavior" (Koch, 2012, p. 53).

Cultures are comparable and efforts have been made to classify them by creating sets "of likely reactions of citizens with a common mental programming" (Hofstede, 1991, p. 112). Hofstede's dimensions (1980) (Power Distance, Individualism versus Collectivism, Masculinity versus Femininity, Uncertainty Avoidance, Long Term Orientation versus Short Term Normative Orientation, and Indulgence versus Restraint) are some of the most applied along with the more recent GLOBE-study from House et al. (2004), which further elaborated the previous body of classifications. Hall (1976) elaborated conceptual factors (context, time, space, the flow of information, and interfacing) to differentiate between cultural characteristics. As described, national cultures are not homogeneous, but given the difficulty of generating data about cultures and the seemingly indefinite number of them, it is easier to compare national cultures in order to understand cultural differences (Hofstede, 1991).

Cultural Intelligence

Cultural Intelligence (CQ, or cultural literacy) refers to detailed knowledge about one's own and others' cultures, the ability to recognize cultural traits, the flexibility to adapt accordingly, and thus function and communicate efficiently within foreign cultures (Engelen & Tholen, 2014; House et al., 2004; Sousa et al., 2015; Vlajčića et al., 2019; Wild et al., 2006). Therefore, a culturally literate person has the "flexibility to respond positively and effectively to practices and values that may be drastically different from what they are accustomed to" (House et al., 2004, p. 5). This includes valuable interpersonal skills such as understanding and interpreting behaviors, responses, and reactions correctly even in unfamiliar situations (Graf, 2004; Sousa et al., 2015; Vlajčića et al., 2019).

There are different dimensions of CQ. The first of four, the metacognitive dimension, refers to the active acquisition and understanding of information, enhancing a mindful perception of culture's impact on an interaction while being able to distinguish between an individual's personal characteristic and mental programming (Ng et al., 2009; Sousa et al., 2015; Vlajčića et al., 2019). The cognitive dimension implies knowing a culture's social, legal, and economic system along with its values, norms, and practices, and structuring the information being prepared to apply it more rapidly to similar situations characterized by cultural diversity (Sousa et al., 2015; Vlajčića et al., 2019). The effective application of the cross-cultural knowledge and its flexible, situationally appropriate usage, including successful verbal and non-verbal communication, refers to the behavioral dimension (Earley & Peterson, 2004; Ng et al., 2009; Sousa et al., 2015). Lastly, the motivational dimension indicates the process of increasing one's intercultural auto-efficiency by directing one's energy and attention to acquiring more cultural knowhow (Earley & Peterson, 2004; Ng et al., 2009; Sousa et al., 2015; Vlajčića et al., 2019).

As globalization has created a seemingly borderless and interdependent world economy and multicultural working environments, cultural factors have been attributed an increasing importance in business (Ang, 2005; Dirlik, 2005; Engelen & Tholen, 2014; Loth, 2006). Research has proven that national cultures influence management practices and are a critical factor in success or failure of internationalization (Engelen & Tholen, 2014; Sousa et al., 2015). Different cultures prefer different management systems and managerial practices do not "transfer across ethnic, cultural, and national boundaries" (Eylon & Au, 1999, p. 374).

CQ for Expatriate Managers

The dynamic environment and competitive circumstances – especially of temporary projects – provoke a necessity for flexibility and permanent adaptation of a group leader combined with high task-orientation (Engelen & Tholen, 2014; Ferreira et al., 2013; Hofstede Insights: Cultural Diversity). A manager has to reduce uncertainties, and manage to extract the most possible potential from the employees (Ferreira et al., 2013; Koch, 2012; Sousa et al., 2015). Leaders of multicultural teams encounter challenges of a different type when, for instance, the locally preferred leadership practice no longer refers to deciding everything, but instead delegating and representing the collective interest (House et al., 2004; Koch, 2012; Loth, 2006; Ng et al., 2009). As managers are confronted with interculturality, CQ has become a crucial trait (Gesteland, 2005; Isidor et al., 2011; Vlajčića et al., 2019; Wild et al., 2006). Cultural sensitivity is essential to understand a situation where multiple cultures are present in order to create and profit from synergies (Engelen & Tholen, 2014; Lauginic, 2009; Vlajčića et al., 2019).

Good communication skills (best in the present language(s)) are fundamental to understand the environmental influences through local culture (Deysine & Duboin, 1995; Sousa et al., 2015). Intercultural intelligence facilitates the exchange with Host Country Nationals (HCN), crucial for expatriates to acclimatize to the local ways and socially integrate themselves, especially because a manager who becomes an insider to the collective, is able to provoke more PCB within the team (Rego & Cunha, 2010). The company's policies should therefore emphasize expatriates' CQ and support their adjustment to local cultures reinforcing social integration. The support that expatriates receive from their family, the organization, or any other kind of interpersonal entity throughout the process, can make a big difference (Ali et al., 2019; Feitosa et al., 2014). In extreme cases, expatriates will find themselves in a situation of culture shock, which notably decreases their productivity and can lead to fundamental misunderstandings with local employees, partners, or customers, damaging the project's success and even future relations of the company (Hofstede, 1991; Loth, 2006; Wild et al., 2006). The family and spouse of the expatriate manager are critical factors in a manager's performance and success throughout the expatriation and their personal adjustment is just as crucial to the success of international assignments (Feitosa et al., 2014; Graf, 2004; Vlajčića et al., 2019).

Recapitulating, "knowledge of the culture plus the language will make a great difference in [...] success [and] enjoyment of the experience of working and living abroad" (Hall & Hall, 1990, p. 182). In management and leadership positions, flexible communication strategies are effective tools to overcome differences that otherwise would become invisible barriers (Gesteland, 2005, p. 42). Speaking the language of the host country, pleasing the locals and increasing the cooperation's efficiency, raises the willingness and desire for interaction with HCN, which in its turn enhances learning cultural particularities and local environmental aspects improving the adjustment of the expatriate (Boroditsky, 2010; Lauginic, 2009; Matas-Runquist, 2009). In other words, as CQ enhances social interactions, it increases the intention to share knowhow and enables the manager to decode the information from its cultural embeddedness functioning as the connecting element between the local culture of the subsidiary and the home-office (Ali et al., 2019; Hall & Hall, 1990; Loth, 2006). Simultaneously, creativity and innovation are increased by knowledge transfer, which in their turn increase productivity, and then organizational success (Ali et al., 2019; Loth, 2006; Vlajčića et al., 2019). Metacognitive and motivational CQ are especially important for managers to be more effective with their followers, motivating them and generating trust, while behavioral CQ positively influences performance on the job (Vlajčića et al., 2019).

While the expatriate managers should be culturally literate, the organization needs to create a supportive climate and suitable structures to make it possible for intercultural exchange and knowledge transfer to be experienced even by future generations (Koch, 2012; Sambharya et al., 2005; Trompenaars & Woolliams, 2004). Diversity at the workplace leads to creativity, innovation, and enhanced active learning, thus increasing problem-solving skills and profitability benefitting the company (Ali et al., 2019; Hofstede Insights: Intercultural Management; Skutnabb-Kangas, 2009). The ability to use and benefit from the influences of globalization seems to be dependent on the ability to tolerate different ways and the attitude of a society towards integration (Ali et al., 2019; Hofstede Insights: Cultural Diversity; Loth, 2006).

Cultural Training by Companies

The dynamic of our seemingly borderless world and the lack of defined competencies that are necessary for international assignments, and how to acquire them, raise the difficulty level of preparation for assignments abroad. The expatriate's motivation and willingness to learn can reduce the time needed to adjust to a new environment. Learning Goal Orientation (LGO) is a form of motivation focused upon the learning process and refers to a keenness to learn and advance (Feitosa et al., 2014). LGO is positively related to autonomy, self-management, and solving problems (Feitosa et al., 2014). Technical knowledge, skills, attitudes and other competencies (KSAO), CQ, language skills, and LGO are indicators that have been found most helpful to determine expatriate suitability and are positively related to the candidates' adjustment (Feitosa et al., 2014).

It is in the companies' interest that their employees are successful and have a high performance in order to increase efficiency and future opportunities, which is why they try their best to select and train their employees (Feitosa et al., 2014; Ng et al., 2009; Wild et al., 2006). Cultural literacy depends on cultural exposure, training, socialization, and other experiences and therefore is malleable and can be learned (Ng et al., 2009; Sousa et al., 2015; Vlajčića et al., 2019). Depending on the intensity of the employees' international involvement, different training approaches can be effective and different extents necessary to ensure that managers are culturally literate enough to fulfill the duties required of them (Feitosa et al., 2014; Graf, 2004; Wild et al., 2006). Effective preparation for an international assignment increases the candidates' potential to respond suitably to intercultural situations and adjust properly to new environments (Feitosa et al., 2014).

The employee must present certain personal characteristics such as being open-minded, curious, friendly, tolerant, reliable, sensible, impartial, and having a well-developed empathy, self-confidence, optimism, and ability to reflect on themselves and others are fundamental (Ali et al., 2019; Engelen & Tholen, 2014; Ng et al., 2009). Then, the first step of cultural intelligence acquisition usually consists of environmental briefings (Feitosa et al., 2014; Koch, 2012; Matas-Runquist, 2009). Political, historical, and socio-economic facts should be studied and complemented with culture specific information such as manners, customs, particular taboos, and obligations (Isidor et al., 2011; Koch, 2012; Wild et al., 2006). In addition to being culturally sensitive and knowing characteristics of one's own and others' cultures, a culturally literate person must be able to act and react accordingly (Koch, 2012). Acting flexibly and constructively to manage interculturally requires a lot of respect, tolerance, empathy, sensitivity, and patience spent on communication, adjustment and creating reliable relationships (Koch, 2012; Loth, 2006). When environmental, cultural, and linguistical knowhow have been acquired through various methods, only field experience can teach employees more (Feitosa et al., 2014; Koch, 2012). By socializing and living the experience, the practical experience offers more internal knowledge of the culture and intensifies the learning and acquisition of CQ (Bonavita, 2009; Matas-Runquist, 2009; Ng et al., 2009). Thus, a local mentor is a great adjustment tool and can reduce uncertainties related to the work assignment and to difficulties in expatriates' day-to-day lives. It can be an effective and relatively low-cost method. The better adjusted the expatriates are the more social and intercultural contact they have, and consequently more access to knowhow. Finally, cultural literacy requires the repeatedly flexible and successful managing of intercultural situations.

The model of training approaches of Feitosa et al. (2014), shown in Figure 1, includes different objectives and environmental influences. It illustrates the influences on successful expatriate adjustment which we know are positively related to goal achievement and success.

A rising number of companies invest in providing some sort of cultural training for their employees sent abroad (Wild et al., 2006). Nevertheless, it is not done enough due to the specificity required the involved expenses. On the individual level, cross-cultural training can strongly improve the assignment, and on an organizational level improve the framework for free-flowing information regardless of the original cultural context (Vlajčića et al., 2019).

CASE STUDY

In the following, the specific case of German expatriate managers on assignment in Portugal will be elaborated to exemplify the literature-based research carried out on cultural importance in intercultural

Figure 1. Integrative model of expatriate selection and training
Source: Feitosa et al. (2014, p. 139)

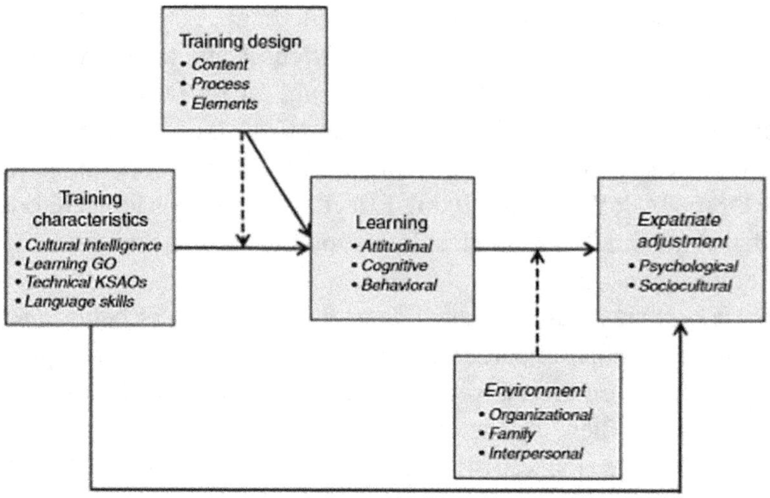

Note: Solid lines indicate best practices drawn from traditional literature, whereas dotted lines indicate novel links that call for empirical testing

business situations. First, the German and the Portuguese national cultures will be analyzed to create a detailed framework for the case. It is to be pointed out that cultures are not uniform, yet for ease of analysis presented as such and subcultures and the different juridical systems, macroeconomics, political, and demographic situations might falsify the data. Notwithstanding these difficulties, the complementary study is intended to show insights into both national cultures and then reveal conflict potentials in the working environment. Hofstede's dimensions as portrayed on Hofstede Insights facilitate the comparison of cultures and build the base of theoretical foundation. Other sources such as Hall and Hall (1990) and House et al. (2004) are referred to complementing the cultural descriptions. Furthermore, a survey has been conducted and interviews carried out, to support (or contradict) theoretical findings and offer additional insights into specific cases.

Portuguese Culture

As a culture, the Portuguese score low to mid-range in all of Hofstede's dimensions, except for a slightly raised Power Distance Index (PDI) and an extremely high score in Uncertainty Avoidance (UA). The GLOBE-study found the Latin Cluster to show a high level of PDI as well and to be high scoring in In-Group Collectivism, especially regarding family. Low scores were obtained for Future Orientation and Gender Egalitarianism; moderate to high scores on UA, Assertiveness, Humane and Performance Orientation, and mid-ranging scores on the remaining dimensions (Jesuino, 2002).

Portugal, in this case coherent with the Latin cluster, has a high PDI and accepts that people in powerful positions are granted privileges and seem unreachable to lower employees (Deysine & Duboin, 1995; Ferreira et al., 2013; Rego & Cunha, 2010). This typical attitude correlates with subordination and obedience – affiliative following (Hofstede Insights: Country Comparison; Loth, 2006; Rodrigues, 2014). The vertical organizational structures and centralized decision making intensify the paternalistic leading and guidance role of supervisors (Ferreira, 2007; Jesuino, 2002; Loth, 2006).

Portugal has a collectivistic culture as people commit to a group and take responsibility for it (Ferreira, 2007; Gesteland, 2005; Rego & Cunha, 2010). Loyalty to a group – consisting of close family, extended family members, and close (family) friends – is an overriding concept within society and is granted unquestioned primacy (Ferreira, 2007; Hofstede Insights: Country Comparison; Jesuino, 2002). In comparison to the very strong In-Group Collectivism the Organizational is rather moderate (Ferreira, 2007; Jesuino, 2002; Rodrigues, 2014). High people-orientation results in the prioritization of the person in charge over procedures (Hofstede Insights: Cultural Diversity; Jesuino, 2002, p. 87). This stress on affiliation is coherent with UA and at the same time, corresponds to a stress on law, a disregard of authorities and an independent attitude (Ferreira, 2007; Hofstede Insights: Country Comparison; Jesuino, 2002).

In temporal matters, Portugal tends towards being on the side of rigid-time cultures, theoretically valuing time and punctuality, especially in comparison to other cultures of the Latin cluster (Gesteland, 2005; Hofstede Insights: Country Comparison). Practically and when compared to more monochronic cultures, they are rather unpunctual, unorganized, and would not be described as good planners. Their agendas and schedules are not as highly prioritized as relationships and therefore often not complied with (Ferreira, 2007; Rodrigues, 2014). They tend to improvisation, and are flexible and innovative, adapting to situations and people (Ferreira, 2007; Rodrigues, 2014).

Consensus is a key word and interpersonal harmony should be striven for – typical for a very Feminine culture (Ferreira, 2007; Hofstede Insights: Country Comparison; Rego & Cunha, 2010). Their desire for harmonious relationships commonly leads to a flexibility in negotiations and compromising with counterparts to reach a solution to everyone's content (Hofstede Insights: Country Comparison; Jesuino, 2002; Rego & Cunha, 2010). Consequently, their use of indirect and high-context language is intensified (Jesuino, 2002; Rego & Cunha, 2010; Rodrigues, 2014). The concept of keeping or saving face is important in Portugal, which is why offending someone (publicly) is to be avoided at all costs (Hofstede Insights: Country Comparison; Rego & Cunha, 2010). Coherent to the desire to keep the others' face, the Portuguese score low in Hofstede's Indulgence dimension (Gesteland, 2005; Hofstede Insights: Country Comparison; Rodrigues, 2014). The combination of this self-demanding attitude and the tendency to avoid public display of emotions due to a high reactiveness to sensitivity results in rarely given feedback (Rego & Cunha, 2010).

Long Term Orientation enhances a past-oriented attitude, a worshipping of traditions, and a commonly granted respect for norms, intensified by the strong presence of Catholicism (Hofstede Insights: Country Comparison; Jesuino, 2002; Loth, 2006). Normative thinking leads to a dislike of change, reflected in the saying '*equipa que ganha não se mexe*' (Rodrigues, 2014, p. 162; 'never change a winning team'). Portugal scores extremely high in the UA dimension. The typically conservative Portuguese tend to be intolerant of unconventional behavior and ideas (Ferreira, 2007; Hofstede Insights: Country Comparison).

An outstanding leader in the Latin Europe Cluster is one who is charismatic and promulgates vision and inspiration to the employees. Being integrated in the team and leading by participation and being a good example is effective and raises their OCB or PCB (Ferreira et al., 2013; Rego & Cunha, 2010; Rodrigues, 2014). It is important that managers earn their employees' trust and loyalty by being fair, respectful, and concerned – even slightly so on a personal level (Ferreira, 2007; Hofstede Insights: Country Comparison; Rego & Cunha, 2010). Portuguese employees desire to feel relevant at their work, considered, and treated with respect and dignity preferably without having to voice their own opinions or even having to take on responsibilities (Ferreira, 2007; Rego & Cunha, 2010). Not wanting to disrupt the harmony in their environment, Portuguese employees seldom raise negative issues or problems with their managers (Ferreira et al., 2013; Rego & Cunha, 2010). Managers are expected to be on top of things

(Hofstede Insights: Country Comparison). A powerful paternalistic leader is more valued than transparency and strict procedures (Ferreira, 2007; Hofstede Insights: Country Comparison; Rego & Cunha, 2010).

There seems to be an ongoing conflict between Portuguese values as modernity and tradition seem to be simultaneously present (Ferreira, 2007; Jesuino, 2002; Rodrigues, 2014). Portugal scores comparatively high in gender egalitarianism, for instance, not giving much importance to gender and not having excessively rigidly defined roles based on gender. Even though the country is theoretically egalitarian, the sense of tradition has a moderating effect. Additionally, the affiliative attitude keeps the country safe, but simultaneously seems to hold the country back. More proactivity could enhance Portugal's competitiveness on the global market.

German Culture

Decentralization and compartmentalization are two key words to describe German culture. Everyone is responsible for themselves and must do their part in the team, working towards the common goal – almost like a social contract everyone is bound to (Deysine & Duboin, 1995; Hall & Hall, 1990; Loth, 2006). The low PDI and decentralization of power imply a compartmentalization of knowledge and knowing one's part is essential to the system, all the more because Germans do not like to share information with others whether it is work related or concerns their private life (Hall & Hall, 1990).

Germans prefer long-term thinking and loyalty in personal and business relationships, offering them reliability and continuity (Hall & Hall, 1990; Hofstede Insights: Country Comparison). Once trust has been earned, friendships are lasting and the most soul-baring feelings and private thoughts will be shared (Gesteland, 2005; Hall & Hall, 1990). Germans are very individualistic, which makes them rather unsocial as they share very little and keep a relatively small social circle, valuing their privacy a lot (Gesteland, 2005; Hall & Hall, 1990; Hofstede Insights: Country Comparison). Their stubborn habits and extremely deal-focused orientation help them to make the best possible deal, and patience and persistency, insisting on their compartmentalization and plans, make them tough negotiation partners (Gesteland, 2005; Hall & Hall, 1990). Manners, formality, and respect are essential in every position in professional contexts and reflect a person's ability to be polite and responsible (Gesteland, 2005; Hall & Hall, 1990).

Deysine and Duboin (1995) and Loth (2006) refer to German business culture as a "*machine bien huilée*" (p. 122; p. 63; well-oiled machine) comparing it to many parts of a machine working efficiently together towards the same objective due to having one of the lowest human-orientations. Typical for a Masculine culture, the environment is very competitive. Informational components are granted more importance than interpersonal harmony, leading to primarily negative criticism (Ferreira et al., 2013; Gesteland, 2005; Rego & Cunha, 2010). Germans are famous for being honest and extremely direct (Gesteland, 2005; Hall & Hall, 1990; Hofstede Insights: Country Comparison). In the German way to communicate facts, background information, historical context, and examples are used in abundance for extra credibility and to ensure their interlocutors' complete and correct understanding; the German culture is extremely low-context (Gesteland, 2005; Hall & Hall, 1990; Loth, 2006).

As a very monochronic culture, Germans tend to plan everything (Hall & Hall, 1990). In combination with their monochronic attitudes focusing on one task at a time, and their severe compartmentalization, business tends to be slow paced. Germans take their time to analyze everything closely, logically, and to the very last detail and then consult with fellow colleagues and superiors to see if they have missed an aspect or are well prepared (Gesteland, 2005; Hall & Hall, 1990; Loth, 2006). German national culture has high UA and likes to avoid it with their urge for detailed and careful analyzation of all facts, and carefully considered and elaborated planning (Ferreira et al., 2013; Hofstede Insights: Country Comparison; House et al., 2004).

The decision-making process in German culture is very elaborate and time consuming, but once a decision is made it is final and they stand firmly behind it, giving it all their energy (Hall & Hall, 1990; Deysine & Duboin, 1995). The German way of carving things into stone and the need to put stamps on documents hinder them from being flexible in business management and everyday work (Hall & Hall, 1990). German culture tends to be hesitant towards change and irritated by it, but once people realize it leads to increased efficiency, they encourage it; they are rather pragmatic (Hofstede Insights: Country Comparison). The irritation is not directly based on the change itself, but on the time that was wasted – and time is highly valued in Germany. Being punctual is the golden rule in Germany (Gesteland, 2005; Smith & Zagelmeyer, 2010). Schedules are made far ahead and must always be respected (Deysine & Duboin, 1995; Hall & Hall, 1990; Gesteland, 2005).

Cultural Comparison and Conflict Potentials

Figure 2 illustrates the difference between the German and Portuguese national cultures portraying differences that could potentially lead to difficulties for German managers going to Portugal. Portugal classifies as a culture with a high PDI and where socially accepted hierarchical discrepancies lead to a single person being in charge. In German business culture, power is decentralized, and a participative environment leads to numerous contributions when decisions are being taken. This rather lengthy process of getting to the bottom of things, considering everything that might help in making the right decisions, may seem interminable to the Portuguese who wait for their superiors to make the decision and them adapt to it.

While both national cultures are considered to have a high UA Index – Portugal very high (99) and Germany (65) – the Portuguese plan and then adapt if needed. Germany's culture is less flexible and more skeptical when it comes to change. Everything is planned in detail and one could even use the expression 'control freak' in combination with a German's obsession to obtain all information, organize it, and apply it according to a strict plan. The Portuguese enjoy a plan, but really only care that the final result is carried out with precision. Their affiliative attitude and orientation towards interpersonal relationships instead of informative factors correspond to their general flexible and adaptive attitude. Conflict

Figure 2. Comparing Germany (l.) to Portugal (r.)
Source: Hofstede Insights: Country Comparison

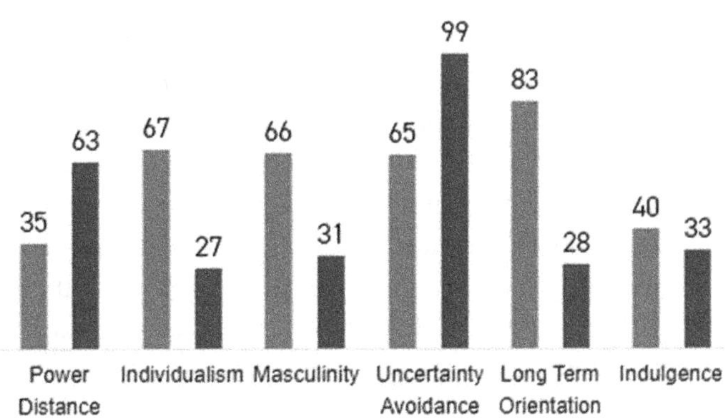

potential arises here as the Portuguese enjoy the guiding hand of participative leadership and working cooperatively, while Germans tend to trust in themselves and compartmentalize by distributing tasks.

The different perception of time is the next contentious issue. The adaptiveness of Portuguese culture corresponds to their tendency of neglecting to plan to the last detail before starting and often leads to last-minute effort and missing deadlines. This is something that makes Germans furious. The effective use of time and being punctual is expected of everyone, and schedules, deadlines, and agendas are to be rigorously followed. That things do not go according to plans in Portugal corresponds to the fact that their highest priority are harmonious interpersonal relationships. They prefer doing business with people they know and trusting their business partners is fundamental, while Germans do not mind doing business with strangers and avoid small talk. Portugal ranks high in Collectivism (especially In-Group Collectivism), contrary to the Germans' high individualistic character that may seem cold hearted, and distant. In the dimension of Organizational Collectivism, they rather show for the contrary: Germans identify themselves with the company and the Portuguese sense of responsibility remains rather with the individuals.

Sensitivity towards other peoples' feelings and the desire for a harmonious environment are important to the Portuguese, while in Germany competing to be the best performer is more common. Toughness and insensitivity rule a world where function is imperative and people's feelings almost seem to be non-existent. Communication reinforces these differences. Germans being low-context are extremely direct, honest, and very literally. The people-oriented Portuguese are the opposite: moderately high-context and indirect, avoiding confrontation. The concept of 'face' is crucial. On an organizational level, the high assertiveness of Germans clashes with the low assertiveness levels of the Portuguese. When working together, the different manners of giving rather negative feedback – very directly or not at all – are bound to lead to contentious situations.

Survey

A questionnaire was developed to receive more specific information regarding the management of projects based in Portugal managed by Germans. In total there were twelve responses to the survey and the heterogeneity of the survey respondents permitted only limited results. There were managers who had been with their employer for ten years and more and others only two years or less. Three participants had a previous relationship with the country that exceeded the intensity of summer vacation trips. Portuguese language skills were very poor with a third not having any previous skills, three basic skills and only one having had a working proficient language level. On the contrary, the managers' English skills were well developed. The participants' companies' were very passive before the project's start. Only two indicated having received cultural training before their expatriation. Nevertheless, the majority felt culturally prepared and capable enough before going on assignment. There was only one manager who indicated that he wished to have been more prepared and two admitted not having thought about their capabilities to cope with the cultural differences before. The projects' planned duration differed between half a year and two years. The companies usually provided aid with the moving process, after arrival provided language classes and sometimes financial compensation, especially when families or spouses where involved. The majority brought their family or spouse with them to Portugal who would also receive language classes. The positions filled abroad often corresponded to the ones in Germany and were mostly related to team and project management, except one working in production management and one in HRM.

The projects' teams were mostly consisting of Portuguese, Brazilians, and Germans. English was the main language used often alongside with Portuguese. The expatriates were asked to compare the personal attributes of their team members in Portugal to those of the team members in Germany (Figure 3). Team members in Portugal score higher in categories regarding personal interaction and are indicated to be more friendly, helpful, willing to compromise, flexible, and respectful. The participants of the survey thought that people in Germany were more reliable, punctual, goal-oriented, and efficient, scoring higher in adjectives related to working efficiency and discipline.

Figure 3. Comparison of German and Portuguese team members

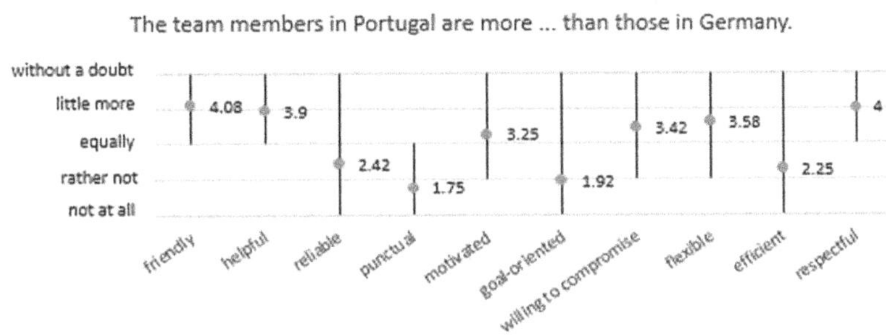

In relation to the team, the expatriate managers indicated that they had the many difficulties communicating with the employees and with building a strong sense of teamwork. Issues motivating, guiding and leading, and giving feedback were each indicated by three expatriates and issues with controlling employees by four. Only one of the twelve could say that the team was always on the same page and everyone knew what to do, just as only one other person confirmed the statement that there were neither confusions nor delays. Time factors like scheduling and keeping deadlines seem to have been the most frequent problem for the German managers in Portugal. Half of them indicated that the time was not efficiently used. Four expatriates experienced a culture shock of whom one seriously considered going home.

Some of the expatriate managers have not returned or finished their projects (yet): one retired in Portugal, two are still on site, one has just not gone back, and one has temporarily returned to Germany due to Covid-19, but still works for his project. Those who have already returned indicated having acquired some sort of knowledge specific to the Portuguese culture. Most have also developed different communication strategies and improved the general coping with intercultural situations and increased their flexibility in relation to time management.

The expatriates English language skills increased only slightly compared to previously high scores prior to the assignments. The non-existent Portuguese language skills from before expatriation show a variety of change. Three indicated still having no Portuguese skills. Having basic skills or those that are enough to cope with daily life were each selected by three of the managers. The three highest of the six levels of language skills were each marked by one expatriate. Very popular skills that were advised for the next generation to have were patience, persistence, an open mind, language skills, flexibility, and being actively interested in other people and cultures. Marked as beneficial by half of the participants were developing cross-cultural communication strategies and time management specific to the Portuguese culture. All agreed that being superficially acquainted with the local culture beforehand was advisable.

Interviews

In addition to the survey, three interviews were conducted. The interviewees were chosen based on indications regarding company's involvement and keeping in mind personal connections. In the following, the interviewees will be referred to as IP-1, IP-2, and IP-3. It can be stated that IP-2 and IP-3 are both from the same company and were stationed in the same subsidiary. All three managers were sent to Portugal for two years and all are men. IC-3 has returned, IC-2 is still in Portugal, and IC-3 prolonged his two year stay repeatedly until finally retiring in Portugal after a total of twelve years. All identified themselves with German culture; IP-2's additionally with the Russian culture as his parents are Russian-Germans.

IP-2 and IP-3 applied to go to Portugal after having already commuted to the project before wishing to be stationed there. IP-1 was asked and spontaneously accepted. All three managers moved with their spouses and IP-2 with children. The previous management experience ranged from one, to four, to over ten years. All had been with their company for ten years and more. When asked about their cultural competencies prior to the foreign assignment, IP-1 felt the most literate and IP-3 the least. While everyone's English skills were already evolved before, the managers' Portuguese language skills all started at zero. The biggest improvement was made by IP-3. IP-1's skills have not reached conversational levels, but he is not interested in improving them either not seeing the necessity. IP-2 has basic skills after being in Portugal for approximately nine months. The positions of IP-2 and IP-3 involved regular contact with workers on the shop floor putting them in situations where Portuguese would be useful.

All employers provided the expatriate managers and their spouses with weekly one-to-one Portuguese lessons and helped with the moving process. For IP-1 and IP-2 this also applied to cultural training. The companies organized a one-day event, where the interviewees learned about differences such as conversational taboos and local food culture. Both pointed out that it did not have anything to do with the working context and was rather focused upon differences to be encountered in private life. The employer of IP-2 and IP-3 went the extra mile, offering the spouses support for educational purposes or starting a professional life abroad, and providing the children with a spot at a private German school. IP-2 was satisfied with the service he received and IP-3 was not, which can be explained by the replacement of the company's external relocation agency.

At work, the three participants reported that Germans tend to be more ambitious and goal- and performance-oriented. IP-3 complained about the Portuguese lack of efficiency and autonomy at work. They seemed impulsive and were not examining the whole situation before acting, bringing about (according to IP-2 and IP-3) an unnecessary amount of chaos. Meetings were also perceived as chaotic: the Portuguese were too late, unproductive yet eventually expedient, and too emotionally loaded, leading to emotionally heated discussions. Chaos was again mentioned by the managers because the employees did not take responsibility for tasks. Typically, emails were sent to everyone and no one felt directly approached leaving no one in charge of the problem. And even if an employee was directly attributed to a task "'Yes' meant something else than in Germany". In relation to giving feedback, the managers experienced the expected difficulties between low- and high-context cultures. Being criticized by their German manager seems to have made the Portuguese feel like they had failed personally. IP-1, who was responsible for HRM, had fewer problems with his meetings. His experience was that meetings and deadlines were less postponed and usually complied with.

When asked about the team members in Portugal (Portuguese and Brazilians) compared to those in Germany only IP-1 clearly indicated preferring his new team members and the other two preferred the Germans. They all agreed that during their time abroad the people were more friendly and helpful on a private basis. At work they had difficulties building a strong sense of teamwork. The lack of autonomy and ambition reportedly led to lower individual and team performance. The emotional identification with their work hinders the Portuguese to admit to having problems and to ask for help. IP-3 pointed out that this difference might come from anxiety felt by Germans about not getting their work done on time, so that the Germans are rather willing to ask colleagues for help.

None of the three reported having a lot of personal relations outside work. IP-2, who has moved abroad the most recently, has a bit more contact with locals due to his children's school and leisure activities. IP-3 talked about contacts through work with whom he went out to eat or for a beer after work sometimes, but only referred to one colleague as a 'friend'. Even IP-1, who has been in Portugal for twelve years now, talks about having "sort of a circle of friends, which … well [he does] not meet regularly, but keeps contact with".

We know that IP-1 clearly enjoyed his work in Portugal, because he finished his professional career there. IP-2 has already made it clear he would like to try to stay longer. From the survey, interviews, and personal impressions, he seems to be the most apt for a life abroad. His open-mindedness and flexibility are high, and his awareness that he cannot change the Portuguese but must adapt to them are advantages. IP-3 and his wife had thought about and planned to extend their stay even though the manager had considered to abort the project at one point. Agreeing with his own assessment, he had not been culturally prepared enough to work in Portugal. They eventually returned to Germany as planned indicating three reasons: his wife's pregnancy, her lack of social integration in Portugal, and being asked to return by the employer.

DISCUSSION

There was no data collected for the selection process of expatriate candidates. Nevertheless, it is interesting to see how the interviewees' cultural assessment from before the assignment is coherent with the course of their posting abroad. Yet, it cannot be denied that their assessment is influenced in hindsight by their subsequent experience. The only one of the participants who indicated having experienced a culture shock was the one who had the most difficulties with social integration in Portugal despite being the only one who learned the language (so far).

It could be confirmed that social integration in Portugal was difficult to achieve for the German interviewees. Germans are very private and do not make new friends easily. The Portuguese, on the contrary, are very in-group collectivistic but might see their group as already established and closed while their friendliness and hospitality make outsiders feel welcomed. This behavior provides a difficult context for outsiders to establish a harmonious social life, leaving our three interviewees with great difficulties integrating themselves socially. At work, the harmony and keeping face on the Portuguese side collides with the Germans' performance-oriented thinking.

Conflict potential between the national cultures was found in the contradicting behavior of Germans being extremely low-context and direct and the Portuguese moderately high-context communicators. English skills in Portugal are widespread and elevated, facilitating communicating among the participants. None of the managers questioned had any relevant Portuguese language skills before going to

Portugal, leaving it undetectable whether language skills would have improved the experience. Usually the misunderstandings were not due to linguistic problems, but because of who was addressed and who felt addressed. IP-2 and IP-3 both indicated noticing a lack of autonomy and feeling responsible among their Portuguese colleagues. Giving feedback seemed to be a conflictive task as well, as managers felt they had personally insulted the employees without knowing how.

Another problematic issue that could be traced back to cultural differences was time. Complaints about deadlines not being met, meetings starting late, and time not being efficiently used were referred to within the survey and in the interviews. While IP-1 was positively impressed by the punctuality and compliance with scheduled staff meetings, the other two managers were frustrated by people showing up late and deadlines being postponed again and again. IP-2 learned that if he would indirectly let his colleagues know he had been waiting for them to start meetings – counting on their desire for harmony – they would feel bad and arrive less late.

There was no supporting or contradictory evidence for the assumption that previous management skills or experiences abroad facilitate the management of an international assignment. Regarding the three interviewees, there was a very clear difference between IP-1 and the other two managers. While the latter were both (voluntarily) sent abroad by the same company to the same project (production management, yet not the exact same positions), IP-1 asked to be responsible for HRM. He indicated that he had had fewer problems both with time perceptions and communication. It would be enlightening to understand the reason for these opposite experiences. Production is a relatively competitive field, relying on performance (Germany is a masculine and deal-focused collective), while HR is centered on interpersonal relations (Portugal has a feminine culture with high humane orientation). Being confronted with the local culture on 'their territory' could facilitate integration and adjustment, instead of trying to promote one's own mental programming.

CONCLUSION

It became clear, that the role of all involved employers was rather passive not having invested enough in the expatriates' preparation. For the majority of participants, the help provided by the organization was limited to language classes, relocation and financial support. IP-2 and IP-3's families would have been supported if they had actively asked for (financial) help, but that did not improve their integration. Having a family with children has made it easier for IP-2 to integrate himself establishing contacts through his children's activities underlining the importance of family adjustment. The cultural training, if provided, was extremely insufficient. All three interviewees could have benefitted from a cultural training specifically designed for interactions with Portuguese, especially so because the cultural heterogeneity at their workplace and in their teams was relatively small. Additionally, the training was limited to the predeparture period or the beginning phase. A multifocal support system was not available to the managers. IP-2 and IP-3 were assigned mentors, but it remains only to assume they were not carefully selected or matched. The expatriates tried to look for helpful local contacts, but not all successfully. Simultaneously to making others' experiences available for the expatriate to learn and benefit from, a well-paired mentor could have increased social interaction and thus facilitated social integration in the foreign environment. Social networks (outside the family and the organization) could become an additional motivational force and provide an outlet and support for the employee.

FUTURE RESEARCH DIRECTIONS

Future investigations should try to provide more internal consistency among participants, reducing the influence of the specific nature of the companies represented, the extent of the project, and other situational factors. By accompanying expatriate managers posted abroad throughout the different stages of their assignment, more personal characteristics could be considered, and the development of their cultural intelligence studied. It would also be enlightening to know more about the organizational influence as well, such as selection processes and subsequent project success. Furthermore, the perception of the Portuguese employees could also provide additional information, especially about aspects related to leadership practices. This study has demonstrated the influence of CQ in business environments, shed light on how diverse the perceptions of cultural factors can be, and how there is still work to be done in convincing industry of the potential benefits of investing more in testing for CQ and training to improve it.

REFERENCES

Ali, I., Ali, M., Leal-Rodríguez, A. L., & Albort-Morant, G. (2019). The role of knowledge spillovers and cultural intelligence in enhancing expatriate employees' individual and team creativity. *Journal of Business Research*, *101*, 561–573. doi:10.1016/j.jbusres.2018.11.012

Ang, I. (2005). Who needs cultural research? In P. Leistyna (Ed.), *Cultural Studies: From Theory to Action* (pp. 477–483). Blackwell. doi:10.4324/9780203990810

Banai, M., & Sama, L. A. (2000). Ethical dilemmas in MNCs' international staffing policies: A conceptual framework. *Journal of Business Ethics*, *25*(3), 221–235. doi:10.1023/A:1006079511331

Bonavita, A. (2009). La mobilité professionnelle en Europe: Témoignage d'une guide-interprète italienne à Paris. In F. X. Aligny, A. Guillaume, B. Nieder, F. Rastier, C. Tremblay, & H. Wismann (Eds.), *Plurilinguisme, Interculturalité et Emploi: Défis pour l'Europe* (pp. 89–92). L'Harmattan.

Boroditsky, L. (2010, July 24). Lost in Translation. *Wall Street Journal.*

Boroditsky, L. (2017). How language shapes the way we think. *TEDWomen 2017.* https://www.ted.com/talks/lera_boroditsky_how_language_shapes_the_way_we_think/up-next

Business Dictionary. (n.d.). http://www.businessdictionary.com/definition/expatriate.html

Deysine, A., & Duboin, J. (1995). *S'Internationaliser: Stratégies et Techniques.* Dalloz.

Dirlik, A. (2005). The Postcolonial Aura: Third World Criticism in the Age of Global Capitalism. In P. Leistyna (Ed.), *Cultural Studies: From Theory to Action* (pp. 29–55). Blackwell.

Earley, P. C., & Peterson, R. S. (2004). The elusive cultural chameleon: Cultural intelligence as a new approach to intercultural training for the global manager. *Academy of Management Learning & Education*, *3*(1), 100–115. doi:10.5465/amle.2004.12436826

Economist. (n.d.). https://www.economist.com/graphic-detail/2019/12/04/where-are-the-worlds-best-english-speakers

Engelen, A., & Tholen, E. (2014). *Interkulturelles Management*. Schäffer-Poeschel Verlag.

Eylon, D., & Au, Y. K. (1999). Exploring empowerment cross-cultural differences along the power distance dimension. *International Journal of Intercultural Relations*, *23*(3), 373–385. doi:10.1016/S0147-1767(99)00002-4

Feitosa, J., Kreutzer, C., Kramperth, A., Kramer, W. S., & Salas, E. (2014). Expatriate adjustment: Considerations for selection and training. *Journal of Global Mobility*, *2*(2), 134–159. doi:10.1108/JGM-06-2013-0042

Ferreira, A. I., Braun, T., & Sydow, J. (2013). Citizenship behavior in project-based organizing: Comparing German and Portuguese project managers. *International Journal of Human Resource Management*, *24*(20), 3772–3793. doi:10.1080/09585192.2013.777937

Ferreira, J. A. A. (2007). *Concepções de liderança excepcional em Portugal: Um estudo exploratório* (Unpublished Master Dissertation). University of Aveiro, Aveiro, Portugal.

Gesteland, R. R. (2005). *Cross-Cultural Business Behavior: Negotiating, Selling, Sourcing and Managing Across Cultures* (4th ed.). Business School Press.

Graf, A. (2004). *Interkulturelle Kompetenzen im Human Resource Management. Empirische Analyse konzeptioneller Grundfragen und der betrieblichen Relevanz*. Deutscher Universitäts-Verlag. doi:10.1007/978-3-322-82025-9

Hall, E. T. (1976). *Beyond Culture*. Anchor Books/Doubleday.

Hall, E. T., & Hall, M. R. (1990). *Understanding Cultural Differences: Germans, French and Americans*. Intercultural Press.

Harris, M. M., & Lievens, F. (2005). Selecting employees for global assignments: Can assessment centers measure cultural intelligence? In A. Rahim & R. T. Golembiewski (Eds.), *Current Topics in Management, 10* (pp. 221–240). Research Collection Lee Kong Chian School Of Business.

Hofstede, G. (1991). *Cultures and Organizations: Software of the Mind* (2nd ed.). McGraw-Hill.

Hofstede Insights. (n.d.a). *Country Comparison*. https://www.hofstede-insights.com/country-comparison/germany,portugal/

Hofstede Insights. (n.d.b). *Cultural Diversity*. https://news.hofstede-insights.com/news/why-is-managing-cultural-diversity-important

Hofstede Insights. (n.d.c). *Intercultural Management*. https://hi.hofstede-insights.com/intercultural-management-programmes

Hofstede Insights. (n.d.d). *National Culture*. https://hi.hofstede-insights.com/national-culture

House, R. J., Hanges, P. J., Javidan, M., Dorfman, P. W., & Gupta, V. (Eds.). (2004). *Culture, Leadership, and Organizations: The GLOBE Study of 62 Societies*. Sage.

Isidor, R., Schwens, C., & Kabst, R. (2011). Human resource management and early internationalization: Is there a leap-frogging in international staffing? *International Journal of Human Resource Management, 22*(10), 2167–2184. doi:10.1080/09585192.2011.580186

Jesuino, J. C. (2002). Latin Europe cluster: From South to North. *Journal of World Business, 37*(1), 81–89. doi:10.1016/S1090-9516(01)00076-1

Kivisto, P. (2002). *Multiculturalism in a Global Society*. Blackwell. doi:10.1002/9780470694916

Koch, E. (2012). *Interkulturelles Management: Für Führungspraxis, Projektarbeit und Kommunikation*. UVK Verlagsgesellschaft.

Lauginic, J.-M. (2009). L'efficacité entrepreneuriale passe par le plurilinguisme. In F. X. Aligny, A. Guillaume, B. Nieder, F. Rastier, C. Tremblay, & H. Wismann (Eds.), *Plurilinguisme, Interculturalité et Emploi: Défis pour l'Europe* (pp. 135–139). L'Harmattan.

Lexico. (n.d.). https://www.lexico.com/definition/expatriate

Loth, D. (2006). *Le management interculturel*. L'Harmattan.

Matas-Runquist, N. (2009). Une expérience plurilingue en milieu professionnel: L'anglais ne suffit pas! In F. X. Aligny, A. Guillaume, B. Nieder, F. Rastier, C. Tremblay, & H. Wismann (Eds.), *Plurilinguisme, Interculturalité et Emploi: Défis pour l'Europe* (pp. 156–161). L'Harmattan.

Morence, C., Esteves, M., Silva, N., & Moreira, A. C. (2020). Types and challenges of expatriation. In M. Khosrow-Pour (Ed.), *Encyclopedia of Organizational Knowledge, Administration, and Technologies*. IGI Global.

Ng, K.-Y., Van Dyne, L., & Ang, S. (2009). Developing global leaders: The role of international experience and cultural intelligence. *Advances in Global Leadership, 5*, 225–250. doi:10.1108/S1535-1203(2009)0000005013

Rego, A., & Cunha, M. P. (2010). Organisational Justice and Citizenship Behaviors: A Study in the Portuguese Cultural Context. *Applied Psychology, 29*(3), 404–430. doi:10.1111/j.1464-0597.2009.00405.x

Ribau, C. P., Moreira, A. C., & Raposo, M. (2018). SME internationalization research: Mapping the state of the art. *Canadian Journal of Administrative Sciences, 35*(2), 280–303. doi:10.1002/cjas.1419

Rodrigues, A., Lopes, R., Almeida, R., Coutinho, A., & Moreira, A. C. (2020). Challenges of the repatriation process. In M. Khosrow-Pour (Ed.), *Encyclopedia of Organizational Knowledge, Administration, and Technologies*. IGI Global.

Rodrigues, J. J. (2014). *Influência cultura portuguesa na cultura organizações estrangeiras em Portugal* (Unpublished Master Dissertation). University of Aveiro, Aveiro, Portugal.

Sambharya, R. B., Kumaraswamy, A., & Banerjee, S. (2005). Information technologies and the future of the multinational enterprise. *Journal of International Management, 11*(2), 143–161. doi:10.1016/j.intman.2005.03.005

Skutnabb-Kangas, T. (2009). Diversities or homogenization and dumbing-down: Some arguments. In F. X. Aligny, A. Guillaume, B. Nieder, F. Rastier, C. Tremblay, & H. Wismann (Eds.), *Plurilinguisme, Interculturalité et Emploi: Défis pour l'Europe* (pp. 105–109). L'Harmattan.

Smith, M., & Zagelmeyer, S. (2010). Working time management and SME performance in Europe. *International Journal of Manpower, 31*(4), 392–409. doi:10.1108/01437721011056994

Sousa, C., Gonçalves, G., Reis, M., & Santos, J. V. (2015). Evidências métricas da adaptação da escala de inteligência cultural numa amostra portuguesa. *Psychology. Psicologia: Reflexão e Crítica, 28*(2), 232–241. doi:10.1590/1678-7153.201528203

Standifer, R. L., Raes, A. M. L., Peus, C., Passos, A. M., Marques Santos, C., & Weisweiler, S. (2014). Time in teams: Cognitions, conflict and team satisfaction. *Journal of Managerial Psychology, 30*(6), 692–708. doi:10.1108/JMP-09-2012-0278

Trompenaars, F., & Woolliams, P. (2004). *Marketing Across Cultures*. Capstone Publishing.

Varner, I., & Beamer, L. (2005). *Intercultural Communication in the Global Workplace* (3rd ed.). Irwin.

Vlajčića, D., Caputo, A., Marzi, G., & Dabića, M. (2019). Expatriates managers' cultural intelligence as promoter of knowledge transfer in multinational companies. *Journal of Business Research, 94*, 367–377. doi:10.1016/j.jbusres.2018.01.033

Wild, J. J., Wild, K. L., & Han, J. C. Y. (2006). *International Business: The Challenges of Globalization* (3rd ed.). Pearson Education.

Williams, R. (1983). *Keywords: A Vocabulary of Culture and Society*. Oxford University Press.

World Trade Organization. (2019). *World Trade Statistical Review 2019*. https://www.wto.org/english/res_e/statis_e/miwi_e/miwi_e.htm

KEY TERMS AND DEFINITIONS

Cultural Intelligence: The capability to understand and interpret verbal and nonverbal messages as meant by the counterpart of a foreign culture and act accordingly and appropriately to local standards.

Cultural Training: A program offered by a company to increase cultural intelligence of its employees in order to prepare them for international working environments.

Culture: The unconscious and constantly evolving set of personal characteristics that differentiate a person from a certain social group from another.

Expatriate: A person who works abroad for a defined period of time.

Expatriation: A staffing policy applied by international companies to maintain control and implement organizational culture in foreign subsidiaries by sending a current employee from the home-office.

Intercultural Management: The development, implementation, and control of processes and practices within a culturally diverse team in order to reach previously defined goals.

Project Citizenship Behavior: A sense of belonging to a project and its team triggering loyalty and supportive behavior, which fosters a strong sense of teamwork.

Chapter 9
International Effect on Family SME Financial Distress Prediction

Ines Lisboa
https://orcid.org/0000-0003-2802-2589
CARME, School of Technology and Management, Polytechnic Institute of Leiria, Portugal

Magali Costa
CEFAGE, School of Technology and Management, Polytechnic Institute of Leiria, Portugal

EXECUTIVE SUMMARY

Understanding the reasons of default risk is crucial to avoid the firm's bankruptcy. The purpose of this work is to analyze the impact of internationalization on firm's probability of distress. For it, this chapter aims to propose a model to predict default specific to family SMEs (small and medium enterprises). An unbalanced panel of 10,832 firms over the period from 2012-2018 is analyzed. Ex-ante criteria to classify firms in default or compliant is used. International SMEs have lower probability of default than domestic firms, and compliant firms export more. Results show that export ratio is an important determinant of the probability of default. Moreover, the ratios of liquidity, profitability, size, leverage, efficiency, cash flow, and age are also relevant. Moreover, these ratios explain default risk of both groups international and domestic SMEs. The proposed model has an accuracy of 92.9%, which increases to 95.6% if only export SMEs are analyzed.

INTRODUCTION

Globalization has brought several challenges that a firm has to face today. It includes increased pressure and global competition that has forced many firms to look for new business opportunities. Firms have moved from competing locally to competing worldwide (Roy, Sekhar, & Vyas, 2016). Globalization has led to a change in corporate strategies, which have come to view going abroad as a growth and survival strategy, especially when domestic markets are tight.

DOI: 10.4018/978-1-7998-4387-0.ch009

Singh, Pathak, and Naz (2010) consider that firms internationalize to surpass the disadvantages of operating only in the domestic market. According to these authors, these disadvantages are namely the domestic market saturation and the increased competition, especially critical for SMEs.

The internationalization brings diverse opportunities as firms can increase their sales volume, benefiting from cost efficiency and economies of scale, and reduce the risk to sell only to one country (Gupta, Wilson, Gregoriou, & Healy, 2014). Firms can also benefit from tax saving and can have easier access to capital, particularly when it comes to integrated financial markets. Although, internationalization also brings some uncertainties, not only because firms are exposed to multiple political environments and foreign exchange risk, but also because their financial needs are different (Arslan & Karan, 2009), which can impact the firm's probability of distress.

Firm size has always been considered to play an important and decisive role for a firm to decide to internationalize. However, with globalization, the SMEs also felt the need to internationalize to assure the business success and growth (Roy et al., 2016). In fact, SME are more vulnerable not only to globalization, but also to the speed of technological change and the scarcity of resources (Valentim, Lisboa, & Franco, 2016).The point is that these firms have capital and often knowledge constraints that affect the internationalization process and the potential benefits.

Family firms are a specific group of firms, with singular characteristics that also have some constrains and benefits that can influence its internationalization process. Basly (2007) argues that family firms' internationalization depends on its tolerance to external financial intervention. These firms have valuable knowledge that is passed down from generation to generation which can help in the internationalization process.

In this context, given the advantages and disadvantages of internationalization and the particularities of family SMEs, this chapter aims: 1) to define a way to classify distress specific to SMEs, that can be used by future researchers; 2) to establish a model to predict financial distress accurate to family SMEs; 3) to analyze the impact of internationalization on firm's probability of distress.

Ex-ante criteria are used to classify firms in solvent or distress. A Logit model is applied to develop the distress prediction model for family SMEs. Eight financial ratios (liquidity; profitability; size; indebtedness; efficiency; cash flows; age; and exports intensity) are analyzed. A sample of Portuguese SMEs, more precisely from Leiria region, over the period from 2012 till 2018 is studied. It is a non-balanced panel data analysis over 10,832 non-financial SMEs.

In 2017, Portugal was the 44° world country with more exportations (OEC, 2019). Moreover, in 2015, exports represented 40% of the Gross Domestic Product (AICEP, 2016). Hence, understanding the effect of internationalization is particularly relevant for Portuguese firms.

There is an extensive empirical literature on detecting firm's default risk (e.g. Altman, 1968; Ohlson, 1980; Altman, Iwanicz-Drozdowska, Laitinen, & Suvas, 2017). Although, most studies focus on public or large size firms, and not include the impact of internationalization. SMEs represent the majority of firms all over the world and correspond to two-third of the total employment (Gupta et al., 2014). In Portugal, SMEs represent 99.9% of Portuguese firms (Pordata, 2020a). Moreover, the sample focuses on a specific group of SMEs, family-owned firms. Family firms are around 70%-80% of Portuguese firms (Felicidade, 2019) and about 90% of firms from Leiria region (Lisboa, 2019a).

This work contributes to the literature in several aspects. Namely in the literature on SMEs by analyzing the impact of internationalization on the distress risk of family SMEs in the Portuguese market. Few studies focus on the analysis of this impact, but conclusions are relevant to help managers and shareholders on their decision-making process. Particularly, it is important to analyze if the internationalization decision/process will work as an engine of financial sustainability or if, on the contrary, it will increase the default probability due to the investment required. The impact of internationalization is not only analyzed through the ratio of percentage of export sales, but also, the impact of export sales to European and non-European countries as the risk to export for these markets is singular. Moreover, the main differences with regards to factors that explain default risk of international firms and the ones that only sell to the domestic market. The final sample is divided into two: firms that export (international) and firms that only sell to the domestic market (domestic), to detect the main differences regarding default probabilities when a firm decide to internationalize. Studies analyzing this impact are almost inexistent. Furthermore, a homogeneous group is analyzed, family-owned firms, which allow a deeper knowledge about this specific firms. Family firms have singular characteristics which make them apart from non-family ones, so to understand this specific group of firms is crucial.

An ex-ante criterion of default is used in order to classify firms in distress or compliant. This work uses criteria adapted to SMEs, namely the criteria purposed by SIREVE (Company' Recovery System through Extrajudicial Agreements) which is a set of procedures that aim to recover firms through a non-judicial way. An ex-ante approach allows to detect and correct situations of default before the firm's failure. Then, the factors that specifically explain distress probability of family SMEs are detected. Therefore, family SMEs can understand which factors may lead to distress, in order to control them and promote the firm's solvency.

This chapter is organized into six sections. After this first introductory section, the second one presents a theoretical context, followed by the sample characterization and the description of the methodology and variables to be used in the analysis of default risk. In section four the results are discussed. The main conclusions are presented after it, and in the last section future lines of research are addressed.

LITERATURE REVIEW

Default risk is the probability of a firm not being able to meet its debt covenants (Ashraf, Félix, & Serrasqueiro, 2019). It is not a persistent situation as the bankruptcy risk, when a firm no longer has financial recovery. Default risk can be related with a punctual lack of liquidity or the difficulty to obtain credit in a moment (CIRE, 2019).

To identify if a firm is in default there are diverse methods, which can be divided into two groups: ex-post and ex-ante criteria. An ex-post criterion is usually related with the legal classification. Altman (1968), Ohlson (1980), Blums (2003), Martinho and Antunes (2012), and Altman, Iwanicz-Drozdowska, Laitinen and Suvas (2017) used this approach. Although, this criterion depends on the country analyzed, since the legislation may be different. Moreover, it may change through the years to be adapted to the market changes (Pindado & Rodrigues, 2005; Tinoco & Wilson, 2013).

An ex-ante criterion allows firms to identify financial problems and to make decisions to surpass difficulties, avoiding the probability of bankruptcy. Pindado, Rodrigues, and de la Torre (2008) consider that a firm has financial problems if, during two consecutive years, EBITDA (Earnings before interests, taxes, depreciations and amortizations) is smaller than interest expenses, and the firm's market value decreases. To Rosner (2003), a firm has financial problems when has: a) negative working capital in the current year, b) negative earnings before interests and taxes in one of the three years before bankruptcy, c) negative retained earnings in the third year previous to bankruptcy, or d) negative net profit in one of the three years before bankruptcy. Nagar and Sen (2018) added to these criteria an additional one e) negative earnings before interests and taxes in the last two consecutive years. To Salloum, Schmitt, and Bouri (2012) a firm has financial problems when net profit divided by interests expenses in less than 0.8.

In Portugal, in the year of 2012, and with the aim to help firms to recover from financial problems, the Government creates the program SIREVE (Company' Recovery System through Extrajudicial Agreements). This program was in effect until 2018. It was created for non-distress firms, it means, firms with probability of recovery. Compliant firms are the ones that, in the previous three years had: a) capital ratio greater than 5%, b) earnings before interests, taxes, depreciations and amortizations greater than 1.3 of interest expenses, c) net debt ratio greater than 0 and smaller than 10. Every ratio should be fulfilled at least in one of the three previous years, and 50% of all possible combinations should be meet every year. These criteria can be applied to SME and are more demanding than the previous criteria listed.

Using one of these criteria, firms are classified as default or compliant firms. Then, the prediction model will validate this classification of firms. Two errors can occur: Type I, which happens when the form is in default and is classified by the model as a compliant firm; Type II, which occurs when a compliant firm is classified as being in default (Lin, 2009).

In the literature there are several prediction models. Although, there is no ideal model. Beaver, in 1966, has created a univariate model to predict the firm's bankruptcy from one to five years before it happens. From an initial list of thirty ratios, the author identified five with greater prediction power. The success rate of the model was 87% in the year before bankruptcy and 78% in the analysis made five years before it. Although, analyzing individual ratios can lead to some misreading interpretation.

In 1968, Altman, using de multiple discriminant analysis statistic model, detect the five ratios that greater explain the firm's probability of bankruptcy. The model created was known as Z-score. It was created to listed firms, and its success rate was 95% for the year previous to bankruptcy and 83% for two years before. Based on the Altman's z-score model, two new versions were created: Z'-score (Altman, 1983), which was adapted to unlisted firms, and Z''-score (Altman, 1983), that was adapter to different industries. In 1977, Altman, Haldeman and Narayanan have adapted the Z-score model to increase its success rate for two years before bankruptcy. The developed Zeta model considers the size effect, the stability of earnings and the debt service to predict the firm's bankruptcy.

The Z-score and the Zeta models use multiple discriminant analysis statistic model. Although for it is needed to have a group of bankruptcy and compliant firms with similar characteristics, which is very difficult to obtain. To surpass this problem, Ohlson (1980) suggests the use of the logit regression technique. The author detects four ratios to predict bankruptcy probability and achieved 96% of success rate. In 1984, Zmijewsky suggests the use of the probit regression technique, that has similar attributes as the logit model. Although, the probit is more difficult to apply due to its complexity.

The Hazard model was proposed, in 2001, by Shumway. The author has combined different accounting ratios and market variables and reaches a success rate of 75%.In 2003, Blums created the D-Score using the notional theory. This model had a success rate of 90%.

Later on, diverse researchers have adapted these models, including other ratios in order to predict bankruptcy. Table 1 shows a synthesis of the main determinants of default risk used by researchers and that can be applied to SME. These determinants are subdivided in groups: liquidity, profitability, size, leverage, efficiency, financial expenses, and exports intensity.

The first group of variables is liquidity, and it is expected that liquidity has a negative impact on the default probability, i.e. the lower the firm's liquidity, the higher its default probability. A firm may have more difficulties in fulfill its debt covenants when it has insufficient current assets (Mselmi et al.,

Table 1. Determinants of default risk: expected impact, proxies and main studies

Variables	Expected Impact	Proxies	Main References
Liquidity	-/+	WC_t / TA_t CA_t / CD_t CA_t / TA_t (Cash and Equivalents$_t$) / CD_t CD_t / CA_t	Alaminos, Del Castillo, and Fernandez (2016); Altman (1968); Altman et al. (1977); Altman (1983); Beaver (1966); Cheng, Su and Li (2009); Gottardo and Moisello (2017); Lin (2009); Mselmi, Lahiani and Hamza (2017); Ohlson (1980); Zmijewski (1984)
Profitability	-	$EBITDA_t / TA_t$ $EBIT_t / TA_t$ $EBIT_t / RVC_{t-1}$ RE_t / TA_t RE_t / RVC_{t-1} NI_t / TA_t	Alaminos et al. (2016); Altman (1968); Altman (1983); Altman et al. (1977); Altman and Sabato (2007); Beaver (1966); Blums (2003); Gottardo and Moisello (2017); Gupta et al. (2014); Lin (2009); Lohe and Calabrò (2017); Martinho and Antunes (2012); Manzaneque et al. (2016); Pindado et al. (2008); Ohlson (1980); Shumway (2001); Zmijewski (1984).
Size	+/-	$Ln (TA_t)$	Altman et al. (1977); Donker, Santen, and Zahir (2009); Gottardo and Moisello (2017).
Leverage	+/-	D_t / TA_t D_t / E_t NCD_t / TA_t E_t / D_t E_t / TA_t	Alaminos et al. (2016); Beaver (1966); Cheng et al. (2009); Donker et al. (2009); Gottardo and Moisello (2017); Lin (2009); Md-Rus, Mohd, Latif, and Alassan (2013); Mselmi et al. (2017); Ohlson (1980); Salloum et al. (2012); Shumway (2001); Tinoco and Wilson (2013); Udin, Khan, and Javid (2017); Zmijewski (1984).
Efficiency	-	S_t / TA_t	Alaminos et al. (2016); Altman (1968); Altman (1983); Lin (2009); Martinho and Antunes (2012).
Interest Expenses	+/-	IE_t / RVC_{t-1} $EBITDA_t / IE_t$	Altman et al. (1977); Altman and Sabato (2007); Gupta et al. (2014); Manzaneque et al. (2016); Pindado et al. (2008); Tinoco and Wilson (2013).
Cash Flow	-	OCF_t / D_t CF_t / TA_t	Beaver (1966); Ohlson (1980); Tinoco and Wilson (2013).
Age	+/-	$Ln(Age_t)$	Chancharat, Tina, Davy, MacGrae, and Lodh (2010)
Exports	+/-	$Export_t/S_t$	Arslan and Karan (2009), Gupta et al. (2014)

CA– Current Asset; CD – Current Debt; D– Total Debt; E – Equity; EBITDA – Earnings before Interest, Taxes, Depreciation and Amortization; EBIT – Earnings before Interest, and Taxes; GDP – gross domestic product; IE – Interest Expenses; OCF –Operating Cash Flow; NCD – Noncurrent Debt; NI – Net Income; RE –Retained Earnings; S – Sales; TA –Total Asset; WC – Working Capital

Source: Own Source

2017). A positive impact is expected to the variable CD/CA since it is the inverse of the current ratio (liquidity ratio).

Regarding profitability, higher values mean that the firm is generating profits that can be used to pay its credits. Therefore, a negative sign is expected (Blums, 2003).

The firm's size can have an ambiguous impact in the probability of default. Smaller firms have higher probability of default since they have more difficulties to lead to market changes (Chancharat et al., 2010). On the other hand, large-size firms can have communication problems, which can lead to financial problems.

More indebt leads to an increase of default probability since firms need to pay interest expenses and have a higher financial risk (Tinoco & Wilson, 2013). When leverage is measured by total equity divided by total liabilities the expected sign is the inverse.

Regarding efficiency, the higher the firm's efficiency the smallest the probability of default, since the firm managed assets in a properly way (Brito & Neto, 2008).

The higher the firm's interest expenses the greater the probability of default since the firm must generate more earnings to pay this cost (Pindado et al., 2008). The opposite sign is expected when the ratio of EBITDA divided by interest expenses is used.

Firms with higher free cash flow have lower probability of default since have more cash and similar to pay its credits (Tinoco & Wilson, 2013).

The firm age has an ambiguous impact on the probability of default (Lohe & Calabrò, 2017). For one side, new firm have not enough knowledge about the market and may have difficulties in adapt the business to the market changes. For another side, old firms can be in a maturity lifecycle, having difficulties to increase its market share, which can lead to annual losses and financial difficulties. Some researchers, as Costa (2016) and Pérez, Llopis, and Llopis (2010) found a non-linear effect with regards to age.

The impact of internationalization on firm's risk of default is less explored in the literature. Although, the internationalization affects the firm's performance and its capital structure, so it is expected to also affect the probability of default. The decision of internationalize is a high-risk decision (Pacheco, 2016). Internationalization can bring more additional costs, not only transportation costs, but also due to foreign exchange. SMEs have problems to finance at a low-cost capital, and this situation persist in its internationalization process (Roy et al., 2016). Moreover, internationalization increases the business' volatility, at least in the beginning, since the firm as few knowledges about the market, the culture and competition (Lisboa, 2019b). The multiple political and financial frameworks can also increase the firm's risk (Arslan & Karan, 2009). Additionally, firms can have some problems to collect payment on time from a far-off country (Roy et al., 2016). Although, on the other hand the internationalization allows firms to diversify their revenues, and increase its cash flows, which can decrease the firm's risk, and the default risk as well (Gupta et al., 2014). Moreover, these firms can benefit from economies of scale, costs efficiency due to high production volume, and tax savings. They can also have easier access to capital (Lisboa, 2019b). Finally, SMEs benefit from knowledge management practices, which are transferred to all in the firm, which helps to launch new products and services, new markets or new opportunities (Valentim et al., 2016). This situation is more evident in family firms since these group is known for their long-term relationship between all stakeholders, the commitment of employees and the celerity in the decision-making process (Lisboa, 2019a).

METHODOLOGY

Sample

The sample analyzes Portuguese family SME for the Leiria Region. Portugal is a small-size country almost unexplored. It is an interesting case study regarding default risk, since with the international crisis of 2007/2008, the country had some solvency problems, with an increase in the public deficit. Diverse firms went to bankruptcy and others had serious financial problems. From 2008 till 2012 the firms' death rate was superior than its birth rate (in 2010 the difference between the 2 rates was around 3.4%). The death rate achieves its high value in 2011 (around 16%), and only after 2012, the Portuguese economy have started to recovery from this crisis (Pordata, 2020b).

SMEs were chosen since this type of firms represent around 99.9% of the Portuguese firms (Pordata, 2020a). The classification of SME follows the European Union classification, i.e., firms with annual sales less than 50 million and with less than 250 employees.

Moreover, this work analyzes a specific group of firms: family firms. This type of firms represents around 70%-80% of Portuguese firms (Felicidade, 2019), and around 90% of firms in the Leiria Region (Lisboa, 2019a).

Leiria region was selected since this region, although being the 16th largest Portuguese region, was, in 2017 (last year with data available), the 4th region with higher gross domestic product per habitant (INE, 2020). This region has valuable natural resources, a diversified sector structure, focused on innovation and exports. In 2018, Leiria Region was the 7th region with the highest contribution to Portuguese exports. Moreover, the ratio of exports over imports was 134%, whether the national average was 77% (Pordata, 2020c). Although, not all firms and industries export. For this reason, the final sample is divided into two subsamples: international firms, which include all firms that export, and domestic firms, firms whose turnover is achieved in the domestic market. This division aims to see if both groups have singularities regarding default risk.

The sample is analyzed from 2012 till 2018. 2012 was the year when the SIREVE was implemented in Portugal (criteria used to classify firms in default or compliant).

All data was collected from SABI Databases, from Bureau Van Dijk. To select family firms, we consider firms whose shareholders have more than 25% of the firm shares. This criterion follows the one used by Kristanti, Rahayu, and Huda (2016). There are several classifications of family firms, but the more relevant factors are ownership and impact in the firm's management. In Leiria, most of the firms are family firms and have the family ownership concentration as it was found by Lisboa (2019a).

To be in the sample, firms need to have at least four consecutive years with information. Moreover, outliers were deleted to avoid biases in the analysis. The final sample is an unbalanced panel data of 10,832 firms.

Proposed Model

In this work, the logit regression model was used since previous researchers, as Altman and Sabato (2007) and Pindado *et al.* (2008), argued that has a better performance than multiple discriminant analysis. A panel data methodology was applied to eliminate unobservable heterogeneity, to solve the problem of choosing the estimation year before default, and to increase the accuracy of the model (Costa, 2016, Pindado & Rodrigues, 2005, Pindado et al., 2008).

Variables

Dependent Variables

The dependent variable is a binary variable, which is 1 if the firm is in default and 0 if it is a compliant firm. To do this classification we followed the criteria proposed by SIREVE, it means: a firm is classified as compliant if the following criteria are meet at least once in the last three years previous to classification, and at least every year 50% of possible combinations are met:

1. capital ratio is greater than 5%;
2. earnings before interests, taxes, amortizations and depreciations is greater than 1.3 of interests expenses;
3. net debt ratio is greater than 0 and smaller than 10.

Independent Variables

The independent variables were selected from the list of variables presented in table 1.

RESULTS

Sample Characterization

Table 2 presents the percentage of default and compliant firms per year subdividing by international and domestic firms.

Table 2. Firms Classification

Year	2012	2013	2014	2015	2016	2017	2018	Mean
Panel 1: Default Firms								
International	7.44%	7.75%	7.77%	6.84%	5.51%	5.23%	4.88%	6.37%
Domestic	12.35%	11.32%	11.21%	10.25%	9.01%	8.53%	7.55%	9.86%
Total	**11.19%**	**10.44%**	**10.34%**	**9.22%**	**7.95%**	**7.61%**	**6.88%**	**8.93%**
Panel 2: Compliant Firms								
International	92.56%	92.25%	92.23%	93.16%	94.49%	94.77%	95.12%	93.63%
Domestic	87.65%	88.68%	88.79%	89.75%	90.99%	91.47%	92.45%	90.14%
Total	**88.81%**	**89.56%**	**89.66%**	**90.78%**	**92.05%**	**92.39%**	**93.12%**	**91.07%**

Source: Own Source

Analyzing table 2, it can be concluded that the percentage of compliant family SMEs is higher than the percentage of default. However, there is a downward trend in the number of default firms. The recovery program SIREVE was applied from 2012 till 2018, which can explain the decrease of the percentage of default firms. Moreover, from the year of 2013/2014, the Portuguese economy began to recover from the international crisis of 2007/2008.

Analyzing international and domestic firms, it can be concluded that exporting firms are able to more easily fulfill their obligations. The percentage of compliant international firms is greater than those of non-exporting firms. Moreover, both groups of compliant firms have increase since 2014.

In table 3 the descriptive statistics for both groups (default and compliant) are presented. The variables selected were obtained in the stepwise method and through the analysis of the correlation matrix. The variables chosen are the ones that better explain default risk of this sample. From the group of variables presented in table 1, only variables that measure interest expenses are not determinants of the probability of default.

Additionally, the Mann-Whitney Test (MW) nonparametric test was performed to test if the medians for both groups of firms are equal.

Regarding the variable that measure the firm's liquidity (CD/CA), default companies exhibit higher values. Note that the higher the value of this variable, the lower the liquidity, since it is the inverse of the current ratio. When firm's liquidity is low, the firm has more difficulty to fulfil debt obligations, since

Table 3. Descriptive statistics

Variables		Group of Firms	Mean	Median	SD	Min.	Max.	MW Test
Liquidity	CD/CA	Default	2.664	0.999	13.529	0.000	744.732	0.000
		Compliant	0.828	0.526	4.245	0.000	341.966	
Profitability	EBITDA/TA	Default	-0.067	0.003	0.728	-30.088	9.472	0.000
		Compliant	0.098	0.081	0.139	-12.238	1.952	
	RE/TA	Default	-1.260	-0.373	5.576	-233.580	0.965	0.000
		Compliant	0.192	0.188	0.366	-9.134	0.996	
Size	Ln(TA)	Default	12.162	12.024	1.634	7.262	20.776	0.000
		Compliant	13.052	12.904	1.469	6.958	20.530	
Leverage	D/TA	Default	1.727	1.063	4.384	0.000	185.441	0.000
		Compliant	0.580	0.606	0.231	0.000	7.196	
	D/E	Default	5.062	-1.522	40.650	-200.911	492.099	0.000
		Compliant	2.615	1.530	5.751	-123.888	341.350	
Efficiency	S/TA	Default	125.223	81.147	147.939	0.000	1067.227	0.000
		Compliant	116.934	96.969	98.647	0.000	1092.101	
Cash Flow	CF/D	Default	-0.084	-0.010	2.109	-129.547	2.457	0.000
		Compliant	0.218	0.107	0.933	-20.602	46.942	
Age	Age	Default	14.857	13.000	10.296	2.000	94.000	0.000
		Compliant	17.360	15.000	11.110	2.000	129.000	
Exportation Intensity	%EXP	Default	0.048	0.000	0.174	0.000	1.000	0.000
		Compliant	0.107	0.000	0.244	0.000	1.000	

CA: current assets; CD: current debt; CF: Cash Flow, D: Debt, E: Equity; %EXP: Percentage of exportation, EBITDA: earnings before depreciation amortization, interests and taxes, RE: Retained Earnings;, S: Sales, TA: Total Asset.

Source: Own Source

the amount of payables is too high, which leads to an increase in the probability of default. The median difference among the two groups is also significant.

At a profitability level (EBITDA/TA and RE/TA) default firms present negative values, in mean, contrary to compliant firms. This result suggests that less profitable firms have difficulties in generating earnings and, therefore, in meet financial obligations, which in turn leads to an increase in its distress. The medians of both groups are significantly different, as it can be observed in the Mann-Whitney test.

Analyzing size (ln(TA)), default firms are smaller than compliant firms, in mean (12.162 vs 13.052). Smaller firms have more difficulties in surpass financial problems since these firms have more difficulties in adapted to changes in the market and the business.

Default firms are more indebted (D/TA and D/E), and the indebtedness is statistically different between the two groups. Higher leverage leads to an increase of default probability since firms need to pay interest expenses and have a higher financial risk.

Despite default firms present higher efficiency ratio (S/TA) mean, in terms of median they can be considered less efficient. Compliant firms are so better managers of their assets. This is reflected in the cash flows available for payment of debts. Default firms present a lower cash flow ratio, and the difference between groups is statistically significant, as it can be observed in the Mann-Whitney test.

Default firms are, in mean, younger than those of compliant firms (15 vs 17 years), suggesting that younger firms have higher probability of default due to the lack of enough experience about the market. The median difference is significative among both groups which means that the age between default and compliant is statistic different.

The U Mann-Whitney test allow us to verify the impact of internationalization on firm's probability of distress, namely if default and compliant firms have different exportation intensity.

By analyzing Table 3 we can conclude that compliant companies have, in mean, a higher export ratio (0.048 vs 0.107).

Model

In order to analyze if the internationalization, using the exportation intensity variable, is an important determinant of the probability of default, the model presented in equation 1 was tested by running a panel data. All relevant variables were used in the estimation according to the stepwise method and to the correlations' analysis (Model 1) as shown in the following equation:

$$P = \left(1 + \exp\left\{-\begin{bmatrix}\beta_0 + \beta_1 X_1 + \beta_2 X_2 + \beta_3 X_3 + \beta_4 X_4 + \beta_5 X_5 + \beta_6 X_6 \\ +\beta_7 X_7 + \beta_8 X_8 + \beta_9 X_9 + \beta_{10} X_{10} + \beta_{11} X_{11}\end{bmatrix}\right\}^{-1}\right) \quad (1)$$

With

$$X_1 = \frac{CD_t}{CA_t}; X_2 = \frac{EBITDA_t}{TA_t}; X_3 = \frac{RE_t}{TA_t}; X_4 = Ln(TA_t);$$
$$X_5 = \frac{D_t}{TA_t}; X_6 = \frac{D_t}{E_t};\ X_7 = \frac{S_t}{TA_t}; X_8 = \frac{CF_t}{TA_t};$$
$$X_9 = Ln(age_t); X_{10} = Ln(age_t)^2; X_{11} = \%Exp$$

In which: CA: Current Asset; CD: Current Debt; CF: Cash Flow; D: Debt; E: Equity; %Exp: Percentage of exports; RR: Retained Earnings; S: Sales; TA: Total Asset.

An analysis was carried out by group, namely using international firms (Model 2) and domestic firms (Model 3) in order to verify whether the determinants remained the same.

The results of the proposed model to predict default are shown in table 4.

Table 4. Results of the final proposed model

	Expected Sign	Model 1 Total	Model 2 International	Model 3 Domestic
Constant		−9.800 ***	−4.348***	−4.946***
CD/CA	-/+	0.008**	0.274 ***	0.003
EBITDA/TA	-	−1.518***	0.605	−1.422 ***
RE/TA	-	−1.106***	−2.082***	−1.086***
Ln(TA)	+/-	−0.114***	−0.250 ***	0.011
D/TA	+/-	6.437***	9.237***	6.538***
D/E	+/-	0.004***	0.007***	0.003***
S/TA	-	−0.002***	−0.002***	−0.002***
CF/TA	-	−0.465**	−2.196***	−0.817***
Ln(Age)	+/-	−1.362***	−1.787 ***	−1.336 ***
$Ln(Age)^2$	-	0.282***	0.379***	0.275***
%EXP	+/-	−0.741***	−0.279*	
No. Observ.		27,864	9,549	18,942
McFadden R^2		55.33%	56.39%	53.74%
Adjusted R^2		55.23%	56.01%	53.63%

*** Significant at level 1%; ** Significant at level 5%; * Significant at level 10%;

CA: current assets; CF: Cash Flow, D: Debt, E: Equity; %EXP: Percentage of exportation, EBITDA: earnings before depreciation amortization, interests and taxes, NCD: Noncurrent Debt, RE: Retained Earnings, S: Sales, TA: Total Asset.

Source: Own Source

McFadden R^2 and Adjusted R^2 are higher than 50%, a higher value than the one found by Donker *et al.* (2009), Manzaneque *et al.* (2016), and Uddin *et al.* (2017), which proves the accuracy of the model.

Analyzing results of model 1, we can conclude that all the determinants present the expected impact. Regarding liquidity ratio, since the CD/CA ratio was used, a positive relationship was found, which is line with Blums (2003) and Mselmi et al. (2017). The regression estimation results show that less liquidity leads to higher probability of default since a firm may have more difficulties in fulfill its debt obligations.

The EBITDA/TA and RE/TA variables, which measures the firm's profitability, have a negative impact to explain firms' probability of default. This result is similar with those obtain by Brito and Neto (2008), and Lin (2009). Lower earnings and, in turn retained earnings, mean that firms were not efficient in generating results in the past, and thus have more difficulties in fulfil financial obligations. This is related to efficiency and the creation of cash flows, both with negative impact. Since firms that are unable to properly manage their assets (low efficiency), will not be able to obtain cash flows that it will allow them to meet their obligations so they will be more likely to default. This result is in line with Tinoco and Wilson (2013) conclusion.

Smaller firms (Ln (TA)) have higher default probability since they have not enough experience and knowledge about the market and have more difficulties to adapt to new business models or market demands (Chancharat, 2008). Moreover, large-size firms have more collateral that can be used in case of failure.

Total indebtedness, measured by D/TA and D/E, have a positive impact in the probability of default. More indebt firms may find more difficult to repay contract obligations, leading to a greater probability of failure. Similar results were found by Tinoco and Wilson (2013).

Age presents an U-shape relationship to explain the probability of default. Younger firms have higher probability of default as these firms have less experience and resilience, less retained earnings, which lead to more difficulties in meeting financial obligations (Altman, 1968). Although, as firms acquire more experience, their adaption to market and business changes, and so the probability of distress decreases (Pérez et al., 2010). After a certain age, older firms have more difficulties to change older habits and to do a financial restructure when it is needed. This in turn leads to an increase in financial problems

The internationalization negatively impacts the default risk, which means that, when a firm diversify their revenues, increasing the exportation intensity, the default risk decreases (Gupta et al., 2014). Valentim et al. (2016) argument that Portuguese SMEs use their management practice knowledge in their new opportunities to achieve its goal. In fact, internationalizations bring advantages to firms that prevail, given possible disadvantages, namely economies of scale, costs efficiency, tax savings and better capital access conditions (Lisboa, 2019b). This result proves that SMEs internationalization assures the business growth and survival, as argued by Roy *et al.* (2016).

We also analyze if exports to European or other countries have different impact in default risk. Although results prove that the effect is the same, meaning that exports intensity, independent on the countries to whether the company exports, decreases the probability of default. These additional results are available upon request.

When the sample is subdivided into two: firms that internationalize and the others, results show that the factors and its impact on default risk to international SMEs is similar to those of domestic firms. Similar results were found by Gupta *et al.* (2014) who suggest that these groups should not be analyzed in separate when modelling risk. The exceptions are with regards to liquidity (CD/CA), and size (ln(A)), which are not relevant factors to explain default risk of domestic firms, and EBITDA/TA which is not a relevant factor to international SME.

Table 5 presents the success rate of the model, exhibiting errors Type I and Type II.

The estimated model has a success rate of 92.9%, which is similar of those found by the original model of Altman z-score model (1968) – 95%, and the Ohlson O-score (1980) – 96%. Moreover, it is greater than the success rate of Gupta *et al.* (2014) - 65% that also analyze the impact of internationaliza-

Table 5. Success rate of final proposed model

			Prevision Model		Total	Correct Percentage
			Compliant	Default		
Actual Position	Compliant	**Total**	**22,427**	**269**	**22,696**	**92,9%**
		International	8,517	63	8,580	95,9%
		Domestic	14,160	276	14,436	91,8%
	Default	**Total**	**1,716**	**3,452**	**5,168**	**92,8%**
		International	360	609	969	90,6%
		Domestic	1,268	3,238	4,506	92,1%
	Total	**Total**	**24,143**	**3,721**	**27,864**	**92,9%**
		International	8,877	672	9,549	95,6%
		Domestic	15,428	3,514	18,942	91,8%

Source: Own Source

tion. The model classifies better international compliant firms and domestic default companies, which represents a small error Type 1 and Type 2.

CONCLUSION

This chapter aims to analyze the impact of exports intensity on the firm's probability of default. A default model specific to family SMEs was proposed to understand which factors contribute to increase the firm's risk of distress. For it, an unbalance panel data of 10,832 family SMEs from Leiria region - Portugal, over the period from 2012 till 2018, was analyzed.

First, we use ex-ante criteria to classify firms in distress or compliant firms. This type of criteria helps to understand the firm's financial situation before situation of bankruptcy. Results show that there are more compliant firms, and over the period the percentage of compliant firms increased. Moreover, export firms have less probability of default, than firms that only sell to the domestic market. This result suggests that family SMEs internationalization is to assure the business growth and financial sustainability.

Then, to predict the more accurate variables to explain default risk, the stepwise analysis was used. From the initial list of variables, 13 variables were selected, but due to high correlation between two variables, the final model includes 11 variables, the ones with the highest prediction power to explain firm's probability of default. The prediction model of default risk, specific to family SMEs was established.

Results prove that exports intensity is relevant to explain firm's default risk. Few works include this variable to explain firm's probability of default risk, but our results prove its relevance. International firm have their risk more diversified, which reduces the default risk. Exporting to European or other countries has the same impact on default risk. Although, the variables used to explain default risk of export SMEs is similar to those of domestic SMEs, suggesting that these two groups can be analyzed together regarding risk.

The determinants that were important in determining the default probability of family SMEs present the expected impact. The analysis of liquidity, profitability, efficiency, age, indebtedness is crucial to the success of a firm. A firm with low liquidity and profitability, with higher indebtedness, which has efficiency problems, and which consequently cannot generate cash flows will be more likely to be unable to meet its obligations.

Our findings are relevant to literature and practice. First, literature about SMEs and default risk is enlarged. Few studies analyze SMEs probability of default. Although this type of firms is the majority of firm all over the world. Moreover, we introduce a new variable, exports intensity, almost unexplored, and results prove the impact of this variable to explain the risk of default.

To practice results are also relevant since help firm's managers to take action to control the firm's financial situation and to avoid default risk. Moreover, results show that exports have a positive impact to SMEs risk, due to economies of scale and diversification of risk. Therefore, managers may try to diversify its activity to reduce uncertainties. Creditors can also understand that lending money to export firms is not negative since these firms have less risk. Finally, policymakers and all the community can understand how firms can have a sustainable situation.

LIMITATIONS AND FUTURE RESEARCH DIRECTIONS

This chapter shows the relevance of exports intensity on the risk ode default of family SME to the Portuguese market. Since similar analyzes are scarce. We have analyzed family SMEs of a specific region of Portugal. Therefore, results cannot be extrapolated since the sample analyze cannot represent all firms all over the world. Therefore, we suggest that this study should be replicated using other markets to see if our results are corroborated.

Moreover, the success of internationalization may depend on the economic, political and even cultural context of the country where the firm is located. In this study we have not included macroeconomic variables, but only economic and financial variables. It would be interesting to include macroeconomic variables to see the impact on the financial distress. Moreover, we suggest future researches to analyze if internationalization continues to be a crucial variable in the success of firms for different economies, with different levels of development.

The present study uses a homogeneous group of firms, family SMEs. Even if family firms are persistent all over the world, they do not represent all firms. Moreover, this group of firms have some specificities which turn them apart from non-family firms. Thus, it would be interesting to extend the analysis by comparing family and non-family firms. Moreover, additional variables regarding corporate governance as percentage of ownership, the type of the largest owners (family, institutional, banks, blockholders, among others), manager's characteristics, and others should be insert in the model to see if these variables are relevant to explain default's probability.

ACKNOWLEDGMENT

This research was supported by National Funds of the FCT – Portuguese Foundation for Science and Technology within the project [UIDB/04928/2020].

REFERENCES

AICEP (2016). Portugalglobal. *Revista Portugal Global, AICEP, 90.*

Alaminos, D., Del Castillo, A., & Fernandez, M. A. (2016). A global model for bankruptcy prediction. *PLoS One, 11*(11), 1–18. doi:10.1371/journal.pone.0166693 PMID:27880810

Altman, E. I. (1968). Financial ratios, discriminant analysis and the prediction of corporate bankruptcy. *The Journal of Finance, 23*(4), 589–609. doi:10.1111/j.1540-6261.1968.tb00843.x

Altman, E. I. (1983). *Corporate financial distress: a complete guide to predicting, avoiding, and dealing with bankruptcy.* Wiley Interscience, John Wiley and Sons.

Altman, E. I., Haldeman, R. G., & Narayanan, P. (1977). ZETA Analysis - A new model to identify bankruptcy risk corporations. *Journal of Banking & Finance, 1*(1), 29–54. doi:10.1016/0378-4266(77)90017-6

Altman, E. I., Iwanicz-Drozdowska, M., Laitinen, E. K., & Suvas, A. (2017). Financial distress prediction in an international context: A review and empirical analysis of Altman's Z- Score model. *Journal of International Financial Management & Accounting, 28*(2), 131–171. doi:10.1111/jifm.12053

Altman, E. I., & Sabato, G. (2007). Modelling credit risk for SMEs: Evidence from the U.S. market. *Abacus, 43*(3), 332–357. doi:10.1111/j.1467-6281.2007.00234.x

Arslan, O., & Karan, M. (2009). Credit risks and internationalization of SMEs. *Journal of Business Economics and Management, 10*(4), 361–368. doi:10.3846/1611-1699.2009.10.361-368

Ashraf, S., Félix, E. G. S., & Serrasqueiro, Z. (2019). Do Traditional Financial Distress Prediction Models Predict the Early Warning Signs of Financial Distress? *Journal of Risk and Financial Management, 12*, 1–17. doi:10.3390/jrfm12020055

Basly, S. (2007). The internationalization of family SME: An organizational learning and knowledge development perspective. *Baltic Journal of Management. Emerald, 2*(2), 154–180.

Beaver, W. H. (1966). Financial Ratios as Predictors of Failure. *Journal of Accounting Research, 4*, 71–111. doi:10.2307/2490171

Blums, M. (2003). *D-Score: Bankruptcy Prediction Model for Middle Market Public Firms.* Academic Press.

Brito, G. A. S., & Neto, A. A. (2008). Modelo de classificação de risco de crédito de empresas. *Revista Contabilidade & Finanças, 19*(46), 18–29. doi:10.1590/S1519-70772008000100003

Chancharat, N., Tina, G., Davy, P., MacGrae, M., & Lodh, S. (2010). Multiple States of Financially Distressed Companies: Tests using a Competing-Risks Model. *Australasian Accounting Business and Finance Journal, 4*(4), 27–49.

Cheng, W.-Y., Su, E., Li, S.-J., Fen, Y.-G., & Dong, G.-M. (2009). Corporate governance and financial distress: Evidence from public- listed electronics companies in Taiwan. *Journal of Statistics and Management Systems, 12*(5), 813–827. doi:10.1080/09720510.2009.10701424

CIRE - Código da Insolvência e da Recuperação de Empresas. Decreto Lei 53/2004 de 18 de março. Diário da República Nª 66/2004. http://www.dre.pt

Costa, M. P. (2016). *Three Essays on Firms' Financial Distress* (PhD Thesis). Évora University.

Donker, H., Santen, B., & Zahir, S. (2009). Ownership structure and the likelihood of financial distress in the Netherlands. *Applied Financial Economics*, *19*(21), 1687–1696. doi:10.1080/09603100802599647

Felicidade, M. (2019). Gestão RH em Empresas Familiares. *RH Magazine*, *121*, 14–17.

Gottardo, P., & Moisello, A. M. (2017). Family firms, risk-taking and financial distress. *Problems and Perspectives in Management*, *15*(2), 168–177. doi:10.21511/ppm.15(2-1).2017.01

Gupta, J., Wilson, N., Gregoriou, A., & Healy, J. (2014). The effect of internationalisation on modelling credit risk for SMEs: Evidence from UK market. *Journal of International Financial Markets, Institutions and Money*, *31*(C), 397–413. doi:10.1016/j.intfin.2014.05.001

INE. (2020). *Produto interno bruto por habitante e NUTS III*. Instituto Nacional de Estatísticas.

Kristanti, F. T., Rahayu, S., & Huda, A. N. (2016). The determinant of financial distress on indonesian family firm. *Procedia: Social and Behavioral Sciences*, *219*, 440–447. doi:10.1016/j.sbspro.2016.05.018

Lin, T.-H. (2009). A cross model study of corporate financial distress prediction in Taiwan: Multiple discriminant analysis, logit, probit and neural networks models. *Neurocomputing*, *72*(16-18), 3507–3516. doi:10.1016/j.neucom.2009.02.018

Lisboa, I. (2019a). Sucessão nas empresas familiares e o impacto no endividamento. Evidência para as PME da região de Leiria. *Revista de Gestão dos Países de Língua Portuguesa*, *17*(2), 24. doi:10.12660/rgplp.v17n2.2018.78223

Lisboa, I. (2019b). Capital Structure Choices and Exports: The Case of the Portuguese Mold Industry. *Australasian Accounting. Business and Finance Journal*, *13*(4), 23–45. doi:10.14453/aabfj.v13i4.3

Lohe, F.-W., & Calabrò, A. (2017). Please do not disturb! Differentiating bord tasks in family and non-family during financial distress. *Scandinavian Journal of Management*, *33*(1), 33–49. doi:10.1016/j.scaman.2017.01.001

Manzaneque, M., Priego, A. M., & Merino, E. (2016). Corporate governance effect on financial distress likelihood: Evidence from Spain. *Revista de Contabilidad*, *19*(1), 111–121. doi:10.1016/j.rcsar.2015.04.001

Martinho, R., & Antunes, A. (2012). Um Modelo De Scoring Para As Empresas Portuguesas. *Banco de Portugal - Relatório de Estabilidade Financeira*, 117–131. doi:10.1063/1.342458

Md-Rus, R., Mohd, K. N. T., Latif, R. A., & Alassan, Z. N. (2013). Ownership Structure and Financial Distress. *Journal of Advanced Management Science*, *1*(4), 363–367. doi:10.12720/joams.1.4.363-367

Mselmi, N., Lahiani, A., & Hamza, T. (2017). Financial distress prediction: The case of French small and medium-sized firms. *International Review of Financial Analysis*, *50*, 67–80. doi:10.1016/j.irfa.2017.02.004

Nagar, N., & Sen, K. (2018). Earnings Management Strategies During Financial Distress. *The IUP Journal of Accounting Research & Audit Practices*, *17*(3), 52–79.

OEC. (2019). *Observatory of Economic Complexity*. Retrieved from https://oec.world/pt/profile/country/prt/

Ohlson, J. A. (1980). Financial Ratios and the Probabilistic Prediction of Bankruptcy. *Journal of Accounting Research*, *18*(1), 109–131. doi:10.2307/2490395

Pacheco, L. (2016). Capital structure and internationalization: The case of Portuguese industrial SMEs. *Research in International Business and Finance*, *38*, 531–545. doi:10.1016/j.ribaf.2016.07.014

Pérez, S., Llopis, A., & Llopis, J. (2010). A competing risks analysis of firms exit. *Empirical Economics*, *38*(2), 281–304. doi:10.100700181-009-0266-x

Pindado, J., & Rodrigues, L. (2005). Determinants of Financial Distress Costs. *Financial Markets and Portfolio Management*, *19*(4), 343–359. doi:10.100711408-005-6456-4

Pindado, J., Rodrigues, L., & de la Torre, C. (2008). Estimating financial distress likelihood. *Journal of Business Research*, *61*(9), 995–1003. doi:10.1016/j.jbusres.2007.10.006

PORDATA. (2020a). *Número de PME*. Lisboa, Portugal: PORDATA, Fundação Francisco Manuel dos Santos.

PORDATA. (2020b). *Taxa de natalidade, mortalidade e sobrevivência das empresas*. Lisboa, Portugal: PORDATA, Fundação Francisco Manuel dos Santos.

PORDATA. (2020c). *Valor dos bens importados e exportados pelas empresas*. Lisboa, Portugal: PORDATA, Fundação Francisco Manuel dos Santos.

Rosner, R. L., & University, L. I. (2003). Earnings Manipulation in Failing Firms. *Contemporary Accounting Research*, *20*(2), 361–408. doi:10.1506/8EVN-9KRB-3AE4-EE81

Roy, A., Sekhar, C., & Vyas, V. (2016). Barriers to internationalization: A study of small and medium enterprises in India. *Journal of International Entrepreneurship*, *14*(4), 513–538. doi:10.100710843-016-0187-7

Salloum, C., Schmitt, C., & Bouri, E. (2012). Does board structure affect financial distress? A study with reference to family firms in Lebanon. *Investment Management and Financial Innovations*, *9*(4), 113–123.

Shumway, T. (2001). Forecasting Bankruptcy More Accurately: A Simple Hazard Model. *The Journal of Business*, *74*(1), 101–124. https://www.jstor.org/stable/10.1086/209665. doi:10.1086/209665

Singh, G., Pathak, D., & Naz, R. (2010). Issues faced by SMEs in the internationalization process: Results from Fiji and Samoa. *International Journal of Emerging Markets*, *5*(2), 153–182. doi:10.1108/17468801011031801

SIREVE - Sistema de Recuperação de Empresas por Via Extrajudicial. Decreto Lei 178/2012 de 3 de agosto. Diário da República Nª 150/2012. Acedido a 24 jan. 2019. www.dre.pt

Tinoco, M. H., & Wilson, N. (2013). Financial distress and bankruptcy prediction among listed companies using accounting, market and macroeconomic variables. *International Review of Financial Analysis*, *30*, 394–419. doi:10.1016/j.irfa.2013.02.013

Udin, S., Khan, M. A., & Javid, A. Y. (2017). The effects of ownership structure on likelihood of financial distress: An empirical evidence. *Corporate Governance: The International Journal of Business in Society*, *17*(4), 589–612. doi:10.1108/CG-03-2016-0067

Valentim, L., Lisboa, J. V., & Franco, M. (2016). Knowledge management practices and absorptive capacity in small and medium-sized enterprises: Is there really a linkage? *R & D Management*, *46*(4), 711–725. doi:10.1111/radm.12108

Zmijewski, M. E. (1984). Methodological Issues Related to the Estimation of Financial Distress Prediction Models. *Journal of Accounting Research*, *22*, 59–82. doi:10.2307/2490859

KEY TERMS AND DEFINITIONS

Bankruptcy Risk: When a firm no longer has financial recovery.

Company's Internationalization: Companies that sell or provide services to external markets.

Default Risk: The probability of a firm not being able to meet its debt covenants.

Ex-Ante Criterion of Default Risk: Criterion used to identify company's financial problems to classify companies in default or compliant.

Ex-Post Criterion of Default Risk: Legal classification of companies in default or compliant.

Family Firms: Firms whose shareholders have more than 25% of the firm shares, and the family control's the firm's management.

Small and Medium Enterprises (SME): Companies with less than 250 employees and which turnover is smaller than 50 million of euros or total assets is less than 43 million of euros.

Chapter 10
Assessing the Relationship Between Brand Image, Market Orientation, and Competitive Advantage

Orlando Lima Rua
ISCAP, CEOS, Polytechnic of Porto, Portugal & NECE, University of Beira Interior, Portugal & UNIAG, Associação dos Politécnicos do Norte de Portugal, Portugal

Catarina Santos
ISCAP, Polytechnic of Porto, Portugal

EXECUTIVE SUMMARY

This study aims to analyze the relationship between intangible resources, namely the brand image, and competitive advantage through differentiation and market orientation. To this end, using a quantitative methodological approach, an empirical study was carried out with Portuguese companies exporting the footwear industry, to which a questionnaire survey was applied, resulting in a sample of 86 companies. Findings show that (1) the brand image has a direct, positive, and significant impact on market orientation and on competitive advantage through differentiation and that (2) market orientation has a significant impact on competitive advantage through differentiation.

INTRODUCTION

We go back to the 20th century to find the first scientific references to the *Resourced-Based View* (RBV) theory, which according to Penrose (1959) argues that the competitive advantage of any organization is based on the set of resources it has and the role they play in its strategy.

It can then be said that the competitive advantage is based not only on the final product or service placed on the market, but mostly on a clear identification of the available resources (Wernerfelt, 1984) and on the way they are optimized (Penrose, 1959).

DOI: 10.4018/978-1-7998-4387-0.ch010

Foss (1997) concluded that the wealth of the markets and the power over them is based on the heterogeneity of resources between competitors, more specifically on the causes of this asymmetry and the ability to maintain this advantage (Miller, 2003). That is, the Theory establishes a market hierarchy based exclusively on the inherent capacities and resources of each organization (Bouncken et al., 2014).

Barney (1991) defines these resources as "all assets, capabilities, organizational processes, company characteristics, information, knowledge, etc. controlled by the organization and allowing it to develop and implement strategies that improve its efficiency and effectiveness" (p. 101), which can be divided between physical, organizational, financial and human resources.

The degree of organizational productivity achieved will then be directly dependent on the cross-cutting relationship of creating resource-based opportunities, as well as on the ability to create synergies in the current opportunities for more resources to come from them (Madhok & Keyhani, 2012).

Thus, the degree of flexibility and responsiveness to external change comes mostly from internal efforts to create a resource-centric organisational structure (Fredericks, 2005), thus becoming the central purpose of any organisation to "coordinate these resources, and combine them to create new value" (Bouncken, Schuessler & Kraus, 2015, p. 42).

Therefore, the resource-structure-performing model emerges (Barney, Wright & Ketchen, 2011; Brouthers et al., 2008; Ray, Barney & Muhanna, 2004), consisting this one on the "alignment of organizational structure with capabilities/resources will result in superior performance" (He et al., 2012, p. 14). Therefore, from a contingency perspective where there are no irrefutably superior resources or strategies, but rather a manifestly high alignment between an organizational profile and external conditioning (Venkatraman, 1989), and efficient response to market orientation also emerges (Barney et al., 2001).

Nakatani and Teixeira (2009) go further, and argue that the organisational structure can itself become a resource since it allows "establishing relationships with and between workers (internal architecture) and with suppliers and customers (external architecture), or with a group of companies with correlated activities" (p. 66), as well as the reuse of resources and capabilities in various products and services (Wernerfelt, 1984). This approach complements the importance of resources with the growing centrality of partnerships, introducing the concept of resource networks as a new foundation for Resource-Based Theory (Bouncken et al., 2015).

For organisations to gain an advantage over the rest of the market it is crucial that their resources and the way they operate among themselves "are not reproducible, transferable or accessible" (Nalcaci & Yagci, 2014, p. 672), but rather "valuable, rare, difficult or impossible to imitate and irreplaceable" (Bouncken et al., 2015, p.41). This is the VRIO model (Hussain & Terziovski, 2016), depending its value on its ability to "exploit and/or neutralise threats" (Greco et al., 2013, p. 56).

Baker and Nelson (2005) add an external resources component, advocating a corporate "bricolage", where organizations should be on constant alert to new competitive strategies because they may translate into internal optimization opportunities that otherwise would not be developed.

This perspective is in line with the Asymmetry-based Theory (Miller, 2003), which advocates changing the prism of the competitive advantage of resources to an angle with a greater focus on the future and development possibilities (Shane & Venkataraman, 2000), relating precisely to Stevenson & Jarillo's (1990, p. 23) definition of opportunity, "a desired and achievable future situation (...) that is beyond the organization's current activities".

In other words, there is an evolution of focus from an internal perspective of the organisation, to a dynamic prism, where more than identifying and developing capabilities, the organization should have the ability to adapt them to an increasingly volatile and demanding environment and this will determine its market competitiveness (Teece, 2007; Barney et al., 2011).

The high demand for the markets and the diversification of competition, both based on a flat world without geographical barriers, has reformulated the Portuguese business perspective, where most traditional sectors, such as the footwear industry, saw internationalization as a response to the arduous task of remaining competitive (APICCAPS, 2020). One of the major difficulties facing the industry is its inability to respond to the low-price strategy of other competitors, especially those of Asian origin. It then became necessary to focus on quality and innovation instead of prices (Rua & França, 2018; APICCAPS, 2020).

The research question of this study is to analyse the role that intangible resources, specifically the brand, have in the creation and management of competitive advantage through differentiation in an international context, to present strategic guides to the footwear sector but with transversal validity, considering the mediating effect of market orientation.

This study gains special relevance by filling a research gap given the intangible resources still suffer from a huge inattention of the academic sector, but especially due to the export trend that the footwear sector has been experiencing.

In conclusion, although there are various perspectives on the subject of resources and their role in the development, implementation and control of business strategy, the main idea is that they are assigned an increasingly relevant mission (Madhok et al., 2012). However, for the objectives to be achieved, the organisation has to ensure the development and implementation of a structure-oriented to the resources, creating synergies between them (Nalcaci et al., 2014).

THEORETICAL FRAMEWORK

Intangible Resources

The Industrial Revolution created a market where the success and value of a company were established by its ability to obtain, use and sell physical resources (Tsai, Lu & Yen, 2012). However, the Information Society has brought with it a new reality in which physical assets give rise to intangible values such as knowledge, culture and technology (Fakhrutdinova, Kolesnikova, Yurieva & Kamasheva, 2014), and in which the main source of market value creation rests on immaterial pillars (Tsai et al., 2012).

Thus, intangible resources begin to gain a central place in organizational strategies (Rauh & Sufi, 2010; Rampini & Viswanathan, 2010), "representing opportunities for future growth" (Tsai et al., 2012, p. 68) and becoming exponentially a crucial area for the survival of any company (Li & Liu, 2012).

Wernerfelt (1984) advocates the existence of two types of organizational resources: tangible, all that can be touched, and intangible, which in contrast are immaterial assets related to the history and culture of the organization itself.

Fakhrutdinova et al. (2014), generalizing, argue that intangible resources are "all intangible products with the potential to respond to needs and generate profits" (p. 83), such as trademarks, patents, or knowledge (Dyer & Singh, 1998).

According to Economic Theory, intangible resources are based on the relationship between society and property, which in itself has neither a material form nor recognizable value, but can generate profit and competitive advantage (Fakhrutdinova et al., 2014).

These resources are created through core competencies such as "organisational structure, employee knowledge, employer centripetal strength, innovation and development capacity, consumer dimension, brand recognition and market share", originating "the dynamic capacity of the organisation" (Tsai et al., 2012, p. 67).

Kayo (2002, p.19) argued that intangible resources can then be classified in the following categories:

1. Human resources: knowledge, talent, skills, experience, top management, key employees and training;
2. Innovation resources: research and development, patents, secret formulas, and technological knowledge; and
3. Relational resources: brand value, trademarks, copyright, customer relations, suppliers, licensing contracts and franchising.

Tsai et al. (2012) propose a more developed and detailed evaluation:

1. Intangible capital: research and development intensity (Gleason & Klock, 2006; Fukui & Ushijima, 2007; Jo & Harjoto, 2011; Boujelben & Fedhila, 2011), and advertising intensity (Gleason & Klock, 2006; Fukui & Ushijima, 2007; Boujelben et al., 2011);
2. Organisation structure: family (Wiwattanakantang, 2001; Jo & Harjoto, 2011), relationship with government (Wiwattanakantang, 2001), the cultural influence of foreign investors (Wiwattanakantang, 2001; Oxelheim & Randoy, 2003), management interests (Wiwattanakantang, 2001; Lins, 2003), non-participations in the management (Lins, 2003), managers (Wiwattanakantang, 2001; Lins, 2003), hierarchy (Wiwattanakantang, 2001; Lins, 2003) and business group (Wiwattanakantang, 2001);
3. Corporate management: management dimension (Oxelheim et al., 2003; Xie, Davidson & Dadalt, 2003), management independence (Oxelheim et al, 2003; Xie et al., 2003; Jo & Harjoto, 2011), block holder (Lins, 2003; Jo & Harjoto, 2011), centralization of control (Wiwattanakantang, 2001; Lins, 2003) and foreign participation (Oxelheim et al., 2003; Lang, Lins & Miller, 2003);
4. Organizational characteristics: influence (Fukui & Ushijima, 2007; Bozec et al., 2010; Jo & Harjoto, 2011) and differentiation (Allayannis et al., 2001; Fukui & Ushijima, 2007; Jo & Harjoto, 2011);
5. Industry characteristics: level of concentration and market position (Anderson, Fornell & Mazvancheryl, 2004; Rao, Agarwal & Dahlhoff, 2004; Oxelheim et al., 2003; Lang et al., 2003); and
6. Relations with analysts and clients: interest of analysts and proximity to the public (Lang et al., 2003; Jo & Harjoto, 2011).

On the other hand, there is an academic current that advocates the use of intangible resources as a measure of future performance evaluation (Fukui & Ushijima, 2007; Gleason et al., 2006; Rao et al., 2004) in which they play an equitable role to the tangible in terms of developing brand value, and in which "innovation and brand loyalty are seen as investments that (...) have the potential to positively affect future cash flows" (Tsai et al., 2012, p. 68).

Fakhrutdinova et al. (2014) state that a strategy based on intangible resources represents the solution to many of the problems that companies face today, such as:

1. Gaining competitive advantage: by reducing costs, developing a more positive image and offering more effective products and services;
2. Increased external investment: by focusing on immaterial resources the organisation can reduce costs with physical materials, becoming more attractive to potential investors;
3. Human resource involvement: it has been proven that there is greater employee involvement in organizations that the intangible component has a greater impact; and
4. Prevention of opportunistic behavior: intangible resources, besides being an integral part of the external development process, may play a central role in internal management, such as in the distribution of dividends, making the process fairer and benefiting the most altruistic employees.

About intangible resources, due to their strong emotional component and personal connection to consumers, they are inseparable from the context in which they are inserted (Capra, 1996). Thus, it is necessary to analyze the value and potential of each intangible component according to its specific context (Fukui & Ushijima, 2007; Gleason et al., 2006) and variables such as the technical characteristics of the industry (Tsai et al., 2012) and market concentration (Anderson et al., 2004).

Thus, "intangible brand associations represent valuable sources of brand equity (...) and differentiation" (Keller, 2000, p. 124) and, according to Resource Theory, the most important sources of competitive advantage (Omar, Williams & Lingelbach, 2009), provided they ensure their inimitability and rarity (Abratt & Kleyn, 2012) and establish an emotional connection with consumers (Balmer & Gray, 2003).

However, although currently intangible resources are considered one of the most critical factors for obtaining competitive advantage (Tsai et al., 2012), the existing information is still quite dubious and confused and cannot act as a strategic guideline for organizations (Lins, 2003; Wiwattanakantang, 2001), essentially because the concept is a difficult quantitative transition (Niebel, O'Mahony & Saam, 2013).

To answer this problematic question, the latest studies have opted for an integrated approach where the role of resources is analysed from the presumption of the interrelationship of intangible and tangible resources (Moeller, 2009).

Brand Image

The current consumer at the time of his choices considers much more than simply the physical characteristics of the product or service, looking for brands with which he identifies as a consumer, but also as a human being (Popoli, 2015).

Thus, companies live in an increasingly competitive and demanding reality, where there is increasing pressure for them to maintain the behaviour demanded by their consumers, and that their assessment depends on all existing information according to external filters and criteria (van Gelder, 2003).

The competitive advantage and perceived differentiation are then decreasingly focused on "technological and performance characteristics, and increasingly on the value resulting from intangible resources" (Popoli, 2015, p. 24).

Since the 1950s, the concepts of brand image and company image have been gaining relevance (Gardner & Levy, 1955; Martineau, 1958; Park, Jaworski & MacInnis, 1986; Spector, 1961; Patterson, 1999; Stern, Zinkhan & Jaju, 2001), but their true meaning remains a subject of great debate and high difficulties (Patterson, 1999; Franzen & Bouwman, 2001; Stern et al., 2001).

Briefly, brands are "the perceptions reflected through associations in the memory of the consumer" (Keller, 1993, p. 3). The America Marketing Association defines a brand as a name, term, sign, symbol, design or combination of these, to identify goods and services and differentiate them from the competition. Kotler (2000, p. 426) adds "a trademark is a name, term, symbol, design or all the foregoing, and is used to differentiate a company's products and services from those of its competitors".

Contrary to previous concepts, there is a view that the brand has no tangible component (Alwi & Kitchen, 2014; Azoulay & Kapferer, 2003; Keller & Richey, 2006; Slaughter, Zickar, Highhouse & Mohr, 2004;), i.e., it is created internally through advertising campaigns, but essentially by the clients themselves (Wang & Tsai, 2014), serving as criteria in the evaluation of options at the time of purchase (Zeithaml, 1988; Richardson, Dick & Jain, 1994; Keegan, Moriarty & Duncan, 1995).

In short, although there are several definitions for the concept of a brand, they all incorporate the idea of globality, i.e., the brand is always related to the total impression of the organisation shared by a group of external members (Franzen et al., 2001).

This global dimensionality was summarized by Dimofte, Johansson and Ronkainen (2008) in five factors: social and environmental responsibility, availability and visibility, a symbol of achievement, safety and time savings, local characteristics versus standardization. Alwi and Kitchen (2014) add that the idea of brand as a global perception is defined by both affective and cognitive attributes.

Howard (1977) argues that the possibility of creating a competitive advantage based on the value of the brand lies precisely in the components of perception, both emotionally and cognitively, and that the development of trust by the organization will be based precisely on these elements.

The perceived brand can then be evaluated through the Attitude Model based on the interaction of three components: cognition, affectivity and connectivity (Schiffman & Kanuk, 2007; Rosenberg & Hoveland, 1960).

Brand Image Value

As mentioned above, a strong brand image is an important factor in market differentiation and superiority over the competition (Hsieh & Li, 2008), and consequently in the behavior of current customers as well as potential new markets (Burmann, Schaefer & Maloney, 2008).

Through informal clues, consumers create their opinions about brands (Wang & Tsai, 2014), and consequently define their hierarchy of preferences, transferring these criteria to their purchasing and consumption choices (Simonian, Forsythe, Kwon & Chattaraman, 2012), i.e., the more positive a brand image is, the greater the chances of buying (Simonian et al., 2012; Keller, 2003). These buying probabilities will translate into buying intentions, that is, "at the conscious level of an individual's efforts to buy a brand" (Spears & Singh, 2004, p. 63).

There is a dependent relationship between the brand value and its image, where together with performance, services, aesthetic and functional characteristics, durability, reliability and compliance, define the achieved levels of quality perceived by the public (Garvin, 1987).

Therefore, the stronger the brand image, the lower the perceived risks (Akaah & Korgaonkar, 1988; Rao & Monroe, 1988) and the higher the value attributed (Loudon & Bitta, 1988; Fredericks & Slater, 1998; Romaniuk & Sharp, 2004); and, considering the latter with the determining factor in intentions to purchase, the greater the probability of achieving competitive advantage (Zeithaml, 1988; Dodds, Monroe & Grewal, 1991; Cronin, Brady & Hult., 2000).

The brand image in establishing the direct link from the necessity to demand represents an intangible resource that is central to differentiation (Popoli, 2015), making it essential to understand the psychology of consumption behind the responses to the different stimuli of companies (Franzen et al., 2001).

The brand then represents much more than simply the marketing mix (Popoli, 2015). It is a set of feelings based on personal, intrinsic and extrinsic clues that come to fill the gap between consumers' current life and personality and their ideals (Olson, 1977).

Therefore, there is currently a relentless search by brands to dematerialize the products or services they sell and instead develop strategies that allow them to become affective, emotional and behavioral symbols to reach levels that are not comparable with other competitors in the market (Popoli, 2015).

Brand Image Size

Brands today live in a world without borders, and consequently their reality has also become transversal, where their value does not depend exclusively on their target audiences, but on all the direct and indirect relationships they establish in the various phases of their development (Lambin, 2008).

This expanded perspective is based on the impact of stakeholders on the development of competitive advantage (Carroll, 1989; Clarkson, 1995; Donaldson & Dunfee, 1994; Jawahar & McLaughlin, 2001), which uses Systems Theory as its starting point (Capra, 1996; Golinelli, 2000) and adds the importance of the analysis and development of all external relations that the company maintains for the development of the competitive advantage in the long term, defending that this will be its capacity of relational management responsible for the maximization of the resources and the effective response to the expectations and demands of the market (Popoli, 2015).

Similarly, Holt, Quelch & Taylor (2004) argue that the importance of image increases in an international context, representing 64% of the purchase decision and that any brand operating in the international arena should take into account its perceived image in a global and unified way.

Market Orientation

The concept of market orientation relates to "the set of processes and routines that encourage companies to produce, disseminate and respond to information about customers, competitors and the external environment" (Kohli & Jaworski, 1990, p. 28).

It focuses on the internal processes that allow the organization to understand and respond effectively to all its surrounding context, including customers, competitors and suppliers (Kohli et al., 1990), through a corporate structure based on market intelligence and which privileges the satisfaction and loyalty of its consumers (Kirca, Jayachandran & Bearden, 2005).

In an international context, such an idea is particularly important as it makes it possible to reduce part of the risk associated with identifying and comparing the original products and services with international needs and expectations, and then make the necessary adjustments and corrections (He, Brouthers & Filatotchev, 2012).

In other words, we see a progression where internationalization is defined by the "specific priorities of a country, institution or specific group of stakeholder*s*" (Knight, 2015, p.2), and where the success of its implementation depends not exclusively on transaction costs, but on the ability of organizations to understand the differences between the home market and the international market, as well as to develop competitive advantage and responses to the difficulties arising from this heterogeneity (Brouthers, Brouthers & Werner, 2008; Hitt et al., 2007; He, 2012).

The following research question emerge from this: - *Does the brand image influence the market orientation and competitive advantage through differentiation? - Does the market orientation influence the competitive advantage through differentiation?*

RESEARCH HYPOTHESES

According to Keller (2000) the brand is the main source for the creation of associations between consumers and organisations, and therefore the fundamental basis for the creation of "brand equity (...) and differentiation" (p. 124)

On the other hand, knowing that the brand is one of the most fundamental intangible resources (Kayo, 2002), Fakhrutdinova et al. (2014) state that it should be the pillar of a sustained and differentiated international strategy, capable of ensuring competitive advantage to the organization and communicating its positioning to its audiences (Morgan & Pritchard, 2004).

Holt, Quelch and Taylor (2004) argue that brand value gains even more relevance in an international context, where levels of competitiveness are equally higher. In this way, it should convey a unified and coherent idea, but it should also be adapted to local specificities, i.e. it should be geared to the markets in which it operates (Kirca et al., 2005), ensuring an effective response to consumer needs and requirements (Kohli et al., 1990). The intention was then to test the following hypotheses:

H1: The brand image has a positive influence on market orientation.
H2: The brand image has a positive influence oncompetitive advantage through differentiation.

The orientation for the market is designated by the concern of an organization in understanding and responding to the characteristics of the market where it acts (Kohli et al., 1990), altering the focus of its attention from an internal perspective to an external perspective (Kirca, Jayachandran & Bearden, 2005). Popoli (2015) defends that the direct link of the organization to the necessities of its markets is central for the effective and full accomplishment of a strategy employing the differentiation, therefore the present study intended to test the following hypothesis:

H3: Market orientation has a positive influence on competitive advantage through differentiation.

METHODOLOGY

Regarding the research's decision of the method, Fachin (2001) identifies two decisive factors: the nature of the objective and the objective itself.

Inevitably, this same work needs mental and technical checks to be given scientific value, and consequently to achieve results considered original knowledge (Prodanov & Freitas, 2013) and practicality in solving everyday problems (Lakatos & Marconi, 2007).

Respectively, scientific research emerges from a "set of intellectual and technical procedures" (Gil, 2008, p. 8), and derives from a "set of intellectual and technical procedures adopted to achieve knowledge" (Prodanov et al., 2013, p. 24).

For this study, the quantitative methodology was used through the distribution of a questionnaire (Bryman & Cramer, 2012). The answers will be assessed on a Likert scale, allowing qualitative answers to be translated into quantitative data, one of the main reasons for their popularity within academia (Lindwall et al., 2012; Rodebaugh, Woods, & Heimberg, 2007; Roszkowski & Soven, 2010; Sonderen, Sanderman, & Coyne, 2013)

As regards data collection and subsequent analysis, based on Mintzberg (1979, p. 585) "regardless of sample size or area of interest", it is essential that an analysis is carried out in an effective and structured manner.

Pre-Test

The questionnaire was subject to a pre-test to minimize the difficulties in its completion and interpretation, having been tested with 17 companies with export activity. In this pre-test no difficulties were detected in the interpretation of the questions incorporated in the questionnaire.

Structure of the Survey by Questionnaire, Operationalisation and Measurement of Variables

The instrument used was the questionnaire survey, in the sense that no variable was manipulated and all data related to the variables were collected at the same time (Bryman & Cramer, 2012).

Regarding the brand image, taking into account the work of Kayo (2002), who argues that one of the most relevant aspects in the identification and analysis of the intangible resources of an organization are the relational resources, which the author characterizes as the value of the brand and the relationship it establishes and maintains with its customers. Furthermore, the categories of intangible resources adapted by Tsai et al. (2012) were taken as a reference, namely: organizational characteristics, such as the influence of differentiation (Allayannis et al., 2001; Fukui & Ushijima, 2007; Jo et al., 2011), and the relationship with analysts and clients (Lang et al., 2003; Jo et al., 2011), in this case exclusively with clients (Table 1).

Table 1. Brand image's survey items

Items	Source
• Brand recognition. • Connecting consumers to the culture and personality of the brand.	Adapted from Kayo (2002) and Tsai et al. (2012)

The market orientation was based on the vast majority of the categories of the two authors (Table 2). Kayo (2002) states that in the category of resources and innovation, innovation efforts are implicit, and consequently the concern to launch new products; furthermore, in the category of human resources, knowledge and skills, as well as the decisions of top management, play a central role; finally, in its category of relational resources, the value of the relationships established with all the partners in the value chain is mentioned, which will determine the speed and effectiveness of the organisation's response.

As for the analysis of Tsai et al. (2002), the categories of intangible capital are the following:

1. innovation of new models,
2. structure of the organization, more specifically the verticality of the hierarchy (Gleason & Klock, 2006; Fukui & Ushijima, 2007; Jo & Harjoto, 2011; Boujelben & Fedhila, 2019),
3. decisions of top management (Wiwattanakantang, 2001) are taken into account; Lins, 2003; Ellili, 2011),
4. corporate management, in terms of fluidity of response and centralization of control among the various hierarchical levels (Wiwattanakantang, 2001; Lins, 2003) and, finally,
5. customer relations, to be able to identify and analyze changes in behavior (Lang et al., 2003; Jo et al., 2011).

Table 2. Market orientation's survey items

Items	Source
• You consider that your company frequently launches new models. • You feel that the company has the ability to quickly analyze market changes and respond effectively to them.	Adapted from Kayo (2002) and Tsai et al. (2012)

Sample and Data Collection Process

Portuguese companies that made footwear or footwear components were considered for the sample, with the majority of Portuguese share capital, due to the representativeness of this group in Portugal's exports (3.6%) (Portugal Global, 2017).

In this first selection, no account was taken of whether the company exports or not, since part of the study was intended to clarify the percentage of companies that have international activity. Therefore, a mandatory question was inserted in the questionnaire to segment companies that do not export at the moment, in which case the questionnaire is given as completed.

A database previously provided by the Portuguese Association of the Footwear, Components, Leather Goods and their Successors Industries (APICCAPS) with the contact of 231 companies was then used. Questionnaires were also distributed to other companies through the personal knowledge of the author of workers in the area, with a total of about 280 companies being contacted.

The companies were contacted by e-mail, with a link to a googledoc, to answer the questionnaire, these e-mails being addressed to the top management and/or the person responsible for the export. The confidentiality of the respondents was assured, not containing any question that could identify the respondent, nor the employer.

Two weeks after the first email was sent, a second contact was sent to get a higher response rate. The application of the questionnaire began on October 10, 2017, and ended on November 7, 2017, and during this period it proceeded with two insistences.

According to the Portuguese Association of Footwear, Components, Leather Goods and their Successors (APICCAPS, 2017), there are 1473 companies in the footwear industry, of which 380 have an export profile and 367 with share capital held in more than 50% by Portuguese companies.

We used a non-probabilistic and convenience sample and obtained 102 responses, of which 86 companies replied that they had an export profile. The response rate was 23.4% (Table 3).

Table 3. Research datasheet

Universe of Analysis	Portuguese footwear manufacturers exporters
Type of Sampling	Non-probabilistic and convenience sample
Population's Size	367 companies
Sample's Size	86 companies
Response Rate	23.4%
Valid Answers	86
Data Collection Period	October 10, 2017, to November 7, 2017

RESULTS

Reliability Analysis

Initially, an Alpha de Cronbach analysis was carried out to ensure the consistency and stability of the responses gathered, taking into account the heterogeneity of the respondents and consequently their opinions.

For this, the scale proposed by Pestana and Gageiro (2008) was used. The sample reliability is very good (0.866) for all variables.

Exploratory Factorial Analysis

The extraction of the factors was performed through the analysis of main components (PCA), with Varimax rotation that allows obtaining factors easier to interpret and, theoretically, with more meaning. This extraction followed the recommendations of Pestana and Gageiro (2008).

Tables 4 and 5 show that 3 factors were extracted: 1) competitive advantage – differentiation; 2) brand image; and 3) market orientation.

After concluding the reliability analysis, and according to statistical practices, Kaiser-Meyer-Olkin (KMO) analysis was performed to test the adequacy of the variables and consistency of the collected data, as well as to establish covariance relations between variables in hidden factors, and Bartlett's sphericity test (Maroco, 2011). For KMO assessment we used the scale proposed by Pestana and Gageiro (2008).

Table 6 show a KMO=0.793, presenting a mean data consistency for a 99% significance level, α=0.001, the *p* value (Sig.).000<0.001. Bartlett's sphericity test was used to assess the adequacy, resulting in a Chi-square approximation of 447.556, with 78 degrees of freedom, for a significance level of 99%, α=0.001, the *p*-value (Sig.).000<0.001. Therefore, factor analysis is considered appropriate.

Table 4. Total variance explained

Componente	Valores próprios iniciais			Somas de extração de carregamentos ao quadrado			Somas rotativas de carregamentos ao quadrado		
	Total	% de variância	% cumulativa	Total	% de variância	% cumulativa	Total	% de variância	% cumulativa
1	4,736	36,433	36,433	4,736	36,433	36,433	2,366	18,201	18,201
2	1,928	14,828	51,261	1,928	14,828	51,261	2,300	17,690	35,891
3	1,324	10,187	61,448	1,324	10,187	61,448	2,262	17,403	53,294
4	1,018	7,829	69,277	1,018	7,829	69,277	2,078	15,983	69,277
5	,743	5,713	74,990						
6	,699	5,381	80,371						
7	,653	5,020	85,391						
8	,395	3,039	88,430						
9	,388	2,983	91,412						
10	,334	2,567	93,980						
11	,305	2,344	96,323						
12	,263	2,019	98,343						
13	,215	1,657	100,000						

Método de Extração: Análise de Componente Principal.

Table 5. Rotating component matrix[a]

Items	Components		
	(1) Competitive Advantage	(2) Brand Image	(3) Market Orientation
Product quality	.873		
Differentiation	.658		
Innovation	.674		
Brand recognition		.726	
Connecting consumers to brand culture and personality		.715	
Do you consider that your company often launches new models			.827
Feels that the company can quickly analyze market changes and respond effectively to them			.461

Extraction Method: Main Component Analysis.
Rotation Method: Varimax with Kaiser Normalization.
a. Convergent rotation in 13 iterations.
Source: Own.

Table 6. KMO and Bartlett's sphericity test

Kaiser-Meyer-Olkin Sample Suitability Measure		.793
Bartlett's Sphericity Test	Approx. Chi-square	447.556
	df	78
	Sig.	.000

Source: Own.

Partial Least Squares

The structural equation model is designated as a multiple regression method to establish relations between variables (Marôco, 2010, 2011), have as a minimum relational value 0.7 to ensure that it is higher than the error variance (Carmines & Zeller, 1979).

The partial regression of least squares is a method of exploratory analysis that allows the development of theory, currently little tested. This method is capable of generating structural models based on small samples of less than 250 observations as is the case of the present study (Reinartz, Haenlein & Henseler, 2009). And simultaneously it allows maximizing the variance of the various dependent variables (Chin & Newsted, 1999; Reinartz, Haenlein & Henseler, 2009), as well as calculating formative and reflective calculus models (Chin, 2010).

Through Cronbach's alpha-based stability and internal consistency, the reliability of the variables used in the research is calculated, with a minimum required level of 0.7 (Chin, 2010).

In the present study, Alpha de Cronbah levels between 0.702 and 0.792 were reached, as can be seen in Table 7, which is considered acceptable (Pestana & Gageiro, 2008).

Table 7. Cronbach's alpha of the multidimensional variables

Constructs	Cronbach's Alpha	*p Values*
Brand image	.781	.000
Market orientation	.702	.000
Competitive advantage - Differentiation	.792	.000

Source: Own.

The reliability coefficient was also used to test the constructs' validity (Chin, 1998). As can be seen in Table 8 the variables exceed the reference value exponentially (0.6).

Table 8. Composite reliability of the multidimensional variables (ρc)

Constructs	Composite Reliability	*p Values*
Brand image	.861	.000
Market orientation	.756	.000
Competitive advantage - Differentiation	.876	.000

Source: Own.

In this test, both convergent validity analysis, where indicators represent only one construction (Reinartz, Haenlein & Henseler, 2009), and discriminant validity are usually carried out.

The method proposed by Fornell and Larcker (1981) was used in this research study, which proposes the use of the average extracted variance (AVE) with a minimum value of 0.5 to prove convergent validity. As can be seen in the next table, the values exceed the previously mentioned (Table 9).

The discriminative validity is determined by construction and is related to the level at which it differs and stands out from the other constructions of the model, thus making it necessary to have no correlations with other latent variables.

Table 9. Convergent validity

Constructs	AVE	*p Values*
Brand image	.756	.000
Market orientation	.613	.000
Competitive advantage - Differentiation	.702	.000

Source: Own.

It can be gauged from the principle that all cross loads cannot be greater than the loading of each indicator. On the other hand, the Fornell-Larcker criterion (1981) states that AVE must be greater than the variance between the constructions of the same model.

Referring to the separation of Chin (1998)'s explanatory power between moderate and substantial, it can be seen in Table 10 that satisfactory results have been obtained regarding the validity of discrimination and consequently that constructions are significantly diverse.

Table 10. Discriminatory validity

Fornell-Larcker Criterion	Brand Image	Market Orientation	Competitive Advantage - Differentiation
Brand image	.869		
Market orientation	.240	.783	
Competitive advantage - Differentiation	.440	.358	.838

Source: Own.

According to Table 11, only two hypotheses were not significant according to Chin (1998) that advocates a minimum structural coefficient of 0.2. The *bootstrapping* technique was used to calculate the relative strength of each exogenous constructs.

DISCUSSION

This study aims to analyse how the brand image has contributed to the achievement of international market orientation and competitive advantage through differentiation.

H1 was supported, hence the brand image has a positive and significant influence on market orientation, given that the brand should not only convey the personality of an organisation, product or service (Keller, 2000), but should also establish an emotional and behavioural link with its consumers (Popoli, 2015). In other words, brands should progressively adopt an extrinsic, market-oriented focus and their

Table 11. Path coefficients

Hypotheses	Original Sample (O)	Sample Mean (M)	Standard Error (STERR)	T Statistics (|O/STERR|)	*p* Values	Results
H1: BI --> +MO	.243	.258	.124	2.089	.050***	Supported
H2: BI --> +CA-DIF	.377	.389	.076	4.953	.000*	Supported
H3: MO --> +CA-DIF	.271	.277	.125	2.180	.029**	Supported

Legend:
BI – Brand image; MO - Market orientation; CA-DIF - Competitive advantage (differentiation).
* p<0.001
** p<0.05
*** p<0.1
Source: Own.

desires, needs and requirements (Kirca, Jayachandran & Bearden, 2005), enabling exponential levels of loyalty to be achieved (Hsieh & Li, 2008).

H2 was supported, in line to what was previously argued. However, it was not proven that brand image as an intangible resource promotes a strategy of competitive advantage through differentiation.

H3 was also supported, i.e., there was positive and significant link between market orientation and differentiation. The study then showed that the fact that the organisation seeks to understand the needs and wishes of the markets and then adapt to them (Popoli, 2015), does not ensure that it can do so uniquely about other competitors and therefore achieve competitive advantage through differentiation.

The present study allows us to conclude that many ideas established in general in the academic environment were not supported, underlining the need for more research in a theme that is itself overwhelmed with subjectivity and dubiousness, such as intangible resources.

However, it has been proven that there is currently a moment of revitalisation of the footwear industry, which as a way to respond proactively to the crisis has bet on international markets, initially relying on destinations of greater proximity, but a growing desire to explore more and greater distant destinations, such as Oceania and Asia.

This geographical movement should, however, be accompanied by constant analyses that are quite specific to the markets, where the crops and valences of those markets should be considered as starting points for the development of possible new or at least hybrid positions.

It has also been proven that the brand plays a central role in international strategy, where it will enable deeper links to be established with the various consumers, and consequently result in higher levels of loyalty, which will be even more crucial when acting in an international arena.

However, and although the brand is often associated as an intangible resource directed at differentiation strategies, this has not been supported, which may, on the one hand, hinder the performance of Portuguese brands, since they seek, essentially due to the difficulty in competing with prices in Asian exporting markets, to focus on target markets that value quality and innovation at the expense of attractive prices.

Precisely because of the very high level of competition in the international footwear sector, not only because of the ability to lower prices but also because of the international experience that some exporting countries already have, the national sector faces a great challenge. And for this reason, it is crucial that this revitalization that has been proven in this study continues, not only through the import destinations but mainly through continued investment in training and education of resources, which as we know is characterized as one of the poorest in the country.

CONCLUSION

This research can be attributed theoretical and practical contributions, since it explores the complementarity between academic value and the study of current business cases, allowing a closer link between the development of knowledge and its application. In this way, the same work can stimulate easily visible improvements in the footwear industry.

Besides, this study deepened the study of intangible resources, which is still rather neglected by both academia and the business world. Therefore, this study represents a deep contribution to the academic sector, but mainly to the footwear industry.

As the footwear industry is characterized by clusters, the current sample is extremely centralized in the North, corresponding to a non-probabilistic and convenience sample which may bias the responses obtained.

Future research efforts will have to reach a more significant sample as well as a more geographically dispersed one.

REFERENCES

Abratt, R., & Kleyn, N. (2012). Corporate identity, corporate branding and corporate reputations: Reconciliation and integration. *European Journal of Marketing*, *46*(8), 1048–1063. doi:10.1108/03090561211230197

Akaah, I. P., & Korgaonkar, P. K. (1988). A Conjoint Investigation of the Relative Importance of Risk Relievers in Direct Marketing. *Journal of Advertising Research*, *28*(2), 38–44.

Allayannis, G., & Weston, J. P. (2001). The Use of Foreign Currency Derivatives and Firm Market Value. *Review of Financial Studies*, *14*(1), 243–276. doi:10.1093/rfs/14.1.243

Alwi, S. F., & Kitchen, P. J. (2014). Projecting corporate brand image and behavioral response in business schools: Cognitive or affective brand attributes? *Journal of Business Research*, *67*(11), 2324–2336. doi:10.1016/j.jbusres.2014.06.020

Anderson, E. W., Fornell, C., & Mazvancheryl, S. K. (2004). Customer Satisfaction and Shareholder Value. *Journal of Marketing*, *68*(4), 172–185. doi:10.1509/jmkg.68.4.172.42723

APICCAPS. (2020). Footure – Plano Estratégico Cluster do Calçado. Porto: APICCAPS (Associação Portuguesa dos Industriais de Calçado, Componentes e Artigos de Pele e seus Sucedâneos).

Azoulay, A., & Kapferer, J.-N. (2003). Do brand personality scales really measure brand personality? *Journal of Brand Management*, *11*(2), 143–155. doi:10.1057/palgrave.bm.2540162

Baker, T., & Nelson, R. E. (2005). Creating something from nothing: Resource construction through entrepreneurial bricolage. *Administrative Science Quarterly*, *50*(3), 329–366. doi:10.2189/asqu.2005.50.3.329

Balmer, J. M., & Gray, E. R. (2003). Corporate brands: What are they? What of them? *European Journal of Marketing*, *37*(8), 972–997. doi:10.1108/03090560310477627

Barney, J. B. (1991). Firm resources and sustainable competitive advantage. *Journal of Management*, *17*(1), 99–120. doi:10.1177/014920639101700108

Barney, J. B., Ketchen, D. J. Jr, & Wright, M. (2011). The future of resource-based theory - Revitalization or decline? *Journal of Management*, *37*(5), 1299–1315. doi:10.1177/0149206310391805

Bouncken, R. B., & Pesch, R. (2014). New product performance through channeling in supply chain innovation alliances. In T. K. Das (Eds.), Strategic alliances for innovation and R&D (pp. 85-106). Carolina do Norte: Information Age Publishing.

Bouncken, R. B., Schuessler, J., & Kraus, S. (2015). Coopetition: A systematic review, synthesis, and future research directions. *Review of Managerial Science*, *9*(3), 577–601. doi:10.100711846-015-0168-6

Brouthers, K. D., Brouthers, L. E., & Werner, S. (2008). Resource-based advantages in an international context. *Journal of Management*, *34*(2), 189–217. doi:10.1177/0149206307312508

Bryman, A., & Cramer, D. (2012). *Quantitative Data Analysis with IBM SPSS 17, 18 & 19: A Guide for Social Scientists. Abingdon-on-Thames*. Routledge. doi:10.4324/9780203180990

Burmann, C., Schaefer, K., & Maloney, P. (2008). Industry image: Its impact on the brand image of potential employees. *Brand Management*, *15*(3), 157–176. doi:10.1057/palgrave.bm.2550112

Capra, F. (1996). The web of life: a new scientific understanding of living systems. Nova Iorque: Anchor Books.

Carmines, E. G., & Zeller, R. A. (1979). *Reliability and validity assessment*. Sage Publications. doi:10.4135/9781412985642

Carroll, A. B. (1989). *Business and society: ethics and stakeholder management*. South–Western Publishing Company.

Chin, W. (2010). Bootstrap cross-validation indices for PLS path model assessment. In V. Esposito Vinzi, W. Chin, J. Henseler, & H. Wang (Eds.), Handbook of Partial Least Squares: Concepts, Methods and Applications (pp. 83-97). Nova Iorque: Springer Publishing Company. doi:10.1007/978-3-540-32827-8_4

Chin, W. W. (1998). The partial least squares approach for structural equation modeling. In G. A. Marcoulides (Ed.), *Modern methods for business research* (pp. 295–236). Lawrence Erlbaum Associates.

Chin, W. W., & Newsted, P. R. (1999). Structural equation modeling analysis with small samples using partial least squares. In R. H. Hoyle (Ed.), *Statistical strategies for small sample research* (pp. 307–341). Sage.

Clarkson, M. (1995). A Stakeholder Framework for Analyzing and Evaluating Corporate Social Performance. *Academy of Management Review*, *20*(1), 92–117. doi:10.5465/amr.1995.9503271994

Cronin, J. J. Jr, Brady, M. K., & Hult, G. T. (2000). Assessing the effects of quality, value, and customer satisfaction on consumer behavioral intentions in service environments. *Journal of Retailing*, *76*(2), 193–218. doi:10.1016/S0022-4359(00)00028-2

Dimofte, C. V., Johansson, J. K., & Ronkainen, I. A. (2008). Cognitive and Affective Reactions of U.S. Consumers to Global Brands. *Journal of International Marketing*, *16*(4), 113–135. doi:10.1509/jimk.16.4.113

Dodds, W. B., Monroe, K. B., & Grewal, D. (1991). Effects of price, brand, and store information on buyers' product evaluations. *JMR, Journal of Marketing Research*, *28*(3), 307–319.

Donaldson, T., & Dunfee, T. (1994). Toward a Unified Conception of Business Ethics: Integrative Social Contracts Theory. *Academy of Management Review*, *19*(2), 252–284. doi:10.5465/amr.1994.9410210749

Dos Reis, F. (2010). *Como elaborar uma dissertação de mestrado, segundo Bolonha*. Pactor.

Dyer, J. H., & Singh, H. (1998). The Relational View: Cooperative Strategy and Sources of Interorganizational Competitive Advantage. *Academy of Management Review*, *23*(4), 660–679. doi:10.5465/amr.1998.1255632

Fachin, O. (2001). *Fundamentos de Metodologia*. Saraiva.

Fakhrutdinova, E., Kolesnikova, J., & Yurieva, O. K. (2014). Current trends of realization of the intellectual capital and problems of intellectual migration. *Procedia Economics and Finance*, *14*(1), 326–332.

Fornell, C., & Larcker, D. (1981). Evaluating structural equation models with unobservable variables and measurement error. *JMR, Journal of Marketing Research*, *18*(1), 39–50. doi:10.1177/002224378101800104

Foss, N. J. (1997). *Resources, firms, and strategies: a reader in the resource-based perspective*. Oxford: Oxford Management Readers.

Franzen, G., & Bouwman, M. (2001). *The mental world of brands: Mind, memory and brand Success*. NTC Publications.

Fredericks, J. O., & Slater, J. M. (1998). What Does Your Customer Really Want? *Quality Progress*, *31*(1), 63–65.

Fukui, Y., & Ushijima, T. (2007). Corporate diversification, performance, and restructuring in the largest Japanese manufacturers. *Journal of the Japanese and International Economies*, *21*(3), 303–323. doi:10.1016/j.jjie.2006.06.002

Gardner, B., & Levy, S. (1955). The product and the brand. *Harvard Business Review*, (Março-Abril), 33–39.

Garvin, D. (1987). Competing in the Eight Dimensions of Quality. *Harvard Business Review*, *87*(1), 101–109.

Gefen, D., & Straub, D. (2005). A Practical Guide To Factorial Validity Using PLS-Graph: Tutorial And Annotated Example. *Communications of the Association for Information Systems*, *16*(1), 91–109. doi:10.17705/1CAIS.01605

Gil, A. C. (2008). *Métodos e Técnicas de Pesquisa Social*. Atlas.

Gleason, K. (2006). Intangible capital in the pharmaceutical and chemical industry. *The Quarterly Review of Economics and Finance*, *46*(2), 300-314.

Golinelli, G. M. (2000). *L' approccio sistemico al Governo dell' impresa*. Cedam.

He, X., Brouthers, K. D., & Filatotchev, I. (2012). Resource-based and institutional perspectives on export channel selection and export performance. *Journal of Management*, *39*(1), 27–47. doi:10.1177/0149206312445926

Hitt, M. A., Ireland, R. D., & Hoskisson, R. E. (2007). *Strategic management: competitiveness and globalization*. Mason: Thomson SouthWestern.

Holt, D. B., Quelch, J. A., & Taylor, E. L. (2004). How global brands compete. *Harvard Business Review*, (September), 1–9. PMID:15449856

Howard, D. (1977). Technology transfer trhough commercial transations. *The Journal of Industrial Economics*, *16*(2), 161–175.

Hsieh, A.-T., & Li, C.-K. (2008). The moderating effect of brand image on public relations perception and customer loyalty. *Marketing Intelligence & Planning*, *26*(1), 26–42. doi:10.1108/02634500810847138

Jawahar, I. M., & McLaughlin, G. L. (2001). Toward a descriptive stakeholder theory: An organizational life-cycle approach. *Academy of Management Review*, *26*(1), 397–414. doi:10.5465/amr.2001.4845803

Jo, H., & Harjoto, M. A. (2011). Corporate governance and firm value: The impact of corporate social responsibility. *Journal of Business Ethics*, *103*(3), 351–383. doi:10.100710551-011-0869-y

Kayo, E. K. (2002). *A estrutura de capital e o risco das empresas tangível e intangível-intensivas: uma contribuição ao estudo da valoração de empresas* (PhD thesis). FEA/USP.

Keegan, W., Moriarty, S., & Duncan, T. (1995). *Marketing*. Prentice Hall.

Keller, K. (1993). Conceptualizing, measuring, and managing customer-based brand equity. *Journal of Marketing*, *57*(1), 1–22. doi:10.1177/002224299305700101

Keller, K. (2000). Building and managing corporate brand equity. In M. Schultz, M. Hatch, & M. Larsen (Eds.), *The expressive organisation. Linking identity, reputation, and the corporate brand* (pp. 115–137). Oxford University Press.

Keller, K. L., & Richey, K. (2006). The importance of corporate brand personality traits to a successful 21st century business. *Journal of Brand Management*, *14*(1), 74–81. doi:10.1057/palgrave.bm.2550055

Kirca, A. H., Jayachandran, S., & Bearden, W. O. (2005). Market orientation: A meta-analytic review and assessment of its antecedents and impact on performance. *Journal of Marketing*, *69*(1), 24–41. doi:10.1509/jmkg.69.2.24.60761

Kohli, A. K., & Jaworski, B. J. (1990). Market orientation: The construct, research propositions and managerial implications. *Journal of Marketing*, *54*(2), 1–18. doi:10.1177/002224299005400201

Kotler, P. (2000). Administração de Marketing: a edição do novo milénio (Vol. 10). Prentice Hall.

Lakatos, E. M., & Marconi, M. D. (2007). *Metodologias Científicas*. Atlas.

Lakatos, E. M., & Marconi, M. D. (2007). *Metodologias Científicas*. Atlas.

Lambin, J. (2008). *Market Driven Management*. Nova Iorque: McGrawHil.

Lang, M. H., Lins, K. V., & Miller, D. P. (2003). ADRs, analysts, and accuracy: Does cross listing in the United States Improve a firm's information environment and increase market value? *Journal of Accounting Research*, *41*(2), 317–345. doi:10.1111/1475-679X.00106

Li, E. X., & Liu, L. X. (2012). *Intangible assets and cross-sectional stock returns: Evidence from structural estimation*. Reunião Anual da Associação Económica America. Retrievied from https://ssrn.com/abstract=1560014

Lins, K. V. (2003). Equity ownership and firm vaiue in emerging markets. *Journal of Financial and Quantitative Analysis*, *38*(1), 159–184. doi:10.2307/4126768

Loudon, D. L., & Bitta, A. J. (1988). *Consumer Behavior: Concepts and Applications. Nova Iorque*. McGraw-Hill.

Madhok, A., & Keyhani, M. (2012). Acquisitions as entrepreneurship: Asymmetries, opportunities, and the internationalization of multinationals from emerging economies. *Global Strategy Journal*, *2*(1), 26–40. doi:10.1002/gsj.1023

Maroco, J. (2010). *Análise de Equações Estruturais: Fundamentos teóricos, Software e Aplicações*. Pêro Pinheiro: ReportNumber.

Maroco, J. (2011). *Análise Estatistica com o SPSS Statistics* (Vol. 5). Pêro Pinheiro: ReportNumber.

Martineau, P. (1958). The personality of the retail store. *Harvard Business Review*, *36*(1), 47–55.

Miller, D. (2003). An asymmetry-based view of advantage: Towards an attainable sustainability. *Strategic Management Journal*, *24*(10), 961–976. doi:10.1002mj.316

Mintzberg, H. (1979). *The Structuring of Organizations: a synthesis of the research. Nova Jérsia*. Prentice Hall.

Moeller, K. (2009). Intangible and financial performance: Causes and effects. *Journal of Intellectual Capital*, *10*(2), 224–245. doi:10.1108/14691930910952632

Morgan, N., & Pritchard, A. (2004). Meeting the destination branding challenge. In N. Morgan, A. Pritchard, & R. Pride (Eds.), *Destination branding: Creating the unique destination proposition* (Vol. 2, pp. 59–78). Elsevier Butterworth-Heinemann.

Nakatani, M. S., & Teixeira, R. M. (2009). Resource- Resource-based View as a ased View as a ased View as a Perspective for Public Tourism erspective for Public Tourism Management R Management Research: esearch: esearch: Evidence Evidence Evidence from Two Brazilian Brazilian Tourism Destinations. *Brazilian Admininstration Review*, *6*(1), 62–77. doi:10.1590/S1807-76922009000100006

Nalcacia, G., & Yagcib, M. I. (2014). The Effects of Marketing Capabilities on Export Performance Using Resource-based View: Assessment on Manufacturing Companies. *Procedia: Social and Behavioral Sciences*, *148*(1), 671–679. doi:10.1016/j.sbspro.2014.07.012

Niebel, T., O'Mahony, M., & Saam, M. (2013). *The contribution of intangible assets to sectoral productivity growth in the EU*. doi:10.2139srn.2319362

Olson, J. C. (1977)). Price as an Informational Cue: Effects on Product Evaluations. In A. G. Woodside, J. N. Sheth, & P. D. Bennett (Eds.), Consumer and Industrial Buying Behavior (pp. 267-286). Nova Iorque: North Holland.

Omar, M., Williams, R. Jr, & Lingelbach, D. (2009). Global brand market-entry strategy to manage corporate reputation. *Journal of Product and Brand Management*, *18*(3), 177–187. doi:10.1108/10610420910957807

Oxelheim, L., & Randoy, T. (2003). The impact of foreign board membership on firm value. *Journal of Banking & Finance*, *27*(12), 2369–2392. doi:10.1016/S0378-4266(02)00395-3

Park, C. W., Jaworski, B. J., & Macinnis, D. J. (1986). Strategic Brand Concept-Image Management. *Journal of Marketing*, *50*(1), 135–145. doi:10.1177/002224298605000401

Patterson, M. (1999). Re-appraising the concept of brand image. *Journal of Brand Management*, *6*(6), 409–426. doi:10.1057/bm.1999.32

Pestana, M. H., & Gageiro, J. N. (2008). *Análise de dados para ciências sociais: a complementaridade do SPSS* (Vol. 5). Sílabo.

Popoli, P. (2015). Reinforcing Intangible Assets through CSR in a Globalized World. *Journal of Management Policies and Practices*, *3*(1), 23–30. doi:10.15640/jmpp.v3n1a4

Portugal Global (2017). *Portugal Ficha País – Outubro 2017*. Lisboa: Agência para o Investimento e Comércio Externo de Portugal, E.P.E.

Prodanov, C. C., & Freitas, E. C. (2013). *Metodologia do Trabalho Científico: Métodos e Técnicas da Pesquisa e do Trabalho Acadêmico*. Novo Hamburgo: Editora Feevale.

Rao, A. R., & Monroe, K. B. (1988). The Moderating Effect of Prior Knowledge on Cue Utilization in Product Evaluations. *The Journal of Consumer Research*, *15*(2), 253–264. doi:10.1086/209162

Rao, V., Agarwal, M., & Dahlhoff, D. (2004). How Is Manifest Branding Strategy Related to the Intangible Value of a Corporation? *Journal of Marketing*, *68*(1), 126–141. doi:10.1509/jmkg.68.4.126.42735

Rauh, J. D., & Sufi, A. (2010). Capital structure and debt structure. *Review of Financial Studies*, *23*(12), 4242–4280. doi:10.1093/rfs/hhq095

Reinartz, W., Haenlein, M., & Henseler, J. (2009). An Empirical Comparison of the Efficacy of Covariance-Based and Variance-Based SEM. *International Journal of Research in Marketing*, *26*(4), 332–344. doi:10.1016/j.ijresmar.2009.08.001

Richardson, P. S., Dick, A., & Jain, A. K. (1994). Extrinsic and intrinsic cue effects on perceptions of store brand quality. *Journal of Marketing*, *58*(1), 28–36. doi:10.1177/002224299405800403

Rodebaugh, T. L., Woods, C. M., & Heimberg, R. G. (2007). The reverse of social anxiety is not always the opposite: The reverse-scored items of the Social Interaction Anxiety Scale do not belong. *Behavior Therapy*, *38*(1), 192–206. doi:10.1016/j.beth.2006.08.001 PMID:17499085

Romaniuk, J., & Sharp, B. (2004). Conceptualising and measuring brand salience. *Marketing Theory*, *4*(4), 327–342. doi:10.1177/1470593104047643

Rosenberg, M. J., & Hovland, C. I. (1960). *Attitude Organization and Change: An Analysis of Consistency Among Attitude Components*. Yale University Press.

Roszkowski, M. J., & Soven, M. (2010). Shifting gears: Consequences of including two negatively worded items in the middle of a positively worded questionnaire. *Assessment & Evaluation in Higher Education, 35*(2), 113–130. doi:10.1080/02602930802618344

Rua, O. L., & França, A. (2018). Linking entrepreneurial orientation to brand reputation. *Global Business and Economics Review, 20*(5/6), 667–678. doi:10.1504/GBER.2018.094451

Schiffman, L. G., & Kanuk, L. L. (2007). Consumer Behavior (Vol. 9). Prentice Hall.

Shane, S., & Venkataraman, S. (2000). The promise of entrepreneurship as a field of research. *Academy of Management Review, 25*(1), 217–226. doi:10.5465/amr.2000.2791611

Simonian, M. A., Forsythe, S., Suk Kwon, W., & Chattaraman, V. (2012). The role of product brand image and online store image on perceived risks and online purchase intentions for apparel. *Journal of Retailing and Consumer Services, 19*(3), 325–331. doi:10.1016/j.jretconser.2012.03.006

Slaughter, J. E., Zickar, M. J., Highhouse, S., & Mohr, D. C. (2004). Personality Trait Inferences about Organizations: Development of a Measure and Assessment of Construct Validity. *The Journal of Applied Psychology, 89*(1), 85–103. doi:10.1037/0021-9010.89.1.85 PMID:14769122

Sonderen, E. V., Sanderman, R., & Coyne, J. C. (2013). Ineffectiveness of reverse wording of questionnaire items: Let's learn from cows in the rain. *PLoS One, 8*(7), e68967. doi:10.1371/journal.pone.0068967 PMID:23935915

Spears, N., & Singh, S. N. (2004). Measuring attitude toward the brand and purchase intentions. *Journal of Current Issues and Research in Advertising, 26*(2), 53–66. doi:10.1080/10641734.2004.10505164

Spector, A. J. (1961). Basic dimensions of the corporate image. *Journal of Marketing, 25*(1), 47–51. doi:10.1177/002224296102500608

Stern, B., Zinkhan, G. M., & Jaju, A. (2001). Marketing images: Construct definition, measurement issue, and theory development. *Marketing Theory, 1*(2), 201–224. doi:10.1177/147059310100100203

Stevenson, H. H., & Jarillo, J. C. (1990). A paradigm of entrepreneurship: Entrepreneurial management. *Strategic Management Journal, 11*(1), 17–27.

Teece, D. J. (2007). Explicating dynamic capabilities: The nature and microfoundations of (sustainable) enterprise performance. *Strategic Management Journal, 28*(13), 1319–1350. doi:10.1002mj.640

Tsai, C., Lu, Y., & Yen, D. C. (2012). Determinants of intangible assets value: The data mining approach. *Knowledge-Based Systems, 31*(1), 67–77. doi:10.1016/j.knosys.2012.02.007

van Gelder, S. (2003). *Global brand strategy: Unlocking brand potential across countries, cultures and markets*. Sterling.

Wang, E. S., & Tsai, B.-K. (2014). Consumer response to retail performance of organic food retailers. *British Food Journal, 116*(2), 212–227. doi:10.1108/BFJ-05-2012-0123

Wernerfelt, B. (1984). A resource-based view of the firm. *Strategic Management Journal*, *5*(2), 171–180. doi:10.1002mj.4250050207

Wiwattanakantang, Y. (2001). Controlling shareholders and corporate value: Evidence from Thailand. *Pacific-Basin Finance Journal*, *9*(4), 323–362. doi:10.1016/S0927-538X(01)00022-1

Zeithaml, V. A. (1988). Consumer perceptions of price, quality, and value: A means-end model and synthesis of evidence. *Journal of Marketing*, *52*(1), 2–22. doi:10.1177/002224298805200302

ADDITIONAL READING

Aulakh, P. S., Kotabe, M., & Teegen, H. (2000). Export strategies and performance of firms from emerging economies: Evidence from Brazil, Chile, and Mexico. *Academy of Management Journal*, *43*(3), 342–361.

Barney, J. (1991). Firm Resources and Sustained Competitive Advantage. *Journal of Management*, *17*(1), 99–120. doi:10.1177/014920639101700108

Monteiro, A. P., Soares, A. M., & Rua, O. L. (2017). Linking intangible resources and export performance: The role of entrepreneurial orientation and dynamic capabilities. *Baltic Journal of Management*, *12*(3), 329–347. doi:10.1108/BJM-05-2016-0097

Penrose, E. T. (1959). *The Theory of the Growth of the Firm*. John Wiley.

Peteraf, M. (1993). The cornerstones of competitive advantage: A resource-based view. *Strategic Management Journal*, *14*(3), 179–191. doi:10.1002mj.4250140303

Rua, O. L., & Alves, H. (2019). Linking municipal best value and market performance: The Portuguese experience. *Public Money & Management*. Advance online publication. doi:10.1080/09540962.2019.1651036

Rua, O. L., & França, A. (2018). The Linkage Between Intangible Resources and Export Performance: The mediating effect of Innovation. *International Journal of Innovation*, *5*(3), 399–410. Advance online publication. doi:10.5585/iji.v5i3.190

KEY TERMS AND DEFINITIONS

Brand Image: The perceptions reflected through associations in the memory of the consumer.

Competitive Advantage: Based on the strategies of broad cost leadership, broad differentiation, cost focus and differentiation focus.

Intangible Resources: Considered strategic resources, including six dimensions: reputational resources; access to financial resources; human resources; cultural resources; relational resources; and informational resources.

Market Orientation: The set of processes and routines that encourage companies to produce, disseminate and respond to information about customers, competitors, and the external environment.

Resource-Based View: Theory based on the assumption that the source of competitive advantage is obtained from firms' resources.

SME: Small and medium-sized enterprises.

Chapter 11
Internationalization of Family Businesses:
Does Size Really Matter?

Joana Costa
https://orcid.org/0000-0001-7514-9836
University of Aveiro, Portugal

EXECUTIVE SUMMARY

Worldwide, family businesses are one of the cornerstones of the entrepreneurial fabric, being as a consequence central to growth and development. In a globalized era, these institutions require the attention of businessmen, practitioners, and policymakers. The chapter seeks to examine if the internationalization performance does vary according to firm size, and its link to the innovative performance in multiple dimensions along with conventional characteristics such as age and turnover. Theoretical research evidences the interest in understanding the patterns and determinants of the internationalisation performance, given its importance in firm growth and survival; however, this strategical option brings advantages and problems. Empirical evidence demonstrates that the determinants do change according to firm dimension; estimations provide valuable insights about the connection between globalized operation and innovation, for the different organisations.

INTRODUCTION

Family-owned businesses are central in most of the economies around the world, and most of them contribute with a substantial part to national income generation. According to the information presented by the Portuguese Family Business Association, presently, this type of companies represents nearly 70% of firms in operation, contributing with two thirds of the GDP. In Portugal their estimated impact in the job market encompasses half of the labor force and represents four fifths of the firms in operation. According to the INE and Pordata, the average number of workers per firm fell from 6.3 in 1990 to 3.1 in 2015 (see "inquérito anual às empresas" and "sistema de contas integradas das empresas"[1]); meaning

DOI: 10.4018/978-1-7998-4387-0.ch011

that most organizations in Portugal are likely to be family businesses and in most cases they are small organizations (see previous studies and articles such as Freire, 2008 and Marques & Couto[2]).

According to the European Commission for Industry Research and Energy, 85% of all firms operating in Europe are family owned businesses, being responsible for 60% of the total jobs in the private sector[3]. According to the European authorities (COM, 2008)[4], there is a need to collect, systematize and publicize detailed and reliable information about this type of organizations as it is mostly inexistent. In the theoretical dimension, despite being omnipresent, only recently, this type of organizations grasped the attention of academics, and most of the empirical evidence relies empirical evidence from the United States (Botero et al., 2015), which is expectably different from Europe, due to a dissimilar business environment.

It is of worth understanding that these firms are undeniably heterogeneous concerning their structure and their Governance; still, in most cases they are small or even micro entities (up to 9 workers), which play a major role in the protection of employment during crisis and promote sustainable and inclusive growth.

Encompassing family and business is often a complex task; still it will often produce powerful results. Instead of separating the family and the business, putting both together enhance success and the creation of competitive advantages impossible to find in other kinds of organizations. Family firms have established a unique area in research that witnessed exponential growth in the past few years because family firms represent many businesses worldwide (Tsao & Lien 2013; Holt 2012; Piva et al. 2013; Arregle et al. 2012). However, this field is somehow recent in terms of the literature available.

There is a common belief that these organizations are usually small or medium sized; however, important organizations quoted on the stock exchange are controlled by families. These players are central in terms of job opportunities, local development, long term knowledge transfer, tradition and territorial cohesion. They organize and lead complex outsourcing networks which streamline niche markets and small communities generating high value added and singular identities (Tsao & Lien 2013). They are pillars of the economic activity at the regional, sectoral and national level. Despite numerous, these organizations cannot fit a single character as their essence is plasticity.

Family firms are singular in the way they operate, in their internationalization and innovation attitude. Family ownership does influence the way these organizations perform, which has been appraised in different perspectives across the literature (Anderson & Reeb, 2003).

Family businesses (FBs) are scattered across all economic sectors, being multi-featured. In their business model, they generate value for both their entrepreneurs and their communities; they generate technological take-offs, promote knowledge transfer, combining tradition and modernity exploiting new business ideas. FBs promote self-employment and job creation inside and outside the firm borders promoting the development of human capital and innovation (Botero et al., 2015).

Designing and engaging internationalization processes is a key factor for a competitive economy. Moreover, the world has been witnessing a trend towards internationalization not only by large multinationals but also by small businesses, yet it exposes firms to increased risks (Marin, 2017). With the mainstreaming of globalization, firms and markets have become more prone to take advantages from the external environment, which favors the acknowledgement and exploitation of new ideas and methods to gain competitiveness and survive (Giovanetti et al., 2013).

FBs are often considered as conservative and risk adverse, resisting change. They prefer relying on internal factors rather than opening to the external environment, which may endanger their future. As a consequence, no straightforward evidence can be found in tying internationalization with FBs. As on the one hand, there is a strong belief that FBs have a reduced propensity to approach new markets due to their embedded culture; on the other hand, and due to values as loyalty, trust and informal networks, they will be more prone to develop either individual or collective internationalization strategies with solid roots (Marin, 2017).

Existing literature points towards the existence of heterogeneous trends concerning FBs in their operations. In this vein, one line of research states that this type of organizations as unwilling to invest in new missions abroad due to skeptical views towards new challenges (Eddleston & Kellermanns, 2007); others consider that family ownership may lead to a more innovative and open to new market business strategy (Gómez-Mejía et al., 2007). The internationalization process is often beneficial for firms in the long run, given the importance for the firm long-term survival as this practice consolidates competitive advantages, which leads to the expansion to new markets, economies of scale and a greater diversification of production inputs. However, the internationalization process demands flexibility and plasticity from the organization; for FBs there is a greater need to change their hierarchical structure in order to gain competitiveness in the new markets. Another element that consolidates the internationalization process in FBs is their long-term commitment; they lean to have continuity in their business strategies instead of short term objectives (Gallo & Sveen, 1991). The economic performance of a company is improved in the presence of a higher participation in international markets (Giovanetti, et al., 2013). International presence underpins business operations and opens up new possibilities such as economies of scale, nonetheless when deciding to internationalize FBs are exposed to greater and tougher competition than local agents, so they have to create new solutions in order to counter this effect (Kafourus et al., 2008).

According to the Portuguese Family Businesses Association [Associação Empresas Familiares][5], in 2016, FBs represented more than 70% of the total firms operating in Portugal, generating nearly two thirds of the GDP and providing one half of the total job opportunities. The dataset encompasses different firm sizes, sectors of activity, age, internationalization and governance.

Firstly, this chapter aims systematizing the determinants of internationalization of FBs as notwithstanding their abundance these structures are scantly analyzed, mostly in what concerns critical success factors and advisable structural characteristics. Besides this characterization, the second objective is to understand if these characteristics do hold regarding the firm size. Finally, and based upon empirical evidence, policy recommendations will be offered to reinforce the performance of FBs so that these entities can be properly addressed from the economy and policy perspective.

Using a dataset of 1148 family businesses located in the North of Portugal, the aim of the study is twofold: identify the determinants of internationalization among FBs; and address the role of size in the propensity to internationalize. Binary count models were estimated to provide evidence on the determinants of internationalization, controlling for relevant firm characteristics, henceforth firms will be separated in sub-sample according to their size and the analysis will focus on the maintenance of change of the determinants and the test of the statistical differences among them. The econometric estimations prove that the firm internationalization performance relies much more on the innovation strategy in its different dimensions, rather than on conventional structural characteristics such as governance, family equity or age.

A deep understanding about the role of size in the internationalization process and the identification of other structural characteristics that are relevant to the internationalization processes will shed some light to the effective policy schemes that should to be implemented. Hence, the chapter aims to provide empirical evidence and policy recommendation which can be helpful for entrepreneurs, investors, managers and policy makers.

The remainder of the chapter is structured as follows. Section 2 presents the theoretical background of FBs and their structural characteristics. It also discusses the role of innovation and internationalization along with firm size. In Section 3 database, methodology and econometric modeling are defined. Section 4 presents the econometric estimations, and the discussion of the results. Finally, Section 5 concludes presenting some policy recommendations.

LITERATURE REVIEW

Every so often, FBs are considered as the most complex and challenging type of organization to analyze both in the theoretical and empirical perspective. This type of business arrays from non-technological activities to technologically intensive sectors; being present in different economic sectors; operating either in local markets or internationally, and presenting dimensions from micro-sized to large corporations; in sum, they are multifaceted.

All over the world, the most important companies are FBs, or, they have started as so, due to their particular features, combining economic and emotional aspects this firms are far different from their non-family counterparts (Gómez-Mejía,et al. 2007, 2011).

An important part of the multinational companies we know today started as small family businesses (Swoboda & Olejnik, 2013). The concept of FB is too broad, needing to be narrowed to obtain a coherent set of organizations which present singular features in terms of their characteristics and governance that provides relevant insights for the deepening of their understanding.

This particular type of firms is common in many countries across the globe, being identified as organizations in which the founding family has intense ownership and active participation in management (Barbera & Moores 2013; Chung 2012). In these organizations, one or more family members have significant bestowed interests in ownership.

Being considered essential for economic growth and sustainability, as they are the most common type of firm in the different economic activities, (Anderson & Reeb, 2003), There is no single universal definition for FFBs (Miller et al., 2007, Siebels & Aufseß, 2012). Despite the inexistence of consensus (the literature point towards 90 or more different definitions), it is critical to set the boundaries of what is and what is not a FB (e.g. Astrachan & Shanker, 1996; Miller et al., 2007; Siebels & Aufseß, 2012), as the differences in the conceptual framework will change the empirical evidence presented (Chrisman et al., 2003).

Quite consensually, one may state that in these firms some family members have relevant managerial positions, which means that the company is wielded by family management; in other words, these organizations are those in which the "family" leads the governance (Miller & Le Breton-Miller, 2006).

In a simpler perspective, a firm is labeled as FB if the majority of equity is in possession of the family (Chrisman et al., 2003; Claver et al., 2008; Kontinen & Ojala, 2010; Swoboda & Olejnik, 2013; Piva et al., 2013). Shanker and Astrachan (1996) evidence the direct involvement in daily decision making processes as a request of FBs, being responsible for the management. To Tsang (2002), this decision making process can be shared between the family and external members and still having a FB classification. To the European Commission (2009) four different dimensions need to be fulfilled to identify a FB: a) most of the decisions are taken by the founder or by those representing his/her legacy, which normally is the natural heirs or indirect relatives; b) most of the decision-making can be direct or indirect; c) at least one family member apart from the founder is involved in the firm control; and d) the founder and his family own 25% or more of the equity.

Regardless of the equity structure, all forms of business aim to maximize profit. However, there are elements which separate family-owned businesses from their counterparts in terms of the decision-making process in the sense as they have a different *mindset* and ethical concerns towards wealth creation (Berrone et al., 2010). Given their long-term orientation, these corporations focus on survival, and tend to avoid higher financial risks; their risk aversion will also be reflected in their internationalization processes (Zahra, 2004; Berrone et al., 2010; Alessandri et al., 2018). On the contrary, non-family firms seek for immediate profits, focusing on short and medium-term income generation, which makes them more likely to take risks, namely in the internationalization process (Berrone et al., 2010; Alessandri et al., 2018). As a consequence, FBs are more prone to act locally, which brings security for their legacy. As a consequence they will avoid or neglect the operation in foreign markets. This aversion may hinder their expansion process (Zahra, 2004; Gómez-Mejía et al., 2007; Gómez-Mejía et al., 2010).

Two theoretical proposals are widely accepted in the academic community: the first relies on the components-of-involvement approach, classifying firms as FBs according to the percentage of shares in possession by family members, regardless their managerial role (Siebels & Aufseß, 2012); in this vein, Chrisman et al. (2003) state that the threshold is half of the equity. Indeed, presently in Europe, a firm is classified as FB if 25% or more of its shares are controlled by the family.

The second definition connects to the essence approach model, stating that direct involvement in day-to-day operations is mandatory (Shanker & Astrachan, 1996). To Eddleston et al. (2012), a business can be considered as family if members have everyday involvement in managerial decisions, strategic planning, direct involvement and emotional bonds (Chua et al., 1999).

When relying on different conceptual frameworks, the empirical results may diverge (Chrisman et al., 2003), So, in most cases, authors restrict the label 'Family Business' to those firms in which the family owns equity in such a proportion that allows family members to control the strategic and managerial decisions in a continuous perspective, playing active roles on operations and management in a daily basis. However, it becomes relevant to analyze their business strategies as well as how they act towards foreign markets.

Internationalization Strategy of FBs

For decades internationalization process is considered as a pathway to economic sustainability and businesses expansion. A strategy oriented towards foreign markets is a valuable asset for organizations as it blurs risk, reinforces market penetration and increases economic power, avoiding country-level downturns. The economic performance is boosted when involved in international markets (Johanson & Vahlne, 1977). Being involved in international markets improves the economic performance of the company (Kontinen & Ojala, 2010; Hagemejer & Kolasa, 2011; Swoboda & Olejnik, 2013; Piva et al., 2013). Operating abroad or dealing with multiple markets reinforces competitiveness and introduces the organization to globalized markets; still it requires plasticity in the organizational structure and the ability to accommodate a more demanding community of buyers. Being exposed to increased competition, both internally and internationally, pushes the firms towards the constant seek for improvement and efficiency gains. International placement enhances commercial opportunities; nevertheless, globalized operations put firms into higher exposure to worldwide competition in comparison to local markets, so they need to come up with new solutions to overcome this outcome (Kafouros et al., 2008). Often, FBs will internationalize their operation after consolidating their influence within their domestic market, as once they have built up resources and capabilities for growth in domestic market, they will feel capable to scale up for further expansion abroad (Huang et al., 2014).

In the same manner that it does with other types of organizations, internationalization processes may leverage FBs into long term success, as they allow for the penetration into new markets, the scaling of the operation and the exploitation of economies of scale and the access to diversified tangible and intangible resources, knowledge and culture. As all firms operate in globalised markets, the only decision to be taken is approaching multi-cultural market actively or passively; those actively intervening in this process may take advantage of it rather than simply protecting themselves from fierce international competition. This process is hard, still, the involvement of family members will help overcoming its difficulties; as FBs are committed to longevity, they will be more likely to succeed in this effort (Gallo & Sveen, 1991).

Industry conditions and competitive forces are crucial for family business international expansion (Kontinen & Ojala 2010; Hu & Shieh 2013). To Gallo and Sveen (1991), the success of the internationalization process in FBs relies on the structure flexibility, meaning that the previous awareness of the external markets' characteristics will give them time to adapt to the new environment, and, as a consequence leveraging the potential success of the operation.

The ability to take advantage of the formal and the informal knowledge, the tradition and the legacy is a natural advantage found within the family. This involvement, when transferred to the entrepreneurial venture, will raise the probability to succeed. Moreover, inside the family, there will be and increased probability to self-finance the project with family funds; generating uniqueness to the venture, singular involvement and intrinsic competitive advantages compared to their counterparts (Habbershon & Pistrui, 2002). However, the family involvement is potentially dangerous as emotional reasons may endanger continuity. As a consequence, disentangling the roles is as difficult as necessary. Managerial strategies may need to go in opposite directions from family matters. External finance operates rationally, demanding profitability and nothing else. Furthermore, when facing self-funding constraints, family members may believe that the financial system brings more than increased costs.

Empirical research supports that firm characteristics enable them to accentuate the importance of performance influenced by internationalization (Benito-Hernández et al., 2014). The chapter contributes to build a deeper understanding about FBs as well as international venturing; seeking for explanations on the way equity ownership affects this process. An important branch of the literature in this field identifies FBs as resistant to change, being closed to the external ecosystem, rigid and scantly prone to accept the challenge of operating in unknown markets (Bettinelli et al., 2014; Nordquist & Melin, 2002).

To Gallo and Sveen (1991), the internationalization process is above all a method of transformation within the organization. Additionally, it is explored the potential mediating role of social capital, strategic participative process and strategic flexibility in internationalization of family businesses; however, the determinant factors in internationalization of family enterprises are interconnected to other structural characteristics. The internationalization process is embodied not only by the required changes within the company but also by the necessary knowledge and adjustment to the foreign markets. Thus capital ownership does impact the whole process since different types of companies have different business strategies (Gallo & Sveen, 1991; Gómez-Mejía et al, 2007).

Although the process of internationalization generates a major competitive advantage for businesses, due to market inexperience, it is risky, generating agency costs and requiring specific management structures. Investing in external markets exposes the business to higher competition, these and the elements mentioned above can have negative consequences in the internationalization process and can put the organization in a chance of financial failure (Tallman and Li, 1996; Marin, 2017). Targeting the organization into a new market requires flexibility and adaptation that can be vital to its success, in the case of FBs there is a greater need for plasticity due to the hierarchical and ownership characteristics which make them different (Gallo & Sveen, 1991).

The internationalization success mainly depends on two factors: external and internal factors. External factors are not controlled by the firm, such as the economic environment, the legislative measures and exchange rate. Regarding internal factors, ownership structure becomes one of the most significant (Marin, 2017). Thus internationalization processes differ between family and non-family businesses (Gallo & Sveen, 1991). The literature suggests that there is a negative relationship between family businesses and the internationalization process (Fernandez & Nieto, 2005; Gallo & Sveen, 1991; Graves & Thomas, 2008). However, if the company identifies the internationalization process as vital to its survival there will be a pursuit of this strategy even with the associated risks (Zahra, 2004).

FBs have developed distinctive behaviors connected to the socio-emotional wealth. This concept highlights emotional and non-economic behaviors that family businesses develop to protect their identity, family influence and legacy. This concept may be central to understand the singularities of FBs in their business strategies and also their internationalization process (Gomez-Mejia et al., 2007). Internationalization processes demand important financial and organizational investments, with uncertain returns; being perceived as a risky; as FBs are willing to protect their socio-emotional wealth the entry to new markets may be considered as a threat to legacy and survival thereby pledging new business opportunities (Gomez-Mejia et al., 2007). The inherent risks in the internationalization process impact FBs and non-FBs differently being a challenge for the first to adapt their organizational structure without losing family control (Gomez-Mejia et al., 2011; Kraus et al., 2016; Alessandri et al., 2018).

Depending on the generation in control the FBs may have different strategies; often, founders are more averse to organizational change; the centralization of control may lead to lower propensity to invest in internationalization strategies (Marin, 2017). Expectably, future generations will have greater intention to internationalize the business as they will combine their expertise in business with the awareness of the developments of the global context; as a consequence the entry of new generations is seen as an enhancer of the internationalization process (Fernandez & Nieto, 2005; Graves & Thomas, 2008; Marin, 2017).

Unwillingness to approach the new markets throughout the penetration in multinational networks and value chains will jeopardize the success of the operation in any firm, and in FBs in particular (Gomez-Mejia et al., 2011; Pukall & Calabrò, 2014). It is doubtful whether FBs are more internationalized than their non-family counterparts, as they may be uncomfortable in this process, fearing the loss of identity and control during this process. Preserving themselves as singular entities will be determinant for the success of the internationalization process itself (Alessandri et al., 2018). As a result, it is desirable that FB's approach internationalization processes with solid strategies and identity preservation as this will on the one hand the probability of success, and on the other hand the efficiency and longevity of the business.

Notwithstanding, the business strategies pursued by FBs are different, such that, it has to be implemented encompassing this diversity (Alessandri et al., 2018). Due to *familyness*, the behavior of the company is more cautious in what concerns business strategies, focusing in the avoidance of control loss and the preservation of legacy. Therefore, they are less likely to move forward with high investment projects with highly uncertain returns. Since most FBs are controlled by manager-owners there is a greater precaution the business activities and their potential dangers (Fernández & Nieto, 2005). Studies highlight that in the case of manager-owners, internationalization processes are less dynamic; conversely, if the manager is a non-family member internationalization goes faster (D'Angelo et al.,

2016). Given these features, the internationalization strategies performed by FBs and the connection to their dimension becomes an important research issue.

Innovation Strategy of FBs

There is widespread consensus that innovative firms grow more rapidly in terms of employment and profitability (Geroski et al., 1993), and firm and industry particular features may accelerate or deter innovation outcomes (Acs & Audretsch, 1987). It is however an undeniable factor of growth and economic performance in FBs (Nieto et al., 2015; de Massis et al., 2015). As beyond boosting performance, innovation reinforces through the creation of comparative advantages allows for profit maximization (de Massis et al., 2016). Hence, innovation will reinforce the long term performance of FBs and, as a consequence their survival (Alberti & Pizzurno, 2013). The generation of successful innovation cycles is therefore positive at both micro and macroeconomic level. Innovative activities, connected to emerging products or improved processes will raise efficiency, productivity, reduce costs, generating competitive advantages.

The fact that Portugal recently shifted to a Strong Innovator score (European Innovation Scoreboard, 2019), generates increased interest on its entrepreneurial fabric as a case study, as a way to understand the importance of the innovation practices, to be disseminated among companies in operation, being a generalized practice to leverage the overall performance of firms. Innovation is structural to economic performance, as the introduction of new products and practices boosts the present and the future productive potential. Experience enables organizations to experience upon learning-by-doing and learning-by-failing effects. The first improves the firm's R&D efficiency, the second works as self-reinforcement (Maidique & Zirger, 1985; Zirger, 1997 García-Vega & López, 2010).

There is common acceptance that FBs are highly conservative in their managerial strategies, so, more averse to risky projects and changes. It is therefore expectable that they tend to innovate less, even though this option may jeopardize their performance (Canepa & Stoneman, 2002). Innovative projects are uncertain by nature, running out of the control of managers. Very often hindering factors appear from inside or outside the firm. These activities have moral hazard problems, becoming unattractive to external investors. Information asymmetries chase away venture capital due to uncertainty, and also, intangible assets are not accepted as collaterals (Costa et al., 2018). Unavailability of external finance, combined with increased risks will decrease the intentions to innovate among FBs, moreover, reliance on internal finance which is needed for core activities will expose them to perhaps unnecessary risks (Claver et al., 2008).

Understanding the full dimension of innovation on FBs and its connection to the internationalization process is an important gap to be fulfilled as the literature is ambiguous. On one hand, due to the conservativeness argument there is an expectation for them to innovate less. On the other hand, due to flexibly, FBs have enhanced capabilities to open formal and informal innovation channels with the entire ecosystem. The appraisal of the impact of innovation will be performed in a threefold way: firstly throughout the effect of internal R&D, secondly by the analysis on innovation as an output, and finally through the connection with the University.

Given the positive effect of innovation on FBs economic performance, efforts should be made to nourish the innovative milieu inside the FBs community and their connection to other players.

The Role of Size in FBs Performance

Young and and small and medium-sized enterprises pursuing risky actions such as innovation or internationalization processes may fall in severe financial problems (Hadjimanolis, 1999). Larger firms have an increased capability to take risks, to exploit new ideas, to dilute fixed costs connected to innovation and internationalization, greater financial possibilities. In the existing literature, the number of paid employees is the natural proxy of firm size (Zahra, 2004; Marin, 2017).

Organisations with a larger number of workers will have more potential to benefit from economies of scale, therefore being more interested in innovation along with market expansion abroad (Piva et al., 2013). Their potential in terms of the staff skills is also enlarged (Giovannetti et al., 2013) and due to the organizational structure, the workers have the possibility to concentrate on particular tasks, enhancing the learning effect. This fact will raise productivity due to repetition boosting the overall firm performance.

For most of authors, firm size positively influences the internationalization performance (Giovannetti et al. 2013; Piva et al., 2013). Here this structural characteristic is proxied by the number of employees, is also directly connected to firm performance and internationalization, as larger firms have more availability of internal finance and are more willing and able to take risks, namely those associated with internationalization and the implementation of new challenges, ideas, putting the available knowledge in use to exploit new possibilities and scale up the activity; they have more awareness of the new markets with a simplified process to overcome the sunk costs related to the entry in new markets (Eickelpash & Vogel, 2011).

Firm size is consistently positively correlated to internationalization strategies across the studies in FBs (Zahra, 2004; Hernández & Nieto, 2005; Perri & Peruffo, 2017). Empirical evidence highlights that larger companies, due to greater availability of resources, tend to become more active towards internationalization processes (Benito-Hernández et al., 2014).

Also, it is more prone to find R&D departments in large firms, these infrastructures will develop new ideas, promoting innovation which will boost efficiency and retro-fed the internationalization process (Narula & Zanfei, 2003). It is expectable that larger firms are more prone to benefit from economies of scale, scaling up the production will reduce the cost of production which will generate comparative advantages to compete in the foreign markets; the penetration in new markets will enhance market power and consolidate profit maximization. Additionally, this process will leverage the expertise of the human capital which will indirectly increase the productivity levels (Koellinger, 2008; Ganotakis, 2012).

Other Structural Characteristics of FBs

Being established in the market is normally connected to economic stability, availability of internal finance, existing stocks of knowledge, market awareness and maturity. As a consequence, the literature considers firm age as an important factor in firm performance (Zahra, 2004; Gomez-Mejia et al., 2010; De Massis et al., 2018); as a consequence younger companies tend to postpone internationalization plans (Benito-Hernández et al., 2014). Nonetheless, recently the born global phenomenon contradicts this belief, as some ventures are born operating globally (Ribau, Moreira, & Raposo, 2015).

Innovation depends on the stock of knowledge, the absorptive and cumulative capacity. Efficiency along the process requires the recognition of relevant of knowledge collected in the ecosystem its assimilation and its commercial application (Dosi, 1988; Cohen et al., 1990; Lall, 1992). The role of education on economic growth is widely acknowledged (Ganotakis, 2012); when moving to the micro level, it is also highlighted the positive connection between human capital intensity and firm survival (Collier et al., 2011; Herstad et al. 2013).

Mainstream literature on human capital reinforces the desirability of educated personnel to raise added value, consequently profitability; the existence diversified competences delivers the manager a powerful tool to deal with business challenges and adversity (Koellinger, 2008). As a result, high endowments of educated employees along with managerial competences will consolidate firm performance. Often, successful managers lead working teams with broad typologies of skills (West & Noel, 2009), albeit, the success of R&D projects strongly relies on the managers' competences (Chen et al., 2012).

Extant literature has three streamlines: the first, tying the manager's competences to project success; the second, relying on firm characteristics; and the third, connecting the performance with the business environment. As a consequence the econometric estimations will encompass variables that capture the manager's skills, firm structural characteristics and the innovation ecosystem

The understanding of the determinants of FBs' internationalization ventures is of major interest as the traditional literature focus on performance or on internationalization as a result of availability of resources. FBs have singularities in their governance and their scale which make them different from other organizational structures.

Table 1. FBs appraisal according to their characteristics

Strengths	Weaknesses
relevance on the entrepreneurial fabric	weak professional governance
multi-sectoral presence	legacy issues
economic dynamism	risk aversion
local embededness	talent attraction and retention
familyness	
Opportunities	**Threats**
smoothing of the economic activity	definition of FB
segmentation on sub-types	lack of political relevance
promotion of entrepreneurial initiative	neglection of the singularities
sustainable growth	resistance to change
achievement of smart specialization goals	closedness and aversion to cooperation
territorial cohesion	exposure to family conflicts

METHODOLOGY

The empirical part of the present chapter relies on a database gathered by the project Roadmap for Portuguese Family Firms[6]. Therefore, it is a primary source of information which was purposefully conducted to fulfill the inexistence of microdata in the sector of family firms. A particularly singular feature of this chapter is that it gathers a sample of 1148 firms operating in different economic sectors, with different technological intensities and sizes. The analysis of the internationalization performance is run considering the innovative performance along with other structural characteristics, and it aims to clarify the role of size in this process and produce policy recommendations to incentive and finance the innovative activities and internationalization, given its importance in enhancing their profitability and survival. Moreover given that FBs are the backbone of the economic activity in most of the sectors, it is important to get a deep understanding about their singularities and provide the policy instruments to allow the improvement of their performance exploiting the market opportunities and promoting sustainable growth.

Database and Exploratory Analysis

This study was based on the analysis of family businesses industry located in the Northern region of Portugal. The aim of the study is twofold: to identify the determinants of internationalization among FBs; and to address the role of size in the propensity to internationalize. The database provides direct information about the economic performance of FBs, their internationalization strategy, a set of firm structural characteristics such as firm size, SIC code, economic sector, technological intensity, education intensity, R&D intensity which will be used to run the econometric estimations.

The database represents 10.4% of the Northern FBs identified by Statistics Portugal (INE[7]). This region is particularly dynamic in what concerns venture creation, and, as a consequence it is important to identify their strategies, mostly in what relates to the presence in foreign markets, to understand what has to be done to leverage these organizations to higher levels, producing synergies in their regional ecosystems.

In what relates to size, SMEs, and following the Recommendation of the European Commission (2003/361/CE)[8], these firms employ less than 250 employees, their turnover is below 50 million euros and the total balance sheet does not exceed 43 million. These organizations are the most prevalent type of firm in both Portugal and Europe; according to Statistics Portugal and Pordata, in 2016 these firms represented 99.9% of the total firms in operation, in Europe this percentage, on average, 99%: Among those, 95.4% are micro-firms, 3.9% were small and only 0.6% are medium. Here, micro-firms have less than 10 employees. In the database, nearly 70% of the firms have this profile. Due to the over-representation of this segment, and in the expectation of remarkable differences, firms with up to 3 employees were classified as *nano*-firms and those with 4 to 9 were kept as micro. Small firms (with up to 49 workers) represent 16.3% and the remaining are medium or large.

Dependent Variable Revisited

In order to reach sustainability and survival, SME's need to consider internationalization strategies as a way to acquire competitive advantages and reach the external markets, thus becoming globalized. According to the Insight Observatory[9] (2018), the internationalization process means export, which means that there is a significant difference between secondary and tertiary sectors. To Insight observatory for SMEs in the year of 2017, one fourth of the total SMEs are strongly internationalized; nearly one third of them have less than 30% of exports. Most of them intend to continue in exporting and they forecast an increase. As a consequence, time seems to play a determinant role in the internationalization process. Internationalization is determinant in the context of FBs, however, in the database, nearly three quarters of them do export and among the remaining quarter, only nearly 5% of them export three quarters of the total turnover. When connecting export intensity to age, two alternative profiles are found: exporting up to 25% of the total turnover often happens in older firms and among those who sell abroad almost the total production there is a prevalence of younger corporations, evidencing the "born global" phenomenon.

Here the dependent variable is dichotomous; meaning that the value takes the value 1 if the firm does mention the existence of sales abroad, regardless its intensity. As a consequence the focus relies upon propensity, neglecting intensity. This proxy is being used in several studies (e.g. Fernández & Nieto, 2005; Benito-Hernández et al., 2014).

Descriptive Analysis, Correlations and Tests

In order to understand the connection among the variables in use, descriptive statistics were run along with the correlation matrix. The results provide consistency to perform the econometric estimations, which will be performed in the following section. Except for the case of family equity, which is uncorrelated with the rest of the variables, all predictors are moderately correlated.

Table 2. Descriptive Statistics and Correlations

	Descriptive Statistics					Correlations								
	N	Min	Max	Mean	S-D	1	2	3	4	5	6	7	8	9
Internationalization (1)	1148	0	1	0.35	0.479		.157**	.379**	.397**	.215**	.171**	.150**	-.015	.087**
Age (2)	1022	1	172	24.70	18.376			.358**	.370**	.154**	.179**	.002	.073*	.028
Turnover (3)	1148	1	6	2.48	1.525				.789**	.289**	.199**	.063*	-.007	.085**
Size (4)	1148	1	4	2.27	1.018					.287**	.209**	.065*	-.035	.082**
Internal R&D (5)	1148	0	1	0.11	0.316						.343**	.263**	-.044	.078**
Innovation (6)	1148	0	1	0.16	0.369							.201**	.006	.069*
Univ_links (7)	1148	0	1	0.03	0.170								-.046	.090**
Family_equity (8)	1148	0	1	0.94	0.231									.026
Managerial_skills (9)	1146	0	5	3.04	1.355									

**. Significant at 0.01 (2 tails); *. Significant at 0.05 (2-tails)

Given the heterogeneous expectations of the behavior of the variables in use, non-parametric tests were implemented to address the statistical differences of the sub-sample. When performing the Kruskall-Wallis test for independent samples, the results are shown in Table 3.

Considering the variables in use, the null hypothesis was rejected, in the case of Internationalization, Age and Turnover. This rejection means that there are significant differences between the size groups. This result statistically demonstrates that the determinants of internationalization do vary according to firm size. According to the results of the Kruskall–Wallis tests, there is strong evidence supporting the fact that size does matter in terms of internationalization strategy.

Table 3. Kruskall-Wallis test

	Significance	Decision
Internationalization (1)	0.000	rej H0
Age (2)	0.000	rej H0
Turnover (3)	0.000	rej H0
Internal R&D (5)	cannot be performed	
Innovation (6)	cannot be performed	
Univ_links (7)	cannot be performed	
Family_equity (8)	0.371	do not rej H0
Managerial_skills (9)	cannot be performed	

Asymptotic significances displayed ($p < 0.05$)

ECONOMETRIC ESTIMATIONS

Several models were run to address the internationalization determinants and the asymmetries according to size. In our study we use logit models and analyze their marginal effects. The first model encompasses the entire sample with size considered as an explanatory variable. The second and third models consider two sub-samples according to size with the purpose of testing if the determinants are the same or if they do change according to firm size. Doing so allows us to observe the effects of independent variables on the dependent variable and on the control variables which are the size of the business and its age. The estimations are shown in Table 4.

In what concerns Model (1) the entire sample was considered. As previously mentioned, there is no connection between the firm age and the propensity to export. This result was expectable as there was no strong correlation between the variables. As a consequence, there is a reinforcement of a dual reality of firms which wait for their maturity to internationalize and those who are born global. Extending the analysis to models (2) and (3) one can observe that age appears as an enhancer to internationalization for SMEs; for them, each additional year raises the probability to export by 1 percentage point. As a consequence, it seems that smaller FBs do not need a consolidation period in the local market to move on to foreign markets.

Regardless the firm size, sales turnover does influence export propensity; firms with higher levels of revenue will become more prone to operate in international markets.

The variable size was considered only in model 1, as the other logit estimations only considered one firm size. In the sample, larger firms are more prone to develop activities in foreign markets.

Given the importance of innovation as a booster of firm growth and the acquisition of competitive advantages, the model encompasses three alternative proxies: the existence of an internal R&D department, performing innovative activities and the establishment of links with the University. For the first case, the existence of an internal R&D department, the variable is significant for SMEs; in that case, performing internal R&D raises the probability to export. Concerning the second dimension (having performed innovative activities), the variable is significant for the entire sample and for *nano* and micro firms; innovative firms in these cases are more likely to sell abroad.

In a very similar way, the establishment of links with the University enhances internationalization propensity only in Models (1) and (2), seeming that Universities are more helpful for *nano* and micro

Table 4. Econometric Estimations

Variables	Entire Sample (1)	Nano and Micro (2)	Small and Medium (3)
Age (2)	-0.000	-0.009	0.010*
	(0.004)	(0.007)	(0.006)
Turnover (3)	0.233***	0.399***	0.380***
	(0.073)	(0.106)	(0.092)
Size (4)	0.526***	n.a.	n.a.
	(0.116)		
Internal R&D (5)	0.315	0.171	0.554*
	(0.238)	(0.469)	(0.285)
Innovation (6)	0.363*	0.970***	0.007
	(0.197)	(0.293)	(0.257)
Univ_links (7)	1.469***	1.476**	1.041
	(0.464)	(0.616)	(0.681)
Family_equity (8)	0.066	0.495	-0.123
	(0.324)	(0.556)	(0.420)
Managerial_skills (9)	0.063	0.161**	-0.029
	(0.054)	(0.079)	(0.076)
Constant	-2.811***	-2.813***	-1.514***
	(0.401)	(0.642)	(0.535)
Observations	1020	583	437

Standard errors in parentheses
*** $p<0.01$, ** $p<0.05$, * $p<0.1$

entities rather than for SMEs. It should be of interest to further analyze the underlying reasons of the loss of significance of this variable for larger corporations.

Here, the existence of control from the family fails to be statistically significant. From the sample in analysis, the fact of being controlled or not by the family does not affect the internationalization strategy.

There is a common expectation that the profile of the founder (here proxied by the educational degree) influences the internationalization strategy. The variable appears as significant only for *nano* and micro firms. A higher level of education of the manager raises the propensity to internationalize the operation.

CONCLUSION AND POLICY RECOMMENDATIONS

The main objective of the chapter was to empirically contribute to the literature on FBs and their internationalization strategies with a size threshold.

In Portugal FBs are a pillar of the economy in terms of income generation and job creation as they are the basis of the entrepreneurial fabric being highly represented in the entire territory and in the Northern region in particular. Empirical results reinforce the dynamism of the FBs in the database, illustrating to the possible extent the entire region. As the data relates to a post-crisis period, with the present moment we are living, the results may be of help to learn from the positive aspects and avoid past errors. FBs play a central role in local communities, accelerating the recovery, and, at present, this is certainly in the agenda of businessman and policy makers. Being responsible for more than a half of the jobs offered in the private sector, these organizations are facing a huge challenge to nail the present crisis.

These organizations are traditionally characterized for their low risk propensity, preferring internal sources of finance as an insurance of control maintenance. In doing so, they will have a stronger managerial control which will work as an advantage during downturns and crisis.

The empirical findings evidence that export propensity is not influenced by the firm age, which is an interesting finding as it reinforces the heterogeneity of the group and creates a warning to policy makers when designing policy packages which tend to favor mature firms. The skills of the manager have a dissimilar effects regarding firm size. For *nano* and micro firms more skilled managers raise export propensity, still, in the case of small and medium sized firms this variable becomes insignificant.

However, the sales turnover is relevant when opting for pursuing an internationalization strategy. This reinforces the former argument that FBs focus in maintaining the control of their operations and choose internal finance for supporting exports. Still, it is overlooked if this option is voluntary or compulsory, and perhaps some credit lines or public support should be targeted to these organizations.

FBs are often identified as laggards in terms of the innovation dynamics. The innovation dimension was appraised in different vectors with dissimilar results which should be carefully interpreted. Innovation and internationalization are commonly considered as an inextricable binomial, and the empirical evidence reinforces this connection mostly for smaller firms. Still the availability of finance may hamper their coexistence despite the awareness that both are strong engines of growth.

The internationalization challenge is determinant for FBs notwithstanding this is a very risky strategy, mainly in the case of smaller organizations, due to the financial constraints, the exiguous endowments of resources and the difficulty in diluting sunk costs. This fact may explain the significance of internal R&D only to larger firms. Relying upon external sources of knowledge to innovate, such as the University, enhances internationalization mostly for smaller organizations. These results request for further discussion as larger firms shift from the use of Universities to the internal R&D departments, contradicting the open innovation frameworks. It is not consensual that FBs are more dynamic in innovative strategies than their non-family counterparts. It is believed that they are conservative, risk averse, resisting change; on the contrary, the loyalty and the trust of *familyness* will allow building the loyalty and trust of the long term relations, allowing the establishment of formal and informal innovation networks.

It seems of central importance understanding the changing roles of the innovation sources as it is mandatory to understand what has to be done to include FBs in the innovation ecosystem to fully benefit from their spillovers.

The empirical findings aim to shed a light on the importance of empowering the smaller organizations towards innovation strategies in multiple dimensions. The importance of the R&D departments is undeniable for innovation processes; as a consequence, shared infrastructures may enhance the results. Stronger involvements with the University favor knowledge share are required to exploit the advantages of the network.

The development of smart policies which respect and seize the singularities of these organizations will permit the enhancement of their social capital, their relational and symbolic capital encompassing ethical values, tradition and the reinforcement of *familyness*. These corporations are the epicenter of local development, social inclusion and the development of sustainable communities which will combine tradition and modernity preserving job erosion and the exposure to external crisis.

REFERENCES

Acs, Z., & Audretsch, D. (1987). Innovation, market structure, and firm size. *The Review of Economics and Statistics*, *69*(4), 567–575. doi:10.2307/1935950

Alberti, F., & Pizzurno, E. (2013). Technology, innovation and performance in family firms. *International Journal of Entrepreneurship and Innovation Management, 17*(1/2/3).142-161.

Alessandri, G., Consiglio, C., Luthans, F., & Borgogni, L. (2018). Testing a dynamic model of the impact of psychological capital on work engagement and job performance. *Career Development International*, *23*(1), 33–47. doi:10.1108/CDI-11-2016-0210

Anderson, R., & Reeb, D. (2003). Founding-family ownership and firm performance: Evidence from the S&P 500. *The Journal of Finance*, *58*(3), 1301–1328. doi:10.1111/1540-6261.00567

Arregle, J., Naldi, L., Nordqvist, M., & Hitt, M. A. (2012). Internationalization of family-controlled firms: A study of the effects of external involvement in governance. *Entrepreneurship Theory and Practice*, *36*(6), 1115–1143. doi:10.1111/j.1540-6520.2012.00541.x

Barbera, F., & Moores, K. (2013). Firm ownership and productivity: A study of family and non-family SMEs. *Small Business Economics*, *40*(4), 953–976. doi:10.100711187-011-9405-9

Benito-Hernández, S., Priede-Bergamini, T., & López-Cózar-Navarro, C. (2014). Factors determining exportation and internationalization in family businesses: The importance of debt. *South African Journal of Business Management*, *45*(1), 13–25. doi:10.4102ajbm.v45i1.114

Berrone, P., Cruz, C., & Gomez-Mejia, L. (2010). Socioemotional wealth in family firms. *Family Business Review*, *25*(3), 258–279. doi:10.1177/0894486511435355

Bettinelli, C., Fayolle, A., & Randerson, K. (2014). Family entrepreneurship: A developing field. *Foundations and Trends in Entrepreneurship*, *10*(3), 161–236. doi:10.1561/0300000049

Botero, I. C., Cruz, C., De Massis, A., & Nordqvist, M. (2015). Family business research in the European context. *European Journal of International Management*, *9*(2), 139–159. doi:10.1504/EJIM.2015.067858

Canepa, A., & Stoneman, P. (2002). *Financial constraints on innovations: A European cross-country study.* Working Paper no. 02–11. Kiel Institute of World Economics.

Chen, Y., Chang, K., & Chang, C. (2012). Nonlinear influence on R&D project performance. *Technological Forecasting and Social Change*, *79*(8), 1537–1547. doi:10.1016/j.techfore.2012.04.007

Chrisman, J., Chua, J., & Sharma, P. (2003). *Current trends and future directions in family business management studies: toward a theory of the family business,* Coleman White Paper Series.

Chua, J., Chrisman, J., & Sharma, P. (1999). Defining the family business by behavior. *Entrepreneurship Theory and Practice*, *23*(4), 19–39. doi:10.1177/104225879902300402

Chung, H. (2012). The role of family management and family ownership in diversification: The case of family business groups. *Asia Pacific Journal of Management, 30*(3), 871–891. doi:10.100710490-012-9284-x

Claver, E., Rienda, L., & Quer, D. (2008). Family firms' risk perception: Empirical evidence on the internationalization process. *Journal of Small Business and Enterprise Development, 15*(3), 457–471. doi:10.1108/14626000810892283

Cohen, W., & Levinthal, D. (1990). Absorptive capacity: A new perspective on learning and innovation. *Administrative Science Quarterly, 35*(1), 128–152. doi:10.2307/2393553

Collier, W., Green, F., Kim, Y., & Peirson, J. (2011). Education, training and economic performance: Evidence from establishment survival data. *Journal of Labor Research, 32*(4), 336–361. doi:10.100712122-011-9116-7

COM – European Commission. (2008). *Think Small First- Um Small Business Act para a Europa 394.* Author.

Costa, J., Botelho, A., & Matias, J. (2018). Hindering Factors to Innovation: A Panel Data Analysis In Entrepreneurship along the Industry Life Cycle: The changing role of Entrepreneurial Activities and Knowledge Competencies. Springer.

D'Angelo, A., Majocchi, A., & Buck, T. (2016). External managers, family ownership and the scope of SME internationalization. *Journal of World Business, 51*(4), 534–547. doi:10.1016/j.jwb.2016.01.004

de Massis, A., Frattini, F., Kotlar, J., Messeni-Petruzzelli, A., & Wright, M. (2016). Innovation through tradition: Lessons from innovative family businesses and directions for future research. *The Academy of Management Perspectives, 30*(1), 93–116. doi:10.5465/amp.2015.0017

de Massis, A., Frattini, F., Majocchi, A., & Piscitello, L. (2018). Family firms in the global economy: Toward a deeper understanding of internationalization determinants, processes, and outcomes. *Global Strategy Journal, 8*(1), 3–21. doi:10.1002/gsj.1199

de Massis, A., Frattini, F., Pizzurno, E., & Cassia, L. (2015). Product innovation in family versus non family firms: An exploratory analysis. *Journal of Small Business Management, 53*(1), 1–36. doi:10.1111/jsbm.12068

Eddleston, A., Rodrigo-Alarcón, J., Parra-Requena, G., García-Villaverde, P., Bolo, A., Muchemi, A., & Gomez-Mejia, L. (2012). The succession process from a resource- and knowledge-based view of the family firm. *Family Business Review, 2*(1), 328–353.

Eddleston, K., & Kellermanns, F. (2007). Destructive and productive family relationships: A stewardship theory perspective. *Journal of Business Venturing, 22*(4), 545–565. doi:10.1016/j.jbusvent.2006.06.004

Eickelpasch, A., & Vogel, A. (2011). Determinants of export behaviour of German business services companies. *Service Industries Journal, 31*(4), 513–526. doi:10.1080/02642069.2010.504304

European Commission. (2019). *European Innovation Scoreboard.* Author.

Fernández, Z., & Nieto, M. (2005). Internationalization strategy of small and medium-sized family businesses: Some influential factors. *Family Business Review*, *18*(1), 77–89. doi:10.1111/j.1741-6248.2005.00031.x

Freire, J. (2008). *Economia e sociedade. Contributos para uma sociologia da vida económica em Portugal na viragem do século*. Celta Editora.

Gallo, M., & Sveen, J. (1991). Internationalizing the family business: Facilitating and restraining factors. *Family Business Review*, *4*(2), 181–190. doi:10.1111/j.1741-6248.1991.00181.x

Ganotakis, P. (2012). Founders' human capital and the performance of UK new technology based firms. *Small Business Economics*, *39*(2), 495–515. doi:10.100711187-010-9309-0

García-Vega, M., & López, A. (2010). Determinants of abandoning innovative activities: Evidence from Spanish Firms. *Cuadernos de Economía y Dirección de la Empresa*, *13*(45), 69–91. doi:10.1016/S1138-5758(10)70024-4

Geroski, P., Machin, S., & van Reenen, J. (1993). The profitability of innovating firms. *The Rand Journal of Economics*, *24*(2), 198–211. doi:10.2307/2555757

Giovannetti, G., Ricchiuti, G., & Velucchi, M. (2013). Location, internationalization and performance of firms in Italy: A multilevel approach. *Applied Economics*, *45*(18), 2665–2673. doi:10.1080/00036846.2012.665597

Gomez-Mejia, L., Berrone, P., & de Castro, J. (2011). The Bind that ties: Socio-emotional wealth preservation in family firms. *The Academy of Management Annals*, *5*(1), 653–707. doi:10.5465/19416520.2011.593320

Gómez-Mejía, L., Haynes, K., Núñez-Nickel, M., Jacobson, K., & Moyano-Fuentes, J. (2007). Socioemotional wealth and business risks in family-controlled firms: Evidence from Spanish olive oil mills. *Administrative Science Quarterly*, *52*(1), 106–137. doi:10.2189/asqu.52.1.106

Graves, C., & Thomas, J. (2008). Determinants of the internationalization pathways of family firms: An examination of family influence. *Family Business Review*, *21*(2), 151–167. doi:10.1111/j.1741-6248.2008.00119.x

Habbershon, T., & Pistrui, J. (2002). Enterprising families domain: Family-influenced ownership groups in pursuit of transgenerational wealth. *Family Business Review*, *15*(3), 223–237. doi:10.1111/j.1741-6248.2002.00223.x

Hadjimanolis, A. (1999). Barriers to innovation for SMEs in a small less developed country (Cyprus). *Technovation*, *19*(9), 561–570. doi:10.1016/S0166-4972(99)00034-6

Hagemejer, J., & Kolasa, M. (2011). Internationalization and economic performance of enterprises: Evidence from polish firm-level data. *World Economy*, *34*(1), 74–100. doi:10.1111/j.1467-9701.2010.01294.x

Herstad, S., Sandven, T., & Solberg, E. (2013). Location, education an enterprise growth. *Applied Economics Letters*, *20*(10), 1019–1022. doi:10.1080/13504851.2013.772287

Holt, D. (2012). The Journey of a 'Green' Micro-Enterprise – The Green Planet. *Corporate Social Responsibility and Environmental Management*, *19*(2), 90–101. doi:10.1002/csr.290

Hu, R., & Shieh, C.-H. (2013). High-tech industries overseas investment performance evaluation - Application of Data Envelopment Analysis. *South African Journal of Economic and Management Sciences*, *16*(5), 67–73. doi:10.4102ajems.v16i5.670

Huang, K., Chung Lo, S., Liu, C., & Tung, J. (2014). Internationalization of family business: The effect of ownership and generation involvement. *The Anthropologist*, *17*(3), 757–767. doi:10.1080/09720073.2014.11891490

Johanson, J., & Vahlne, J. (1977). The Internationalization process of the firm—A model of knowledge development and increasing foreign market commitments. *Journal of International Business Studies*, *8*(1), 23–32. doi:10.1057/palgrave.jibs.8490676

Kafouros, M., Buckley, P., Sharp, J., & Wang, C. (2008). The role of internacionalization in explaining innovation performance. *Technovation*, *28*(1-2), 63–74. doi:10.1016/j.technovation.2007.07.009

Koellinger, P. (2008). Why are some entrepreneurs more innovative than others? *Small Business Economics*, *31*(1), 21–37. doi:10.100711187-008-9107-0

Kontinen, T., & Ojala, A. (2010). Internationalization pathways of family SMEs: Psychic distance as a focal point. *Journal of Small Business and Enterprise Development*, *17*(3), 437–454. doi:10.1108/14626001011068725

Kraus, S., Mensching, A., Calabrò, A., Cheng, C., & Filsera, M. (2016). Family firm internationalization: A configurational approach. *Journal of Business Research*, *69*(11), 5473–5478. doi:10.1016/j.jbusres.2016.04.158

Lall, S. (1992). Technological capabilities and industrialisation. *World Development*, *20*(2), 165–186. doi:10.1016/0305-750X(92)90097-F

Maidique, A., & Zirger, B. (1985). The new product learning cycle. *Research Policy*, *14*(6), 299–313. doi:10.1016/0048-7333(85)90001-0

Marin, Q., Hernández-Lara, A. B., Campa-Planas, F., & Sánchez-Rebull, M. V. (2017). Which factors improve the performance of the internationalization process? Focus on family firms. *Applied Economics*, *49*(32), 3181–3194. doi:10.1080/00036846.2016.1257103

Miller, D., & Le Breton-Miller, I. (2006). Family Governance and Firm Performance: Agency, Stewardship, and Capabilities. *Family Business Review*, *19*(1), 73–87. doi:10.1111/j.1741-6248.2006.00063.x

Miller, D., Le Breton-Miller, I., Lester, R., & Cannella, A. Jr. (2007). Are family firms really superior performers? *Journal of Corporate Finance*, *13*(5), 829–858. doi:10.1016/j.jcorpfin.2007.03.004

Narula, R., & Zanfei, A. (2003). *Globalisation of Innovation The Role of Multinational Enterprises*. No 03-15, DRUID Working Papers, DRUID, Copenhagen Business School, Department of Industrial Economics and Strategy/Aalborg University, Department of Business Studies.

Nieto, M. J., Santamaria, L., & Fernandez, Z. (2015). Understanding the innovation behavior of family firms. *Journal of Small Business Management, 53*(2), 382–399. doi:10.1111/jsbm.12075

Nordqvist, M., & Melin, L. (2002). The dynamics of family firms: An institutional perspective on corporate governance and strategic change. In D. Fletcher (Ed.), *Understanding the Small, Family Firm*. Routledge.

Perri, A., & Peruffo, E. (2017). *Family Business and Technological Innovation*. Empirical Insights from the Italian Pharmaceutical Industry. Palgrave. doi:10.1007/978-3-319-61596-7

Piva, E., Rossi-Lamastra, C., & De Massis, A. (2013). Family firms and internationalization: An exploratory study on high-tech entrepreneurial ventures. *Journal of International Entrepreneurship, 10*(1), 109–129.

Pukall, T., & Calabrò, A. (2014). The internationalization of family firms: A critical review and integrative model. *Family Business Review, 27*(2), 103–125. doi:10.1177/0894486513491423

Ribau, C., Moreira, A. C., & Raposo, M. (2015). Internationalisation of the firm theories: A schematic synthesis. *International Journal of Business and Globalisation, 15*(4), 528–554. doi:10.1504/IJBG.2015.072535

Shanker, M., & Astrachan, J. (1996). Myths and realities: Family businesses' contribution to the US economy – A framework for assessing family business statistics. *Family Business Review, 9*(2), 107–123. doi:10.1111/j.1741-6248.1996.00107.x

Siebels, J.-F., & Aufseß, D. (2012). A Review of theory in family business research: The implications for corporate governance. *International Journal of Management Reviews, 14*(3), 280–304. doi:10.1111/j.1468-2370.2011.00317.x

Swoboda, B., & Olejnik, E. (2013). A taxonomy of small and medium-sized international family firms. *Journal of International Entrepreneurship, 11*(2), 130–157. doi:10.100710843-012-0101-x

Tallman, S., & Li, J. (1996). Effects of international diversity and product diversity on the performance of multinational firms. *Academy of Management Journal, 39*(1), 179–196.

(1988). The nature of the innovative process. InDosi, G. (Ed.), *Technical Change and Economic Theory* (pp. 221–238). Pinter Publishers.

Tsang, E. (2002). Learning from overseas venturing experience, the case of Chinese family businesses. *Journal of Business Venturing, 17*(1), 21–40. doi:10.1016/S0883-9026(00)00052-5

Tsao, M., & Lien, W.-H. (2013). Family management and internationalization: The impact on firm performance and innovation. *Management International Review, 53*(2), 189–213. doi:10.100711575-011-0125-9

West, G. III, & Noel, T. (2009). The impact of knowledge resources on new venture performance. *Journal of Small Business Management, 47*(1), 1–22. doi:10.1111/j.1540-627X.2008.00259.x

Zahra, S., Hayton, J., & Salvato, C. (2004). Entrepreneurship in family vs. non–family firms: A resource–based analysis of the effect of organizational culture. *Entrepreneurship Theory and Practice, 28*(4), 363–381. doi:10.1111/j.1540-6520.2004.00051.x

Zirger, B. (1997). The influence of development experience and product innovativeness on product outcome. *Technology Analysis and Strategic Management*, *9*(3), 287–297. doi:10.1080/09537329708524285

ADDITIONAL READING

Ribau, C. P., Moreira, A. C., & Raposo, M. (2017). Export performance and the internationalisation of SMEs. *International Journal of Entrepreneurship and Small Business*, *30*(2), 214–240. doi:10.1504/IJESB.2017.081438

Ribau, C. P., Moreira, A. C., & Raposo, M. (2018). SME internationalization research: Mapping the state of the art. *Canadian Journal of Administrative Sciences*, *35*(2), 280–303. doi:10.1002/cjas.1419

KEY TERMS AND DEFINITIONS

Family Business: A firm, of any size, is a family business, if 1) The majority of decision-making rights is in the possession of the natural person(s) who established the firm, or in the possession of the natural person(s) who has/have acquired the share capital of the firm, or in the possession of their spouses, parents, child or children's direct heirs. 2) The majority of decision-making rights are indirect or direct. 3) At least one representative of the family or kin is formally involved in the governance of the firm. 4) Listed companies meet the definition of family enterprise if the person who established or acquired the firm (share capital) or their families or descendants possess 25 per cent of the decision-making rights mandated by their share capital. (Following the European Commission proposal: https://ec.europa.eu/growth/smes/promoting-entrepreneurship/we-work-for/family-business_lt)

Firm Economic Performance: Consists in the appraisal of the firm ability to generate revenue based on the endowments of resources used to run the business models. It usually *proxies* firm's financial health and potential growth.

Innovation: Consists in the introduction of something (tangible or intangible) new or significantly modified, to the market, within the enterprise or a new or significantly improved process. It is based on the results of technological developments, technology combinations, or the use of other knowledge, developed or acquired by the enterprise (Following the Community Innovation Survey definition).

Internationalization: The process of initiating firm involvement within international markets. In doing so, there will be an increase in the interaction and integration among firms, markets, and governments.

SMEs: Firms with a staff headcount lower than 250 workers and either turnover lower than 50 million € or balance sheet total lower than 43 million € (According to the European Commission proposal: https://ec.europa.eu/growth/smes/business-friendly-environment/sme-definition_en).

ENDNOTES

1 https://www.ine.pt/xportal/xmain?xpid=INE&xpgid=ine_publicacoes&PUBLICACOESpub_boui=358546042&PUBLICACOESmodo=2&xlang=pt

2 https://www.roadmapef.pt/archive/doc/Artigo_APM_E_AIC.pdf

3 http://ec.europa.eu/enterprise/policies/sme/promoting-entrepreneurship/familybusiness/family_business_expert_group_report_en.pdf.

4 https://ec.europa.eu/commission/presscorner/detail/en/IP_08_1003

5 On-line document 27/5/2015

6 Project: Roadmap para as empresas familiares Portuguesas

7 Economic indicators of non-financial firms in Portugal, 2008-2016.

8 https://op.europa.eu/en/publication-detail/-/publication/5849c2fe-dcd9-410e-af37-1d375088e886

9 Knowledge Platform created to understand the reality of SMEs and their present and future internationalization perspectives

Chapter 12
Predictive Strategic Factors in Export Performance in the Automotive Industry:
The Mediating Effect of Innovation

Orlando Lima Rua
ISCAP, CEOS, Polytechnic of Porto, Portugal & NECE, University of Beira Interior, Portugal & UNIAG, Associação dos Politécnicos do Norte de Portugal, Portugal

Ana Ferreira
ISCAP, Polytechnic of Porto, Portugal

EXECUTIVE SUMMARY

The purpose of this chapter is to analyze the linkage between intangible resources and export performance, considering the mediating effect of innovation on it. The authors have adopted a quantitative methodological approach applied to a sample of Portuguese exporting companies from the automotive industry. The application of the structural equation model is highlighted, using partial least squares (PLS). The results allow us to conclude from the existence of a positive and direct impact of intangible resources on export performance and the mediator effect of innovation in this relationship. The main contribution of this study is the mediating effect of innovation on the relationship established between intangible resources and export performance concerning companies from the automotive industry.

DOI: 10.4018/978-1-7998-4387-0.ch012

INTRODUCTION

Globalisation has brought emerging challenges of productivity, flexibility and responsiveness of companies, with internationalisation presenting itself as a way to meet the challenges inherent to this process. Morgan, Vorhies and Schlegelmilch (2006) maintain that operating in international markets represents considerable challenges for companies and calls for their best capabilities.

The success of a company, expressed in its competitive advantage, therefore depends on the ability to detect and seize opportunities, on the combination of internal and external innovations, on the efficient transfer of technology between and within companies, on the protection of intellectual property, on the improvement of benchmarking, on the adoption of new business models, on conscious decision making, on the development of forms of imitation protection and on new ways of leading the global market (Porter, 2000). Innovation and knowledge transfer can thus be considered as competitiveness enhancers (Silva, 2007). In turn, Arbix, Salerno and Negri (2004) concluded from the existence of evidence that the competitiveness of companies would be positively influenced by technological innovations, following processes of internationalization. Some authors (Miller, 1983; Covin & Slevin, 1989) point out the fact that to achieve a sustainable competitive advantage it is necessary that the company continuously reinvents processes and strategies, launching new products, is proactive in the market and willing to take risks.

Starting from *Resource-Based View* (RBV) (Penrose, 1959; Amit & Schoemaker, 1993; Barney, 1995), this study aims to understand the impact of resources, specifically intangible resources, on export performance, as well as to analyze the mediation effect of innovation in these relationship. The strategic role of resources and capabilities and their impact on competitive advantage and performance has been emphasized by several contributions in the area (Morgan et al., 2006; Bakar & Ahmad, 2010).

In this context, exporting is a strategic option to access and diversify international markets for many companies (Monteiro, Soares & Rua, 2017, Rua, 2018a,b). The performance of exports has been studied in the context of RBV and DCV, which focus on strategic resources and capabilities (Rua, 2018a,b).

Stouraitis et al. (2017) state that the factors that trigger the growth of SMEs (including exports) still need to be investigated. On the other hand, the survival and expansion of companies and the consequent economic growth of many countries depend heavily on a better understanding of the determinants that influence export performance, which is still insufficiently investigated (Sousa et al., 2008). These authors go even further, stating that such an investigation should privilege the study of mediating variables. The present study is thus an answer to the challenge of these scholars.

The automotive industry, as one of the decisive engines for the country's development, through the significant boost to national exports, needs that in addition to productivity improvements, strong innovation policy is implemented to products, production and commercial processes.

Therefore, the purpose of this paper is to broad the boundaries of strategic management literature and test the following research questions: *(1) Does intangible resources positively influence small business' innovation? (2) Does intangible resources and innovation positively influence small business' export performance? (3) Does innovation mediate the relationship between intangible resources and export performance?*

THEORETICAL FRAMEWORK

Resouce-based View

It was in the '50s that the foundations of RBV were created with the works of Penrose (1959). This economist was one of the pioneers to conceive the idea of a company as a "resource bundle". She focused on the issue of the growth of organizations, adopting a different perspective from neoclassical economists. For the economist, the firm was seen as an administrative entity and a set of resources, rather than as an abstract function of turning inputs into products.

Penrose (1959) values the company's internal attributes as a source of sustainable competitive advantage, noting that the skills of organizations are in their resources and capabilities and identifies these productive resources as tangible and intangible assets. The economist also argues that the essential facts in the production process are not only the resources themselves but also the services that the resources yield, i.e. the same resource, employed for different purposes in combination with other types of resources, originates different services.

Resources, for Amit and Schoemaker (1993), are a set of specific factors owned and controlled by the company and are later converted into products or services through the use of technology mechanisms, information management systems, incentive systems and trust between the different social partners. These resources consist of commercial know-how (patents and licenses); financial or physical assets (real estate, facilities and equipment) and human resources.

In this sense, Barney (1995) classifies resources into 1) Human Resources - experiences, knowledge, value judgments, risk propensity and individual wisdom associated with the company; 2) Physical Resources - machinery, equipment and facilities; 3) Financial Resources - debts, profits and shares; and 4) Organisational Resources - history, relationships, trust, organisational culture (attributes of groups of individuals linked to the company), formal and informal communication, control systems and compensation policies. This author considers resources all assets, competencies, organizational processes, attributes and information controlled by the organization to enable strategies to increase its efficiency and effectiveness.

Table 1. VRIS Model

Resources	Description
Valuable	Resources that enable a company to design strategies that improve its efficiency and effectiveness by seizing opportunities or minimizing threats.
Rare	Valuable resources cannot be a source of sustainable competitive advantage if they are accessible to several competitors since each of their holders will have the capacity to exploit them, implementing common strategies, which would lead to obtaining only average returns.
Imperfectly imitated	Even if they are valuable and rare, resources are only a source of sustainable competitive advantage if organizations that do not already have them cannot obtain them too easily.
Not Replaceable	Resources must be non-replaceable, i.e., they must not have an equivalent that is not infrequently and imperfectly imitable. For imitation or replacement by another strategic resource is a threat to the sustainability of the strategic advantage, making the original resource obsolete and losing its ability to generate value.

Source: Adapted from Barney (1991).

RBV builds its theory on two assumptions: that resources are heterogeneous, that is, firms that compete within the same industry may have different sets of resources; and that resources are immovable, that is, resources are immovable between firms, thus enabling the perpetuation in time of heterogeneity (Barney, 1991; Barney, 2001). Based on these assumptions, the author defined resources in his VRIS model (Table 1) as value (because resources have the potential), rarity, imitability and not substitutability.

However, Barney, in continuing his studies with Wright, found that instead of the "S" for VRIS it should have an "O" (for Organisation), as they considered that the company has to be organised to make its resources profitable. This was called the VRIO model (Table 1). The company's resources should be valuable, rare and not easily imitated, and may generate a source of sustained competitive advantage, but only if the company is organized to capitalize on its resources (Barney & Wright, 1998).

Intangible Resources

In the last 20 years, the world has progressively changed to a knowledge-based, rapidly changing, a technology-intensive economy in which investments in human resources, information technology, research and development, advertising are essential for a company to maintain its competitive position and ensure its future viability (Cañibano, Garcia-Ayuso & Sanchez, 2000)

Intangible resources are those that are more likely to generate a sustainable competitive advantage because they are often rare and complex, making it difficult for others to imitate them and are characterized by being very distinct between companies (Barney, 1991; Hitt, Bierman, Shimizu & Kochhar, 2001).

According to the existing literature, in exporting firms it is possible to obtain an important source of competitive advantage from six types of intangible resources (Morgan et al., 2006):

1. Reputation: can be differentiation factors in the target market (Hall, 1992) and are related to the company's image. Since they are rare and difficult to imitate they can be understood as a source of competitive advantage (Barney, 1991);
2. Financial: companies with financial resources tend to respond more quickly to market changes and obtain a competitive advantage more easily (Chesbrough & Teece, 2002). Access to capital allows companies to overcome challenges and/or invest in capital-intensive projects to protect themselves in existing markets or enter new markets (Westhead, Wright & Ucbasaran, 2001);
3. Human: Human capital allows the company to create an opportunity to achieve a competitive advantage. Human resources are extremely valuable and rare due to the unique capabilities that individuals provide, especially in the more specialized areas (Coff & Kryscynski, 2011);
4. Cultural: consists of the sharing of values, beliefs and assumptions that provide behavioral norms that shape strategic competitive planning and achievement, representing an important source of competitive advantage (Barney, 1986);
5. Relational: they are considered a source of competitive advantage because, according to Barney (1991), the relationship resources that consist of the relationships between companies and the various stakeholders are distributed asymmetrically among companies, imperfectly mobile, difficult to imitate and have no substitutes available (Davis & Mentzer, 2008); and
6. Information and Knowledge: information is a resource that concerns the acquisition and dissemination of information and/or knowledge about the various *stakeholders*, distribution channels and internal or external markets (Katsikeas & Morgan, 1994). It is a source of competitive advantage because it results from transformation processes, on the part of companies, of changing the structure

of the industry, as well as the rules of competition between them, allowing companies to perceive new ways of acting towards rivals or even create new business, often within the same company (Porter & Millar, 1985).

Innovation

Innovation is a complex technological, sociological and economic process, involving an extremely intricate web of interactions both within the company and between the company and its economic, technical, competitive and social environments. It is a concept that can be defined as the achievement of new combinations, encompassing the introduction of new products, the creation of new forms of production, the emergence of new markets, the availability of new raw materials and the emergence of new companies. Schumpeter has the appropriate terms for the process of implementing these new combinations, as well as for those responsible for making them. In his words, "the execution of the new combinations we cal *enterprise*; the individuals whose function is to carry it out we cal *entrepreneurs*" (Schumpeter, 1961, p. 74).

Atuahene-Gima and Ko (2001) investigated the effect of entrepreneurial orientation on the innovative performance of small business products and found that it positively affects business performance. Baker and Sinkula (2009) examined the entrepreneurial orientation and identified a direct effect on profitability in a sample of small and medium-sized companies in the US. They found that profitability was driven by the successful innovation of new products launched on the market. Liu, Luo and Shi (2003) found that a higher level of entrepreneurial orientation increases the competitive advantage of Chinese state-owned companies. Hult, Hurley and Knight (2004) found in large companies, on an industrial scale, the positive relationship between entrepreneurial orientation and innovation and performance. In studies by Li, Liu and Zhao (2006) and Li (2005), Chinese entrepreneurially oriented companies, showed that there was a positive relationship with the innovation dimension. These companies showed positive effects on new products' performance. Subsequently, Li, Zhao, Tan and Liu (2008) also presented a study that analyzed the entrepreneurial dimensions of innovation and proactivity, which demonstrated strengthening business performance.

According to Cavusgil and Knight (2004), innovation is the way to create new solutions and meet the challenges posed by competitors, including creating new products and markets, often trying to be a leader and not just following what competitors do. It is noticeable that the *born globals*' studies, which use the concept of innovation, in general, adopt a broad perspective of this concept.

Knight considers a global born company the one that starts its export activity until its third year of existence, as well as the one that accumulates 25% of minimum revenues in its international markets. Knight and Cavusgil (2004), later explain the concept and assume the *born globals* as companies with a high culture of innovation, capacity and knowledge. They also explain that these companies, despite scarce resources, succeed in adopting a differentiated mix of guidelines and strategies for a multiplicity of international markets.

Carvalho et al. (2009) classify innovation in four types:

1. Product innovation is the introduction of a new or significantly improved good or service concerning its characteristics or intended uses;
2. Process innovation is the implementation of a new or significantly improved production or distribution method;

3. Market (marketing or position) innovation is the change or even creation of a new marketing method with significant changes in product design or packaging, product positioning, promotion, development of new distribution channels, or pricing; and
4. Organizational innovation refers to the implementation of a new organizational method in the company's business practices, in the organization of its workplace or in its external relations.

The nature of innovation can be classified in 3 different ways: incremental innovation, radical or distinctive innovation, disruptive or revolutionary innovation (Gaynor, 2002; InnoSkills, 2013; Taborda, 2012).

1. Incremental innovation consists of the incorporation of new and improved elements about the previous process, product, service or production or distribution activity that already existed, and their basic functions have been modified, simplified or consolidated;
2. Distinctive/radical innovation implies launching in the market something that involves a great effort on the part of the organization and workers in various areas, major marketing decisions as well as state-of-the-art technology and that has a great impact on results over a long period of time. This effort leads to the creation of something that may exist, but that incorporates functions that did not exist before. These innovations have a great impact on the industry and may even develop new businesses; and
3. Disruptive/revolutionary innovation takes on a revolution in existing markets since it is something never before achieved and so different that it cannot be compared with any existing knowledge or practice. This type of innovation arises in response to a need that has not existed up to now. Sometimes a disruptive innovation may not satisfy the customer's needs at the moment since the population does not need the innovation because it has not yet discovered the need that the product/service satisfies (Christensen, 1997).

In recent years, we have witnessed an important growth of innovation in the competitiveness of companies, is increasingly present in all sectors of activity. In this sense, it is important to understand the concept of technological innovation to enhance the knowledge about which factors help or hinder the innovation processes in organizations. Innovation implies the development of new methods, ideas or objects to satisfy needs, to strengthen the competitive position and increase the performance of the company in question. Its main objective is the creation and optimization of products, systems or services that generate value for customers. It is a process of technical activities, development or management to create new or better products.

In the business paradigm, technology is used to achieve objectives, which allow ideas to be transformed into goods or services, boosting competitiveness. We can conclude that the main objectives of technological innovation are to reduce costs, increase the profit margin and meet customer needs.

According to Tidd, Bessant and Pavitt (2003), companies that use innovation to improve and differentiate their products and services perform better than their competitors by measuring "market share, profitability, growth or market capitalisation". It is therefore expected that companies will achieve sustainable competitive advantages through differentiation. This may involve incremental improvements, which may dictate their "capacity for differentiation and local innovation" (Godinho, 2003a).

Innovation "has an incomparable power to create profound and lasting changes in terms of competitive advantages" (Hamel, 2007, p. 33), thus appearing as a way for companies to differentiate themselves from the competition in an increasingly demanding market through a distinctive offer (Freire, 2002).

For Sarkar (2010), the concepts of "innovation" and "differentiation" are related to the degree of competitive pressure. Innovation is then associated with markets with little competitive pressure and differentiation with very competitive markets.

Therefore, we can define technological innovation as the main driver of economic activity. Technological innovation can be considered as the process by which ideas/knowns are transformed into new products or processes for their successful introduction in the market (Amorim, 2005). In this sense, technological innovation arises as to the application of new technological knowledge, which results in new products, processes or services, or the significant improvement of some of its attributes. Changing market conditions lead to the introduction of new products and services. Technological change creates opportunities and sometimes changes in market structure. Consequently, the more intense the changes in the two currents of factors, the greater the pressure for firms to innovate.

Internationalisation and Export

Globalisation is the phenomenon of the interdependence of markets and producers from different countries; it is the process of creating a world market. It brings with it challenges of productivity, flexibility and responsiveness to companies, to which they must constantly respond. The strengthening of new channels of communication, such as the Internet, means that the circulation of information is increasingly rapid. Thus, the distance between countries, people and businesses is increasingly influenced by the circulation of information.

Internationalisation cannot be considered as a recent event. If we go back a few hundred years, we see that exchanges between nations are lost in time. Interest in international economics is one of the oldest in economic science. During the 18th and 19th centuries, international trade grew significantly and foreign investment reached very significant amounts.

According to Ghemawat (2001), markets are more open and competitive, making the economic, financial, environmental, social and technological pressures facing companies increasingly global. All of these factors influence the decision to go international. It is a complex challenge that absorbs financial and human resources, which should not be a response to a one-off failure in the national market or the availability of abundant financial resources. Entry into new markets must have the purpose of exploiting advantages exploited in the national market or in other markets. Besides, the company's expansion may also be based on access to resources and/or strategic assets (Dunning & Lundan, 2008).

The concept of internationalisation has long been a subject of discussion and there is no consensus on its definition. Czinkota and Ronkainen (2007) define internationalisation as the planning and conduct of transactions across national borders for exchanges that meet individual and organisational objectives. This process improves the current situation of companies, and for some companies, internationalization is a gradual process, particularly in small markets. Welch and Luostarinen (1988) define internationalization as the process of increasing participation in international operations while Calof and Beamish (1995) consider internationalization as the process of adapting companies (strategy, structure, resources, etc) to international environments.

The process of internationalszation of companies has evolved, and instead of companies seeking to gradually reach different international markets, they reach a certain degree of internationalization of their business a few years after its creation.

According to Johanson and Vahlne (2009), the Uppsala's model explains the characteristics of a company's internationalisation process. The authors, though some studies of Swedish companies in international markets, concluded that the process is developed taking into account a sequential evolution, with an increasing level of commitment. These authors identify the internationalization process with the establishment chain concept, referring to four stages:

1. Non-regular exports - allow the company to establish the first contact with the market without the commitment of resources;
2. Exports through an agent - generate greater market knowledge and greater demand for the commitment of resources;
3. Creation of a commercial subsidiary - which functions as a controlled information channel; and
4. Establishment of a productive subsidiary - implies greater knowledge of resources and sufficient knowledge of the market.

One of the particularities of the model is that companies begin to internationalize their business in markets that are closer to the domestic market in terms of psychological distance (Johnson & Vahlne, 2009). The authors consider that companies enter successively into markets with greater psychological distance, being a gradual process in which psychological distance is inversely proportional to market knowledge.

The Uppsala model took into account two internationalisation mechanisms. The first concerns the changes that take place in companies through the knowledge acquired with experiences in international markets. When a company starts its internationalization process, it increases its level of knowledge about the practices of that market.

The second has to do with the changes that occur due to compromise decisions, which make it possible to strengthen the company's position in the international market. Thus, after a knowledge of the market, it is through the allocation of resources to international operations that new commitment decisions are established, which increases the number of activities and contacts in the international market.

The model is based on the assumption that a company, which seeks to internationalize, invests in resources gradually, its level of knowledge acquired and its involvement with the international market is increasing.

According to the model review in 2009, companies focus on a network of relationships and contacts. Networking has a considerable impact on a company's decision to enter a given market, as it allows opportunities to be identified and explored. It is through these networks that it is possible to acquire knowledge and that commitment decisions arise, based on the trust of the relationships established by companies. Thus, the great difference from the initial model lies in the fact that the internationalisation of a company depends on the network.

According to the authors, as in the initial model, the process of internationalization takes into account a gradual process of knowledge level, based on two mechanisms. However, in the new model, instead of considering that the change arises from the knowledge acquired with the experience, it takes into account that the knowledge acquired arises from the opportunities that arise from integrating a network of contacts. As far as commitment decisions are concerned, they arise from the relationships established, to strengthen the company's position in the international market.

In the study of Falize and Courderoy (2012) it is possible to verify that Small and Medium Enterprises (SMEs) can exploit global market opportunities more quickly and efficiently, according to the concept of *Born Global*. There are several definitions in the literature for this concept, as it is relatively recent.

The concept emerged in 1989 with McDougall's study, which recognized a new standard of internationalization, in which he identified that the strategies of companies of the *Born Global* type are different from those defined by companies operating in the domestic market. For Oviatt and McDougall (2005), *Born Global* consists of business organizations that, since their conception or beginning of activities, seek business in the foreign market to obtain a significant competitive advantage from the use of their resources and the sale of their products in different countries.

Born Global are companies that use their high know-how to gain competitive advantage and achieve internationalization in the first years of life. Also, managers have a pivotal role when it comes to defining an international strategy in a *Born Global* company. More than a global vision, they have a high capacity to adapt to markets with different organizational cultures, which makes the difference when looking for opportunities beyond the domestic market. Now, through their knowledge and global vision, these are companies that, from a very early age, perceive the world as their market and quickly reach a high percentage of exports (Knight & Cavusgil, 2004). According to Hitt et al. (2018, p. 227), "the most usual methods of internationalisation of a company are export, licensing, strategic alliances, acquisition and new wholly-owned subsidiaries".

Export is the entry strategy responsible for the massive trade movement that constitutes global trade (Dias, 2007). When a company formulates, as a development strategy, the internationalization of the business, it is confronted with the first obstacle that consists in overcoming the anxiety that arises from its doubts as to the competencies to compete in foreign markets (Root, 1994). This evidence is particularly visible for SMEs because, for example:

1. the limited knowledge of the markets;
2. the lack of experience in external contacts;
3. the shortage of qualified human resources with specific skills for internationalisation; and
4. to weak bargaining power.

Thus, for companies at an early stage of the internationalisation process, the greatest concerns go more towards minimising the risks of entering unknown markets than maximising the control of their international operations. Thus, export operations appear to be the best way to start the internationalization process. According to Root (1994) and Kelly (2009) starting the internationalization process, via exports, is a powerful learning process to later adopt more sophisticated and risky forms of internationalization, mainly because it enables lower initial operation costs, fewer risks and higher profits.

Gradually, the company is acquiring experience and knowledge in the *modus operandi* of new markets, allowing the adoption of an exploratory and experimental behavior to obtain knowledge and adapt its structure to improve its competitive position in these markets.

The mode of entry into foreign markets via export can be done in three distinct ways: direct export, which occurs when the company sells to an importer from a foreign country, indirect export when it involves the use of intermediaries (import-export agents, trading company, sub-contractor, central purchasing of large distribution chains, among others), located in the country of origin, and own export, which consists of direct sale to final customers in the country of destination (Simões et al., 2013).

Although indirect export involves less risk in the process of internationalisation and is therefore initially the easiest way to enter foreign markets, it restricts the degree of freedom to the company in developing its own market entry strategy and, at the same time, delays the process of knowing the target markets.

This allows learning both in terms of production efficiency and in terms of design and marketing, which can act as a lever for other forms of entry into target markets (Simões, 1997).

In its own export, contrary to the previous ones, there are no intermediaries, since the company sells directly to customers located in other countries. In this case, the exporting company is responsible for marketing (product promotion and customer acquisition) and the distribution of its products.

This type of export is not feasible for mass consumption products and is used in the case of industrial goods - intermediate and, above all, capital goods were establishing direct relations with the customer is often a technical imperative. The automobile components industry is a good example of export itself (Simões et al, 2013).

Export Performance

Export performance is increasingly important within any strategic perspective of the company. By assessing performance, the efficiency and effectiveness of an organization are being evaluated, which allows the analysis of its situation within the competitive context in which the company is inserted. To evaluate the export performance of a company that has decided to compete in the international market, it is necessary to make an analysis of its development and background such as internationalization strategies used, vision and perception of external market orientation, entrepreneurial orientation, available resources and its ability to innovate products and services, processes and organizational and management arrangements, among others (Mugnol, 2013).

The company's export performance is determined by its financial and strategic performance in international markets, as well as its satisfaction with this performance (Zou, Taylor & Osland, 1998). Some studies identify several ways to measure performance, including sales growth, market share, profit, overall performance and stakeholder satisfaction (Lumpkin & Dess, 1996). Others have used profit, sales volume and market share (Dhanaraj & Beamish, 2003; Piercy et al., 1998).

In turn, Okapara (2009) evaluates export performance through five variables: profit, sales growth, growth in the number of employees, expansion in the foreign market and the company's overall performance.

RESEARCH MODEL AND HYPOTHESES

Baker and Sinkula (2009) innovation and identified a direct effect on profitability in a sample of small and medium enterprises in the US. They found that profitability was driven by the successful innovation of new products launched in the market. Liu, Luo and Shi (2003) found that a higher level of entrepreneurial orientation increases the competitive advantage of Chinese state-owned enterprises. Hult, Hurley and Knight (2004) found, in large companies, on an industrial scale, the positive relationship between innovation and performance. Studies by Li, Liu and Zhao (2006) and Li (2005), on entrepreneurial-oriented Chinese companies, showed that there was a positive relationship with the dimension of innovation. These companies had positive effects on the performance of new products. Subsequently, Li, Zhao, Tan and Liu (2008) also presented a study that analyzed the entrepreneurial dimensions of innovation and proactivity, which have been shown to strengthen business performance.

Intangible resources are responsible for an organization's ability to innovate. It encompasses the whole body of tacit and explicit knowledge accumulated in the company. Thus, it involves, in addition to the competencies incorporated in their individuals and groups, the knowledge assets encoded in the internal records, whether or not they are appropriated in the form of intellectual property (Quadros, 2008). For Burlamarqui and Proença (2003), companies are increasingly articulating in favour of the development of strategies, which focus primarily on innovation and competition, which corroborates RBV's assumptions. In this context, we intend to confirm the following hypothesis:

H1: *Intangible resources positively influence innovation.*

Export performance is increasingly important from any strategic perspective of the company. By assessing performance, you are evaluating the efficiency and effectiveness of an organization, which allows to analyze the situation within the competitive context in which the company operates. To evaluate the export performance of a company that has decided to compete in the international market, it is necessary to analyze its development and antecedents such as: internationalization strategies used, vision and perception of orientation to the external market, entrepreneurial orientation, available resources and its ability to innovate products and services, processes and organizational and management arrangements, among others (Mugnol, 2013).

The company's export performance is determined by its financial and strategic performance in international markets, as well as its satisfaction with this performance (Zou, Taylor & Osland, 1998).

There are studies that identify various ways to measure performance, including sales growth, market share, profit, overall performance and stakeholder satisfaction (Lumpkin & Dess, 1996). Others used profit, sales volume and market share (Dhanaraj & Beamish, 2003; Piercy et al., 1998). On the other hand, Okapara (2009) assesses export performance through five variables: profit, sales growth, headcount growth, foreign market expansion and overall company performance.

The essence of resource-based insight (Barney, 1991) links superior-than-average performance in an industry with the quality of its strategic resources. The performance of companies is explained by the presence of valuable, rare, difficult to imitate, hardly substitutable strategic resources for competitors, enabling the creation of sustainable asymmetries and competitive advantages for the organizations that have them, that is, the result of heterogeneous resources. Thus, heterogeneous resource ownership and capabilities directly affect firm performance (Makadok, 2001; Teece et al., 1997). Finally, we aim to test the following hypotheses:

H2: *Intangible resources positively influence export performance.*

Atuahene-Gima and Ko (2001) investigated the effect of entrepreneurial orientation on innovative small business product performance and found that it positively affects business performance. Liu, Luo and Shi (2003) found that a higher level of entrepreneurial orientation increases the competitive advantage of Chinese state-owned enterprises. Hult, Hurley and Knight (2004) found, in large companies on an industrial scale, the positive relationship between innovation and performance. Thus, we have as hypotheses of work:

H3: *Innovation positively influences export performance.*

Innovation is the ability to simultaneously pursue both exploration and exploitation, efficiency and flexibility, or alignment and adaptability (De Clercq, Thongpapanl & Dimov, 2013). Innovation requires different strategic orientations, technological resources and processes. Innovation provides a mechanism to effectively manage change by repeatedly pursue and achieve both disruptive and incremental innovation (Andriopoulos & Lewis, 2009). For some scholars (e.g., Andriopoulos & Lewis, 2009; Jansen et al., 2005), innovation requires different strategic orientations, technological resources and processes. It provides a mechanism for managing change effectively and can achieve both disruptive and incremental innovation.

This research tests the mediating effect of innovation in the relationship between intangible resources and export performance. The significance of the variables' mediating effect was assessed by Aroian test (Baron & Kenny, 1986). This test is used to determine whether the indirect effect of the independent variable on the dependent variable via the mediator is significantly different from zero (Aroian, 1947). Thus we propose:

Thus, based on the above, the following hypotheses are:

H4: *Intangible resources positively influence export performance through the mediating effect of innovation.*

Figure 1 shows the research model.

Figure 1. Research model
Source: Own.

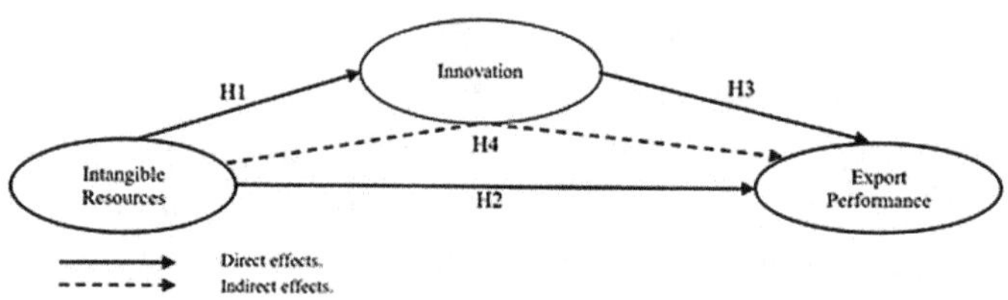

METHODOLOGY

Sample and Data Collection Process

The population of this study corresponds to the Portuguese automobile industry exporting companies. To this end, we collected data by sending the survey by e-mail to companies belonging to the sector "15 - Vehicles and components" of AICEP's website - "Buy From Portugal - Catalogue of Portuguese Suppliers" - excluding sub-sectors of two-wheeled vehicles, railway and naval equipment - and those of AFIA associates not listed.

The questionnaire was applied from 1 August 2018 to 31 January 2019, with a total of 54 responses from 179 companies, corresponding to a response rate of around 44,69%, and was done by email, linking a link to the survey that was online. The answer to the questionnaire was anonymous, containing no confidentiality or identifying information from the respondent or company, and the IP was conditional on only one answer.

Measurement Instrument

The study instrument used will be the questionnaire survey, in that no variable will be manipulated and all data related to the variables will be collected at the same time (Bryman & Cramer, 2012). This data collection method is best suited for this type of research (Sousa, Martínez-López & Coelho, 2008), as there is a need to interrogate a large number of companies (Campenhoudt & Quivy, 2008).

We measured using Morgan, Vorhies and Schlegelmich's (2006) measurement scale for reputational, (access to) financial, human, relational, cultural and informational/knowledge resources. For the analysis of innovation, the scales of Hurley and Hult (1998) and Atuahene-Gima (1996) were used. Finally, to assess export performance we used the Okapara (2009) scale, evaluating export performance through five profitability indicators: sales growth, profit, activities and operations, and overall company performance.

RESULTS

Partial Least Squares

Table 2. Cronbach's alpha and composite reliability coefficients of multidimensional variables

Constructs	Cronbach's Alpha	Composite Reliability	*p* Values
Intangible resources	.948	.954	0.000
Innivation	.887	.893	0.000
Export Peformance	.811	.871	0.000

Source: Own.

Partial Least Squares (PLS) is a technique that best fits predictive applications (exploratory analysis) and theory development when it is not soundly established (Cepeda & Roldán, 2014). This technique, on one hand, maximize the explained variance of the dependent variables (latent or observed, or both) and estimate structural models with small samples (Chin & Newsted, 1999; Reinartz, Haenlein & Henseler, 2009). On the other hand, it estimates reflective and formative measurement models without identification problems (Chin, 2010). PLS appear to be a preferable option for researchers with samples below 250 observations (247 in this study) (Reinartz et al., 2009).

Table 3. Convergent validity

Constructs	AVE	p Values
Intangible resources	.584	.000
Innovation	.546	.000
Export performance	.578	.000

Source: Own.

In order to verify the reliability of overall variables, we estimated the stability and internal consistency through Cronbach's alpha (α). Generally, an instrument or test is classified with appropriate reliability when α is higher or equal to 0.70 (Nunally, 1978; Chin, 2010). The result of 0.965 achieved for all variables is considered excellent, confirming the sample's internal consistency (Pestana & Gageiro, 2008).

We also use the composite reliability coefficient to assess construct validity (Chin, 1998). This coefficient reflects construct adequacy for a level higher than 0.6 using confirmatory factor analysis (Gefen & Straub, 2005), as in our case.

Table 2 illustrates that the studied constructs (all multidimensional) highly exceeded the minimum required for a good fit.

For validity assessment, two subtypes are usually examined: convergent and discriminant validity. Convergent validity implies that a set of indicators represents one and the same underlying construct (Henseler et al., 2009). Fornell and Larcker (1981) suggest using the *Average Variance Extracted* (AVE) criterion and that an AVE value of at least 0.5 indicates sufficient convergent validity (Table 3).

Discriminant validity is the degree to which any single construct is different from the other constructs in the model. To have discriminant validity a construct must exhibit weak correlations with other latent variables that measure different phenomena. There are two measures of discriminant validity in PLS. The Fornell–Larcker criterion (1981) recommends that the AVE should be greater than the variance between a given construct and the other with which it shares the model. The second criterion suggests that the loading of each indicator is expected to be greater than all of its cross-loadings (Henseler et al., 2009).

We can observe the explanatory power of each variable in the model. Entrepreneurial orientation is the only purely explanatory variable and reputational resources and absorptive capacity of knowledge exploitation the explained variables. Chin (1998) distinguishes the explanatory power from moderate to substantial. Table 4 expresses the good results in terms of discriminant validity of the research model, confirming that constructs do differ significantly.

Table 4. Discriminant validity

Fornell-Larcker Criterion	Export Performance	Innovation	Intangible Resources
Export performance	**.760**		
Innovation	.596	**.667**	
Intangible resources	.752	.526	**.696**

Source: Own.

In order to determine the significance of the studied relationships and the confidence intervals of the path coefficients, we used bootstrapping technique. The weighted coefficients indicate the relative strength of each exogenous construct. According to Hair Jr., Hult, Ringle and Sarstedt (2014), relationships between constructs, with structural coefficients higher than 0.2, are considered robust. From Table 5, we thus conclude that the original model does not present non-significant paths.

All research hypotheses are supported.

Table 5. Path coefficients effects

Hypotheses	Original Sample (O)	Sample Mean (M)	Standard Error (STERR)	T Statistics (|O/ STERR|)	*p* Values
H1: IR -> +1	.526	.575	.098	5.363	.000 *
H2: IR -> +EP	.607	.608	.093	6.550	.000 *
H3: I -> +EP	.276	.275	.109	2.537	.011 **
H4: IR -> +1 -> +EP	.145	.158	.072	2.029	.043 **

Key:
IR – Intangible resources; I – Innovation; EP – Export performance.
* $p < 0.001$.
** $p < 0.05$.
Source: Own.

DISCUSSION AND CONCLUSION

The aim of this study was to analyze the impact of intangible resources on the export performance of automotive companies, considering the mediating effect of innovation in this relationship.

54 companies responded to the study through a questionnaire survey to collect data that would allow us to test the research hypotheses formulated using statistical procedures and tests. The companies in this questionnaire assessed export performance, innovation and performance against their main competitor(s).

The relationship between intangible resources and innovation has been supported, corroborating the fact that these types of resources are responsible for the innovativeness of an organization. This result is in line with the conclusions of Burlamarqui and Proença (2003), who state that companies are increasingly articulating themselves in favour of developing strategies aimed primarily at innovation and competition. Export performance is explained by the presence of valuable, rare, difficult to imitate, hardly substitutable strategic resources for competitors, enabling the creation of sustainable asymmetries and competitive advantages for the organizations that own them, that is, the result of heterogeneous resources. This runs counter to the essence of the resource-based view (Barney, 1991), which links higher than average performance in an industry with the quality of its strategic resources. The relationship between innovation and export performance was further confirmed by meeting Liu, Luo and Shi (2003), who found that a higher level of innovation increases competitive advantage. On the other hand, the relationship between intangible resources and export performance, taking into account the mediating effect of innovation, is valid. Some scholars (e.g., Andriopoulos & Lewis, 2009; Jansen et al., 2005) argue that innovation requires different strategic orientations, technological resources and processes. It provides a mechanism for managing change effectively and can achieve both disruptive and incremental innovation. This result was also corroborated by Rua (2018a,b) and Rua and França (2018).

There is not only one way to define the best strategy for a company in the global business world. For exceptional performance, companies need to distinguish themselves from the competition with unique management and superior performance. These companies that have (or use) strategic resources tend to have superior performance as these are valuable, rare, hardly imitable, hardly replaceable by competitors (Barney, 1991), adding that innovation, while variable mediator, regardless of their type, allow the optimization of resources in order to boost superior performance (Andriopoulos & Lewis, 2009; Jansen et al., 2005).

In this sense, the present study reinforces the contribution of intangible resources to leverage innovation, in order to improve and differentiate their products and services, so that their superior performance can be enhanced (Tidd, Bessant & Pavitt, 2003).

All research work has limitations, either in terms of methodology, procedures used or even analysis and interpretation of study results. The size of the sample was the most difficult limitation we found, as not all companies were available to cooperate in this investigation. The fact that it is a non-probabilistic sample for convenience may also be considered as a limitation. Throughout this investigation, we used the 1 to 5 point Likert scale to evaluate the constructs. However, it should be noted that most responses to the questionnaire were based on the subjective opinion of the respondent. Therefore, it can be said that some of the answers do not represent the reality regarding companies' performance in international markets.

Whenever scientific research is carried out, it is possible to leave the way clear so that this subject can be approached in other ways, with different perspectives, with different techniques or until new knowledge on the subject is added.

In future studies, we suggest that the industry construct 4.0 be considered empirically as a mediating variable of the relationship between intangible resources and absorptive capacities. We also suggest extending the scope of the study to other upstream and downstream industries, drawing on other sectors of the automotive industry than the one that was the subject of the present study. Finally, we suggest to promote future comparative studies between the Portuguese industry and those of other countries.

REFERENCES

Amit, R., & Schoemaker, P. (1993). Strategic assets and organizational rent. *Strategic Management Journal*, *14*(1), 33–46. doi:10.1002mj.4250140105

Andriopoulos, C., & Lewis, M. W. (2009). Exploitation-exploration tensions and organizational ambidexterity: Managing paradoxes of innovation. *Organization Science*, *20*(4), 696–717. doi:10.1287/orsc.1080.0406

Arbix, G., Salerno, M., & Negri, J. (2004). *Inovação via internacionalização, faz bem para as exportações brasileiras. In Comunicação apresentada no XVI Fórum Nacional Economia do Conhecimento.* CrescimentoSustentado e Inclusão Social.

Aroian, L. A. (1947). The probability function of the product of two normally distributed variables. *Annals of Mathematical Statistics*, *18*(2), 265–271. doi:10.1214/aoms/1177730442

Atuahene-Gima, K. (1996). Market orientation and innovation. *Journal of Business Research*, *35*(2), 93–103. doi:10.1016/0148-2963(95)00051-8

Atuahene-Gima, K., & Ko, A. (2001). An empirical investigation of the effect of market orientation and entrepreneurship orientation alignment on product innovation. *Organization Science*, *12*(1), 54–74. doi:10.1287/orsc.12.1.54.10121

Bakar, L. J. A., & Ahmad, H. (2010). Assessing the relationship between firm resources and product innovation performance: A resource-based view. *Business Process Management*, *16*(3), 420–435. doi:10.1108/14637151011049430

Baker, W. E., & Sinkula, J. M. (2009). The complementary effects of market orientation and entrepreneurial orientation on profitability in small businesses. *Journal of Small Business Management*, *47*(4), 443–464. doi:10.1111/j.1540-627X.2009.00278.x

Barney, J. (1986). Organizational culture: Can it be a source of sustained competitive advantage? *Academy of Management Review*, *11*(3), 656–665. doi:10.5465/amr.1986.4306261

Barney, J. (1991). Firm Resources and Sustained Competitive Advantage. *Journal of Management*, *17*(1), 99–120. doi:10.1177/014920639101700108

Barney, J. (1995). Looking inside for competitive advantage. *The Academy of Management Perspectives*, *9*(4), 49–61. doi:10.5465/ame.1995.9512032192

Barney, J. B. (2001). Is the Resource-Based "View" a Useful Perspective for Strategic Management Research? Yes. *Academy of Management Review*, *26*(1), 41–56.

Barney, J. B., & Wright, P. M. (1998). On becoming a strategic partner: The role of human resources in gaining competitive advantage. *Human Resource Management*, *37*(1), 31–46. doi:10.1002/(SICI)1099-050X(199821)37:1<31::AID-HRM4>3.0.CO;2-W

Baron, R. M., & Kenny, D. A. (1986). The moderator-mediator variable distinction in social psychological research: Conceptual, strategic, and statistical considerations. *Journal of Personality and Social Psychology*, *51*(6), 1173–1182. doi:10.1037/0022-3514.51.6.1173 PMID:3806354

Barreto, I. (2010). Dynamic Capabilities: A Review of Past Research and an Agenda for the Future. *Journal of Management*, *36*(1), 256–280. doi:10.1177/0149206309350776

Bryman, A., & Cramer, D. (2012). *Quantitative Data Analysis with IBM SPSS 17, 18 & 19: A Guide for Social Scientists*. Routledge. doi:10.4324/9780203180990

Campenhoudt, L. V., & Quivy, R. (2008). *Manual de investigação em Ciências Sociais*. Gradiva Publicações.

Cañibano, L., Garcia-Ayuso, M., & Sanchez, P. (2000). Accounting for Intangibles: A Literature Review. *Journal of Accounting Literature*, *19*, 102–130.

Carmines, E. G., & Zeller, R. A. (1979). *Reliability and Validity Assessment*. Sage. doi:10.4135/9781412985642

Cavusgil, T., & Knight, G. (2009). *Born global firms: a new international enterprise*. Business Experts Press. doi:10.4128/9781606490136

Chesbrough, H., & Teece, D. (2002). Organizing for innovation: when is virtual virtuous? *The Innovative Enterprise*, (August), 127–134.

Chin, W. W. (1998). The partial least squares approach to structural equation modelling. In G. A. Marcoulides (Ed.), *Modern methods for business research* (pp. 295–336). Lawrence Erlbaum Associates.

Chin, W. W. (2010). How to write up and report PLS analyses. In V. E. Vinzi, W. W. Chin, J. Henseler, & H. Wang (Eds.), *Handbook of partial least squares: Concepts, methods and applications in marketing and related fields* (pp. 655–690). Springer. doi:10.1007/978-3-540-32827-8_29

Chin, W. W., & Newsted, P. R. (1999). Structural equation modelling analysis with small samples using partial least squares. In R. H. Hoyle (Ed.), *Statistical strategies for small sample research* (pp. 307–341). Sage.

Coff, R., & Kryscynski, D. (2011). Invited Editorial: Drilling for Micro-Foundations of Human CapitalBased Competitive Advantages. *Journal of Management*, *37*(5), 1429–1443. doi:10.1177/0149206310397772

Correia, M. J. & Rua, O. L. (2016). Innovation in the Portuguese health sector organizations: Empirical evidence from the Community Innovation Survey. *Tékhne - Review of Applied Management Studies*, *14*, 2-9.

Covin, J. G., & Slevin, D. P. (1989). Strategic management of small firms in hostile and benign environments. *Strategic Management Journal*, *10*(1), 75–87. doi:10.1002mj.4250100107

Davis, D., & Mentzer, J. (2008). Relational Resources in Interorganizational Exchange: The Effects of Trade Equity and Brand Equity. *Journal of Retailing*, *84*(4), 435–448. doi:10.1016/j.jretai.2008.08.002

De Clercq, D., Thongpapanl, N. T., & Dimov, D. (2013). Shedding new light on the relationship between contextual ambidexterity and firm performance: An investigation of internal contingencies. *Technovation*, *33*(4), 119–132. doi:10.1016/j.technovation.2012.12.002

Dhanaraj, C., & Beamish, P. W. (2003). A Resource-Based Approach to the Study of Export Performance. *Journal of Small Business Management*, *41*(3), 242–261. doi:10.1111/1540-627X.00080

Dias, M. (2007). *A internacionalização e os fatores de competitividade: o caso Adira* (Master's thesis). Faculdade de Economia da Universidade do Porto. Retrieved from https://hdl.handle.net/10216/7548

Fornell, C., & Larcker, D. F. (1981). Structural Equation Models with Unobservable Variables and Measurement Error: Algebra and Statistics. *JMR, Journal of Marketing Research*, *18*(3), 382–388. doi:10.1177/002224378101800313

Gefen, D., & Straub, D. (2005). A practical guide to factorial validity using PLS-graph: Tutorial and annotated example. *Communications of the Association for Information Systems*, *16*(1), 91–109.

Hall, R. (1992). The strategic analysis of intangible resources. *Strategic Management Journal*, *13*, 135–144. Retrieved from de http://onlinelibrary.wiley.com/doi/10.1002/smj.4250130205/abstract

Hill, A., & Hill, M. M. (2008). Investigação por Questionário (2a ed.). Edições Silabo.

Hitt, M., Bierman, L., Shimizu, K., & Kochhar, R. (2001). Direct and moderating effects of human capital on strategy and performance in professional service firms: A resource-based perspective. *Academy of Management Journal*, *44*(1), 13–28.

Hult, G. T., Hurley, R. F., & Knight, G. A. (2004). Innovativeness: Its Antecedents and impact on Business Performance. *Industrial Marketing Management*, *33*(5), 429–438. doi:10.1016/j.indmarman.2003.08.015

Hurley, R. F., & Hult, G. T. (1998). Innovation, Market Orientation, and Organizational Learning: An Integration and Empirical Examination. *Journal of Marketing*, *62*(3), 42–54. doi:10.1177/002224299806200303

Jansen, J. J. P., Van Den Bosch, F. A. J., & Volberda, H. W. (2005). Managing Potential and Realized Absorptive Capacity: How Do Organizational Antecedents Matter? *Academy of Management Journal*, *48*(6), 999–1015. doi:10.5465/amj.2005.19573106

Katsikeas, C. S., & Morgan, R. E. (1994). Differences in perceptions of exporting problems based on firm size and export market experience. *European Journal of Marketing*, *28*(5), 17–35. doi:10.1108/03090569410062014

Kelly, P. (2009). *International business and management*. South-Western, Cengage Learning, EMEA.

Knight, G., & Cavusgil, S. T. (2004). Innovation, organizational capabilities, and the born-global firm. *Journal of International Business Studies*, *35*(2), 124–141. doi:10.1057/palgrave.jibs.8400071

Lee, J. (1992). Quantitative versus qualitative research methods two approaches to organization studies. *Asia Pacific Journal of Management*, *9*(1), 87–94. doi:10.100710490-015-9454-8

Li, L. (2005). Is Regional Strategy More Effective Thanglobal Strategy in the US Service Industries? *Management International Review*, *45*(1), 37–57.

Li, Y., Liu, Y., & Zhao, Y. (2006). The role of market and entrepreneurship orientation and internal control in the new product development of Chinese firms. *Industrial Marketing Management*, *35*(3), 336–347. doi:10.1016/j.indmarman.2005.05.016

Li, Y., Zhao, Y., Tan, J., & Liu, Y. (2008). Moderating Effects of Entrepreneurial Orientation on Market Orientation-Performance Linkage: Evidence from Chinese Small Firms. *Journal of Small Business Management*, *46*(1), 113–133. doi:10.1111/j.1540-627X.2007.00235.x

Liu, S. S., Luo, X., & Shi, Y. Z. (2003). Market oriented organizations in an emerging economy: A study of missing links. *Journal of Business Research*, *56*(6), 481–491. doi:10.1016/S0148-2963(01)00265-X

López, S. V. (2005). Competitive advantage and strategy formulation: The key role of dynamic capabilities. *Management Decision*, *43*(5), 661–669. doi:10.1108/00251740510597699

Lumpkin, G., & Dess, G. (1996). Clarifying the entrepreneurial orientation construct and linking it to performance. *Academy of Management Review*, *21*(1), 135–172. http://amr.aom.org/content/21/1/135.short. doi:10.5465/amr.1996.9602161568

Makadok, R. (2001). Toward a synthesis of the resource-based and dynamic-capability views of rent creation. *Strategic Management Journal*, *22*(5), 387–401. doi:10.1002mj.158

Marconi, M., & Lakatos, E. (2011). *Metodologia Científica*. Editora Atlas.

Marôco, J. (2011). Análise estatística com o SPSS Statistics (5a ed.). ReportNumber, Lda.

Miller, D. (1983). The correlates of entrepreneurship in three types of firms. *Management Science*, *29*(7), 770–791. doi:10.1287/mnsc.29.7.770

Monteiro, A. P., Soares, A. M., & Rua, O. (2017). Linking intangible resources and export performance: The role of entrepreneurial orientation and dynamic capabilities. *Baltic Journal of Management*, *12*(3), 329–347. doi:10.1108/BJM-05-2016-0097

Morgan, N., Vorhies, D. W., & Schlegelmilch, B. B. (2006). Resource–performance relationships in industrial export ventures: The role of resource inimitability and substitutability. *Industrial Marketing Management*, *35*(5), 621–633. doi:10.1016/j.indmarman.2005.05.018

Mugnol, R. (2013). *A performance exportadora e os seus antecedentes. O papel da orientação para o mercado externo, empreendedorismo, recursos e inovação: um estudo em empresas exportadoras do sul do Brasil.* Tese de Doutoramento. Coimbra: Universidade de Coimbra. Retrieved from https://estudogeral.sib.uc.pt/handle/10316/25112

Nunnally, J. C. (1978). *Psychometric theory*. McGraw-Hill.

Penrose, E. (1959). *The Theory of the Growth of the Firm* (4th ed.). Oxford University Press., doi:10.1093/0198289774.001.0001

Pestana, M. H., & Gageiro, J. N. (2008). Análise de Dados para Ciências Sociais - A complementaridade do SPSS (5a ed.). Edições Silabo.

Piercy, N., Kaleka, A., & Katsikeas, C. (1998). Sources of competitive advantage in high performing exporting companies. *Journal of World Business*, *33*(4), 378–393. doi:10.1016/S1090-9516(99)80081-9

Porter, M. (2000). Location, competition, and economic development: Local clusters in a global economy. *Economic Development Quarterly*, *1*(14), 15–34. doi:10.1177/089124240001400105

Porter, M., & Millar, V. (1985). How information gives you competitive advantage. *Harvard Business Review*, *63*(4), 149–160.

Quadros, R. (2008). Aprendendo a inovar: padrões de gestão da inovação tecnológica em empresas industriais brasileiras. In *Relatório de pesquisa Padrões de gestão da inovação tecnológica em empresas brasileiras, apresentado ao CNPq*. Universidade Estadual de Campinas.

Reinartz, W., Haenlein, M., & Henseler, J. (2009). An Empirical Comparison of the Efficacy of Covariance-Based and Variance-Based SEM. *International Journal of Research in Marketing*, *26*(4), 332–344. doi:10.1016/j.ijresmar.2009.08.001

Richardson, R. (1989). *Pesquisa Social: métodos e técnicas*. Atlas.

Roldán, J. L., Cegarra, J. G., & Cepeda, G. (2014). Building organisational agility through an unlearning Context. *European Conference on Knowedge Management*, *2*, 834-842.

Rua, O. L. (2018a). From intangible resources to export performance: Exploring the mediating effect of absorptive capabilities and innovation. *Review of International Business and Strategy*, *28*(3/4), 373–394. doi:10.1108/RIBS-02-2018-0012

Rua, O. L. (2018b). Absorptive Capabilities and Export Performance: The Mediating Effect of Innovation. *International Journal of Advances in Management and Economics*, *7*(5), 28–37.

Rua, O. L., & França, A. (2018). The Linkage Between Intangible Resources and Export Performance: The mediating effect of Innovation. *International Journal of Innovation*, *5*(3), 399–410. Advance online publication. doi:10.5585/iji.v5i3.190

Sarkar, S. (2010). *Empreendedorismo e Inovação* (2nd ed.). Escolar Editora.

Schumpeter, J. A. (1961). *The Theory of Economic Development: An Inquiry Into Profits, Capital, Credit, Interest, and the Business Cycle*. Oxford University Press.

Silva, M. J. (2007). O papel da inovação e do conhecimento na construção da competitividade regional. Actas da 4.ª Conferência de Engenharia 'Engenharia' 2007 – Inovação e Desenvolvimento. Covilhã, 433-438.

Sousa, C. M. P., Martínez-López, F. J., & Coelho, F. (2008). The determinants of export performance: A review of the research in the literature between 1998 and 2005. *International Journal of Management Reviews*, *10*(4), 343–374. doi:10.1111/j.1468-2370.2008.00232.x

Stouraitis, V., Harris, M., Harun, M., & Kyritsis, M. (2017). Motivators of SME initial export choice and the European Union regional effect in manufacturing. *International Journal of Entrepreneurial Behaviour & Research*, *23*(1), 35–55. doi:10.1108/IJEBR-05-2015-0120

Teece, D. J. (2007). Explicating dynamic capabilities: The nature and microfoundations of (sustainable) enterprise performance. *Strategic Management Journal*, *1350*(August), 1319–1350. doi:10.1002mj.640

Teece, D. J., Pisano, G., & Shuen, A. (1997). Dynamic capabilities and strategic management. *Strategic Management Journal*, *18*(7), 509–533. doi:10.1002/(SICI)1097-0266(199708)18:7<509::AID-SMJ882>3.0.CO;2-Z

Tidd, J., Bessant, J., & Pavitt, K. (2003). *Gestão da Inovação*. Monitor.

Westhead, P., Wright, M., & Ucbasaran, D. (2001). The internationalization of new and small firms: A resource-based view. *Journal of Business Venturing*, *9026*(99), 333–358. doi:10.1016/S0883-9026(99)00063-4

Wu, L.-Y. (2010). Applicability of the resource-based and dynamic-capability views under environment volatility. *Journal of Business Research*, *63*(1), 27–31. doi:10.1016/j.jbusres.2009.01.007

Zou, S., Taylor, C. R., & Osland, G. E. (1998). The EXPERF scale: A cross-national generalized export performance measure. *Journal of International Marketing*, *6*(3), 37–58. doi:10.1177/1069031X9800600307

ADDITIONAL READING

Aulakh, P. S., Kotabe, M., & Teegen, H. (2000). Export strategies and performance of firms from emerging economies: Evidence from Brazil, Chile, and Mexico. *Academy of Management Journal*, *43*(3), 342–361.

Monteiro, A., Soares, A. M., & Rua, O. L. (2017). Entrepreneurial orientation and export performance: The mediating effect of organisational resources and dynamic capabilities. *Journal of International Business and Entrepreneurship Development*, *10*(1), 3–19. doi:10.1504/JIBED.2017.082749

Penrose, E. T. (1959). *The Theory of the Growth of the Firm*. John Wiley.

Peteraf, M. (1993). The cornerstones of competitive advantage: A resource-based view. *Strategic Management Journal*, *14*(3), 179–191. doi:10.1002mj.4250140303

Peteraf, M., & Barney, J. (2003). Unravelling the resource-based tangle. *Managerial and Decision Economics, 24*(1), 309–323. doi:10.1002/mde.1126

Rua, O. L., & França, A. (2017). Assessing the relationship between Entrepreneurial Orientation, Reputational Resources and Absorptive Capability: A resource-based approach. *Periodica Polytechnica Social and Management Sciences, 26*(1), 30–37. doi:10.3311/PPso.10206

KEY TERMS AND DEFINITIONS

Exports Performance: Strategic performance in international markets, as well as its satisfaction with this performance.

Innovation: New combinations, encompassing the introduction of new products, the creation of new forms of production, the emergence of new markets, the availability of new raw materials and the emergence of new companies.

Intangible Resources: Considered strategic resources, including six dimensions: reputational resources; access to financial resources; human resources; cultural resources; relational resources; and informational resources.

Resource-Based View: Theory based on the assumption that the source of competitive advantage is obtained from firms' resources.

SME: Small and medium-sized enterprises.

Chapter 13
Using Main Courante and Daily Revenue Report Methods in Accounting of Daily Revenues in Touristic Accomodation Enterprises

Engin Meriç
https://orcid.org/0000-0002-0965-3089
Trakya University, Turkey

EXECUTIVE SUMMARY

In today's globalised world, internationalisation is an obligation beyond being a choice and it is inevitable for the small and medium-sized accommodation enterprises to take place in this process. Since utilising from global opportunities depends on the protection of themselves from threats, their incomes should be tracked daily, and their internal control mechanism must be strengthened. With this purpose, the study aims to realise the room revenues of SMEs with Main Courante and other unit revenues with DRRs. For the accounting of the revenues Main Courante offset is given place, whereas for the control accounts the daily revenue report offset is preferred. Documents related to income record that can be used in the flow of the process in SMEs have been included. With this method, it is aimed to prevent losses and leaks, provide data flow towards accounting internal control system, sustain competitive advantage and contribute to the internationalization efforts.

INTRODUCTION

Due to the fact that there are many income units and labour-intensive services that continue 24/7 in the touristic accommodation establishments (TAEs), the possibility of erroneous and fraudulent transactions is higher when compared to the other kinds of enterprises. In order to avoid and minimize problems, an effective internal control with an accounting organization which can meet all the needs of enterprises is inevitable. However, in order to manage this process effectively, TAEs require more personnel recruit-

DOI: 10.4018/978-1-7998-4387-0.ch013

ment, which increases the costs and thereby weakens the competitiveness of the TAEs in micro and medium sized enterprises.

One of the most crucial units of an effective internal control is the front-desk office unit. In addition to the many periodic works that should be carried out in the front office of TAEs, front-desk offices are also responsible for welcoming guests, making guest check-in processes, baggage-related transactions, preparing incoming and outgoing guest lists, making reservations in a healthy way, delivering messages to guests on time, opening folios, charging folios, organizing daily-weekly reports, ensuring that the guests leave with good impressions and facilitating good communication and relations between other units of the facility. The front office executes all the relations with the departments of reception, reservation, front cash, and concierge.

In the small and medium-sized hospitality businesses (especially in the small-scale ones), the front office works are carried out by a single staff, making the procedures extremely intense and difficult. This situation often weakens the effectiveness of internal control processes in small and medium-sized enterprises (SMEs). As a result of the incomplete records, businesses have difficulties in estimating their revenues and spending costs precisely, which results in losing their power in terms of competition and internationalization.

Nevertheless, keeping in mind the fact that today's globalized world favours internationalized or multinational businesses over the others, and that tourism sector necessitates it even more than the other sectors, it would be appropriate to state that internationalization has become an imperative beyond being a choice. Out of this necessity, there occurred an obligation for small and medium sized accommodation enterprises to take their places in this process too. In their way to internationalization, to provide protection of themselves from threats is of great importance for small and medium-sized accommodation enterprises so that these threats would not minimize their better use of global opportunities. Thus, TAEs need to take a safer position to compete with global developments. For this reason, enterprises need to track their incomes daily as a whole, and their internal control mechanism must be strengthened.

Moving from this necessity, it has been aimed in this study to use Main Courante offset in the accounting of revenues, and to control accounts in the Daily Revenue Report (DRR) offset. In the flow of the process, documents related to income record that can be used in SMEs were included. The overall purposes of using this method are to prevent losses and leaks, to provide data flow towards accounting internal control system, to sustain competitive advantage and to contribute to the internationalization efforts.

The method of the study has been chosen after a meticulous preliminary examination. The fact that front desk missions are executed by a single staff in most of the small and medium-sized businesses, the manual or semi-automative usability of the system, and the lack of necessity for a capital cost required for a complete software system as well as the easily applicable feature of this method have been effective in choosing it for this study. A boutique accommodation facility with 40 rooms was chosen as the application facility, and Main Courante and DRRs were prepared according to the daily revenue data of the enterprise.

In developing countries, some tools are needed to be used for the survival of the businesses in the long term. One of these tools is the internal control system (ICSs). When an effective ICS is mentioned, corporate accounting order comes to the front. The accounting system is important in terms of increasing the efficiency of enterprises and of the effective operation of ICSs (Aktürk, 2015). The effective functioning of the accounting system in TAEs will contribute to operational efficiency in different ways and of significant quantity. As a result, businesses' competitiveness and contribution to the economic development of countries will accelerate (Yilanci, 2001). At this point, it is inevitable to increase the awareness of investors, managers and responsible stakeholders on ICSs. One of the fields in which such an awareness should be increased is the tourism sector.

Today, tourism industry in Turkey is in a continuous rapid growth and has significant contributions to the gross national product and employment. According to 2019 data, contribution of tourism sector to gross national product is 4.6% while it provided 34.520.3 billion dollars foreign currency input (TURSAB, 2020). Investments and expenditures in the sector of tourism provide high employment when compared to other sectors. According to the data provided by The World Travel & Tourism Council (WTTC), direct employment in tourism sector in Turkey increased 7% between the years 2010 to 2017 and reached 484 thousand of employees. In the same period, indirect employment increased from 1 million 152 thousand employee to 1 million 624 thousand people. The share of the tourism sector in total employment was generally around 8% in Turkey. Along with these, according to the estimates of WTTC, direct employment in tourism sector will have 915 thousand employees in 2025, whereas indirect employment is expected to reach 1 million 902 thousand of workers. According to Bahar and Bilen (2020), total employment in the tourism sector is estimated to reach 2 million 817 thousand people.

Considering the significant contributions of the sector to Turkey's gross national product, it would not be erroneous to state that tourism is one of the most significant sectors in the Turkish economy. Thereby, Turkey embodies a great number of touristic facilities and different types of accommodation enterprises each of which requires distinct legal procedures. There are two types of registration documents for accommodation enterprises in Turkey: (a) certified facilities which are registered by local administrations (municipalities), and (b) accommodation establishments that have a business document registered by the Ministry of Tourism. In Turkey, there are 4,053 facilities (with 992,544 beds) which have a tourism operation certificate, and there are 727 facilities (with 183.992 beds) which have a tourism investment license. Total number of facilities that have Ministry of Tourism License is 4.780 with 1.176.536 beds. The bed average per facility certified by the Ministry of Tourism can be calculated as 246. The number of facilities with a municipality certificate is 8.211, with a capacity of 553,439 beds (Ministry of Culture and Tourism-MCT, 2020). This can be estimated as an average of 67 beds per facility, or 30 rooms per facility. A large part of the operating certificates including TAEs registered by ministries and municipalities in Turkey consists of small and medium-sized TAEs. 90% of accommodation businesses in the UK, similarly, is made up of small businesses that employs 10 people (European Commission, 2019). Likewise, more than 90% of the accommodation enterprises in Europe are small and medium-sized accommodation enterprises (European Commission, 2019).

Taking this high percentage into consideration, for providing income accrual and recording method system especially in small and medium sized TAEs, application of Main Courante and DRRs was given place. In addition, in practice, the accounting of revenues is intended to contribute to the context of the establishment of internal control system of the enterprise.

LITERATURE REVIEW

There are several studies about accounting of incomes in accommodation establishments and about the contributions of the internal control to the enterprises in the accounting and finance literature which are given below, but limited research is available in tourism literature.

In one of these studies, Türedi (2008) emphasized the fact that effectiveness of ICSs in TAEs depends on the effectiveness of the accounting information system of the enterprises. Turedi also stated that managers should determine financial and accounting risks of the businesses, and develop some methods and procedures accordingly, in order to avoid these risks. In another study belonging to Kurniadi and

Zio (2011), the role of the internal control systems in the operations of international and local hotel businesses in Sweden and Indonesia was examined. Their study indicated that implementation of the internal control systems helps ensuring the effectiveness of inner operations. It is also emphasized in their study that the internal control system is a guide for protecting assets, preventing losses and generating accurate and reliable financial reports. Karagiorgos, Drogalas and Giovanis (2011) discussed the interaction between the various components of ICSs and performance of internal control system in hotel businesses in Greece in their study and they concluded that all the components of the ICSs are vital for the effectiveness and success of internal control. They also stated that internal audit has the ability of influencing survival and success of businesses. In the study conducted by Mndzebele (2013), the use of Accounting Information Systems (AIS) was analysed to determine whether they improve the internal control systems in the hotels or not. As a result, it was determined that there is a relationship between accounting information systems and ICSs. Mndzebele also stated that hotel managements use accounting information systems in internal control for providing lower cost and up to date information. Juen and Mustapha (2015) surveyed department managers at 100 hotel businesses in Malaysia to evaluate the effectiveness of internal control systems in hotel establishments; and it was revealed in the study that control environment, risk assessment, information and communication are the important components of the internal control effectiveness of the TAEs. Yemer and Chekol (2017) investigated the relationship and effect of all components of internal control in hotel revenues. As a result of the study, it was determined that internal control components had a positive effect on increasing hotel revenues. Particularly, it was emphasized that components of control activities and information and communication practices can guide the estimation of hotel revenues.

As it has been mentioned in the preceding parts of the study, internationalization, defined as the geographical expansion of a company's research and development activities, production, sales or other business functions outside the national borders of the country, is important in terms of companies' growth and competitiveness strategies (Hollensen, 2014; Ruzzier et al., 2006). Company resources and their management skills, strategic orientation and individual characteristics of the founders, partners and managers play an important role on the internationalization degree and size of the companies. According to Hollensen (2014), these factors also cause differentiation in internationalization approaches and strategies of small enterprises from multinational companies.

Internationalization activities of both multinational and SMEs are of great importance for economic development of companies. Especially outward-oriented internationalization efforts provide significant competitive advantage to companies, regions and countries in many perspectives. The most important of these activities can be listed as developments in products and innovation processes, efficient and productive use of resources, high level of technological and economic progresses and increase in welfare at the country level (Ruzzier et al., 2006).

When the internationalization activities are analysed, it is observed that these operations are not only dominated by multinational firms, and that the internationalization of SMEs also grows proportionally and volumetrically (Bal & Kunday, 2014; Lu & Beamish, 2006).

Despite the differences in definitions of concepts, internationalization constitutes one of the most important growth strategies not only for large companies but also for SMEs. Hollansen (2014) emphasized that there are important differences between multinational companies and SMEs in terms of structural and resource diversity, amount and access. Since it has been stated in the literature by many researchers that these small enterprises are not small-sized models of large and corporate companies, but they have their own behaviour and strategies (Knight & Liesch, 2016), it is advocated that it requires differentiation in internationalization approaches and theories related to these companies (Meckl & Schramm, 2005). Therefore, by addressing internationalization at the enterprise level, an answer is sought for how businesses can gain and sustain their competitive advantage in the international trade. According to Haghighti and Albayrak (2016), if a business expects a long-term and substantial benefit from the foreign market, and there is a market structure that will meet its expectations, it may be appropriate to invest directly in that country. Tourism sector is a good example for such an internationalization procedure since there is a tendency towards globalization in the tourism sector. Many tourism organizations are global organizations operating across national borders (Reisinger, 2009).

CONCEPTUAL FRAMEWORK

Significant developments which made international businesses important can be qualified as the technological developments, increasing competitive environment, standardization activities, business environment, political influence of national businesses, economic integration, and globalization (Koparal, 2010). Enterprises should execute their management functions strategically in order to increase their efficiency and effectiveness as well as to ensure both national and international sustainability. Taş and Zengin (2019) highlighted that business executives should act together for the purposes of increasing the public welfare by producing goods and services, maintaining employment in business, ensuring the continuity of the business, increasing production and sales, increasing market share of business, ensuring growth of business, maximizing the profit of business and maximizing the value of the business. Today, the importance of SMEs is accepted all over the world in terms of their number in total enterprises, their great contribution to employment, their role in balanced regional development and their share in production (OECD, 2019).

According to Wanhill (2000), benefits of developing SMEs in tourism businesses was discussed earlier and their importance in the country's economy was revealed a long time ago. Rapid changes occurring in markets where many accommodation businesses are located are the factors that can change the tourism market and competition environment. With the effect of these changes, some hotel businesses in the market lose their advantages, while others gain some. However, no matter under what market conditions TAEs operate, accommodation enterprises can have a chance to increase their competitiveness by determining their strategies and management methods accordingly (Bahar & Kozak, 2012). In terms of achieving this goal, a strictly controlled accounting system is of great significance.

Hall (2013) defines accounting systems in accommodation establishments as a part of the business information systems, which record activities that can be described as data; qualify the data as information; convert data to basic financial reports that are required, and prepare the special financial reports in line with the management's request.

The accounting system in the accommodation enterprises carries out basic activities stated below (Çetiner, 2009):

- It ensures continuous recording and control of value movements expressed in money related to assets and resources in the enterprise,
- It determines the income and expenses of each business segment separately, and as a result determines the income and expenses of the whole business,
- It determines costs of goods and services offered to guests,
- It ensures that necessary measures are taken according to the results obtained from the accounting records.

Deduced from the activities and responsibilities given above, it can clearly be concluded that accounting in hospitality and accommodation businesses in tourism sector is an important element that aims to record and track the financial transactions of those using the business facilities and services of guests. Although it seems difficult at the application stage, it is actually based on a simple logic, and above all, requires basic mathematical skills, responsibility, accuracy and great attention (Kapiki, 2015).

Main Courante is an application that covers the daily room and board revenues and extra expenses that customers make as room accounts in other units that they would pay at the time of the check-out (Karaxontzitis & Sarlis, 1989).The DRRs, on the other hand, collect and present all business information from the previous day. In accordance with the business, it can also be called as the "daily income reports" (DIRs) or "gross income reports" (GIRs). DRRs are prepared in the form of daily income statements according to the department (Hales, 2005).

Revenue is the income resulting from the ordinary activities of businesses, and carries various titles such as sales, wages, interest, dividends and name rights. It is recognized in cases where future economic benefits are likely to become operational and such benefits can be measured reliably (Gökgöz & Özdemir, 2015).

The revenue of a facility should be accrued when it is determined that the business will provide economic benefits in the future and these benefits can be measured reliably (Dursun &Yalnız, 2013).

Measurement of revenue according to the Turkish Accounting Standart-18 (TMS-18) is categorized under three headings: (a) Measurement of Revenue in Sales of Goods; (b) Measurement of Revenue in Service Sales; (c) Measurement of Revenue of Interest, Dividend and Name Rights. In this study, only the measurement of revenue in service sales is scrutinized. TMS-18 revenue standard describes the situations where the criteria are met, and the revenue is recognized as a result. Additionally, this standard provides practical guidance on the implementation of these criteria (Şenel, 2009).The purpose of TMS-18 revenue standard is to explain how the items obtained as a result of the ordinary transactions and covered by revenue should be accounted for (Gökçen, Ataman, & Çakıcı, 2006). The most important issue here is when the revenue should be counted and when it will be recorded as revenue. This standard aims to determine when and to what extent the revenue arising in different situations will be accrued (Dursun & Yalnız, 2013).

Due to the sectoral differences in accommodation establishments, the facts such as the 24/7 service in the facility, labour intensive businesses, high amount of monetary transactions, high income centres, employment of unqualified personnel and sales of ordinary products with high unit value should be taken into consideration in the establishment of the internal control system (Kaya & Köse, 2013). In this study, room revenues and pension (breakfast, lunch and dinner in BB, HB, FB accommodations) revenues were realized with Main Courante, whereas other unit (restaurant, bar, beach-swimming pool, laundry, sports activities etc.) revenues were realized with the DRRs.

METHOD

It is of great significance that TAEs document their daily income completely and dominate the reporting revenues in the registration process from check-in to check-out. It is necessary to manage (a) accommodation expenditures of customers whose accommodation is continuing; and (b) extra account expenses of room account they make in other units being paid at check-out with a controllable recording method. In addition to these, it would be appropriate to make revenues with accrual systems in order to document actual profit (or loss) of the accommodation enterprises for each month.

In practice, daily accommodation units of business and the registration and tracking of the extra expenses that customers make to pay at check-out are realized with the Main Courante method, which will cover all the processes until the collection stage.

Main Courante method has 7 sections:

1. Document and customer information
2. Transfer of the balance of receivables from the previous day's reception (from customers),
3. Room income, breakfast income and meal income related to Bed & Breakfast, Half board, Full board (BB, HB and FB) accommodation,
4. Extra spending by customers on other units as room account to pay at the check-out
5. The sum of daily expenses and the total sum obtained with the transfer,
6. Payment transactions of customers leaving the business,
7. Ongoing customer account balances

In the scope of the study, The DDRs were used in accounting of food and beverage units and other units (such as beach-swimming pool, laundry, sports activities).

FINDINGS

A group of 56 people, encapsulating 4 single 26 double rooms, with the date of 19.07.2019 entry and 02.08.2019 exit, has been booked to the TAE which is subject to application in this study. The booking is a half board (HB) with breakfast check in and accommodation group reservation. The room prices are as follows:

- Single room 80,00 $
- Double room 120,00 $

Let's assume that the income of this group was not made through the accrual system during the stay, and income record was made on 02.08.2019 at the time of check-out. In this case, 12 days of July 2019 revenues will be recorded in August 2019. The calculation of the situation is given in Box 1.

Box 1.

Calculation	Amount
Single 4 room*12 nights* 80,00 $	= 3.840,00 $
Double 26 room*12 nights*120,00 $	= 37.440,00 $
TOTAL	**41.280,00 $**
Total Gross Income	= 41.280,00 $
Total Net Income = 41.280,00 $ / 1.08	= 38.222,22 $
TAX	= 3.057,78 $

The fact that the net income of 38.222,22 $ for July 2019 will be included in the revenues of August 2019 can be seen in this calculation given above.

In this case, for example, the company, which is expecting a 30.000,00 $ budgeted profit in July, will encounter a 8.222,22 $ loss because of the fact that 38.222,22 $ profit in the income statement of July was recorded in August. This situation will cause the enterprise's targeted costs-based income to be out of control as well as an inability to analyse the budget deviations because of the inadequate internal control. This shows that accommodation companies' recording all their income on a daily basis with the accrual method and to report the income target controls and deviations per budget in overnight stays in favour of deviations is of great importance in terms of taking necessary precautions.

In the light of the above explanations, while the accommodation section of the business is granted to the application of the folio, Main Courante in the income accruals, the accounting was performed with the Main Courante offset. Food and beverage units and other unit revenues, application examples of issuing cashier reports have been completed. The control of these reports by the accounting officer resulted in the preparation of the DRRs and the issuance of the DRR offset of the daily revenues. It is adopted as the main purpose in this study, and it is expected that the application of this method contributes to the related sector and study has been executed in this context.

Table 1. Group Folio

Folio				
Folio no:		001816		
Voucher no:		0626718		
Room no:		210-290 / 310-352		
Customer name:		Grup / X		
Room type:		4 Single 26 Double		
Accommodation type:		HB		
Check in date:		19.07.2019 Breakfast Check in		
Check out date:		02.08.2019		
HB single room price:		80,00 $		
HB double room price:		120,00 $		
Item No	**Date**	**Explanations**	**Amount**	**Balance**
1		001809 – 001801 no folio balance transfer		41.280,00
2	31.07.2019	Breakfast	448,00	
3	31.07.2019	Dinner	840,00	
4	31.07.2019	Room	2.152,00	44.720,00
5				
6				
7				
TOTAL				
CASH				
CREDIT CARD/ CHECK				
CURRENT ACCOUNT				
BALANCE				

Table 2. Group Folio Calculation

Room Type	Number of Rooms	Number of Customers	Room Costs	Breakfast Cost	Food Cost
Single Room	4	4	4 room*57,00 = 228,00 $	4 people*8,00 = 32,00 $	4 people*15,00 = 60,00 $
Double Room	26	52	26 room*74,00 = 1.924,00 $	52 people*8,00 = 416,00 $	52 people*15,00 = 780,00 $
TOTAL	**30**	**56**	**2.152,00 $**	**448,00 $**	**840,00 $**

As it can be seen, Group HB prices, service costs expansion and calculation are made above. As of 19.07.2019 entry date for group folio, 4 Single 26 Double rooms for 56 people until 02.08.2019 release day, daily price of 2.152,00 $ per day, 448,00 $ pension (breakfast) and 840,00 $ pension (meal) fee will be charged and transferred to Main Courante daily.

Table 3. Individual Customer Folio

Folio				
Folio no:		**001818**	**Individual Customer Folio Calculation**	
Room no:		428	Room 84,00 $	
Customer name:		Customer A	Breakfast 2 people* 8,00 $ 16,00 $	
Room type:		Double	Dinner 2 people*15,00 $ 30,00$	
Accommodation type:		HB		
Check in date:		30.07.2019 Dinner Check in		
Check out date:		31.07.2019		
HB double room price:		130,00 $		
Item No	**Date**	**Explanation**	**Amount**	**Balance**
1	30.07.2019	Dinner	30,00	
2	30.07.2019	Room	84,00	
3	30.07.2019	Bar	10,00	124,00
4	31.07.2019	Breakfast	16,00	140,00
5				
6				
7				
TOTAL				**140,00 $**
CASH				
CREDIT CARD/ CHECK				
CURRENT ACCOUNT				**140,00 $**
BALANCE				

Given above, the Half Pension accommodation of 2 customers who make entrance with dinner on 30.07.2019 will leave the establishment with breakfast on 31.07.2019 can be seen. For these customers, the folio number 001818 was charged 30,00 $, the room price 84,00 $ and the extra expenses they made in other departments to be paid at the exit on 30.07.2019. On 31.07.2019 breakfast charge was made as 16,00 $ and finally folio was closed.

Table 4. Individual Customer Folio

Folio				
Folio no:		001819	**Individual Customer Folio Calculation**	
Room no:		402	Room 84,00 $	
Customer name:		Customer B	Breakfast 2 people* 8,00 $ 16,00 $	
Room type:		Double	Dinner 2 people*15,00 $ 30,00 $	
Accommodation type:		HB		
Check in date:		31.07.2019 Dinner Check in		
Check out date:		03.08.2019		
HB double room price:		130,00 $		
Item No	**Date**	**Explanations**	**Amount**	**Balance**
1	31.07.2019	Dinner	30,00	
2	31.07.2019	Room	84,00	
3	31.07.2019	Bar	43,00	
4	31.07.2019	Bar	20,00	177,00
5				
6				
7				
TOTAL				
CASH				
CREDIT CARD/ CHECK				
CURRENT ACCOUNT				
BALANCE				

In Table 4, Half Pension accommodation of 2 customers who enter with dinner on 31.07.2019 will leave the establishment with breakfast on 03.08.2019 is demonstrated. For these customers, the folio number 001819 was charged 30,00 $, the room price 84,00 $ and the extra expenses they made in other departments to be paid at the exit on 31.07.2019. On 01.08.2019 and 02.08.2019 for each day; the price of breakfast is 16,00 $, the meal price is 30,00 $ and the room price is 84,00 $. On 03.08.2019, 16,00 $ breakfast charge will be made, and the folio will be closed.

Table 5. Individual Customer Folio

Folio				
Folio no:		**001817**	**Individual Customer Folio Calculation**	
Room no:		411	Room 67,00 $	
Customer name:		Customer C	Breakfast 1 person* 8,00$ 8,00 $	
Room type:		Single	Dinner 1 person*15,00 $ 15,00 $	
Accommodation type:		HB		
Check in date:		30.07.2019 Dinner Check in		
Check out date:		03.08.2019		
HB single room price:		90,00 $		
Item No	**Date**	**Explanation**	**Amount**	**Balance**
1	30.07.2019	Dinner	15,00	
2	30.07.2019	Room	67,00	82,00
3	31.07.2019	Breakfast	8,00	
4	31.07.2019	Dinner	15,00	
5	31.07.2019	Room	67,00	
6	31.07.2019	Bar	32,00	
7	31.07.2019	Laundry	12,00	
8	31.07.2019	Restaurant	40,00	
9	31.07.2019	Bar	16,00	272,00
10				
11				
12				
TOTAL				
CASH				
CREDIT CARD/ CHECK				
CURRENT ACCOUNT				
BALANCE				

Table 5 gives the record of an individual with half board accommodation who entered with dinner on 30.07.2019 and will leave the facility on 03.08.2019. Folio number 001817 was charged for this customer on 30.07.2019 with a meal price of 15,00 $ and a room price of 67,00 $. Again, on 31.07.2019, 8,00 $ breakfast price, 15,00 $ food price, 67,00 $ room price, and the extra expenses customer made to pay at the check-out spent at the other units were charged. On 01.08.2019 and 02.08.2019, 8,00 $ breakfast fee, 15,00 $ meal price and 67,00 $ room price will be charged for each day. Folio will be closed after the charge of 8,00 $ breakfast fee on 03.08.2019.

In the folio charges belonging to the group and individual customers, room income was included separately as breakfast and meal income in order to record favourable income for the customers' stay with HB accommodation. In addition, the extra expenses made by the customers in the food and beverage units and other units of the business (such as beach-swimming pool, laundry, sports activities) to be collected at the exit by the reception and the room account in the Cashier Reports and Daily Revenue Reports were charged to the folios in detail to balance the expenses.

Table 6. Main Courante Table (31.07.2019)

A							B	C			D				E		F					G
Check In Date	Check Out Date	Folio No	Room Number	Number of Rooms	Number of Customers	Customer Name and Surname	Transfer	Room Income	Breakfast Income	Dinner Income	Restaurant	Bar	Laundry	Paid-Out	Daily Total	General Total	Discounts	Cash	Credit Card	Check	Current Account	Balance
19.07. 2019		001816		30	56	Group X	41.280,00	2.152,00	448,00	840,00	-	-	-		**3.440,00**	44.720,00		-			-	44.720,00
31.07. 2019		001819	402	1	2	Customer B	-	84,00	-	30,00	-	63,00	-		**177,00**	177,00		-			-	177,00
30.07. 2019		001817	411	1	1	Customer C	82,00	67,00	8,00	15,00	40,00	48,00	12,00		**190,00**	272,00		-			-	272,00
30.07. 2019	31.07. 2019	001818	428			Customer A	124,00	-	16,00	-	-	-	-		**16,00**	140,00		-			140,00	-
TOTAL				**32**	**59**		**41.486,00**	**2.303,00**	**472,00**	**885,00**	**40,00**	**111,00**	**12,00**		**3.823,00**	**45.309,00**		**-**			**140,00**	**45.169,00**
Room Income																						2.303,00 / 1.08 = 2.132,40 $
Breakfast Income																						2.472,00 / 1.08 = 437,03 $
Dinner Income																						885,00 /1.08 = 819,44 $
TAX																						271,13 $
Room Customers Control Account																						163,00 $
TOTAL																						**3.823,00 $**

In this Main Courante dated 31.7.2019, there are current room revenues, pension (breakfast, food) revenues related to the customers staying at the establishment, and on the same date, extra spending of the customers in the departments such as restaurant, bar, laundry included. In addition, the amounts related to the account segments belonging to the expenditure amounts of the customers who have checked out from the company are included.

Accounting of daily transactions in Main Courante of 31.07.2019 was made with the offset receipt number M0419, which is demonstrated in Table 7.

Table 7. Main Courante Offset

Offset Voucher 31/07/2019 Offset No: M.0419							
Accounts Payable				**Accounts Receivables**			
Account No	**Account Title**	**Amount**		**Account No**	**Account Title**	**Amount**	
120	CUSTOMERS		140,00	136	OTHER RECEİVABLES		140,00
.00	Customer 1	140,00		.00	Receivables from Reception	140,00	
136	OTHER PAYABLES		3.823,00	182	ROOM CUSTOMER CONTROL ACCOUNT		163,00
.00	Payables from Reception	3.823,00		.01	Room Control Account	163,00	
				391	CALCULATED TAX		271,13
				.01	Collected Tax	271,13	
				600	DOMESTIC SALES		3.388,87
				.00.01	Room Income	2.132,40	
				.10.01	Breakfast Income	437,03	
				.10.02	Dinner Income	819,44	
TOTAL			**3.963,00 $**	**TOTAL**			**3.963,00 $**

EXPLANATION: Accounting for Main Courante records dated 31.07.2019

Documents such as addition / sales receipts for customer expenditures related to food and beverage units and other units in addition to accommodation units in the enterprise were issued and these documents were transferred to cashier reports. In the cashier reports, the income and income types related to these units are detailed in a way that allows them to see the cost controls and the revenues of each department separately. In addition, the accommodation account expenditures of the customers whose accommodation has not been collected yet continue to pay at check-out are included. After this stage, DRRs were created from cashier reports. The generated revenue report has been accounted for using revenue and control accounts related to the revenue report offset. Cashier reports, revenue report, revenue report offset, and other accounting application slips related to the application are listed below.

Table 8. Restaurant Cashiers Report (31.07.2019)

Room No	Customer Name	Voucher No	Service		Food Income	Beverage Income	Other Income	Total	Food Discounts	Beverage Discounts	Other Discounts	Cash	Credit Card	Room Account	Current Account
			Food	Beverage											
		614181	2	2	57,00	32,00	-	**89,00**				-	89,00		
411	Customer C	614182	3	3	36,00	4,00		**40,00**				-	-	40,00	
		614183	1	1	29,00	7,00		**36,00**				36,00	-		
		614184	2	2	50,00	32,00		**82,00**				-	82,00		
		614185	4	4	62,00	35,00	4,00	**101,00**				-	101,00		
		614186	2	2	20,00	11,00		**31,00**				31,00	-		
		614187	3	3	13,00	25,00		**38,00**				38,00	-		
		614188	-	2	-	35,00		**35,00**					35,00		
		614189	-	2	-	13,00		**13,00**				13,00	-		
		614190	4	4	82,00	57,00		**139,00**				139,00	-		
TOTAL			**21**	**25**	**349,00**	**251,00**	**4,00**	**604,00**				**257,00**	**307,00**	**40,00**	**-**
Food Income															349,00/1.08 = 323,15 $
Beverage Income															251,00 / 1.08 = 232,41 $
Other Income															4,00 / 1.08 = 3,70 $
TAX															44,74 $
TOTAL															**604,00 $**

Table 9. Bar Cashier Report (31.07.2019)

Room No	Customer Name	Voucher No	Service		Food Income	Beverage Income	Other Income	Total	Food Discounts	Beverage Discounts	Other Discounts	Cash	Credit Card	Room Account	Current Account
			Food	Beverage											
	Customer Z	B 612401	2	2	27,00	52,00	-	**79,00**				-	-	-	79,00
		B 612402	3	3	15,00	102,00	-	**117,00**				-	117,00	-	-
		B 612403	-	5	-	110,00	-	**110,00**				-	110,00	-	-
411	Customer C	B 612404	-	2	-	48,00	-	**48,00**				-	-	48,00	-
		B 612405	1	1	13,00	16,00	-	**29,00**				29,00	-	-	-
		B 612406	-	1	-	12,00	-	**12,00**				12,00	-	-	-
402	Customer B	B 612407	-	3	-	63,00	-	**63,00**				-	-	63,00	-
TOTAL			**6**	**17**	**55,00**	**403,00**		**458,00**				**41,00**	**227,00**	**111,00**	**79,00**
Food Income															55,00 / 1.08 = 50,93 $
Beverage Income															403,00 / 1.08 = 373,15 $
TAX															33,92 $
TOTAL															**458,00 $**

Table 10. Laundry Cashiers Report (31.07.2019)

Room No	Customer Name	Voucher No	Laundry Income	Other Income	Total	Other Discounts	Cash	Credit Card	Room Account	Current Account
411	Customer C	314121	12,00		**12,00**				12,00	
		314122	21,00		**21,00**		**21,00**			
		314123	11,00		**11,00**			11,00		
		314124	20,00		**20,00**			20,00		
TOTAL			**64,00**		**64,00**		**21,00**	**31,00**	**12,00**	
Dry Cleaning Income			64,00 / 1.08 = 59,26 $							
TAX			4,74 $							
TOTAL			**64,00 $**							

Table 11. Daily Revenue Report (31.07.2019)

Department	Service		Food Income	Beverage Income	Laundry Income	Beach& Pool Income	Other Income	Tax	Total	Food Discounts	Beverage Discounts	Other Discounts	Cash	Credit Card/ Check	Room Account	Current Account	Explanation
	Food	Beverage															
RESTAURANT	21	25	323,15	232,41			3,70	44,74	**604,00**				257,00	307,00	40,00	-	Customer C
BAR	6	17	50,93	373,15				33,92	**458,00**				41,00	227,00	111,00	79,00	Customer Z
LAUNDRY					59,26			4,74	**64,00**				21,00	31,00	12,00	-	Customer C
BEACH & POOL									-								
OTHER UNITS									-								
TOTAL $	**27**	**42**	**374,08**	**605,56**	**59,26**		**3,70**	**83,40**	**1.126,00**				**319,00**	**565,00**	**163,00**	**79,00**	

Cashier reports regarding the expenditures made by the customers in the units such as restaurants, bars and laundries of the business have been prepared and these reports have generated the Daily Revenue Report.

Table 12. Offset Daily Revenue Report

Offset Voucher 31/07/2019									
Accounts Payable				Accounts Receivables					
Account No	Account Title	Amount		Account No	Account Title	Amount			
108	OTHER READY VALUES		565,00	391	CALCULATED TAX		83,40		
.01	Credit Card Account	565,00		.01	Collected TAX	83,40			
182	ROOM CUSTOMER CONTROL ACCOUNT		163,00	600	DOMESTIC SALES		1.042,60		
.01	Room Control Account	163,00		.10.03	Restaurant Extra Food Income	323,15			
120	CUSTOMERS		79,00	.10.04	Bar Extra Food Income	50,93			
.00.121	Customer 10	79,00		.20.01	Restaurant Beverage Income	232,41			
136	OTHER RECEIVABLES		319,00	.20.02	Bar Beverage Income	373,15			
.10	Receivables from Cashier	319,00		.50.01	Laundry Income	59,26			
				.60.01	Other Income	3,70			
TOTAL			1.126,00 $	TOTAL			1.126,00 $		

EXPLANATIONS: Accounting of the expenses in accordance with the Daily Revenue Report

Figure 1. Front Cashier Charged Vouchers

Voucher No: 14210 FRONT CASHIER CHARGED 31.07.2019

257,00 $

Only: Two hundred fifty-seven $.

Explanation: Collected as the cash Restaurant revenue on 31.07.2019.

FRONT CASHIER

Sign

Voucher No: 14211 FRONT CASHIER CHARGED 31.07.2019

41,00 $

Only: Forty-one $.

Explanation: Collected as Bar cash revenue on 31.07.2019.

FRONT CASHIER

Sign

Voucher No: 14212 FRONT CASHIER CHARGED 31.07.2019

21,00 $

Only: Twenty-one $.

Explanation: Collected as Laundry cash revenue on 31.07.2019.

FRONT CASHIER

Sign

With the Daily Revenue Report, the cashier collections amounting to TL 319,00 $, which is lent to the receivables from the cashiers, is received by the front desk with the receipts no. 14210, 14211 and 14212 as can be observed above. This amount received was delivered to the accounting department by the reception with the cash receipt number T-00124 and the account was closed.

Figure 2. Cash Receipt Voucher

CASH RECEIPT VOUCHER

No: T-00124 31/07/2019

100	CASH

ACCOUNT NO	ACCOUNT TITLE	AMOUNT	
136	OTHER RECEİVABLES		319,00
.10	Receivables from Cashier	319,00	
TOTAL			319,00 $

EXPLANATION:

14210, 14211, 14212 with Front Cash receipts, Restaurant 257,00 $, Bar 41,00 $ and Laundry 21,00 $ collected from the front deposit due to cash revenue.

Prepared by **Authorized Signatures**

DISCUSSION

The importance of the internal control systems for the businesses have been discussed in various studies in the literature. In one of these studies, for instance, Aktaş (1995), while asserting that there are two main elements which are subject to income in hotel businesses- the room incomes, food and beverage incomes, and other incomes-, simultaneously emphasizes the fact that businesses should take these two main elements under control in order to compete with the other businesses and to survive. The main aim in the income control, in his view, is to determine whether the room and food and beverage incomes are collected completely and whether the sales records are kept regularly or not.

In parallel with this aim, in the scope of this study, for providing the income accrual and a recording method system of a boutique accommodation facility, Main Courante method was used in the accrual of the accommodation units (such as room incomes and pension incomes) whereas the incomes of food and beverage and other units (beach-swimming pool, laundry, sports activities) were accrued via Daily Revenue Report. In terms of the accounting of the incomes, the control accounts of the Main Courante and Daily Revenue Report offsets have been presented as well as other documents related to income records which can be used in the flow of the business in SMEs. Daily analysis of these reports by the business management would be directive and of great use in terms of detecting the deviations in the targeted overnight stays, income and costs and taking correction decisions in favour of the facility when necessary.

With the purpose of determining the income of the business, Main Courante and Daily Revenue Report documents have been generated, by adhering to the current departmental structure of the facility. With these reports, a uniform chart of accounts has been constituted under the main accounts and a recording system was organized available for analysis. By using the method, it was made possible to see the daily incomes of each department of the business separately and a substructure was set up for the cost controls.

About the significance of the internal control systems in businesses, Michael M. Coltman (1998) asserts that, internal control is less necessary in the small-scale hotels since the manager can control the cash flow himself, unlike the large-scale hotels in which a single staff control remains insufficient and therefore application of an effective internal control system is required. However, he also emphasizes that the costs of this effort to provide a successful internal control should never exceed the possible benefits that the system would bring together with it.

In this study, with the successful daily recording of the incomes via this method, data flow towards accounting internal control system was targeted. The fact that in the most of the small and medium-sized hospitality businesses, front-desk works are executed by a single staff (such as the reception officer, reservation officer and front desk cashier), that the method has no capital cost, and that the easy applicability of the method in SMEs in manual or semi-automative way are the reasons for choosing this particular method for the study. Main Courante and Daily Revenue Reports have been organized in accordance with the daily revenue data in the boutique hospitality facility with 40 rooms of accommodation capacity chosen for application. The findings attained at the end of the study have demonstrated the fact that the method is an effective function/method in the correct recording of the incomes in the business. This is also affirmative of the statement of Michael M. Coltman concerning the costs and benefits of the system.

In Hancer's view (2003), businesses in the service industry who have succeeded in gaining customer loyalty have many advantages such as the sustainability of profit, decrease of the management costs and outmanoeuvring in competitiveness and in Michael L. Kasavana and M. Brooks's view (1995), this depends on the faultless and unadulterated execution of the operations in hotel businesses which is closely related to the effectiveness of the internal control system.

Attained results would make contributions to the businesses in terms of enabling them to compare their situations with their budget targets and to take necessary precautions. Additionally, within the framework of the study, the accommodation and extra spendings of the customers such as food and beverage have been internally controlled via the recording method and the data flow among business departments, thus, leading the business to see its daily incomes clearly. With the control accounts, the internal control system has been empowered which has also directly empowered the accounting internal control system. In this context, the activities realized within the scope of the study and the results attained are supportive of this fact.

CONCLUSION

The contributions and other benefits of SMEs to employment and national economies have more severely been recognized worldwide recently. Just like the fact that majority of the accommodation establishments in Turkey consists of SMEs, 90% of the accommodation businesses in the UK is also made up of small business that employs 10 people (European Commission, 2019). This shows that, due to the increase in competition among SMEs, businesses are obliged to sell their services or products at lower prices although this situation reduces their profits.

In today's globalized modern world, internationalization has become an imperative for small and medium-sized TAEs, in order to increase their competitive power and maintain their stability. Small and medium-sized TAEs will achieve their growth targets by realising the most important factor of growing- internationalization-; so that they will be able to gain more shares from the foreign market, expansion in the geographical area, competitive advantage, more customers and more profits. However, they can be able to maintain their sustainability by performing their management functions correctly, maintaining their employment capacity, ensuring business continuity, and maximizing the value of the business. To cope with the competition brought by the changes experienced in the market where many accommodation enterprises are located; competitor analysis, better recognition of competitors, quality of service, low cost, flexibility, and managerial functions are necessary, which can be realized by providing control with an accurate and reliable recording system as well as achieving internationalization. In this proposed study, an easy-to-apply method has been proposed to recognize the revenues in a correct and timely manner, to prevent losses, to contribute to the strengthening of internal control, and to create an infrastructure for the control of costs, which is a very important factor in competition.

As a result of the application carried out within the framework of the proposed method, on 31.07.2019, 2.303,00 $ Room Revenue, 472,00 $ Breakfast Revenue, 885,00 $ Meal income and 163,00 $ Restaurant, Bar and Laundry revenues room account customer expenses for a total of 32 rooms accommodating 59 people were charged to the folio and took place in Main Courante on 31.07.2019. When the Main Courante is analysed, the transfer amount belonging to revenues before 31.07.2019 appears to be 41.486,00 $. When the accounting records are analysed after the end of 31.07.2019, the receivables account balance from the reception, which is in the Main Courante balance, is 45.169,00 $. This balance will be reset by lending to the relevant accounts that will be received from the group / customer issues and receivables from the reception. Main Courante balance dated 31.07.2019 is also the amount of 45.169,00 $ expenditure, which is included in the accounting records as the account receivables from the reception, and the expenditures belonging to the customers whose check-out transaction has not been carried out yet should be balanced with the total of the folio balances in the front office.

With the Main Courante method, the accommodation unit revenues, room revenues and pension (breakfast and food) revenues were recorded on the date of the service, and the extra expenditures that the customers made as room accounts in the other units of the enterprise to pay at the exit were also recorded. With the Main Courante offset, the accounts receivable from the reception are accounted for using the VAT and related income accounts collected from the room customers control account. Additionally, income realizations related to food and beverage units and other service units (such as beach-swimming pool, laundry and sports activities) were compiled with cashier reports, and a DRRs were created. In these DRRs that have been generated, receivables were given to the daily revenue report offset, related income accounts and collected VAT account, whereas credit card account was accounted by borrowing from the accounts receivable from the room customers control account, buyers and cashiers. Transactions after this stage, cash collections, credit card collections, check collections, collections from buyers will be credited to the relevant control accounts, while the cash deposit is closed by lending to bank accounts. It is seen that with this method, while all revenues of the company are recorded in revenues with Main Courante and Daily Revenue Offset, contribution is made to the accounting internal control system by using control accounts such as room customer control account, receivables from cashiers account, receivables from reception.

The results obtained will contribute to the business management to compare their budget targets and take measures in favour of the business. In addition to all these, the method of recording the extra expenditures made by the customers as room accounts to pay at the check-out have been ensured to control the interdepartmental collection deliveries within the enterprise. In addition, it has been ensured that the company can track its income on a daily basis.

REFERENCES

Aktaş, A. (1995). *Yiyecek ve Içecek Yönetimi*. Livane Matbaası.

Aktürk, A. (2015). Konaklama işletmelerinde etkin bir iç kontrol sisteminin tesisi bağlamında muhasebe sistem organizasyonu: Bir vaka analizi. *Journal of Accounting. Finance and Auditing Studies, 1*(4), 108–127.

Association of Turkish Travel Agencies (TURSAB). (2020). *Tourism income, distribution of average spend by years share of tourism revenues in GDP*. https://www.tursab.org.tr/istatistikler-icerik/turizm-geliri

Bahar, O., & Bilen, K. (2020). Turizmde güvenlik algısının Türkiye ekonomisine etkisi. *Güvenlik Bilimleri Dergisi, UGK Özel Sayısı,* 185-206.

Bahar, O., & Kozak, M. (2012). *Turizm ve Rekabet*. Detay Yayıncılık.

Bal, E., & Kunday, A. Ö. (2014). Investigating the role of entrepreneurial traits and human capital on the internationalization degree of small and medium enterprises in Turkey. *International Journal of Business and Social Science, 5*(8), 192–201.

Çetiner, E. (2009). *Otel işletmeleri muhasebesi*. Gazi Kitapevi.

Coltman, M. M. (1998). *Hospitality Management Accounting*. John Wiley&Sons, Inc.

Drogalas, G., Karagiorgos, T., Christodoulou, P., & Euaggelidou, A. (2006). Theoretical approach in an Internal Control System: A conceptual framework and usability of internal audit in hotel business. *1st International Conference on Accounting and Finance. Conference Proceedings*.

Dursun, A., & Yalnız, S. (2013). Konaklama işletmelerinde hizmet üretim maliyetleri-TMS 2 stoklar ve TMS 18 hasılat standartları açısından değerlendirilmesi. *Atatürk Üniversitesi İktisadi ve İdari Bilimler Dergisi, 27*(1), 139–157.

European Commission, (2019). *Annual Report on European SMEs 2018/2019*. SME Annual report 2018-2019.pdf

Gökçen, G., Ataman Akgül, B., & Çakıcı, C. (2006). *Türkiye muhasebe standartları uygulamaları (uluslararası muhasebe standartları ile uyumlu)*. Beta Basım Yayın Dağıtım.

Gökgöz, A., & Özdemir, H. (2015). Dış ticarette teslim ve ödeme şekillerinin TMS 18 hasılat standardı çerçevesinde incelenmesi. *Journal of Accounting. Finance and Auditing Studies, 1*(3), 105–122.

Haghighti, E., & Albayrak, M. (2016). Küresel doğan işletmeler ve uluslararasılaşma süreci. *Isparta: 12. Tarım Ekonomisi Kongresi*, 2173-2182.

Hales, J. A. (2005). *Accounting and Financial Analysis in the Hospitality Industry*. Elsevier Butterworth–Heineman.

Hall, J. A. (2013). *Accounting Information Systems*. South-Western Cengage.

Hancer, M. (2003). Konaklama endüstrisinde müşteri sadakati: Anlam, önem, etki ve sonuçlar. *Seyahat ve Turizm Araştırmaları Dergisi*, *3*(1-2), 39–45.

Hollensen, S. (2014). *Global marketing*. Pearson Education.

Juen, C. S., & Mustapha, M. (2015). An assessment of internal controls in budget hotels in Malaysia, proceedings of the international conference on natural resources. *Tourism and Services Management*, 405-412.

Kapiki, S. (2015). *Τήρηση Λογαριασμών Πελατών: Main-Courante Ξενοδοχείων* [Front Office Accounting-Table of Contents]. doi:10.2139srn.2690782

Karagiorgos, T., Drogalas, G., & Giovanis, N. (2011). Evaluation of the effectiveness of internal audit in Greek hotel business. *International Journal of Economic Sciences and Applied Research*, *4*(1), 19–34.

Karaxontzitis, D., & Sarlis, K. (1989). *Hotel Accounting*. Interbooks.

Kasavana, M., & Brooks, R. (1995). *Front Office Procedures*. Educational Institute of the American Hotel & Motel Association.

Kaya, E. & T. Köse. (2013). *Konaklama Işletmelerinde Muhasebe Uygulamaları*. Anadolu Üniversitesi Yayın No: 2816.

Knight, G. A., & Liesch, P. W. (2016). Internationalization: From incremental to born global. *Journal of World Business*, *51*(1), 93–102. doi:10.1016/j.jwb.2015.08.011

Koparal, C. (2010). *Uluslararası Işletmeciliğe Giriş*. Uluslararası Işletmecilik, Eskişehir, Anadolu Üniversitesi Yayınları.

Kurniadi, L., & Zio, L. (2011). *The role of internal control in the operation of hotels* (Unpublished master dissertation). Lund University, Sweden.

Lu, J. W., & Beamish, P. W. (2006). Partnering strategies and performance of SMEs' international joint ventures. *Journal of Business Venturing*, *21*(4), 461–486. doi:10.1016/j.jbusvent.2005.02.002

Meckl, R., & Schramm, R. (2005). *Empirical evidence for a theory of international new ventures*. Univ., Wirtschaftswiss. Fak.

Ministry of Culture and Tourism-MCT. (2020). *Tourism Certified Facilities*. https://ktb.gov.tr/TR-9860/turizm-belgeli-tesisler.html

Mndzebele, N. (2013). The usage of accounting information systems for effective internal controls in the hotels. *International Journal of Advancements in Computing Technology*, *2*(5), 1–3.

OECD. (2019). *OECD SME and Entrepreneurship Outlook 2019*. http://www.oecd.org/industry/smes/SME-Outlook-Highlights-FINAL.pdf

Reisinger, Y. (2009). *International Tourism Cultures and Behavior*. Routledge Taylor & Francis Group.

Ruzzier, M., Hisrich, R. D., & Antoncic, B. (2006). SME internationalization research: Past, present, and future. *Journal of Small Business and Enterprise Development*, *13*(4), 476–497. doi:10.1108/14626000610705705

Şenel, S. A. (2009). TMS 18 hasılat standardı kapsamında mal satışından kaynaklanan hasılatın muhasebeleştirilmesi. *E-Journal of New World Sciences Academy*, *4*, 389–405.

Taş, M., & Zengin, B. (2019). Seyahat işletmelerinde uluslararasılaşma sorunları ve çözüm önerilerinin kavramsal çerçevede incelenmesi. *Ekonomi, İşletme ve Maliye Araştırmaları Dergisi*, *1*(3), 205–216. doi:10.38009/ekimad.568728

Türedi, S. (2008). Konaklama işletmelerinde muhasebe bilgi sistemi ile iç kontrol sistemi arasındaki ilişkiler. *Mevzuat Dergisi*, *11*(126).

Wanhill, S. (2000). Small and medium tourism enterprises. *Annals of Tourism Research*, *27*(1), 132–147. doi:10.1016/S0160-7383(99)00072-9

Yemer, M., & Chekol, F. (2017). The effect of internal controls systems on hotels revenue. A case of hotels in Bahir Dar and Gondar cities. *Arabian Journal of Business and Management Review*, *6*(6), 19–37.

Yilanci, M. (2001). Muhasebe bilgi sistemi, iç kontrol ve verimlilik üçgeni. *Muhasebe Bilim ve Dünya Dergisi*, *3*(3), 37-50.

KEY TERMS AND DEFINITIONS

Accounting Internal Control: All the methods and procedures used with the purpose of recording accounting records such as revenue, cost, debit and credits properly; of depicting the errors and frauds and of preparing the accounting tables on time and confidentially by the enterprises.

Competitive Advantages: Circumstances which are provided to a company as a result of producing a product or service with a lower price when compared to its competitors.

Daily Revenue Report: A report which embodies the revenues of various units such as the restaurant, bar, beach, swimming pool, sports activities, and laundry in accommodation enterprises.

Internationalization: Carrying the activity area of the enterprises overseas, to carry on the business overseas.

Main Courante: A report which is used in the accommodation enterprises to follow the room revenues, breakfast, lunch, dinner revenues and other extra spendings which would be paid at the check-out.

Small and Medium Enterprises (SMEs): Enterprises which are smaller when compared to the large-scale enterprises in terms of employee number, indorsement, and balance; and whose limits are predetermined.

Tourism Accommodation Enterprises: Enterprises in which accommodations take place during domestic or international holidays, culture tours, thermal health services, business trips and hunting tourism, etc.

Compilation of References

(1988). The nature of the innovative process. InDosi, G. (Ed.), *Technical Change and Economic Theory* (pp. 221–238). Pinter Publishers.

Abell, P., Felin, T., & Foss, N. (2008). Building micro-foundations for the routines, capabilities, and performance links. *Managerial and Decision Economics*, *29*(6), 489–502. doi:10.1002/mde.1413

Abratt, R., & Kleyn, N. (2012). Corporate identity, corporate branding and corporate reputations: Reconciliation and integration. *European Journal of Marketing*, *46*(8), 1048–1063. doi:10.1108/03090561211230197

Acs, Z. J., & Audretsch, D. B. (2005). Entrepreneurship, innovation and technological change. *Foundations and Trends in Entrepreneurship*, *1*(4), 1–65. doi:10.1561/0300000004

Acs, Z., & Audretsch, D. (1987). Innovation, market structure, and firm size. *The Review of Economics and Statistics*, *69*(4), 567–575. doi:10.2307/1935950

AEVI. (2018). *El sector de los videojuegos en España: impacto económico y escenarios fiscales*. Madrid, Spain: AEVI. http://www.aevi.org.es/web/wp-content/uploads/2018/01/1801_AEVI_EstudioEconomico.pdf

AEVI. (2020). *La industria del videojuego en España. Anuario 2019*. Madrid, Spain: AEVI. http://www.aevi.org.es/web/wp-content/uploads/2020/04/AEVI-ANUARIO-2019.pdf

Agarwal, S., & Ramaswami, S. N. (1992). Choice of foreign market entry mode: Impact of ownership, location and internalization factors. *Journal of International Business Studies*, *23*(1), 1–27. doi:10.1057/palgrave.jibs.8490257

Aguzzoli, R., Lengler, J., Sousa, C. M. P., & Benito, G. R. G. (2020). Here We Go Again: A Case Study on Re-entering a Foreign Market. *British Journal of Management*, *00*, 1–19. doi:10.1111/1467-8551.12407

AICEP (2016). Portugalglobal. *Revista Portugal Global, AICEP, 90.*

Akaah, I. P., & Korgaonkar, P. K. (1988). A Conjoint Investigation of the Relative Importance of Risk Relievers in Direct Marketing. *Journal of Advertising Research*, *28*(2), 38–44.

Akhter, S. H., & Choudry, Y. A. (1993). Forced withdrawal from a country market managing political risk. *Business Horizons*, *36*(3), 47–54. doi:10.1016/S0007-6813(05)80148-X

Aktaş, A. (1995). *Yiyecek ve Içecek Yönetimi*. Livane Matbaası.

Aktürk, A. (2015). Konaklama işletmelerinde etkin bir iç kontrol sisteminin tesisi bağlamında muhasebe sistem organizasyonu: Bir vaka analizi. *Journal of Accounting. Finance and Auditing Studies*, *1*(4), 108–127.

Alaminos, D., Del Castillo, A., & Fernandez, M. A. (2016). A global model for bankruptcy prediction. *PLoS One*, *11*(11), 1–18. doi:10.1371/journal.pone.0166693 PMID:27880810

Alberti, F., & Pizzurno, E. (2013). Technology, innovation and performance in family firms. *International Journal of Entrepreneurship and Innovation Management, 17*(1/2/3).142-161.

Alessandri, G., Consiglio, C., Luthans, F., & Borgogni, L. (2018). Testing a dynamic model of the impact of psychological capital on work engagement and job performance. *Career Development International, 23*(1), 33–47. doi:10.1108/CDI-11-2016-0210

Ali, I., Ali, M., Leal-Rodríguez, A. L., & Albort-Morant, G. (2019). The role of knowledge spillovers and cultural intelligence in enhancing expatriate employees' individual and team creativity. *Journal of Business Research, 101*, 561–573. doi:10.1016/j.jbusres.2018.11.012

Allayannis, G., & Weston, J. P. (2001). The Use of Foreign Currency Derivatives and Firm Market Value. *Review of Financial Studies, 14*(1), 243–276. doi:10.1093/rfs/14.1.243

Alon, I., Mersland, R., Musteen, M., & Randy, T. (2020). The research frontier on internationalization of social enterprises. *Journal of World Business, 55*(5), 101091. doi:10.1016/j.jwb.2020.101091

Altman, E. I. (1968). Financial ratios, discriminant analysis and the prediction of corporate bankruptcy. *The Journal of Finance, 23*(4), 589–609. doi:10.1111/j.1540-6261.1968.tb00843.x

Altman, E. I. (1983). *Corporate financial distress: a complete guide to predicting, avoiding, and dealing with bankruptcy.* Wiley Interscience, John Wiley and Sons.

Altman, E. I., Haldeman, R. G., & Narayanan, P. (1977). ZETA Analysis - A new model to identify bankruptcy risk corporations. *Journal of Banking & Finance, 1*(1), 29–54. doi:10.1016/0378-4266(77)90017-6

Altman, E. I., Iwanicz-Drozdowska, M., Laitinen, E. K., & Suvas, A. (2017). Financial distress prediction in an international context: A review and empirical analysis of Altman's Z- Score model. *Journal of International Financial Management & Accounting, 28*(2), 131–171. doi:10.1111/jifm.12053

Altman, E. I., & Sabato, G. (2007). Modelling credit risk for SMEs: Evidence from the U.S. market. *Abacus, 43*(3), 332–357. doi:10.1111/j.1467-6281.2007.00234.x

Alwi, S. F., & Kitchen, P. J. (2014). Projecting corporate brand image and behavioral response in business schools: Cognitive or affective brand attributes? *Journal of Business Research, 67*(11), 2324–2336. doi:10.1016/j.jbusres.2014.06.020

Amit, R., & Schoemaker, P. (1993). Strategic assets and organizational rent. *Strategic Management Journal, 14*(1), 33–46. doi:10.1002mj.4250140105

Anderson, E. W., Fornell, C., & Mazvancheryl, S. K. (2004). Customer Satisfaction and Shareholder Value. *Journal of Marketing, 68*(4), 172–185. doi:10.1509/jmkg.68.4.172.42723

Anderson, R., & Reeb, D. (2003). Founding-family ownership and firm performance: Evidence from the S&P 500. *The Journal of Finance, 58*(3), 1301–1328. doi:10.1111/1540-6261.00567

Andreu, R., Claver, E., Quer, D., & Rienda, L. (2020). Family ownership and Spanish hotel chains: An analysis of their expansion through internationalization. *Current Issues in Tourism.* Advance online publication. doi:10.1080/13683500.2019.1620186

Andriopoulos, C., & Lewis, M. W. (2009). Exploitation-exploration tensions and organizational ambidexterity: Managing paradoxes of innovation. *Organization Science, 20*(4), 696–717. doi:10.1287/orsc.1080.0406

Ang, I. (2005). Who needs cultural research? In P. Leistyna (Ed.), *Cultural Studies: From Theory to Action* (pp. 477–483). Blackwell. doi:10.4324/9780203990810

Apetrei, A., Kureshi, N. I., & Horodnic, I. A. (2015). When culture shapes international business. *Journal of Business Research*, *68*(7), 1519–1521. doi:10.1016/j.jbusres.2015.01.044

APICCAPS. (2020). Footure – Plano Estratégico Cluster do Calçado. Porto: APICCAPS (Associação Portuguesa dos Industriais de Calçado, Componentes e Artigos de Pele e seus Sucedâneos).

Arbix, G., Salerno, M., & Negri, J. (2004). *Inovação via internacionalização, faz bem para as exportações brasileiras. In Comunicação apresentada no XVI Fórum Nacional Economia do Conhecimento.* CrescimentoSustentado e Inclusão Social.

Arenius, P., Sasi, V., & Gabrielsson, M. (2005). Rapid internationalisation enabled by the internet: The case of a knowledge intensive company. *Journal of International Entrepreneurship*, *3*(4), 279–290. doi:10.100710843-006-7856-x

Argote, L., & Ren, Y. (2012). Transactive memory systems: A microfoundation of dynamic capabilities. *Journal of Management Studies*, *49*(8), 1375–1382. doi:10.1111/j.1467-6486.2012.01077.x

Armario, J., Ruiz, D., & Armario, E. (2008). Market Orientation and Internationalization in Small and Medium Sized Enterprises. *Journal of Small Business Management*, *46*(4), 485–511. doi:10.1111/j.1540-627X.2008.00253.x

Aroian, L. A. (1947). The probability function of the product of two normally distributed variables. *Annals of Mathematical Statistics*, *18*(2), 265–271. doi:10.1214/aoms/1177730442

Arregle, J., Naldi, L., Nordqvist, M., & Hitt, M. A. (2012). Internationalization of family-controlled firms: A study of the effects of external involvement in governance. *Entrepreneurship Theory and Practice*, *36*(6), 1115–1143. doi:10.1111/j.1540-6520.2012.00541.x

Arslan, O., & Karan, M. (2009). Credit risks and internationalization of SMEs. *Journal of Business Economics and Management*, *10*(4), 361–368. doi:10.3846/1611-1699.2009.10.361-368

Ashoka. (2016). *the Ashoka Globalizer Program.* Author.

Ashoka. (2017). *Institutional Report - Ashoka Brazil.* Author.

Ashoka. (2019). www.ashoka.org

Ashraf, S., Félix, E. G. S., & Serrasqueiro, Z. (2019). Do Traditional Financial Distress Prediction Models Predict the Early Warning Signs of Financial Distress? *Journal of Risk and Financial Management*, *12*, 1–17. doi:10.3390/jrfm12020055

Association of Turkish Travel Agencies (TURSAB). (2020). *Tourism income, distribution of average spend by years share of tourism revenues in GDP.* https://www.tursab.org.tr/istatistikler-icerik/turizm-geliri

Atuahene-Gima, K. (1996). Market orientation and innovation. *Journal of Business Research*, *35*(2), 93–103. doi:10.1016/0148-2963(95)00051-8

Atuahene-Gima, K., & Ko, A. (2001). An empirical investigation of the effect of market orientation and entrepreneurship orientation alignment on product innovation. *Organization Science*, *12*(1), 54–74. doi:10.1287/orsc.12.1.54.10121

Australian Government: Department of Industry, Innovation and Science. (2020). *Australian Automotive Industry: Transition following the end of Australian motor vehicle production.* https://www.industry.gov.au/sites/default/files/2020-01/australian-automotive-industry-transition-following-the-end-of-australian-motor-vehicle-production.pdf

Australian Government: Department of Industry, Science, Energy and Resources. (2020). *Industry Growth Centers.* https://www.industry.gov.au/strategies-for-the-future/industry-growth-centres

Australian Industry Group. (2019). *Australian manufacturing in 2019: local and global opportunities.* Author.

Autio, E. (2005). Creative tension: The significance of Ben Oviatt's and Patricia McDougall's article 'toward a theory of international new ventures'. *Journal of International Business Studies, 36*(1), 9–19. doi:10.1057/palgrave.jibs.8400117

Autio, E., George, G., & Alexy, O. (2011). International entrepreneurship and capability development—qualitative evidence and future research directions. *Entrepreneurship Theory and Practice, 35*(1), 11–37. doi:10.1111/j.1540-6520.2010.00421.x

Autio, E., Nambisan, S., Thomas, L. D., & Wright, M. (2018). Digital affordances, spatial affordances, and the genesis of entrepreneurial ecosystems. *Strategic Entrepreneurship Journal, 12*(1), 72–95. doi:10.1002ej.1266

Axinn, C., & Matthyssens, P. (2002). Limits of internationalization theories in an unlimited world. *International Marketing Review, 19*(5), 436–449. doi:10.1108/02651330210445275

Ayob, A., & Freixanet, J. (2014). Insights into public export promotion programs in an emerging economy: The case of Malaysian SMEs. *Evaluation and Program Planning, 46*, 38–46. doi:10.1016/j.evalprogplan.2014.05.005 PMID:24907593

Ayuso, S., & Navarrete-Báez, F. E. (2018). How does entrepreneurial and international orientation influence SMEs' commitment to sustainable development? Empirical evidence from Spain and Mexico. *Corporate Social Responsibility and Environmental Management, 25*(1), 80–94. doi:10.1002/csr.1441

Azoulay, A., & Kapferer, J.-N. (2003). Do brand personality scales really measure brand personality? *Journal of Brand Management, 11*(2), 143–155. doi:10.1057/palgrave.bm.2540162

Bacq, S., & Eddleston, K. A. (2018). A resource-based view of social entrepreneurship: How stewardship culture benefits scale of social impact. *Journal of Business Ethics, 152*(3), 589–611. doi:10.100710551-016-3317-1

Bahar, O., & Bilen, K. (2020). Turizmde güvenlik algısının Türkiye ekonomisine etkisi. *Güvenlik Bilimleri Dergisi, UGK Özel Sayısı,* 185-206.

Bahar, O., & Kozak, M. (2012). *Turizm ve Rekabet*. Detay Yayıncılık.

Bakar, L. J. A., & Ahmad, H. (2010). Assessing the relationship between firm resources and product innovation performance: A resource-based view. *Business Process Management, 16*(3), 420–435. doi:10.1108/14637151011049430

Baker, T., & Nelson, R. E. (2005). Creating something from nothing: Resource construction through entrepreneurial bricolage. *Administrative Science Quarterly, 50*(3), 329–366. doi:10.2189/asqu.2005.50.3.329

Baker, W. E., & Sinkula, J. M. (2009). The complementary effects of market orientation and entrepreneurial orientation on profitability in small businesses. *Journal of Small Business Management, 47*(4), 443–464. doi:10.1111/j.1540-627X.2009.00278.x

Bal, E., & Kunday, A. Ö. (2014). Investigating the role of entrepreneurial traits and human capital on the internationalization degree of small and medium enterprises in Turkey. *International Journal of Business and Social Science, 5*(8), 192–201.

Balmer, J. M., & Gray, E. R. (2003). Corporate brands: What are they? What of them? *European Journal of Marketing, 37*(8), 972–997. doi:10.1108/03090560310477627

Banai, M., & Sama, L. A. (2000). Ethical dilemmas in MNCs' international staffing policies: A conceptual framework. *Journal of Business Ethics, 25*(3), 221–235. doi:10.1023/A:1006079511331

Barbera, F., & Moores, K. (2013). Firm ownership and productivity: A study of family and non-family SMEs. *Small Business Economics, 40*(4), 953–976. doi:10.100711187-011-9405-9

Barney, J. B., & Clark, D. N. (2007). Resource-Based Theory: Creating and Sustaining Competitive Advantage. Oxford University Press. doi:10.1362/026725708X382046

Barney, J. (1986). Organizational culture: Can it be a source of sustained competitive advantage? *Academy of Management Review, 11*(3), 656–665. doi:10.5465/amr.1986.4306261

Barney, J. (1995). Looking inside for competitive advantage. *The Academy of Management Perspectives, 9*(4), 49–61. doi:10.5465/ame.1995.9512032192

Barney, J. B. (1991). Firm resources and sustained competitive advantage. *Journal of Management, 17*(1), 99–120. doi:10.1177/014920639101700108

Barney, J. B. (2001). Is the Resource-Based "View" a Useful Perspective for Strategic Management Research? Yes. *Academy of Management Review, 26*(1), 41–56.

Barney, J. B. (2001). Resource-based theories of competitive advantage: A ten-year retrospective on the resource-based view. *Journal of Management, 27*(6), 643–650. doi:10.1177/014920630102700602

Barney, J. B., Ketchen, D. J. Jr, & Wright, M. (2011). The future of resource-based theory - Revitalization or decline? *Journal of Management, 37*(5), 1299–1315. doi:10.1177/0149206310391805

Barney, J. B., Wright, M., & Ketchen, D. (2001). The resource-based view of the firm: Ten years after. *Journal of Management, 16*(3), 171–174.

Barney, J. B., & Wright, P. M. (1998). On becoming a strategic partner: The role of human resources in gaining competitive advantage. *Human Resource Management, 37*(1), 31–46. doi:10.1002/(SICI)1099-050X(199821)37:1<31::AID-HRM4>3.0.CO;2-W

Barney, J., & Felin, T. (2013). What are microfoundations? *The Academy of Management Perspectives, 27*(2), 138–155. doi:10.5465/amp.2012.0107

Baron, R. M., & Kenny, D. A. (1986). The moderator-mediator variable distinction in social psychological research: Conceptual, strategic, and statistical considerations. *Journal of Personality and Social Psychology, 51*(6), 1173–1182. doi:10.1037/0022-3514.51.6.1173 PMID:3806354

Barreto, I. (2010). Dynamic Capabilities: A Review of Past Research and an Agenda for the Future. *Journal of Management, 36*(1), 256–280. doi:10.1177/0149206309350776

Basly, S. (2007). The internationalization of family SME: An organizational learning and knowledge development perspective. *Baltic Journal of Management. Emerald, 2*(2), 154–180.

Battisti, S. (2012). Social innovation: The process development of knowledge-intensive companies. *International Journal of Services Technology and Management, 18*(3-4), 224–244. doi:10.1504/IJSTM.2012.052860

Baum, M., Schwens, C., & Kabst, R. (2011). A typology of international new ventures: Empirical evidence from high–technology industries. *Journal of Small Business Management, 49*(3), 305–330. doi:10.1111/j.1540-627X.2011.00328.x

Baum, M., Schwens, C., & Kabst, R. (2015). A latent class analysis of small firms' internationalization patterns. *Journal of World Business, 50*(4), 754–768. doi:10.1016/j.jwb.2015.03.001

Bayfield, R., Dana, L. P., & Stewart, S. (2009). Firm characteristics and internationalisation strategies: An empirical investigation of New Zealand exporters. *International Journal of Globalisation and Small Business, 3*(3), 275–287. doi:10.1504/IJGSB.2009.024571

Beaver, W. H. (1966). Financial Ratios as Predictors of Failure. *Journal of Accounting Research, 4*, 71–111. doi:10.2307/2490171

Beckerman, W. (1956). Distance and the pattern of intra-European trade. *The Review of Economics and Statistics, 38*(1), 31–40. doi:10.2307/1925556

Belak, J., & Duh, M. (2012). Integral Management: Key Success Factors in the MER Model. *Acta Polytechnica Hungarica, 9*(3), 5–26.

Bell, J., McNaughton, R., & Young, S. (2001). 'Born-again global' firms: An extension to the 'born global' phenomenon. *Journal of International Management, 7*(3), 173–189. doi:10.1016/S1075-4253(01)00043-6

Bell, J., McNaughton, R., Young, S., & Crick, D. (2003). Towards an Integrative Model of Small Firm internationalization. *Journal of International Entrepreneurship, 1*(4), 339–362. doi:10.1023/A:1025629424041

Benito, G. R. G., & Welch, L. S. (1994). Foreign market servicing: Beyond choice of entry mode. *Journal of International Marketing, 2*(2), 7–27. doi:10.1177/1069031X9400200202

Benito-Hernández, S., Priede-Bergamini, T., & López-Cózar-Navarro, C. (2014). Factors determining exportation and internationalization in family businesses: The importance of debt. *South African Journal of Business Management, 45*(1), 13–25. doi:10.4102ajbm.v45i1.114

Berrone, P., Cruz, C., & Gomez-Mejia, L. (2010). Socioemotional wealth in family firms. *Family Business Review, 25*(3), 258–279. doi:10.1177/0894486511435355

Bettinelli, C., Fayolle, A., & Randerson, K. (2014). Family entrepreneurship: A developing field. *Foundations and Trends in Entrepreneurship, 10*(3), 161–236. doi:10.1561/0300000049

Bingham, C. B., Howell, T., & Ott, T. E. (2019). Capability creation: Heuristics as microfoundations. *Strategic Entrepreneurship Journal, 13*(2), 121–153. doi:10.1002ej.1312

Blums, M. (2003). *D-Score: Bankruptcy Prediction Model for Middle Market Public Firms*. Academic Press.

Bonavita, A. (2009). La mobilité professionnelle en Europe: Témoignage d'une guide-interprète italienne à Paris. In F. X. Aligny, A. Guillaume, B. Nieder, F. Rastier, C. Tremblay, & H. Wismann (Eds.), *Plurilinguisme, Interculturalité et Emploi: Défis pour l'Europe* (pp. 89–92). L'Harmattan.

Boroditsky, L. (2010, July 24). Lost in Translation. *Wall Street Journal.*

Boroditsky, L. (2017). How language shapes the way we think. *TEDWomen 2017*. https://www.ted.com/talks/lera_boroditsky_how_language_shapes_the_way_we_think/up-next

Bossom, A., & Dunning, B. (2015). *Video games: an introduction to the industry*. Bloomsbury Publishing.

Botero, I. C., Cruz, C., De Massis, A., & Nordqvist, M. (2015). Family business research in the European context. *European Journal of International Management, 9*(2), 139–159. doi:10.1504/EJIM.2015.067858

Bouncken, R. B., & Pesch, R. (2014). New product performance through channeling in supply chain innovation alliances. In T. K. Das (Eds.), Strategic alliances for innovation and R&D (pp. 85-106). Carolina do Norte: Information Age Publishing.

Bouncken, R. B., Muench, M., & Kraus, S. (2015). Born globals: Investigating the influence of their business models on rapid internationalization. *International Business & Economics Research Journal, 14*(2), 247–256.

Bouncken, R. B., Schuessler, J., & Kraus, S. (2015). Coopetition: A systematic review, synthesis, and future research directions. *Review of Managerial Science, 9*(3), 577–601. doi:10.100711846-015-0168-6

Braga, A., Marques, C. S., & Serrasqueiro, Z. (2018). Internationalisation strategy of knowledge-intensive business services. *Journal of the Knowledge Economy*, *9*(2), 359–377. doi:10.100713132-017-0461-5

Brito, G. A. S., & Neto, A. A. (2008). Modelo de classificação de risco de crédito de empresas. *Revista Contabilidade & Finanças*, *19*(46), 18–29. doi:10.1590/S1519-70772008000100003

Brouthers, K. D., Brouthers, L. E., & Werner, S. (2008). Resource-based advantages in an international context. *Journal of Management*, *34*(2), 189–217. doi:10.1177/0149206307312508

Brown, T. (2009). *Change by design: How design thinking creates new alternatives for business and society*. Collins Business.

Bruneel, J., d'Este, P., & Salter, A. (2010). Investigating the factors that diminish the barriers to university–industry collaboration. *Research Policy*, *39*(7), 858–868. doi:10.1016/j.respol.2010.03.006

Bryman, A., & Cramer, D. (2012). *Quantitative Data Analysis with IBM SPSS 17, 18 & 19: A Guide for Social Scientists. Abingdon-on-Thames*. Routledge. doi:10.4324/9780203180990

Bunz, T., Casulli, L., Jones, M. V., & Bausch, A. (2017). The dynamics of experiential learning: Microprocesses and adaptation in a professional service INV. *International Business Review*, *26*(2), 225–238. doi:10.1016/j.ibusrev.2016.07.001

Burmann, C., Schaefer, K., & Maloney, P. (2008). Industry image: Its impact on the brand image of potential employees. *Brand Management*, *15*(3), 157–176. doi:10.1057/palgrave.bm.2550112

Business Dictionary. (n.d.). http://www.businessdictionary.com/definition/expatriate.html

Butler, J. E., Doktor, R., & Lins, F. A. (2010). Linking international entrepreneurship to uncertainty, opportunity discovery, and cognition. *Journal of International Entrepreneurship*, *8*(2), 121–134. doi:10.100710843-010-0054-x

Cabras, I., Goumagias, N. D., Fernandes, K., Cowling, P., Li, F., Kudenko, D., Devlin, S., & Nucciarelli, A. (2017). Exploring survival rates of companies in the UK video-games industry: An empirical study. *Technological Forecasting and Social Change*, *117*, 305–314. doi:10.1016/j.techfore.2016.10.073

Campenhoudt, L. V., & Quivy, R. (2008). *Manual de investigação em Ciências Sociais*. Gradiva Publicações.

Canepa, A., & Stoneman, P. (2002). *Financial constraints on innovations: A European cross-country study*. Working Paper no. 02–11. Kiel Institute of World Economics.

Cañibano, L., Garcia-Ayuso, M., & Sanchez, P. (2000). Accounting for Intangibles: A Literature Review. *Journal of Accounting Literature*, *19*, 102–130.

Cantwell, J., Dunning, J. H., & Lundan, S. M. (2010). An evolutionary approach to understanding international business activity: The co-evolution of MNEs and the institutional environment. *Journal of International Business Studies*, *41*(4), 567–586. doi:10.1057/jibs.2009.95

Capra, F. (1996). The web of life: a new scientific understanding of living systems. Nova Iorque: Anchor Books.

Carmines, E. G., & Zeller, R. A. (1979). *Reliability and validity assessment*. Sage Publications. doi:10.4135/9781412985642

Carrasqueira, H., Garcia, C., & Carrasqueira, M. (2018). A internacionalização da hotelaria portuguesa para os mercados emergentes. *Revista Investigaciones Turísticas*, *15*(15), 34–48. doi:10.14198/INTURI2018.15.02

Carroll, A. B. (1989). *Business and society: ethics and stakeholder management*. South–Western Publishing Company.

Cavusgil, S., & Knight, G. (2015). The born global firm: An entrepreneurial and capabilities perspective on early and rapid internationalization. *Journal of International Business Studies*, *46*(1), 3–16. doi:10.1057/jibs.2014.62

Cavusgil, T., & Knight, G. (2009). *Born global firms: a new international enterprise*. Business Experts Press. doi:10.4128/9781606490136

Central Reserve Bank of El Salvador. (2020). Retrieved from https://www.bcr.gob.sv/comex/

CEPALSTAT. (2019). Retrieved from https://estadisticas.cepal.org/cepalstat/WEB_CEPALSTAT/estadisticasIndicadores.asp?idioma=e

Cerviño, J., Arteaga-Ortiz, J., & Fernández-del Hoyo, A. (2017). Marketing internacional. In J. Arteaga Ortiz (Ed.), *Manual de internacionalización. Técnicas, herramientas y estrategias necesarias para afrontar con éxito el proceso de internacionalización* (pp. 218–372). ICEX-CECO.

Çetiner, E. (2009). *Otel işletmeleri muhasebesi*. Gazi Kitapevi.

Chancharat, N., Tina, G., Davy, P., MacGrae, M., & Lodh, S. (2010). Multiple States of Financially Distressed Companies: Tests using a Competing-Risks Model. *Australasian Accounting Business and Finance Journal*, *4*(4), 27–49.

Chandler, G. N., DeTienne, D. R., McKelvie, A., & Mumford, T. V. (2011). Causation and effectuation processes: A validation study. *Journal of Business Venturing*, *26*(3), 375–390. doi:10.1016/j.jbusvent.2009.10.006

Chandra, A. A., Paul, J., & Chavan, M. (2020). Internationalization challenges for SMEs: Evidence and theoretical extension. *European Business Review*, *ahead-of-print*(ahead-of-print). Advance online publication. doi:10.1108/EBR-08-2019-0164

Cheng, H. L., & Yu, C. M. J. (2008). Institutional pressures and initiation of internationalization: Evidence from Taiwanese small and medium-sized enterprises. *International Business Review*, *17*(3), 331–348. doi:10.1016/j.ibusrev.2008.01.006

Cheng, W.-Y., Su, E., Li, S.-J., Fen, Y.-G., & Dong, G.-M. (2009). Corporate governance and financial distress: Evidence from public- listed electronics companies in Taiwan. *Journal of Statistics and Management Systems*, *12*(5), 813–827. doi:10.1080/09720510.2009.10701424

Chen, J., Saarenketo, S., & Puumalainen, K. (2018). Home country institutions, social value orientation, and the internationalization of ventures. *International Business Review*, *27*(2), 443–454. doi:10.1016/j.ibusrev.2017.09.011

Chen, Y., Chang, K., & Chang, C. (2012). Nonlinear influence on R&D project performance. *Technological Forecasting and Social Change*, *79*(8), 1537–1547. doi:10.1016/j.techfore.2012.04.007

Chesbrough, H., & Teece, D. (2002). Organizing for innovation: when is virtual virtuous? *The Innovative Enterprise*, (August), 127–134.

Chetty, S. (1996). The case study method for research in small- and medium-sized firms. *International Small Business Journal*, *15*(l), 73–85. doi:10.1177/0266242696151005

Chetty, S., & Campbell-Hunt, C. (2003). Paths to internationalisation among small to medium-sized firms: A global versus regional approach. *European Journal of Marketing*, *37*(5/6), 796–820. doi:10.1108/03090560310465152

Chetty, S., & Campbell-Hunt, C. (2004). A strategic approach to internationalization: A traditional versus a 'born-global' approach. *Journal of International Marketing*, *12*(1), 57–81. doi:10.1509/jimk.12.1.57.25651

Cheuk, S., Liew-Tsonis, J., Ing, G. P., & Razli, I. A. (2010). An Establishment Of The Role Of Private And Public Sector Interests In The Context Of Tourism Transport Planning And Development: The Case Of Malaysia. I*nternational Business &. Economic Research Journal*, *9*(2), 59–68. doi:10.19030/iber.v9i2.522

Child, J., Hsieh, L., Elbanna, S., Karmowska, J., Marinova, S., Puthusserry, P., Tsai, T., Narooz, R., & Zhang, Y. (2017). SME international business models: The role of context and experience. *Journal of World Business*, *52*(5), 664–679. doi:10.1016/j.jwb.2017.05.004

Chin, W. (2010). Bootstrap cross-validation indices for PLS path model assessment. In V. Esposito Vinzi, W. Chin, J. Henseler, & H. Wang (Eds.), Handbook of Partial Least Squares: Concepts, Methods and Applications (pp. 83-97). Nova Iorque: Springer Publishing Company. doi:10.1007/978-3-540-32827-8_4

Chin, W. W. (1998). The partial least squares approach for structural equation modeling. In G. A. Marcoulides (Ed.), *Modern methods for business research* (pp. 295–236). Lawrence Erlbaum Associates.

Chin, W. W. (1998). The partial least squares approach to structural equation modelling. In G. A. Marcoulides (Ed.), *Modern methods for business research* (pp. 295–336). Lawrence Erlbaum Associates.

Chin, W. W. (2010). How to write up and report PLS analyses. In V. E. Vinzi, W. W. Chin, J. Henseler, & H. Wang (Eds.), *Handbook of partial least squares: Concepts, methods and applications in marketing and related fields* (pp. 655–690). Springer. doi:10.1007/978-3-540-32827-8_29

Chin, W. W., & Newsted, P. R. (1999). Structural equation modeling analysis with small samples using partial least squares. In R. H. Hoyle (Ed.), *Statistical strategies for small sample research* (pp. 307–341). Sage.

Chin, W. W., & Newsted, P. R. (1999). Structural equation modelling analysis with small samples using partial least squares. In R. H. Hoyle (Ed.), *Statistical strategies for small sample research* (pp. 307–341). Sage.

Chrisman, J., Chua, J., & Sharma, P. (2003). *Current trends and future directions in family business management studies: toward a theory of the family business,* Coleman White Paper Series.

Chua, J., Chrisman, J., & Sharma, P. (1999). Defining the family business by behavior. *Entrepreneurship Theory and Practice*, *23*(4), 19–39. doi:10.1177/104225879902300402

Chung, H. (2012). The role of family management and family ownership in diversification: The case of family business groups. *Asia Pacific Journal of Management*, *30*(3), 871–891. doi:10.100710490-012-9284-x

CIRE - Código da Insolvência e da Recuperação de Empresas. Decreto Lei 53/2004 de 18 de março. Diário da República Nª 66/2004. http://www.dre.pt

Ciszewska-Mlinarič, M. (2016). Foreign Market Knowledge and SME's International Performance: Moderating Effects of Strategic Intent and Time-to-Internationalization. *Entrepreneurial Business and Economics Review*, *4*(4), 51–66. doi:10.15678/EBER.2016.040404

Clarkson, M. (1995). A Stakeholder Framework for Analyzing and Evaluating Corporate Social Performance. *Academy of Management Review*, *20*(1), 92–117. doi:10.5465/amr.1995.9503271994

Claver, E., Rienda, L., & Quer, D. (2008). Family firms' risk perception: Empirical evidence on the internationalization process. *Journal of Small Business and Enterprise Development*, *15*(3), 457–471. doi:10.1108/14626000810892283

Coff, R., & Kryscynski, D. (2011). Invited Editorial: Drilling for Micro-Foundations of Human CapitalBased Competitive Advantages. *Journal of Management*, *37*(5), 1429–1443. doi:10.1177/0149206310397772

Cohen, M. D. (2012). Perceiving and remembering routine action: Fundamental micro-level origins. *Journal of Management Studies*, *49*(8), 1383–1388. doi:10.1111/j.1467-6486.2012.01078.x

Cohen, W., & Levinthal, D. (1990). Absorptive capacity: A new perspective on learning and innovation. *Administrative Science Quarterly*, *35*(1), 128–152. doi:10.2307/2393553

Collier, W., Green, F., Kim, Y., & Peirson, J. (2011). Education, training and economic performance: Evidence from establishment survival data. *Journal of Labor Research*, *32*(4), 336–361. doi:10.100712122-011-9116-7

Colombo, S., & Perujo-Villanueva, M. (2017). Analysis of the spatial relationship between small olive farms to increase their competitiveness through cooperation. *Land Use Policy*, *63*, 226–235. doi:10.1016/j.landusepol.2017.01.032

Coltman, M. M. (1998). *Hospitality Management Accounting*. John Wiley&Sons, Inc.

COM – European Commission. (2008). *Think Small First- Um Small Business Act para a Europa 394*. Author.

Comi, S., & Resmini, L. (2019). Are export promotion programs effective in promoting the internalization of SMEs? *Economics and Politics*, 1–35.

Contractor, F., Foss, N. J., Kundu, S., & Lahiri, S. (2019). Viewing global strategy through a microfoundations lens. *Global Strategy Journal*, *9*(1), 3–18. doi:10.1002/gsj.1329

Correia, M. J. & Rua, O. L. (2016). Innovation in the Portuguese health sector organizations: Empirical evidence from the Community Innovation Survey. *Tékhne - Review of Applied Management Studies*, *14*, 2-9.

Costa, J., Botelho, A., & Matias, J. (2018). Hindering Factors to Innovation: A Panel Data Analysis In Entrepreneurship along the Industry Life Cycle: The changing role of Entrepreneurial Activities and Knowledge Competencies. Springer.

Costa, M. P. (2016). *Three Essays on Firms' Financial Distress* (PhD Thesis). Évora University.

Coudounaris, D. N. (2018). Export promotion programmes for assisting SMEs. *Review of International Business and Strategy*, *28*(1), 77–109. doi:10.1108/RIBS-06-2017-0050

Coviello, N. E. (2006). The network dynamics of international new ventures. *Journal of International Business Studies*, *37*(5), 713–731. doi:10.1057/palgrave.jibs.8400219

Coviello, N. E., & Cox, M. P. (2006). The resource dynamics of international new venture networks. *Journal of International Entrepreneurship*, *4*(2–3), 113–132.

Coviello, N., & McAuley, A. (1999). Internationalisation and the smaller firm: A review of contemporary empirical research. *Management International Review*, *39*(3), 223–256.

Covin, J. G., & Slevin, D. P. (1989). Strategic management of small firms in hostile and benign environments. *Strategic Management Journal*, *10*(1), 75–87. doi:10.1002mj.4250100107

Cresswell, J. W. (2003). *Research design: Qualitative, quantitative, and mixed methods approaches* (2nd ed.). Sage Publications.

Crick, D. (2004). U.K. SMEs' decision to discontinue exporting: An exploratory investigation into practices within the clothing industry. *Journal of Business Venturing*, *19*(4), 561–587. doi:10.1016/S0883-9026(03)00032-6

Cronin, J. J. Jr, Brady, M. K., & Hult, G. T. (2000). Assessing the effects of quality, value, and customer satisfaction on consumer behavioral intentions in service environments. *Journal of Retailing*, *76*(2), 193–218. doi:10.1016/S0022-4359(00)00028-2

CSIRO. (2020). *SME Connect - where business meets research*. https://www.csiro.au/en/Do-business/

D'Angelo, A. (2012). Innovation and export performance: A study of Italian high-tech SMEs. *The Journal of Management and Governance*, *16*(3), 393–423. doi:10.100710997-010-9157-y

D'Angelo, A., Majocchi, A., & Buck, T. (2016). External managers, family ownership and the scope of SME internationalization. *Journal of World Business*, *51*(4), 534–547. doi:10.1016/j.jwb.2016.01.004

Dada, O., & Fogg, H. (2016). Organizational learning, entrepreneurial orientation, and the role of university engagement in SMEs. *International Small Business Journal*, *34*(1), 86–104. doi:10.1177/0266242614542852

Dahlin, K. B., & Behrens, D. M. (2005). When is an invention really radical?: Defining and measuring technological radicalness. *Research Policy*, *34*(5), 717–737. doi:10.1016/j.respol.2005.03.009

Dai, L., Maksimov, V., Gilbert, B. A., & Fernhaber, S. A. (2014). Entrepreneurial orientation and international scope: The differential roles of innovativeness, proactiveness, and risk-taking. *Journal of Business Venturing*, *29*(4), 511–524. doi:10.1016/j.jbusvent.2013.07.004

Dale, G., & Green, C. S. (2017). The changing face of video games and video gamers: Future directions in the scientific study of video game play and cognitive performance. *Journal of Cognitive Enhancement*, *1*(3), 280–294. doi:10.100741465-017-0015-6

Dalmoro, M. (2013). The formation of country wineries networks for internationalization: An analysis of two new world wines regions. *Journal of Wine Research*, *24*(2), 96–111. doi:10.1080/09571264.2012.747086

Damijan, P. J., Knell, M., Majcen, B., & Rojec, M. (2003). The role of FDI, R&D accumulation and trade in transferring technology to transition countries: Evidence from firm panel data for eight transition countries. *Economic Systems*, *27*(2), 189–204. doi:10.1016/S0939-3625(03)00039-6

Davis, D., & Mentzer, J. (2008). Relational Resources in Interorganizational Exchange: The Effects of Trade Equity and Brand Equity. *Journal of Retailing*, *84*(4), 435–448. doi:10.1016/j.jretai.2008.08.002

De Clercq, D., Thongpapanl, N. T., & Dimov, D. (2013). Shedding new light on the relationship between contextual ambidexterity and firm performance: An investigation of internal contingencies. *Technovation*, *33*(4), 119–132. doi:10.1016/j.technovation.2012.12.002

de Correia, R., Lengler, J., & Mohsin, A. (2019). Entrepreneurial approaches to the internationalisation of Portugal's hotel industry. *International Journal of Contemporary Hospitality Management*, *31*(3), 1141–1165. doi:10.1108/IJCHM-09-2017-0567

de Massis, A., Frattini, F., Kotlar, J., Messeni-Petruzzelli, A., & Wright, M. (2016). Innovation through tradition: Lessons from innovative family businesses and directions for future research. *The Academy of Management Perspectives*, *30*(1), 93–116. doi:10.5465/amp.2015.0017

de Massis, A., Frattini, F., Majocchi, A., & Piscitello, L. (2018). Family firms in the global economy: Toward a deeper understanding of internationalization determinants, processes, and outcomes. *Global Strategy Journal*, *8*(1), 3–21. doi:10.1002/gsj.1199

de Massis, A., Frattini, F., Pizzurno, E., & Cassia, L. (2015). Product innovation in family versus non family firms: An exploratory analysis. *Journal of Small Business Management*, *53*(1), 1–36. doi:10.1111/jsbm.12068

De Silva, M., Howells, J., & Meyer, M. (2018). Innovation intermediaries and collaboration: Knowledge–based practices and internal value creation. *Research Policy*, *47*(1), 70–87. doi:10.1016/j.respol.2017.09.011

Del Giudice, M., Arslan, A., Scuotto, V., & Caputo, F. (2017). Influences of cognitive dimensions on the collaborative entry mode choice of small- and medium-sized enterprises. *International Marketing Review*, *34*(5), 652–673. doi:10.1108/IMR-05-2016-0098

Demel, J., & Potužáková, Z. (2012). FDI and the Liberec Region: The Case of the Labour Market. *E&M Economics and Management Journal*, *4*, 4–18.

Demirbag, M., Tatoglu, E., & Glaister, K. W. (2009). Equity-based entry modes of emerging country multinational. *Journal of World Business*, *44*(4), 445–462. doi:10.1016/j.jwb.2008.11.009

Desa, G., & Basu, S. (2013). Optimization or bricolage? Overcoming resource constraints in global social entrepreneurship. *Strategic Entrepreneurship Journal*, *8*(6), 4517–4524. doi:10.1002ej.1150

DEV. (2020a). *Libro blanco del desarrollo español de videojuegos 2019*. Madrid, Spain: DEV. http://www.dev.org.es/images/stories/docs/libro%20blanco%20dev%202019.pdf

DEV. (2020b). *Llibre blanc de la indústria catalana del videojoc 2018*. Barcelona, Spain: Generalitat de Catalunya, Institut Català de les Empreses Culturals. https://issuu.com/icec_generalitat/docs/200625_llibre_blanc

Dew, N., Read, S., Sarasvathy, S. D., & Wiltbank, R. (2011). On the entrepreneurial genesis of new markets: Effectual transformations versus causal search and selection. *Journal of Evolutionary Economics*, *21*(2), 231–253. doi:10.100700191-010-0185-1

Deysine, A., & Duboin, J. (1995). *S'Internationaliser: Stratégies et Techniques*. Dalloz.

Dhanaraj, C., & Beamish, P. W. (2003). A Resource-Based Approach to the Study of Export Performance. *Journal of Small Business Management*, *41*(3), 242–261. doi:10.1111/1540-627X.00080

Di Zhang, D., & Swanson, L. A. (2013). Social entrepreneurship in nonprofit organizations: An empirical investigation of the synergy between social and business objectives. *Journal of Nonprofit & Public Sector Marketing*, *25*(1), 105–125. doi:10.1080/10495142.2013.759822

Dias, M. (2007). *A internacionalização e os fatores de competitividade: o caso Adira* (Master's thesis). Faculdade de Economia da Universidade do Porto. Retrieved from https://hdl.handle.net/10216/7548

DIGESTYC -Dirección General de Estadístico y Censos. (2020). Retrieved from http://www.digestyc.gob.sv/index.php/foro/2-bienvenido-mat/16-pib.html

Dimitratos, P., Amorós, J. E., Etchebarne, M. S., & Felzensztein, C. (2014). Micro-multinational or not? International entrepreneurship, networking and learning effects. *Journal of Business Research*, *67*(5), 908–915. doi:10.1016/j.jbusres.2013.07.010

Dimofte, C. V., Johansson, J. K., & Ronkainen, I. A. (2008). Cognitive and Affective Reactions of U.S. Consumers to Global Brands. *Journal of International Marketing*, *16*(4), 113–135. doi:10.1509/jimk.16.4.113

Dirlik, A. (2005). The Postcolonial Aura: Third World Criticism in the Age of Global Capitalism. In P. Leistyna (Ed.), *Cultural Studies: From Theory to Action* (pp. 29–55). Blackwell.

Djellal, F., & Gallouj, F. (2008). A model for analysing the innovation dynamic in services: The case of 'assembled' services. *International Journal of Services Technology and Management*, *9*(3-4), 285–304. doi:10.1504/IJSTM.2008.019702

Dodds, W. B., Monroe, K. B., & Grewal, D. (1991). Effects of price, brand, and store information on buyers' product evaluations. *JMR, Journal of Marketing Research*, *28*(3), 307–319.

Doherty, B., Haugh, H., & Lyon, F. (2014). Social enterprises as hybrid organizations: A review and research agenda. *International Journal of Management Reviews*, *16*(4), 417–436. doi:10.1111/ijmr.12028

Doherty, R., Matthews, J., Wrigley, C., & Bucolo, S. (2013, December). Early challenges of shifting an Australian manufacturer's utilisation of design. In *2013 IEEE Tsinghua International Design Management Symposium* (pp. 259-267). IEEE. 10.1109/TIDMS.2013.6981246

Dominguez, N., & Mayrhofer, U. (2017). Internationalization stages of traditional SMEs: Increasing, decreasing and re-increasing commitment to foreign markets. *International Business Review, 26*(6), 1051–1063. doi:10.1016/j.ibusrev.2017.03.010

Donaldson, T., & Dunfee, T. (1994). Toward a Unified Conception of Business Ethics: Integrative Social Contracts Theory. *Academy of Management Review, 19*(2), 252–284. doi:10.5465/amr.1994.9410210749

Donker, H., Santen, B., & Zahir, S. (2009). Ownership structure and the likelihood of financial distress in the Netherlands. *Applied Financial Economics, 19*(21), 1687–1696. doi:10.1080/09603100802599647

Dorst, K. (2015). *Frame innovation: Create new thinking by design.* MIT Press. doi:10.7551/mitpress/10096.001.0001

Dos Reis, F. (2010). *Como elaborar uma dissertação de mestrado, segundo Bolonha.* Pactor.

Drogalas, G., Karagiorgos, T., Christodoulou, P., & Euaggelidou, A. (2006). Theoretical approach in an Internal Control System: A conceptual framework and usability of internal audit in hotel business. *1st International Conference on Accounting and Finance. Conference Proceedings.*

Dubois, A., & Gibbert, M. (2010). From complexity to transparency : Managing the interplay between theory, method and empirical phenomena in IMM case studies. *Industrial Marketing Management, 39*(1), 129–136. doi:10.1016/j.indmarman.2009.08.003

Dubravská, M., Mura, L., Kotulič, R., & Novotný, J. (2015). Internationalization of entrepreneurship - Motivating factors: Case study of the Slovak Republic. *Acta Polytechnica Hungarica, 12*, 121–133.

Durão, V., & Moreira, A. C. (2019). Critical and inhibiting success factors in inter-organizational networks: A case study. In S. Teixeira & J. Ferreira (Eds.), *Multilevel Approach to Competitiveness in the Global Tourism Industry* (pp. 63–86). IGI Global. doi:10.4018/978-1-7998-0365-2.ch005

Dursun, A., & Yalnız, S. (2013). Konaklama işletmelerinde hizmet üretim maliyetleri-TMS 2 stoklar ve TMS 18 hasılat standartları açısından değerlendirilmesi. *Atatürk Üniversitesi İktisadi ve İdari Bilimler Dergisi, 27*(1), 139–157.

Dyer, J. H., & Singh, H. (1998). The Relational View: Cooperative Strategy and Sources of Interorganizational Competitive Advantage. *Academy of Management Review, 23*(4), 660–679. doi:10.5465/amr.1998.1255632

Dzikowski, P. (2018). A bibliometric analysis of born global firms. *Journal of Business Research, 85*, 281–294. doi:10.1016/j.jbusres.2017.12.054

Earley, P. C., & Peterson, R. S. (2004). The elusive cultural chameleon: Cultural intelligence as a new approach to intercultural training for the global manager. *Academy of Management Learning & Education, 3*(1), 100–115. doi:10.5465/amle.2004.12436826

Economist. (n.d.). https://www.economist.com/graphic-detail/2019/12/04/where-are-the-worlds-best-english-speakers

Eddleston, A., Rodrigo-Alarcón, J., Parra-Requena, G., García-Villaverde, P., Bolo, A., Muchemi, A., & Gomez-Mejia, L. (2012). The succession process from a resource- and knowledge-based view of the family firm. *Family Business Review, 2*(1), 328–353.

Eddleston, K., & Kellermanns, F. (2007). Destructive and productive family relationships: A stewardship theory perspective. *Journal of Business Venturing, 22*(4), 545–565. doi:10.1016/j.jbusvent.2006.06.004

Egenfeldt-Nielsen, S., Smith, J. H., & Tosca, S. P. (2019). *Understanding video games: the essential introduction.* Routledge. doi:10.4324/9780429431791

Eickelpasch, A., & Vogel, A. (2011). Determinants of export behaviour of German business services companies. *Service Industries Journal, 31*(4), 513–526. doi:10.1080/02642069.2010.504304

Eisenhardt, K. M. (1989). Building theories from case study research. *Academy of Management Review, 14*(4), 532–550. doi:10.5465/amr.1989.4308385

Eisenhardt, K. M., Furr, N. R., & Bingham, C. B. (2010). Microfoundations of performance: Balancing efficiency and flexibility in dynamic environments. *Organization Science, 21*(6), 1263–1273. doi:10.1287/orsc.1100.0564

Elbanna, S., Hsieh, L., & Child, J. (2020). *Contextualizing internationalization decision-making research in SMEs: Towards an integration of existing studies*. European Academy of Management. doi:10.1111/emre.12395

Ellis, P., & Pecotich, A. (2001). Social factors influencing export initiation in small and medium-sized enterprises. *JMR, Journal of Marketing Research, 38*(1), 119–130. doi:10.1509/jmkr.38.1.119.18825

Engelen, A., & Tholen, E. (2014). *Interkulturelles Management*. Schäffer-Poeschel Verlag.

Engelman, R., Zen, A. C., & Fracasso, E. M. (2015). The impact of the incubator on the internationalization of firms. *Journal of Technology Management & Innovation, 10*(1), 29–39. doi:10.4067/S0718-27242015000100003

Engineers Australia. (2009). *Engineering the Future of Australian Manufacturing*. Author.

Eriksson, P., & Kovalainen, A. (2015). *Qualitative methods in business research: a practical guide to social research*. Sage.

Estrin, S., Mickiewicz, T., & Stephan, U. (2016). Human capital in social and commercial entrepreneurship. *Journal of Business Venturing, 31*(4), 449–467. doi:10.1016/j.jbusvent.2016.05.003

Eurofound. (2012). *Born global: The potential of job creation in new international businesses*. Luxembourg: Publications Office of the European Union.

European Commission, (2019). *Annual Report on European SMEs 2018/2019*. SME Annual report 2018-2019.pdf

European Commission. (2019). *European Innovation Scoreboard*. Author.

Evers, N., & Knight, J. (2008). Role of international trade shows in small firm internationalization: A network perspective. *International Marketing Review, 25*(5), 544–562. doi:10.1108/02651330810904080

Expansión. (2019). Retrieved from https://datosmacro.expansion.com/paises/el-salvador

Eylon, D., & Au, Y. K. (1999). Exploring empowerment cross-cultural differences along the power distance dimension. *International Journal of Intercultural Relations, 23*(3), 373–385. doi:10.1016/S0147-1767(99)00002-4

Fachin, O. (2001). *Fundamentos de Metodologia*. Saraiva.

Fakhrutdinova, E., Kolesnikova, J., & Yurieva, O. K. (2014). Current trends of realization of the intellectual capital and problems of intellectual migration. *Procedia Economics and Finance, 14*(1), 326–332.

Fallon-Byrne, L., & Harney, B. (2017). Microfoundations of dynamic capabilities for innovation: a review and research agenda. *The Irish Journal of Management, 36*(1), 21-–1.

Feitosa, J., Kreutzer, C., Kramperth, A., Kramer, W. S., & Salas, E. (2014). Expatriate adjustment: Considerations for selection and training. *Journal of Global Mobility, 2*(2), 134–159. doi:10.1108/JGM-06-2013-0042

Feldman, M. S., & Pentland, B. T. (2003). Reconceptualizing organizational routines as a source of flexibility and change. *Administrative Science Quarterly, 48*(1), 94–118. doi:10.2307/3556620

Felicidade, M. (2019). Gestão RH em Empresas Familiares. *RH Magazine*, *121*, 14–17.

Felin, T., Foss, N. J., Heimeriks, K. H., & Madsen, T. L. (2012). Microfoundations of routines and capabilities: Individuals, processes, and structure. *Journal of Management Studies*, *49*(8), 1351–1374. doi:10.1111/j.1467-6486.2012.01052.x

Felin, T., Foss, N. J., & Ployhart, R. E. (2015). The microfoundations movement in strategy and organization theory. *The Academy of Management Annals*, *9*(1), 575–632. doi:10.5465/19416520.2015.1007651

Felin, T., & Powell, T. C. (2016). Designing organizations for dynamic capabilities. *California Management Review*, *58*(4), 78–96. doi:10.1525/cmr.2016.58.4.78

Fernandes, L., Simões, D., Pereira, C., & Moreira, A. C. (2019). Challenges of the internationalization strategy of a technology-based international new venture. In N. Teixeira, T. Costa, & I. Lisboa (Eds.), *Handbook of Research on Entrepreneurship, Innovation, and Internalization* (pp. 467–489). IGI Global. doi:10.4018/978-1-5225-8479-7.ch018

Fernández-Mesa, A., & Alegre, J. (2015). Entrepreneurial orientation and export intensity: Examining the interplay of organizational learning and innovation. *International Business Review*, *24*(1), 148–156. doi:10.1016/j.ibusrev.2014.07.004

Fernández, Z., & Nieto, M. (2005). Internationalization strategy of small and medium-sized family businesses: Some influential factors. *Family Business Review*, *18*(1), 77–89. doi:10.1111/j.1741-6248.2005.00031.x

Ferreira, J. A. A. (2007). *Concepções de liderança excepcional em Portugal: Um estudo exploratório* (Unpublished Master Dissertation). University of Aveiro, Aveiro, Portugal.

Ferreira, A. I., Braun, T., & Sydow, J. (2013). Citizenship behavior in project-based organizing: Comparing German and Portuguese project managers. *International Journal of Human Resource Management*, *24*(20), 3772–3793. doi:10.1080/09585192.2013.777937

Fletcher, D., & Harris, S. (2012). Knowledge acquisition for the internationalization of the smaller firm: Content and sources. *International Business Review*, *21*(4), 631–647. doi:10.1016/j.ibusrev.2011.07.008

Florida, R. (2011). *The rise of the creative class*. Basic Books.

Foley, C., & McLean, K. (2016, November 16). The Australian manufacturing industry is not dying, it's evolving CSIRO study. *The Conversation*. https://theconversation.com/the-australian-manufacturing-industry-is-not-dying-its-evolving-csiro-study-69398

Fornell, C., & Larcker, D. (1981). Evaluating structural equation models with unobservable variables and measurement error. *JMR, Journal of Marketing Research*, *18*(1), 39–50. doi:10.1177/002224378101800104

Fornell, C., & Larcker, D. F. (1981). Structural Equation Models with Unobservable Variables and Measurement Error: Algebra and Statistics. *JMR, Journal of Marketing Research*, *18*(3), 382–388. doi:10.1177/002224378101800313

Foss, N. J. (1997). *Resources, firms, and strategies: a reader in the resource-based perspective*. Oxford: Oxford Management Readers.

Foss, N. J. (2016). Reflections on a decade of microfoundations research. *Revista ADM*, *51*(1), 117–120.

Foss, N. J., & Linder, S. (2019). *Microfoundations: nature, debate, and promise*. Cambridge University Press. doi:10.1017/9781108685498

Foss, N. J., & Pedersen, T. (2019). Microfoundations in international management research: The case of knowledge sharing in multinational corporations. *Journal of International Business Studies*, *50*(9), 1594–1621.

Francioni, B., Pagano, A., & Castellani, D. (2016). Drivers of SMEs' exporting activity: A review and a research agenda. *Multinational Business Review*, *24*(3), 194–215. doi:10.1108/MBR-06-2016-0023

Francis, J., & Collins-Dodd, C. (2004). Impact of export promotion programs on firm competencies, strategies and performance: The case of Canadian high-technology SMEs June. *International Marketing Review*, *21*(4/5), 474–495. doi:10.1108/02651330410547153

Franco, M., & Haase, H. (2015). University-industry cooperation: Researchers' motivations and interaction channels. *Journal of Engineering and Technology Management*, *36*, 41–51. doi:10.1016/j.jengtecman.2015.05.002

Franzen, G., & Bouwman, M. (2001). *The mental world of brands: Mind, memory and brand Success*. NTC Publications.

Fredericks, J. O., & Slater, J. M. (1998). What Does Your Customer Really Want? *Quality Progress*, *31*(1), 63–65.

Freeman, S. (2007). An integrated framework of de-internationalization strategies for smaller born-globals. *Exploiting the B2B knowledge network: New perspectives and core concepts, 23rd IMP conference proceedings.*

Freeman, S., Deligonul, S., & Cavusgil, T. (2014). Strategic re-structuring by born-globals using outward and inward-oriented activity. *International Marketing Review*, *30*(2), 156–182. doi:10.1108/02651331311314574

Freire, J. (2008). *Economia e sociedade. Contributos para uma sociologia da vida económica em Portugal na viragem do século.* Celta Editora.

Freixanet, J. (2012). Export promotion programs: Their impact on companies' internationalization performance and competitiveness. *International Business Review*, *21*(6), 1065–1086. doi:10.1016/j.ibusrev.2011.12.003

Frishammar, J., & Andersson, S. (2009). The overestimated role of strategic orientations for international performance in smaller firms. *Journal of International Entrepreneurship*, *7*(1), 57–77. doi:10.100710843-008-0031-9

Frost, T. S. (2001). The geographic sources of foreign subsidiaries' innovations. *Strategic Management Journal*, *22*(2), 101–123. doi:10.1002/1097-0266(200101)22:2<101::AID-SMJ155>3.0.CO;2-G

Fukui, Y., & Ushijima, T. (2007). Corporate diversification, performance, and restructuring in the largest Japanese manufacturers. *Journal of the Japanese and International Economies*, *21*(3), 303–323. doi:10.1016/j.jjie.2006.06.002

Furtado, J., Pereira, A., Pereira, I., & Moreira, A. C. (2019). Does theory really fit real life situations?: A case study on the internationalization process of a technological service-based firm. In N. Teixeira, T. Costa, & I. Lisboa (Eds.), *Handbook of Research on Entrepreneurship, Innovation, and Internationalization* (pp. 419–438). IGI Global. doi:10.4018/978-1-5225-8479-7.ch016

Gabrielsson, M., Kirpalani, V. H. M., Dimitratos, P., Solberg, C. A., & Zucchella, A. (2008). Born globals: Propositions to help advance the theory. *International Business Review*, *17*(4), 385–401. doi:10.1016/j.ibusrev.2008.02.015

Galkina, T., & Chetty, S. (2015). Effectuation and networking of internationalizing SMEs. *Management International Review*, *55*(5), 647–676. doi:10.100711575-015-0251-x

Gallo, M., & Sveen, J. (1991). Internationalizing the family business: Facilitating and restraining factors. *Family Business Review*, *4*(2), 181–190. doi:10.1111/j.1741-6248.1991.00181.x

Gandia, R. (2013). The digital revolution and convergence in the video game and animation industries: Effects on the strategic organization of the innovation process. *International Journal of Arts Management*, *15*(2), 32–44.

Ganotakis, P. (2012). Founders' human capital and the performance of UK new technology based firms. *Small Business Economics*, *39*(2), 495–515. doi:10.100711187-010-9309-0

García-Cabrera, A. M., García-Soto, M. G., & Durán-Herrera, J. J. (2016). Opportunity motivation and SME internationalisation in emerging countries: Evidence from entrepreneurs' perception of institutions. *The International Entrepreneurship and Management Journal, 12*(3), 879–910. doi:10.100711365-016-0386-7

García-Cabrera, A. M., García-Soto, M. G., & Suárez-Ortega, S. M. (2017). Macro-level spillovers and micro-level capabilities as antecedents of young SMEs' propensity to export and to become a born global. *The International Entrepreneurship and Management Journal, 13*(4), 1199–1220. doi:10.100711365-017-0451-x

García-Vega, M., & López, A. (2010). Determinants of abandoning innovative activities: Evidence from Spanish Firms. *Cuadernos de Economía y Dirección de la Empresa, 13*(45), 69–91. doi:10.1016/S1138-5758(10)70024-4

Gardner, B., & Levy, S. (1955). The product and the brand. *Harvard Business Review*, (Março-Abril), 33–39.

Garvin, D. (1987). Competing in the Eight Dimensions of Quality. *Harvard Business Review, 87*(1), 101–109.

Gaver, B., & Bowers, J. (2012). Annotated portfolios. *Interaction, 19*(4), 40–49. doi:10.1145/2212877.2212889

Gavetti, G. (2005). Cognition and hierarchy: Rethinking the microfoundations of capabilities' development. *Organization Science, 16*(6), 599–617. doi:10.1287/orsc.1050.0140

Gefen, D., & Straub, D. (2005). A practical guide to factorial validity using PLS-graph: Tutorial and annotated example. *Communications of the Association for Information Systems, 16*(1), 91–109.

Gefen, D., & Straub, D. (2005). A Practical Guide To Factorial Validity Using PLS-Graph: Tutorial And Annotated Example. *Communications of the Association for Information Systems, 16*(1), 91–109. doi:10.17705/1CAIS.01605

Geldres-Weiss, V. V., Etchebarne, M. S., & Bustos, L. H. (2011). The impact of governmental export promotion on the firm's export performance. *Academia (Caracas), 47*, 1–17.

Geldres-Weiss, V. V., & Monreal-Pérez, J. (2018). The effect of export promotion programs on chilean firms' export activity: A longitudinal study on trade shows and trade missions. *Journal of Promotion Management, 24*(5), 660–674. doi:10.1080/10496491.2018.1405519

George, G., Wiklund, J., & Zahra, A. (2005). Ownership and the internationalization of small firms. *Journal of Management, 31*(2), 210–233. doi:10.1177/0149206304271760

Geroski, P., Machin, S., & van Reenen, J. (1993). The profitability of innovating firms. *The Rand Journal of Economics, 24*(2), 198–211. doi:10.2307/2555757

Gerschewski, S., Rose, E. L., & Lindsay, V. J. (2015). Understanding the drivers of international performance for born global firms: An integrated perspective. *Journal of World Business, 50*(3), 558–575. doi:10.1016/j.jwb.2014.09.001

Gesteland, R. R. (2005). *Cross-Cultural Business Behavior: Negotiating, Selling, Sourcing and Managing Across Cultures* (4th ed.). Business School Press.

Ghauri, P. (2004). Designing and conducting case studies in international business research. In R. Marschan-Piekkari & C. Welch (Eds.), *Handbook of Qualitative Research Methods for International Business* (pp. 109–124). Edward Elgar. doi:10.4337/9781781954331.00019

Ghemawat, P. (2001). Distance still Matters. *Harvard Business Review, 79*(8), 137–145. PMID:11550630

Gil, A. C. (2008). *Métodos e Técnicas de Pesquisa Social.* Atlas.

Gil-Barragan, J. M., Belso-Martínez, J. A., & Mas-Verdú, F. (2020). When do domestic networks cause accelerated internationalization under different decision-making logic? *European Business Review*, *32*(2), 227–256. doi:10.1108/EBR-11-2018-0191

Gilmore, A., O'Donnell, A., Carson, D., & Cummins, D. (2003). Factors influencing foreign direct investment and international joint ventures – A comparative study of Northern Ireland and Bahrain. *International Marketing Review*, *20*(2), 195–215. doi:10.1108/02651330310470401

Gioia, D. A., Corley, K. G., & Hamilton, A. L. (2012). Seeking qualitative rigor in inductive research: Notes on the Gioia Methodology. *Organizational Research Methods*, *16*(1), 15–31. doi:10.1177/1094428112452151

Giovannetti, G., Ricchiuti, G., & Velucchi, M. (2013). Location, internationalization and performance of firms in Italy: A multilevel approach. *Applied Economics*, *45*(18), 2665–2673. doi:10.1080/00036846.2012.665597

Gleason, K. (2006). Intangible capital in the pharmaceutical and chemical industry. *The Quarterly Review of Economics and Finance*, *46*(2), 300-314.

Goel, A., & Yang, N. (2015a). Internationalization and performance of Indian born globals. *European Journal of Marketing*, *24*(5), 41–49. doi:10.1108/EL-01-2014-0022

Gökçen, G., Ataman Akgül, B., & Çakıcı, C. (2006). *Türkiye muhasebe standartları uygulamaları (uluslararası muhasebe standartları ile uyumlu)*. Beta Basım Yayın Dağıtım.

Gökgöz, A., & Özdemir, H. (2015). Dış ticarette teslim ve ödeme şekillerinin TMS 18 hasılat standardı çerçevesinde incelenmesi. *Journal of Accounting. Finance and Auditing Studies*, *1*(3), 105–122.

Golinelli, G. M. (2000). *L' approccio sistemico al Governo dell' impresa*. Cedam.

Gomez-Mejia, L.R., Makri, M., & Kintana, M.L. (2010). Diversification decisions in family-owned companies. *Journal of Management Studies*, *4* (2), 223-252. doi:10.1111 / j.1467-6486.2009.00889.x

Gomez-Mejia, L., Berrone, P., & de Castro, J. (2011). The Bind that ties: Socio-emotional wealth preservation in family firms. *The Academy of Management Annals*, *5*(1), 653–707. doi:10.5465/19416520.2011.593320

Gómez-Mejía, L., Haynes, K., Núñez-Nickel, M., Jacobson, K., & Moyano-Fuentes, J. (2007). Socioemotional wealth and business risks in family-controlled firms: Evidence from Spanish olive oil mills. *Administrative Science Quarterly*, *52*(1), 106–137. doi:10.2189/asqu.52.1.106

Gottardo, P., & Moisello, A. M. (2017). Family firms, risk-taking and financial distress. *Problems and Perspectives in Management*, *15*(2), 168–177. doi:10.21511/ppm.15(2-1).2017.01

Govindarajan, V., & Trimble, C. (2010). *The other side of innovation: Solving the execution challenge*. Harvard Business Press.

Graf, A. (2004). *Interkulturelle Kompetenzen im Human Resource Management. Empirische Analyse konzeptioneller Grundfragen und der betrieblichen Relevanz*. Deutscher Universitäts-Verlag. doi:10.1007/978-3-322-82025-9

Grant, R. M. (2016). *Contemporary strategy analysis: Text and cases*. Reino Unido: John Wiley & Sons.

Graves, C., & Thomas, J. (2008). Determinants of the internationalization pathways of family firms: An examination of family influence. *Family Business Review*, *21*(2), 151–167. doi:10.1111/j.1741-6248.2008.00119.x

Gristai, O. (2010). *Promoting creativity and knowledge in the Barcelona Metropolitan Region*. ACRE.

Gupta, J., Wilson, N., Gregoriou, A., & Healy, J. (2014). The effect of internationalisation on modelling credit risk for SMEs: Evidence from UK market. *Journal of International Financial Markets, Institutions and Money, 31*(C), 397–413. doi:10.1016/j.intfin.2014.05.001

Habbershon, T., & Pistrui, J. (2002). Enterprising families domain: Family-influenced ownership groups in pursuit of transgenerational wealth. *Family Business Review, 15*(3), 223–237. doi:10.1111/j.1741-6248.2002.00223.x

Haddoud, M. Y., Jones, P., & Newbery, R. (2017). Export promotion programmes and SMEs' performance: Exploring the network promotion role. *Journal of Small Business and Enterprise Development, 24*(1), 68–87. doi:10.1108/JSBED-07-2016-0116

Hadjikhani, A. (1996). Project marketing and the management of discontinuity. *International Business Review, 5*(3), 319–336. doi:10.1016/0969-5931(96)00013-3

Hadjimanolis, A. (1999). Barriers to innovation for SMEs in a small less developed country (Cyprus). *Technovation, 19*(9), 561–570. doi:10.1016/S0166-4972(99)00034-6

Hagemejer, J., & Kolasa, M. (2011). Internationalization and economic performance of enterprises: Evidence from polish firm-level data. *World Economy, 34*(1), 74–100. doi:10.1111/j.1467-9701.2010.01294.x

Hagen, B., Zucchella, A., Cerchiello, P., & De Giovanni, N. (2012). International strategy and performance—Clustering strategic types of SMEs. *International Business Review, 21*(3), 369–382. doi:10.1016/j.ibusrev.2011.04.002

Haghighti, E., & Albayrak, M. (2016). Küresel doğan işletmeler ve uluslararasılaşma süreci. *Isparta: 12. Tarım Ekonomisi Kongresi*, 2173-2182.

Hakansson, H., & Snehota, I. (2006). "No business is an island" 17 years later. *Strategic Management Journal, 22*(3), 271–274.

Hales, J. A. (2005). *Accounting and Financial Analysis in the Hospitality Industry*. Elsevier Butterworth–Heineman.

Hall, R. (1992). The strategic analysis of intangible resources. *Strategic Management Journal, 13*, 135–144. Retrieved from de http://onlinelibrary.wiley.com/doi/10.1002/smj.4250130205/abstract

Hall, E. T. (1976). *Beyond Culture*. Anchor Books/Doubleday.

Hall, E. T., & Hall, M. R. (1990). *Understanding Cultural Differences: Germans, French and Americans*. Intercultural Press.

Hall, J. A. (2013). *Accounting Information Systems*. South-Western Cengage.

Hambrick, D., & Mason, P. (1984). Upper Echelons: The organization as a reflection of its top managers. *Academy of Management Review, 9*(2), 193–206. doi:10.5465/amr.1984.4277628

Hancer, M. (2003). Konaklama endüstrisinde müşteri sadakati: Anlam, önem, etki ve sonuçlar. *Seyahat ve Turizm Araştırmaları Dergisi, 3*(1-2), 39–45.

Hanner, N., & Zarnekow, R. (2015). Purchasing behavior in free to play games: Concepts and empirical validation. In *2015 48th Hawaii International Conference on System Sciences*. IEEE.

Harmeling, S. (2011). Contingency as an entrepreneurial resource: How private obsession fulfills public need. *Journal of Business Venturing, 26*(3), 293–305. doi:10.1016/j.jbusvent.2009.10.003

Harmeling, S. S., & Sarasvathy, S. D. (2013). When contingency is a resource: Educating entrepreneurs in the Balkans, the Bronx, and beyond. *Entrepreneurship Theory and Practice, 37*(4), 713–744. doi:10.1111/j.1540-6520.2011.00489.x

Harris, M. M., & Lievens, F. (2005). Selecting employees for global assignments: Can assessment centers measure cultural intelligence? In A. Rahim & R. T. Golembiewski (Eds.), *Current Topics in Management, 10* (pp. 221–240). Research Collection Lee Kong Chian School Of Business.

Helfat, C. E., & Peteraf, M. A. (2015). Managerial cognitive capabilities and the microfoundations of dynamic capabilities. *Strategic Management Journal*, *36*(6), 831–850. doi:10.1002mj.2247

Herstad, S., Sandven, T., & Solberg, E. (2013). Location, education an enterprise growth. *Applied Economics Letters*, *20*(10), 1019–1022. doi:10.1080/13504851.2013.772287

He, X., Brouthers, K. D., & Filatotchev, I. (2012). Resource-based and institutional perspectives on export channel selection and export performance. *Journal of Management*, *39*(1), 27–47. doi:10.1177/0149206312445926

Hill, A., & Hill, M. M. (2008). Investigação por Questionário (2a ed.). Edições Silabo.

Hilmersson, M. (2014). Small and medium-sized enterprise internationalisation strategy and performance in times of market turbulence. *International Small Business Journal*, *32*(4), 386–400. doi:10.1177/0266242613497744

Hipp, C. (2008). Service peculiarities and the specific role of technology in service innovation management. *International Journal of Services Technology and Management*, *9*(2), 154–173. doi:10.1504/IJSTM.2008.018433

Hitt, M. A., Ireland, R. D., & Hoskisson, R. E. (2007). *Strategic management: competitiveness and globalization*. Mason: Thomson SouthWestern.

Hitt, M., Bierman, L., Shimizu, K., & Kochhar, R. (2001). Direct and moderating effects of human capital on strategy and performance in professional service firms: A resource-based perspective. *Academy of Management Journal*, *44*(1), 13–28.

Hofstede Insights. (n.d.a). *Country Comparison*. https://www.hofstede-insights.com/country-comparison/germany,portugal/

Hofstede Insights. (n.d.b). *Cultural Diversity*. https://news.hofstede-insights.com/news/why-is-managing-cultural-diversity-important

Hofstede Insights. (n.d.c). *Intercultural Management*. https://hi.hofstede-insights.com/intercultural-management-programmes

Hofstede Insights. (n.d.d). *National Culture*. https://hi.hofstede-insights.com/national-culture

Hofstede, G. (1991). *Cultures and Organizations: Software of the Mind* (2nd ed.). McGraw-Hill.

Hollensen, S. (2014). *Global marketing*. Pearson Education.

Holmlund, M., Sören, K., & Vanyushyn, V. (2007). SMEs' internationalization and the influence of importing on exporting. *International Small Business Journal*, *25*(5), 459–477. doi:10.1177/0266242607080655

Holt, D. (2012). The Journey of a 'Green' Micro-Enterprise – The Green Planet. *Corporate Social Responsibility and Environmental Management*, *19*(2), 90–101. doi:10.1002/csr.290

Holt, D. B., Quelch, J. A., & Taylor, E. L. (2004). How global brands compete. *Harvard Business Review*, (September), 1–9. PMID:15449856

House, R. J., Hanges, P. J., Javidan, M., Dorfman, P. W., & Gupta, V. (Eds.). (2004). *Culture, Leadership, and Organizations: The GLOBE Study of 62 Societies*. Sage.

Howard, D. (1977). Technology transfer trhough commercial transations. *The Journal of Industrial Economics*, *16*(2), 161–175.

Howells, J. (2006). Intermediation and the role of intermediaries in innovation. *Research Policy, 35*(5), 715–728. doi:10.1016/j.respol.2006.03.005

Hron J. (2006). Knowledge and Strategic Management. *Agricultural Economics – Czech, 52*(3), 101-106.

Hsieh, A.-T., & Li, C.-K. (2008). The moderating effect of brand image on public relations perception and customer loyalty. *Marketing Intelligence & Planning, 26*(1), 26–42. doi:10.1108/02634500810847138

Huang, K., Chung Lo, S., Liu, C., & Tung, J. (2014). Internationalization of family business: The effect of ownership and generation involvement. *The Anthropologist, 17*(3), 757–767. doi:10.1080/09720073.2014.11891490

Hult, G. T., Hurley, R. F., & Knight, G. A. (2004). Innovativeness: Its Antecedents and impact on Business Performance. *Industrial Marketing Management, 33*(5), 429–438. doi:10.1016/j.indmarman.2003.08.015

Hu, R., & Shieh, C.-H. (2013). High-tech industries overseas investment performance evaluation - Application of Data Envelopment Analysis. *South African Journal of Economic and Management Sciences, 16*(5), 67–73. doi:10.4102ajems.v16i5.670

Hurley, R. F., & Hult, G. T. (1998). Innovation, Market Orientation, and Organizational Learning: An Integration and Empirical Examination. *Journal of Marketing, 62*(3), 42–54. doi:10.1177/002224299806200303

Hutchinson, K., Quinn, B., & Alexander, N. (2006). The role of management characteristics in the internationalization of SMEs, Evidence of from the UK retail. *Journal of Small Business and Enterprise Development, 13*(4), 513–534. doi:10.1108/14626000610705723

Ietto-Gillies, G. (2012). *Transnational corporations: Fragmentation amidst integration.* Routeldge.

INE. (2020). *Produto interno bruto por habitante e NUTS III.* Instituto Nacional de Estatísticas.

ISES - Instituto Socio Economia Solidária. (2019). http://ises.org.br

Isidor, R., Schwens, C., & Kabst, R. (2011). Human resource management and early internationalization: Is there a leap-frogging in international staffing? *International Journal of Human Resource Management, 22*(10), 2167–2184. do i:10.1080/09585192.2011.580186

Jahdi, K. S., & Acikdilli, G. (2009). Marketing communications and corporate social responsibility (CSR): Marriage of convenience or shotgun wedding? *Journal of Business Ethics, 88*(1), 103–113. doi:10.100710551-009-0113-1

Jalali, S. H. (2012). The effect of export promotion programmes on export performance: Evidence from Iranian food manufacturers. *International Journal of Business and Globalisation, 9*(2), 122–133. doi:10.1504/IJBG.2012.048955

Jansen, J. J. P., Van Den Bosch, F. A. J., & Volberda, H. W. (2005). Managing Potential and Realized Absorptive Capacity: How Do Organizational Antecedents Matter? *Academy of Management Journal, 48*(6), 999–1015. doi:10.5465/amj.2005.19573106

Javalgi, R. G., & Todd, P. R. (2011). Entrepreneurial orientation, management commitment, and human capital: The internationalization of SMEs in India. *Journal of Business Research, 64*(9), 1004–1010. doi:10.1016/j.jbusres.2010.11.024

Javalgi, R., & Martin, C. (2007). Internationalization of services: Identifying the building-blocks for future research. *Journal of Services Marketing, 21*(6), 391–397. doi:10.1108/08876040710818886

Jawahar, I. M., & McLaughlin, G. L. (2001). Toward a descriptive stakeholder theory: An organizational life-cycle approach. *Academy of Management Review, 26*(1), 397–414. doi:10.5465/amr.2001.4845803

Jenssen, J. I., & Nybakk, E. (2013). Inter-organizational networks and innovation in small, knowledge-intensive firms: A literature review. *International Journal of Innovation Management*, *17*(2), 1350008. doi:10.1142/S1363919613500084

Jesuino, J. C. (2002). Latin Europe cluster: From South to North. *Journal of World Business*, *37*(1), 81–89. doi:10.1016/S1090-9516(01)00076-1

Jick, T. J. (1979). Mixing qualitative and quantitative methods: Triangulation in action. *Administrative Science Quarterly*, *24*(4), 602–611. doi:10.2307/2392366

Jo, H., & Harjoto, M. A. (2011). Corporate governance and firm value: The impact of corporate social responsibility. *Journal of Business Ethics*, *103*(3), 351–383. doi:10.100710551-011-0869-y

Johanson, J., & Mattsson, L. G. (2015). Internationalisation in industrial systems — A network approach. In M. Forsgren, U. Holm, & J. Johanson (Eds.), *Knowledge, Networks and Power* (pp. 111–132). Palgrave Macmillan. doi:10.1057/9781137508829_5

Johanson, J., & Vahlne, J. (1977). The internationalization process of the firm: A model of knowledge development and increasing foreign market commitments. *Journal of International Business Studies*, *8*(1), 23–32. doi:10.1057/palgrave.jibs.8490676

Johanson, J., & Vahlne, J. (2009). The Uppsala internationalization process model revisited: From liability of foreignness to liability of outsidership. *Journal of International Business Studies*, *40*(9), 1411–1431. doi:10.1057/jibs.2009.24

Johanson, J., & Vahlne, J.-E. (1990). The mechanism of internationalism. *International Marketing Review*, *7*(4), 11–24. doi:10.1108/02651339010137414

Johanson, J., & Wiedersheim-Paul, F. (1975). The internationalization of the firm - four Swedish cases. *Journal of Management Studies*, *12*(3), 305–323. doi:10.1111/j.1467-6486.1975.tb00514.x

Jones, G., & Khanna, T. (2006). Bringing history (back) into international business. *Journal of International Business Studies*, *37*(4), 453–468. doi:10.1057/palgrave.jibs.8400198

Jornal de Negócios. (2019). *Internacionalização da economia portuguesa: é possível pedir mais?* Retrieved from: https://www.jornaldenegocios.pt/opiniao/colunistas/detalhe/internacionalizacao-da-economia-portuguesa-e-possivel-pedir-mais

Juen, C. S., & Mustapha, M. (2015). An assessment of internal controls in budget hotels in Malaysia, proceedings of the international conference on natural resources. *Tourism and Services Management*, 405-412.

Kafouros, M., Buckley, P., Sharp, J., & Wang, C. (2008). The role of internacionalization in explaining innovation performance. *Technovation*, *28*(1-2), 63–74. doi:10.1016/j.technovation.2007.07.009

Kalafsky, R. V. (2017). Export programs and SME market choice: Evidence from North West England. *GeoJournal*, *82*(6), 1135–1144. doi:10.100710708-016-9733-z

Kalinic, I., & Forza, C. (2012). Rapid internationalization of traditional SMEs: Between gradualist models and born globals. *International Business Review*, *21*(4), 694–707. doi:10.1016/j.ibusrev.2011.08.002

Kapiki, S. (2015). *Τήρηση Λογαριασμών Πελατών: Main-Courante Ξενοδοχείων* [Front Office Accounting-Table of Contents]. doi:10.2139srn.2690782

Karagiorgos, T., Drogalas, G., & Giovanis, N. (2011). Evaluation of the effectiveness of internal audit in Greek hotel business. *International Journal of Economic Sciences and Applied Research*, *4*(1), 19–34.

Karagozoglu, N., & Lindell, M. (1998). Internationalization of small and medium-sized technology-based firms: An exploratory study. *Journal of Small Business Management*, *36*(1), 44–59.

Karaxontzitis, D., & Sarlis, K. (1989). *Hotel Accounting*. Interbooks.

Karlsen, T., Silseth, R., Benito, G., & Welch, L. S. (2003). Knowledge, internationalization of the firm, and inward – outward connections. *Industrial Marketing Management*, *32*(5), 385–396. doi:10.1016/S0019-8501(03)00012-9

Kasavana, M., & Brooks, R. (1995). *Front Office Procedures*. Educational Institute of the American Hotel & Motel Association.

Kastenholz, E., & Almeida, A. (2008). Seasonality in rural tourism – the case of North Portugal. *Tourism Review*, *63*(2), 5–15. doi:10.1108/16605370810883905

Katsikeas, C. S., & Morgan, R. E. (1994). Differences in perceptions of exporting problems based on firm size and export market experience. *European Journal of Marketing*, *28*(5), 17–35. doi:10.1108/03090569410062014

Kaya, E. & T. Köse. (2013). *Konaklama Işletmelerinde Muhasebe Uygulamaları*. Anadolu Üniversitesi Yayın No: 2816.

Kayo, E. K. (2002). *A estrutura de capital e o risco das empresas tangível e intangível-intensivas: uma contribuição ao estudo da valoração de empresas* (PhD thesis). FEA/USP.

Keegan, W., Moriarty, S., & Duncan, T. (1995). *Marketing*. Prentice Hall.

Keller, K. (1993). Conceptualizing, measuring, and managing customer-based brand equity. *Journal of Marketing*, *57*(1), 1–22. doi:10.1177/002224299305700101

Keller, K. (2000). Building and managing corporate brand equity. In M. Schultz, M. Hatch, & M. Larsen (Eds.), *The expressive organisation. Linking identity, reputation, and the corporate brand* (pp. 115–137). Oxford University Press.

Keller, K. L., & Richey, K. (2006). The importance of corporate brand personality traits to a successful 21st century business. *Journal of Brand Management*, *14*(1), 74–81. doi:10.1057/palgrave.bm.2550055

Kelly, P. (2009). *International business and management*. South-Western, Cengage Learning, EMEA.

Kerlin, J. A. (2006). Social enterprise in the United States and Europe: Understanding and learning from the differences. *Voluntas*, *17*(3), 246–262. doi:10.100711266-006-9016-2

Kerlin, J. A. (2010). A comparative analysis of the global emergence of social enterprise. *Voluntas*, *21*(2), 162–179. doi:10.100711266-010-9126-8

Kerlin, J. A. (2013). Defining social enterprise across different contexts: A conceptual framework based on institutional factors. *Nonprofit and Voluntary Sector Quarterly*, *42*(1), 84–108. doi:10.1177/0899764011433040

Kirca, A. H., Jayachandran, S., & Bearden, W. O. (2005). Market orientation: A meta-analytic review and assessment of its antecedents and impact on performance. *Journal of Marketing*, *69*(1), 24–41. doi:10.1509/jmkg.69.2.24.60761

Kivisto, P. (2002). *Multiculturalism in a Global Society*. Blackwell. doi:10.1002/9780470694916

Knight, G. A., & Cavusgil, S. T. (1996). The born global firm: A challenge to traditional internationalization theory. *Advances in International Marketing*, *8*, 11–26.

Knight, G. A., & Cavusgil, S. T. (2004). Innovation, organizational capabilities, and the born-global firm. *Journal of International Business Studies*, *35*(2), 124–141. doi:10.1057/palgrave.jibs.8400071

Knight, G. A., & Liesch, P. W. (2016). Internationalization: From incremental to born global. *Journal of World Business*, *51*(1), 93–102. doi:10.1016/j.jwb.2015.08.011

Koch, E. (2012). *Interkulturelles Management: Für Führungspraxis, Projektarbeit und Kommunikation*. UVK Verlagsgesellschaft.

Koellinger, P. (2008). Why are some entrepreneurs more innovative than others? *Small Business Economics*, *31*(1), 21–37. doi:10.100711187-008-9107-0

Kohli, A. K., & Jaworski, B. J. (1990). Market orientation: The construct, research propositions and managerial implications. *Journal of Marketing*, *54*(2), 1–18. doi:10.1177/002224299005400201

Komorowski, M., & Delaere, S. (2016). Online media business models: Lessons from the video game sector. *Westminster Papers in Communication and Culture*, *11*(1), 103–123. doi:10.16997/wpcc.220

Kontinen, T., & Ojala, A. (2010). Internationalization pathways of family SMEs: Psychic distance as a focal point. *Journal of Small Business and Enterprise Development*, *17*(3), 437–454. doi:10.1108/14626001011068725

Koparal, C. (2010). *Uluslararası Işletmeciliğe Giriş*. Uluslararası Işletmecilik, Eskişehir, Anadolu Üniversitesi Yayınları.

Kotler, P. (2000). Administração de Marketing: a edição do novo milénio (Vol. 10). Prentice Hall.

Kraus, S., Mensching, A., Calabrò, A., Cheng, C., & Filsera, M. (2016). Family firm internationalization: A configurational approach. *Journal of Business Research*, *69*(11), 5473–5478. doi:10.1016/j.jbusres.2016.04.158

Kristanti, F. T., Rahayu, S., & Huda, A. N. (2016). The determinant of financial distress on indonesian family firm. *Procedia: Social and Behavioral Sciences*, *219*, 440–447. doi:10.1016/j.sbspro.2016.05.018

Kruesi, M. A., Hemmington, N. R., & Kim, P. B. (2018). What matters for hotel executives? An examination of major theories in non-equity entry mode research. *International Journal of Hospitality Management*, *70*, 25–36. doi:10.1016/j.ijhm.2017.11.005

Kurniadi, L., & Zio, L. (2011). *The role of internal control in the operation of hotels* (Unpublished master dissertation). Lund University, Sweden.

Kuys, B., & Kyriazis, E. (2015). *It's all about the money: adding value to industry through industrial design-led innovations*. Academic Press.

Lakatos, E. M., & Marconi, M. D. (2007). *Metodologias Científicas*. Atlas.

Lall, S. (1992). Technological capabilities and industrialisation. *World Development*, *20*(2), 165–186. doi:10.1016/0305-750X(92)90097-F

Lambin, J. (2008). *Market Driven Management*. Nova Iorque: McGrawHil.

Lang, M. H., Lins, K. V., & Miller, D. P. (2003). ADRs, analysts, and accuracy: Does cross listing in the United States Improve a firm's information environment and increase market value? *Journal of Accounting Research*, *41*(2), 317–345. doi:10.1111/1475-679X.00106

Laufs, K., & Schwens, C. (2014). Foreign market entry mode choice of small and medium-sized enterprises: A systematic review and future research agenda. *International Business Review*, *23*(6), 1109–1126. doi:10.1016/j.ibusrev.2014.03.006

Lauginic, J.-M. (2009). L'efficacité entrepreneuriale passe par le plurilinguisme. In F. X. Aligny, A. Guillaume, B. Nieder, F. Rastier, C. Tremblay, & H. Wismann (Eds.), *Plurilinguisme, Interculturalité et Emploi: Défis pour l'Europe* (pp. 135–139). L'Harmattan.

Lederman, D., Olarreaga, M., & Payton, L. (2010). Export promotion agencies: Do they work? *Journal of Development Economics*, *91*(2), 257–265. doi:10.1016/j.jdeveco.2009.09.003

Lee, J. (1992). Quantitative versus qualitative research methods two approaches to organization studies. *Asia Pacific Journal of Management*, *9*(1), 87–94. doi:10.100710490-015-9454-8

Leonidou, L. C., Palihawadana, D., & Theodosiou, M. (2011). National export-promotion programs as drivers of organizational resources and capabilities: Effects on strategy. *Journal of International Marketing*, *19*(2), 1–29. doi:10.1509/jimk.19.2.1

Leonidou, L., Samiee, S., & Geldres, V. V. (2015). Using national export promotion programs to assist smaller firms' international entrepreneurial initiatives. In P. N. Ghauri & V. H. M. Kirpalani (Eds.), *Handbook of Research on International Entrepreneurship Strategy: Improving SME Performance Globally* (pp. 239–252). Edward Elgar Publishing Ltd. doi:10.4337/9781783471584.00023

Lexico. (n.d.). https://www.lexico.com/definition/expatriate

Li, E. X., & Liu, L. X. (2012). *Intangible assets and cross-sectional stock returns: Evidence from structural estimation.* Reunião Anual da Associação Económica America. Retrievied from https://ssrn.com/abstract=1560014

Li, F. (2020). The digital transformation of business models in the creative industries: A holistic framework and emerging trends. *Technovation*, *92*, 102012. doi:10.1016/j.technovation.2017.12.004

Li, H., Yi, X., & Cui, G. (2017). Emerging market firms' internationalization: How do firms' inward activities affect their outward activities? *Strategic Management Journal*, *38*(13), 2704–2725. doi:10.1002mj.2679

Li, L. (2005). Is Regional Strategy More Effective Thanglobal Strategy in the US Service Industries? *Management International Review*, *45*(1), 37–57.

Lindemann, U. (2016). Impact of Design Research on Practitioners in Industry. In *Impact of Design Research on Industrial Practice* (pp. 223–232). Springer. doi:10.1007/978-3-319-19449-3_14

Lins, K. V. (2003). Equity ownership and firm vaiue in emerging markets. *Journal of Financial and Quantitative Analysis*, *38*(1), 159–184. doi:10.2307/4126768

Lin, T.-H. (2009). A cross model study of corporate financial distress prediction in Taiwan: Multiple discriminant analysis, logit, probit and neural networks models. *Neurocomputing*, *72*(16-18), 3507–3516. doi:10.1016/j.neucom.2009.02.018

Lipparini, A., & Sobrero, M. (1994). The glue and the pieces: Entrepreneurship and innovation in small-firm networks. *Journal of Business Venturing*, *9*(2), 125–140. doi:10.1016/0883-9026(94)90005-1

Lippitt, M. (1987). *The Managing Complex Change Model. Copyright, 1987, by Dr.* Mary Lippitt, Founder and President of Enterprise Management, Ltd.

Lisboa, I. (2019a). Sucessão nas empresas familiares e o impacto no endividamento. Evidência para as PME da região de Leiria. *Revista de Gestão dos Países de Língua Portuguesa*, *17*(2), 24. doi:10.12660/rgplp.v17n2.2018.78223

Lisboa, I. (2019b). Capital Structure Choices and Exports: The Case of the Portuguese Mold Industry. *Australasian Accounting. Business and Finance Journal*, *13*(4), 23–45. doi:10.14453/aabfj.v13i4.3

Liu, S. S., Luo, X., & Shi, Y. Z. (2003). Market oriented organizations in an emerging economy: A study of missing links. *Journal of Business Research*, *56*(6), 481–491. doi:10.1016/S0148-2963(01)00265-X

Li, Y., Liu, Y., & Zhao, Y. (2006). The role of market and entrepreneurship orientation and internal control in the new product development of Chinese firms. *Industrial Marketing Management*, *35*(3), 336–347. doi:10.1016/j.indmarman.2005.05.016

Li, Y., Zhao, Y., Tan, J., & Liu, Y. (2008). Moderating Effects of Entrepreneurial Orientation on Market Orientation-Performance Linkage: Evidence from Chinese Small Firms. *Journal of Small Business Management, 46*(1), 113–133. doi:10.1111/j.1540-627X.2007.00235.x

Loayza, N., & Pennings, S. (2020). *Macroeconomic Policy in the Time of COVID-19: A Primer for Developing Countries*. Research & Policy Briefs, 28. Washington, DC: World Bank Group. https://documents.worldbank.org/curated/en/951811585836124198/Macroeconomic-Policy-in-the-Time-of-COVID-19-A-Primer-for-Developing-Countries

Lohe, F.-W., & Calabrò, A. (2017). Please do not disturb! Differentiating bord tasks in family and non-family during financial distress. *Scandinavian Journal of Management, 33*(1), 33–49. doi:10.1016/j.scaman.2017.01.001

López, S. V. (2005). Competitive advantage and strategy formulation: The key role of dynamic capabilities. *Management Decision, 43*(5), 661–669. doi:10.1108/00251740510597699

Loth, D. (2006). *Le management interculturel*. L'Harmattan.

Loudon, D. L., & Bitta, A. J. (1988). *Consumer Behavior: Concepts and Applications. Nova Iorque*. McGraw-Hill.

Lu, J. W., & Beamish, P. W. (2006). Partnering strategies and performance of SMEs' international joint ventures. *Journal of Business Venturing, 21*(4), 461–486. doi:10.1016/j.jbusvent.2005.02.002

Luke, B., & Chu, V. (2013). Social enterprise versus social entrepreneurship: An examination of the 'why' and 'how' in pursuing social change. *International Small Business Journal, 31*(7), 764–784. doi:10.1177/0266242612462598

Lumpkin, G., & Dess, G. (1996). Clarifying the entrepreneurial orientation construct and linking it to performance. *Academy of Management Review, 21*(1), 135–172. http://amr.aom.org/content/21/1/135.short. doi:10.5465/amr.1996.9602161568

Luo, Y., & Tung, R. L. (2007). International expansion of emerging market enterprises: A springboard perspective. *Journal of International Business Studies, 38*(4), 481–498. doi:10.1057/palgrave.jibs.8400275

Lydon, J., Dyer, D., & Bradley, C. (2014). *Compete to Prosper: Improving Australia's global competitiveness*. McKinsey Australia.

Maciejewski, M., & Wach, K. (2019). International startups from Poland: Born global or born regional? *Journal of Management and Business Administration. Central Europe, 27*(1), 60–83.

Madhok, A., & Keyhani, M. (2012). Acquisitions as entrepreneurship: Asymmetries, opportunities, and the internationalization of multinationals from emerging economies. *Global Strategy Journal, 2*(1), 26–40. doi:10.1002/gsj.1023

Maidique, A., & Zirger, B. (1985). The new product learning cycle. *Research Policy, 14*(6), 299–313. doi:10.1016/0048-7333(85)90001-0

Mainela, T., Puhakka, V., & Sipola, S. (2018). International entrepreneurship beyond individuals and firms: On the systemic nature of international opportunities. *Journal of Business Venturing, 33*(4), 534–550. doi:10.1016/j.jbusvent.2018.04.002

Mair, J., & Martí, I. (2006). Social Entrepreneurship Research: A Source of Explanation, Prediction, and Delight. *Journal of World Business, 41*(1), 36–44. doi:10.1016/j.jwb.2005.09.002

Makadok, R. (2001). Toward a synthesis of the resource-based and dynamic-capability views of rent creation. *Strategic Management Journal, 22*(5), 387–401. doi:10.1002mj.158

Malhotra, N., & Hinings, C. R. (2010). An organizational model for understanding internationalization processes. *Journal of International Business Studies, 41*(2), 330–349. doi:10.1057/jibs.2009.75

Manzaneque, M., Priego, A. M., & Merino, E. (2016). Corporate governance effect on financial distress likelihood: Evidence from Spain. *Revista de Contabilidad, 19*(1), 111–121. doi:10.1016/j.rcsar.2015.04.001

March, J. G. (1991). Exploration and exploitation in organizational learning. *Organization Science, 2*(1), 71–87. doi:10.1287/orsc.2.1.71

Marconi, M., & Lakatos, E. (2011). *Metodologia Científica.* Editora Atlas.

Marin, D. (1992). Is the export-led growth hypothesis valid for industrialized countries? *The Review of Economics and Statistics, 74*(4), 678–688. doi:10.2307/2109382

Marin, Q., Hernández-Lara, A. B., Campa-Planas, F., & Sánchez-Rebull, M. V. (2017). Which factors improve the performance of the internationalization process? Focus on family firms. *Applied Economics, 49*(32), 3181–3194. doi:10.1080/00036846.2016.1257103

Mariotto, F. L., Zanni, P. P., & Moraes, G. H. S. M. (2014). What is the use of a single-case study in management research? *Revista de Administração de Empresas, 54*(4), 358–369. doi:10.1590/S0034-759020140402

Maroco, J. (2010). *Análise de Equações Estruturais: Fundamentos teóricos, Software e Aplicações.* Pêro Pinheiro: ReportNumber.

Marôco, J. (2011). Análise estatística com o SPSS Statistics (5a ed.). ReportNumber, Lda.

Maroco, J. (2011). *Análise Estatistica com o SPSS Statistics* (Vol. 5). Pêro Pinheiro: ReportNumber.

Martincus, C. V., & Carballo, J. (2010). Beyond the average effects: The distributional impacts of export promotion programs in developing countries. *Journal of Development Economics, 92*(2), 201–214. doi:10.1016/j.jdeveco.2009.02.007

Martineau, P. (1958). The personality of the retail store. *Harvard Business Review, 36*(1), 47–55.

Martinho, R., & Antunes, A. (2012). Um Modelo De Scoring Para As Empresas Portuguesas. *Banco de Portugal - Relatório de Estabilidade Financeira*, 117–131. doi:10.1063/1.342458

Martin, R. L., & Osberg, S. (2007). Social entrepreneurship: The case for definition. *Stanford Social Innovation Review, 5*(2), 28–39.

Matas-Runquist, N. (2009). Une expérience plurilingue en milieu professionnel: L'anglais ne suffit pas! In F. X. Aligny, A. Guillaume, B. Nieder, F. Rastier, C. Tremblay, & H. Wismann (Eds.), *Plurilinguisme, Interculturalité et Emploi: Défis pour l'Europe* (pp. 156–161). L'Harmattan.

McAllister, G., & White, G. R. (2015). Video game development and user experience. In R. Bernhaupt (Ed.), *Game user experience evaluation. Human-computer interaction series* (pp. 11–35). Springer. doi:10.1007/978-3-319-15985-0_2

McDougall, P. P., & Oviatt, B. M. (2000). International entrepreneurship: The intersection of two research paths. *Academy of Management Journal, 43*, 902–908.

McDougall, P. P., & Oviatt, B. M. (2005). Some fundamental issues in international entrepreneurship. *Entrepreneurship Theory and Practice, 29*(5), 537–553.

McKelvie, A., Chandler, G. N., DeTienne, D. R., & Johansson, A. (2019). The measurement of effectuation: Highlighting research tensions and opportunities for the future. *Small Business Economics*, 1–32.

Md-Rus, R., Mohd, K. N. T., Latif, R. A., & Alassan, Z. N. (2013). Ownership Structure and Financial Distress. *Journal of Advanced Management Science, 1*(4), 363–367. doi:10.12720/joams.1.4.363-367

Meckl, R., & Schramm, R. (2005). *Empirical evidence for a theory of international new ventures*. Univ., Wirtschaftswiss. Fak.

Medina, J. F., & Duffy, M. F. (1998). Standardization vs globalization: A new perspective of brand strategies. *Journal of Product and Brand Management, 7*(3), 223–243. doi:10.1108/10610429810222859

Meyskens, M., Robb-Post, C., Stamp, J. A., Carsrud, A. L., & Reynolds, P. D. (2010). Social ventures from a resource-based perspective: An exploratory study assessing global Ashoka fellows. *Entrepreneurship Theory and Practice, 34*(4), 661–680. doi:10.1111/j.1540-6520.2010.00389.x

Miles, I. (2005). Knowledge intensive business services: Prospects and policies. *Foresight, 7*(6), 39–63. doi:10.1108/14636680510630939

Miles, M. B., & Huberman, A. M. (1984). Drawing valid meaning from qualitative data: Toward a shared craft. *Educational Researcher, 13*(5), 20–30. doi:10.3102/0013189X013005020

Miller, D. (1983). The correlates of entrepreneurship in three types of firms. *Management Science, 29*(7), 770–791. doi:10.1287/mnsc.29.7.770

Miller, D. (2003). An asymmetry-based view of advantage: Towards an attainable sustainability. *Strategic Management Journal, 24*(10), 961–976. doi:10.1002mj.316

Miller, D., & Le Breton-Miller, I. (2006). Family Governance and Firm Performance: Agency, Stewardship, and Capabilities. *Family Business Review, 19*(1), 73–87. doi:10.1111/j.1741-6248.2006.00063.x

Miller, D., Le Breton-Miller, I., Lester, R., & Cannella, A. Jr. (2007). Are family firms really superior performers? *Journal of Corporate Finance, 13*(5), 829–858. doi:10.1016/j.jcorpfin.2007.03.004

Minichiello, V., Aroni, R., & Hays, T. (2008). *In-depht interviewing* (3rd ed.). Pearson/Prentice-Hall.

Ministry of Culture and Tourism-MCT. (2020). *Tourism Certified Facilities*. https://ktb.gov.tr/TR-9860/turizm-belgeli-tesisler.html

Ministry of Economy of El Salvador. (2018). *Household survey data*. Retrieved from http://www.digestyc.gob.sv/index.php/temas/des/

Mintzberg, H. (1979). *The Structuring of Organizations: a synthesis of the research. Nova Jérsia*. Prentice Hall.

Mndzebele, N. (2013). The usage of accounting information systems for effective internal controls in the hotels. *International Journal of Advancements in Computing Technology, 2*(5), 1–3.

Moeller, K. (2009). Intangible and financial performance: Causes and effects. *Journal of Intellectual Capital, 10*(2), 224–245. doi:10.1108/14691930910952632

Molina, A., Gómez, M., González-Díaz, B., & Esteban, Á. (2015). Market segmentation in wine tourism: Strategies for wineries and destinations in Spain. *Journal of Wine Research, 26*(3), 192–224. doi:10.1080/09571264.2015.1051218

Monteiro, A. P., Soares, A. M., & Rua, O. (2017). Linking intangible resources and export performance: The role of entrepreneurial orientation and dynamic capabilities. *Baltic Journal of Management, 12*(3), 329–347. doi:10.1108/BJM-05-2016-0097

Moreira, A. C., & Alves, C. (2016). Commitment-trust dynamics in the internationalization process: A case study of market entry in the Brazilian market. In Information Resources Management Association (Ed.), International business: Concepts, methodologies, tools, and applications, (vol. 3, pp. 1206–1229). Hershey, PA: IGI Global. Doi:10.4018/978-1-4666-9814-7.ch057

Moreira, A. C. (2009). The evolution of internationalisation: Towards a new theory? *Global Economics and Management Review, 14*(1), 41–59.

Moreira, A. C., Ferreira, L., & Silva, P. (2018). Inward internationalization. Important challenges among SMEs. In R. Pérez-Uribe, C. Salcedo-Pérez, & D. Ocampo-Guzman (Eds.), *Handbook of Research on Intrapreneurship and Organizational Sustainability in SMEs* (pp. 250–275). IGI Global. doi:10.4018/978-1-5225-3543-0.ch012

Moreira, A. C., Ramos, M., Ferraz, L., & Martins, D. (2018). The internationalization process of a born global: A case study of a beverage firm. In O. Rua (Ed.), *Entrepreneurial Orientation and Opportunities for Global Economic Growth* (pp. 46–68). IGI Global. doi:10.4018/978-1-5225-6942-8.ch003

Moreira, A., & Alves, C. B. (2016). Commitment-trust dynamics in the internationalization process: A case study of market entry in the Brazilian market. In M. Garita & J. Godinez (Eds.), *Business Development Opportunities and Market Entry Challenges in Latin America* (pp. 224–255). IGI Global. doi:10.4018/978-1-4666-8820-9.ch011

Morence, C., Esteves, M., Silva, N., & Moreira, A. C. (2020). Types and challenges of expatriation. In M. Khosrow-Pour (Ed.), *Encyclopedia of Organizational Knowledge, Administration, and Technologies*. IGI Global.

Morgan, N., & Pritchard, A. (2004). Meeting the destination branding challenge. In N. Morgan, A. Pritchard, & R. Pride (Eds.), *Destination branding: Creating the unique destination proposition* (Vol. 2, pp. 59–78). Elsevier Butterworth-Heinemann.

Morgan, N., Vorhies, D. W., & Schlegelmilch, B. B. (2006). Resource–performance relationships in industrial export ventures: The role of resource inimitability and substitutability. *Industrial Marketing Management, 35*(5), 621–633. doi:10.1016/j.indmarman.2005.05.018

Morris, M. H., Webb, J. W., & Franklin, R. J. (2011). Understanding the manifestation of entrepreneurial orientation in the nonprofit context. *Entrepreneurship Theory and Practice, 35*(5), 947–971. doi:10.1111/j.1540-6520.2011.00453.x

Mselmi, N., Lahiani, A., & Hamza, T. (2017). Financial distress prediction: The case of French small and medium-sized firms. *International Review of Financial Analysis, 50*, 67–80. doi:10.1016/j.irfa.2017.02.004

Mugnol, R. (2013). *A performance exportadora e os seus antecedentes. O papel da orientação para o mercado externo, empreendedorismo, recursos e inovação: um estudo em empresas exportadoras do sul do Brasil.* Tese de Doutoramento. Coimbra: Universidade de Coimbra. Retrieved from https://estudogeral.sib.uc.pt/handle/10316/25112

Mühlenhoff, J. (2013). The Role of Intermediaries in Culture-Driven Innovation and Future Orientation of the Organization. In *ISPIM Conference Proceedings* (p. 1). The International Society for Professional Innovation Management (ISPIM).

Munoz, J. M. (2010). *International Social Entrepreneurship: Pathways to Personal and Corporate Impact.* Business E. doi:10.4128/9781606491072

Mura, L., & Rózsa, Z. (2013). The Impact of Networking on the Innovation Performance of SMEs. 7th International Days of Statistics and Economics Location: Prague, 1036-1042.

Musteen, M., Datta, D. K., & Herrmann, P. (2009). Ownership structure and CEO compensation: Implications for the choice of foreign market entry modes. *Journal of International Business Studies, 40*(2), 321–338. doi:10.1057/jibs.2008.63

Nagar, N., & Sen, K. (2018). Earnings Management Strategies During Financial Distress. *The IUP Journal of Accounting Research & Audit Practices, 17*(3), 52–79.

Naidu, G. M., Cavusgil, S., Murthy, B., & Sarkar, M. (1997). An export promotion model for India: Implications for public policy. *International Business Review, 6*(2), 113–125. doi:10.1016/S0969-5931(96)00041-8

Nakatani, M. S., & Teixeira, R. M. (2009). Resource- Resource-based View as a ased View as a ased View as a Perspective for Public Tourism erspective for Public Tourism Management R Management Research: esearch: esearch: Evidence Evidence Evidence from Two Brazilian Brazilian Tourism Destinations. *Brazilian Admininstration Review*, *6*(1), 62–77. doi:10.1590/S1807-76922009000100006

Nalcacia, G., & Yagcib, M. I. (2014). The Effects of Marketing Capabilities on Export Performance Using Resource-based View: Assessment on Manufacturing Companies. *Procedia: Social and Behavioral Sciences*, *148*(1), 671–679. doi:10.1016/j.sbspro.2014.07.012

Naldi, L., & Kuiken, A. (2016). *International market exit and re-entry: An empirical study of export patterns of Swedish SMEs.* Swedish Entrepreneurship Forum.

Nambisan, S., Zahra, S. A., & Luo, Y. (2019). Global platforms and ecosystems: Implications for international business theories. *Journal of International Business Studies*, *50*(9), 1464–1486. doi:10.105741267-019-00262-4

Narula, R., & Zanfei, A. (2003). *Globalisation of Innovation The Role of Multinational Enterprises.* No 03-15, DRUID Working Papers, DRUID, Copenhagen Business School, Department of Industrial Economics and Strategy/Aalborg University, Department of Business Studies.

Nayak, A., Chia, R., & Canales, J. I. (2020). Noncognitive microfoundations: Understanding dynamic capabilities as idiosyncractically refined sensitivities and predispositions. *Academy of Management Review*, *45*(2), 280–303. doi:10.5465/amr.2016.0253

New Department of Industry. (2020). *Boosting Business Innovation.* https://www.business.nsw.gov.au

Ng, K.-Y., Van Dyne, L., & Ang, S. (2009). Developing global leaders: The role of international experience and cultural intelligence. *Advances in Global Leadership*, *5*, 225–250. doi:10.1108/S1535-1203(2009)0000005013

Ngoma, M., Ernest, A., Nangoli, S., & Christopher, K. (2017). Internationalisation of SMEs: Does entrepreneurial orientation matter? *World Journal of Entrepreneurship, Management and Sustainable Development*, *13*(2), 96–113. doi:10.1108/WJEMSD-08-2016-0039

Niebel, T., O'Mahony, M., & Saam, M. (2013). *The contribution of intangible assets to sectoral productivity growth in the EU.* doi:10.2139srn.2319362

Nieto, M. J., Santamaria, L., & Fernandez, Z. (2015). Understanding the innovation behavior of family firms. *Journal of Small Business Management*, *53*(2), 382–399. doi:10.1111/jsbm.12075

Nogueira, R., & Moreira, A. C. (2019). Internationalization and higher education: The case of the University of Aveiro. In C. Machado & P. Davim (Eds.), *Higher Education and the Evolution of Management, Applied Sciences, and Engineering Curricula* (pp. 87–119). IGI Global. doi:10.4018/978-1-5225-7259-6.ch004

Nordqvist, M., & Melin, L. (2002). The dynamics of family firms: An institutional perspective on corporate governance and strategic change. In D. Fletcher (Ed.), *Understanding the Small, Family Firm.* Routledge.

Norman, D. A., & Verganti, R. (2014). Incremental and radical innovation: Design research vs. technology and meaning change. *Design Issues*, *30*(1), 78–96. doi:10.1162/DESI_a_00250

Nunnally, J. C. (1978). *Psychometric theory.* McGraw-Hill.

O'Cass, A., & Weerawardena, J. (2009). Examining the role of international entrepreneurship, innovation and international market performance on sme internationalisation. *European Journal of Marketing*, *43*(11/12), 1325–1348. doi:10.1108/03090560910989911

OEC. (2019). *Observatory of Economic Complexity*. Retrieved from https://oec.world/pt/profile/country/prt/

OECD. (2019). *OECD SME and Entrepreneurship Outlook 2019*. http://www.oecd.org/industry/smes/SME-Outlook-Highlights-FINAL.pdf

Ohlson, J. A. (1980). Financial Ratios and the Probabilistic Prediction of Bankruptcy. *Journal of Accounting Research*, *18*(1), 109–131. doi:10.2307/2490395

Olejnik, E., & Swoboda, B. (2012). SMEs' internationalisation patterns: Descriptives, dynamics and determinants. *International Marketing Review*, *29*(5), 466–495. doi:10.1108/02651331211260340

Olive-Tomas, A., & Harmeling, S. S. (2019). The rise of art movements: An effectual process model of Picasso's and Braque's give-and-take during the creation of Cubism (1908–1914). *Small Business Economics*, 1–24.

Olson, J. C. (1977)). Price as an Informational Cue: Effects on Product Evaluations. In A. G. Woodside, J. N. Sheth, & P. D. Bennett (Eds.), Consumer and Industrial Buying Behavior (pp. 267-286). Nova Iorque: North Holland.

Omar, M., Williams, R. Jr, & Lingelbach, D. (2009). Global brand market-entry strategy to manage corporate reputation. *Journal of Product and Brand Management*, *18*(3), 177–187. doi:10.1108/10610420910957807

Onkelinx, J., Manolova, T. S., & Edelman, L. F. (2016). Human capital and SME internationalization: Empirical evidence from Belgium. *International Small Business Journal*, *34*(6), 818–837. doi:10.1177/0266242615591856

Ormiston, J., & Seymour, R. (2011). Understanding Value Creation in Social Entrepreneurship: The Importance of Aligning Mission, Strategy and Impact Measurement. *Journal of Social Entrepreneurship*, *2*(2), 125–150. doi:10.1080/19420676.2011.606331

Osathanunkul, C. (2015). A classification of business models in video game industry. *International Journal of Management Cases*, *17*(1), 35–44.

Osei, A., Forkuoh, K. S., Shao, Y., & Osei, M. A. (2016). The impact of institutional support in SMEs marketing, and growth—A case study of retail SMEs in Ghana. *Open Journal of Business and Management*, *4*(3), 408–426. doi:10.4236/ojbm.2016.43043

Oviatt, B. M., & McDougall, P. P. (2005). Defining international entrepreneurship and modeling the speed of internationalization. *Entrepreneurship Theory and Practice*, *29*(5), 537–553. doi:10.1111/j.1540-6520.2005.00097.x

Oviatt, B., & McDougall, P. (1994). Toward a theory of international new ventures. *Journal of International Business Studies*, *25*(1), 45–64. doi:10.1057/palgrave.jibs.8490193

Oxelheim, L., & Randoy, T. (2003). The impact of foreign board membership on firm value. *Journal of Banking & Finance*, *27*(12), 2369–2392. doi:10.1016/S0378-4266(02)00395-3

Pacheco, L. (2016). Capital structure and internationalization: The case of Portuguese industrial SMEs. *Research in International Business and Finance*, *38*, 531–545. doi:10.1016/j.ribaf.2016.07.014

Park, C. W., Jaworski, B. J., & Macinnis, D. J. (1986). Strategic Brand Concept-Image Management. *Journal of Marketing*, *50*(1), 135–145. doi:10.1177/002224298605000401

Patterson, M. (1999). Re-appraising the concept of brand image. *Journal of Brand Management*, *6*(6), 409–426. doi:10.1057/bm.1999.32

Patton, M. Q. (2015). *Qualitative Evaluation and Research Methods*. Sage.

Pellegrino, J. M., & McNaughton, R. B. (2015). The co-evolution of learning and internationalization strategy in international new ventures. *Management International Review*, *55*(4), 457–483. doi:10.100711575-015-0246-7

Penrose, E. (1959). *The Theory of the Growth of the Firm* (4th ed.). Oxford University Press., doi:10.1093/0198289774.001.0001

Peredo, A. M., & McLean, M. (2006). Social entrepreneurship: A critical review of the concept. *Journal of World Business*, *41*(1), 56–65. doi:10.1016/j.jwb.2005.10.007

Pérez, S., Llopis, A., & Llopis, J. (2010). A competing risks analysis of firms exit. *Empirical Economics*, *38*(2), 281–304. doi:10.100700181-009-0266-x

Perri, A., & Peruffo, E. (2017). *Family Business and Technological Innovation*. Empirical Insights from the Italian Pharmaceutical Industry. Palgrave. doi:10.1007/978-3-319-61596-7

Pestana, M. H., & Gageiro, J. N. (2008). Análise de Dados para Ciências Sociais - A complementaridade do SPSS (5a ed.). Edições Silabo.

Pestana, M. H., & Gageiro, J. N. (2008). *Análise de dados para ciências sociais: a complementaridade do SPSS* (Vol. 5). Sílabo.

Pickernell, D., Jones, P., Thompson, P., & Packham, G. (2016). Determinants of SME exporting: Insights and implications. *International Journal of Entrepreneurship and Innovation*, *17*(1), 31–42. doi:10.5367/ijei.2016.0208

Piekkari, R., Welch, C., & Paavilainen, E. (2009). The case study as disciplinary convention: Evidence from international business journals. *Organizational Research Methods*, *12*(3), 567–589. doi:10.1177/1094428108319905

Piercy, N., Kaleka, A., & Katsikeas, C. (1998). Sources of competitive advantage in high performing exporting companies. *Journal of World Business*, *33*(4), 378–393. doi:10.1016/S1090-9516(99)80081-9

Pindado, J., & Rodrigues, L. (2005). Determinants of Financial Distress Costs. *Financial Markets and Portfolio Management*, *19*(4), 343–359. doi:10.100711408-005-6456-4

Pindado, J., Rodrigues, L., & de la Torre, C. (2008). Estimating financial distress likelihood. *Journal of Business Research*, *61*(9), 995–1003. doi:10.1016/j.jbusres.2007.10.006

Pinto, L., Ribeiro, M., & Moreira, A. C. (2018). Challenging the theoretical lenses of internationalization: A case study analysis. In C. Machado & P. Davim (Eds.), *Enhancing Competitive Advantage with Dynamic Management and Engineering* (pp. 112–137). IGI Global. doi:10.4018/978-1-5225-5360-1.ch005

Piva, E., Rossi-Lamastra, C., & De Massis, A. (2013). Family firms and internationalization: An exploratory study on high-tech entrepreneurial ventures. *Journal of International Entrepreneurship*, *10*(1), 109–129.

Pla-Barber, J., & Escriba-Esteve, A. (2006). Accelerated internationalisation: Evidence from a late investor country. *International Marketing Review*, *23*(3), 255–278. doi:10.1108/02651330610670442

Popoli, P. (2015). Reinforcing Intangible Assets through CSR in a Globalized World. *Journal of Management Policies and Practices*, *3*(1), 23–30. doi:10.15640/jmpp.v3n1a4

PORDATA. (2020a). *Número de PME*. Lisboa, Portugal: PORDATA, Fundação Francisco Manuel dos Santos.

PORDATA. (2020b). *Taxa de natalidade, mortalidade e sobrevivência das empresas*. Lisboa, Portugal: PORDATA, Fundação Francisco Manuel dos Santos.

PORDATA. (2020c). *Valor dos bens importados e exportados pelas empresas*. Lisboa, Portugal: PORDATA, Fundação Francisco Manuel dos Santos.

Portal[REMOVED HYPERLINK FIELD]. (n.d.).Retrieved from http://www.elsalvadortrade.com.sv/

Porter, M. (2000). Location, competition, and economic development: Local clusters in a global economy. *Economic Development Quarterly*, *1*(14), 15–34. doi:10.1177/089124240001400105

Porter, M. E., & Kramer, M. R. (2006). The link between competitive advantage and corporate social responsibility. *Harvard Business Review*, *84*(12), 78–92. PMID:17183795

Porter, M., & Millar, V. (1985). How information gives you competitive advantage. *Harvard Business Review*, *63*(4), 149–160.

Portugal 2020. (n.d.). *Portugal 2020*. Retrieved from https://www.portugal2020.pt/Portal2020

Portugal Global (2017). *Portugal Ficha País – Outubro 2017*. Lisboa: Agência para o Investimento e Comércio Externo de Portugal, E.P.E.

Prange, C., & Pinho, J. C. (2017). How personal and organizational drivers impact on SME international performance: The mediating role of organizational innovation. *International Business Review*, *26*(1), 1114–1123. doi:10.1016/j.ibusrev.2017.04.004

PretaF. (2019). https://pretahub.com/festival-feira-preta

PricewaterhouseCoopers Australia (PwC). (2019). *Transforming Australian manufacturing: preparing businesses and workplaces for Industry 4.0*. Author.

Prodanov, C. C., & Freitas, E. C. (2013). *Metodologia do Trabalho Científico: Métodos e Técnicas da Pesquisa e do Trabalho Acadêmico*. Novo Hamburgo: Editora Feevale.

PROESA. (2019a). *Directorio Nacional de Empresas Exportadoras*. Retrieved from http://www.proesa.gob.sv/

PROESA. (2019b). *Plan de Eventos El Salvador (2019)*. Retrieved from http://www.proesa.gob.sv/

Programa das Nações Unidas para o Desenvolvimento. (2015). *Mercados inclusivos no Brasil*. Retrieved from http://www.br.undp.org

Pukall, T., & Calabrò, A. (2014). The internationalization of family firms: A critical review and integrative model. *Family Business Review*, *27*(2), 103–125. doi:10.1177/0894486513491423

Quadros, R. (2008). Aprendendo a inovar: padrões de gestão da inovação tecnológica em empresas industriais brasileiras. In *Relatório de pesquisa Padrões de gestão da inovação tecnológica em empresas brasileiras, apresentado ao CNPq*. Universidade Estadual de Campinas.

Quintela, M. M. (2011). Seeking "energy" vs. pain relief in SPAs in Brazil (Caldas da Imperatriz) and Portugal (Termas da Sulfúrea). *Anthropology & Medicine*, *18*(1), 23–35. doi:10.1080/13648470.2010.525875 PMID:21563001

Rao, A. R., & Monroe, K. B. (1988). The Moderating Effect of Prior Knowledge on Cue Utilization in Product Evaluations. *The Journal of Consumer Research*, *15*(2), 253–264. doi:10.1086/209162

Rao, V., Agarwal, M., & Dahlhoff, D. (2004). How Is Manifest Branding Strategy Related to the Intangible Value of a Corporation? *Journal of Marketing*, *68*(1), 126–141. doi:10.1509/jmkg.68.4.126.42735

Rauh, J. D., & Sufi, A. (2010). Capital structure and debt structure. *Review of Financial Studies*, *23*(12), 4242–4280. doi:10.1093/rfs/hhq095

Read, S., Sarasvathy, S. D., Dew, N., & Wiltbank, R. (2016). Response to Arend, Sarooghi, and Burkemper (2015): Co-creating effectual entrepreneurship research. *Academy of Management Review*, *41*(3), 528–536. doi:10.5465/amr.2015.0180

Read, S., Song, M., & Smit, W. (2009). A meta-analytic review of effectuation and venture performance. *Journal of Business Venturing, 24*(6), 573–587. doi:10.1016/j.jbusvent.2008.02.005

Rego, A., & Cunha, M. P. (2010). Organisational Justice and Citizenship Behaviors: A Study in the Portuguese Cultural Context. *Applied Psychology, 29*(3), 404–430. doi:10.1111/j.1464-0597.2009.00405.x

Reinartz, W., Haenlein, M., & Henseler, J. (2009). An Empirical Comparison of the Efficacy of Covariance-Based and Variance-Based SEM. *International Journal of Research in Marketing, 26*(4), 332–344. doi:10.1016/j.ijresmar.2009.08.001

Reisinger, Y. (2009). *International Tourism Cultures and Behavior*. Routledge Taylor & Francis Group.

Rennie, M. W. (1993). Born global. *The McKinsey Quarterly, 45*(4). https://link.gale.com/apps/doc/A15424561/AONE?u=uts&sid=AONE&xid=87dbadf2

Reymen, I. M., Andries, P., Berends, H., Mauer, R., Stephan, U., & Van Burg, E. (2015). Understanding dynamics of strategic decision making in venture creation: A process study of effectuation and causation. *Strategic Entrepreneurship Journal, 9*(4), 351–379. doi:10.1002ej.1201

Rialp, A., Rialp, J., & Knight, G. A. (2015). International entrepreneurship: a review and future directions. In A. Fernhaber & S. Prashantham (Eds.), *The Routledge companion to international entrepreneurship* (pp. 7–28). Routledge.

Rialp-Criado, A. (1999). Los enfoques micro-organizativos de la internacionalización de la empresa: Una revisión y síntesis de la literatura. *Información Comercial Española, ICE. Revista de Economia (Curitiba), 781*, 117–128.

Ribau, C. P., Moreira, A. C., & Raposo, M. (2018a). SME internationalization research: Mapping the state of the art. *Canadian Journal of Administrative Sciences, 35*(2), 280–303. doi:10.1002/cjas.1419

Ribau, C. P., Moreira, A. C., & Raposo, M. (2018b). Categorising the internationalisation of SMEs with social network analysis. *International Journal of Entrepreneurship and Small Business, 35*(1), 57–80. doi:10.1504/IJESB.2018.094264

Ribau, C. P., Moreira, A. C., & Raposo, M. (2019). Multidyadic relationships: A multi-stage perspective. *Global Business and Economics Review, 21*(6), 732–755. doi:10.1504/GBER.2019.102553

Ribau, C., Moreira, A. C., & Raposo, M. (2015). Internationalisation of the firm theories: A schematic synthesis. *International Journal of Business and Globalisation, 15*(4), 528–554. doi:10.1504/IJBG.2015.072535

Ribau, C., Moreira, A. C., & Raposo, M. (2017). SMEs innovation capabilities and export performance: An entrepreneurial orientation view. *Journal of Business Economics and Management, 18*(5), 920–934. doi:10.3846/16111699.2017.1352534

Richardson, P. S., Dick, A., & Jain, A. K. (1994). Extrinsic and intrinsic cue effects on perceptions of store brand quality. *Journal of Marketing, 58*(1), 28–36. doi:10.1177/002224299405800403

Richardson, R. (1989). *Pesquisa Social: métodos e técnicas*. Atlas.

Rietveld, J. (2018). Creating and capturing value from freemium business models: A demand-side perspective. *Strategic Entrepreneurship Journal, 12*(2), 171–193. doi:10.1002ej.1279

Roberts, M. J., & Tybout, J. R. (1997). The decision to export in Columbia: An empirical model of entry with sunk costs. *The American Economic Review, 87*(4), 545–564.

Robertson, M., & Hammersley, G. O. M. (2000). Knowledge management practices within a knowledge-intensive firm: The significance of the people management dimension. *Journal of European Industrial Training, 24*(2-4), 241–253. doi:10.1108/03090590010321205

Rodebaugh, T. L., Woods, C. M., & Heimberg, R. G. (2007). The reverse of social anxiety is not always the opposite: The reverse-scored items of the Social Interaction Anxiety Scale do not belong. *Behavior Therapy*, *38*(1), 192–206. doi:10.1016/j.beth.2006.08.001 PMID:17499085

Rodrigues, J. J. (2014). *Influência cultura portuguesa na cultura organizações estrangeiras em Portugal* (Unpublished Master Dissertation). University of Aveiro, Aveiro, Portugal.

Rodrigues, A., Lopes, R., Almeida, R., Coutinho, A., & Moreira, A. C. (2020). Challenges of the repatriation process. In M. Khosrow-Pour (Ed.), *Encyclopedia of Organizational Knowledge, Administration, and Technologies*. IGI Global.

Roldán, J. L., Cegarra, J. G., & Cepeda, G. (2014). Building organisational agility through an unlearning Context. *European Conference on Knowedge Management*, *2*, 834-842.

Romaniuk, J., & Sharp, B. (2004). Conceptualising and measuring brand salience. *Marketing Theory*, *4*(4), 327–342. doi:10.1177/1470593104047643

Rosenberg, M. J., & Hovland, C. I. (1960). *Attitude Organization and Change: An Analysis of Consistency Among Attitude Components*. Yale University Press.

Rosner, R. L., & University, L. I. (2003). Earnings Manipulation in Failing Firms. *Contemporary Accounting Research*, *20*(2), 361–408. doi:10.1506/8EVN-9KRB-3AE4-EE81

Roszkowski, M. J., & Soven, M. (2010). Shifting gears: Consequences of including two negatively worded items in the middle of a positively worded questionnaire. *Assessment & Evaluation in Higher Education*, *35*(2), 113–130. doi:10.1080/02602930802618344

Roundy, P. T., & Fayard, D. (2019). Dynamic capabilities and entrepreneurial ecosystems: The micro-foundations of regional entrepreneurship. *The Journal of Entrepreneurship*, *28*(1), 94–120. doi:10.1177/0971355718810296

Rowley, J. (2012). Conducting research interviews. *Management Research Review*, *35*(3/4), 260–271. doi:10.1108/01409171211210154

Roy, A., Sekhar, C., & Vyas, V. (2016). Barriers to internationalization: A study of small and medium enterprises in India. *Journal of International Entrepreneurship*, *14*(4), 513–538. doi:10.100710843-016-0187-7

Rua, O. L. (2018a). From intangible resources to export performance: Exploring the mediating effect of absorptive capabilities and innovation. *Review of International Business and Strategy*, *28*(3/4), 373–394. doi:10.1108/RIBS-02-2018-0012

Rua, O. L. (2018b). Absorptive Capabilities and Export Performance: The Mediating Effect of Innovation. *International Journal of Advances in Management and Economics*, *7*(5), 28–37.

Rua, O. L., & França, A. (2018). Linking entrepreneurial orientation to brand reputation. *Global Business and Economics Review*, *20*(5/6), 667–678. doi:10.1504/GBER.2018.094451

Rua, O. L., & França, A. (2018). The Linkage Between Intangible Resources and Export Performance: The mediating effect of Innovation. *International Journal of Innovation*, *5*(3), 399–410. Advance online publication. doi:10.5585/iji.v5i3.190

Rugman, A., & Verbeke, A. (2007). Liabilities of regional foreignness and the use of firm-level versus country-level data: A response to Dunning et al. (2007). *Journal of International Business Studies*, *38*(1), 200–205. doi:10.1057/palgrave.jibs.8400242

Rundh, B. (2007). International marketing behaviour amongst exporting firms. *European Journal of Marketing*, *41*(1/2), 181–198. doi:10.1108/03090560710718175

Ruzzier, M. R., Hisrich, D., & Antoncic, B. (2006). SME internationalization research: Past, present and future. *Journal of Small Business and Enterprise Development*, *13*(4), 476–497. doi:10.1108/14626000610705705

Salloum, C., Schmitt, C., & Bouri, E. (2012). Does board structure affect financial distress? A study with reference to family firms in Lebanon. *Investment Management and Financial Innovations*, *9*(4), 113–123.

Sambharya, R. B., Kumaraswamy, A., & Banerjee, S. (2005). Information technologies and the future of the multinational enterprise. *Journal of International Management*, *11*(2), 143–161. doi:10.1016/j.intman.2005.03.005

Sandqvist, U. (2015). The games they are a changin': New business models and transformation within the video game industry. *Humanities and Social Sciences Latvia*, *23*(2), 4–20.

Sarasvathy, S. D. (2001). Causation and effectuation: Toward a theoretical shift from economic inevitability to entrepreneurial contingency. *Academy of Management Review*, *26*(2), 243–263. doi:10.5465/amr.2001.4378020

Sarasvathy, S. D., & Dew, N. (2005). New market creation through transformation. *Journal of Evolutionary Economics*, *15*(5), 533–565. doi:10.100700191-005-0264-x

Sarasvathy, S. D., Dew, N., Read, S., & Wiltbank, R. (2008). Designing organizations that design environments: Lessons from entrepreneurial expertise. *Organization Studies*, *29*(3), 331–350. doi:10.1177/0170840607088017

Saridakis, G., Idris, B., Hansen, J. M., & Dana, L. P. (2019). SMEs' internationalization: When does innovation matter? *Journal of Business Research*, *96*, 250–263. doi:10.1016/j.jbusres.2018.11.001

Sarkar, S. (2010). *Empreendedorismo e Inovação* (2nd ed.). Escolar Editora.

Schiffman, L. G., & Kanuk, L. L. (2007). Consumer Behavior (Vol. 9). Prentice Hall.

Schott, T., & Jensen, K. W. (2016). Firms' innovation benefiting from networking and institutional support: A global analysis of national and firm effects. *Research Policy*, *45*(6), 1233–1246. doi:10.1016/j.respol.2016.03.006

Schueffel, P., Rico, B., & Amann, W. (2014). Behavioral patterns in born-again global firms: Towards a conceptual framework of the internationalization activities of mature SMEs. *Multinational Business Review*, *22*(4), 418–441. doi:10.1108/MBR-06-2014-0029

Schumpeter, J. A. (1911). The Theory of Economic Development. São Paulo: Cultural April.

Schumpeter, J. A. (1942). Capitalism, Socialism and Democracy. Zahar.

Schumpeter, J. A. (1961). *The Theory of Economic Development: An Inquiry Into Profits, Capital, Credit, Interest, and the Business Cycle*. Oxford University Press.

Seelos, C., & Mair, J. (2005). Social entrepreneurship: Creating new business models to serve the poor. *Business Horizons*, *48*(3), 241–246. doi:10.1016/j.bushor.2004.11.006

Şenel, S. A. (2009). TMS 18 hasılat standardı kapsamında mal satışından kaynaklanan hasılatın muhasebeleştirilmesi. *E-Journal of New World Sciences Academy*, *4*, 389–405.

Seringhaus, F. H., & Rosson, P. J. (1994). International trade fairs and foreign market involvement: Review and research direction. *International Business Review*, *3*(3), 311–329. doi:10.1016/0969-5931(94)90008-6

Shane, S., & Venkataraman, S. (2000). The promise of entrepreneurship as a field of research. *Academy of Management Review*, *25*(1), 217–226.

Shanker, M., & Astrachan, J. (1996). Myths and realities: Family businesses' contribution to the US economy – A framework for assessing family business statistics. *Family Business Review*, *9*(2), 107–123. doi:10.1111/j.1741-6248.1996.00107.x

Shuman, J. C., & Seeger, J. A. (1986). The theory and practice of strategic management in smaller rapid growth firms. *American Journal of Small Business*, *11*(1), 7–18. doi:10.1177/104225878601100101

Shumway, T. (2001). Forecasting Bankruptcy More Accurately: A Simple Hazard Model. *The Journal of Business*, *74*(1), 101–124. https://www.jstor.org/stable/10.1086/209665. doi:10.1086/209665

Siebels, J.-F., & Aufseß, D. (2012). A Review of theory in family business research: The implications for corporate governance. *International Journal of Management Reviews*, *14*(3), 280–304. doi:10.1111/j.1468-2370.2011.00317.x

Silva, M. J. (2007). O papel da inovação e do conhecimento na construção da competitividade regional. Actas da 4.ª Conferência de Engenharia 'Engenharia' 2007 – Inovação e Desenvolvimento. Covilhã, 433-438.

Silva, L. (2007). A procura do turismo em espaço rural. *Etnográfica (Lisboa)*, *11*(1), 141–163. Advance online publication. doi:10.4000/etnografica.1896

Silva, P., & Moreira, A. C. (2019). Subsidiary survival: A case study from the Portuguese electronics industry. *Review of International Business and Strategy*, *29*(3), 226–252. doi:10.1108/RIBS-10-2018-0094

Simonian, M. A., Forsythe, S., Suk Kwon, W., & Chattaraman, V. (2012). The role of product brand image and online store image on perceived risks and online purchase intentions for apparel. *Journal of Retailing and Consumer Services*, *19*(3), 325–331. doi:10.1016/j.jretconser.2012.03.006

Singh, G., Pathak, D., & Naz, R. (2010). Issues faced by SMEs in the internationalization process: Results from Fiji and Samoa. *International Journal of Emerging Markets*, *5*(2), 153–182. doi:10.1108/17468801011031801

Sin, L., Tse, A., Chan, H., Heung, V., & Yim, F. (2006). The effects of relationship marketing orientation on business performance in the hotel industry. *Journal of Hospitality & Tourism Research (Washington, D.C.)*, *30*(4), 407–426. doi:10.1177/1096348006287863

SIREVE - Sistema de Recuperação de Empresas por Via Extrajudicial. Decreto Lei 178/2012 de 3 de agosto. Diário da República Nª 150/2012. Acedido a 24 jan. 2019. www.dre.pt

Skutnabb-Kangas, T. (2009). Diversities or homogenization and dumbing-down: Some arguments. In F. X. Aligny, A. Guillaume, B. Nieder, F. Rastier, C. Tremblay, & H. Wismann (Eds.), *Plurilinguisme, Interculturalité et Emploi: Défis pour l'Europe* (pp. 105–109). L'Harmattan.

Slaughter, J. E., Zickar, M. J., Highhouse, S., & Mohr, D. C. (2004). Personality Trait Inferences about Organizations: Development of a Measure and Assessment of Construct Validity. *The Journal of Applied Psychology*, *89*(1), 85–103. doi:10.1037/0021-9010.89.1.85 PMID:14769122

Smith, M., & Zagelmeyer, S. (2010). Working time management and SME performance in Europe. *International Journal of Manpower*, *31*(4), 392–409. doi:10.1108/01437721011056994

Sonderen, E. V., Sanderman, R., & Coyne, J. C. (2013). Ineffectiveness of reverse wording of questionnaire items: Let's learn from cows in the rain. *PLoS One*, *8*(7), e68967. doi:10.1371/journal.pone.0068967 PMID:23935915

Sousa, C. M. P., Martínez-López, F. J., & Coelho, F. (2008). The determinants of export performance: A review of the research in the literature between 1998 and 2005. *International Journal of Management Reviews*, *10*(4), 343–374. doi:10.1111/j.1468-2370.2008.00232.x

Sousa, C., Gonçalves, G., Reis, M., & Santos, J. V. (2015). Evidências métricas da adaptação da escala de inteligência cultural numa amostra portuguesa. *Psychology. Psicologia: Reflexão e Crítica*, *28*(2), 232–241. doi:10.1590/1678-7153.201528203

Spears, N., & Singh, S. N. (2004). Measuring attitude toward the brand and purchase intentions. *Journal of Current Issues and Research in Advertising*, *26*(2), 53–66. doi:10.1080/10641734.2004.10505164

Spector, A. J. (1961). Basic dimensions of the corporate image. *Journal of Marketing*, *25*(1), 47–51. doi:10.1177/002224296102500608

Spence, L. J. (1999). Does size matter? The state of the art in small business ethics. *Business Ethics: A European Review*, *8*(3), 163-174.

Spence, M. M. (2003). Evaluating export promotion programmes: UK overseas trade missions and export performance. *Small Business Economics*, *20*(1), 83–103. doi:10.1023/A:1020200621988

Stam, E., & Schutjens, V. (2006). *Starting anew: Entrepreneurial intentions and realizations subsequent to business closure*. ERIM Report Series Reference No. ERS-2006-015-ORG. https://ssrn.com/abstract=902744

Standifer, R. L., Raes, A. M. L., Peus, C., Passos, A. M., Marques Santos, C., & Weisweiler, S. (2014). Time in teams: Cognitions, conflict and team satisfaction. *Journal of Managerial Psychology*, *30*(6), 692–708. doi:10.1108/JMP-09-2012-0278

Stern, B., Zinkhan, G. M., & Jaju, A. (2001). Marketing images: Construct definition, measurement issue, and theory development. *Marketing Theory*, *1*(2), 201–224. doi:10.1177/147059310100100203

Stevenson, H. H., & Jarillo, J. C. (1990). A paradigm of entrepreneurship: Entrepreneurial management. *Strategic Management Journal*, *11*(1), 17–27.

Stouraitis, V., Harris, M., Harun, M., & Kyritsis, M. (2017). Motivators of SME initial export choice and the European Union regional effect in manufacturing. *International Journal of Entrepreneurial Behaviour & Research*, *23*(1), 35–55. doi:10.1108/IJEBR-05-2015-0120

Styles, C., & Ambler, T. (1994). Successful export practice: The UK experience. *International Marketing Review*, *11*(6), 23–47. doi:10.1108/02651339410072999

Suarez-Ortega, S. S., & Alamo-Vera, F. (2005). SMES' internationalization: Firms and managerial factors. *International Journal of Entrepreneurial Behaviour & Research*, *11*(4), 258–279. doi:10.1108/13552550510603298

Swoboda, B., & Olejnik, E. (2013). A taxonomy of small and medium-sized international family firms. *Journal of International Entrepreneurship*, *11*(2), 130–157. doi:10.100710843-012-0101-x

Swoboda, B., Olejnik, E., & Morschett, D. (2011). Changes in foreign operation modes: Stimuli for increases versus reductions. *International Business Review*, *20*(5), 578–590. doi:10.1016/j.ibusrev.2010.11.005

Tallman, S., & Li, J. (1996). Effects of international diversity and product diversity on the performance of multinational firms. *Academy of Management Journal*, *39*(1), 179–196.

Tan, W. L., & Yoo, S. J. (2015). Social entrepreneurship intentions of nonprofit organizations. *Journal of Social Entrepreneurship*, *6*(1), 103–125. doi:10.1080/19420676.2014.954260

Taş, M., & Zengin, B. (2019). Seyahat işletmelerinde uluslararasılaşma sorunları ve çözüm önerilerinin kavramsal çerçevede incelenmesi. *Ekonomi, İşletme ve Maliye Araştırmaları Dergisi*, *1*(3), 205–216. doi:10.38009/ekimad.568728

TdB – Turma do Bem. (2019). http://turmadobem.org.br

Teece, D. J. (2007). Explicating dynamic capabilities: The nature and microfoundations of (sustainable) enterprise performance. *Strategic Management Journal*, *28*(13), 1319–1350. doi:10.1002mj.640

Teece, D. J., Pisano, G., & Shuen, A. (1997). Dynamic capabilities and strategic management. *Strategic Management Journal, 18*(7), 509–533. doi:10.1002/(SICI)1097-0266(199708)18:7<509::AID-SMJ882>3.0.CO;2-Z

Tesfom, G., & Lutz, C. (2006). A classification of export marketing problems of small and medium sized manufacturing firms in developing countries. *International Journal of Emerging Markets, 1*(3), 262–281. doi:10.1108/17468800610674480

Thanos, I. C., Dimitratos, P., & Sapouna, P. (2017). The implications of international entrepreneurial orientation, politicization, and hostility upon SME international performance. *International Small Business Journal: Researching Entrepreneurship, 35*(4), 495–514. doi:10.1177/0266242616641749

The World Bank in El Salvador. (2019). Retrieved from https://www.bancomundial.org/es/country/elsalvador/overview#1

Thompson, C. (2011). *Refining Design. U: Magazine*. University of Technology Sydney.

Tidd, J., Bessant, J., & Pavitt, K. (2003). *Gestão da Inovação*. Monitor.

Tinoco, M. H., & Wilson, N. (2013). Financial distress and bankruptcy prediction among listed companies using accounting, market and macroeconomic variables. *International Review of Financial Analysis, 30*, 394–419. doi:10.1016/j.irfa.2013.02.013

Tomić, N. Z. (2018). Economic model of microtransactions in video games. *Journal of Economic Science Research, 1*(1), 17–23.

Torkkeli, L., Saarenketo, S., Salojärvi, H., & Sainio, L.-M. (2017). Sustainability and Corporate Social Responsibility in Internationally Operating SMEs: Implications on Performance. In Value Creation in IB: An SME Perspective (pp 359-373). Vaasa, Finland: Palgrave MacMillan.

Torres, J. P., & Kunc, M. H. (2016). Market opportunity recognition in the Chilean wine industry: Traditional versus relational marketing approaches. *Journal of Wine Research, 27*(1), 19–33. doi:10.1080/09571264.2016.1144584

Trompenaars, F., & Woolliams, P. (2004). *Marketing Across Cultures*. Capstone Publishing.

Tsai, C., Lu, Y., & Yen, D. C. (2012). Determinants of intangible assets value: The data mining approach. *Knowledge-Based Systems, 31*(1), 67–77. doi:10.1016/j.knosys.2012.02.007

Tsang, E. (2002). Learning from overseas venturing experience, the case of Chinese family businesses. *Journal of Business Venturing, 17*(1), 21–40. doi:10.1016/S0883-9026(00)00052-5

Tsao, M., & Lien, W.-H. (2013). Family management and internationalization: The impact on firm performance and innovation. *Management International Review, 53*(2), 189–213. doi:10.100711575-011-0125-9

Tschang, F. T. (2005). Video games as interactive experiential products and their manner of development. *International Journal of Innovation Management, 9*(1), 103–131. doi:10.1142/S1363919605001198

Tukamushaba, E. K., Orobia, L., & George, B. P. (2011). Development of a conceptual model to understand international social entrepreneurship and its application in the Ugandan context. *Journal of International Entrepreneurship, 9*(4), 282–298. doi:10.100710843-011-0079-9

Turcan, J. C. (2019). De-internationalization: A business model perspective. *Journal of Business Models, 7*(4), 39–44.

Türedi, S. (2008). Konaklama işletmelerinde muhasebe bilgi sistemi ile iç kontrol sistemi arasındaki ilişkiler. *Mevzuat Dergisi, 11*(126).

Turunen, H., & Nummela, N. (2017). Internationalisation at home: The internationalisation of location-bound service SMEs. *Journal of International Entrepreneurship, 15*(1), 36–54. doi:10.100710843-016-0167-y

Udin, S., Khan, M. A., & Javid, A. Y. (2017). The effects of ownership structure on likelihood of financial distress: An empirical evidence. *Corporate Governance: The International Journal of Business in Society*, *17*(4), 589–612. doi:10.1108/CG-03-2016-0067

Uzhegova, M., Torkkeli, L., & Saarenketo, S. (2019). Corporate Social Responsibility in SMEs: Implications on Competitive Performance. *Management Review*, *30*(2-3), 232–267.

Valentim, L., Lisboa, J. V., & Franco, M. (2016). Knowledge management practices and absorptive capacity in small and medium-sized enterprises: Is there really a linkage? *R & D Management*, *46*(4), 711–725. doi:10.1111/radm.12108

Valliere, D., & Petterson, R. (2009). Entrepreneurship and economic growth: Evidence from emerging and developed countries. *Entrepreneurship and Regional Development*, *21*(5), 459–480. doi:10.1080/08985620802332723

van Gelder, S. (2003). *Global brand strategy: Unlocking brand potential across countries, cultures and markets*. Sterling.

Varner, I., & Beamer, L. (2005). *Intercultural Communication in the Global Workplace* (3rd ed.). Irwin.

Verganti, R. (2009). *Design driven innovation: changing the rules of competition by radically innovating what things mean*. Harvard Business Press.

Vissak, T., & Francioni, B. (2013). Serial nonlinear internationalization in practice: A case study. *International Business Review*, *22*(6), 951–962. doi:10 1016/j.ibusrev.2013.01.010

Vissak, T. (2010). Nonlinear internationalization: A neglected topic in international business research. In T. Devinney, T. Pedersen, & L. Tihanyi (Eds.), *The past, present and future of international business & management* (pp. 559–580). Emerald. doi:10.1108/S1571-5027(2010)00000230029

Vissak, T., & Francioni, B. (2013). Serial nonlinear internationalization in practice: A case study. *International Business Review*, *22*(6), 951–962. doi:10.1016/j.ibusrev.2013.01.010

VivendasP. (2019). http://programavivenda.com.br

Vlajčića, D., Caputo, A., Marzi, G., & Dabića, M. (2019). Expatriates managers' cultural intelligence as promoter of knowledge transfer in multinational companies. *Journal of Business Research*, *94*, 367–377. doi:10.1016/j.jbusres.2018.01.033

Voss, C., Tsikriktsis, N., & Frohlich, M. (2002). Case research in operations management. *International Journal of Operations & Production Management*, *22*(2), 195–219. doi:10.1108/01443570210414329

Walden, R., Lie, S., Pandolfo, B., & Nemme, A. (2018). Research Prototyping, University-Industry Collaboration and the value of Annotated Portfolios. *Cumulus Paris 2018: To get there together, designing together*.

Walden, R., Lie, S., Pandolfo, B., & Nemme, A. (2020). Developing strategic leadership and innovation capability for manufacturing SMEs transitioning to digital manufacturing technology. In Leadership Styles, Innovation, and Social Entrepreneurship in the Era of Digitalization (pp. 164-189). IGI Global. doi:10.4018/978-1-7998-1108-4.ch007

Walden, R., Pandolfo, B., Lie, S., & Lockhart, C. (2015, September). *The academic design practitioner*. Paper presented at the Creative Practices Conference, Arkitektskolen, Aarhus.

Wang, E. S., & Tsai, B.-K. (2014). Consumer response to retail performance of organic food retailers. *British Food Journal*, *116*(2), 212–227. doi:10.1108/BFJ-05-2012-0123

Wanhill, S. (2000). Small and medium tourism enterprises. *Annals of Tourism Research*, *27*(1), 132–147. doi:10.1016/S0160-7383(99)00072-9

Weber, R. P. (1990). *Basic Content Analysis*. Sage Publications. doi:10.4135/9781412983488

Weerawardena, J., Mort, G. S., Liesch, P. W., & Knight, G. A. (2007). Conceptualizing accelerated internationalization in the born global firm: A dynamic capabilities perspective. *Journal of World Business*, *42*(3), 294–306. doi:10.1016/j.jwb.2007.04.004

Weerawardena, J., Mort, G. S., Salunke, S., Knight, G., & Liesch, P. W. (2015). The role of the market sub-system and the socio-technical sub-system in innovation and firm performance: A dynamic capabilities approach. *Journal of the Academy of Marketing Science*, *43*(2), 221–239. doi:10.100711747-014-0382-9

Welch, C. L., & Welch, L. S. (2009). Re-internationalisation: Exploration and conceptualization. *International Business Review*, *18*(6), 567–577. doi:10.1016/j.ibusrev.2009.07.003

Welch, L. S., & Luostarinen, R. (1988). Internationalization: Evolution of a Concept. *Journal of General Management*, *14*(2), 34–55. doi:10.1177/030630708801400203

Welch, L. S., & Luostarinen, R. K. (1993). Inward-Outward Connections in Internationalization. *Journal of International Marketing*, *1*(1), 44–56. doi:10.1177/1069031X9300100104

Welter, C., Mauer, R., & Wuebker, R. J. (2016). Bridging behavioral models and theoretical concepts: Effectuation and bricolage in the opportunity creation framework. *Strategic Entrepreneurship Journal*, *10*(1), 5–20. doi:10.1002ej.1215

Wernerfelt, B. (1984). A resource-based view of the firm. *Strategic Management Journal*, *5*(2), 171–180. doi:10.1002mj.4250050207

West, G. III, & Noel, T. (2009). The impact of knowledge resources on new venture performance. *Journal of Small Business Management*, *47*(1), 1–22. doi:10.1111/j.1540-627X.2008.00259.x

Westhead, P., Ucbasaran, D., & Binks, M. (2004). Internationalisation strategies selected by established rural and urban SMEs. *Journal of Small Business and Enterprise Development*, *11*(1), 8–22. doi:10.1108/14626000410519065

Westhead, P., Wright, M., & Ucbasaran, D. (2001). The internationalization of new and small firms: A resource-based view. *Journal of Business Venturing*, *16*(4), 333–358. doi:10.1016/S0883-9026(99)00063-4

Wild, J. J., Wild, K. L., & Han, J. C. Y. (2006). *International Business: The Challenges of Globalization* (3rd ed.). Pearson Education.

Wilkinson, T. J., Brouthers, L. E., Salazar, D., & McNally, M. (2009). The strategic impact of international trade shows and trade missions for entrepreneurial firms. *Journal for Global Business Advancement*, *2*(3), 207–220. doi:10.1504/JGBA.2009.028701

Williams, R. (1983). *Keywords: A Vocabulary of Culture and Society*. Oxford University Press.

Wiltbank, R., Dew, N., Read, S., & Sarasvathy, S. D. (2006). What to do next? The case for non-predictive strategy. *Strategic Management Journal*, *27*(10), 981–998. doi:10.1002mj.555

Wiltbank, R., Read, S., Dew, N., & Sarasvathy, S. D. (2009). Prediction and control under uncertainty: Outcomes in angel investing. *Journal of Business Venturing*, *24*(2), 116–133. doi:10.1016/j.jbusvent.2007.11.004

Winter, S. G. (2003). Understanding dynamic capabilities. *Strategic Management Journal*, *24*(10), 991–995. doi:10.1002mj.318

Wiwattanakantang, Y. (2001). Controlling shareholders and corporate value: Evidence from Thailand. *Pacific-Basin Finance Journal*, *9*(4), 323–362. doi:10.1016/S0927-538X(01)00022-1

World Trade Organization. (2019). *World Trade Statistical Review 2019*. https://www.wto.org/english/res_e/statis_e/miwi_e/miwi_e.htm

Wright, M., Westhead, P., & Ucbasaran, D. (2007). Internationalization of small and medium-sized enterprises (SMEs) and international entrepreneurship: A critique and policy implications. *Regional Studies, 41*(7), 1013–1029. doi:10.1080/00343400601120288

Wu, L.-Y. (2010). Applicability of the resource-based and dynamic-capability views under environment volatility. *Journal of Business Research, 63*(1), 27–31. doi:10.1016/j.jbusres.2009.01.007

Yang, X., & Rivers, C. (2009). Antecedents of CSR practices in MNCs' subsidiaries: A stakeholder and institutional perspective. *Journal of Business Ethics, 86*(S2), 155–169. doi:10.100710551-009-0191-0

Yang, Y., & Wu, S. (2015). An exploratory study to understand the internationalization strategies of social enterprises. *Journal of Social Entrepreneurship, 6*(1), 31–41. doi:10.1080/19420676.2014.954255

Yan, Z. J., Zhu, J. C., Fan, D., & Kalfadellis, P. (2018). An institutional work view toward the internationalization of emerging market firms. *Journal of World Business, 53*(5), 682–694. doi:10.1016/j.jwb.2018.03.008

Yemer, M., & Chekol, F. (2017). The effect of internal controls systems on hotels revenue. A case of hotels in Bahir Dar and Gondar cities. *Arabian Journal of Business and Management Review, 6*(6), 19–37.

Yilanci, M. (2001). Muhasebe bilgi sistemi, iç kontrol ve verimlilik üçgeni. *Muhasebe Bilim ve Dünya Dergisi, 3*(3), 37-50.

Yin, R. (2008). *Case Study Research: Design and Methods*. SAGE.

Yin, R. (2014). *Case study research: Design and methods*. Sage Publications.

Yin, R. K. (2014). Applied social research methods series: Vol. 5. *Case study research : Design and methods*. doi:10.1097/FCH.0b013e31822dda9e

Yin, R. K. (2017). *Case study research and applications: design and methods*. Sage.

Zahra, S. A. (2005). A theory of international new ventures: A decade of research. *Journal of International Business Studies, 36*(1), 20–28. doi:10.1057/palgrave.jibs.8400118

Zahra, S. A., Gedajlovic, E., Neubaum, D. O., & Shulman, J. M. (2009). A typology of social entrepreneurs: Motives, search processes and ethical challenges. *Journal of Business Venturing, 24*(5), 519–532. doi:10.1016/j.jbusvent.2008.04.007

Zahra, S. A., Korri, J. S., & Yu, J. F. (2005). Cognition and international entrepreneurship: Implications for research on international opportunity recognition and exploitation. *International Business Review, 14*(2), 129–146. doi:10.1016/j.ibusrev.2004.04.005

Zahra, S. A., Newey, L. R., & Li, Y. (2014). On the frontiers: The implications of social entrepreneurship for international entrepreneurship. *Entrepreneurship Theory and Practice, 38*(1), 137–158. doi:10.1111/etap.12061

Zahra, S. A., Rawhouser, H., Bhawe, N., Neubaum, D., & Hayton, J. (2008). Globalization of social entrepreneurship opportunities. *Strategic Entrepreneurship Journal, 1*, 11–26. doi:10.1002ej

Zahra, S., Hayton, J., & Salvato, C. (2004). Entrepreneurship in family vs. non–family firms: A resource–based analysis of the effect of organizational culture. *Entrepreneurship Theory and Practice, 28*(4), 363–381. doi:10.1111/j.1540-6520.2004.00051.x

Zander, I., McDougall-Covin, P., & Rose, E. L. (2015). Born globals and international business: Evolution of a field of research. *Journal of International Business Studies, 46*(1), 27–35. doi:10.1057/jibs.2014.60

Zeithaml, V. A. (1988). Consumer perceptions of price, quality, and value: A means-end model and synthesis of evidence. *Journal of Marketing, 52*(1), 2–22. doi:10.1177/002224298805200302

Zhang, J., Beatty, S. E., & Walsh, G. (2008). Review and future directions of cross-cultural consumer services research. *Journal of Business Research*, *61*(3), 211–224. doi:10.1016/j.jbusres.2007.06.003

Zirger, B. (1997). The influence of development experience and product innovativeness on product outcome. *Technology Analysis and Strategic Management*, *9*(3), 287–297. doi:10.1080/09537329708524285

Zmijewski, M. E. (1984). Methodological Issues Related to the Estimation of Financial Distress Prediction Models. *Journal of Accounting Research*, *22*, 59–82. doi:10.2307/2490859

Zou, S., Taylor, C. R., & Osland, G. E. (1998). The EXPERF scale: A cross-national generalized export performance measure. *Journal of International Marketing*, *6*(3), 37–58. doi:10.1177/1069031X9800600307

Zucchella, A., Palamara, G., & Denicolai, S. (2007). The drivers of the early internationalization of the firm. *Journal of World Business*, *42*(3), 268–280. doi:10.1016/j.jwb.2007.04.008

About the Contributors

António Moreira obtained a Bachelor's degree in Electrical Engineering and a Master's degree in Management, both from the University of Porto, Portugal. He received his PhD in Management from UMIST-University of Manchester Institute of Science and Technology, England. He has a solid international background in industry leveraged working for a multinational company in Germany as well as in Portugal. He has also been involved in consultancy projects and in research activities. He is Associate Professor at the Department of Economics, Management, Industrial Engineering, and Tourism, University of Aveiro, Portugal, where he headed the Bachelor and Master Degrees in Management for five years. He is member of GOVCOPP research unit.

* * *

Alexandra Alves is from Ovar, a city located in the central region of Portugal. She has a Bachelor's degree in Languages and Business Relations and is finishing a Master's degree in Management, both at the University of Aveiro, Portugal. She is doing a master thesis on internationalization and Export Promotion Programs. She also enjoys learning new languages and studying different cultures.

Carolina Carlos holds a Bachelor's and master's degree in Psychology, from the University of Aveiro, Portugal. Currently, she is undertaking a master's degree in Management, with an specialization in organizational behavior and human resource management. She is keen in exploiting and acknowledging new skills and knowledge, to explore the interdisciplinarity of these two different fields.

Joana Gomes Conceição is a second-year Languages and Business Relations Master's student at the University of Aveiro, Portugal. She received a bachelor's degree in Translation from the same university. She is currently finishing her thesis along with her internship in International Business. Her interests are Languages namely German and English and International trade.

Joana Costa is a Professor at the Economics, Management, Industrial Engineering and Tourism Department (DEGEIT), University of Aveiro, whose professional activities are Economics of Innovation, Structural Change and Innovation, Innovation and Technology, Entrepreneurship and Econometrics. She is also a researcher in GOVCOPP and INESCTEC mostly interested in Innovation Policy, Economic Growth, Entrepreneurship Dynamics, Sustainable Innovation, Innovation Ecosystems and Family Business. Helds a Post-Doc in Economics from FEP Universidade do Porto in the field of "Innovation Persistence and National Innovation Contexts — The Role of Open Innovation". PhD in Public Policy.

Magali Pedro Costa is an Adjunct Professor (Instituto Politécnico de Leiria) Research collaborator (Center for Advanced Studies in Management and Economics- CEFAGE) Ph.D. in Management (U. Évora, 2015), B.A. in Management (I.P. Leiria, 2008). Research interests: Corporate Finance.

Deybbi Cuéllar-Molina is a Professor of Organizational Behaviour and Human Resources Management at the Economic and Business Administration Department of Las Palmas de Gran Canaria University. She has got a PhD in Management and Business. Her research interest covers different aspects of Human Resource Management in profit and non-profit organizations, such as well-being at work, female managers and cross-cultural management. Her works has been published in international journals. She has combined her educational and research activities with consulting services on human resources management. She has professional experience in international projects and working within intercultural teams and have good command of strategic management techniques.

Nicole de Jesus, born in Toronto, Canada, dedicated her childhood and adolescence to volunteering, scouting and ballet. Nicole has a Bachelor's degree in Marketing, where she specializes in Digital Marketing. She is currently completing her master's degree in management at the University of Aveiro, Portugal. She was the runner up in the EDP University Challenge 2018 contest, which had 92 teams, with the "EFOOTPRINT" project, and in the 5th edition of the Mark'it contest with the "Rudá" project.

Marcelo Dionisio is a PhD candidate at COPPEAD, Rio de Janeiro,Brazil, and he is currently writing his thesis on Corporate Social Innovation and how business strategies can achieve both financial and social results. He has published many articles in international journals such as Social Enterprise Journal and International Business Reviews and presented his research at ISIRC, international social innovation research conference.

Luís Farinha holds a PhD in management. He is Assistant Professor and researcher at University of Beira Interior and Assistant Professor at the Polytechnic Institute of Castelo Branco, in Portugal. His research career has focused on the links between entrepreneurship, innovation and regional competitiveness in national and international contexts. He is Founder and Dean of the Regional Helix – International Conference (http://helix.ipcb.pt/). He is the editor of two books (https://www.igi-lobal.com/book/handbook-research-global-competitive-advantage/123114 and http://www.springer.com/gp/book/9783319296753) and journal articles and book chapters. It is also linked to innovation and entrepreneurship programs in cooperation with business incubators and national business associations and sectoral clusters. Previously he was a manager in companies with businesses in the international market.

João J. M. Ferreira is Associate Professor at the University of Beira Interior (UBI), Portugal. He holds a PhD in Entrepreneurship and Small Business Management from the Autonomous University of Barcelona (UAB), Spain. Currently, he is the scientific coordinator of the UBI Research Unit for Business Sciences (NECE), Portugal. He has edited or co-edited several books on strategy, innovation and entrepreneurship and published over 200 papers in premier international journals, including Technological Forecasting & Social Change, Journal of Business Research, Journal of Cleaner Production, Management Decision, and Service Business. He is Associate Editor of Management Decision, and his research interests include strategy, competitiveness, and entrepreneurship.

María Gracia García-Soto is a Professor of Strategic Management of the University of Las Palmas de Gran Canaria. She is PhD in Economics and Business Sciences and Master in Tourism Enterprise Management. Her lines of research are cross-cultural studies and entrepreneurship. Her works have been published in books such as Cases on Information Technology Entrepreneurship (IGI Publishing) or E-Entrepreneurship and ICT Ventures: Strategy, Organization and Technology (IGI Global), and in national and international journals indexed in Social Science Citation Index, including Entrepreneurship & Regional Development, International Journal of Intercultural Relations, International Journal of Human Resource Management and Journal of Small Business Management.

Antonia Mercedes García-Cabrera is a Professor of Strategic Management at the Economic and Business Administration Department of Las Palmas de Gran Canaria University. She received her PhD in Management from this university in 1994 and her areas of academic interest include Entrepreneurship, International Business and Human Resource Management. Her works have been published in international and Spanish journals -i.e., Journal of Small Business Management, Entrepreneurship & Regional Development, European Management Journal, International Journal of Intercultural Relations, Human Resource Development Quarterly, etc.- and in international books -i.e., E-entrepreneurship and ICT ventures: Strategy, Organization and technology (IGI Global Publishing); Cases on Information Technology Entrepreneurship (IGI Global Publishing).

Cristiana Gonçalves is from Barcelos, located in the north of Portugal. Since young developed a passion for Asian culture and languages and she decided to follow a bachelor's degree in Oriental Studies, specifically Chinese and Japanese, at the University of Minho, Portugal. After concluding her studies there, she got interested in business relations and international trade and decided to do a Master's degree at the University of Aveiro on Languages and Business Relations, where she meets her co-writers. Meanwhile, a opportunity to study in China appeared and Cristiana decided to embark on that adventure. She is currently studying International Trade at Hohai University, in the city of Nanjing, Jiangsu Province, China.

Raquel Henriques has a Bachelor's degree in Marketing from the University of Aveiro, Portugal. She was enrolled in the Erasmus program in the Netherlands for one semester where she pursued a minor in Innovation and Creativity at Avans University of Applied Sciences, The Netherlands. She is currently taking a master's degree in Management in the University of Aveiro, Portugal, and is writing her thesis on Socially Responsible Consumption, with the purpose of discovering young consumers' attitudes, intentions, and behaviors on this matter.

Orlando Manuel Lima Rua is an Assistant Professor of Management at the School of Accounting and Administration (ISCAP) of the Polytechnic of Porto (Portugal). Researcher at Center of Business and Legal Studies (CECEJ) (Polytechnic of Porto – ISCAP) and at Management Applied Research Unit (UNIAG) of the Association of Polytechnic Institutes of Northern Portugal (APNOR).

Ines Lisboa is a Professor at the School of Technology and Management of the Polytechnic Institute of Leiria (ESTG/IPLeiria). Coordinator of Master in Management Control of ESTG/IPLeiria. Effective researcher at Centre of Applied Research in Management and Economics (CARME). PhD in Financial Economics and Accounting, with specialization in Family Business, from the University of Extremadura,

Spain (Thesis title: "Differences between Family and Non-Family Companies, Evidence for the Portuguese and Spanish Stock Markets"). Master in Finance, ISCTE, Portugal (Title of dissertation: "Does Ownership Influence Performance? Evidence From Europe."). Degree in Organization and Management of Companies, by the Faculty of Economics of the University of Coimbra, Portugal. She is author of diverse papers published internationally and evaluator of some conferences. She has participated in several national and international conferences.

Rui Centeno Martins is Professor in ISLA-Santarém, Department of Management and Economics and collaborator of the Management Unit of the ISLA Santarém Research Unit. He is also student of a PhD in Management from the University of Beira Interior, Portugal. His research focuses on the strategies of Internationalization of SMEs, entrepreneurship, business networks and business creation.

Engin Meric is a faculty at Trakya University. He has a bachelor's degree in Business Administration; MA with an emphasis on International Business Administration; and PhD with an emphasis on Business Administration. His general research interests focus on Financial Statements Analysis, Cost and Business Budgeting. Prior to his academic career, he worked as a management consultant (in the field of accounting and finance). He advised on budget and cost configurations in many SME-scale production and service enterprises. His research interests include but are not limited to cost and business budgeting in addition to Accounting Recording Systems, Cost and Feasibility, System Efficiency and Effectiveness, Investment Cost Optimization, etc. Finally, his publication studies on budget and cost applications are (especially related to SMEs) ongoing.

Anton Nemme is an industrial designer and graduate of UTS. He began his career in the field of product visualisation producing 3D models and renderings for some of Sydney's leading product design consultancies. Anton has a strong focus on teaching being involved across all the undergraduate year groups. His most recent research themes centre on the value of iteration in design projects, university-industry collaboration, applications for 3D printing and the notion of authenticity in design education.

Antoni Olive-Tomas teaches Strategic Management and Entrepreneurship in the IQS School of Management at the Ramon Llull University in Barcelona. He earned his PhD in Business Management from the Polytechnic University of Catalonia. His areas of specialisation are business opportunities, business models, and effectuation. He has published articles in academic and professional journals and has authored teaching cases. He regularly writes columns in various business newspapers. He has also held management positions in some firms.

José Carlos Martins Rodrigues Pinho, Ph.D., Warwick University, is an Associate Professor of Marketing at School of Economics and Management, University of Minho, Campus of Gualtar, 4710-057, Braga, Portugal (e-mail: jcpinho@eeg.uminho.pt). José Carlos Pinho counts a vast number of publications in peer reviewed journals including Journal of World Business, Technological Forecasting & Social Change, International Business Review, International Marketing Review, International Journal of Project Management, European Journal of Marketing, International Journal of Tourism Research, Journal of International Entrepreneurship, European Business Review, among others. He has also been actively involved in a number of International Projects, published in a number of International Conference Proceedings, served as reviewer for a number of international conferences and journals and has served as Chair, Track Chair and Co-Chair for International Conferences.

Carolina Rodrigues is from Albergaria-a-Velha, Aveiro, Portugal. From a young age, she wanted to learn different languages. She has a Bachelor's degree in Languages and Business Relations at the University of Aveiro, Portugal, where she specializes in Chinese and German. She is finishing a Master's degree in Management, also at the University of Aveiro, where she specializes in business and international business areas.

Yeda Swirski de Souza is a full professor in Organizational Behaviour and Entrepreneurship at Unisinos University (Brazil). Her academic preparation was at the Federal University of RGS (Brazil) and in the Pontificia Catholic University of RS (Brazil). She was a visiting professor at IQS School of Management at the Ramon Llull University in Barcelona. Her research interest is in international entrepreneurship. Her academic contribution in several publications supports understanding how knowledge and creativity based small companies can achieve international reach. Yeda also devoted ten years of her career to academic management positions.

Roderick Walden undertakes research into the contemporary methods and practice of professional industrial design. His academic focus is to develop research intensive design methodologies for knowledge-driven industrial design that situates prototyping as a central research device. He has worked as an industrial designer and production engineer for a range of local and international manufacturers in the commercial office furniture industry including Herman Miller U.S., and Wilkhahn and König + Neurath Germany. His design consultancy, Walden Design Pty Ltd, formed in 2003, designed a range of products for Australian and international companies, working particularly closely with manufacturing SMEs. His academic design practice is disseminated through a series of projects such as the MTB brake-lever multi-tool (2008), leather-moulded office accessories (2008-2010), fire-fighters cooling vest (2009), metal laser sintered SSTL bicycle crank arm (2011 & 2019) and more recently through funded university-industry collaboration projects (2017-2019). Through the study of self-initiated product design projects, he modelled connections between knowledge and practice that he is currently advancing as part of his PhD on knowledge-integration and intellectual agency in industrial design practice. He has co-authored research on topics including university-industry collaboration (UIC), advanced manufacturing systems, design in business, design education and academic design practice. He is a founding member of the UTS-based IPD-R Research Unit that has successfully supported local manufacturing SMEs develop new products and innovation processes.

Index

F

G

H

I

K

L

M

Premier Reference Source
Emerging GIS Applications for Emergency and Disaster Management

Premier Reference Source
Managerial Strategies and Green Solutions for Project Sustainability

Premier Reference Source
Comparative Approaches to Using R and Python for Statistical Data Analysis

Premier Reference Source
Solutions for High-Touch Communications in a High-Tech World

www.ingramcontent.com/pod-product-compliance
Lightning Source LLC
LaVergne TN
LVHW062139300926
849161LV00010B/2574
* 9 7 8 1 7 9 9 8 4 3 8 7 0 *